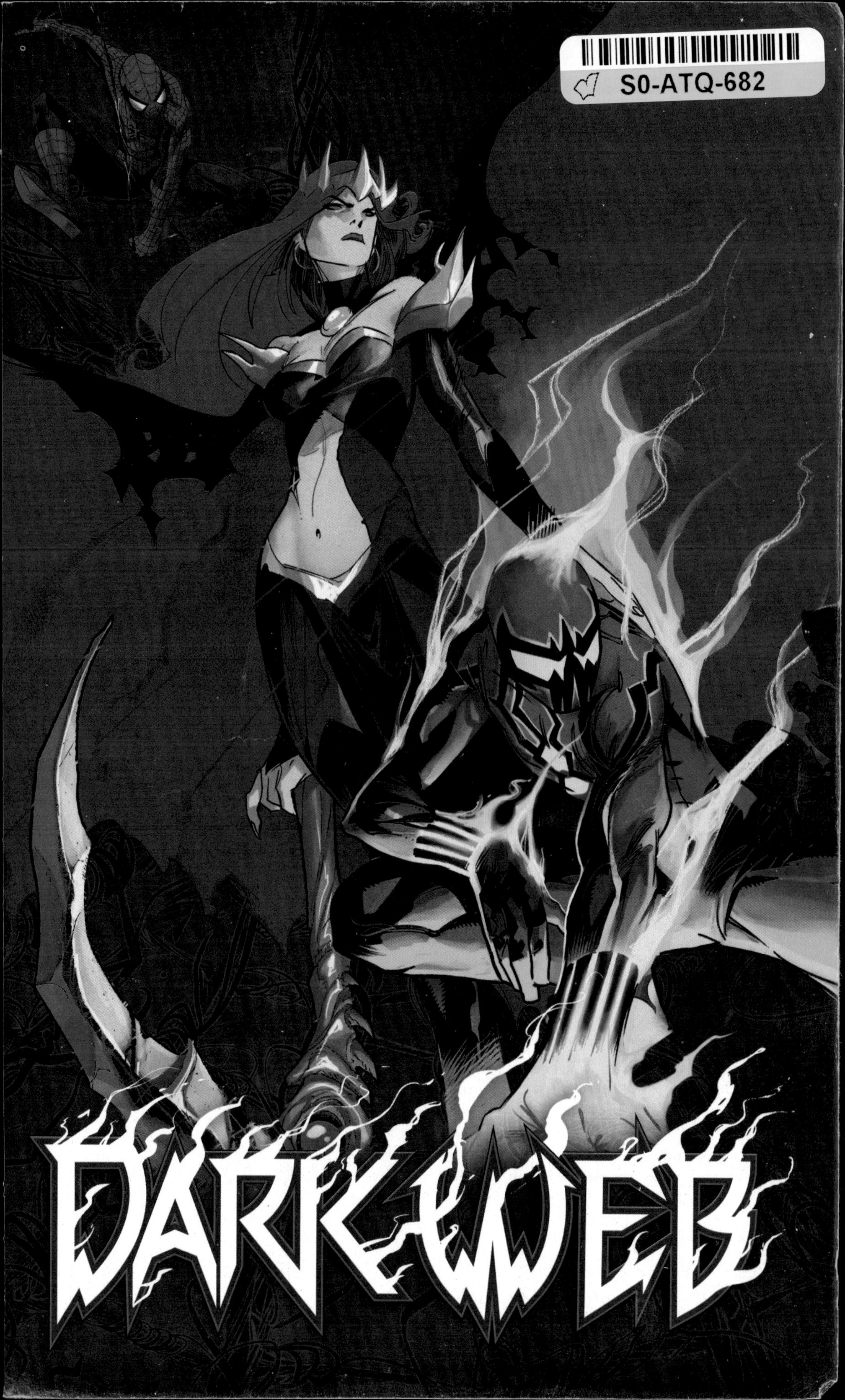
DARK WEB

BEN REILLY is the clone of **PETER PARKER**, A.K.A. **SPIDER-MAN**.

MADELYNE PRYOR is the clone of **JEAN GREY**, A.K.A. **MARVEL GIRL** of the **X-MEN**.

In their long and storied histories, fate has not been kind. Alone, they're the most screwed-over clones in the universe. But together, **CHASM** and the **GOBLIN QUEEN** will have their revenge as they ensnare New York City into their...

FREE COMIC BOOK DAY: SPIDER-MAN/VENOM

WRITER:
ZEB WELLS

PENCILER:
JOHN ROMITA JR.

INKER:
SCOTT HANNA

COLOR ARTIST:
MARCIO MENYZ

LETTERER:
vc's **JOE CARAMAGNA**

COVER ART:
JOHN ROMITA JR., SCOTT HANNA & MARCIO MENYZ

ASSISTANT EDITORS:
LINDSEY COHICK & KAEDEN McGAHEY

EDITOR:
NICK LOWE

DARK WEB #1

WRITER:
ZEB WELLS

ARTIST:
ADAM KUBERT

COLOR ARTIST:
FRANK MARTIN

LETTERER:
vc's **JOE CARAMAGNA**

COVER ART:
ADAM KUBERT & ALEJANDRO SÁNCHEZ

INTERLOCKING-BACKGROUND COVER ART:
FEDERICO VICENTINI & MATTHEW WILSON

ASSISTANT EDITOR:
KAEDEN McGAHEY

EDITOR:
NICK LOWE

AMAZING SPIDER-MAN #15-18

WRITER:
ZEB WELLS

PENCILER:
ED McGUINNESS

INKER:
CLIFF RATHBURN

COLOR ARTISTS:
MARCIO MENYZ WITH **ERICK ARCINIEGA** (#18)

LETTERER:
vc's **JOE CARAMAGNA**

COVER ART:
JOHN ROMITA JR., SCOTT HANNA & MARCIO MENYZ

ASSISTANT EDITOR:
KAEDEN McGAHEY

EDITOR:
NICK LOWE

COLLECTION EDITOR: **JENNIFER GRÜNWALD**
ASSISTANT EDITOR: **DANIEL KIRCHHOFFER**
ASSISTANT MANAGING EDITOR: **MAIA LOY**
ASSOCIATE MANAGER, TALENT RELATIONS: **LISA MONTALBANO**
ASSOCIATE MANAGER, DIGITAL ASSETS: **JOE HOCHSTEIN**
VP PRODUCTION & SPECIAL PROJECTS: **JEFF YOUNGQUIST**
DARK WEB LOGO & BOOK DESIGN: **ADAM DEL RE**
SVP PRINT, SALES & MARKETING: **DAVID GABRIEL**
EDITOR IN CHIEF: **C.B. CEBULSKI**

DARK WEB. Contains material originally published in magazine form as DARK WEB (2022) #1, AMAZING SPIDER-MAN (2022) #15-18, VENOM (2021) #14-16, DARK WEB: X-MEN (2022) #1-3, DARK WEB: MS. MARVEL (2022) #1-2, DARK WEB FINALE (2023) #1 and FREE COMIC BOOK DAY 2022: SPIDER-MAN/VENOM #1. First printing 2023. ISBN 978-1-302-94860-3. Published by MARVEL WORLDWIDE, INC., a subsidiary of MARVEL ENTERTAINMENT, LLC. OFFICE OF PUBLICATION: 1290 Avenue of the Americas, New York, NY 10104. © 2023 MARVEL. No similarity between any of the names, characters, persons, and/or institutions in this book with those of any living or dead person or institution is intended, and any such similarity which may exist is purely coincidental. Printed in Canada. KEVIN FEIGE, Chief Creative Officer; DAN BUCKLEY, President, Marvel Entertainment; DAVID BOGART, Associate Publisher & SVP of Talent Affairs; TOM BREVOORT, VP Executive Editor; NICK LOWE, Executive Editor, VP of Content, Digital Publishing; DAVID GABRIEL, VP of Print & Digital Publishing; SVEN LARSEN, VP of Licensed Publishing; MARK ANNUNZIATO, VP of Planning & Forecasting; JEFF YOUNGQUIST, VP of Production & Special Projects; ALEX MORALES, Director of Publishing Operations; DAN EDINGTON, Director of Editorial Operations; RICKEY PURDIN, Director of Talent Relations; JENNIFER GRÜNWALD, Director of Production & Special Projects; SUSAN CRESPI, Production Manager; STAN LEE, Chairman Emeritus. For information regarding advertising in Marvel Comics or on Marvel.com, please contact Vit DeBellis, Custom Solutions & Integrated Advertising Manager, at vdebellis@marvel.com. For Marvel subscription inquiries, please call 888-511-5480. Manufactured between 2/17/2023 and 3/21/2023 by SOLISCO PRINTERS, SCOTT, QC, CANADA.

10 9 8 7 6 5 4 3 2 1

W E B

VENOM #14-16

WRITERS:
AL EWING (#14, #16) &
RAM V (#15)

PENCILER:
BRYAN HITCH

INKERS:
ANDREW CURRIE WITH
SCOTT HANNA (#15) &
BRYAN HITCH (#16)

COLOR ARTIST:
ALEX SINCLAIR

LETTERER:
vc's **CLAYTON COWLES**

COVER ART:
BRYAN HITCH &
ALEX SINCLAIR

ASSOCIATE EDITOR:
TOM GRONEMAN

EDITOR:
DEVIN LEWIS

DARK WEB: X-MEN #1-3

WRITER:
GERRY DUGGAN

ARTISTS/COLORS:
ROD REIS (#1-3) &
PHIL NOTO (#2-3)

LETTERER:
vc's **CORY PETIT**

COVER ART:
PHIL NOTO

ASSOCIATE EDITOR:
LAUREN AMARO

EDITOR:
JORDAN D. WHITE

DARK WEB: MS. MARVEL #1-2

WRITER:
SABIR PIRZADA

ARTIST:
FRANCESCO MORTARINO

COLOR ARTISTS:
PROTOBUNKER's **DONO**
SÁNCHEZ-ALMARA WITH
FER SIFUENTES-SUJO (#2)

LETTERER:
vc's **ARIANA MAHER**

COVER ART:
MARCO CHECCHETTO &
MATTHEW WILSON

ASSOCIATE EDITOR:
TOM GRONEMAN

EDITOR:
DEVIN LEWIS

DARK WEB FINALE

WRITER:
ZEB WELLS

ARTISTS:
ADAM KUBERT &
FRANCESCO MORTARINO
WITH **SCOTT HANNA**

COLOR ARTISTS:
FRANK MARTIN &
GURU-eFX

LETTERER:
vc's **JOE CARAMAGNA**

COVER ART:
ADAM KUBERT &
FRANK MARTIN

ASSISTANT EDITOR:
KAEDEN McGAHEY

EDITOR:
NICK LOWE

FREE COMIC BOOK DAY:
SPIDER-MAN/VENOM

#1

DARK WEB:
X-MEN #1

AMAZING
SPIDER-MAN #15

DARK WEB:
MS. MARVEL #1

DARK WEB:
X-MEN #2

AMAZING
SPIDER-MAN #16

VENOM #14

AMAZING
SPIDER-MAN #17

DARK WEB:
MS. MARVEL #2

VENOM #15

DARK WEB:
X-MEN #3

AMAZING
SPIDER-MAN #18

VENOM #16

DARK WEB

FINALE

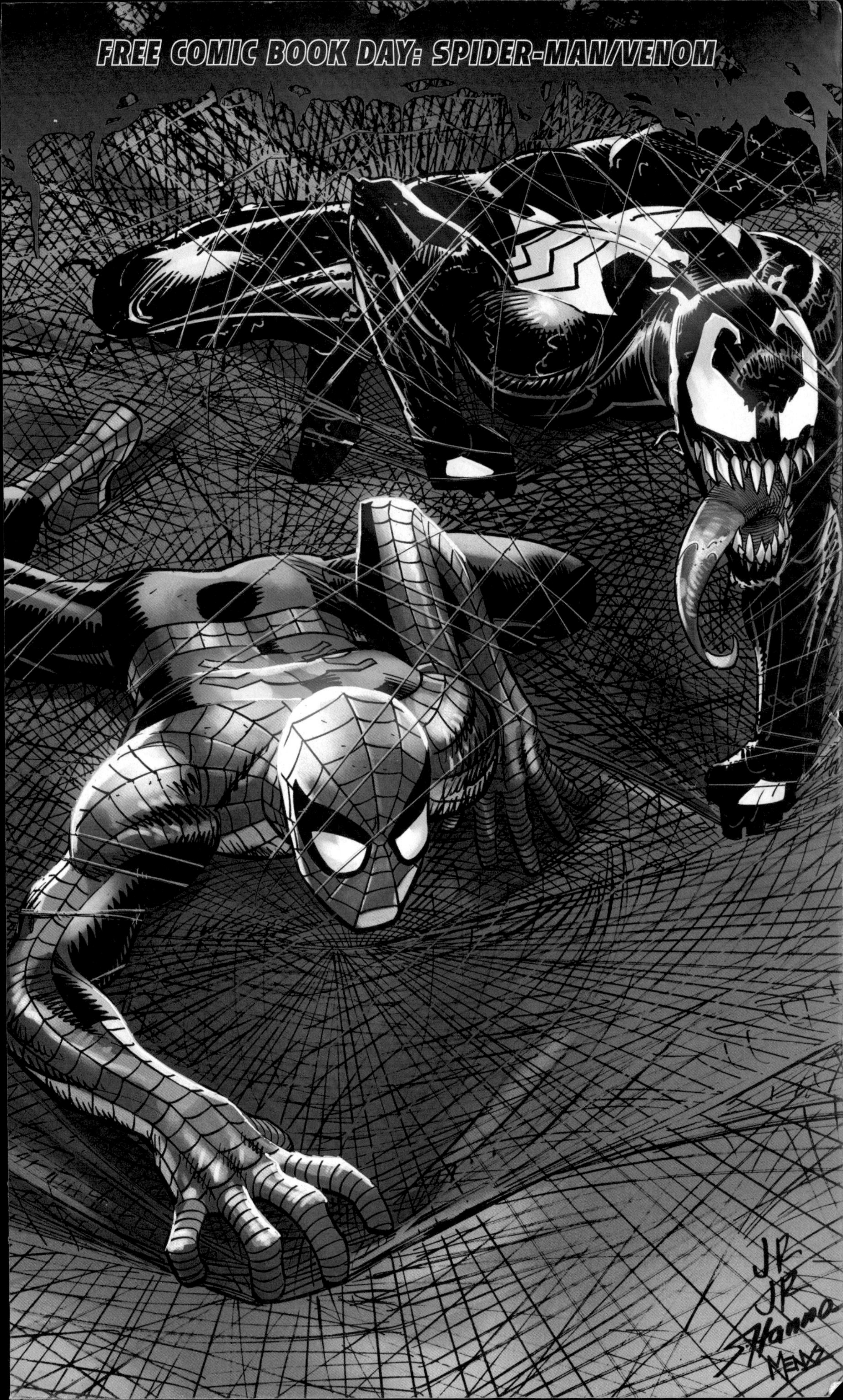
FREE COMIC BOOK DAY: SPIDER-MAN/VENOM

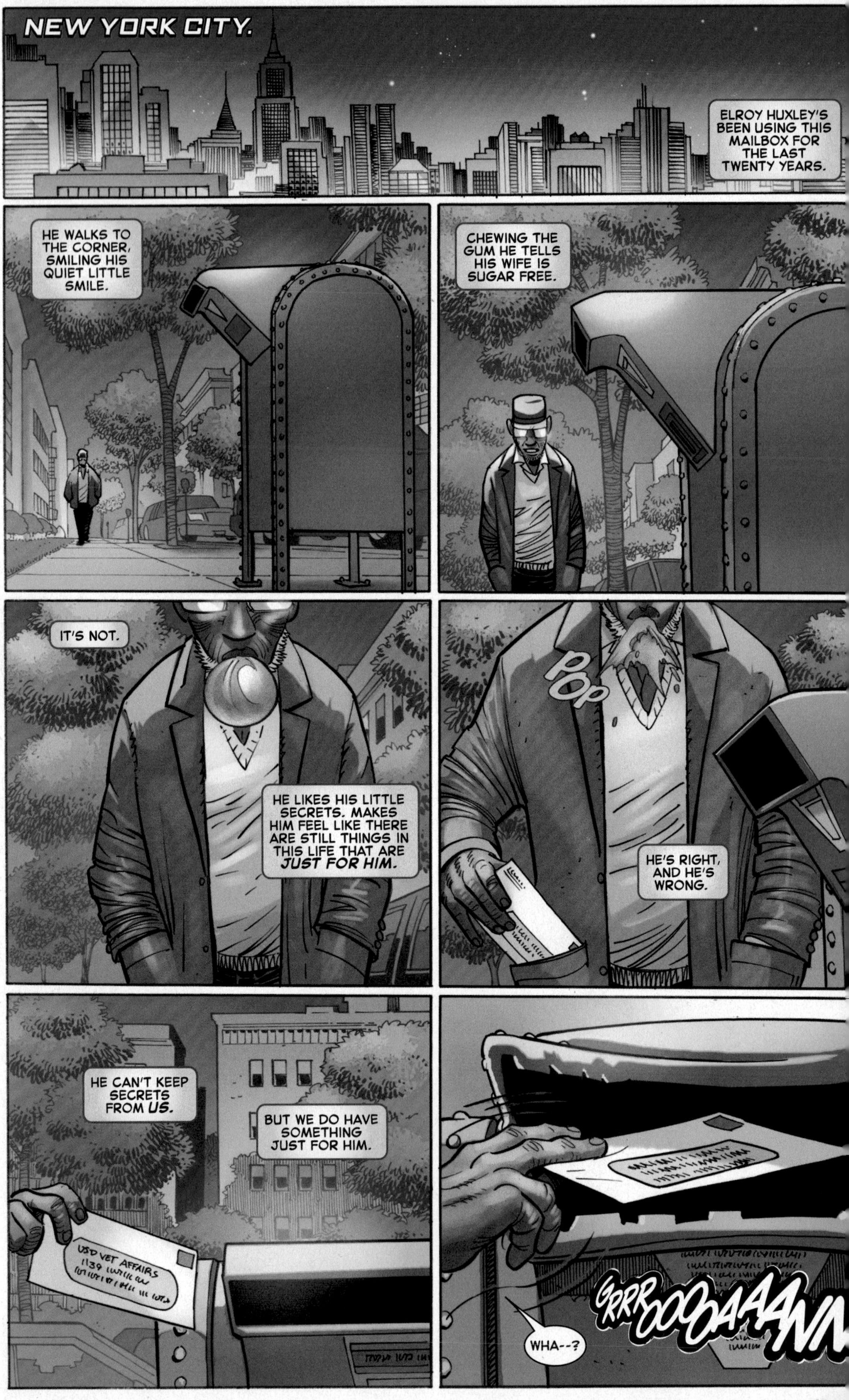

NEW YORK CITY.
ELROY HUXLEY'S BEEN USING THIS MAILBOX FOR THE LAST TWENTY YEARS.
HE WALKS TO THE CORNER, SMILING HIS QUIET LITTLE SMILE.
CHEWING THE GUM HE TELLS HIS WIFE IS SUGAR FREE.
IT'S NOT.
HE LIKES HIS LITTLE SECRETS. MAKES HIM FEEL LIKE THERE ARE STILL THINGS IN THIS LIFE THAT ARE JUST FOR HIM.
POP
HE'S RIGHT, AND HE'S WRONG.
HE CAN'T KEEP SECRETS FROM US.
BUT WE DO HAVE SOMETHING JUST FOR HIM.
USD VET AFFAIRS
WHA--?
GRRROOOAAAW

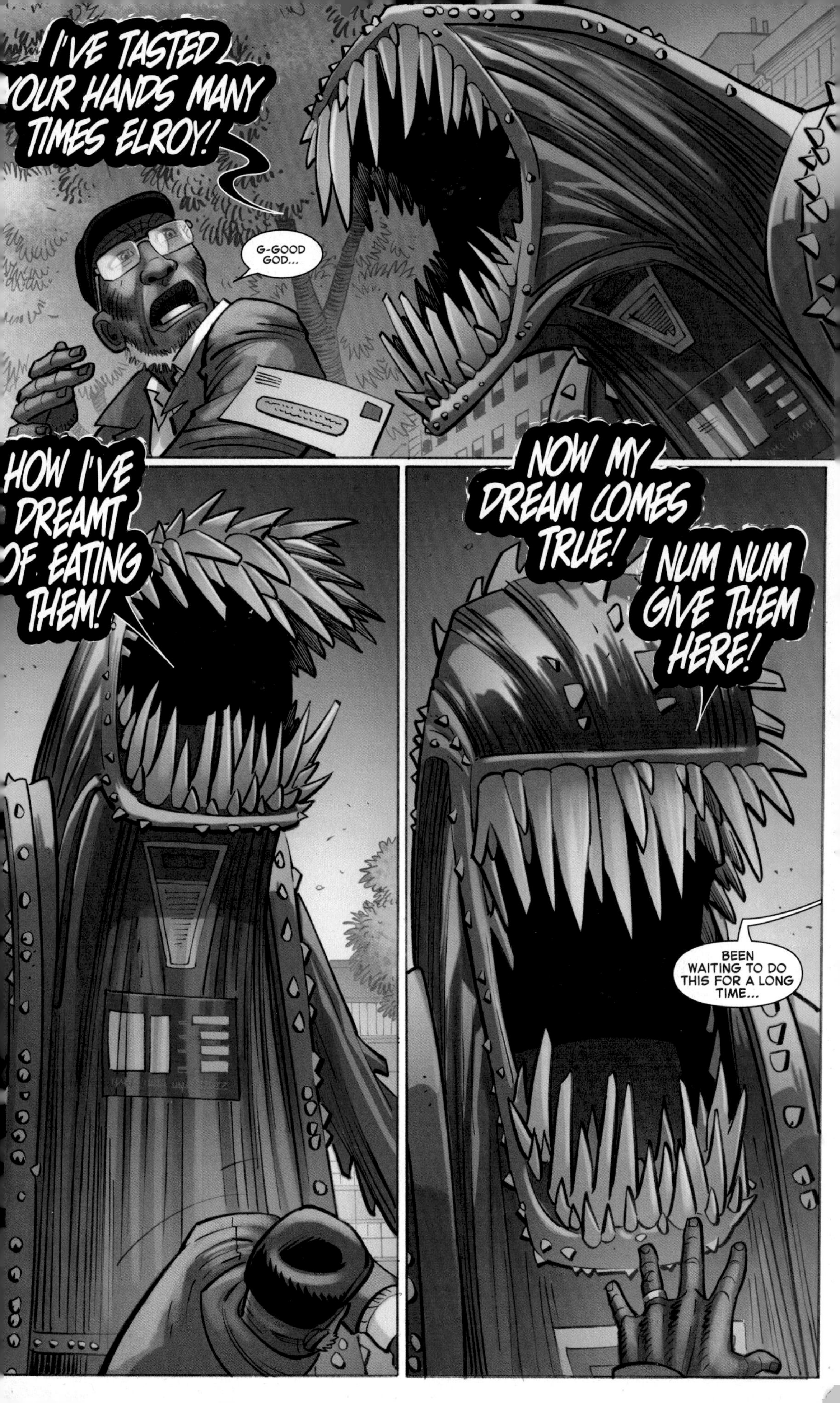
I'VE TASTED YOUR HANDS MANY TIMES ELROY!
G-GOOD GOD...
HOW I'VE DREAMT OF EATING THEM!
NOW MY DREAM COMES TRUE!
NUM NUM GIVE THEM HERE!
BEEN WAITING TO DO THIS FOR A LONG TIME...

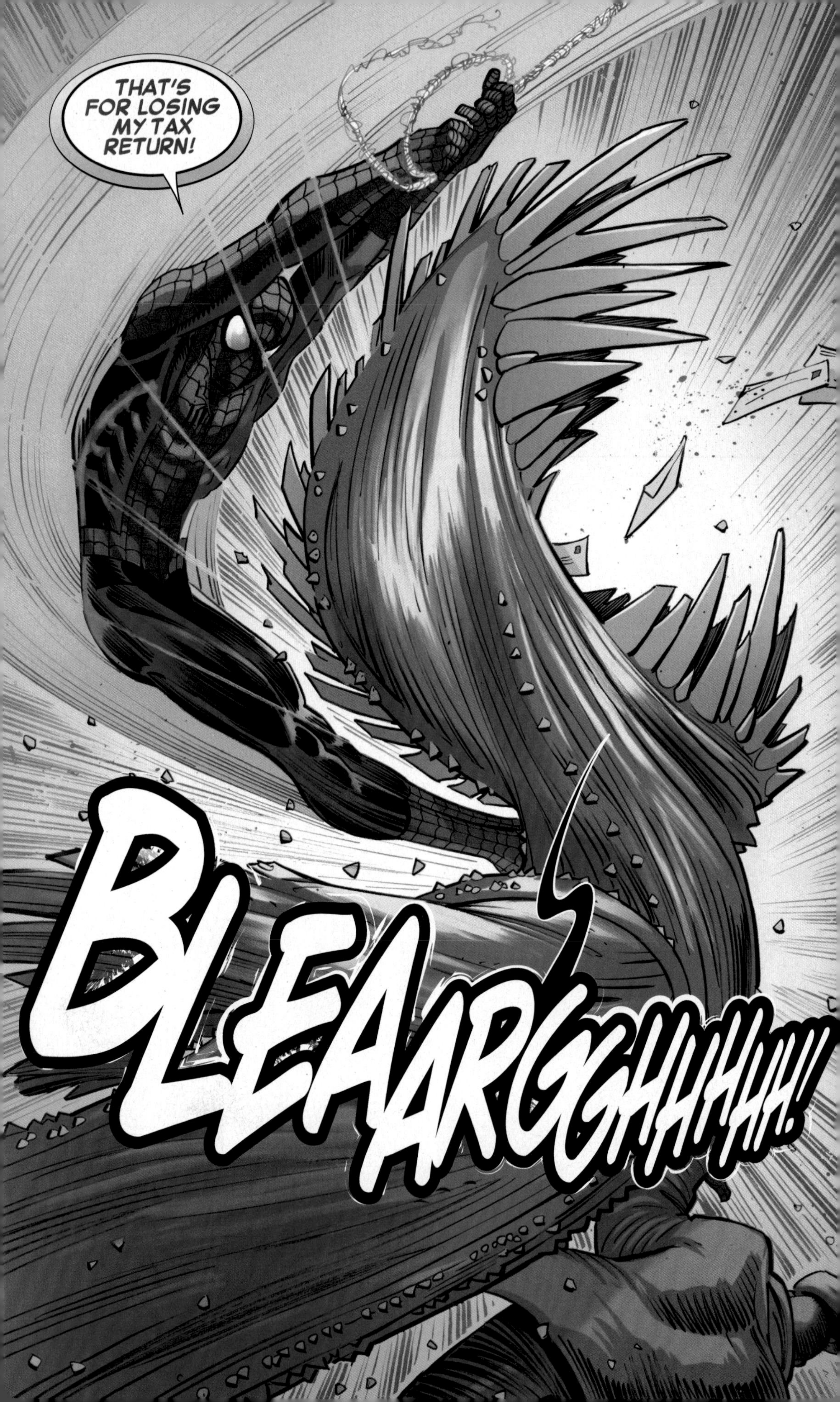
THAT'S FOR LOSING MY TAX RETURN!
BLEAARGGHHHHH!!

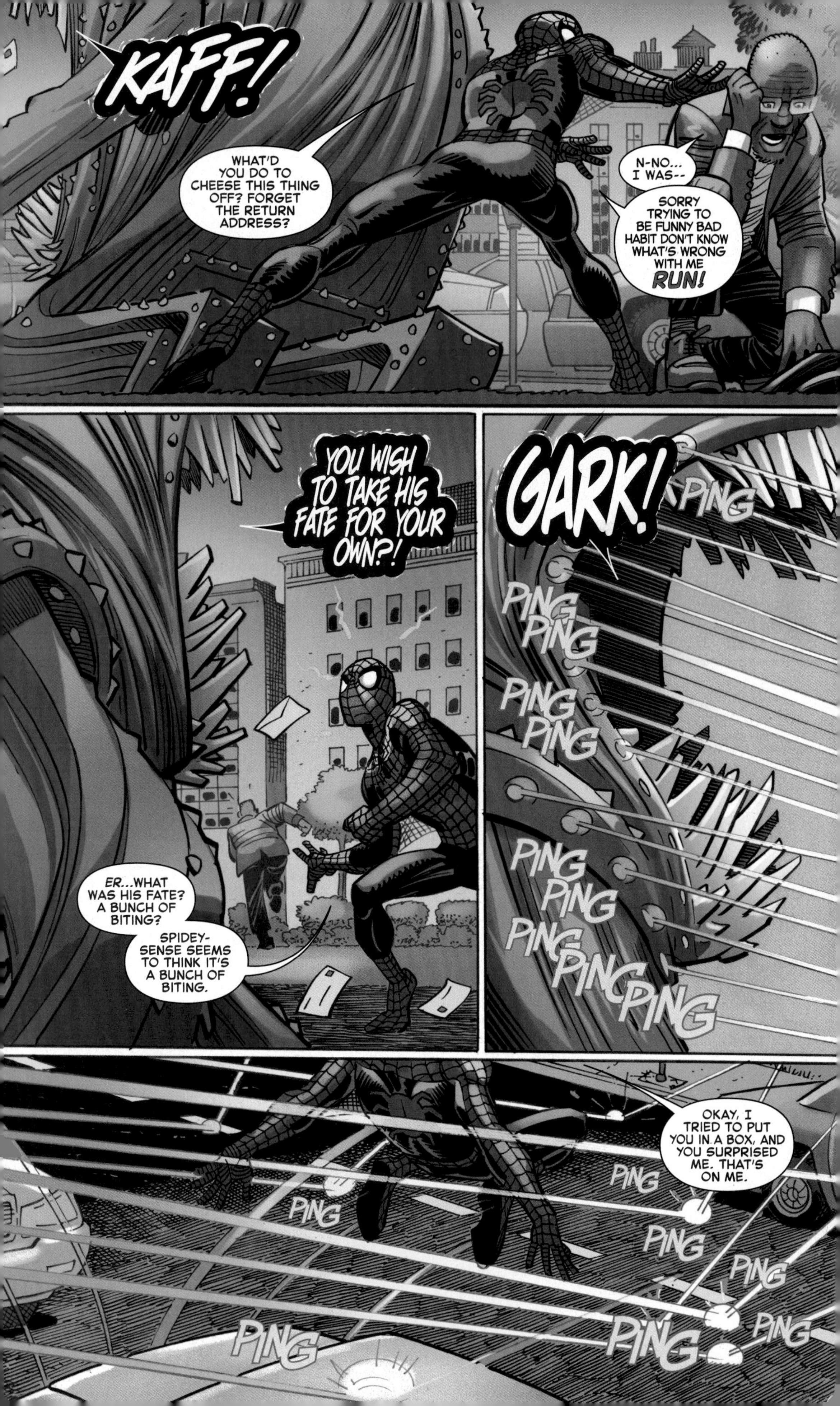
KAFF!
WHAT'D YOU DO TO CHEESE THIS THING OFF? FORGET THE RETURN ADDRESS?
N-NO... I WAS--
SORRY TRYING TO BE FUNNY BAD HABIT DON'T KNOW WHAT'S WRONG WITH ME RUN!
YOU WISH TO TAKE HIS FATE FOR YOUR OWN?!
ER...WHAT WAS HIS FATE? A BUNCH OF BITING?
SPIDEY-SENSE SEEMS TO THINK IT'S A BUNCH OF BITING.
GARK!
PING
PING PING
PING PING
PING PING PING PING PING
OKAY, I TRIED TO PUT YOU IN A BOX, AND YOU SURPRISED ME. THAT'S ON ME.
PING PING PING PING PING PING PING

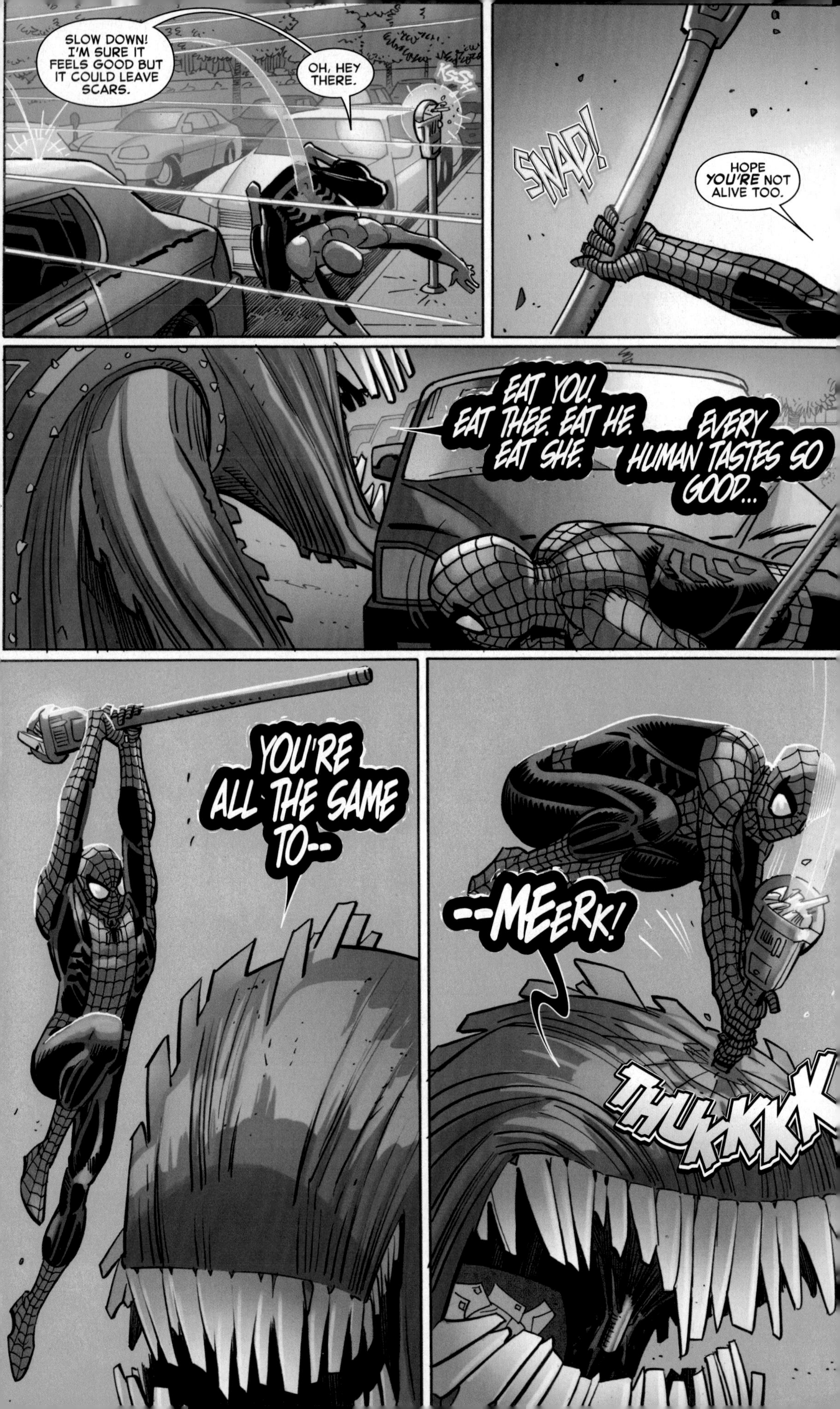
SLOW DOWN! I'M SURE IT FEELS GOOD BUT IT COULD LEAVE SCARS.
OH, HEY THERE.
KSSH
SNAP!
HOPE YOU'RE NOT ALIVE TOO.
EAT YOU. EAT THEE. EAT HE. EAT SHE.
EVERY HUMAN TASTES SO GOOD...
YOU'RE ALL THE SAME TO--
--MEERK!
THUKKKK

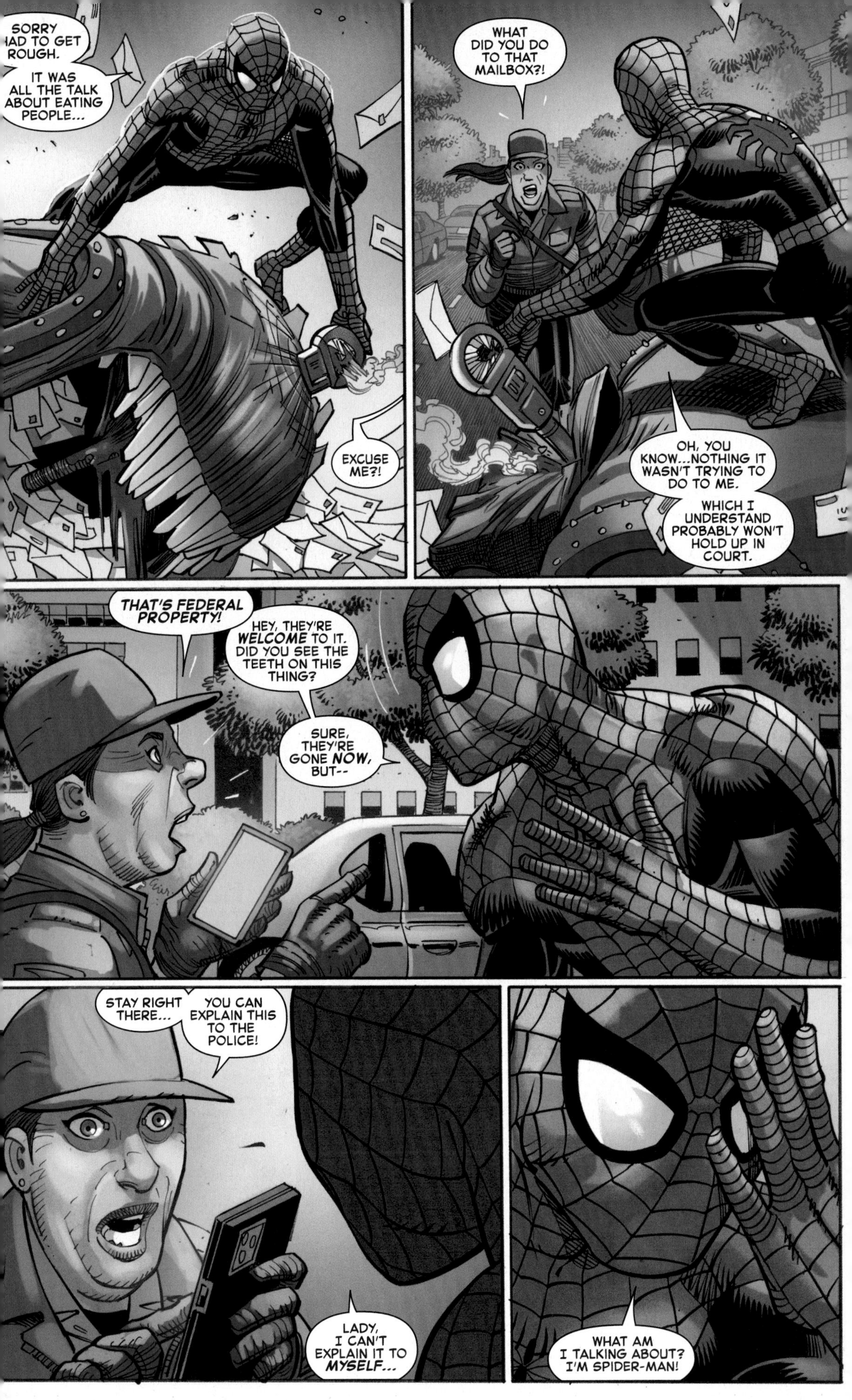
SORRY
IAD TO GET ROUGH.
IT WAS ALL THE TALK ABOUT EATING PEOPLE...
EXCUSE ME?!
WHAT DID YOU DO TO THAT MAILBOX?!
OH, YOU KNOW...NOTHING IT WASN'T TRYING TO DO TO ME.
WHICH I UNDERSTAND PROBABLY WON'T HOLD UP IN COURT.
THAT'S FEDERAL PROPERTY!
HEY, THEY'RE WELCOME TO IT. DID YOU SEE THE TEETH ON THIS THING?
SURE, THEY'RE GONE NOW, BUT--
STAY RIGHT THERE...
YOU CAN EXPLAIN THIS TO THE POLICE!
LADY, I CAN'T EXPLAIN IT TO MYSELF...
WHAT AM I TALKING ABOUT? I'M SPIDER-MAN!

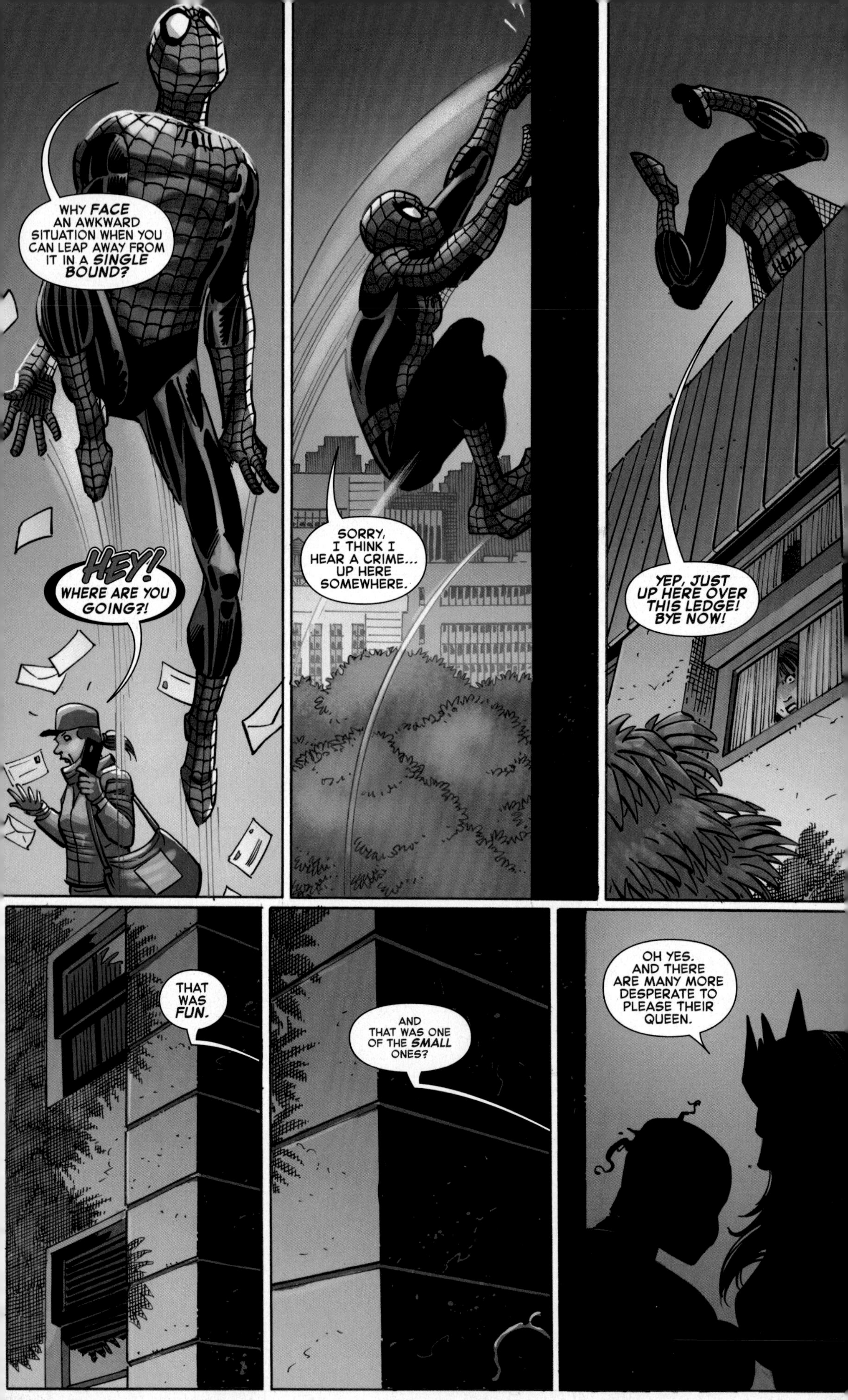
WHY FACE AN AWKWARD SITUATION WHEN YOU CAN LEAP AWAY FROM IT IN A SINGLE BOUND?
HEY! WHERE ARE YOU GOING?!
SORRY, I THINK I HEAR A CRIME... UP HERE SOMEWHERE.
YEP, JUST UP HERE OVER THIS LEDGE! BYE NOW!
THAT WAS FUN.
AND THAT WAS ONE OF THE SMALL ONES?
OH YES. AND THERE ARE MANY MORE DESPERATE TO PLEASE THEIR QUEEN.

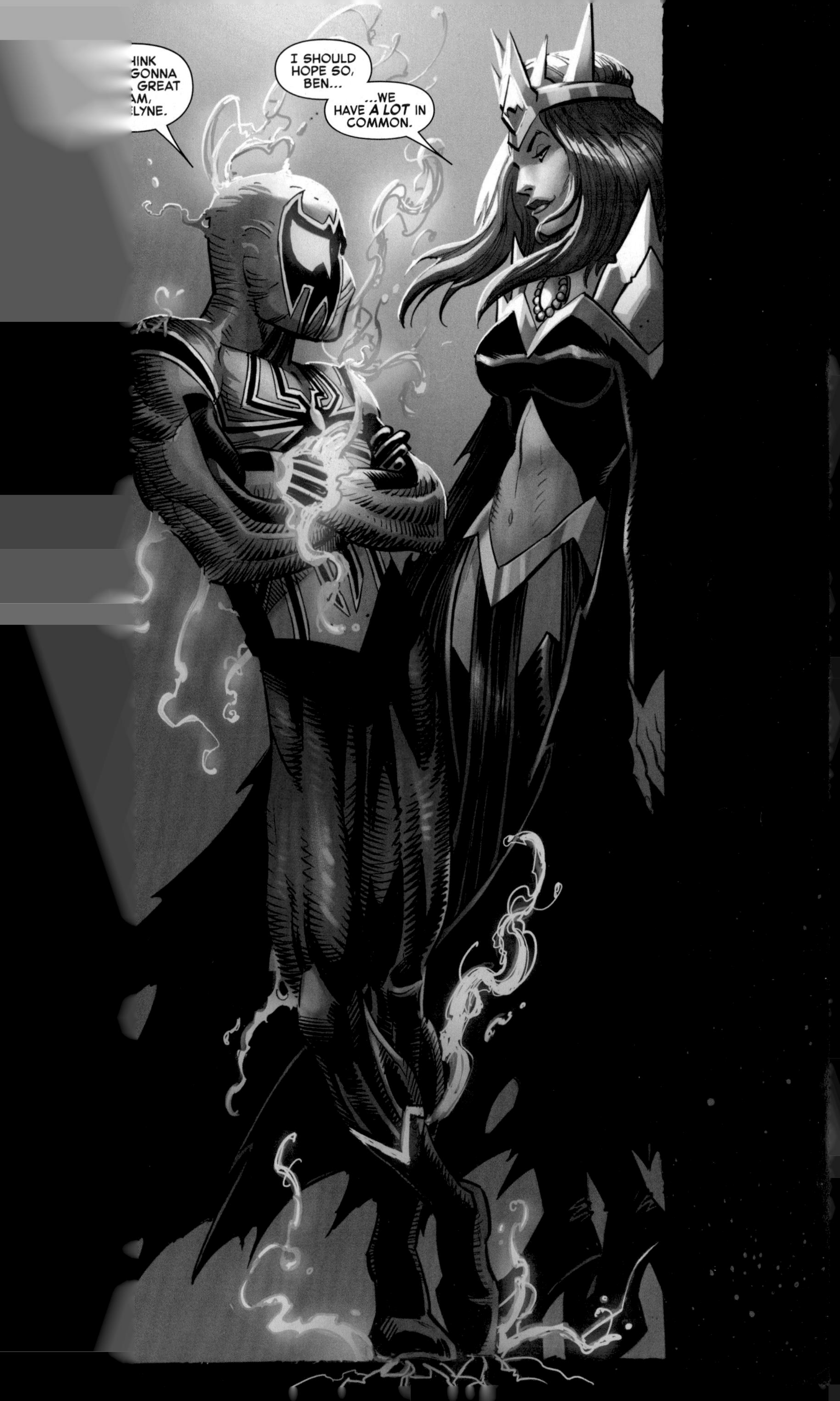
HINK GONNA GREAT AM, ELYNE.
I SHOULD HOPE SO, BEN...
...WE HAVE A LOT IN COMMON.

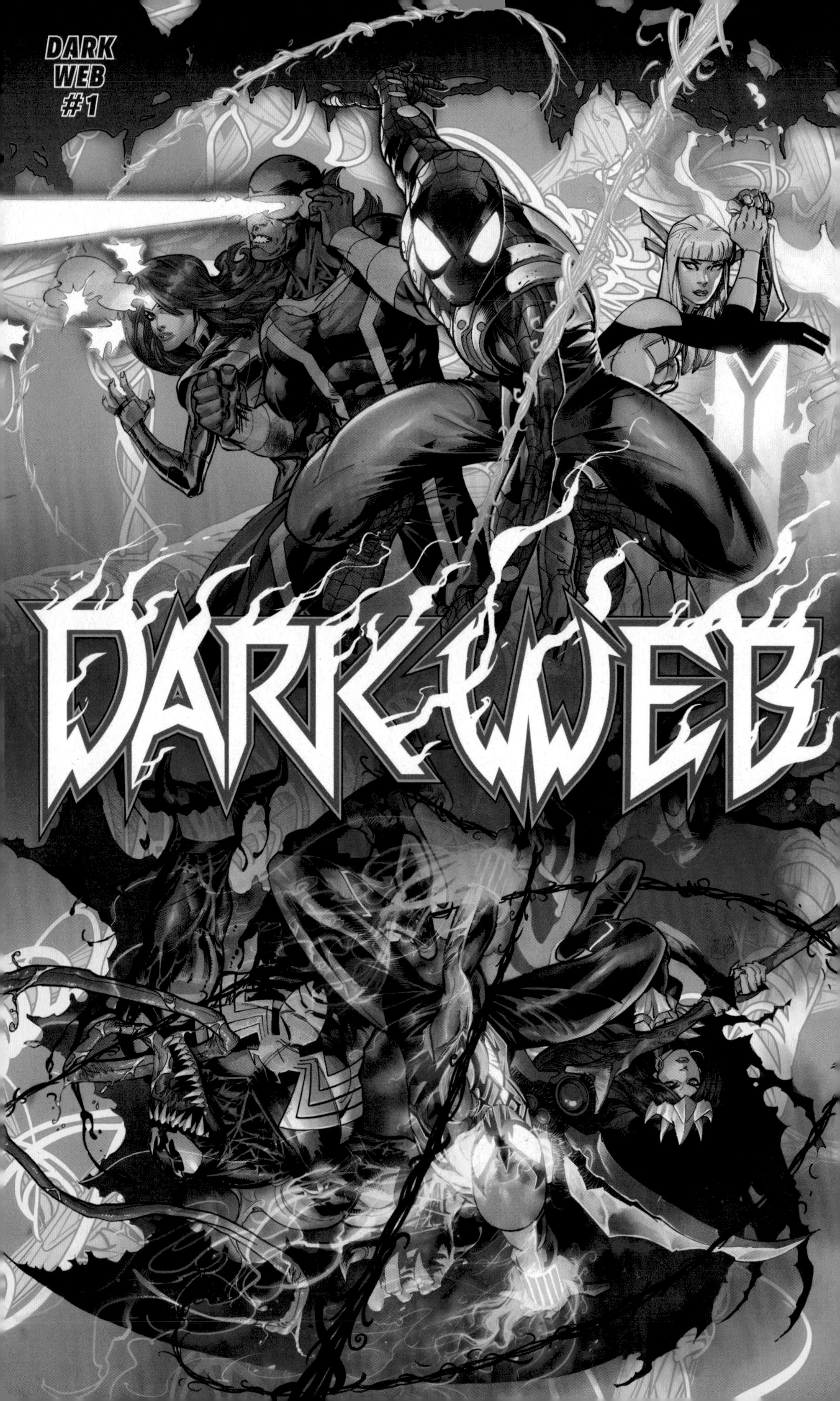

DARK WEB #1
DARK WEB

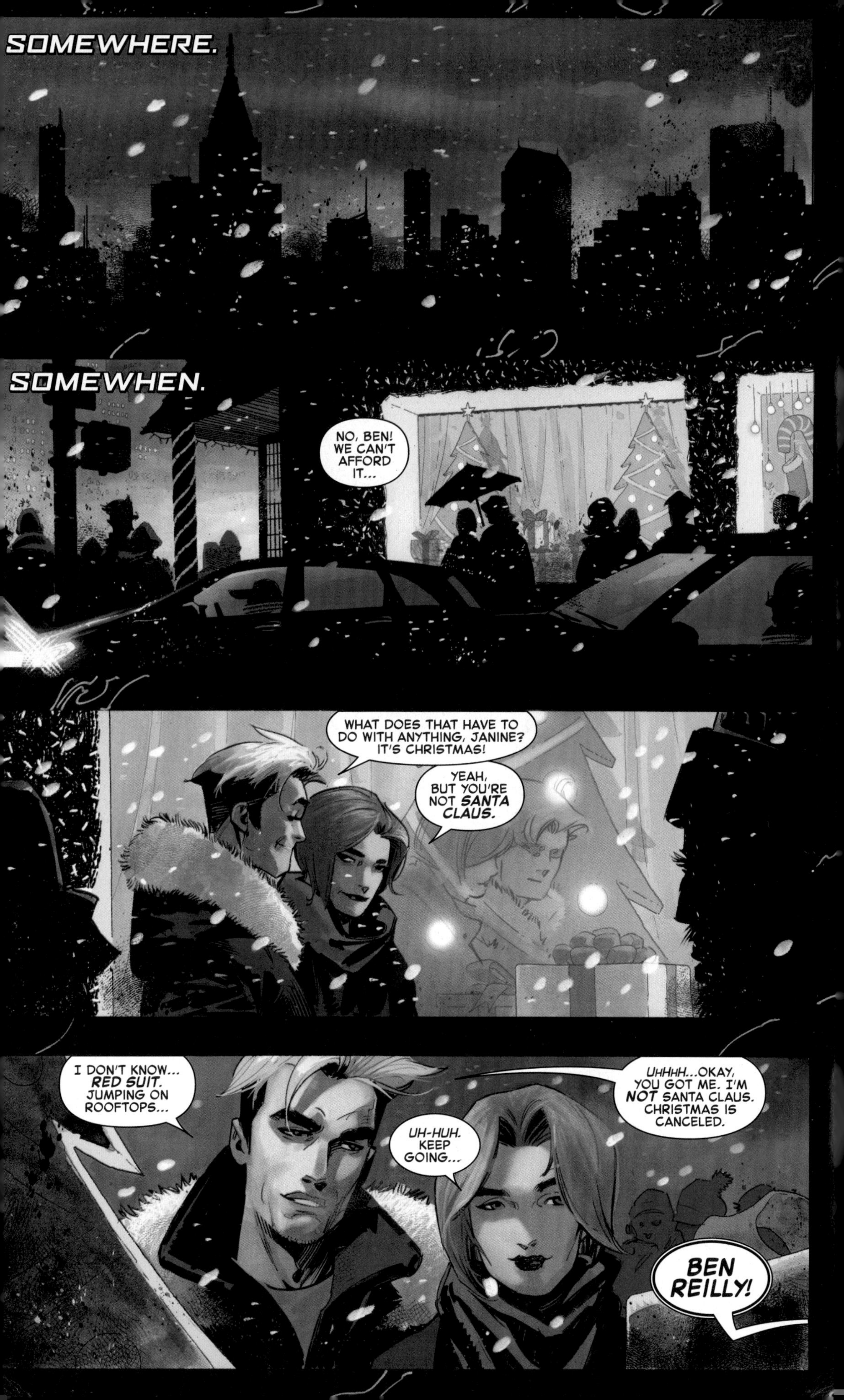
SOMEWHERE.
SOMEWHEN.
NO, BEN! WE CAN'T AFFORD IT...
WHAT DOES THAT HAVE TO DO WITH ANYTHING, JANINE? IT'S CHRISTMAS!
YEAH, BUT YOU'RE NOT SANTA CLAUS.
I DON'T KNOW... RED SUIT. JUMPING ON ROOFTOPS...
UH-HUH. KEEP GOING...
UHHHH...OKAY, YOU GOT ME. I'M NOT SANTA CLAUS. CHRISTMAS IS CANCELED.
BEN REILLY!

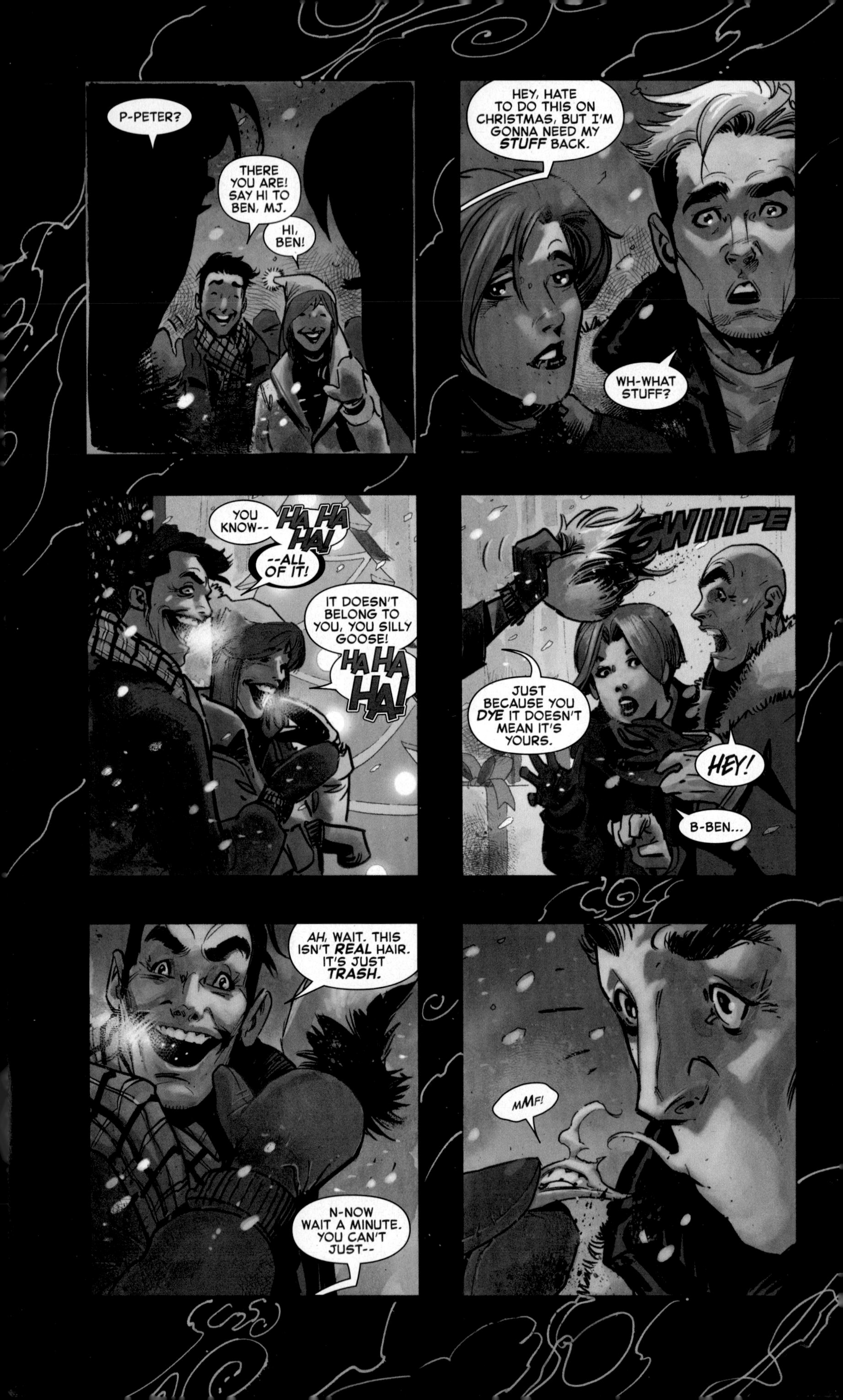
P-PETER?
THERE YOU ARE! SAY HI TO BEN, MJ.
HI, BEN!
HEY, HATE TO DO THIS ON CHRISTMAS, BUT I'M GONNA NEED MY STUFF BACK.
WH-WHAT STUFF?
YOU KNOW--
HA HA HA!
--ALL OF IT!
IT DOESN'T BELONG TO YOU, YOU SILLY GOOSE!
HA HA HA!
SWIIIPE
JUST BECAUSE YOU DYE IT DOESN'T MEAN IT'S YOURS.
HEY!
B-BEN...
AH, WAIT. THIS ISN'T REAL HAIR. IT'S JUST TRASH.
N-NOW WAIT A MINUTE. YOU CAN'T JUST--
MMF!

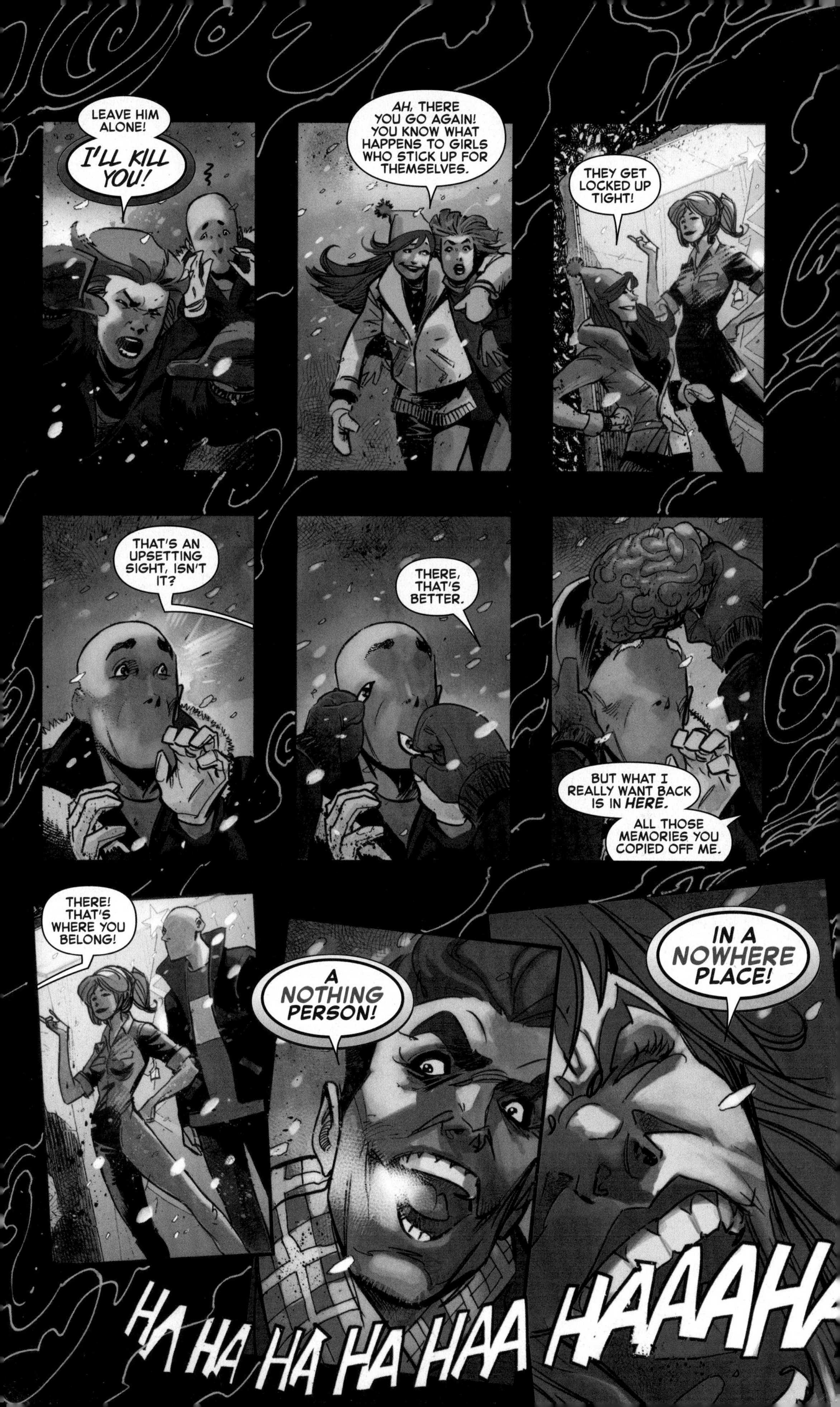

LEAVE HIM ALONE!
I'LL KILL YOU!
AH, THERE YOU GO AGAIN! YOU KNOW WHAT HAPPENS TO GIRLS WHO STICK UP FOR THEMSELVES.
THEY GET LOCKED UP TIGHT!
THAT'S AN UPSETTING SIGHT, ISN'T IT?
THERE, THAT'S BETTER.
BUT WHAT I REALLY WANT BACK IS IN HERE.
ALL THOSE MEMORIES YOU COPIED OFF ME.
THERE! THAT'S WHERE YOU BELONG!
A NOTHING PERSON!
IN A NOWHERE PLACE!
HA HA HA HA HA HAA HAAAHA

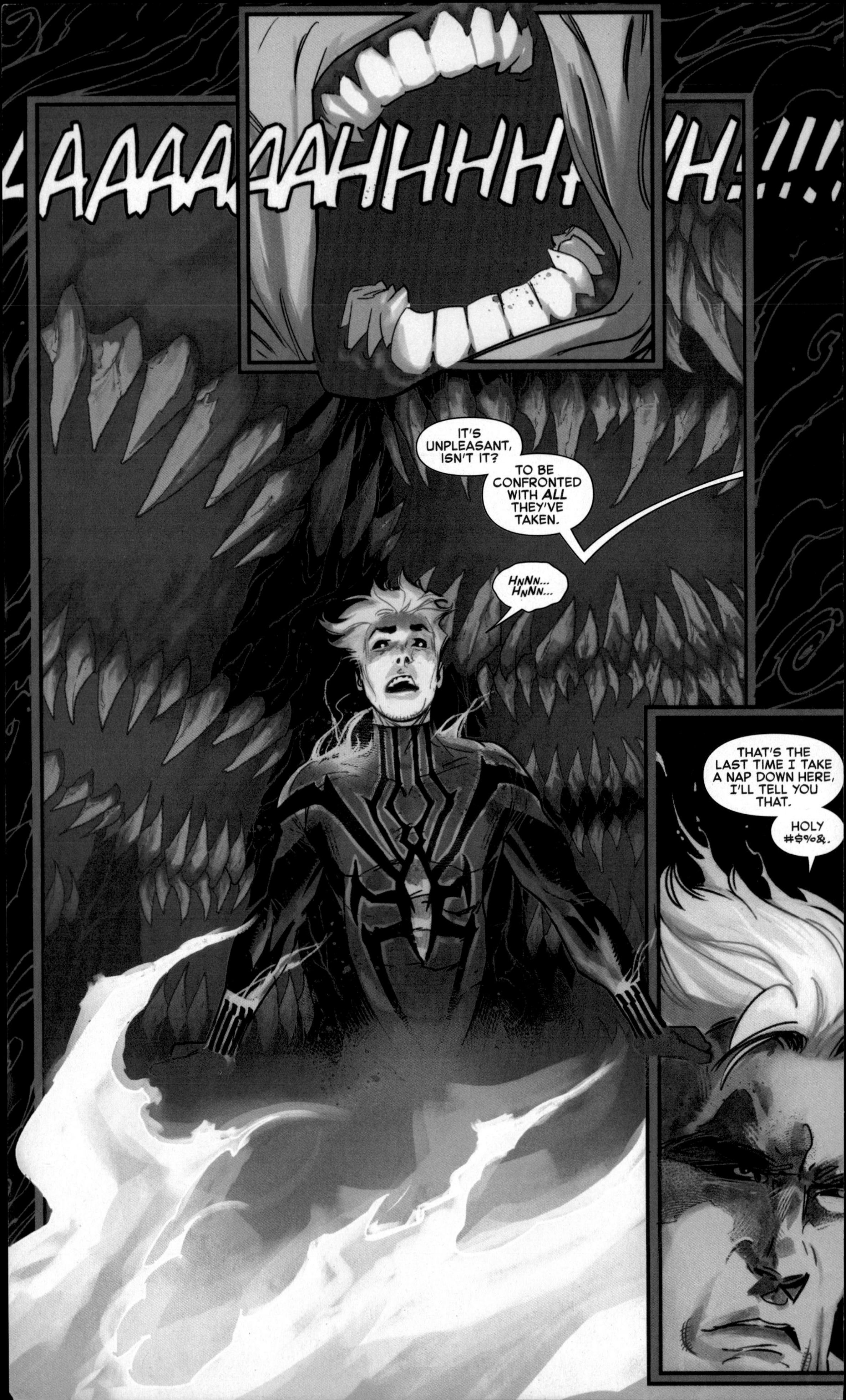

AAAAAAHHHHHHH!!!
IT'S UNPLEASANT, ISN'T IT?
TO BE CONFRONTED WITH *ALL* THEY'VE TAKEN.
HNNN... HNNN...
THAT'S THE LAST TIME I TAKE A NAP DOWN HERE, I'LL TELL YOU THAT.
HOLY #$%&.

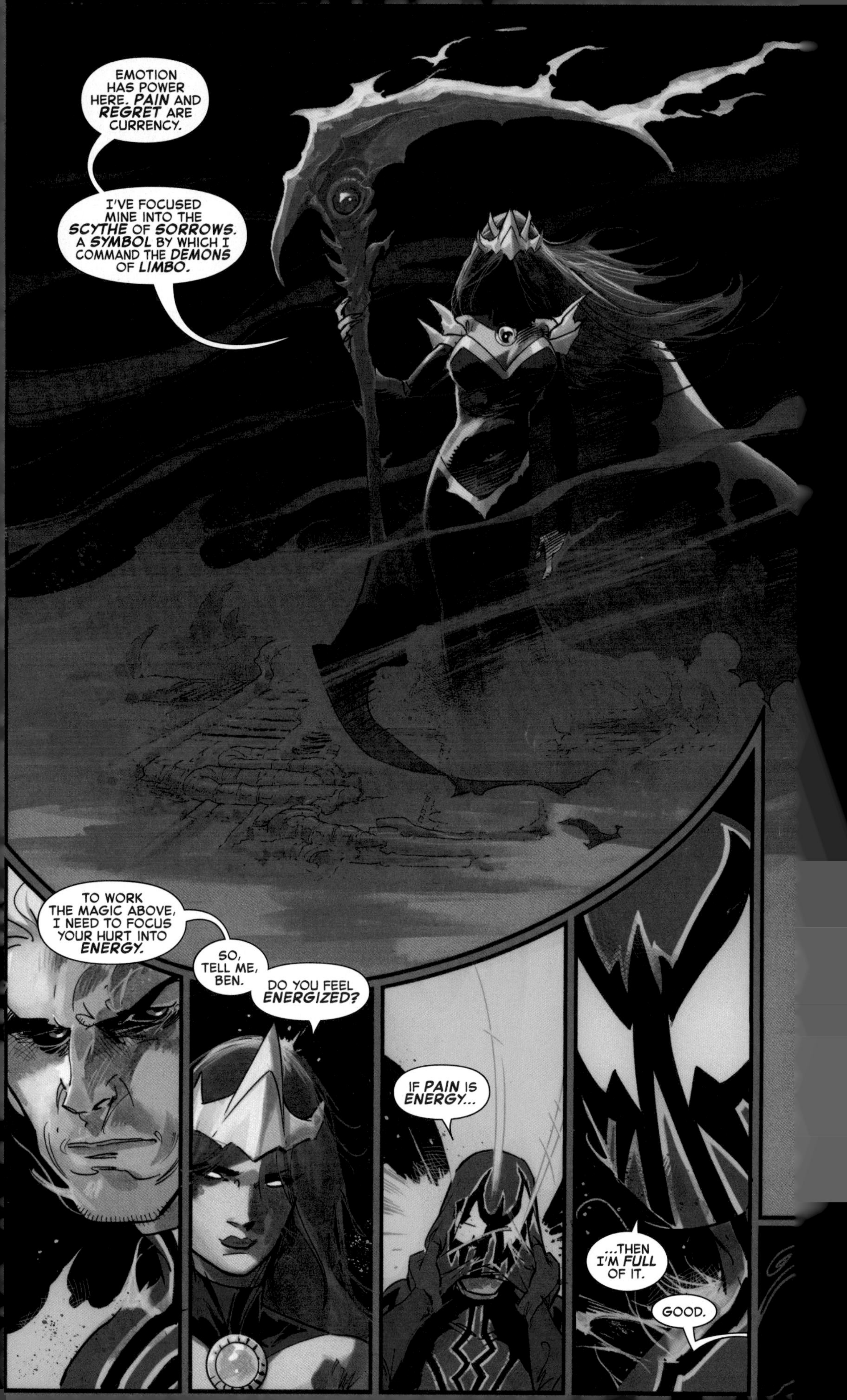
EMOTION HAS POWER HERE. PAIN AND REGRET ARE CURRENCY.
I'VE FOCUSED MINE INTO THE SCYTHE OF SORROWS. A SYMBOL BY WHICH I COMMAND THE DEMONS OF LIMBO.
TO WORK THE MAGIC ABOVE, I NEED TO FOCUS YOUR HURT INTO ENERGY.
SO, TELL ME, BEN.
DO YOU FEEL ENERGIZED?
IF PAIN IS ENERGY...
...THEN I'M FULL OF IT.
GOOD.

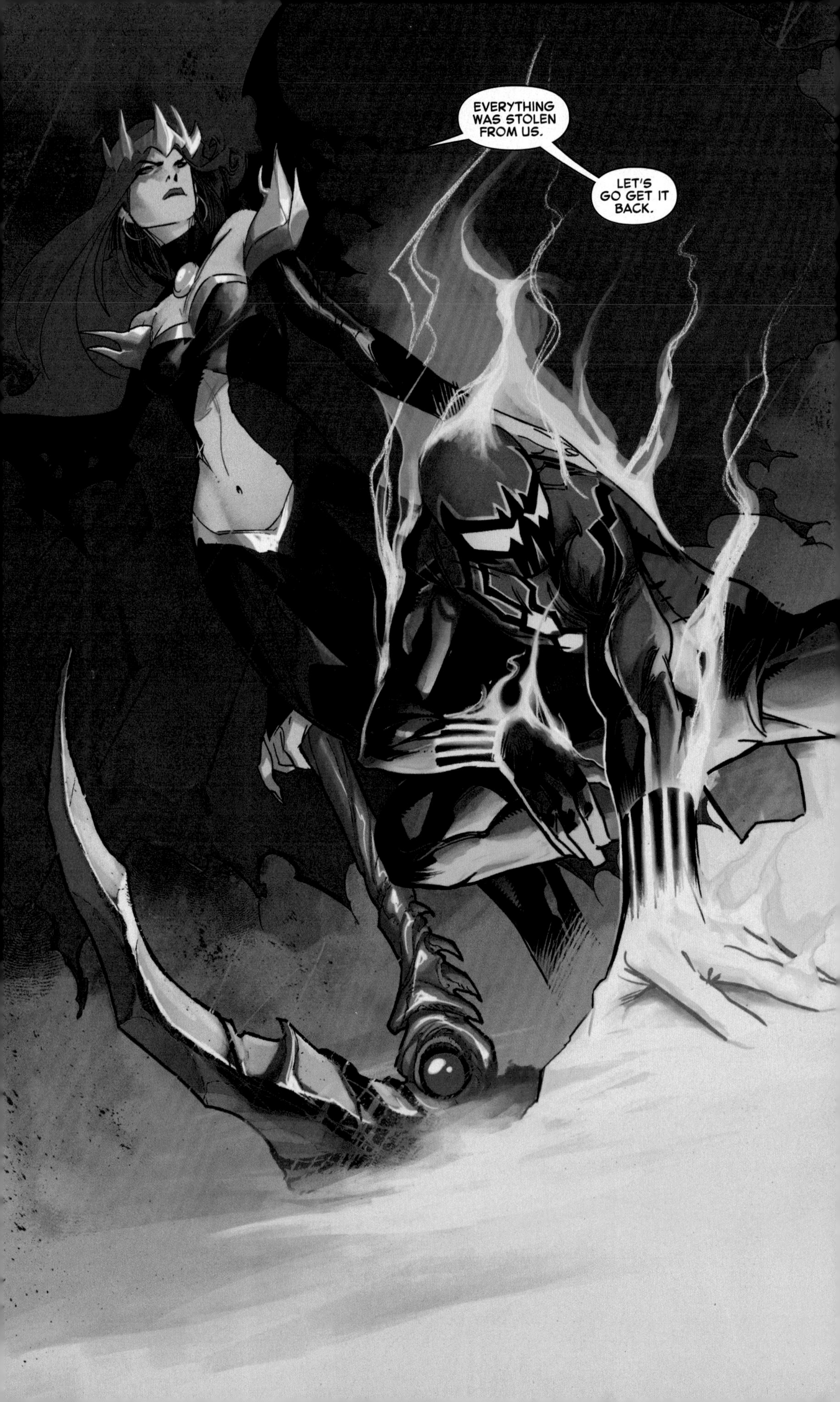
EVERYTHING WAS STOLEN FROM US.
LET'S GO GET IT BACK.

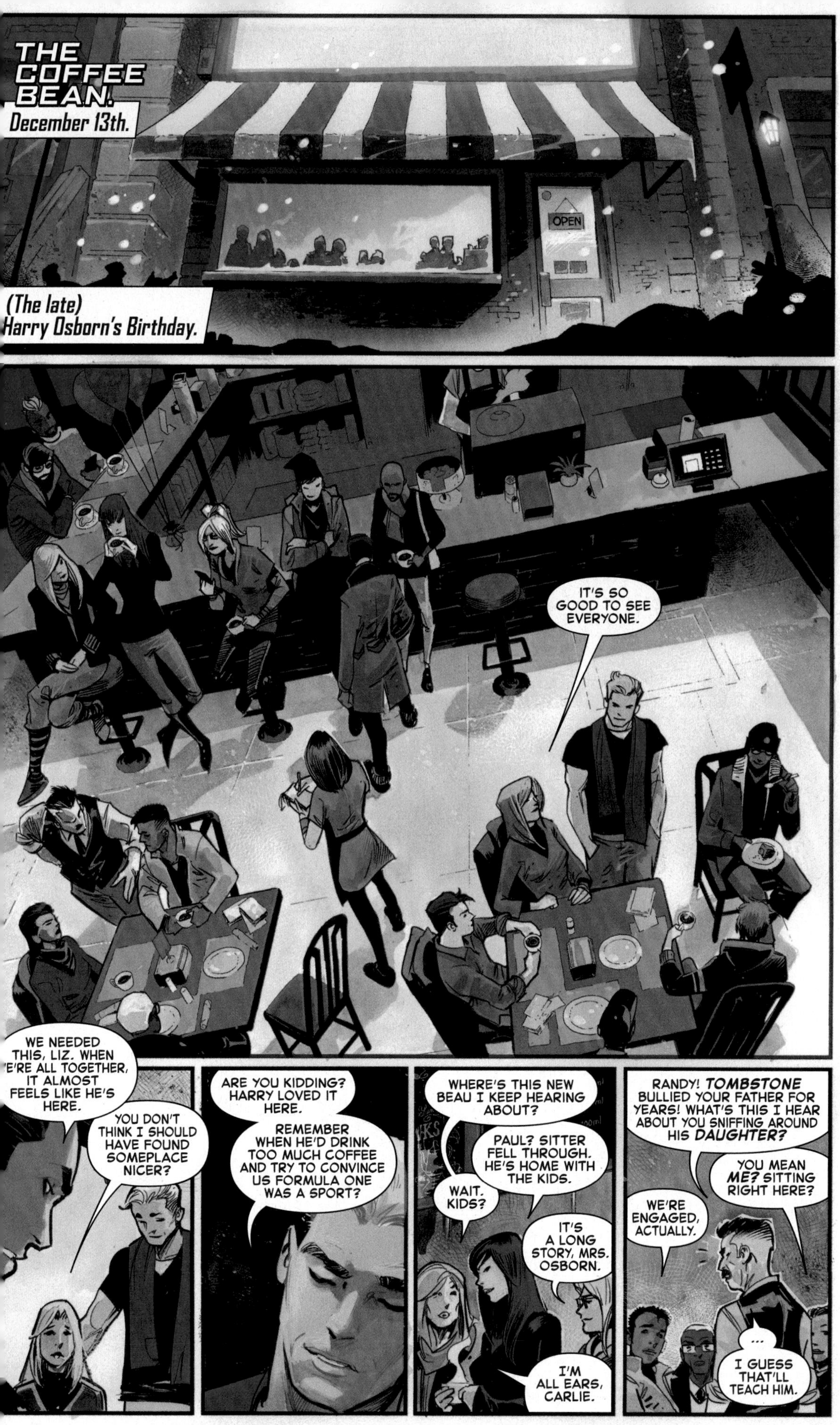

THE COFFEE BEAN.
December 13th.
(The late) Harry Osborn's Birthday.
IT'S SO GOOD TO SEE EVERYONE.
WE NEEDED THIS, LIZ. WHEN WE'RE ALL TOGETHER, IT ALMOST FEELS LIKE HE'S HERE.
YOU DON'T THINK I SHOULD HAVE FOUND SOMEPLACE NICER?
ARE YOU KIDDING? HARRY LOVED IT HERE.
REMEMBER WHEN HE'D DRINK TOO MUCH COFFEE AND TRY TO CONVINCE US FORMULA ONE WAS A SPORT?
WHERE'S THIS NEW BEAU I KEEP HEARING ABOUT?
PAUL? SITTER FELL THROUGH. HE'S HOME WITH THE KIDS.
WAIT. KIDS?
IT'S A LONG STORY, MRS. OSBORN.
I'M ALL EARS, CARLIE.
RANDY! TOMBSTONE BULLIED YOUR FATHER FOR YEARS! WHAT'S THIS I HEAR ABOUT YOU SNIFFING AROUND HIS DAUGHTER?
YOU MEAN ME? SITTING RIGHT HERE?
WE'RE ENGAGED, ACTUALLY.
...
I GUESS THAT'LL TEACH HIM.

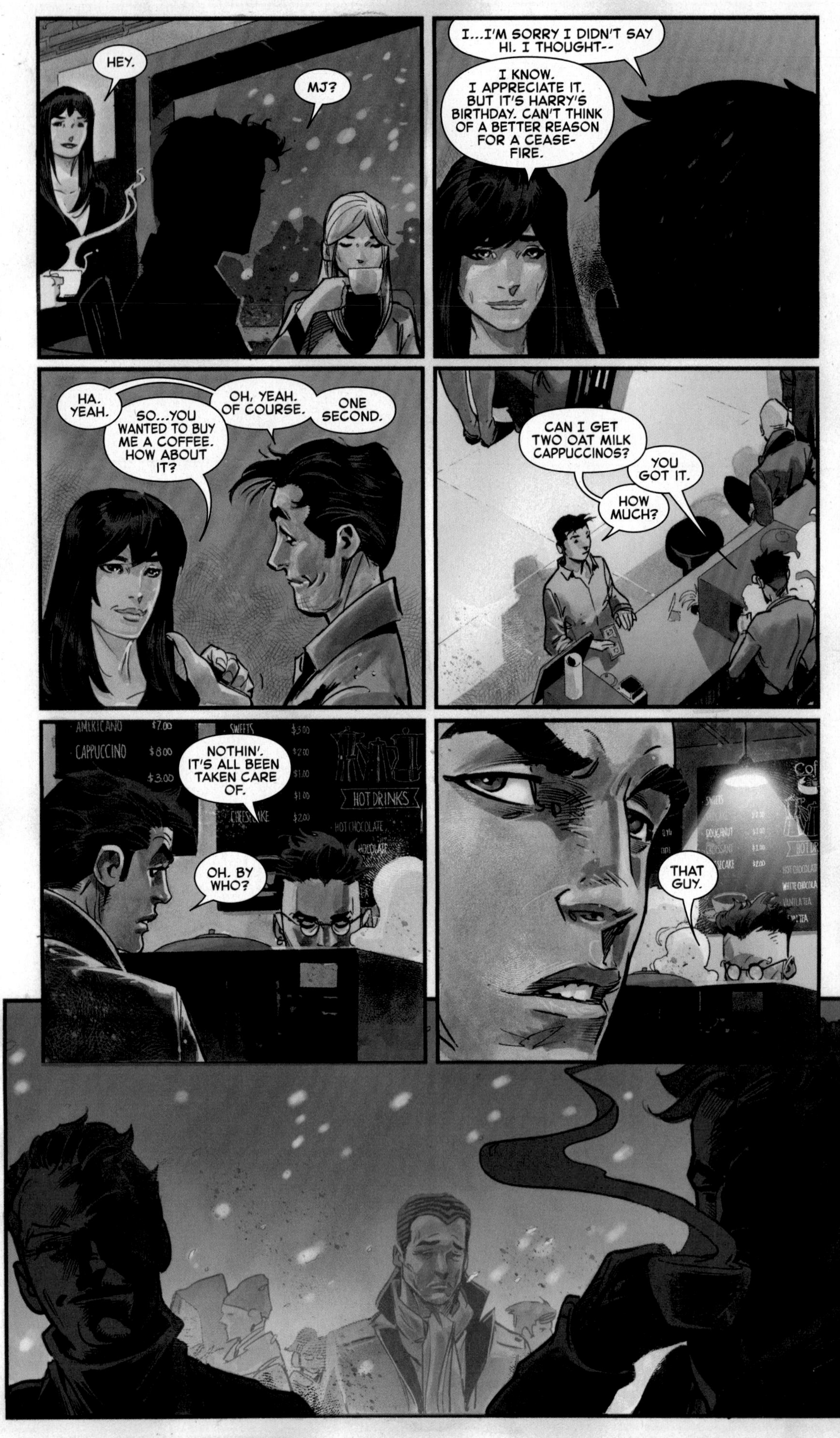
HEY.
MJ?
I...I'M SORRY I DIDN'T SAY HI. I THOUGHT--
I KNOW. I APPRECIATE IT. BUT IT'S HARRY'S BIRTHDAY. CAN'T THINK OF A BETTER REASON FOR A CEASE-FIRE.
HA. YEAH.
SO...YOU WANTED TO BUY ME A COFFEE. HOW ABOUT IT?
OH, YEAH. OF COURSE.
ONE SECOND.
CAN I GET TWO OAT MILK CAPPUCCINOS?
YOU GOT IT.
HOW MUCH?
AMERICANO $7.00
CAPPUCCINO $8.00
$3.00
SWEETS $3.00
HOT DRINKS
CHEESECAKE $2.00
HOT CHOCOLATE
NOTHIN'. IT'S ALL BEEN TAKEN CARE OF.
OH. BY WHO?
THAT GUY.

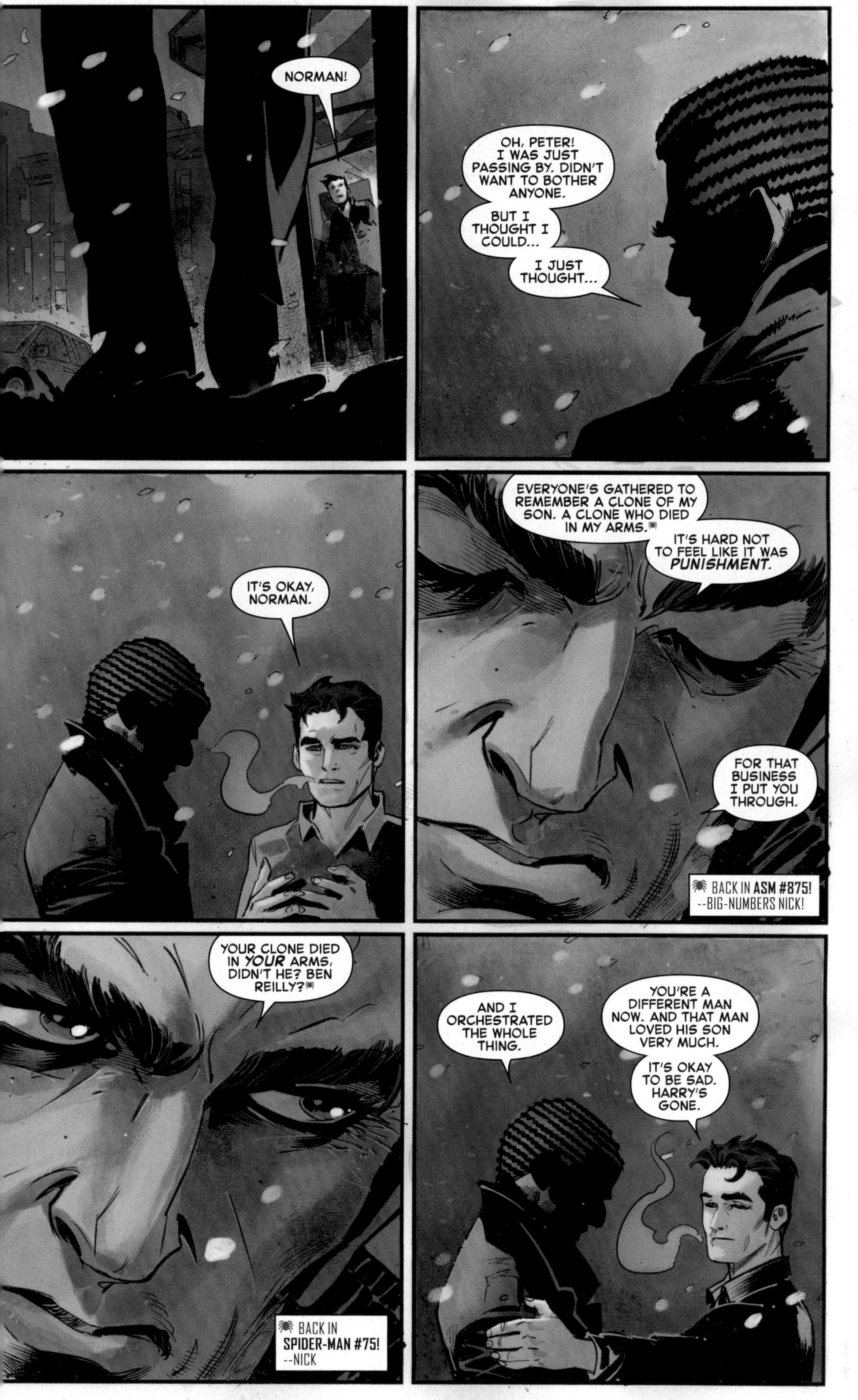

NORMAN!
OH, PETER! I WAS JUST PASSING BY. DIDN'T WANT TO BOTHER ANYONE.
BUT I THOUGHT I COULD...
I JUST THOUGHT...
IT'S OKAY, NORMAN.
EVERYONE'S GATHERED TO REMEMBER A CLONE OF MY SON. A CLONE WHO DIED IN MY ARMS.
IT'S HARD NOT TO FEEL LIKE IT WAS PUNISHMENT.
FOR THAT BUSINESS I PUT YOU THROUGH.
BACK IN ASM #875! --BIG-NUMBERS NICK!
YOUR CLONE DIED IN YOUR ARMS, DIDN'T HE? BEN REILLY?
BACK IN SPIDER-MAN #75! --NICK
AND I ORCHESTRATED THE WHOLE THING.
YOU'RE A DIFFERENT MAN NOW. AND THAT MAN LOVED HIS SON VERY MUCH.
IT'S OKAY TO BE SAD. HARRY'S GONE.

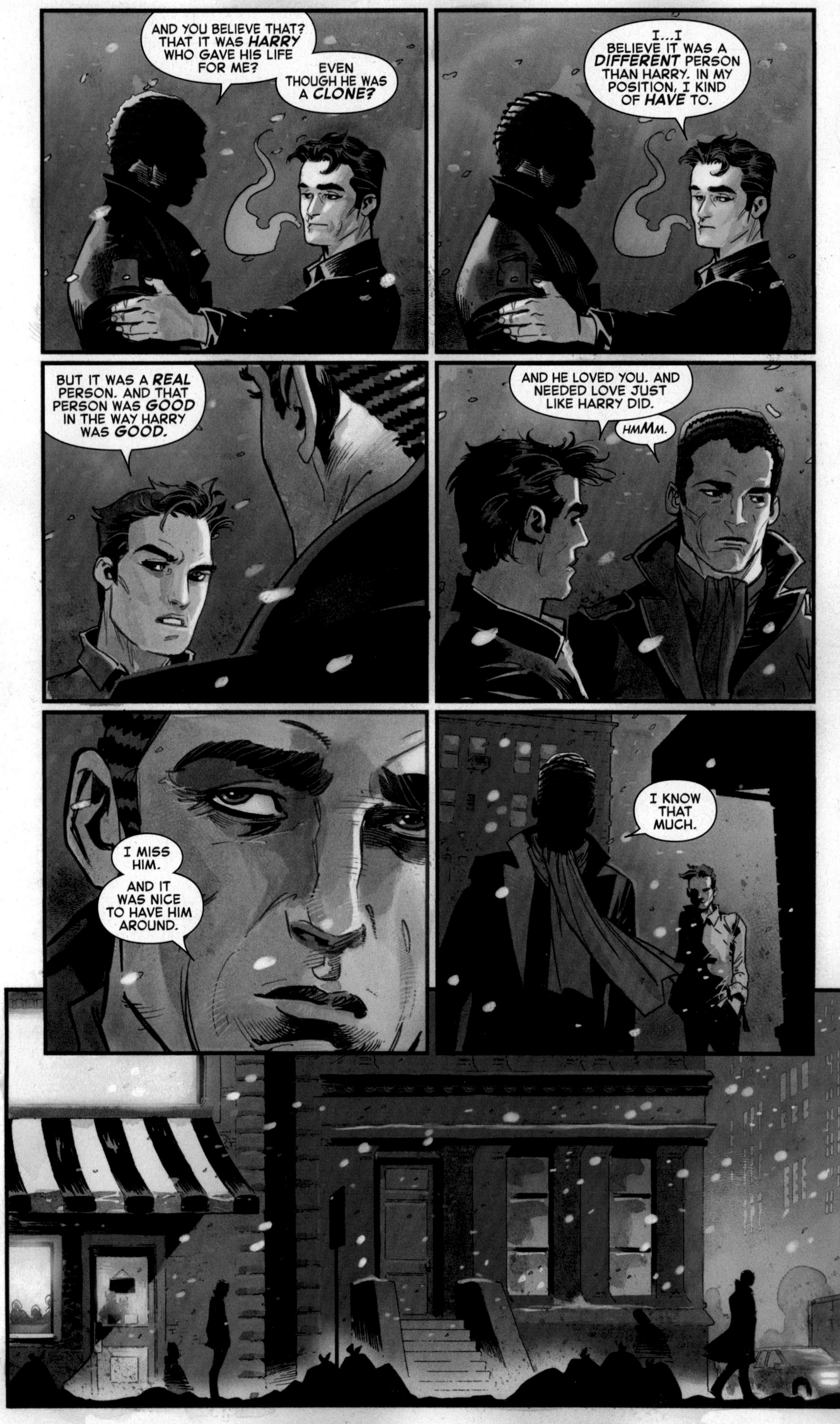

AND YOU BELIEVE THAT? THAT IT WAS HARRY WHO GAVE HIS LIFE FOR ME?
EVEN THOUGH HE WAS A CLONE?
I...I BELIEVE IT WAS A DIFFERENT PERSON THAN HARRY. IN MY POSITION, I KIND OF HAVE TO.
BUT IT WAS A REAL PERSON. AND THAT PERSON WAS GOOD IN THE WAY HARRY WAS GOOD.
AND HE LOVED YOU. AND NEEDED LOVE JUST LIKE HARRY DID.
HMMM.
I MISS HIM.
AND IT WAS NICE TO HAVE HIM AROUND.
I KNOW THAT MUCH.

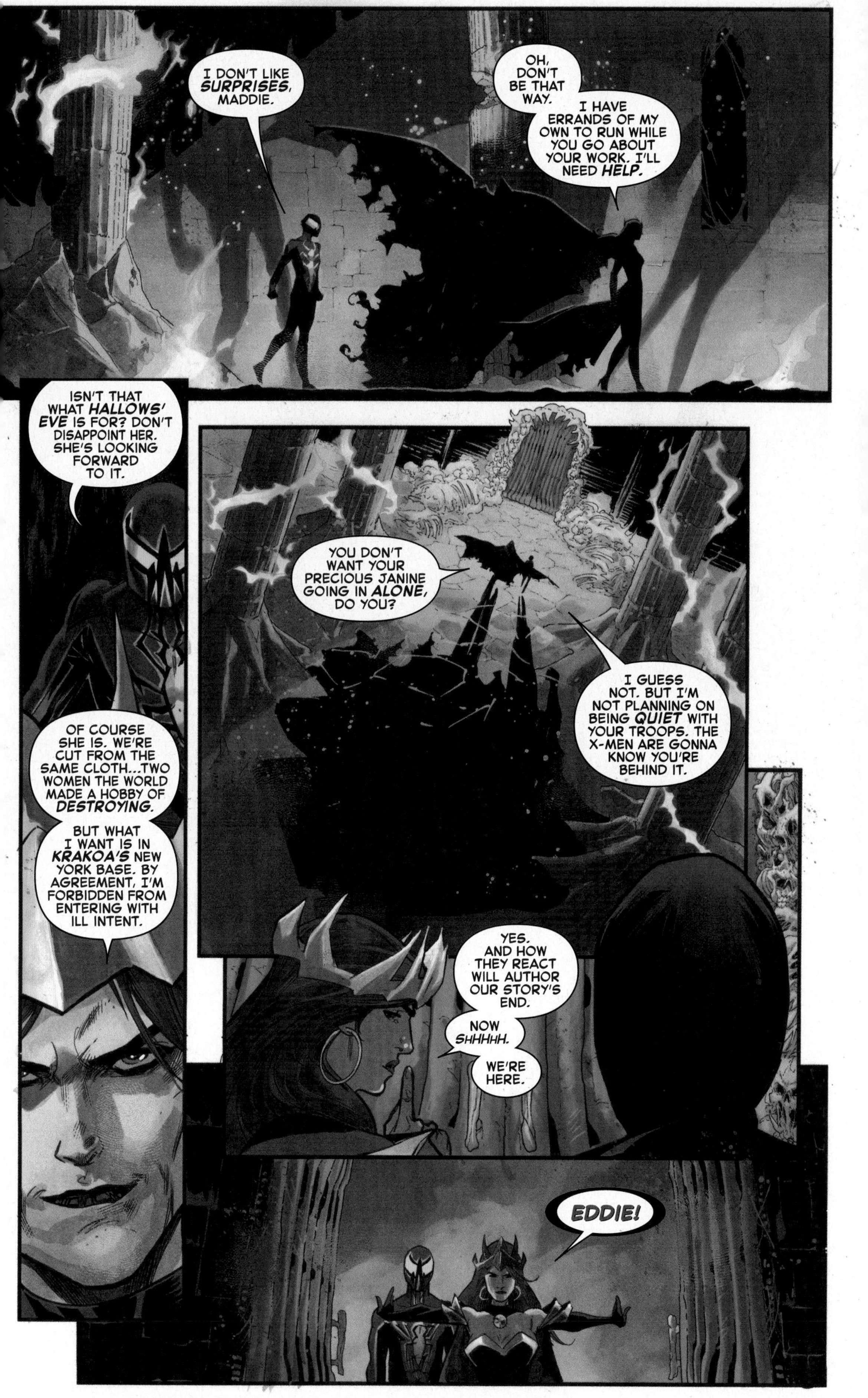
I DON'T LIKE SURPRISES, MADDIE.
OH, DON'T BE THAT WAY.
I HAVE ERRANDS OF MY OWN TO RUN WHILE YOU GO ABOUT YOUR WORK. I'LL NEED HELP.
ISN'T THAT WHAT HALLOWS' EVE IS FOR? DON'T DISAPPOINT HER. SHE'S LOOKING FORWARD TO IT.
OF COURSE SHE IS. WE'RE CUT FROM THE SAME CLOTH...TWO WOMEN THE WORLD MADE A HOBBY OF DESTROYING.
BUT WHAT I WANT IS IN KRAKOA'S NEW YORK BASE. BY AGREEMENT, I'M FORBIDDEN FROM ENTERING WITH ILL INTENT.
YOU DON'T WANT YOUR PRECIOUS JANINE GOING IN ALONE, DO YOU?
I GUESS NOT. BUT I'M NOT PLANNING ON BEING QUIET WITH YOUR TROOPS. THE X-MEN ARE GONNA KNOW YOU'RE BEHIND IT.
YES. AND HOW THEY REACT WILL AUTHOR OUR STORY'S END.
NOW SHHHHH.
WE'RE HERE.
EDDIE!

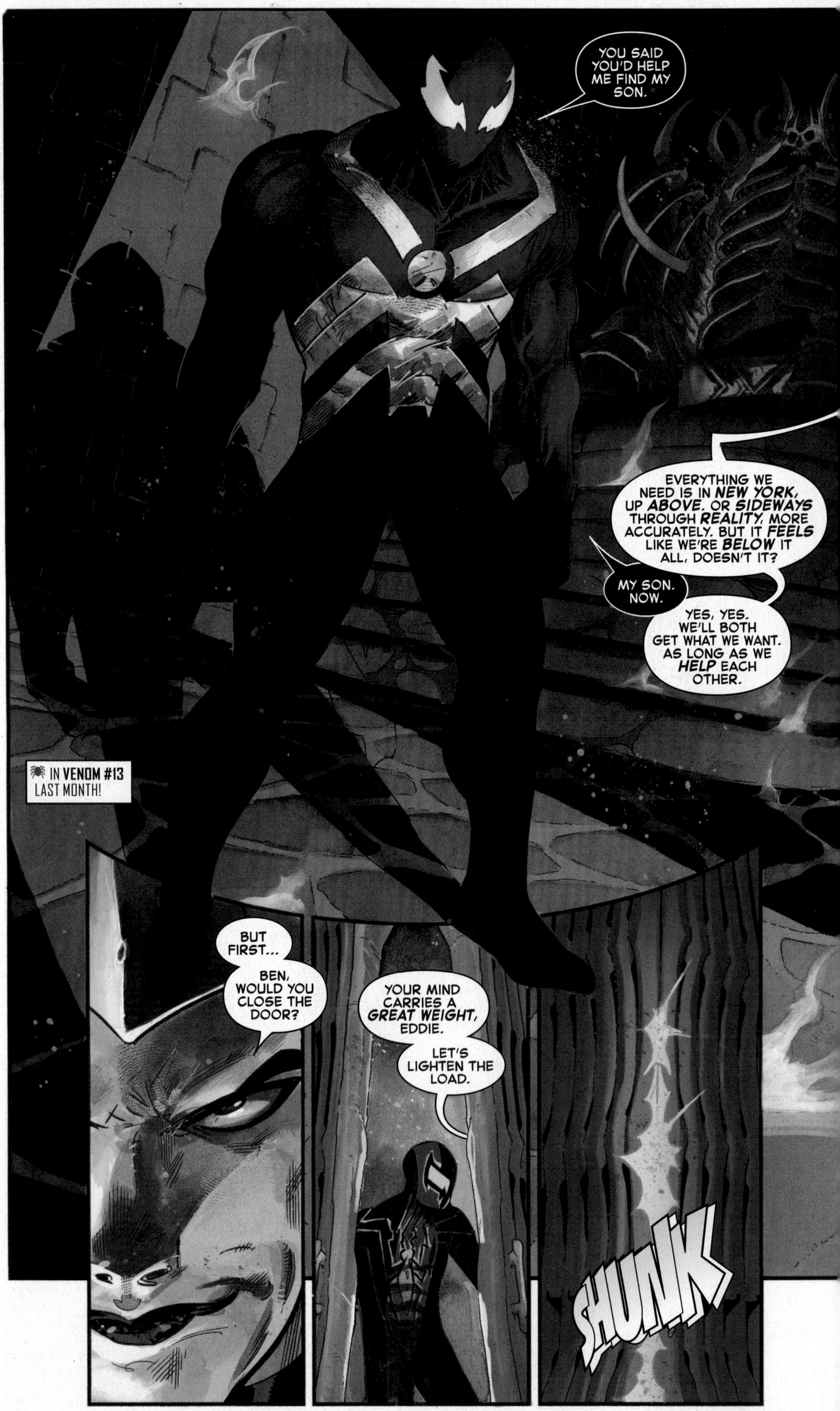

YOU SAID YOU'D HELP ME FIND MY SON.
EVERYTHING WE NEED IS IN NEW YORK, UP ABOVE. OR SIDEWAYS THROUGH REALITY, MORE ACCURATELY. BUT IT FEELS LIKE WE'RE BELOW IT ALL, DOESN'T IT?
MY SON. NOW.
YES, YES. WE'LL BOTH GET WHAT WE WANT. AS LONG AS WE HELP EACH OTHER.
IN VENOM #13 LAST MONTH!
BUT FIRST...
BEN, WOULD YOU CLOSE THE DOOR?
YOUR MIND CARRIES A GREAT WEIGHT, EDDIE.
LET'S LIGHTEN THE LOAD.
SHUNK

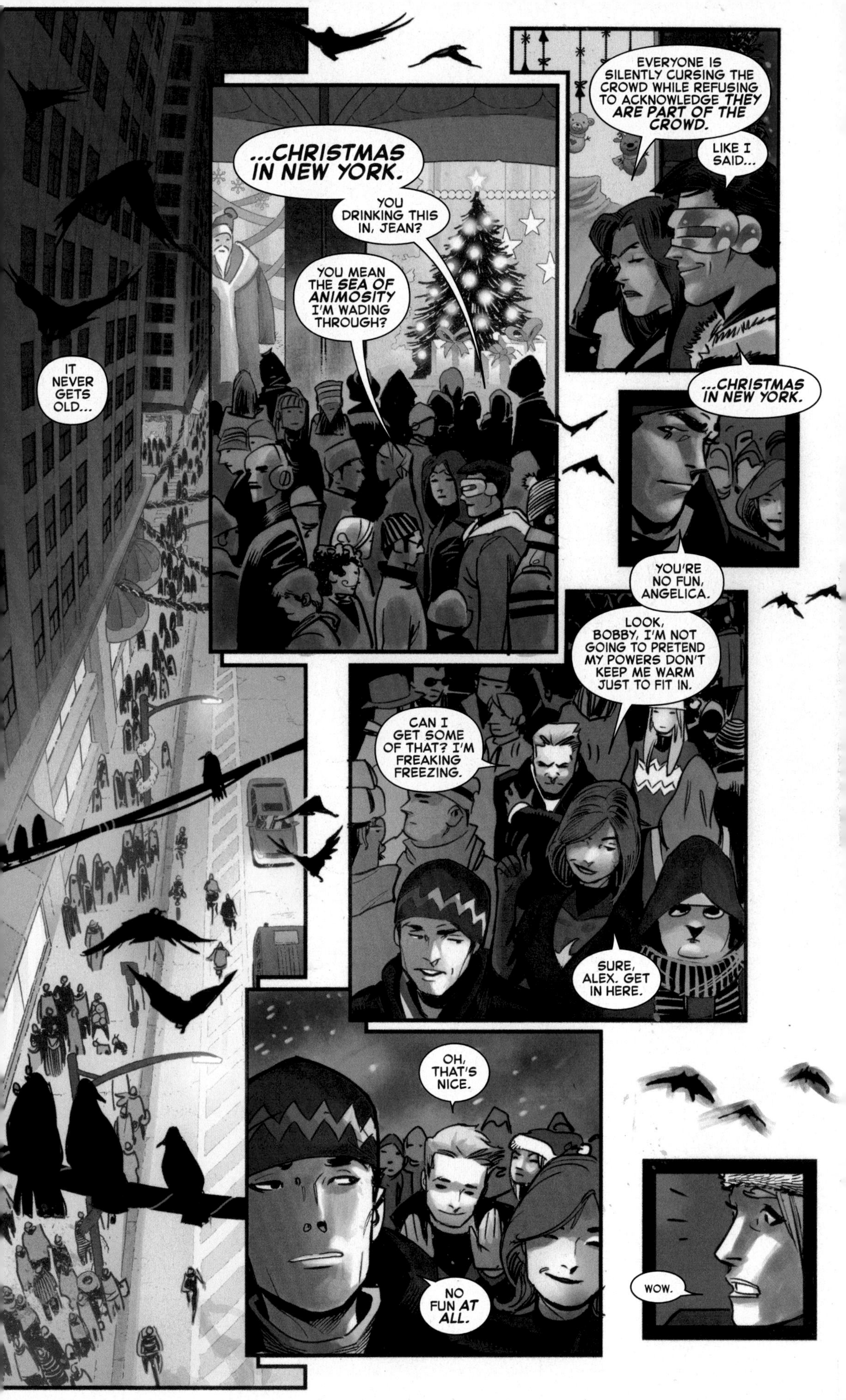

IT NEVER GETS OLD...
...CHRISTMAS IN NEW YORK.
YOU DRINKING THIS IN, JEAN?
YOU MEAN THE SEA OF ANIMOSITY I'M WADING THROUGH?
EVERYONE IS SILENTLY CURSING THE CROWD WHILE REFUSING TO ACKNOWLEDGE THEY ARE PART OF THE CROWD.
LIKE I SAID...
...CHRISTMAS IN NEW YORK.
YOU'RE NO FUN, ANGELICA.
LOOK, BOBBY, I'M NOT GOING TO PRETEND MY POWERS DON'T KEEP ME WARM JUST TO FIT IN.
CAN I GET SOME OF THAT? I'M FREAKING FREEZING.
SURE, ALEX. GET IN HERE.
OH, THAT'S NICE.
NO FUN AT ALL.
WOW.

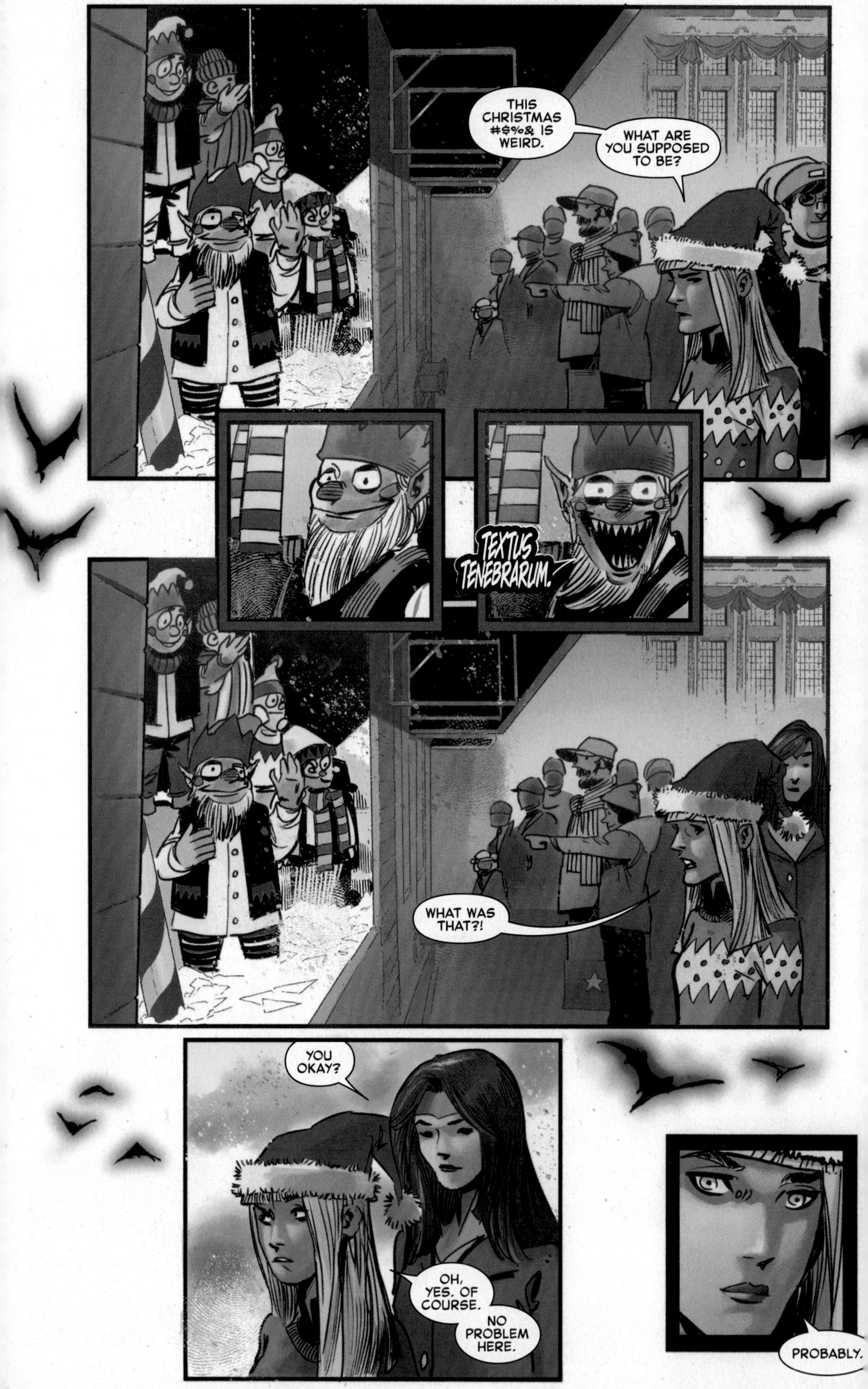
THIS CHRISTMAS #$%& IS WEIRD.
WHAT ARE YOU SUPPOSED TO BE?
TEXTUS TENEBRARUM.
WHAT WAS THAT?!
YOU OKAY?
OH, YES. OF COURSE.
NO PROBLEM HERE.
PROBABLY.

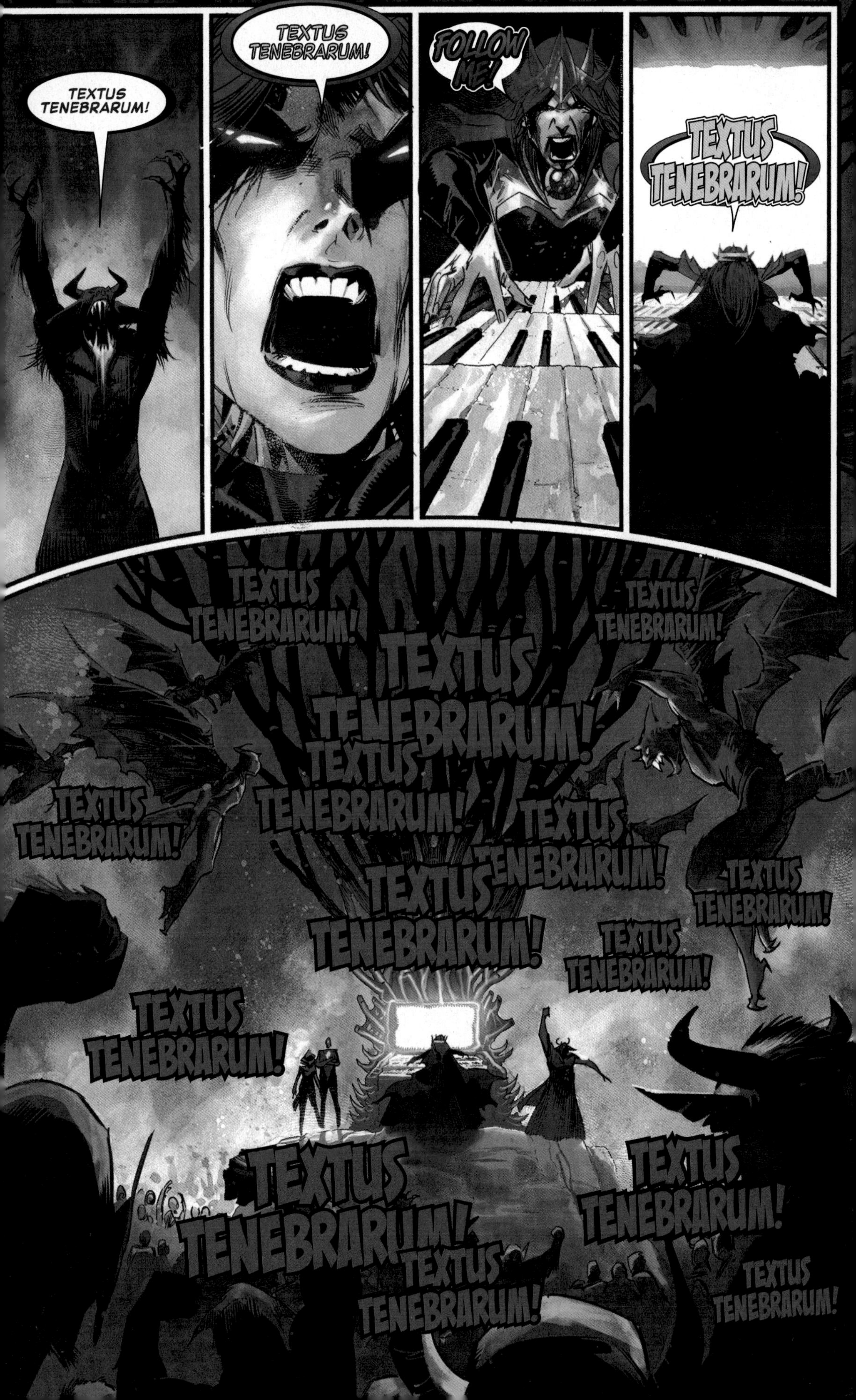
TEXTUS TENEBRARUM!
TEXTUS TENEBRARUM!
FOLLOW ME!
TEXTUS TENEBRARUM!
TEXTUS TENEBRARUM!
TEXTUS TENEBRARUM!
TEXTUS TENEBRARUM!
TEXTUS TENEBRARUM!
TEXTUS TENEBRARUM!
TEXTUS TENEBRARUM!
TEXTUS TENEBRARUM!
TEXTUS TENEBRARUM!
TEXTUS TENEBRARUM!
TEXTUS TENEBRARUM!
TEXTUS TENEBRARUM!
TEXTUS TENEBRARUM!
TEXTUS TENEBRARUM!
TEXTUS TENEBRARUM!

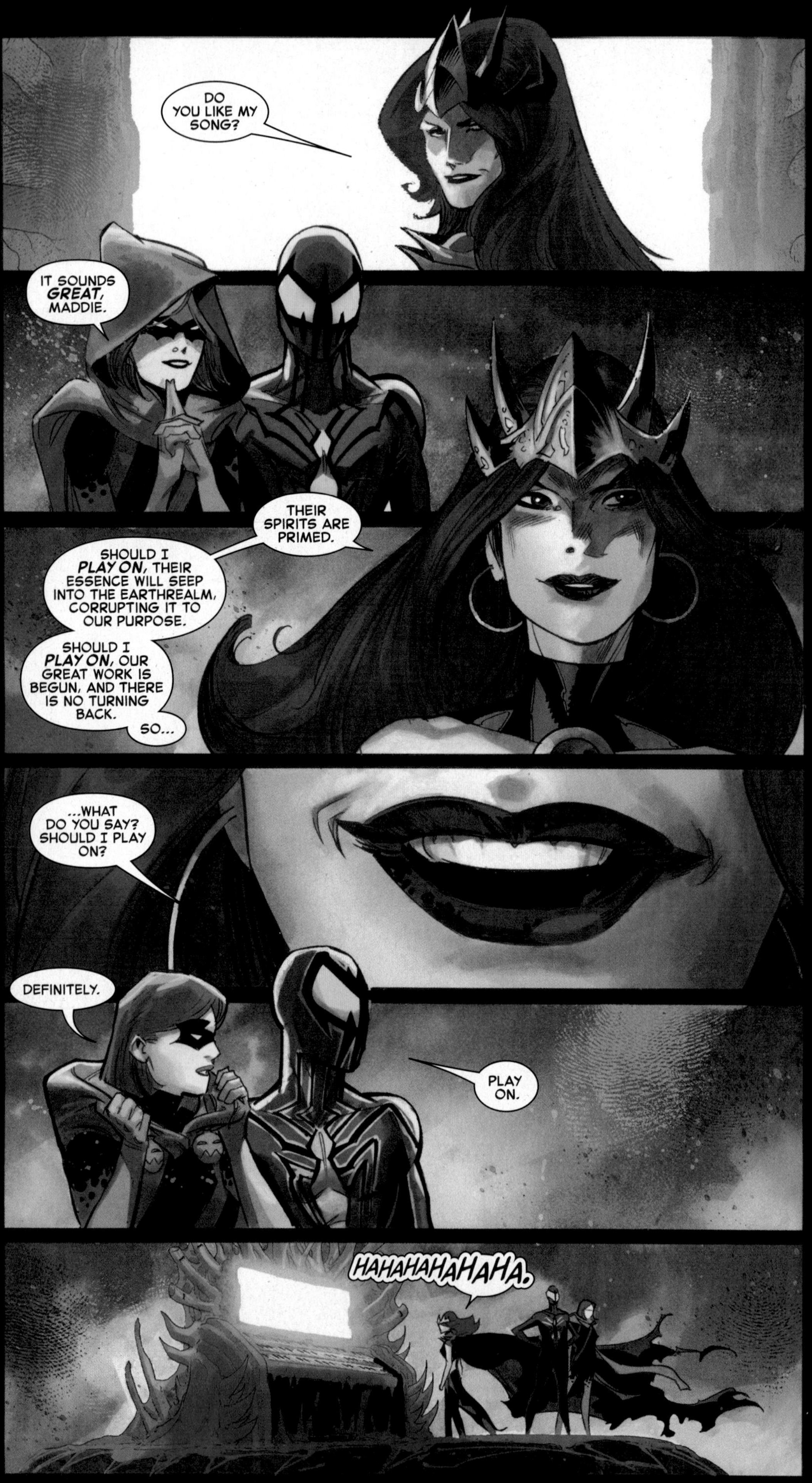
DO YOU LIKE MY SONG?
IT SOUNDS GREAT, MADDIE.
THEIR SPIRITS ARE PRIMED.
SHOULD I PLAY ON, THEIR ESSENCE WILL SEEP INTO THE EARTHREALM, CORRUPTING IT TO OUR PURPOSE.
SHOULD I PLAY ON, OUR GREAT WORK IS BEGUN, AND THERE IS NO TURNING BACK.
SO...
...WHAT DO YOU SAY? SHOULD I PLAY ON?
DEFINITELY.
PLAY ON.
HAHAHAHAHAHAHA.

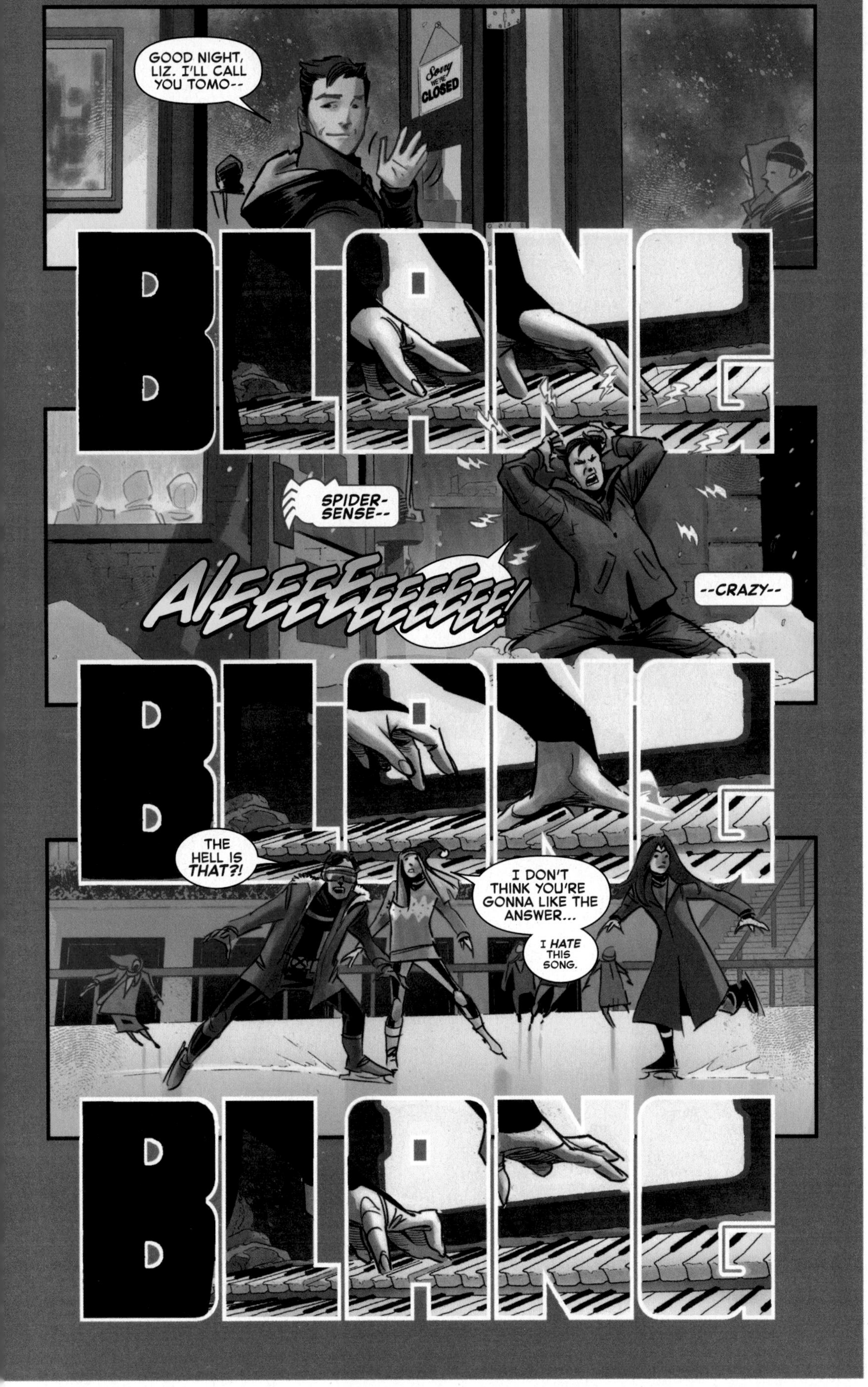
GOOD NIGHT, LIZ. I'LL CALL YOU TOMO--
Sorry WE'RE CLOSED
BLANG
SPIDER-SENSE--
AIEEEEEEEEEE!
--CRAZY--
BLANG
THE HELL IS THAT?!
I DON'T THINK YOU'RE GONNA LIKE THE ANSWER...
I HATE THIS SONG.
BLANG

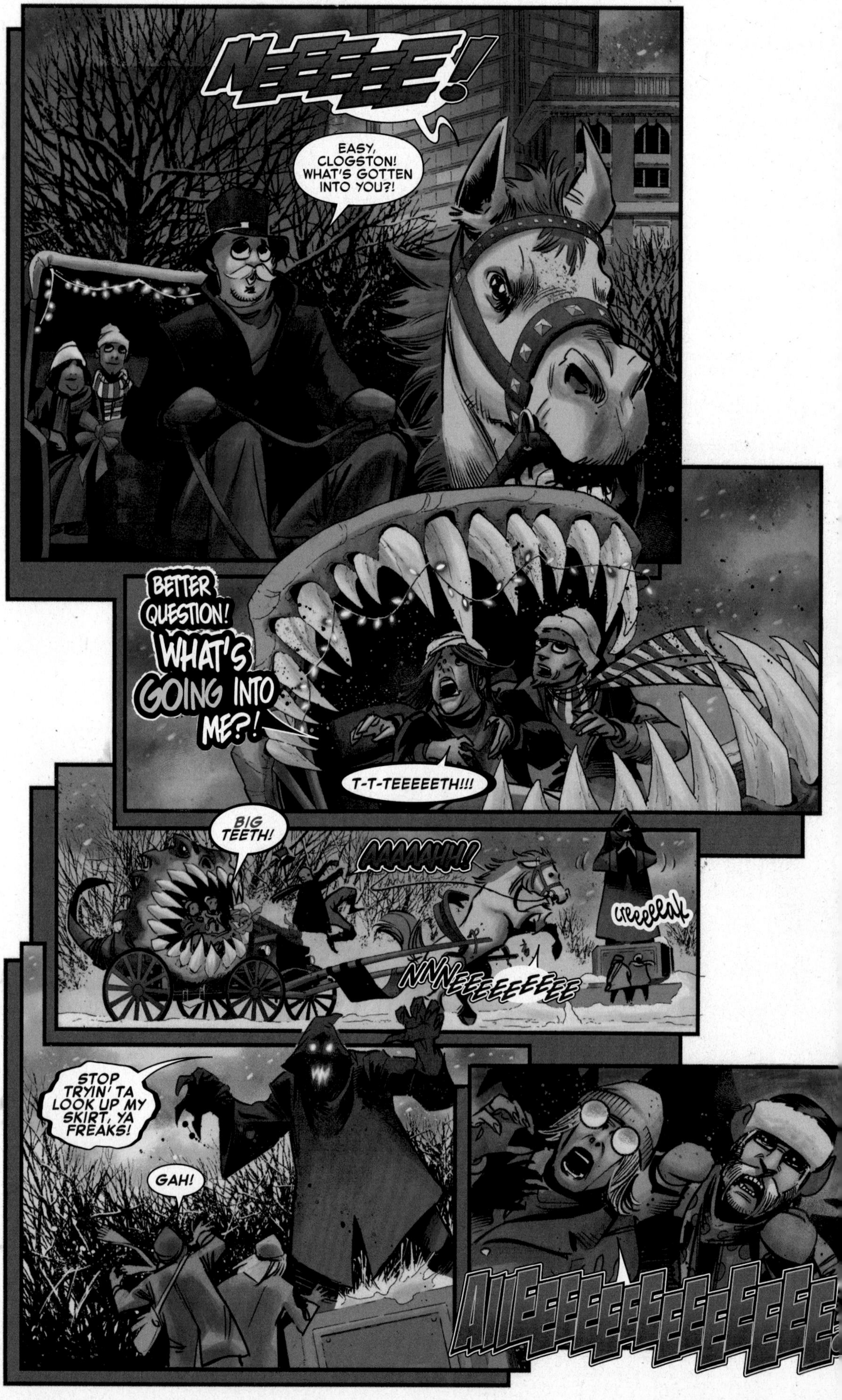

NEEEEE!
EASY, CLOGSTON! WHAT'S GOTTEN INTO YOU?!
BETTER QUESTION! WHAT'S GOING INTO ME?!
T-T-TEEEEETH!!!
BIG TEETH!
AAAAAHH!
CREEEEAK
NNNEEEEEEEEE
STOP TRYIN' TA LOOK UP MY SKIRT, YA FREAKS!
GAH!
AIIEEEEEEEEEEEEEE!

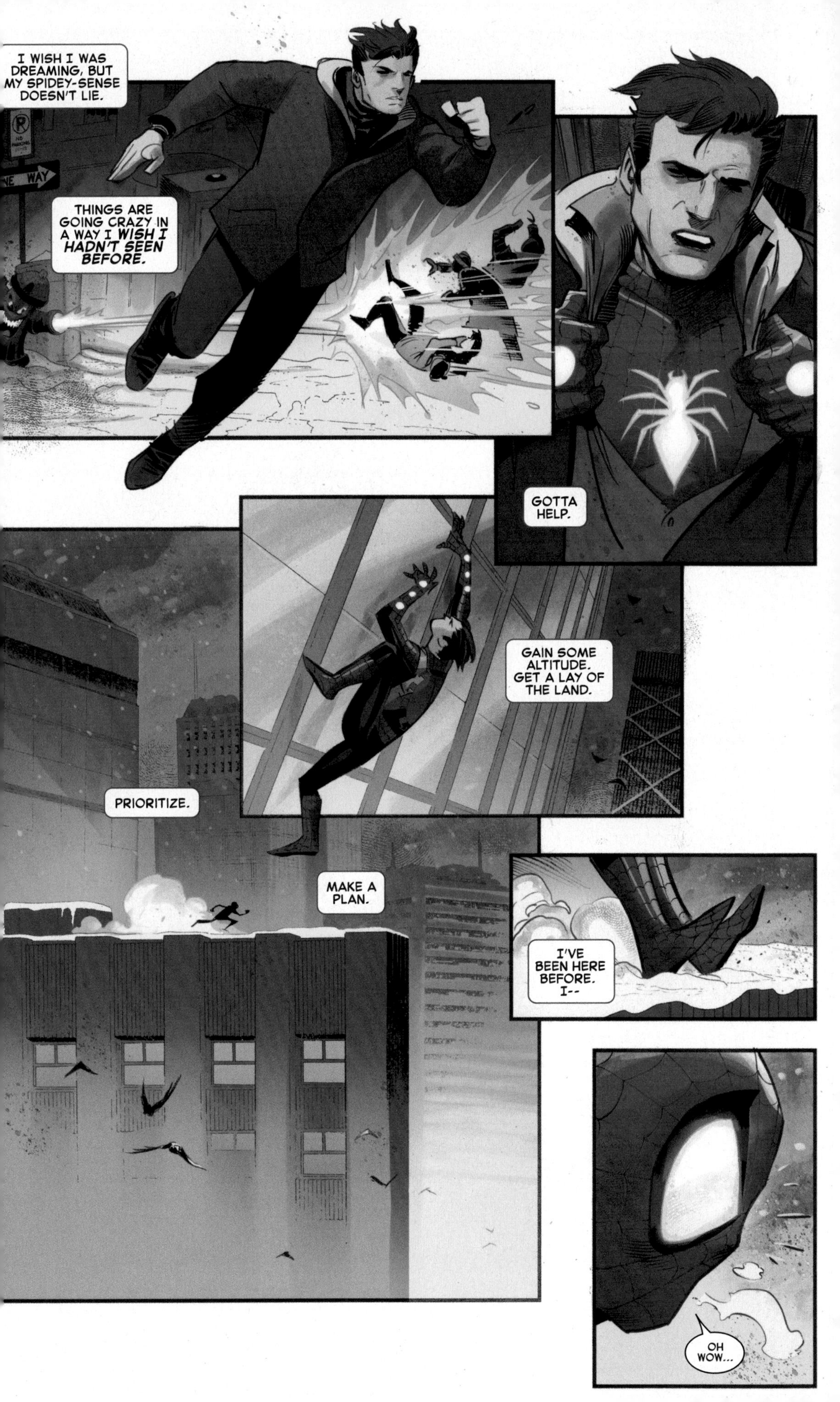

I WISH I WAS DREAMING, BUT MY SPIDEY-SENSE DOESN'T LIE.
ONE WAY
THINGS ARE GOING CRAZY IN A WAY I *WISH I HADN'T SEEN BEFORE.*
GOTTA HELP.
GAIN SOME ALTITUDE. GET A LAY OF THE LAND.
PRIORITIZE.
MAKE A PLAN.
I'VE BEEN HERE BEFORE. I--
OH WOW...

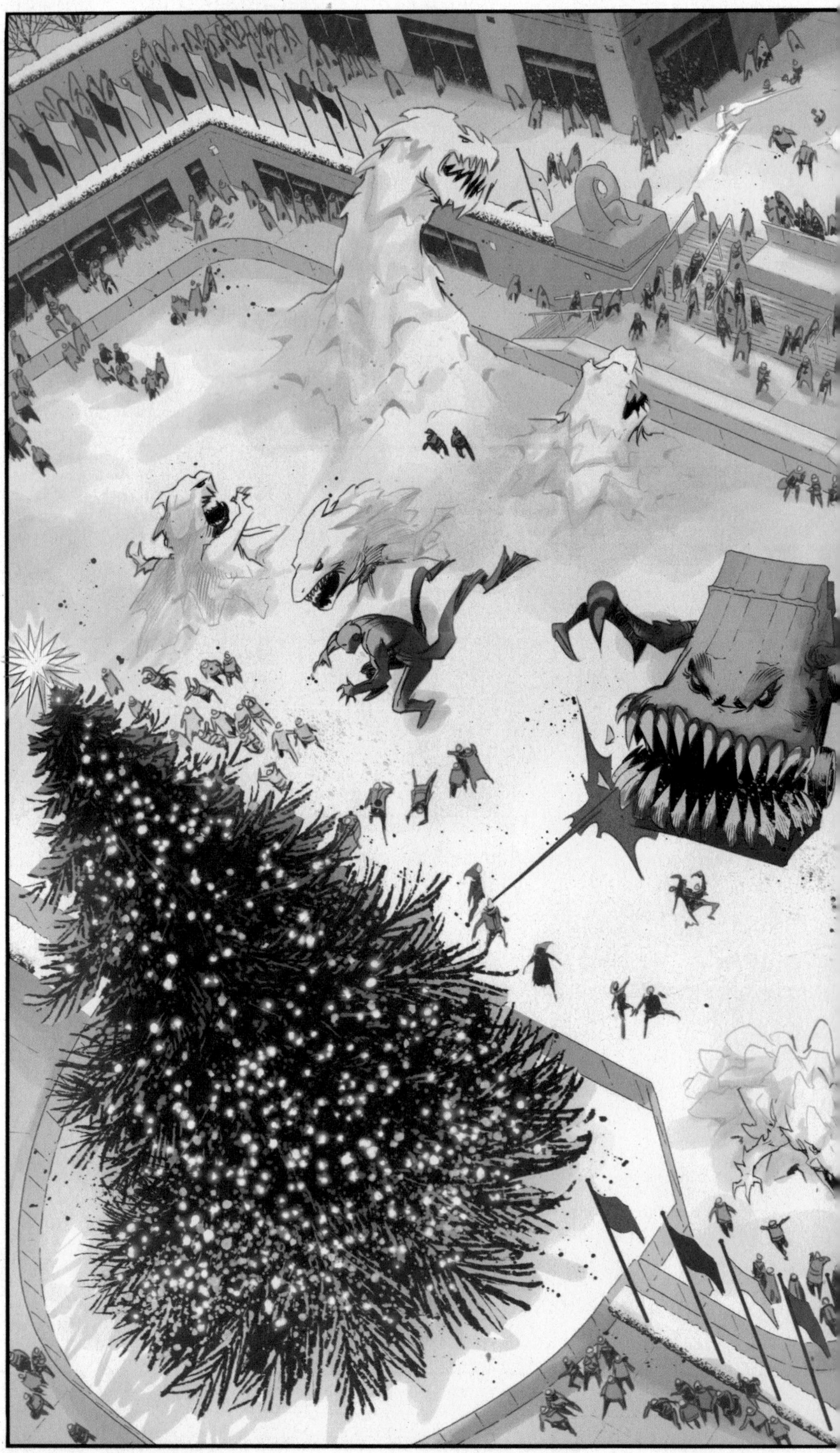

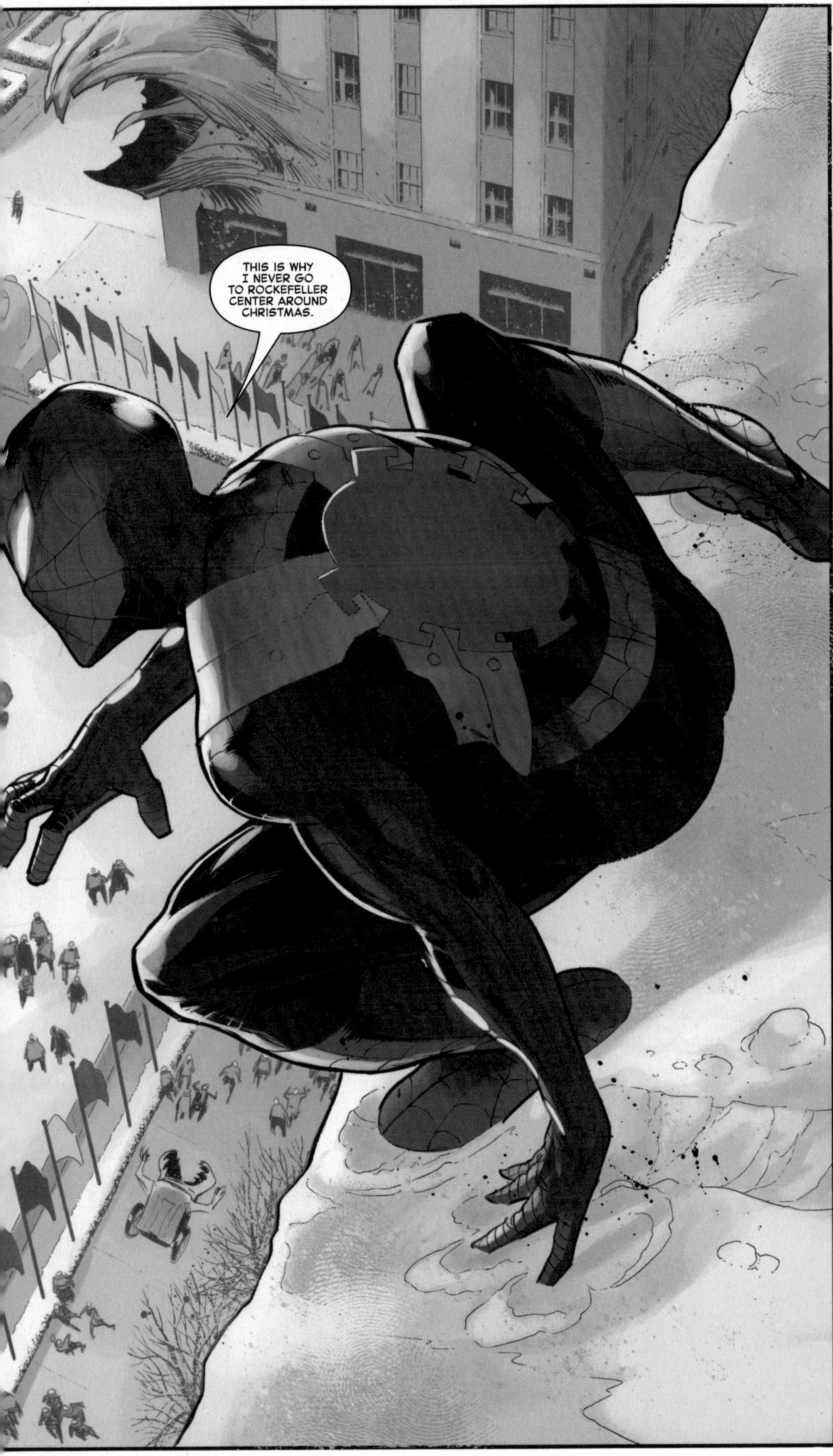
THIS IS WHY I NEVER GO TO ROCKEFELLER CENTER AROUND CHRISTMAS.

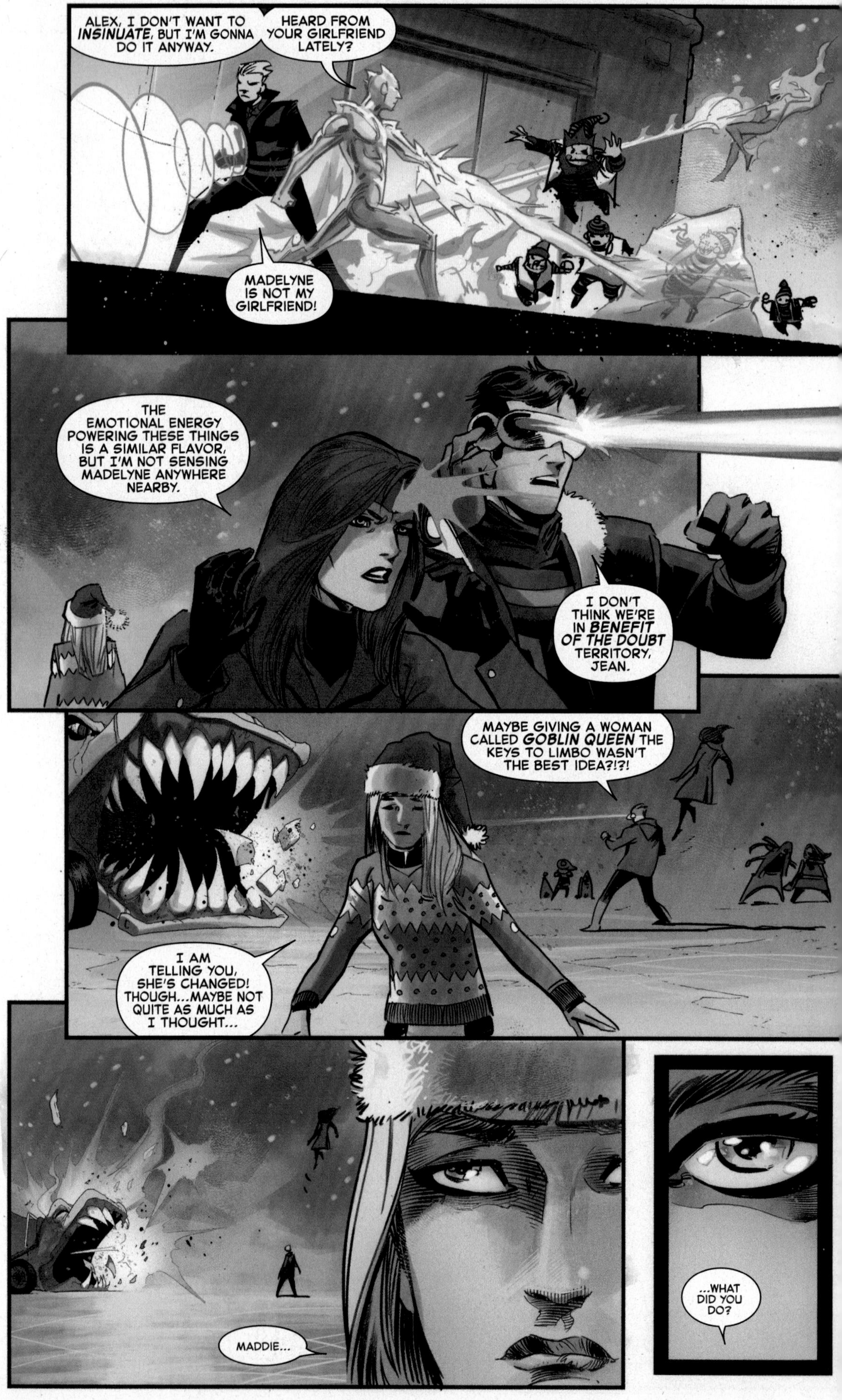

ALEX, I DON'T WANT TO *INSINUATE*, BUT I'M GONNA DO IT ANYWAY.
HEARD FROM YOUR GIRLFRIEND LATELY?
MADELYNE IS NOT MY GIRLFRIEND!
THE EMOTIONAL ENERGY POWERING THESE THINGS IS A SIMILAR FLAVOR, BUT I'M NOT SENSING MADELYNE ANYWHERE NEARBY.
I DON'T THINK WE'RE IN *BENEFIT OF THE DOUBT* TERRITORY, JEAN.
MAYBE GIVING A WOMAN CALLED *GOBLIN QUEEN* THE KEYS TO LIMBO WASN'T THE BEST IDEA?!?!
I AM TELLING YOU, SHE'S CHANGED! THOUGH...MAYBE NOT QUITE AS MUCH AS I THOUGHT...
MADDIE...
...WHAT DID YOU DO?

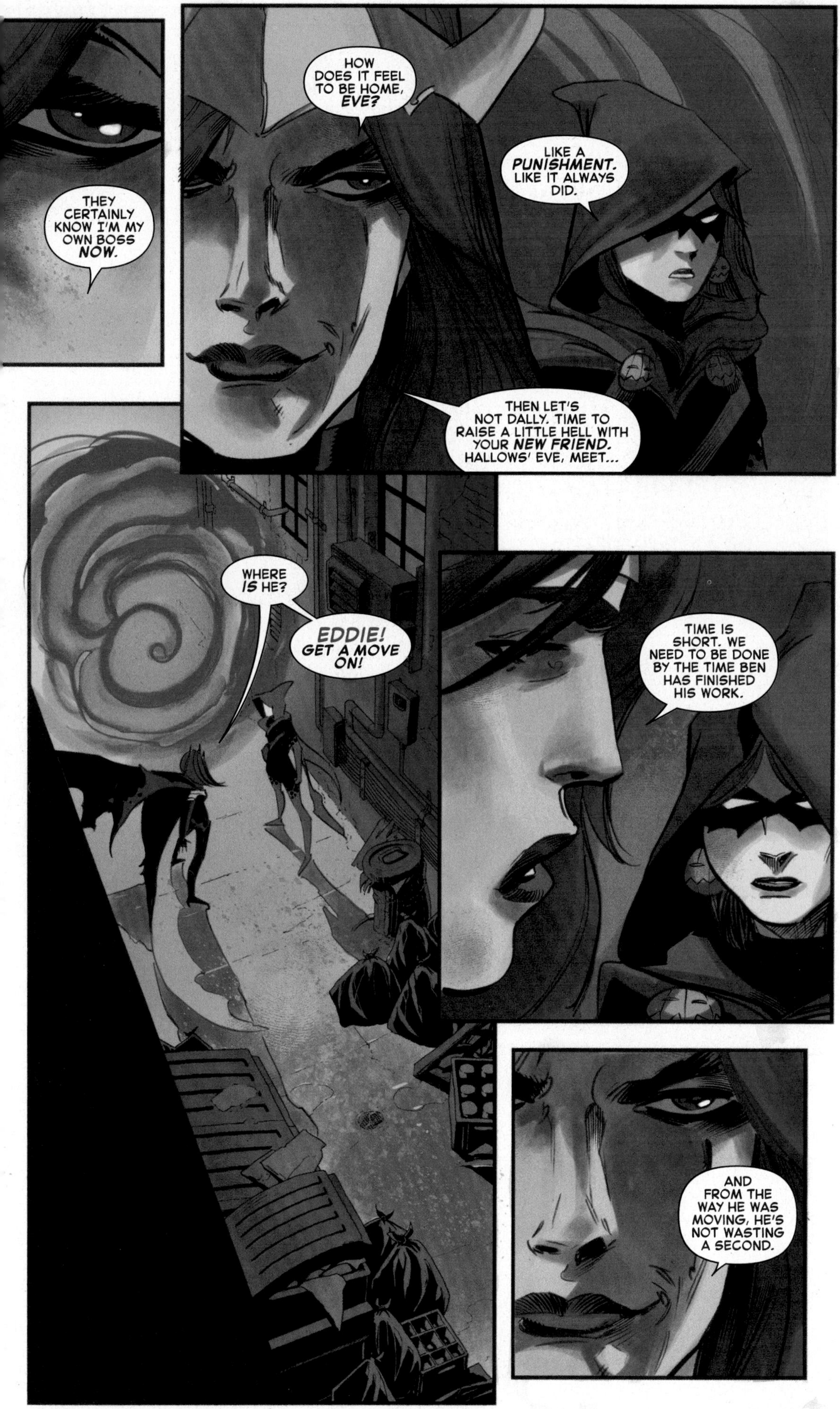
HOW DOES IT FEEL TO BE HOME, EVE?
THEY CERTAINLY KNOW I'M MY OWN BOSS NOW.
LIKE A PUNISHMENT. LIKE IT ALWAYS DID.
THEN LET'S NOT DALLY. TIME TO RAISE A LITTLE HELL WITH YOUR NEW FRIEND. HALLOWS' EVE, MEET...
WHERE IS HE?
EDDIE! GET A MOVE ON!
TIME IS SHORT. WE NEED TO BE DONE BY THE TIME BEN HAS FINISHED HIS WORK.
AND FROM THE WAY HE WAS MOVING, HE'S NOT WASTING A SECOND.

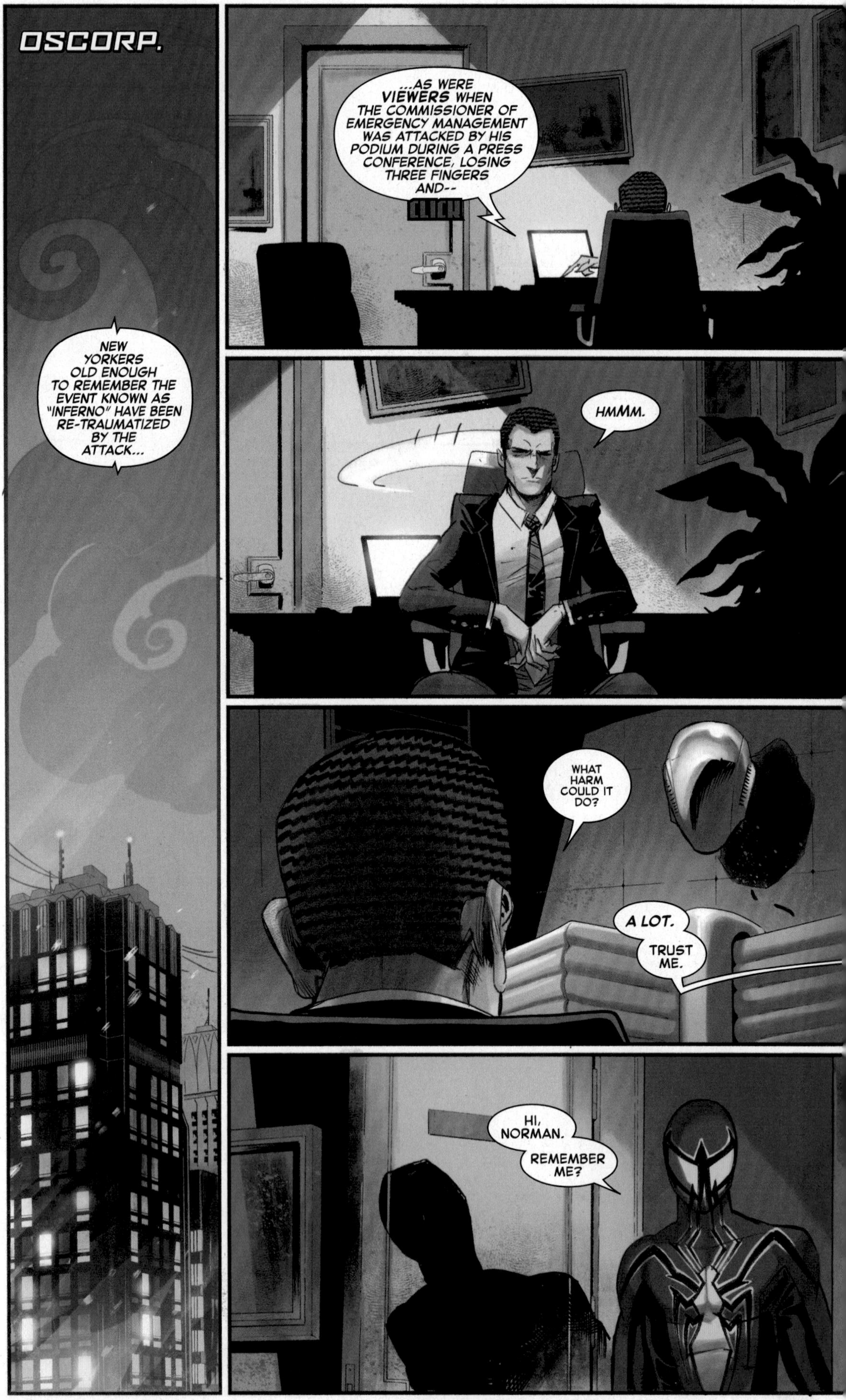
OSCORP.
NEW YORKERS OLD ENOUGH TO REMEMBER THE EVENT KNOWN AS "INFERNO" HAVE BEEN RE-TRAUMATIZED BY THE ATTACK...
...AS WERE VIEWERS WHEN THE COMMISSIONER OF EMERGENCY MANAGEMENT WAS ATTACKED BY HIS PODIUM DURING A PRESS CONFERENCE, LOSING THREE FINGERS AND--
CLICK
HMMM.
WHAT HARM COULD IT DO?
A LOT.
TRUST ME.
HI, NORMAN.
REMEMBER ME?

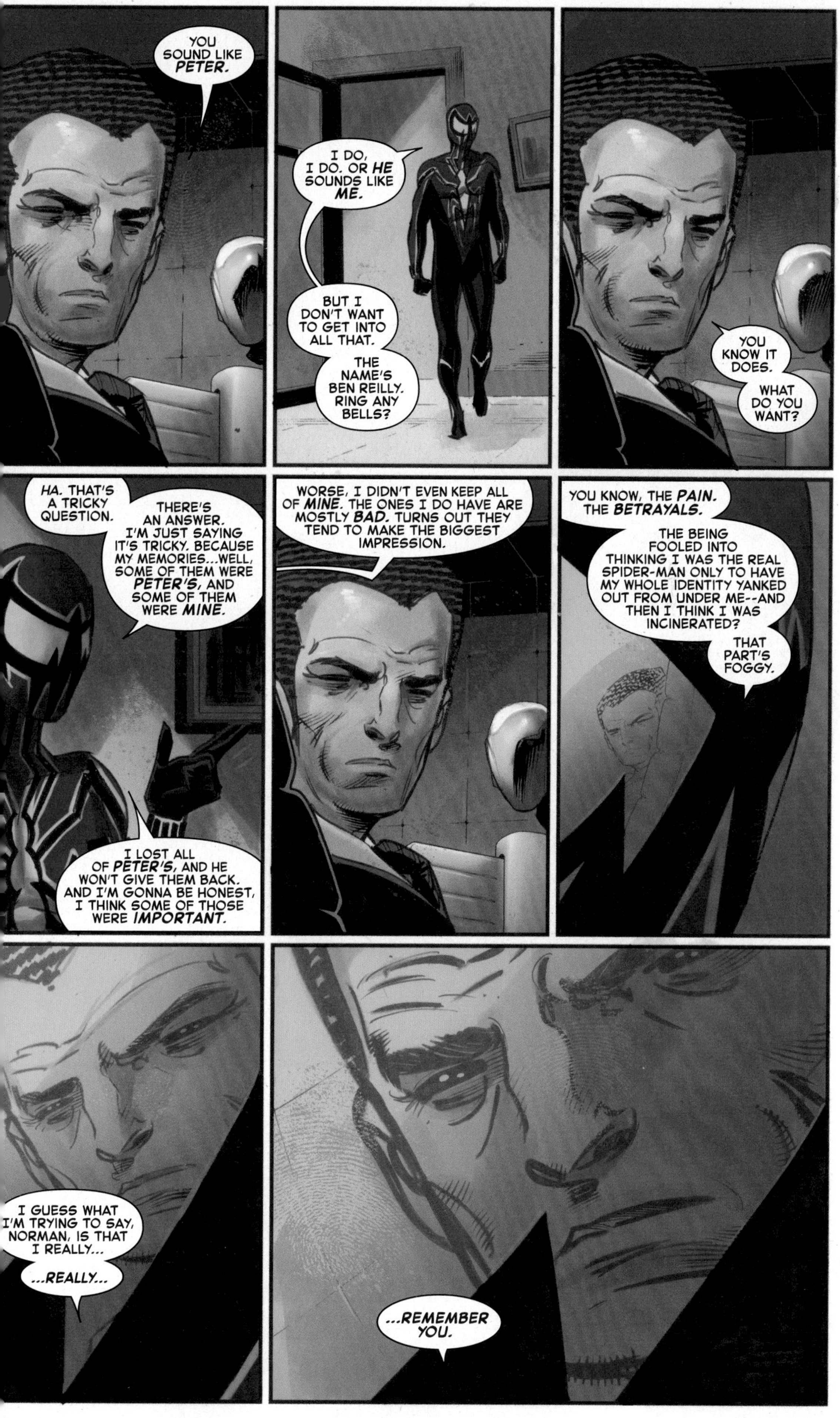
YOU SOUND LIKE PETER.
I DO, I DO. OR HE SOUNDS LIKE ME.
BUT I DON'T WANT TO GET INTO ALL THAT.
THE NAME'S BEN REILLY. RING ANY BELLS?
YOU KNOW IT DOES.
WHAT DO YOU WANT?
HA. THAT'S A TRICKY QUESTION.
THERE'S AN ANSWER. I'M JUST SAYING IT'S TRICKY. BECAUSE MY MEMORIES...WELL, SOME OF THEM WERE PETER'S, AND SOME OF THEM WERE MINE.
I LOST ALL OF PETER'S, AND HE WON'T GIVE THEM BACK. AND I'M GONNA BE HONEST, I THINK SOME OF THOSE WERE IMPORTANT.
WORSE, I DIDN'T EVEN KEEP ALL OF MINE. THE ONES I DO HAVE ARE MOSTLY BAD. TURNS OUT THEY TEND TO MAKE THE BIGGEST IMPRESSION.
YOU KNOW, THE PAIN. THE BETRAYALS.
THE BEING FOOLED INTO THINKING I WAS THE REAL SPIDER-MAN ONLY TO HAVE MY WHOLE IDENTITY YANKED OUT FROM UNDER ME--AND THEN I THINK I WAS INCINERATED?
THAT PART'S FOGGY.
I GUESS WHAT I'M TRYING TO SAY, NORMAN, IS THAT I REALLY...
...REALLY...
...REMEMBER YOU.

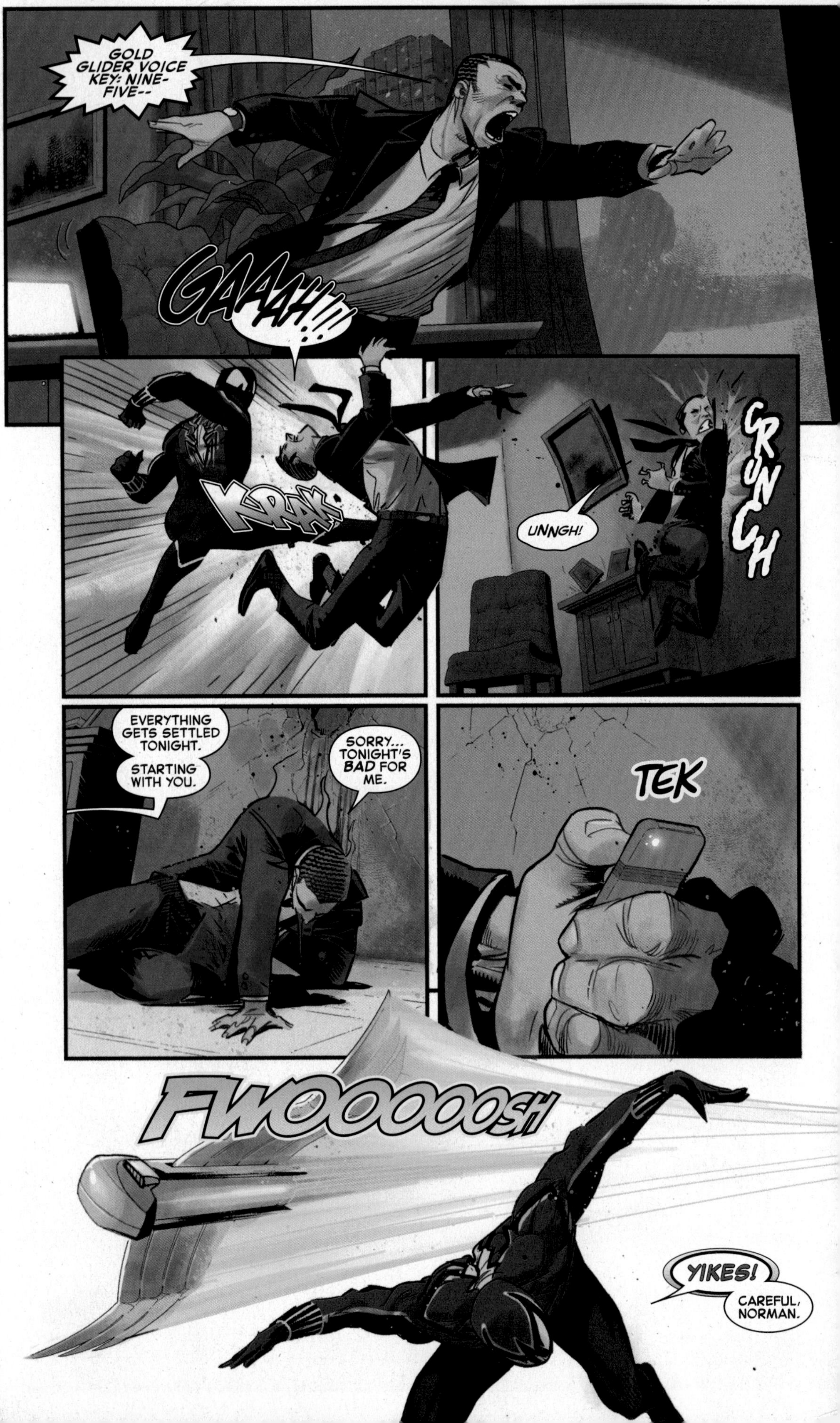
GOLD GLIDER VOICE KEY: NINE-FIVE--
GAAAAH!!!
KRAK
UNNGH!
CRUNCH
EVERYTHING GETS SETTLED TONIGHT.
STARTING WITH YOU.
SORRY... TONIGHT'S BAD FOR ME.
TEK
FWOOOOOSH
YIKES!
CAREFUL, NORMAN.

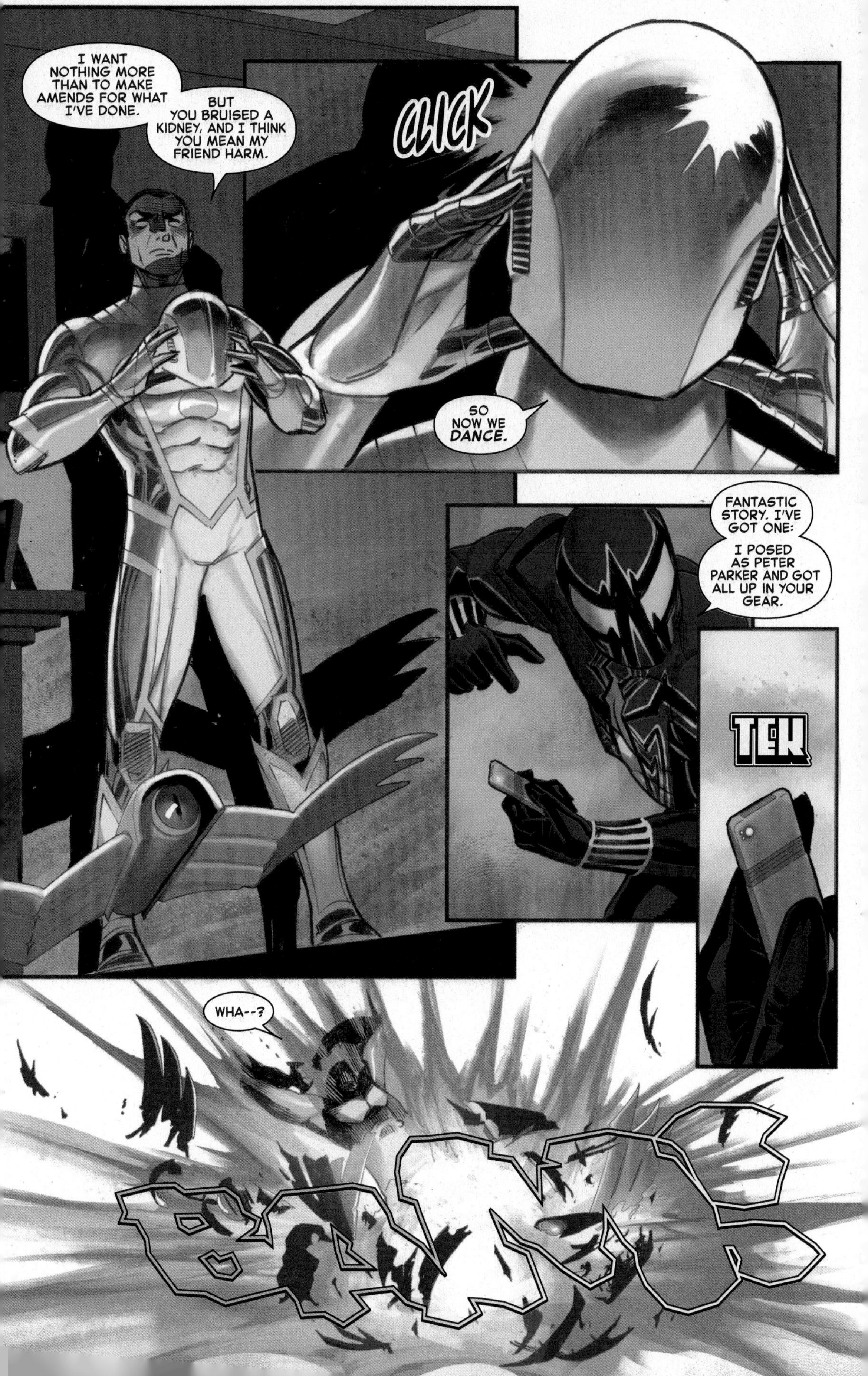
I WANT NOTHING MORE THAN TO MAKE AMENDS FOR WHAT I'VE DONE.
BUT YOU BRUISED A KIDNEY, AND I THINK YOU MEAN MY FRIEND HARM.
CLICK
SO NOW WE DANCE.
FANTASTIC STORY. I'VE GOT ONE:
I POSED AS PETER PARKER AND GOT ALL UP IN YOUR GEAR.
TEK
WHA--?

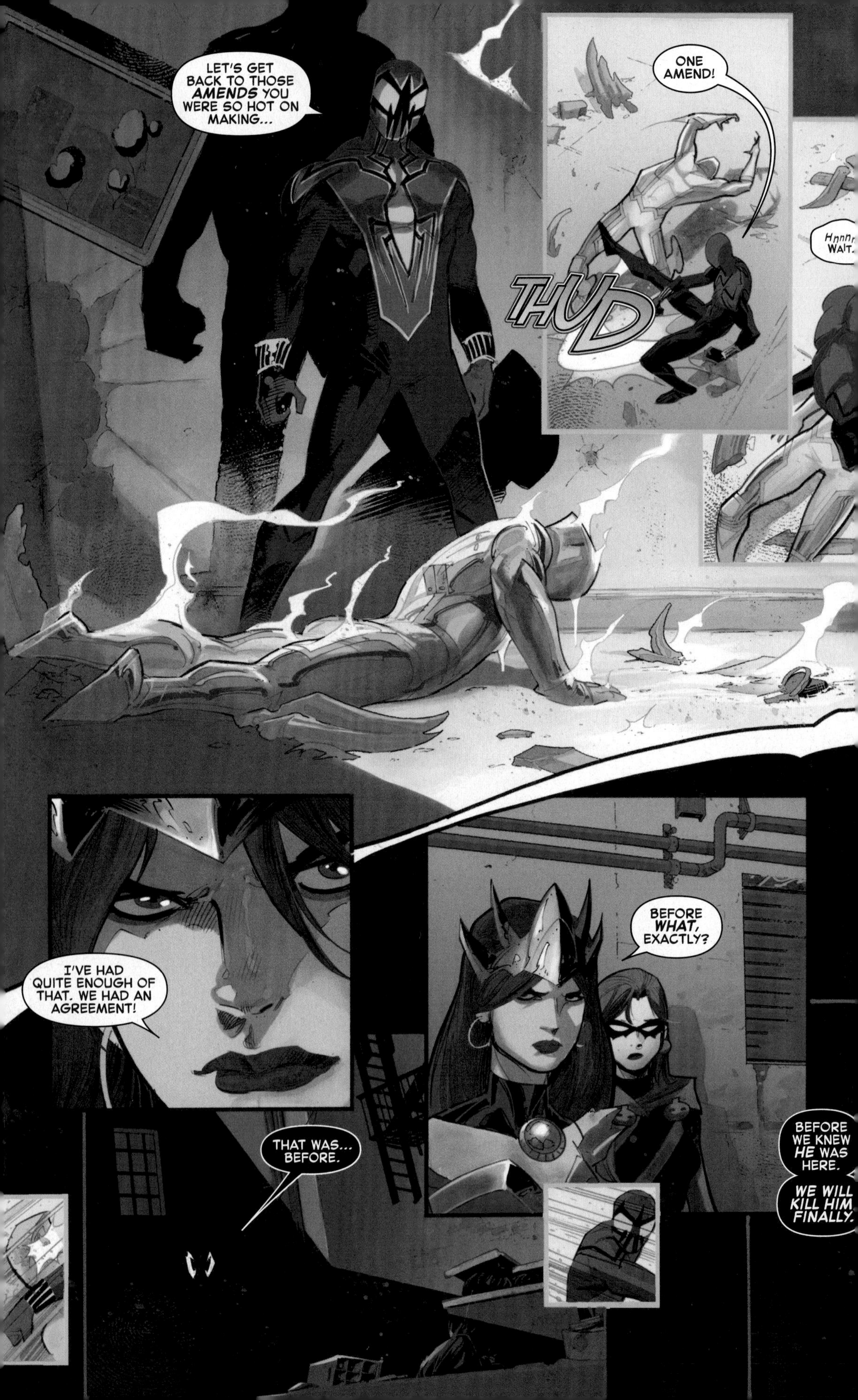
LET'S GET BACK TO THOSE AMENDS YOU WERE SO HOT ON MAKING...
ONE AMEND!
THUD
Hnnn WAIT.
I'VE HAD QUITE ENOUGH OF THAT. WE HAD AN AGREEMENT!
THAT WAS... BEFORE.
BEFORE WHAT, EXACTLY?
BEFORE WE KNEW HE WAS HERE.
WE WILL KILL HIM FINALLY.

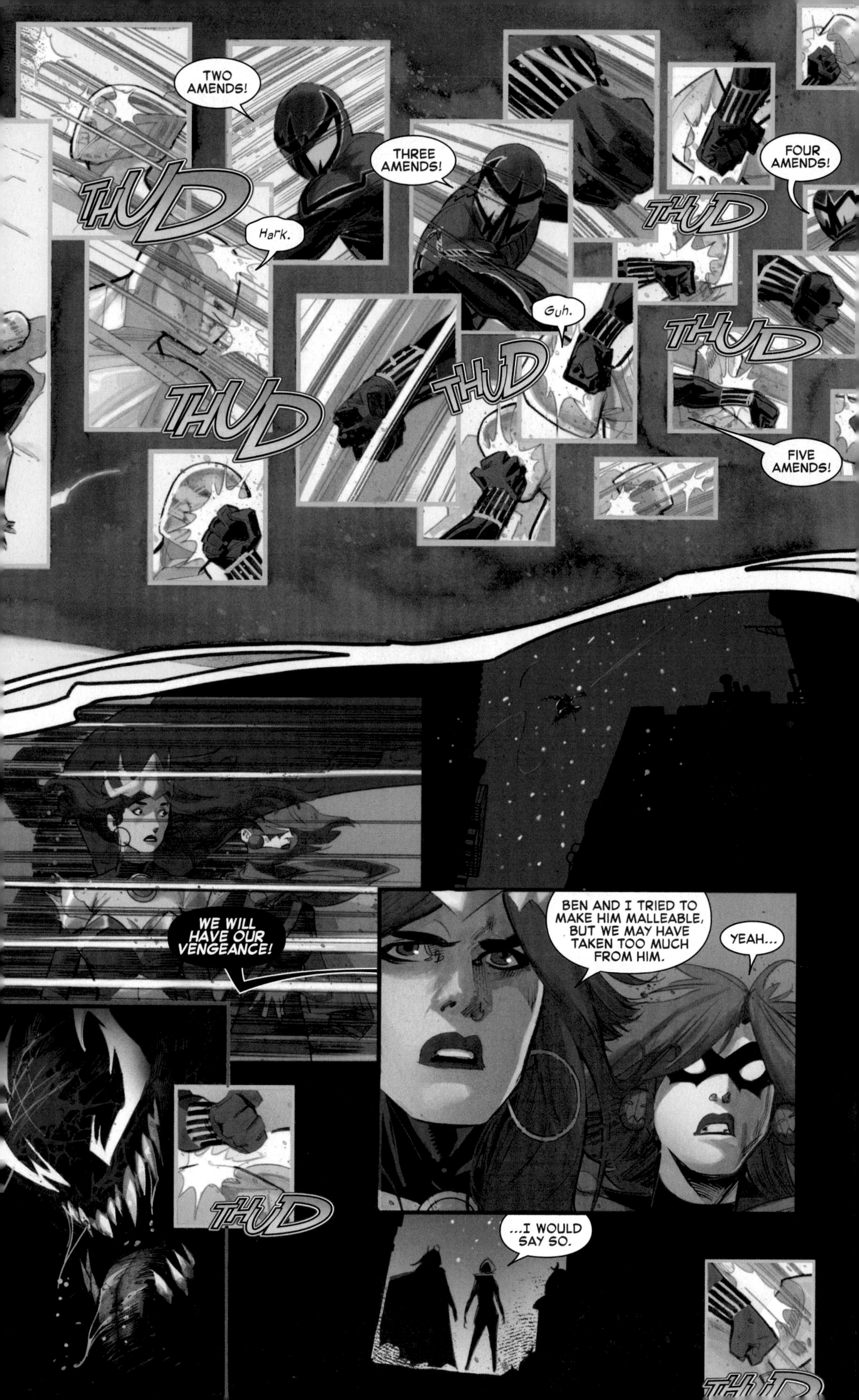
TWO AMENDS!
THUD
Hark.
THREE AMENDS!
THUD
Guh.
THUD
FOUR AMENDS!
THUD
THUD
FIVE AMENDS!
WE WILL HAVE OUR VENGEANCE!
BEN AND I TRIED TO MAKE HIM MALLEABLE, BUT WE MAY HAVE TAKEN TOO MUCH FROM HIM.
YEAH...
THUD
...I WOULD SAY SO.

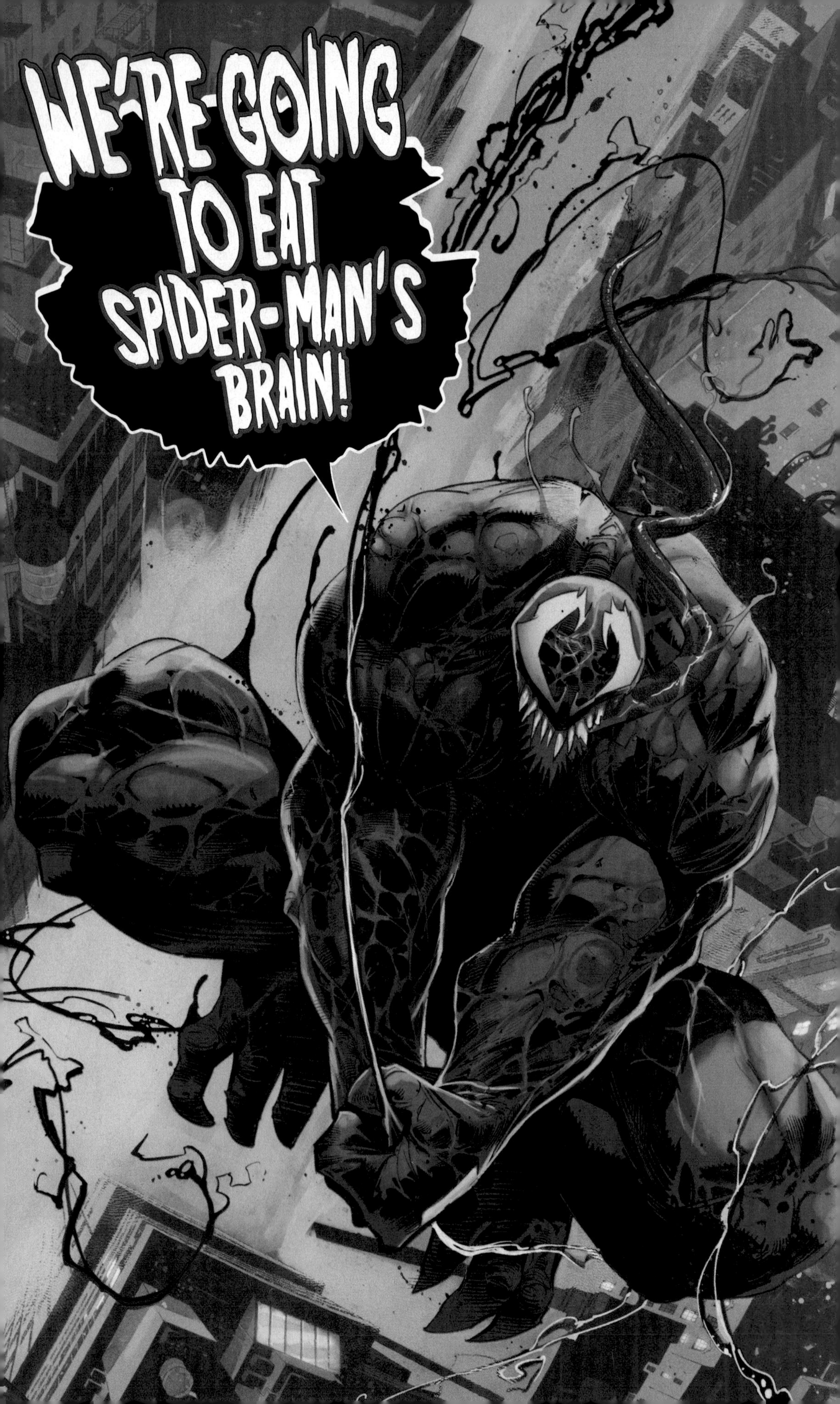
WE'RE GOING TO EAT SPIDER-MAN'S BRAIN!

AMAZING SPIDER-MAN #15

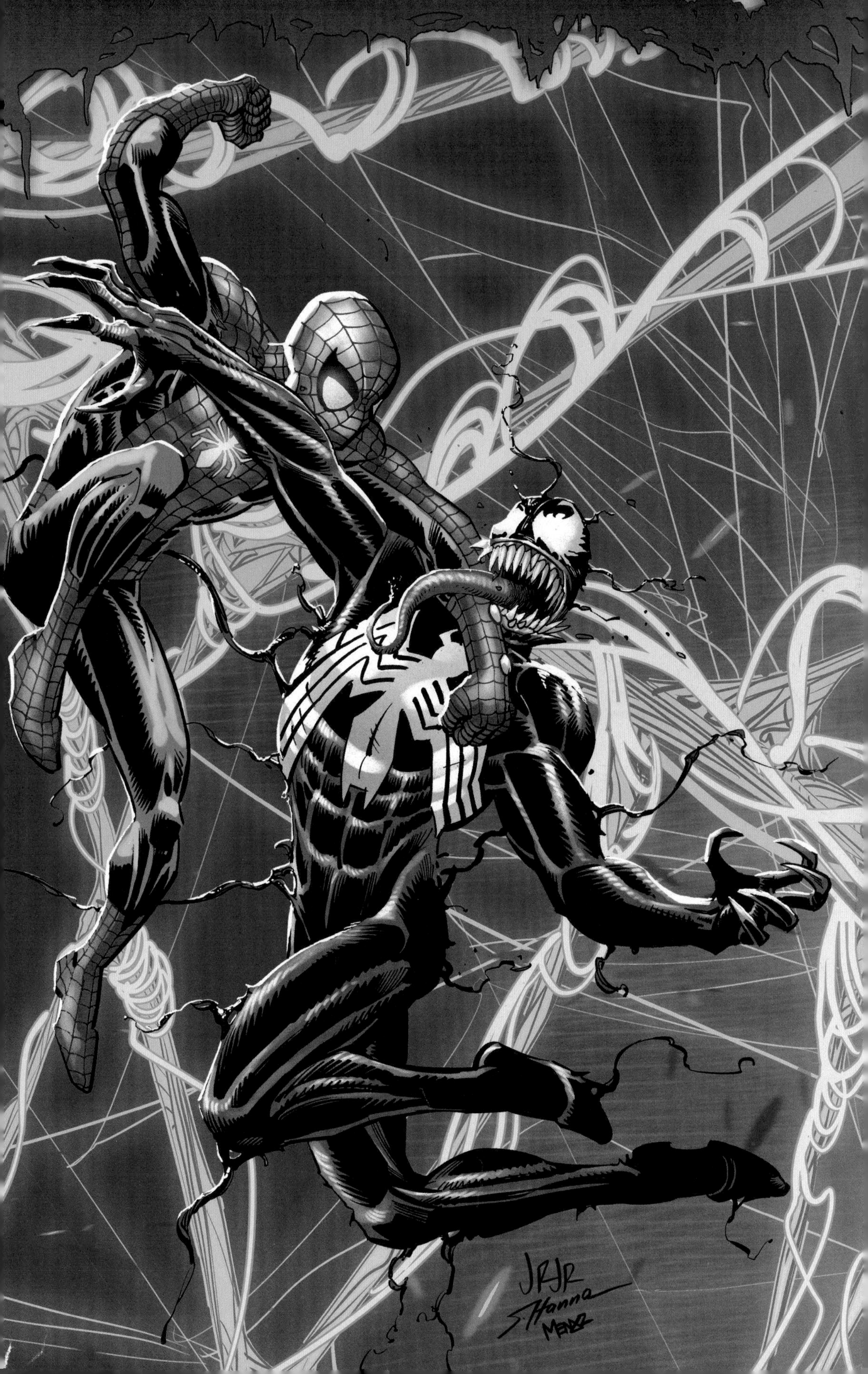

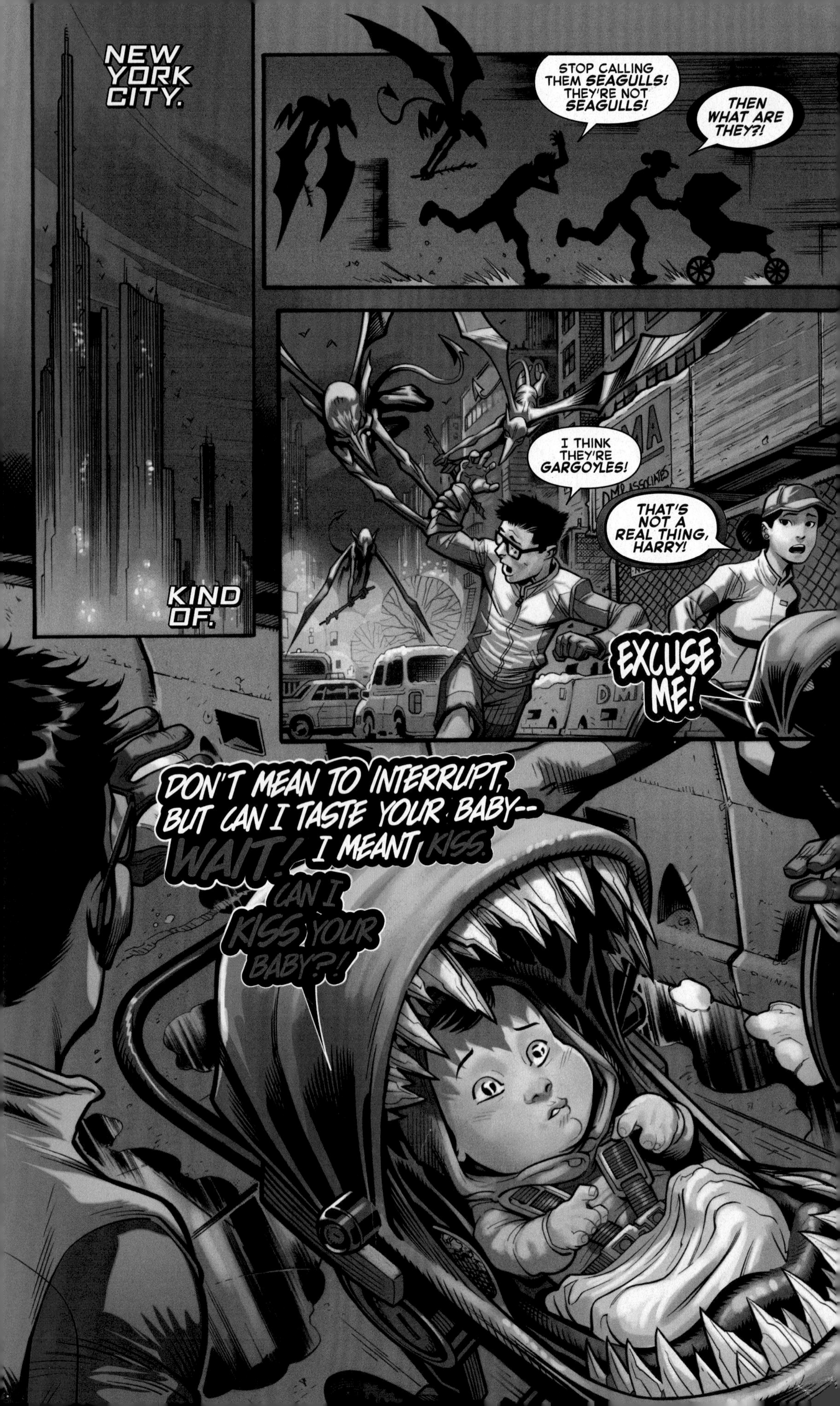
NEW YORK CITY.
KIND OF.
STOP CALLING THEM SEAGULLS! THEY'RE NOT SEAGULLS!
THEN WHAT ARE THEY?!
I THINK THEY'RE GARGOYLES!
THAT'S NOT A REAL THING, HARRY!
EXCUSE ME!
DON'T MEAN TO INTERRUPT, BUT CAN I TASTE YOUR BABY--
WAIT! I MEANT KISS.
CAN I KISS YOUR BABY?!

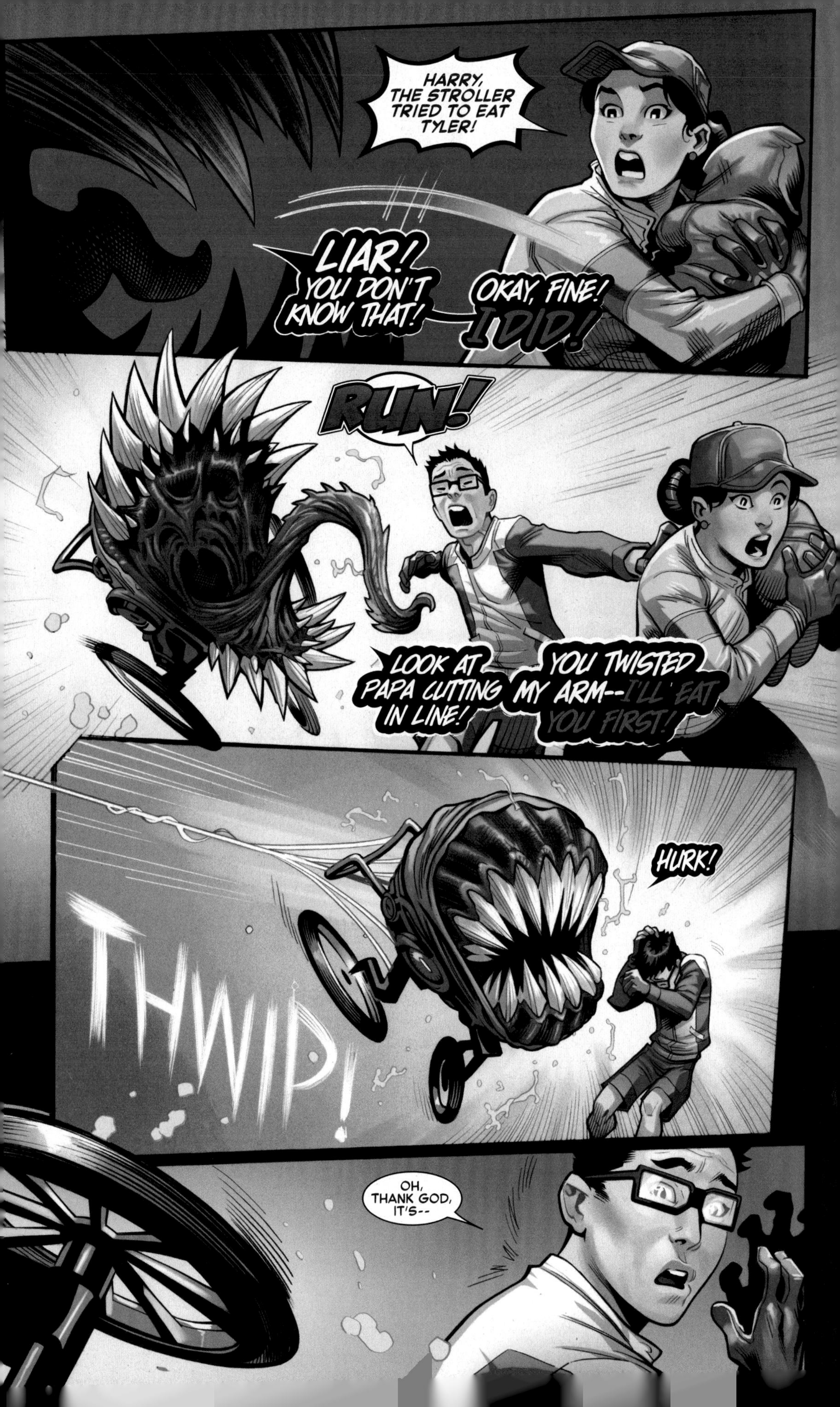
HARRY, THE STROLLER TRIED TO EAT TYLER!
LIAR! YOU DON'T KNOW THAT!
OKAY, FINE! I DID!
RUN!
LOOK AT PAPA CUTTING IN LINE!
YOU TWISTED MY ARM--I'LL EAT YOU FIRST!
HURK!
THWIP!
OH, THANK GOD, IT'S--

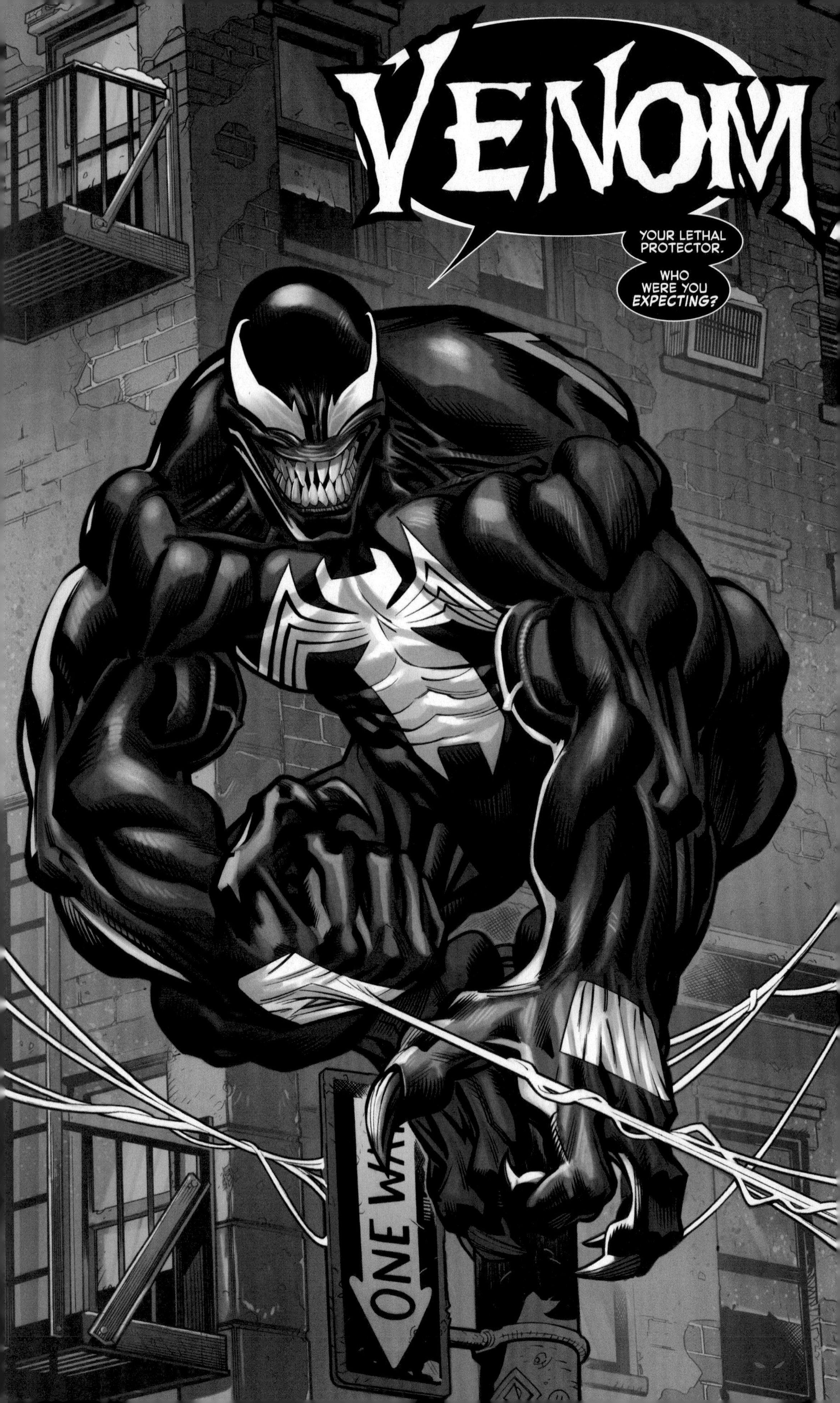
VENOM
YOUR LETHAL PROTECTOR.
WHO WERE YOU EXPECTING?
ONE WAY

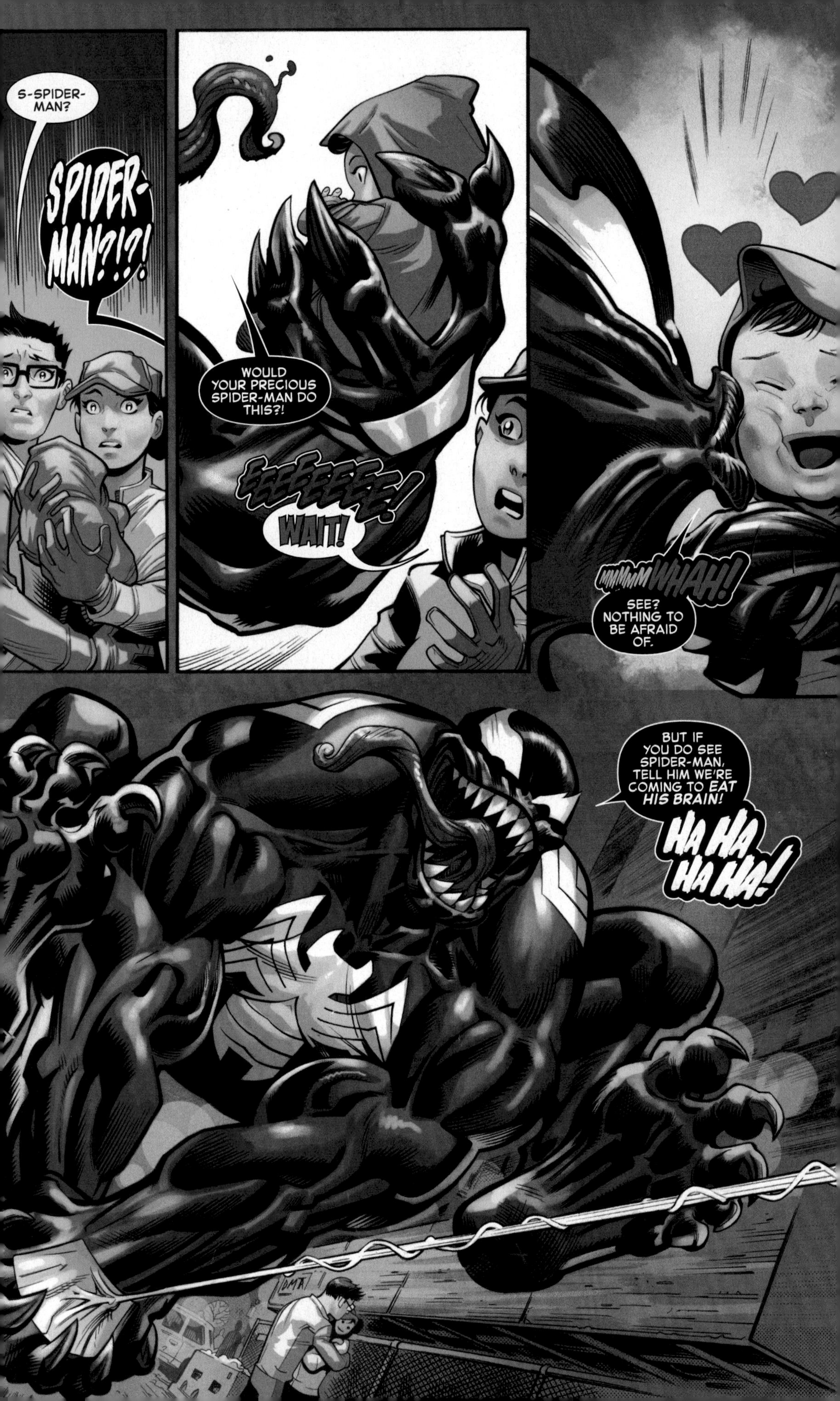

S-SPIDER-MAN?
SPIDER-MAN?!?!
WOULD YOUR PRECIOUS SPIDER-MAN DO THIS?!
EEEEEEEEE!
WAIT!
MMMMMWHAH!
SEE? NOTHING TO BE AFRAID OF.
BUT IF YOU DO SEE SPIDER-MAN, TELL HIM WE'RE COMING TO EAT HIS BRAIN!
HA HA HA HA!

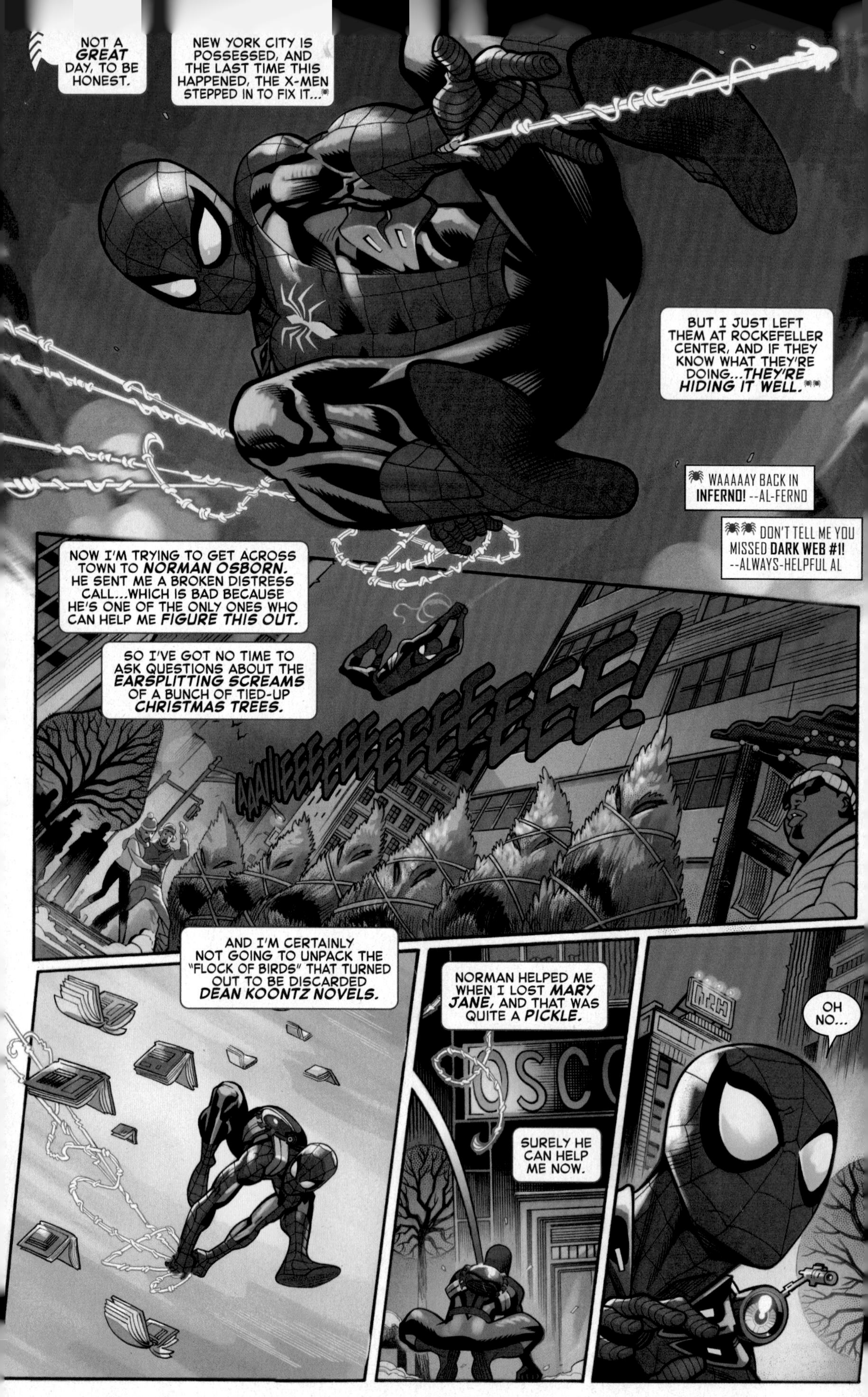
NOT A GREAT DAY, TO BE HONEST.
NEW YORK CITY IS POSSESSED, AND THE LAST TIME THIS HAPPENED, THE X-MEN STEPPED IN TO FIX IT...*
BUT I JUST LEFT THEM AT ROCKEFELLER CENTER, AND IF THEY KNOW WHAT THEY'RE DOING...THEY'RE HIDING IT WELL.**
* WAAAAAY BACK IN INFERNO! --AL-FERNO
** DON'T TELL ME YOU MISSED DARK WEB #1! --ALWAYS-HELPFUL AL
NOW I'M TRYING TO GET ACROSS TOWN TO NORMAN OSBORN. HE SENT ME A BROKEN DISTRESS CALL...WHICH IS BAD BECAUSE HE'S ONE OF THE ONLY ONES WHO CAN HELP ME FIGURE THIS OUT.
SO I'VE GOT NO TIME TO ASK QUESTIONS ABOUT THE EARSPLITTING SCREAMS OF A BUNCH OF TIED-UP CHRISTMAS TREES.
AAAIIEEEEEEEEEEEEE!
AND I'M CERTAINLY NOT GOING TO UNPACK THE "FLOCK OF BIRDS" THAT TURNED OUT TO BE DISCARDED DEAN KOONTZ NOVELS.
NORMAN HELPED ME WHEN I LOST MARY JANE, AND THAT WAS QUITE A PICKLE.
OSCO
SURELY HE CAN HELP ME NOW.
OH NO...

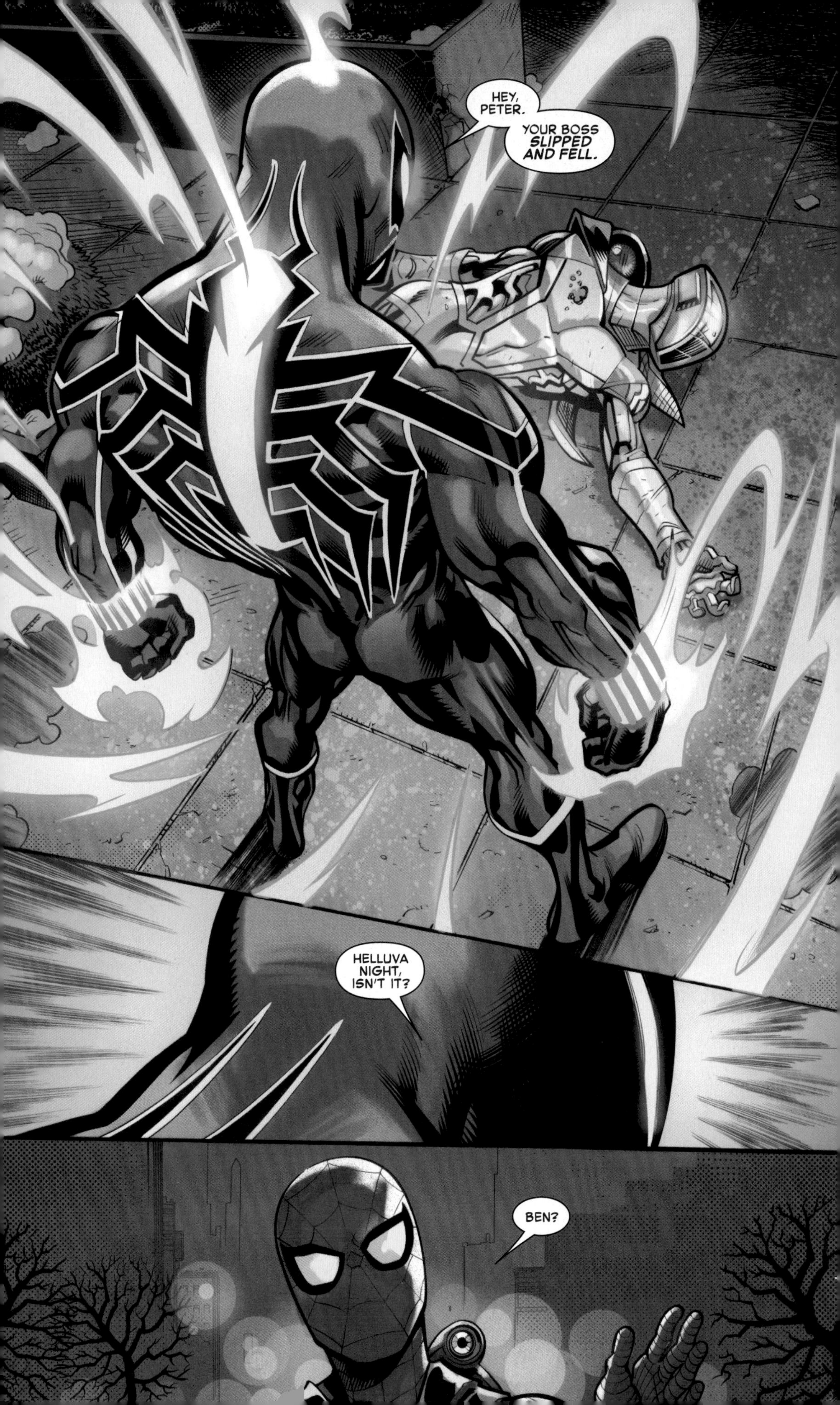
HEY, PETER.
YOUR BOSS SLIPPED AND FELL.
HELLUVA NIGHT, ISN'T IT?
BEN?

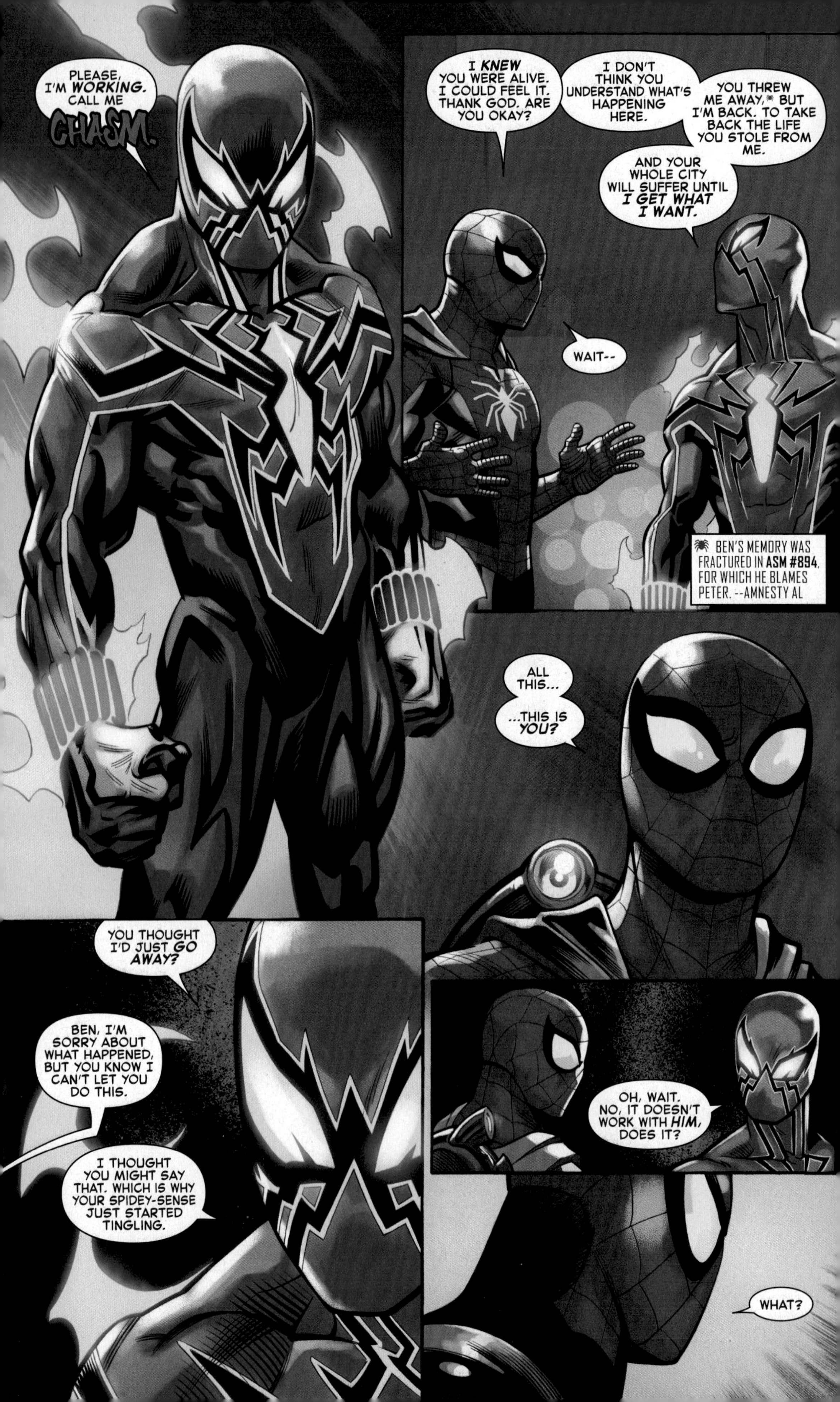
PLEASE, I'M WORKING. CALL ME
CHASM.
I KNEW YOU WERE ALIVE. I COULD FEEL IT. THANK GOD. ARE YOU OKAY?
I DON'T THINK YOU UNDERSTAND WHAT'S HAPPENING HERE.
YOU THREW ME AWAY,* BUT I'M BACK. TO TAKE BACK THE LIFE YOU STOLE FROM ME.
AND YOUR WHOLE CITY WILL SUFFER UNTIL I GET WHAT I WANT.
WAIT--
*BEN'S MEMORY WAS FRACTURED IN ASM #894, FOR WHICH HE BLAMES PETER. --AMNESTY AL
ALL THIS...
...THIS IS YOU?
YOU THOUGHT I'D JUST GO AWAY?
BEN, I'M SORRY ABOUT WHAT HAPPENED, BUT YOU KNOW I CAN'T LET YOU DO THIS.
I THOUGHT YOU MIGHT SAY THAT. WHICH IS WHY YOUR SPIDEY-SENSE JUST STARTED TINGLING.
OH, WAIT. NO, IT DOESN'T WORK WITH HIM, DOES IT?
WHAT?

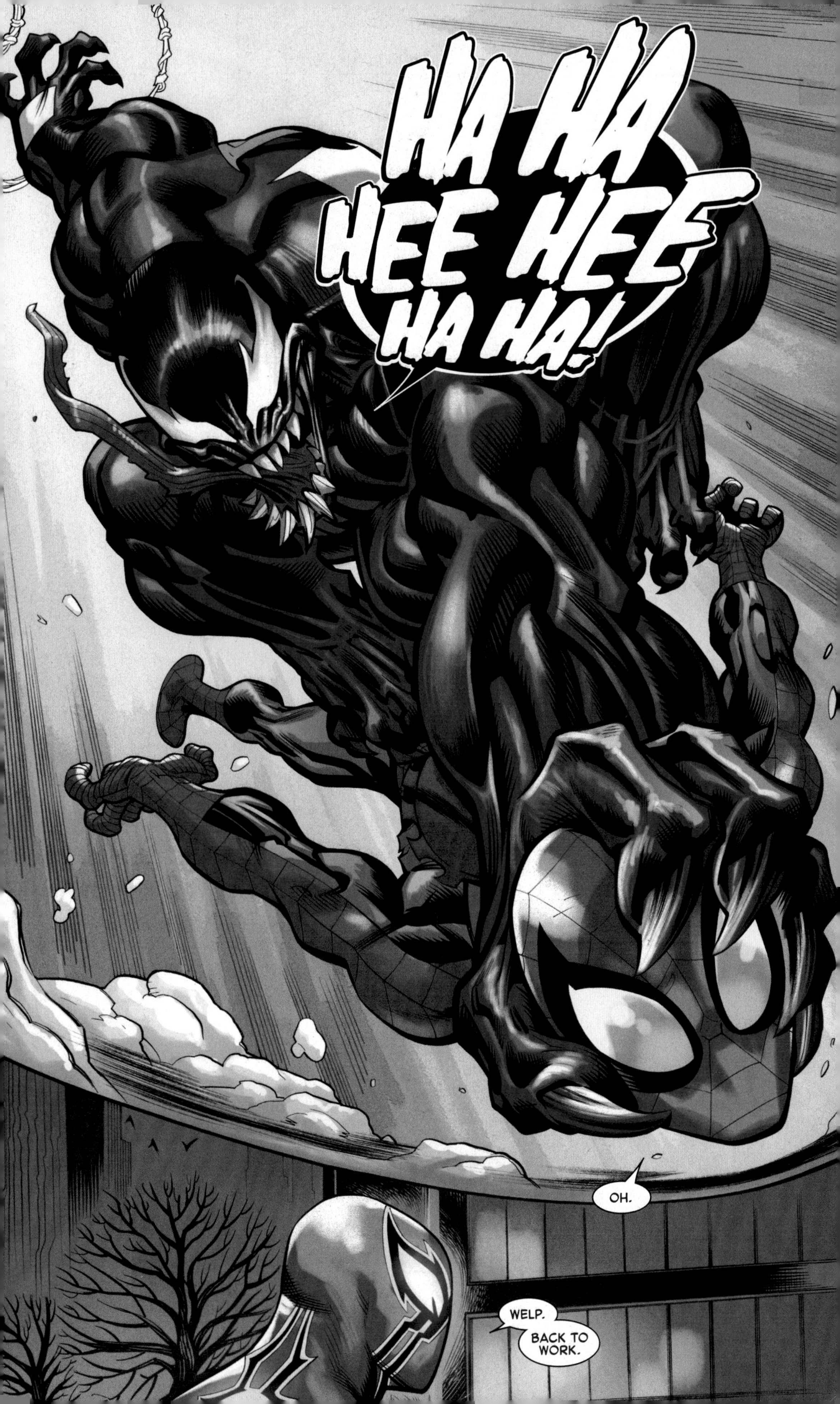
HA HA HEE HEE HA HA!
OH.
WELP.
BACK TO WORK.

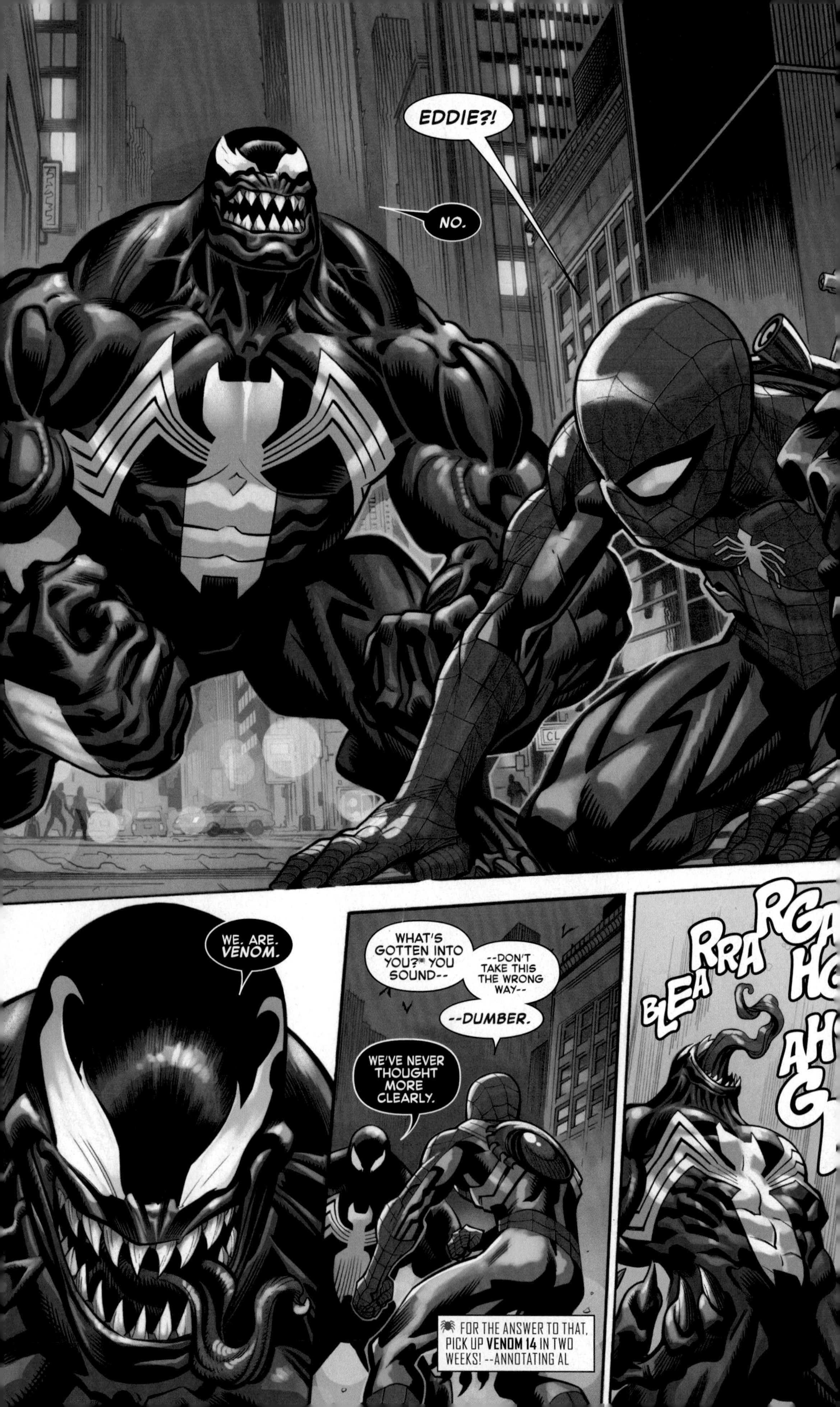

EDDIE?!
NO.
WE. ARE. VENOM.
WHAT'S GOTTEN INTO YOU?* YOU SOUND--
--DON'T TAKE THIS THE WRONG WAY--
--DUMBER.
WE'VE NEVER THOUGHT MORE CLEARLY.
BLEARRARGA
HO
AH
G
*FOR THE ANSWER TO THAT, PICK UP VENOM 14 IN TWO WEEKS! --ANNOTATING AL

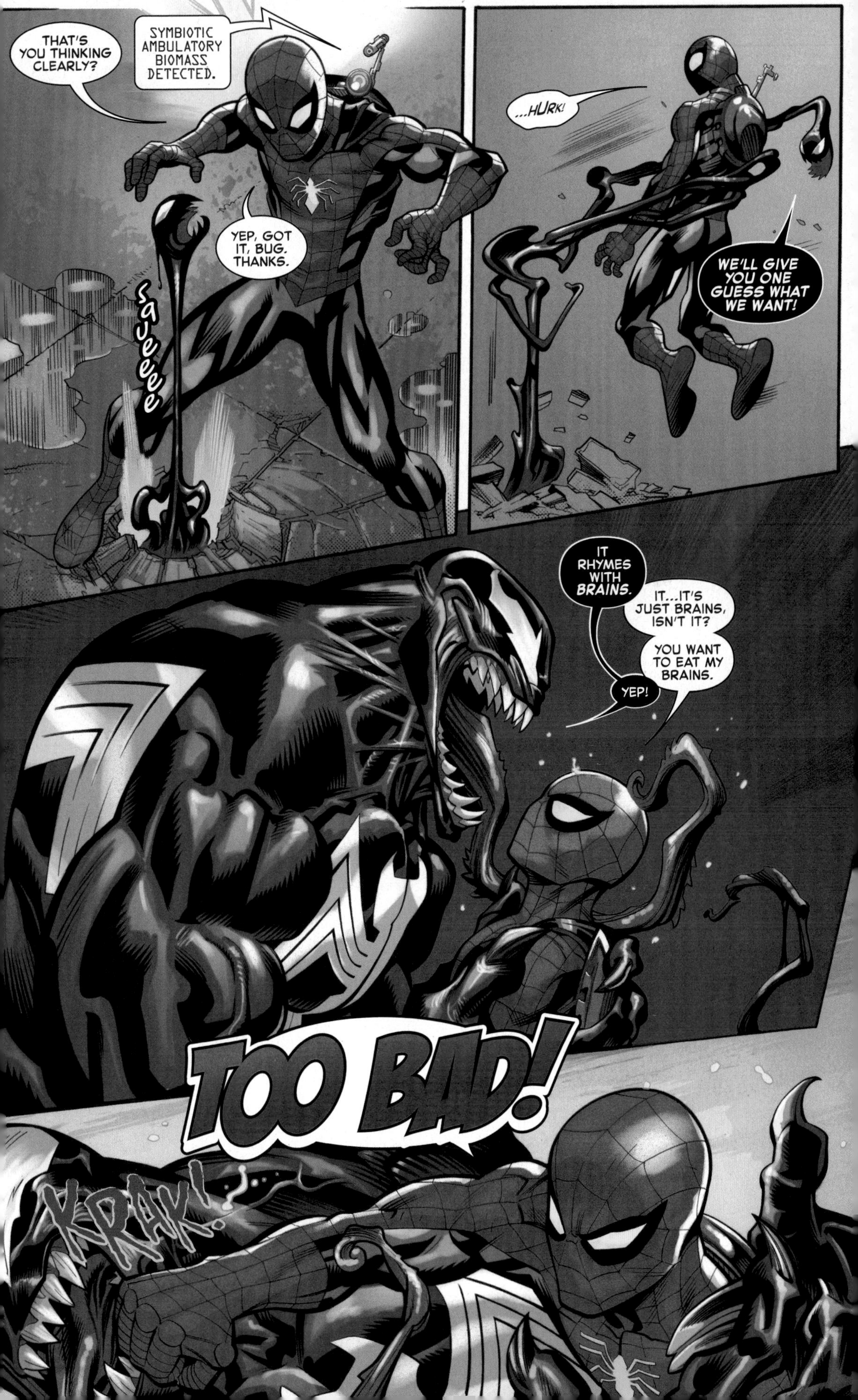
THAT'S YOU THINKING CLEARLY?
SYMBIOTIC AMBULATORY BIOMASS DETECTED.
YEP, GOT IT, BUG. THANKS.
saeeee
...HURK!
WE'LL GIVE YOU ONE GUESS WHAT WE WANT!
IT RHYMES WITH BRAINS.
IT...IT'S JUST BRAINS, ISN'T IT?
YOU WANT TO EAT MY BRAINS.
YEP!
TOO BAD!
KRAK!

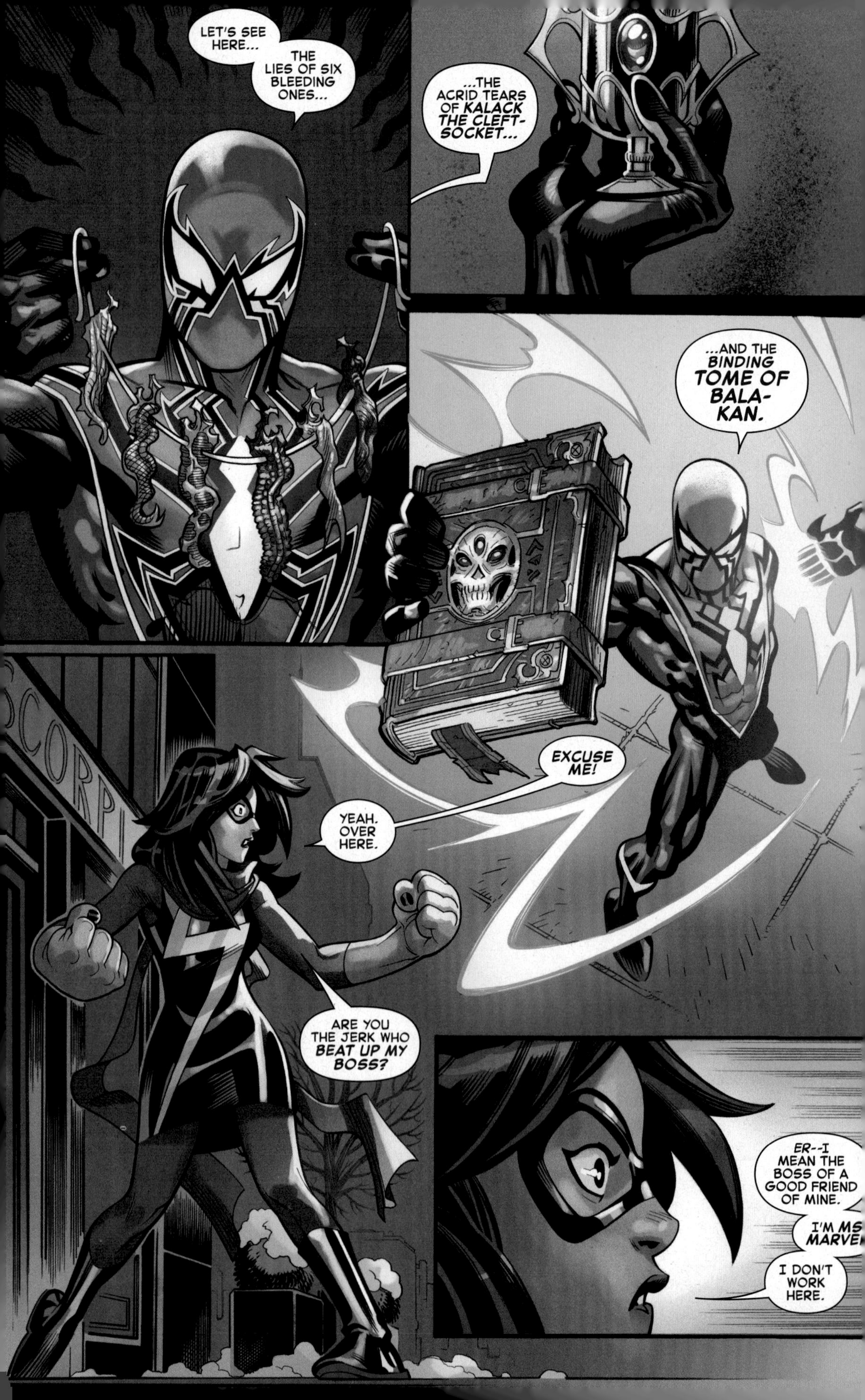

LET'S SEE HERE...
THE LIES OF SIX BLEEDING ONES...
...THE ACRID TEARS OF KALACK THE CLEFT-SOCKET...
...AND THE BINDING TOME OF BALA-KAN.
EXCUSE ME!
YEAH. OVER HERE.
SCORPI
ARE YOU THE JERK WHO BEAT UP MY BOSS?
ER--I MEAN THE BOSS OF A GOOD FRIEND OF MINE.
I DON'T WORK HERE.

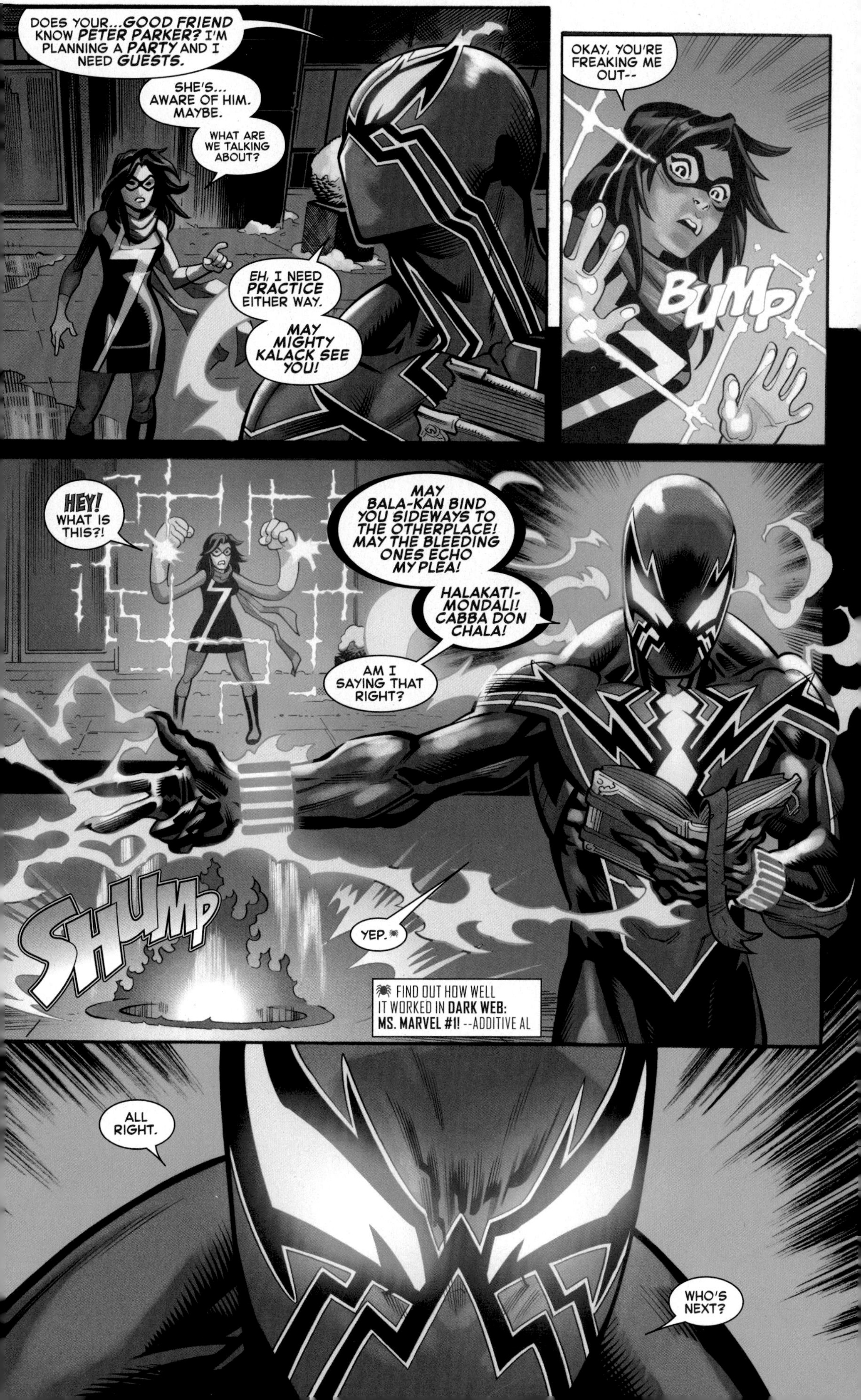

DOES YOUR...GOOD FRIEND KNOW PETER PARKER? I'M PLANNING A PARTY AND I NEED GUESTS.
SHE'S... AWARE OF HIM. MAYBE.
WHAT ARE WE TALKING ABOUT?
EH, I NEED PRACTICE EITHER WAY.
MAY MIGHTY KALACK SEE YOU!
OKAY, YOU'RE FREAKING ME OUT--
BUMP
HEY! WHAT IS THIS?!
MAY BALA-KAN BIND YOU SIDEWAYS TO THE OTHERPLACE! MAY THE BLEEDING ONES ECHO MY PLEA!
HALAKATI-MONDALI! CABBA DON CHALA!
AM I SAYING THAT RIGHT?
SHUMP
YEP.
FIND OUT HOW WELL IT WORKED IN DARK WEB: MS. MARVEL #1! --ADDITIVE AL
ALL RIGHT.
WHO'S NEXT?

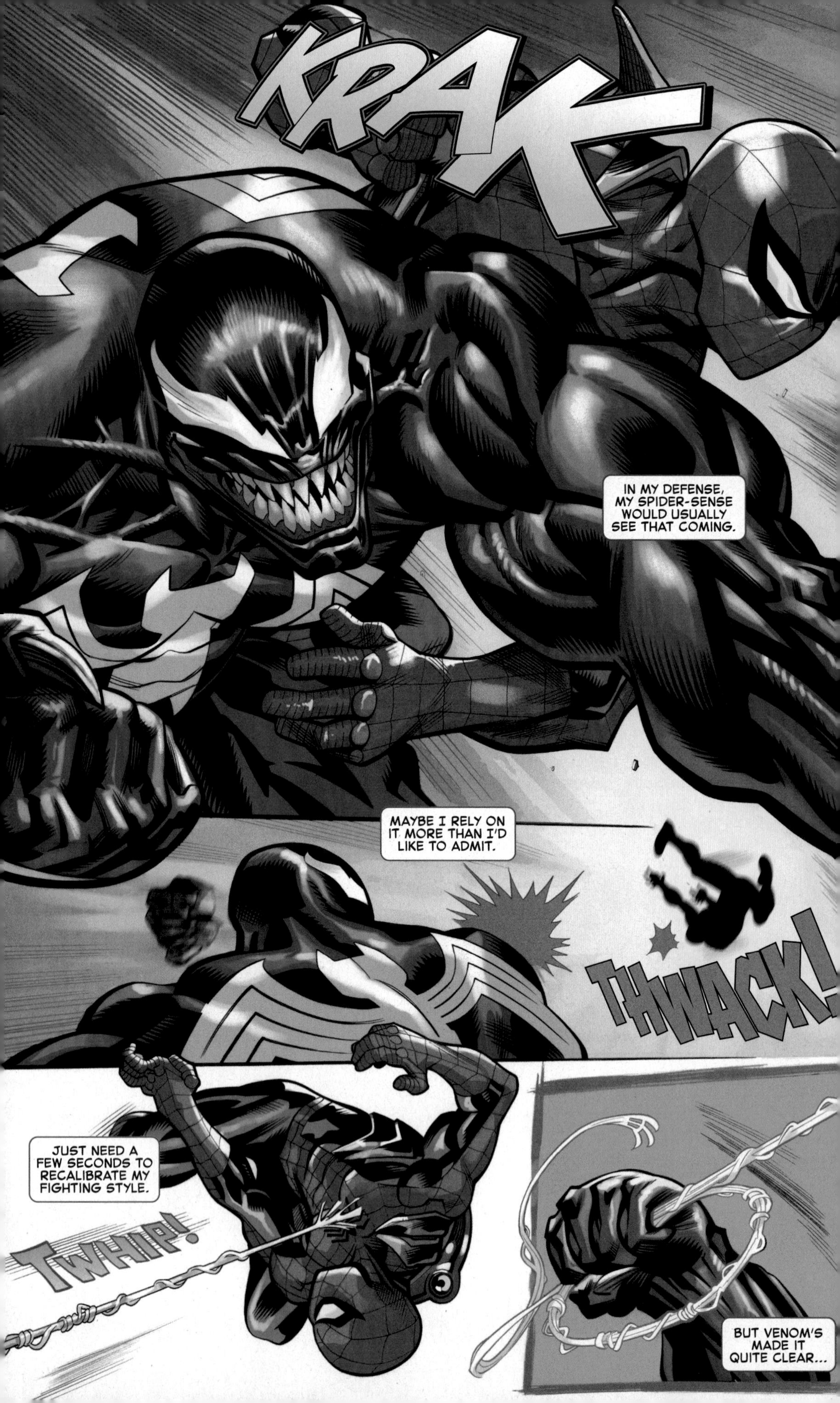
KRAK
IN MY DEFENSE, MY SPIDER-SENSE WOULD USUALLY SEE THAT COMING.
MAYBE I RELY ON IT MORE THAN I'D LIKE TO ADMIT.
THWACK!
JUST NEED A FEW SECONDS TO RECALIBRATE MY FIGHTING STYLE.
TWHIP!
BUT VENOM'S MADE IT QUITE CLEAR...

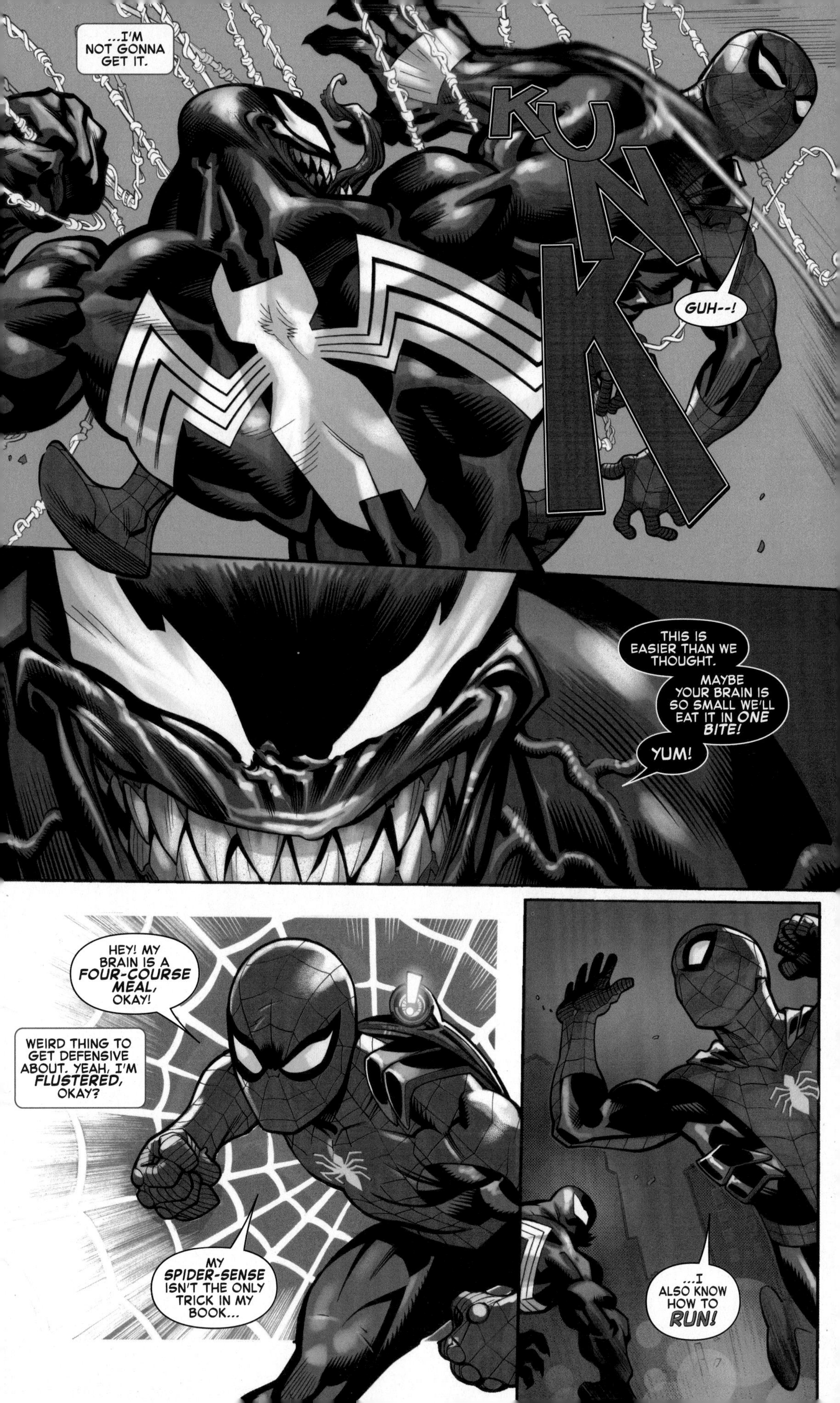
...I'M NOT GONNA GET IT.
KUNK
GUH--!
THIS IS EASIER THAN WE THOUGHT.
MAYBE YOUR BRAIN IS SO SMALL WE'LL EAT IT IN ONE BITE!
YUM!
HEY! MY BRAIN IS A FOUR-COURSE MEAL, OKAY!
WEIRD THING TO GET DEFENSIVE ABOUT. YEAH, I'M FLUSTERED, OKAY?
MY SPIDER-SENSE ISN'T THE ONLY TRICK IN MY BOOK...
...I ALSO KNOW HOW TO RUN!

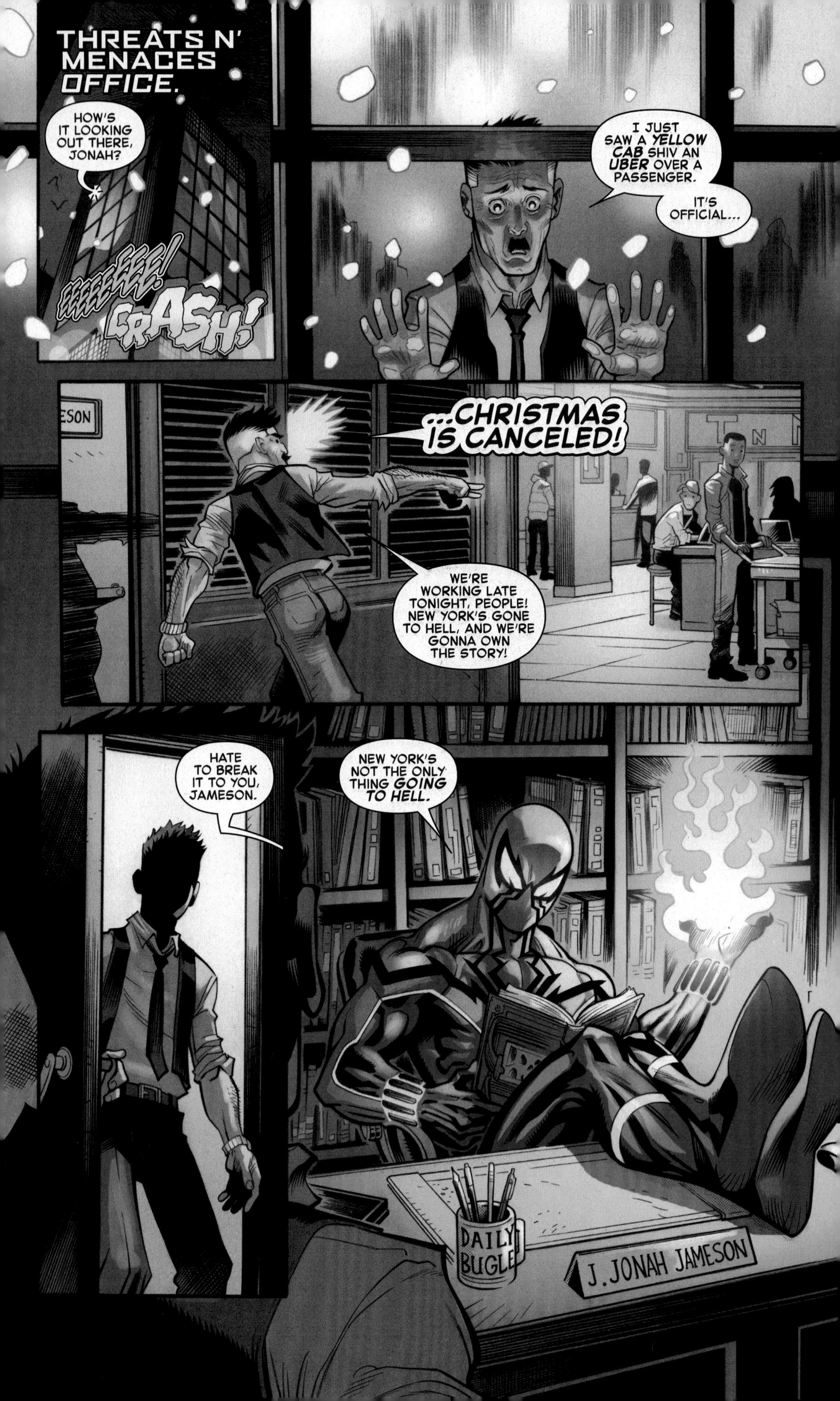
THREATS N' MENACES OFFICE.
HOW'S IT LOOKING OUT THERE, JONAH?
EEEEEEEEE!
CRASH!
I JUST SAW A YELLOW CAB SHIV AN UBER OVER A PASSENGER.
IT'S OFFICIAL...
...CHRISTMAS IS CANCELED!
WE'RE WORKING LATE TONIGHT, PEOPLE! NEW YORK'S GONE TO HELL, AND WE'RE GONNA OWN THE STORY!
HATE TO BREAK IT TO YOU, JAMESON.
NEW YORK'S NOT THE ONLY THING GOING TO HELL.
DAILY BUGLE
J. JONAH JAMESON

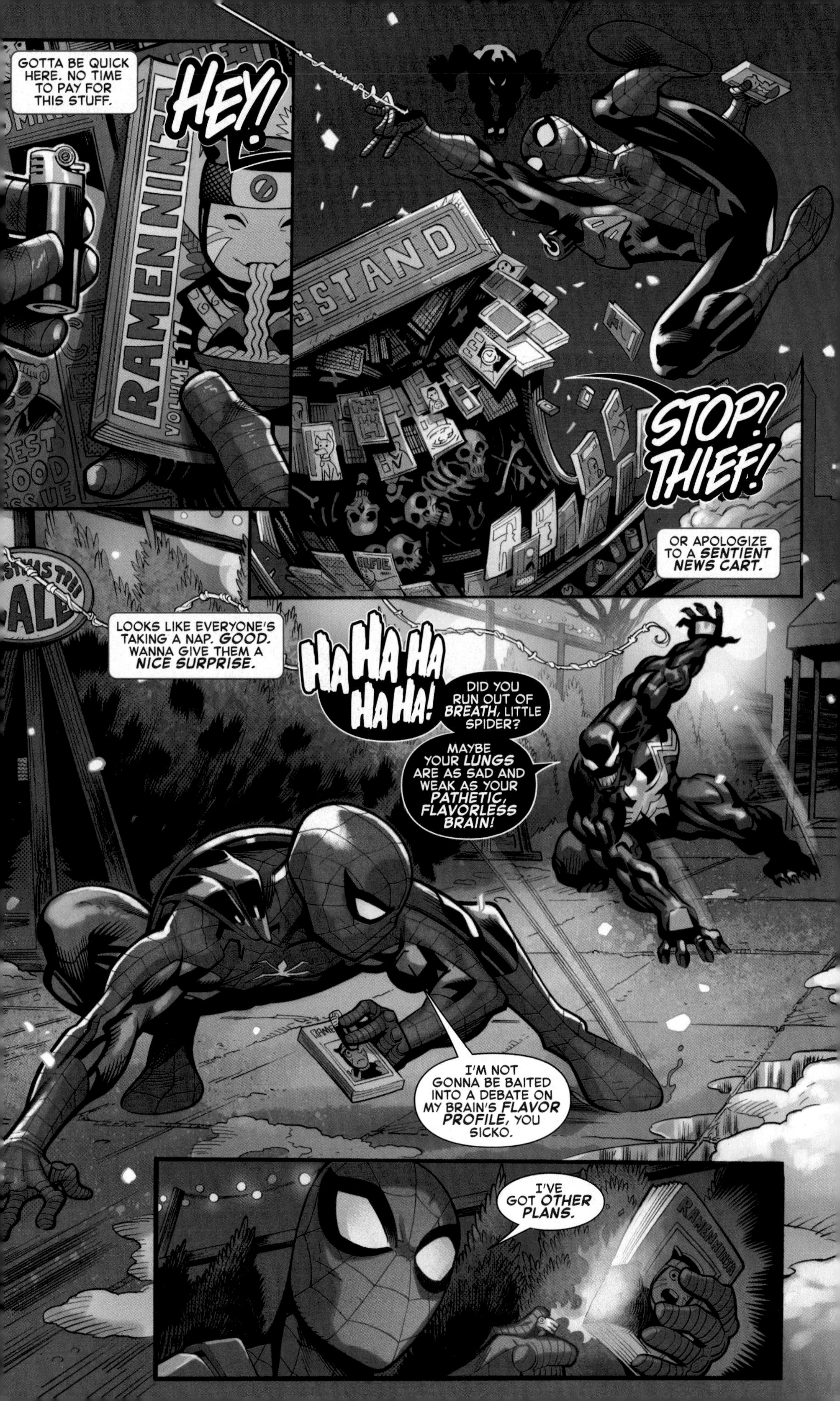

GOTTA BE QUICK HERE. NO TIME TO PAY FOR THIS STUFF.
HEY!
RAMEN NINJA
VOLUME 17
STAND
STOP! THIEF!
OR APOLOGIZE TO A *SENTIENT NEWS CART.*
LOOKS LIKE EVERYONE'S TAKING A NAP. *GOOD.* WANNA GIVE THEM A *NICE SURPRISE.*
HA HA HA HA HA!
DID YOU RUN OUT OF *BREATH,* LITTLE SPIDER?
MAYBE YOUR *LUNGS* ARE AS SAD AND WEAK AS YOUR *PATHETIC, FLAVORLESS BRAIN!*
I'M NOT GONNA BE BAITED INTO A DEBATE ON MY BRAIN'S *FLAVOR PROFILE,* YOU SICKO.
I'VE GOT *OTHER PLANS.*

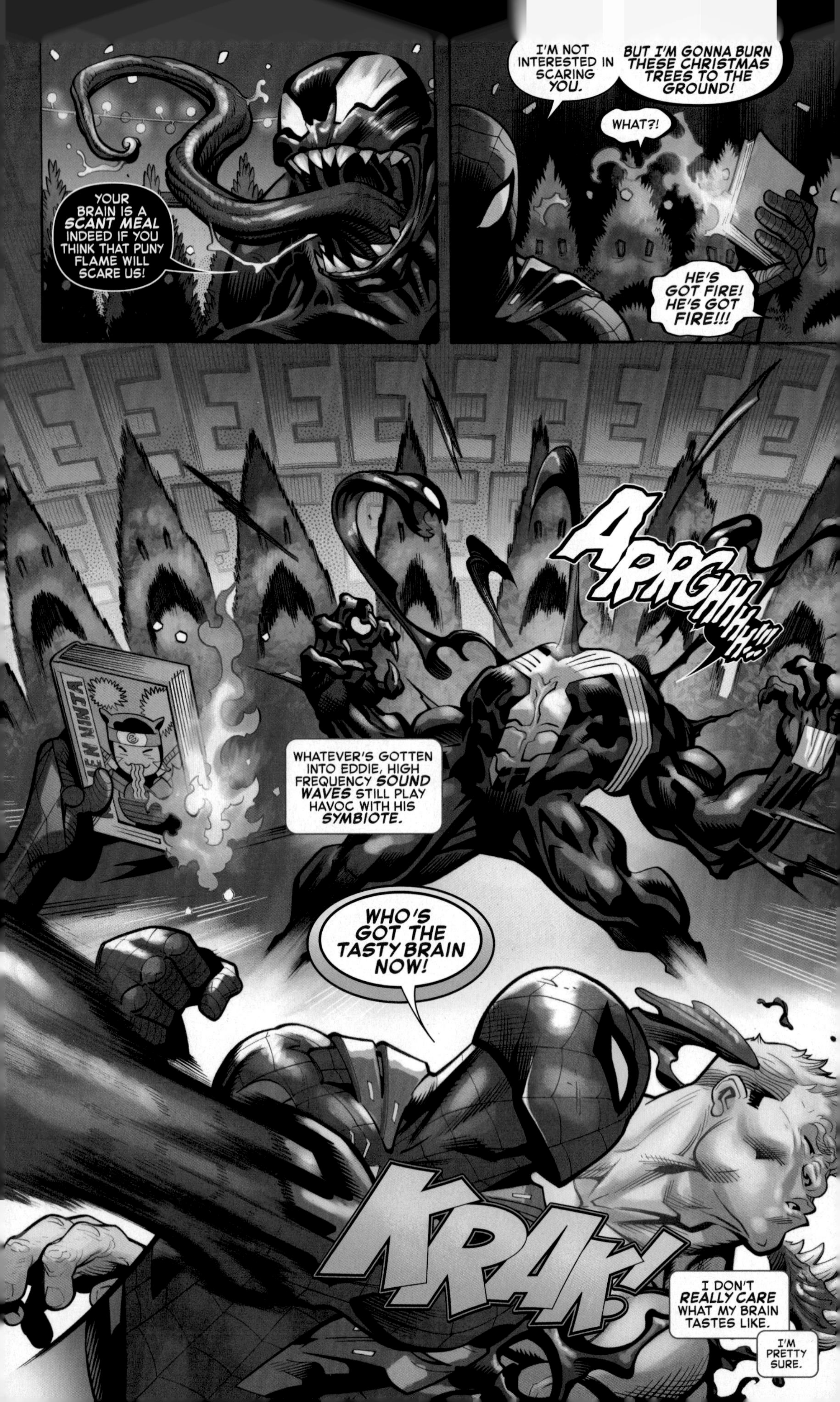
YOUR BRAIN IS A SCANT MEAL INDEED IF YOU THINK THAT PUNY FLAME WILL SCARE US!
I'M NOT INTERESTED IN SCARING YOU.
BUT I'M GONNA BURN THESE CHRISTMAS TREES TO THE GROUND!
WHAT?!
HE'S GOT FIRE! HE'S GOT FIRE!!!
APRGHHH!!
WHATEVER'S GOTTEN INTO EDDIE, HIGH FREQUENCY SOUND WAVES STILL PLAY HAVOC WITH HIS SYMBIOTE.
WHO'S GOT THE TASTY BRAIN NOW!
KRAK!
I DON'T REALLY CARE WHAT MY BRAIN TASTES LIKE.
I'M PRETTY SURE.

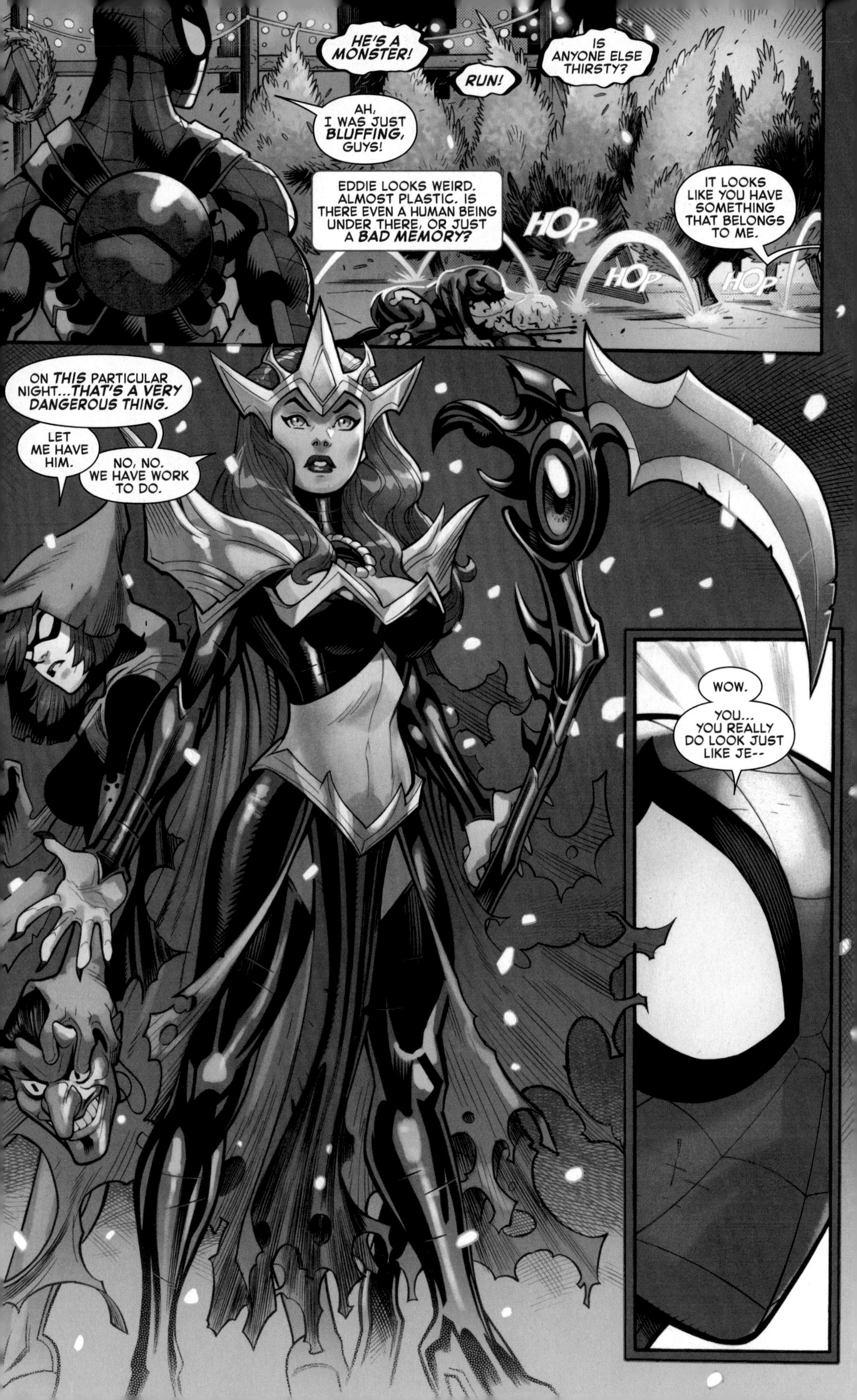
HE'S A MONSTER!
RUN!
IS ANYONE ELSE THIRSTY?
AH, I WAS JUST BLUFFING, GUYS!
EDDIE LOOKS WEIRD. ALMOST PLASTIC. IS THERE EVEN A HUMAN BEING UNDER THERE, OR JUST A BAD MEMORY?
HOP
HOP
HOP
IT LOOKS LIKE YOU HAVE SOMETHING THAT BELONGS TO ME.
ON THIS PARTICULAR NIGHT...THAT'S A VERY DANGEROUS THING.
LET ME HAVE HIM.
NO, NO. WE HAVE WORK TO DO.
WOW.
YOU... YOU REALLY DO LOOK JUST LIKE JE--

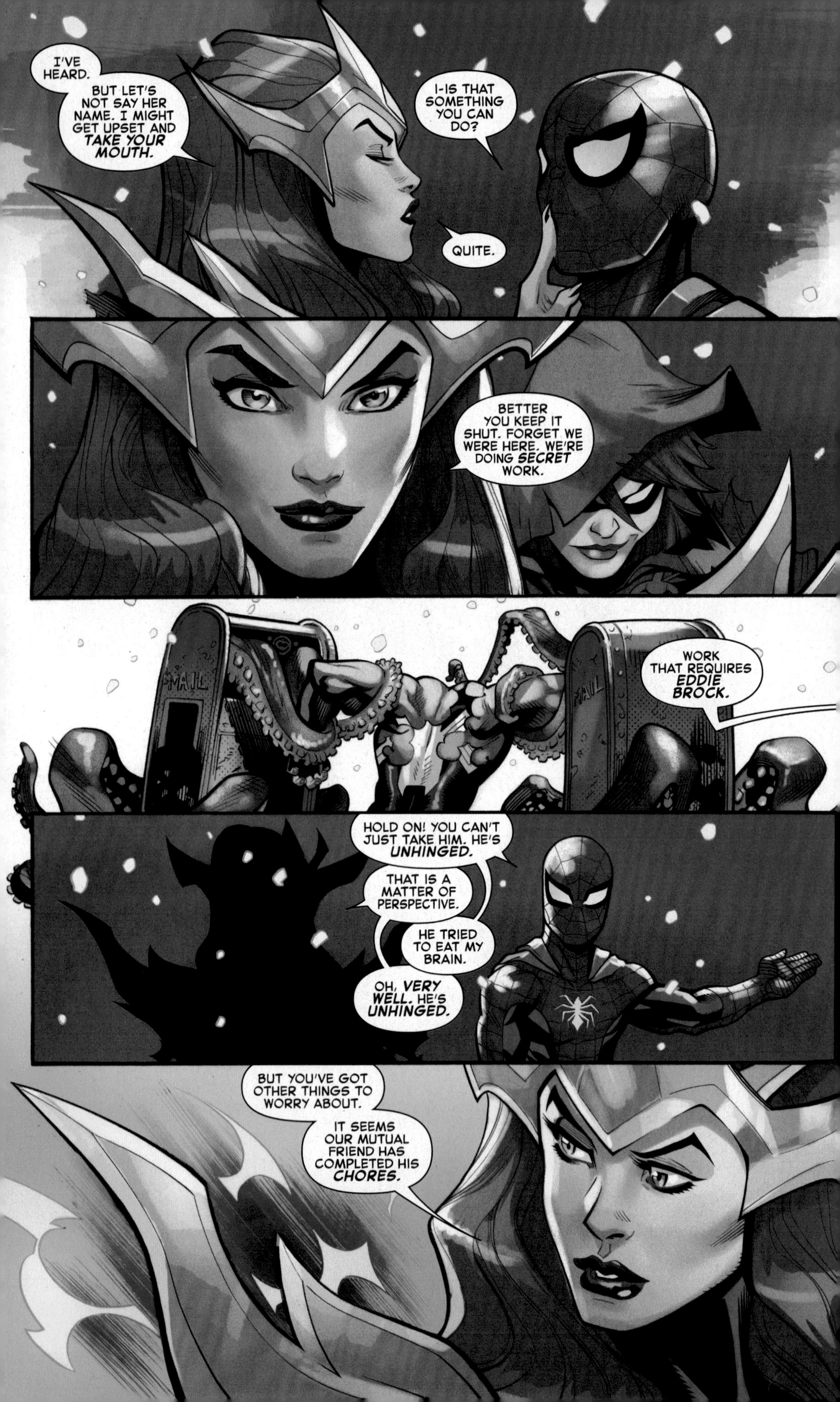
I'VE HEARD.
BUT LET'S NOT SAY HER NAME. I MIGHT GET UPSET AND TAKE YOUR MOUTH.
I-IS THAT SOMETHING YOU CAN DO?
QUITE.
BETTER YOU KEEP IT SHUT. FORGET WE WERE HERE. WE'RE DOING SECRET WORK.
MAIL
MAIL
WORK THAT REQUIRES EDDIE BROCK.
HOLD ON! YOU CAN'T JUST TAKE HIM. HE'S UNHINGED.
THAT IS A MATTER OF PERSPECTIVE.
HE TRIED TO EAT MY BRAIN.
OH, VERY WELL. HE'S UNHINGED.
BUT YOU'VE GOT OTHER THINGS TO WORRY ABOUT.
IT SEEMS OUR MUTUAL FRIEND HAS COMPLETED HIS CHORES.

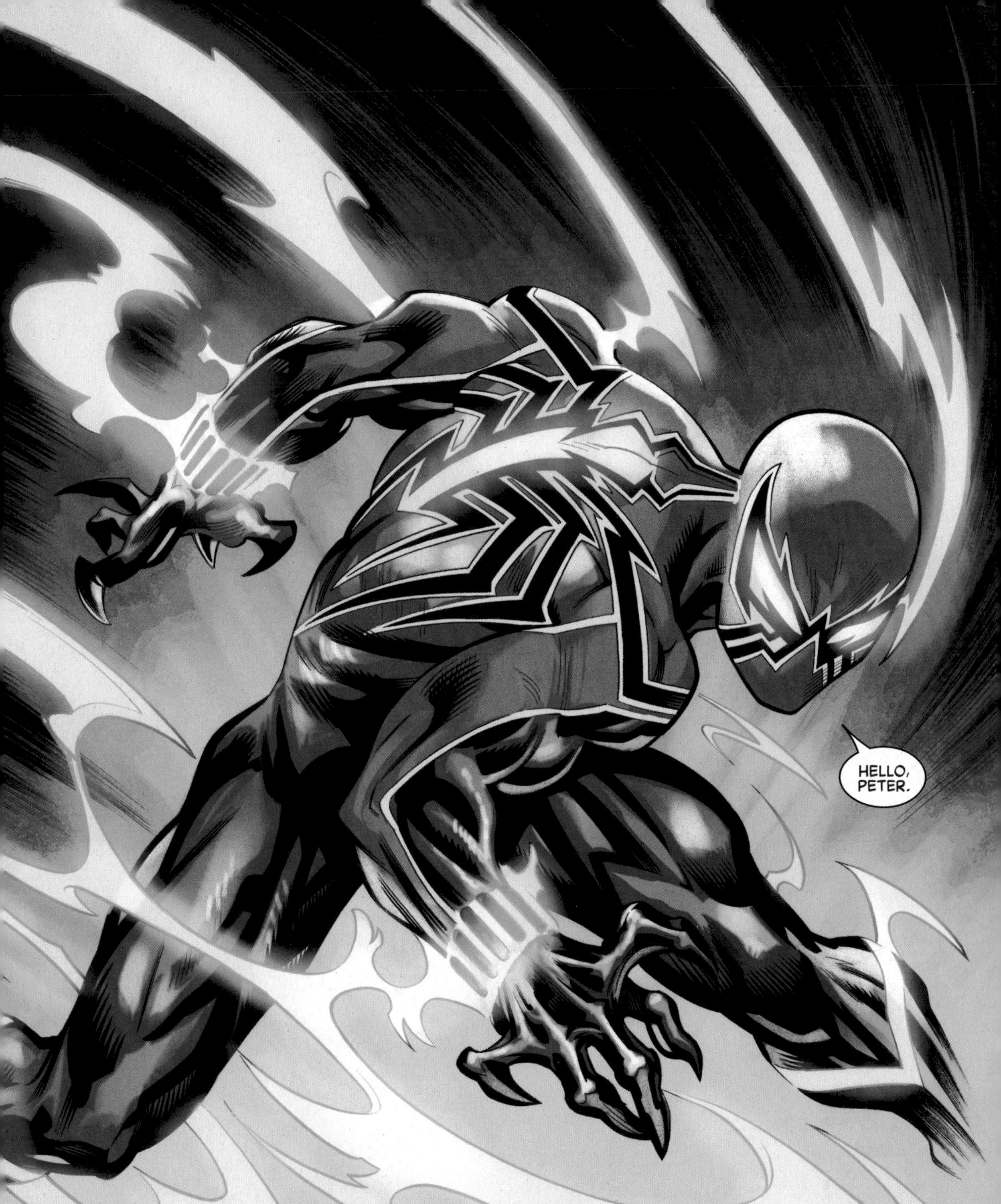
HELLO, PETER.

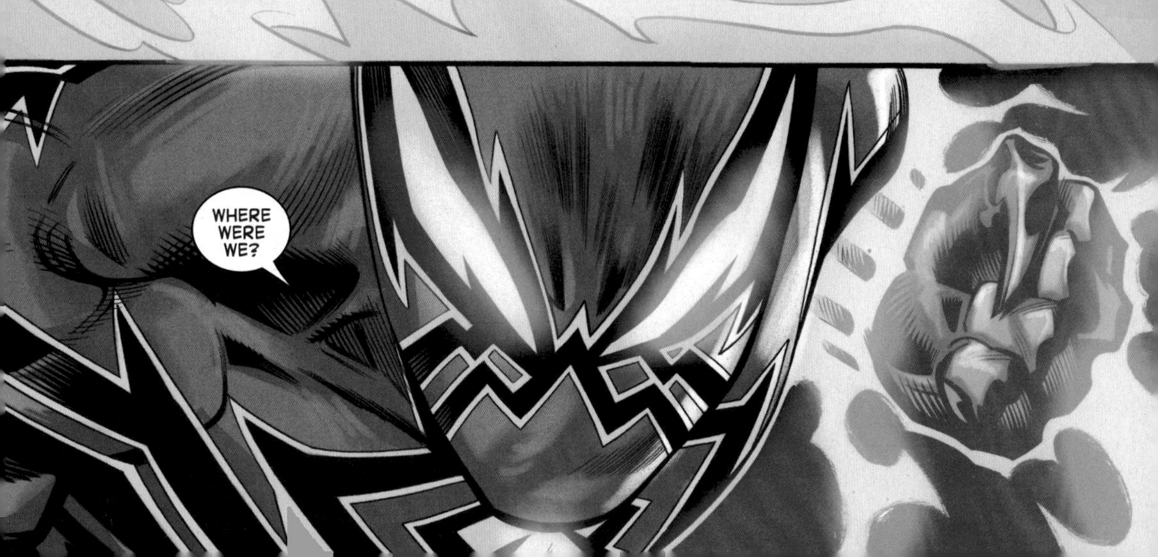
WHERE WERE WE?

AMAZING SPIDER-MAN #16

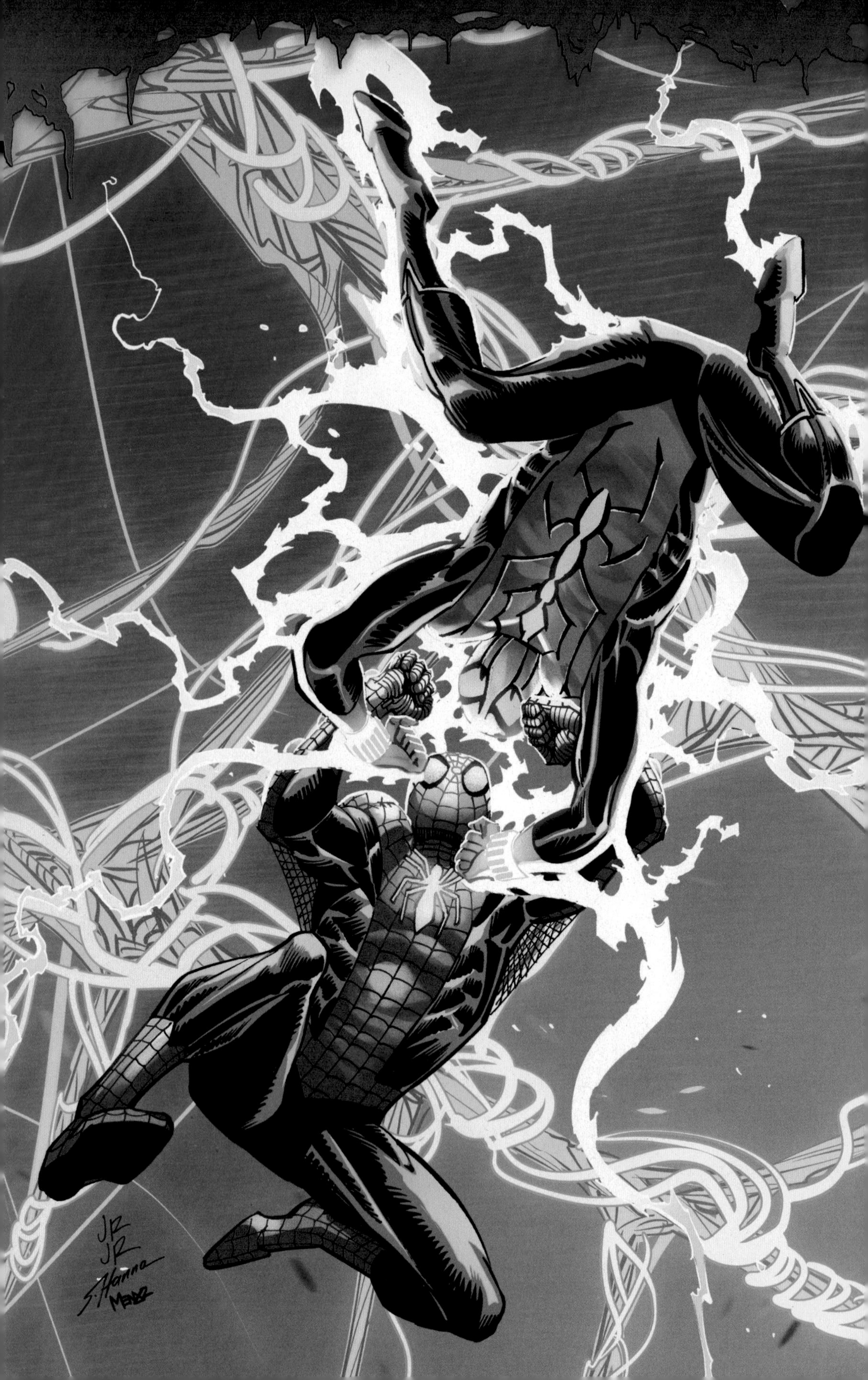

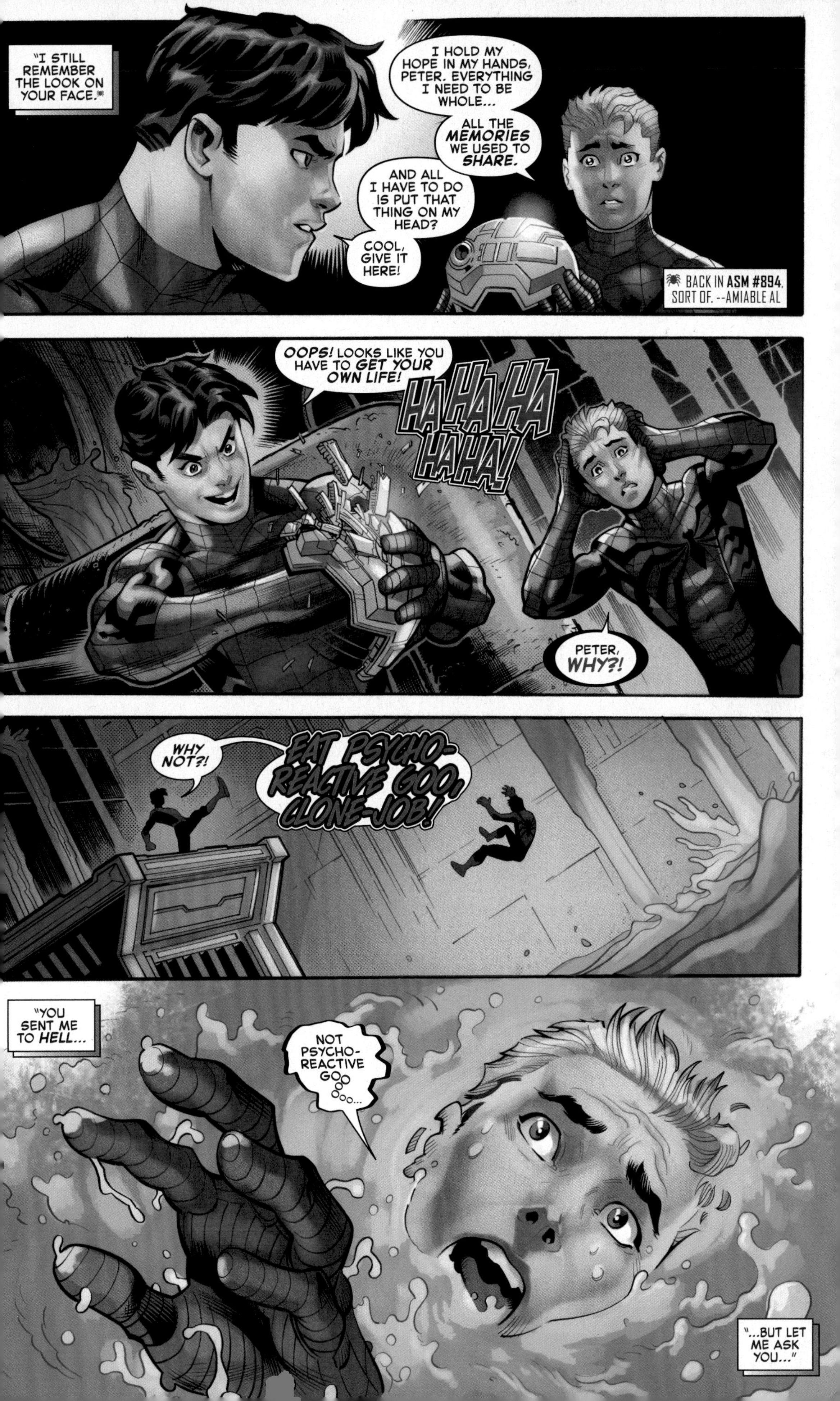
"I STILL REMEMBER THE LOOK ON YOUR FACE.*
I HOLD MY HOPE IN MY HANDS, PETER. EVERYTHING I NEED TO BE WHOLE...
ALL THE MEMORIES WE USED TO SHARE.
AND ALL I HAVE TO DO IS PUT THAT THING ON MY HEAD?
COOL, GIVE IT HERE!
BACK IN ASM #894, SORT OF. --AMIABLE AL
OOPS! LOOKS LIKE YOU HAVE TO GET YOUR OWN LIFE!
HAHAHA HAHA!
PETER, WHY?!
WHY NOT?!
EAT PSYCHO-REACTIVE GOO, CLONE-JOB!
"YOU SENT ME TO HELL...
NOT PSYCHO-REACTIVE GOOOOO...
"...BUT LET ME ASK YOU..."

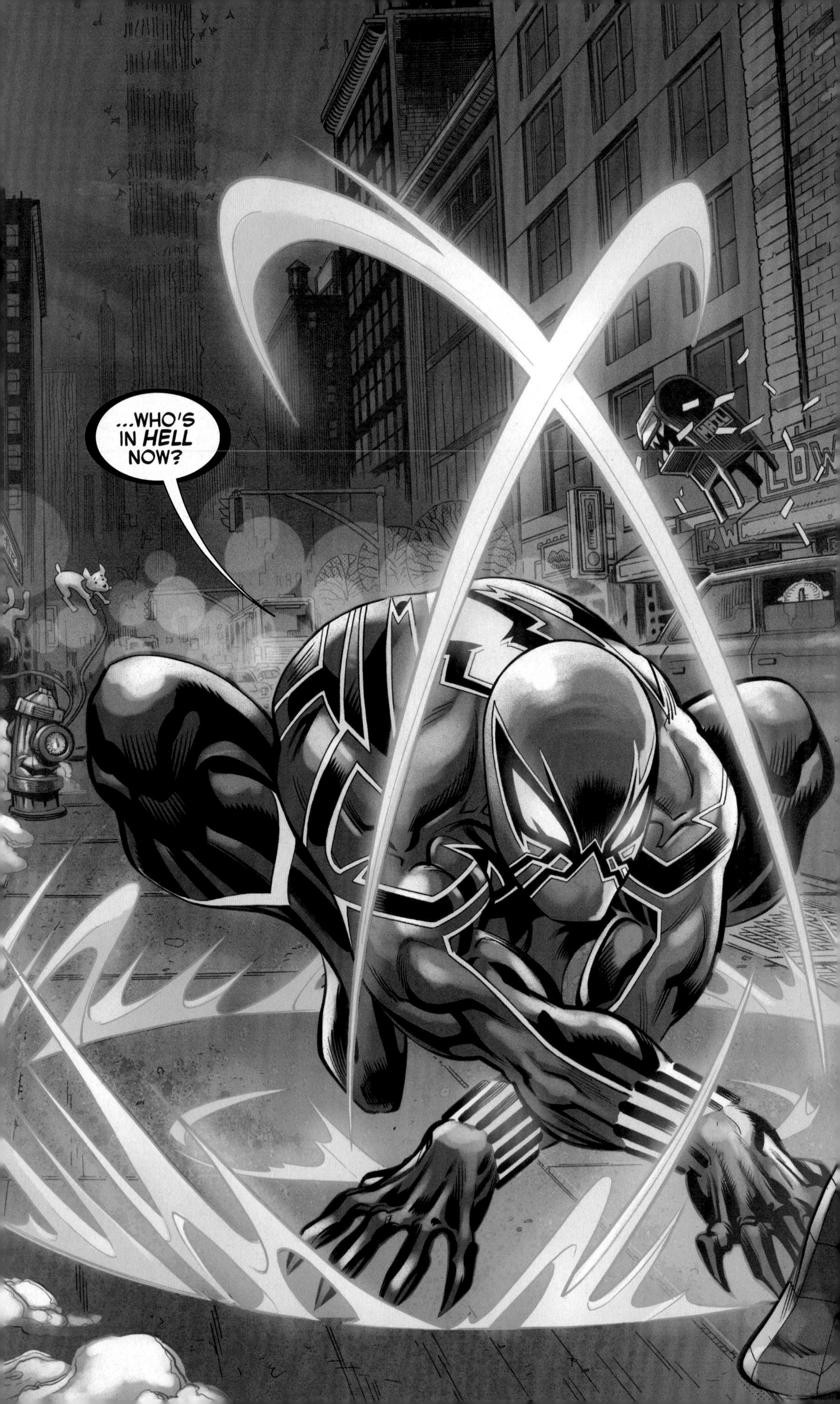

...WHO'S IN HELL NOW?

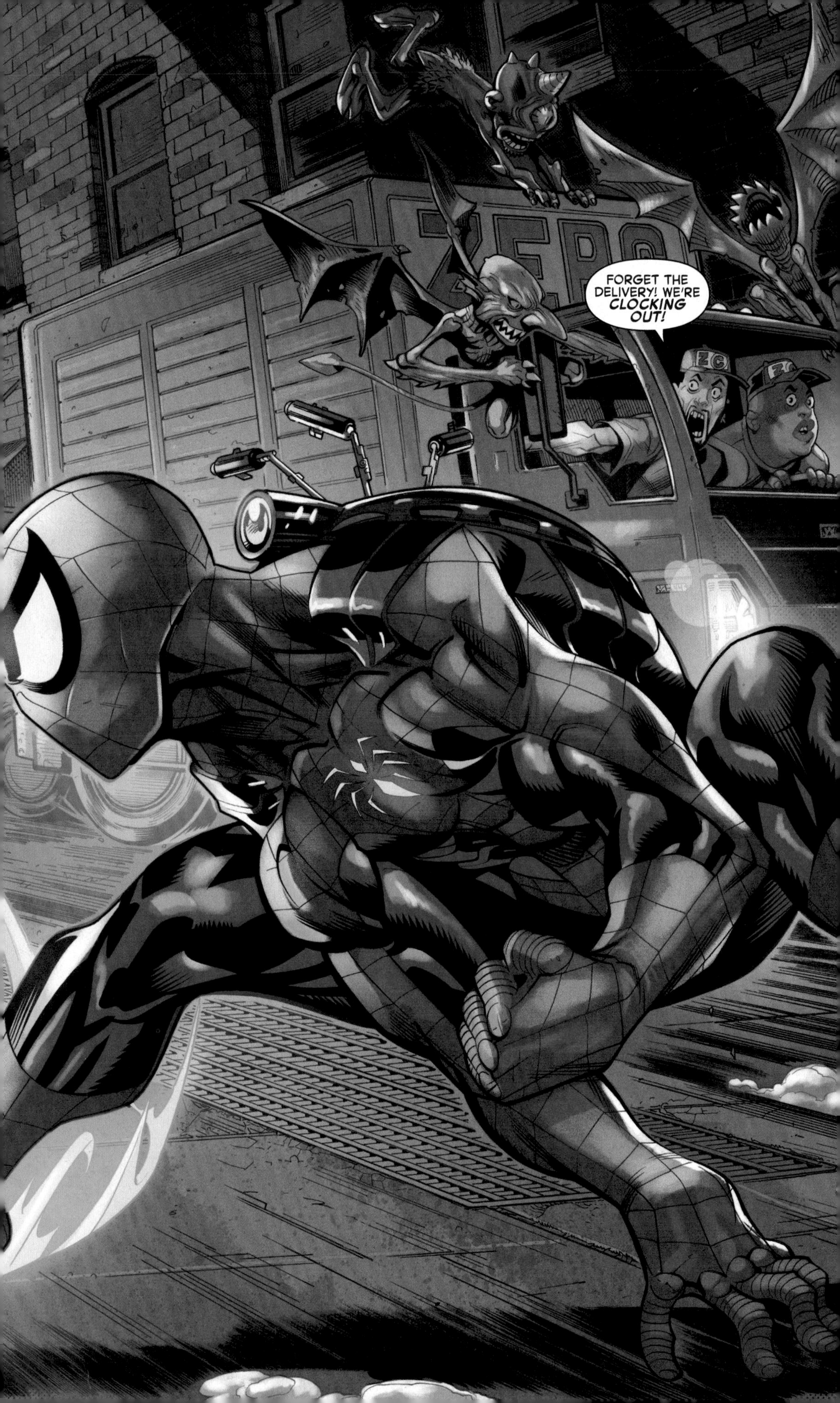
FORGET THE DELIVERY! WE'RE CLOCKING OUT!

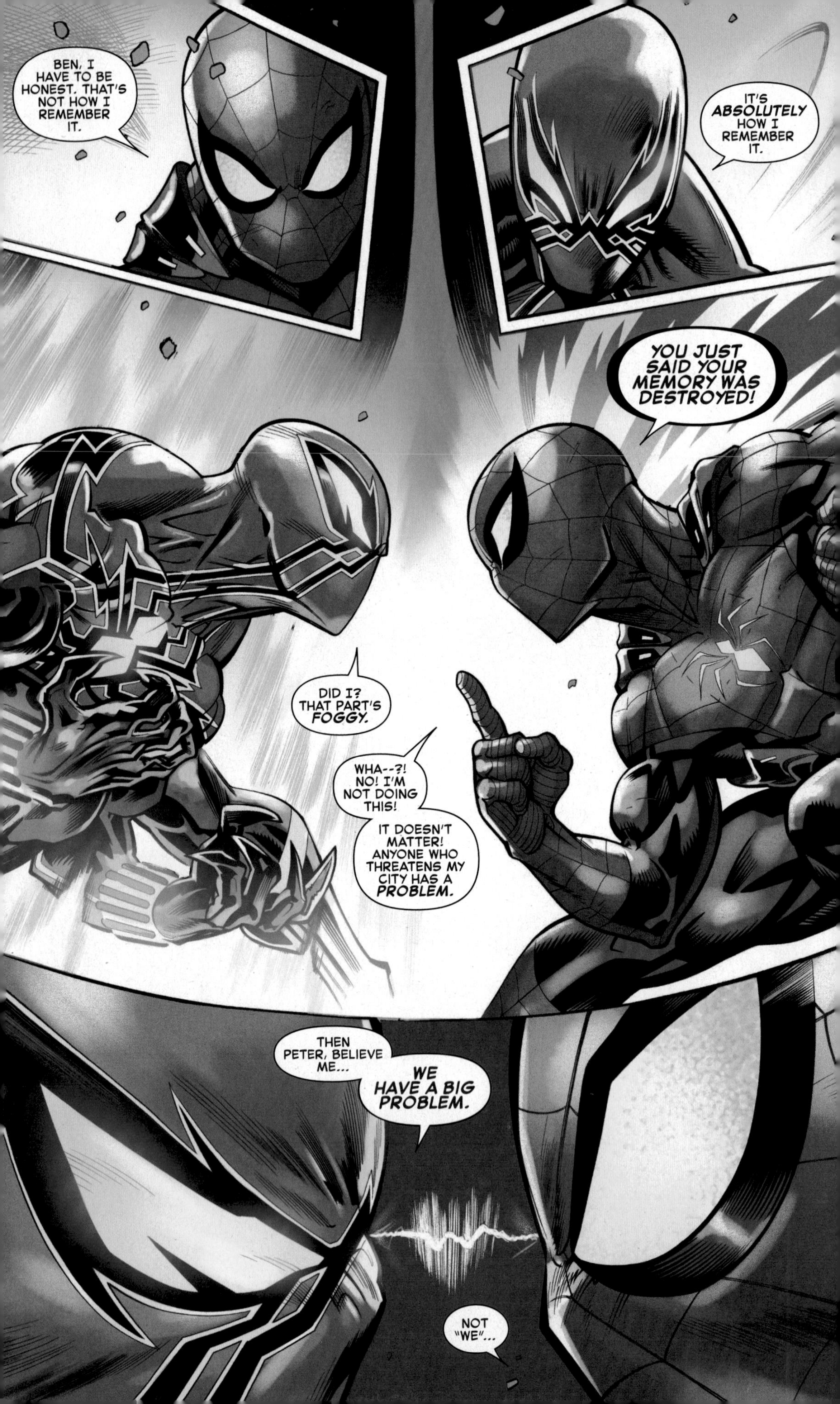
BEN, I HAVE TO BE HONEST. THAT'S NOT HOW I REMEMBER IT.
IT'S ABSOLUTELY HOW I REMEMBER IT.
YOU JUST SAID YOUR MEMORY WAS DESTROYED!
DID I? THAT PART'S FOGGY.
WHA--?! NO! I'M NOT DOING THIS!
IT DOESN'T MATTER! ANYONE WHO THREATENS MY CITY HAS A PROBLEM.
THEN PETER, BELIEVE ME...
WE HAVE A BIG PROBLEM.
NOT "WE"...

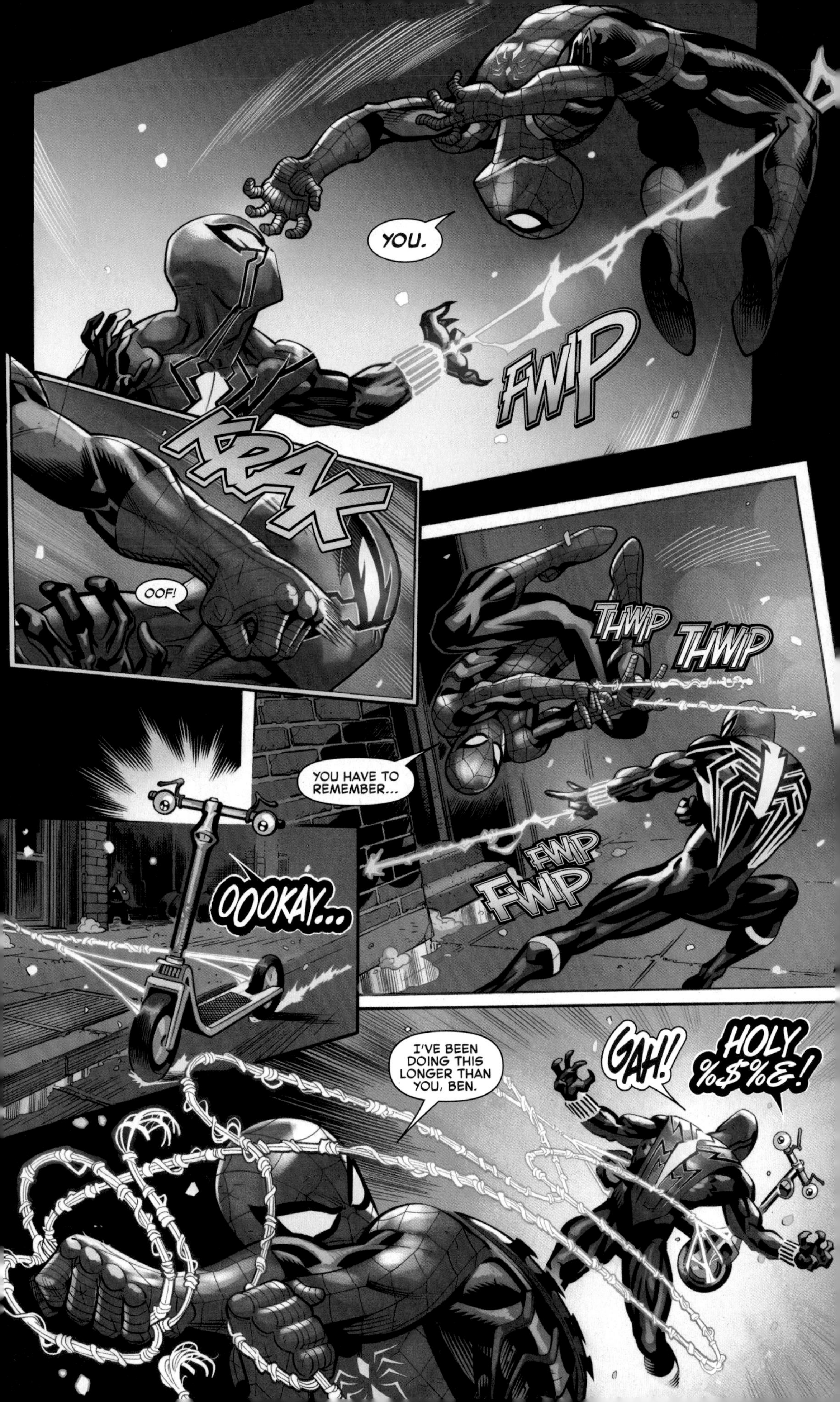

YOU.
FWIP
KRAK
OOF!
THWIP
THWIP
YOU HAVE TO REMEMBER...
FWIP
FWIP
OOOKAY...
I'VE BEEN DOING THIS LONGER THAN YOU, BEN.
GAH!
HOLY %$%&!

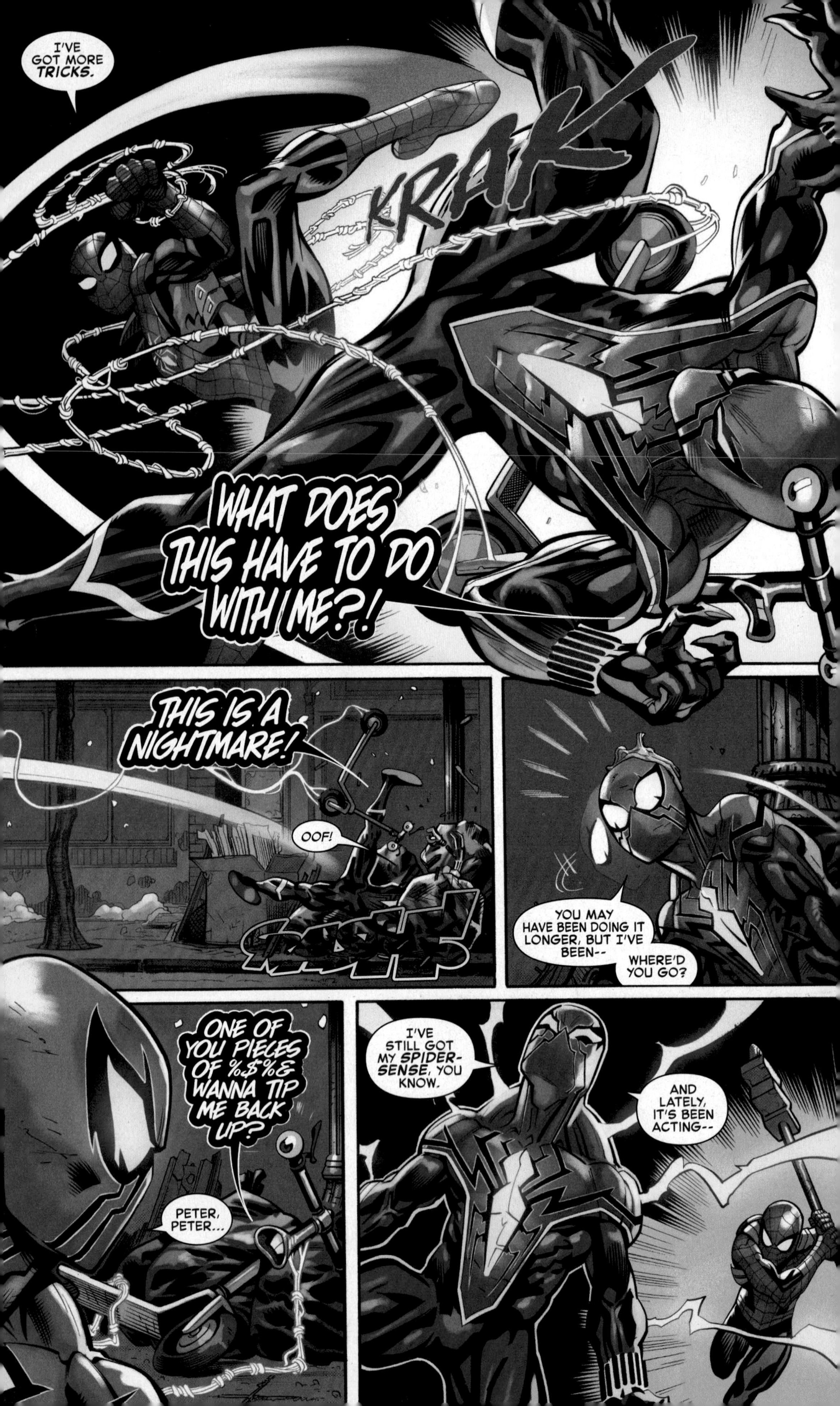
I'VE GOT MORE TRICKS.
KRAK
WHAT DOES THIS HAVE TO DO WITH ME?!
THIS IS A NIGHTMARE!
OOF!
YOU MAY HAVE BEEN DOING IT LONGER, BUT I'VE BEEN--
WHERE'D YOU GO?
ONE OF YOU PIECES OF %$%& WANNA TIP ME BACK UP?
PETER, PETER...
I'VE STILL GOT MY SPIDER-SENSE, YOU KNOW.
AND LATELY, IT'S BEEN ACTING--

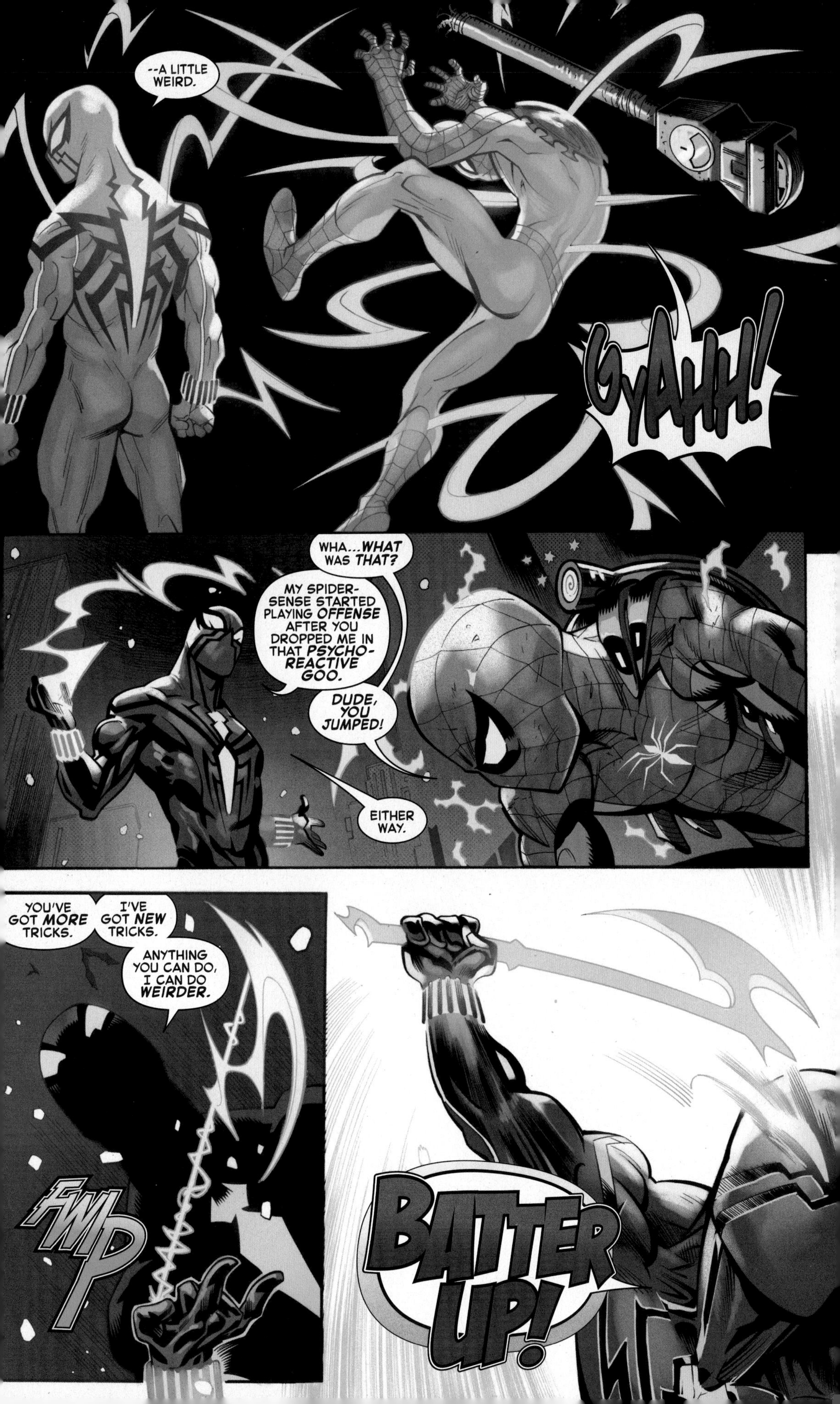
--A LITTLE WEIRD.
GYAHH!
WHA...WHAT WAS THAT?
MY SPIDER-SENSE STARTED PLAYING OFFENSE AFTER YOU DROPPED ME IN THAT PSYCHO-REACTIVE GOO.
DUDE, YOU JUMPED!
EITHER WAY.
YOU'VE GOT MORE TRICKS.
I'VE GOT NEW TRICKS.
ANYTHING YOU CAN DO, I CAN DO WEIRDER.
FWIP
BATTER UP!

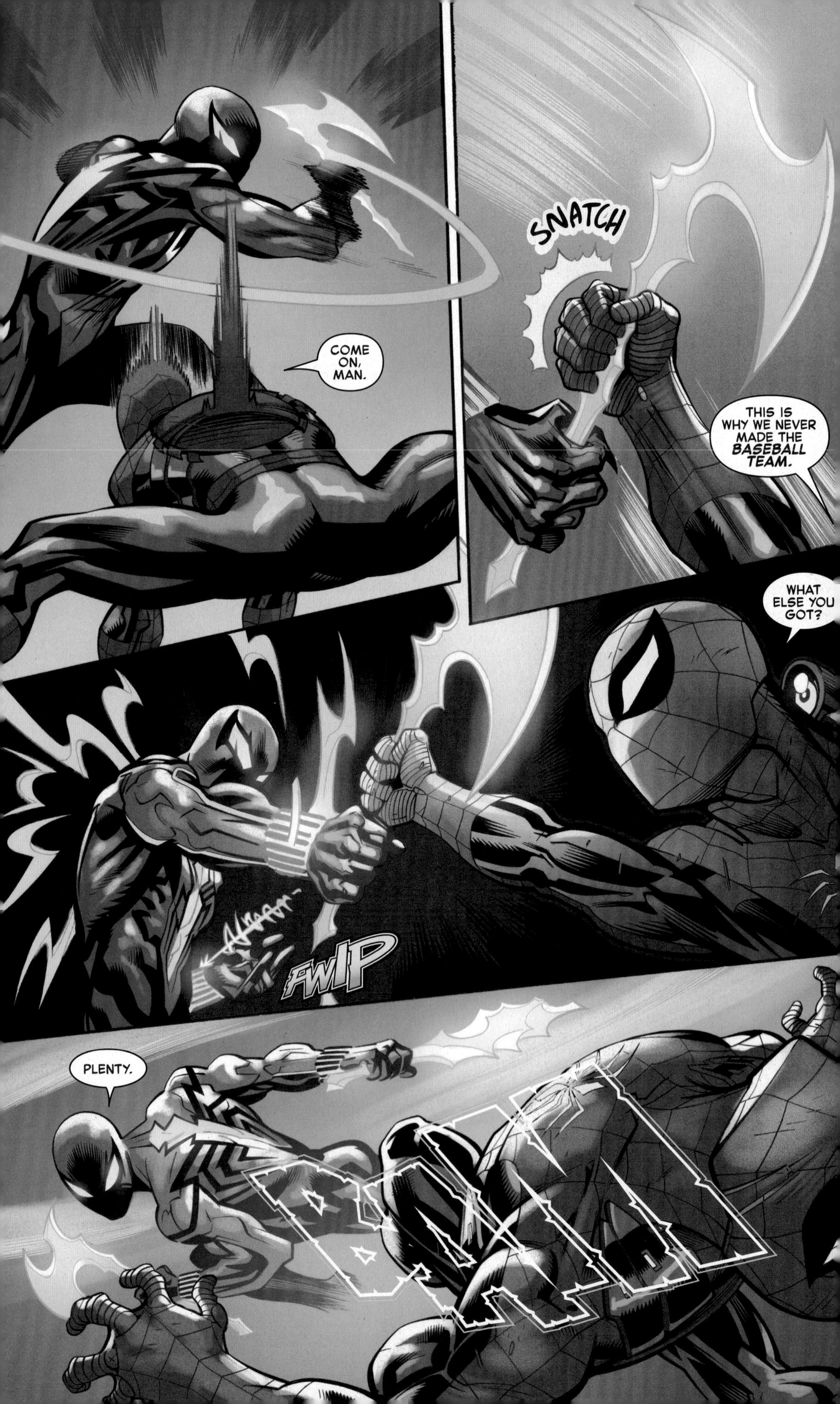
COME ON, MAN.
SNATCH
THIS IS WHY WE NEVER MADE THE BASEBALL TEAM.
WHAT ELSE YOU GOT?
FWIP
PLENTY.

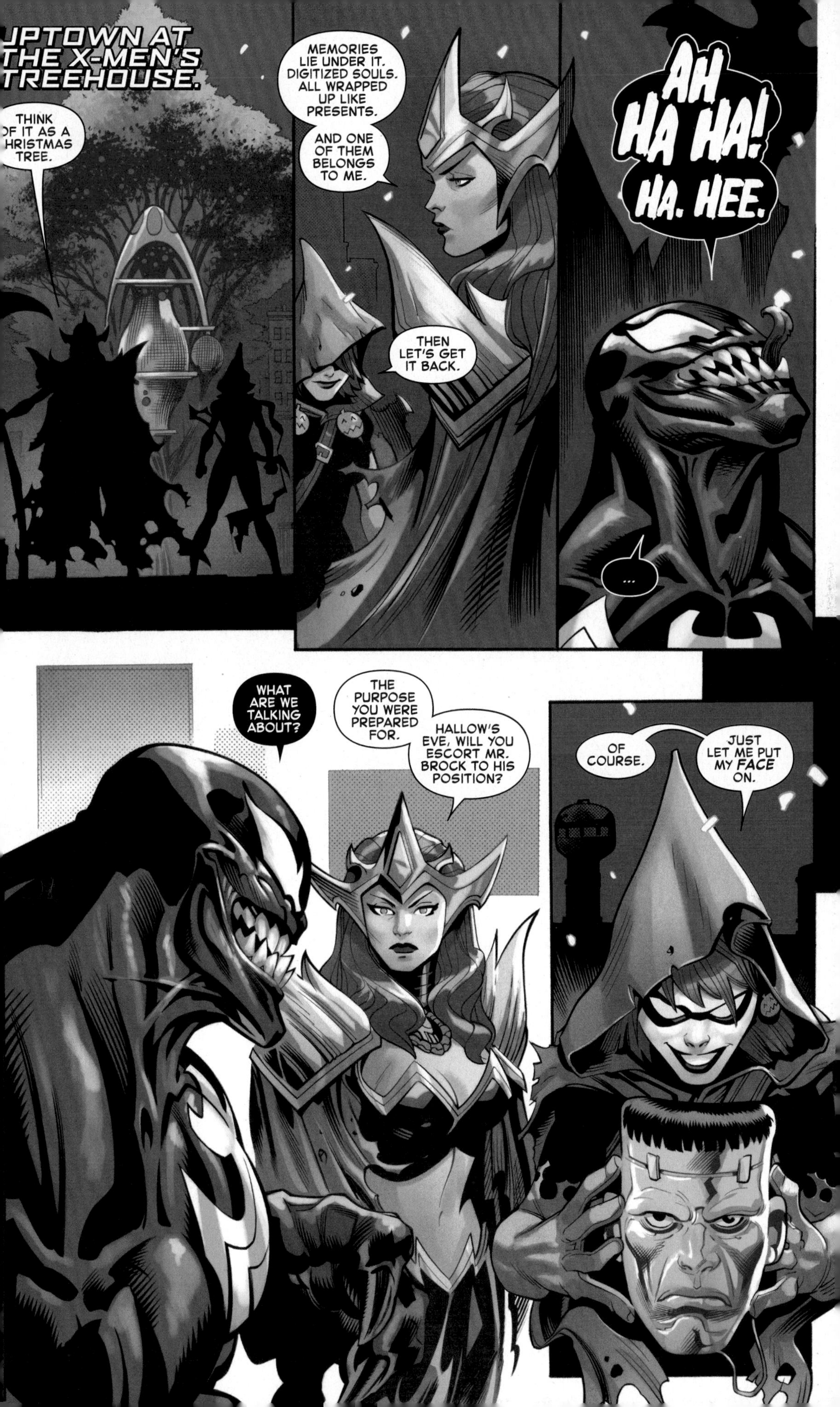
UPTOWN AT THE X-MEN'S TREEHOUSE.
THINK OF IT AS A CHRISTMAS TREE.
MEMORIES LIE UNDER IT. DIGITIZED SOULS. ALL WRAPPED UP LIKE PRESENTS.
AND ONE OF THEM BELONGS TO ME.
THEN LET'S GET IT BACK.
AH HA HA! HA. HEE.
...
WHAT ARE WE TALKING ABOUT?
THE PURPOSE YOU WERE PREPARED FOR.
HALLOW'S EVE, WILL YOU ESCORT MR. BROCK TO HIS POSITION?
OF COURSE.
JUST LET ME PUT MY *FACE* ON.

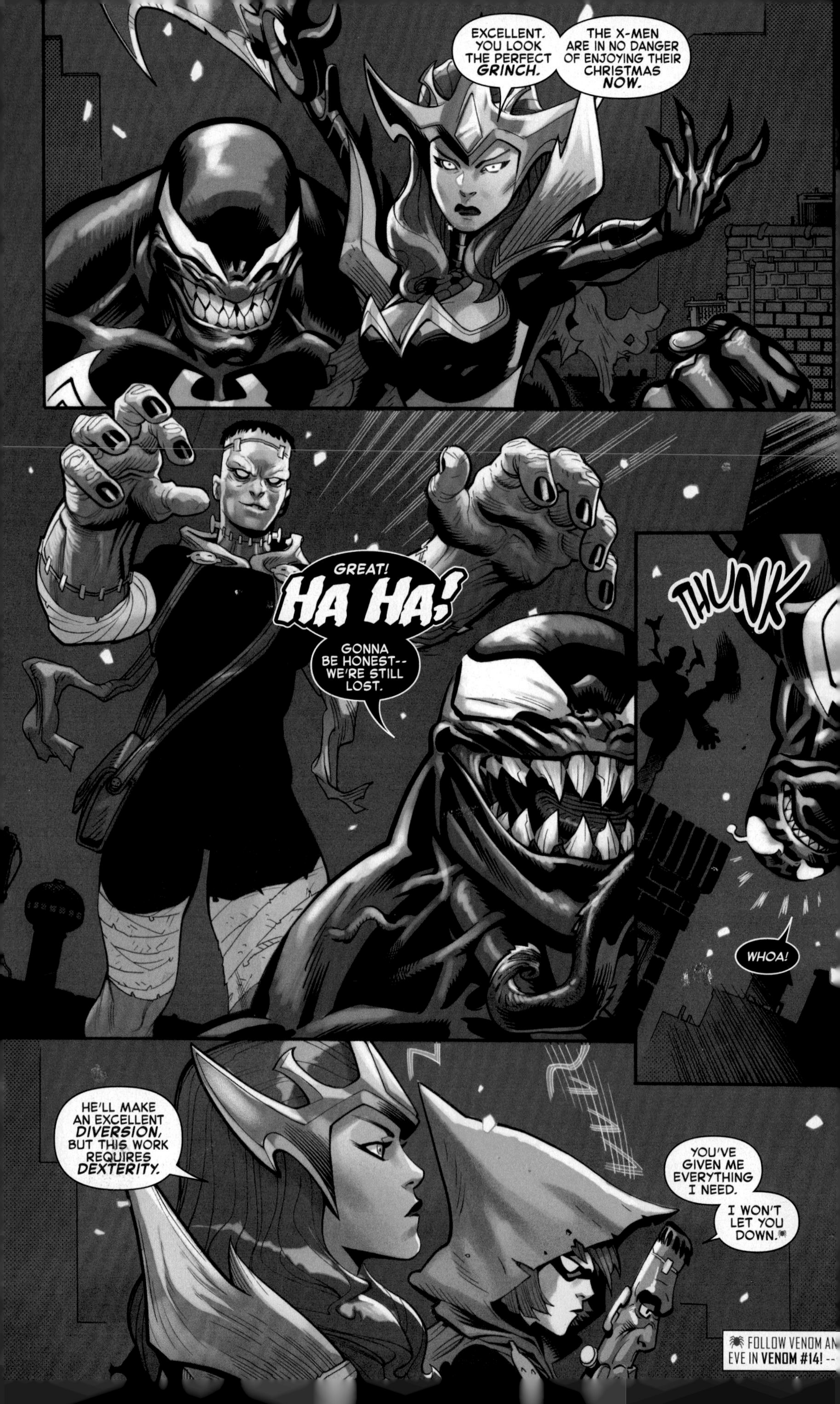
EXCELLENT. YOU LOOK THE PERFECT GRINCH.
THE X-MEN ARE IN NO DANGER OF ENJOYING THEIR CHRISTMAS NOW.
GREAT! HA HA!
GONNA BE HONEST-- WE'RE STILL LOST.
THUNK
WHOA!
HE'LL MAKE AN EXCELLENT DIVERSION, BUT THIS WORK REQUIRES DEXTERITY.
YOU'VE GIVEN ME EVERYTHING I NEED.
I WON'T LET YOU DOWN.
FOLLOW VENOM AN
EVE IN VENOM #14! --

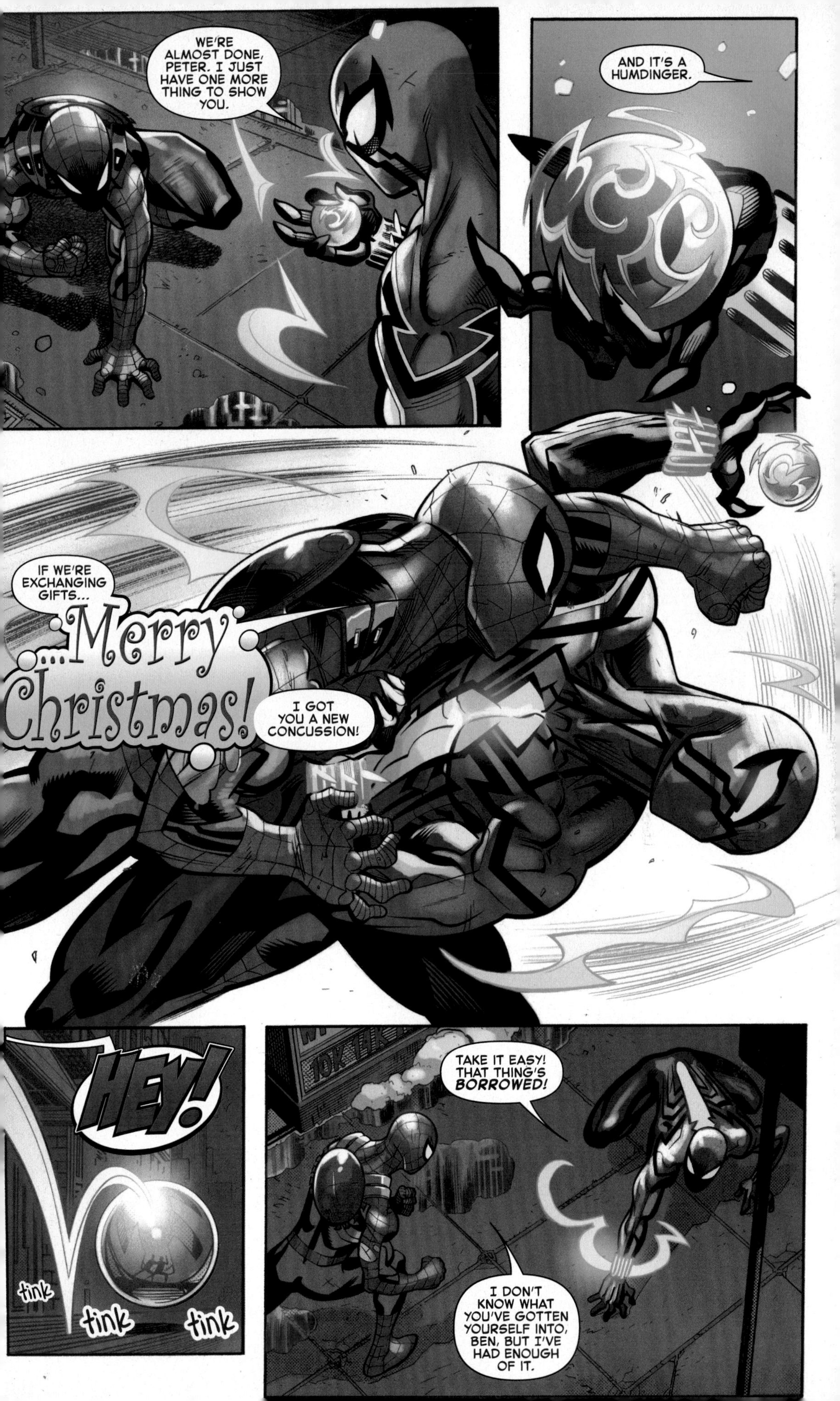

WE'RE ALMOST DONE, PETER. I JUST HAVE ONE MORE THING TO SHOW YOU.
AND IT'S A HUMDINGER.
IF WE'RE EXCHANGING GIFTS...
...Merry Christmas!
I GOT YOU A NEW CONCUSSION!
HEY!
tink
tink
tink
TAKE IT EASY! THAT THING'S BORROWED!
I DON'T KNOW WHAT YOU'VE GOTTEN YOURSELF INTO, BEN, BUT I'VE HAD ENOUGH OF IT.

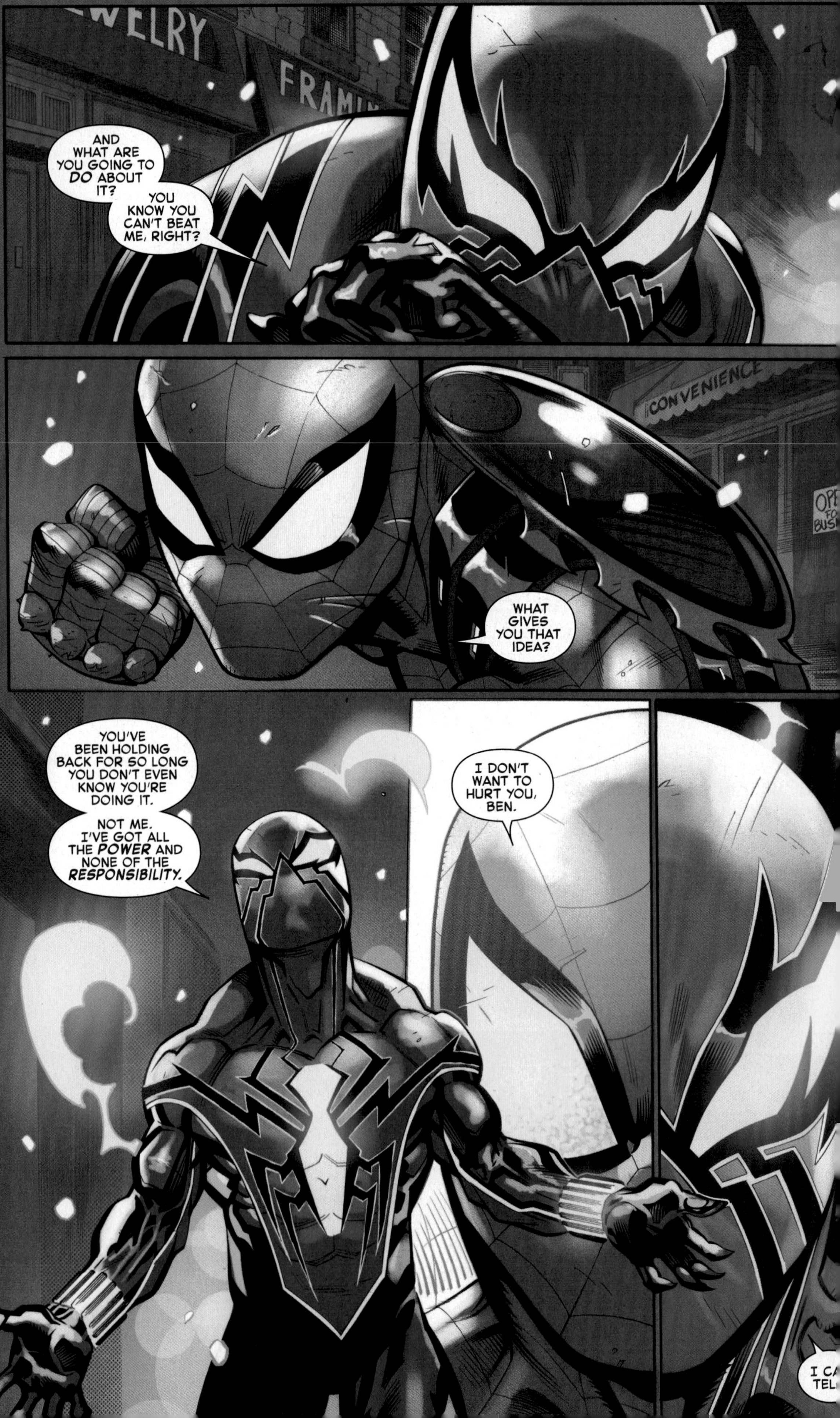

WELRY
FRAMIN
AND WHAT ARE YOU GOING TO *DO* ABOUT IT?
YOU KNOW YOU CAN'T BEAT ME, RIGHT?
CONVENIENCE
WHAT GIVES YOU THAT IDEA?
YOU'VE BEEN HOLDING BACK FOR SO LONG YOU DON'T EVEN KNOW YOU'RE DOING IT.
NOT ME. I'VE GOT ALL THE ***POWER*** AND NONE OF THE ***RESPONSIBILITY.***
I DON'T WANT TO HURT YOU, BEN.

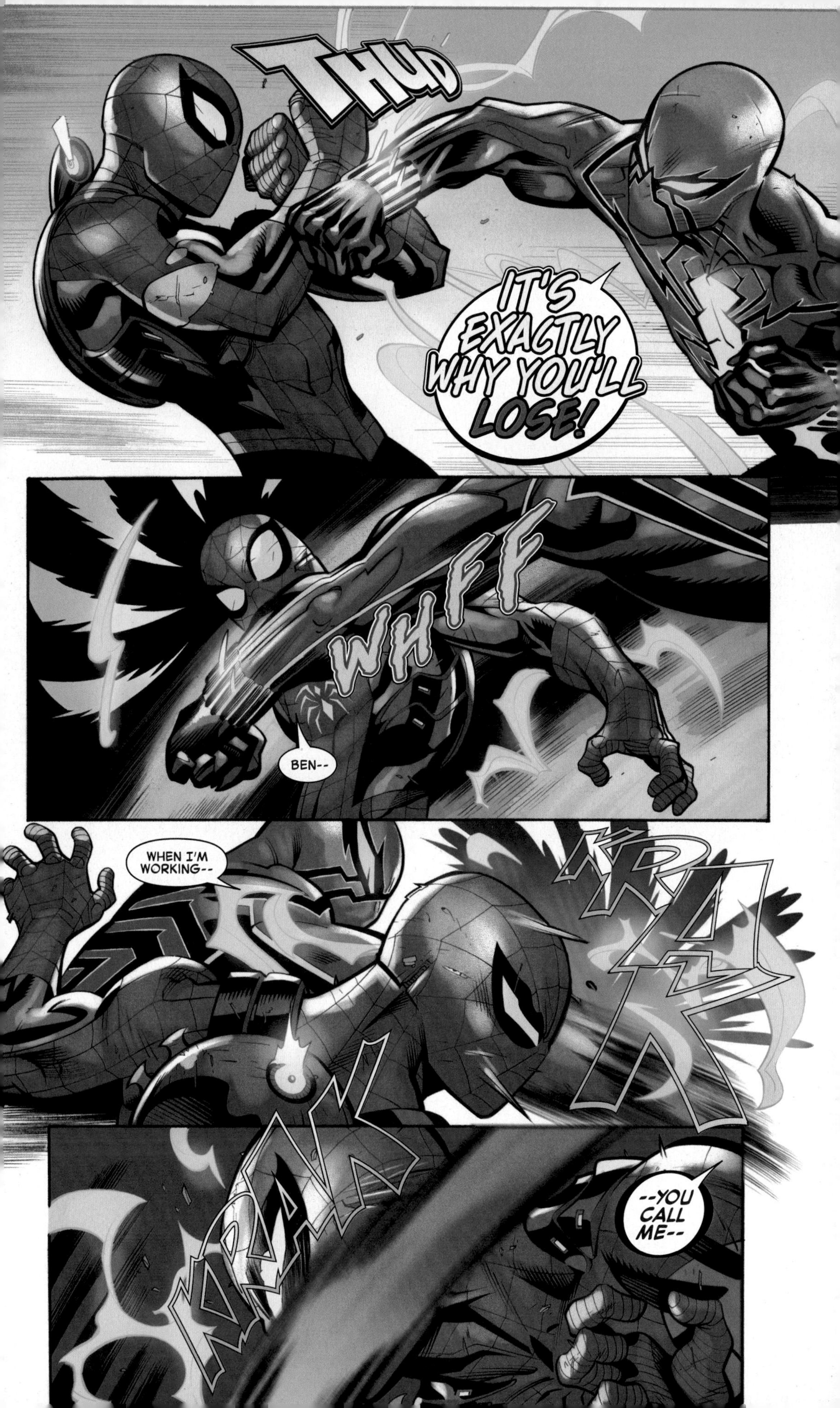
THUD
IT'S EXACTLY WHY YOU'LL LOSE!
WHFF
BEN--
WHEN I'M WORKING--
KRAAK
KRAAK
--YOU CALL ME--

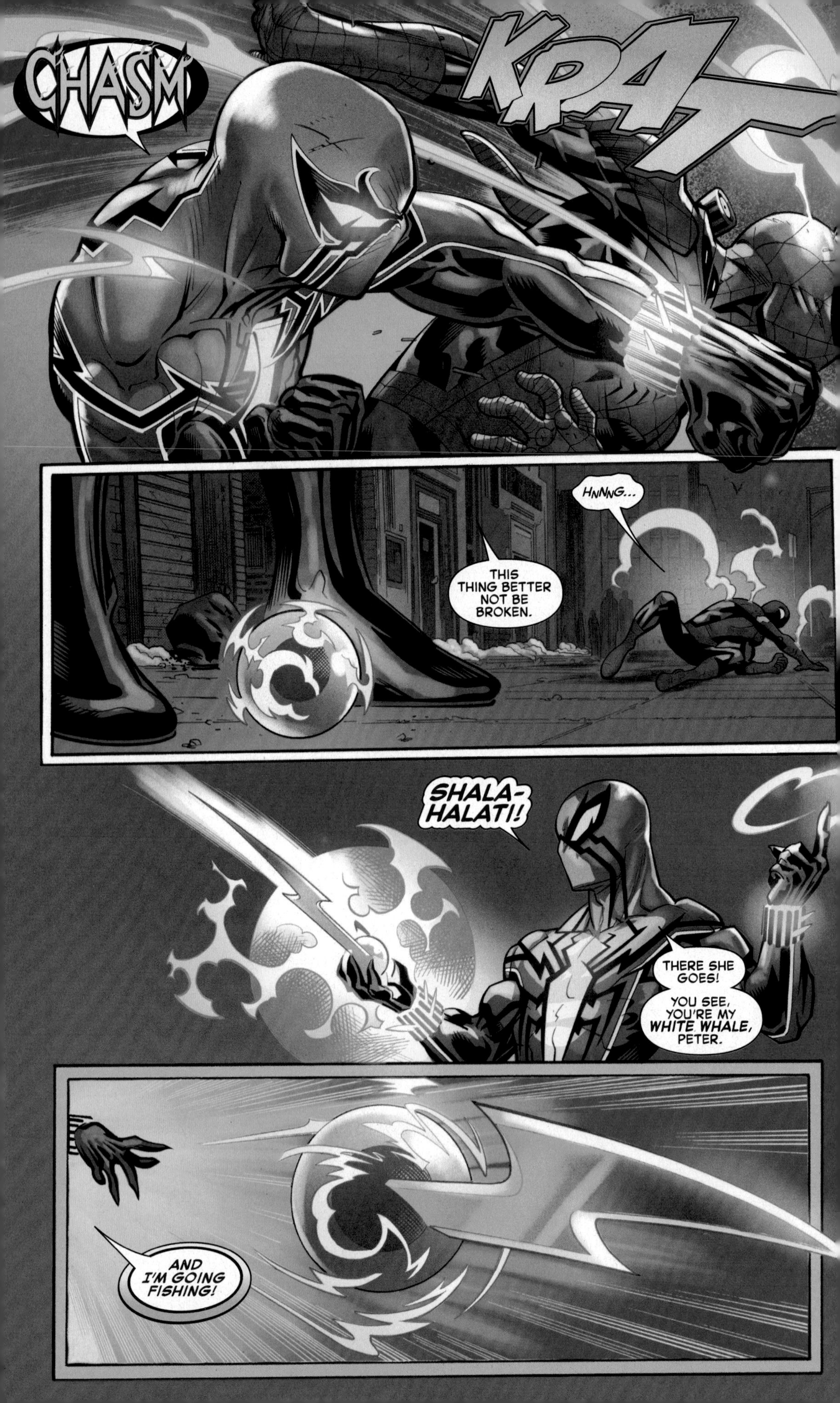
CHASM
KRAT
HNNNG...
THIS THING BETTER NOT BE BROKEN.
SHALA-HALATI!
THERE SHE GOES!
YOU SEE, YOU'RE MY WHITE WHALE, PETER.
AND I'M GOING FISHING!

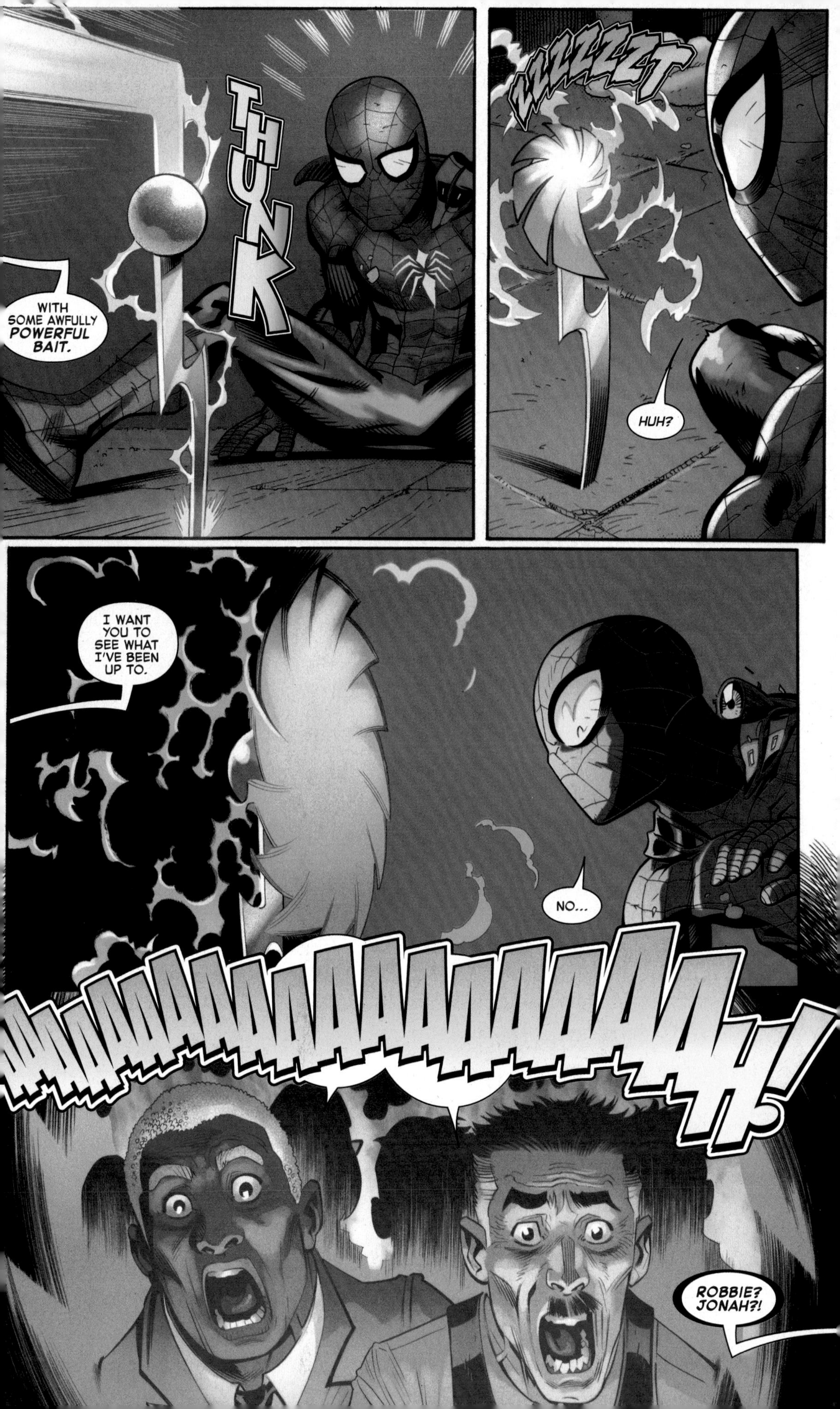
WITH SOME AWFULLY POWERFUL BAIT.
THUNK
ZZZZZZZT
HUH?
I WANT YOU TO SEE WHAT I'VE BEEN UP TO.
NO...
AAAAAAAAAAAAAAAAAAAAAAAAAH!
ROBBIE? JONAH?!

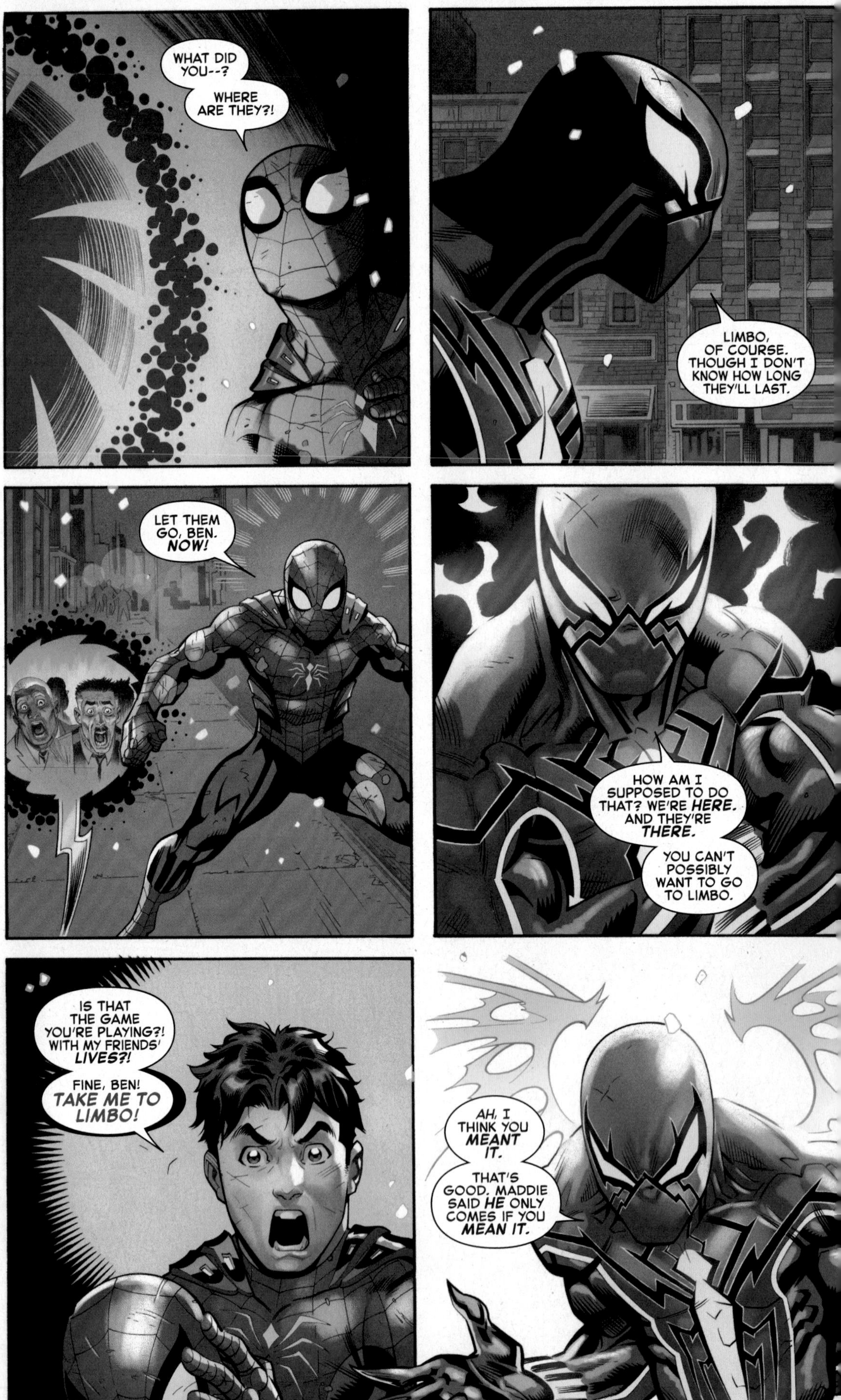
WHAT DID YOU--?
WHERE ARE THEY?!
LIMBO, OF COURSE. THOUGH I DON'T KNOW HOW LONG THEY'LL LAST.
LET THEM GO, BEN. *NOW!*
HOW AM I SUPPOSED TO DO THAT? WE'RE *HERE.* AND THEY'RE *THERE.*
YOU CAN'T POSSIBLY WANT TO GO TO LIMBO.
IS THAT THE GAME YOU'RE PLAYING?! WITH MY FRIENDS' *LIVES?!*
FINE, BEN! *TAKE ME TO LIMBO!*
AH, I THINK YOU *MEANT IT.*
THAT'S GOOD. MADDIE SAID *HE* ONLY COMES IF YOU *MEAN IT.*

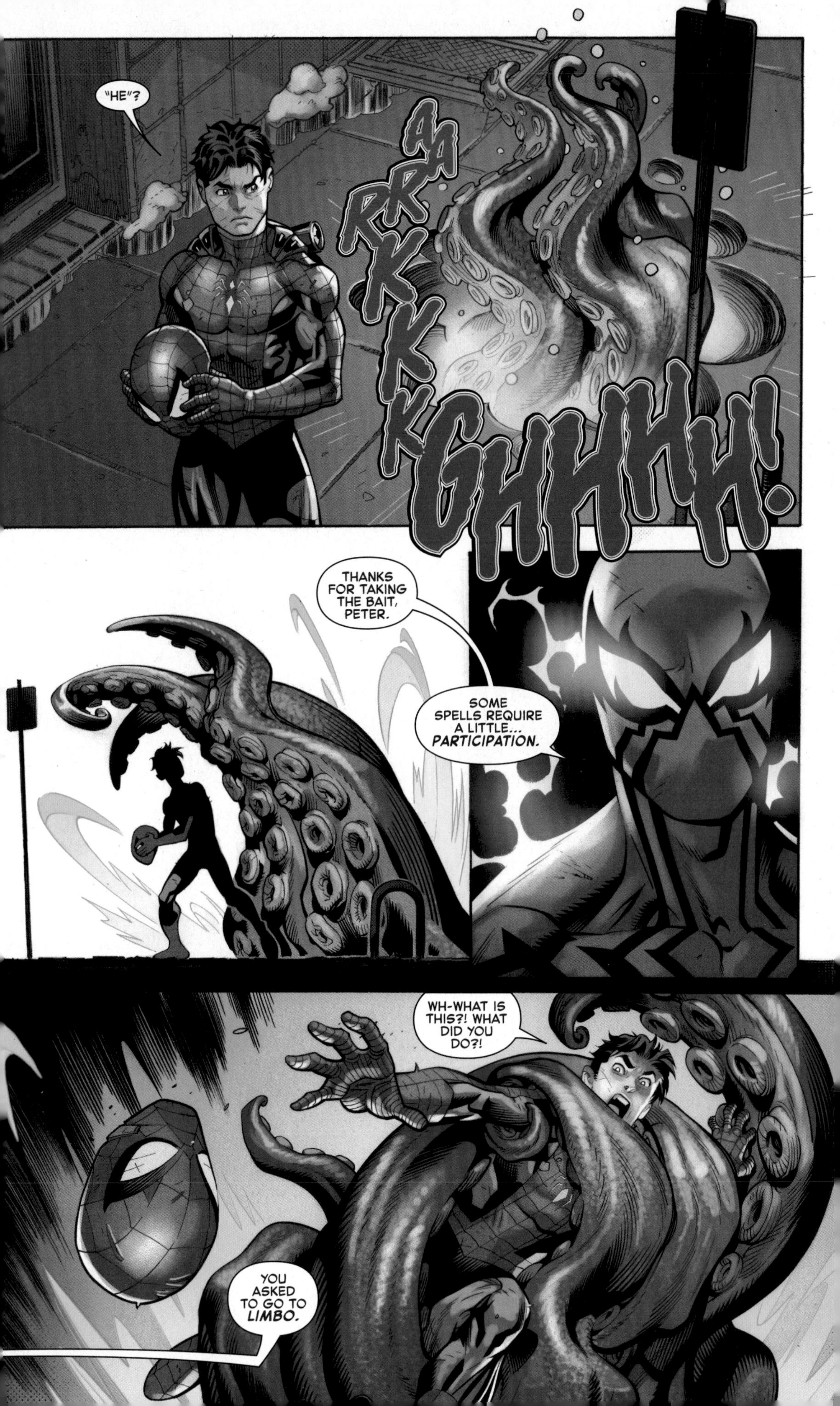
"HE"?
AARRKKKKGHHHH!
THANKS FOR TAKING THE BAIT, PETER.
SOME SPELLS REQUIRE A LITTLE... *PARTICIPATION.*
WH-WHAT IS THIS?! WHAT DID YOU DO?!
YOU ASKED TO GO TO *LIMBO.*

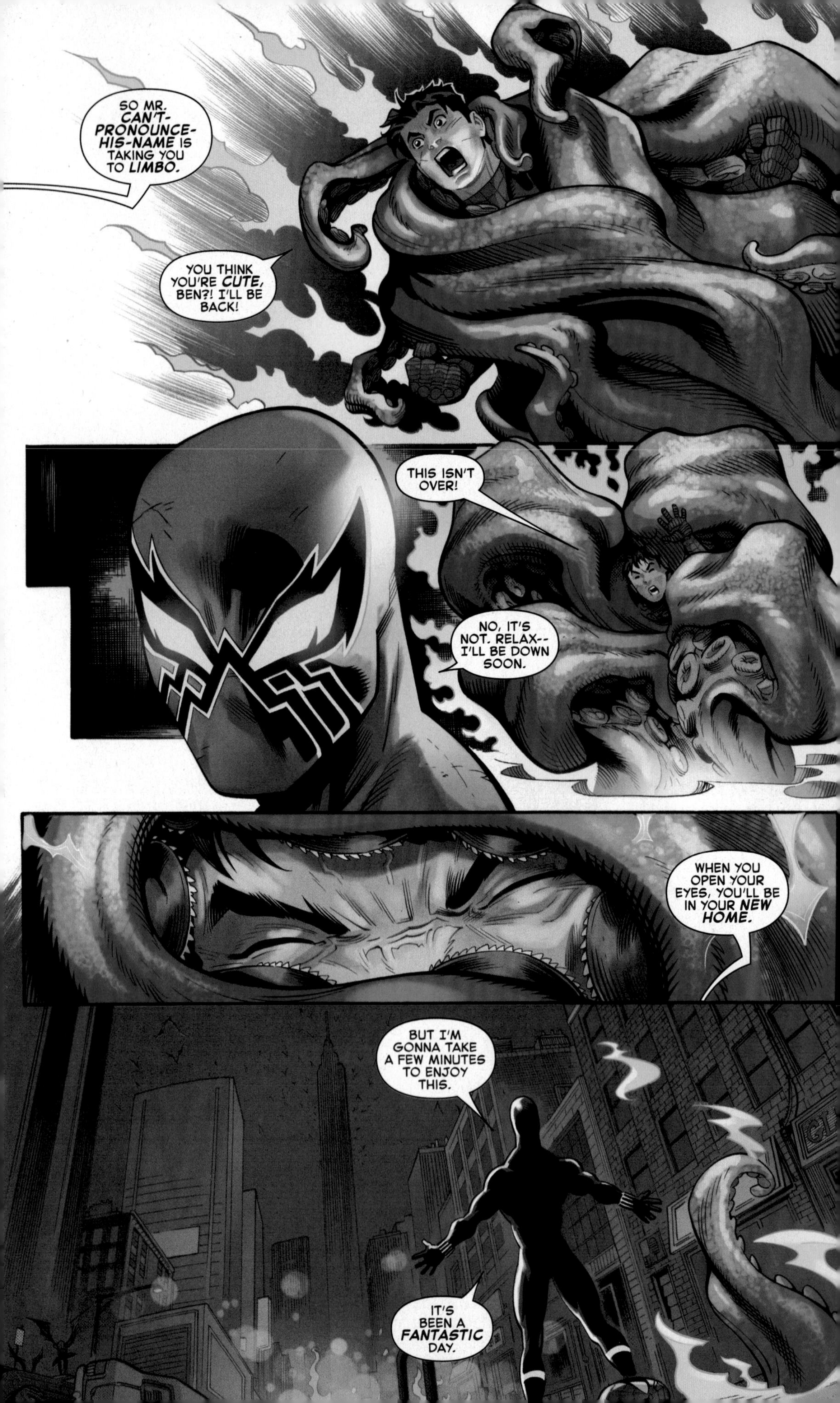
SO MR. CAN'T-PRONOUNCE-HIS-NAME IS TAKING YOU TO LIMBO.
YOU THINK YOU'RE CUTE, BEN?! I'LL BE BACK!
THIS ISN'T OVER!
NO, IT'S NOT. RELAX-- I'LL BE DOWN SOON.
WHEN YOU OPEN YOUR EYES, YOU'LL BE IN YOUR NEW HOME.
BUT I'M GONNA TAKE A FEW MINUTES TO ENJOY THIS.
IT'S BEEN A FANTASTIC DAY.

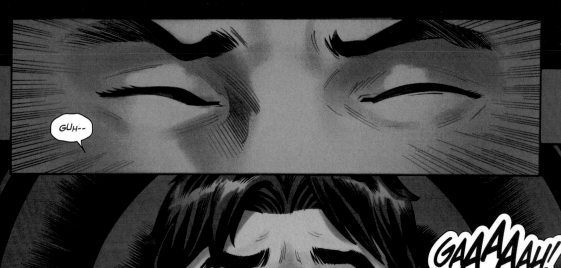

GUH--

GAAAAAH!

PARKER! YOU'RE LATE!

HUH?! WHAT IS THIS?!

DON'T PLAY DUMB, PARKER!

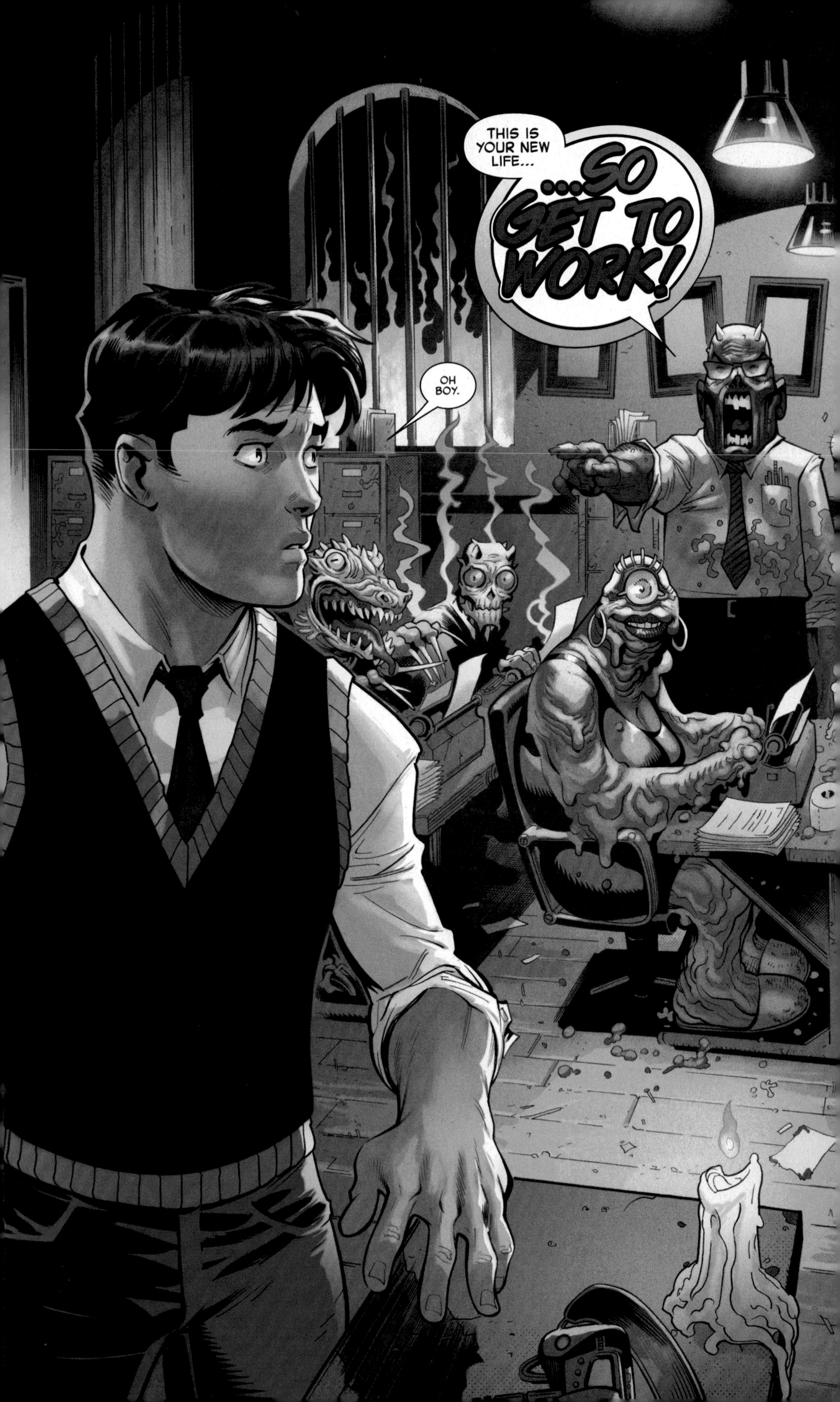
THIS IS YOUR NEW LIFE...
...SO GET TO WORK!
OH BOY.

AMAZING SPIDER-MAN #17

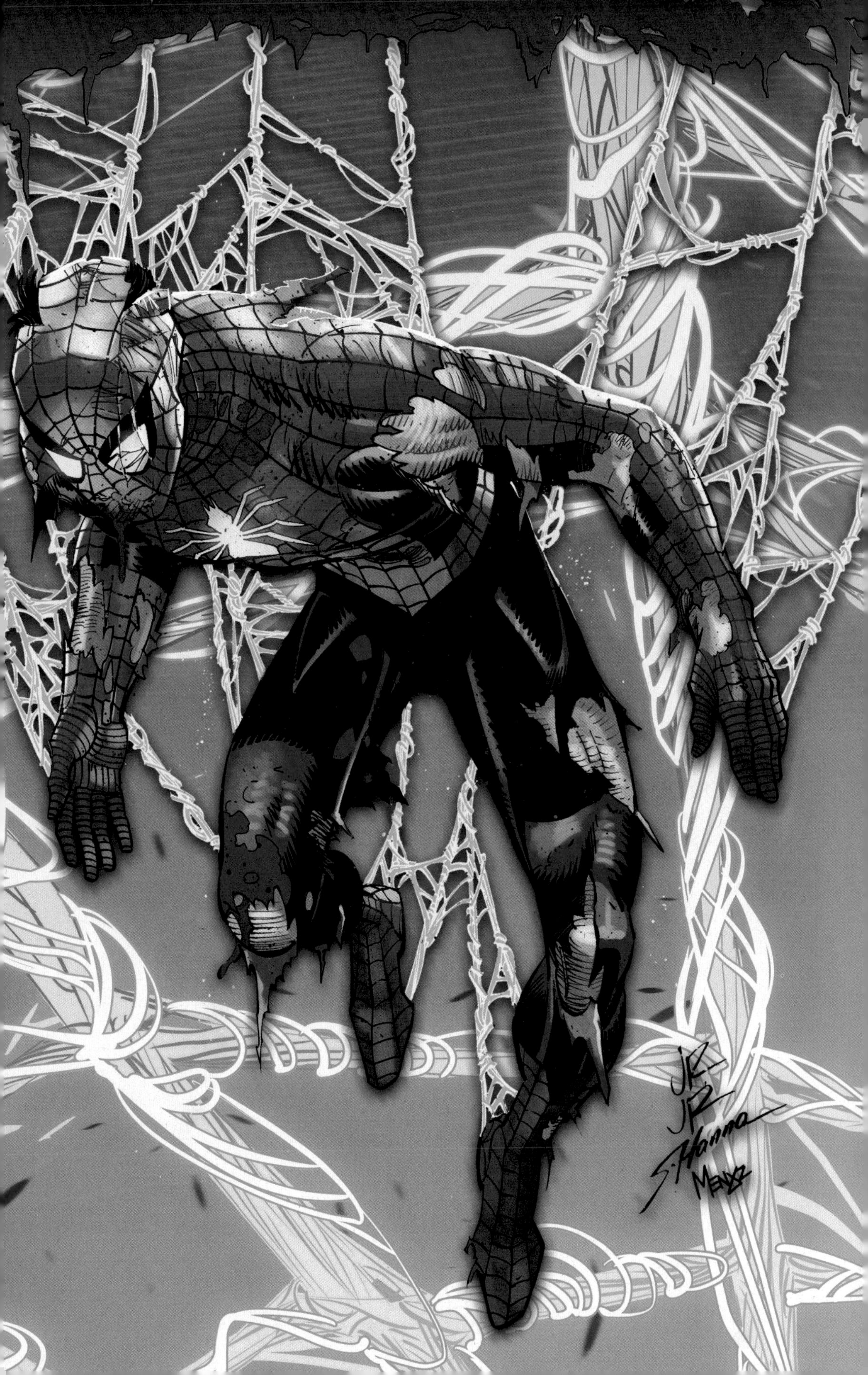

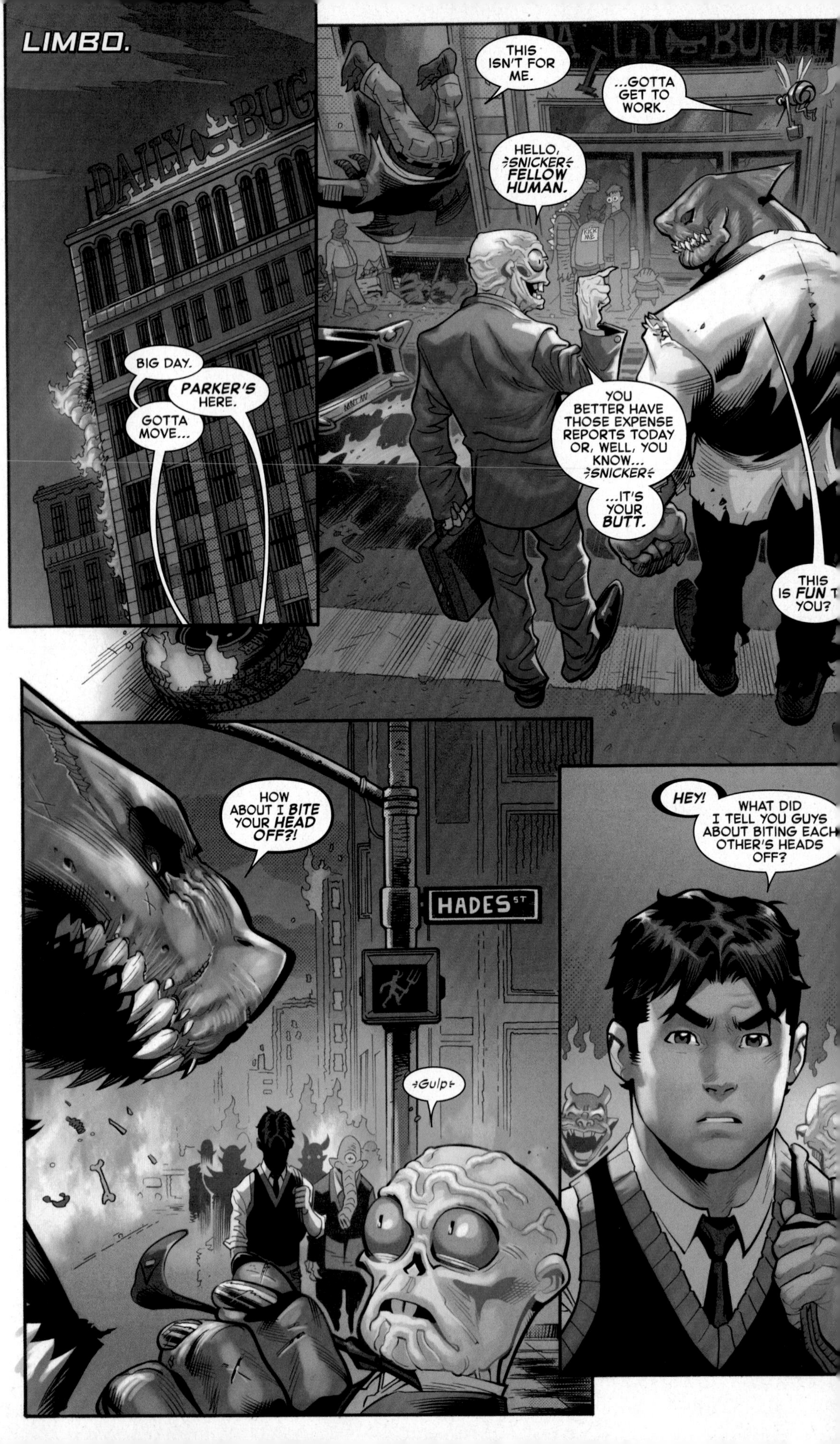
LIMBO.
BIG DAY.
PARKER'S HERE.
GOTTA MOVE...
THIS ISN'T FOR ME.
...GOTTA GET TO WORK.
HELLO, SNICKER FELLOW HUMAN.
YOU BETTER HAVE THOSE EXPENSE REPORTS TODAY OR, WELL, YOU KNOW... SNICKER
...IT'S YOUR BUTT.
THIS IS FUN T YOU?
HOW ABOUT I BITE YOUR HEAD OFF?!
HADES ST
Gulp
HEY!
WHAT DID I TELL YOU GUYS ABOUT BITING EACH OTHER'S HEADS OFF?

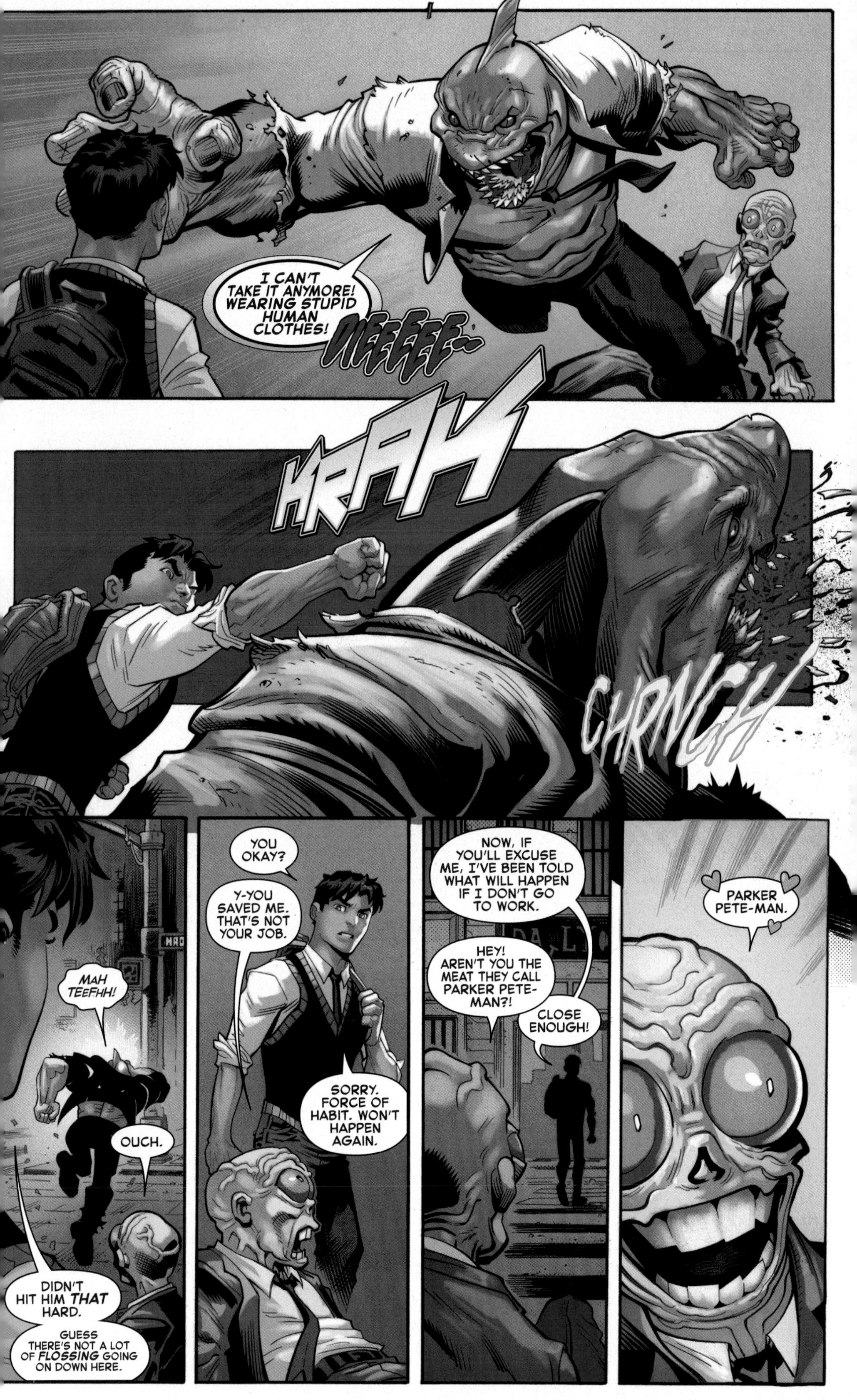
I CAN'T TAKE IT ANYMORE! WEARING STUPID HUMAN CLOTHES!
DIEEEEE--
KRAK
CHRNCH
MAH TEEFHH!
OUCH.
DIDN'T HIT HIM THAT HARD.
GUESS THERE'S NOT A LOT OF FLOSSING GOING ON DOWN HERE.
YOU OKAY?
Y-YOU SAVED ME. THAT'S NOT YOUR JOB.
SORRY. FORCE OF HABIT. WON'T HAPPEN AGAIN.
NOW, IF YOU'LL EXCUSE ME, I'VE BEEN TOLD WHAT WILL HAPPEN IF I DON'T GO TO WORK.
HEY! AREN'T YOU THE MEAT THEY CALL PARKER PETE-MAN?!
CLOSE ENOUGH!
PARKER PETE-MAN.

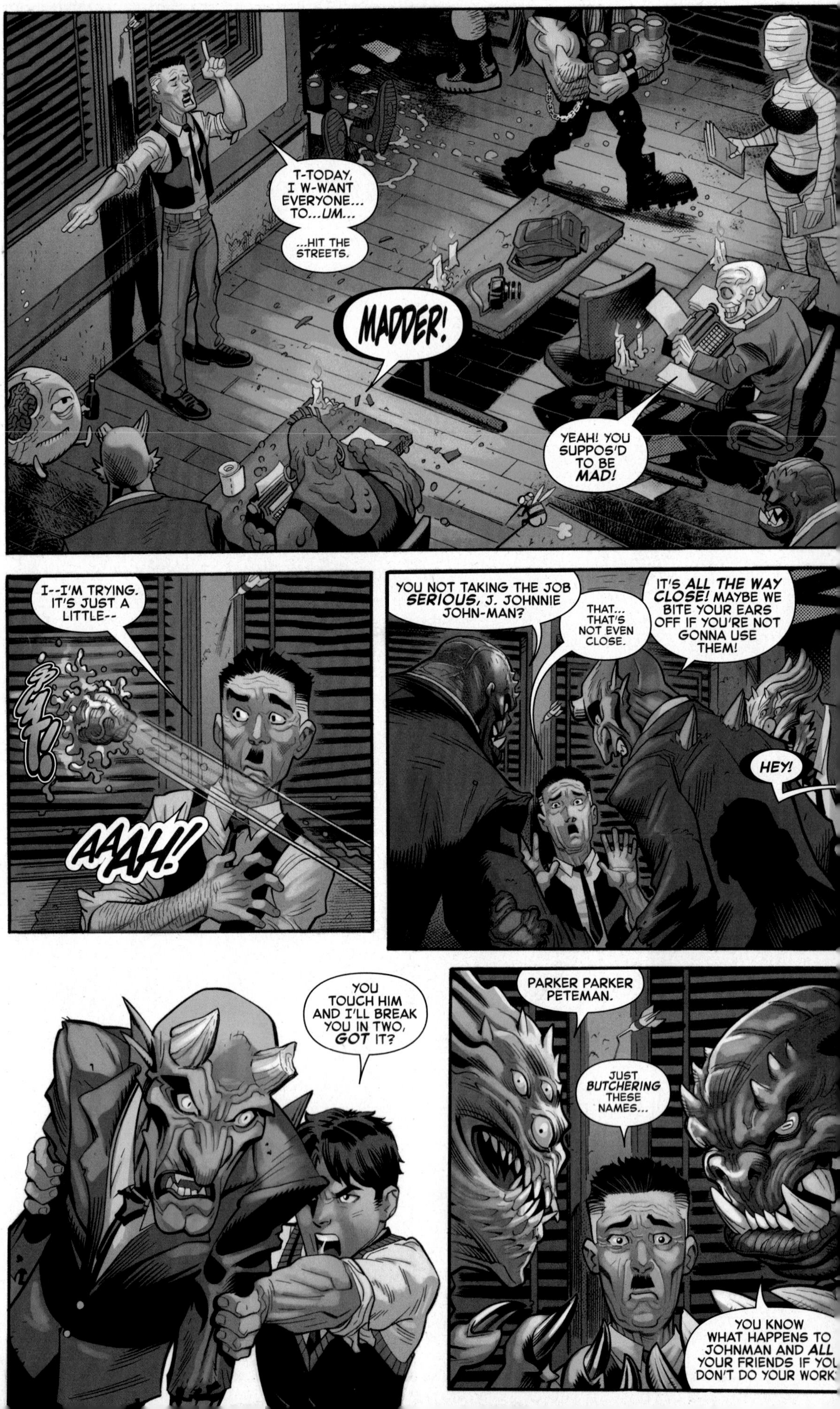

T-TODAY, I W-WANT EVERYONE... TO...UM...
...HIT THE STREETS.
MADDER!
YEAH! YOU SUPPOS'D TO BE MAD!
I--I'M TRYING. IT'S JUST A LITTLE--
AAAH!
YOU NOT TAKING THE JOB SERIOUS, J. JOHNNIE JOHN-MAN?
THAT... THAT'S NOT EVEN CLOSE.
IT'S ALL THE WAY CLOSE! MAYBE WE BITE YOUR EARS OFF IF YOU'RE NOT GONNA USE THEM!
HEY!
YOU TOUCH HIM AND I'LL BREAK YOU IN TWO, GOT IT?
PARKER PARKER PETEMAN.
JUST BUTCHERING THESE NAMES...
YOU KNOW WHAT HAPPENS TO JOHNMAN AND ALL YOUR FRIENDS IF YOU DON'T DO YOUR WORK

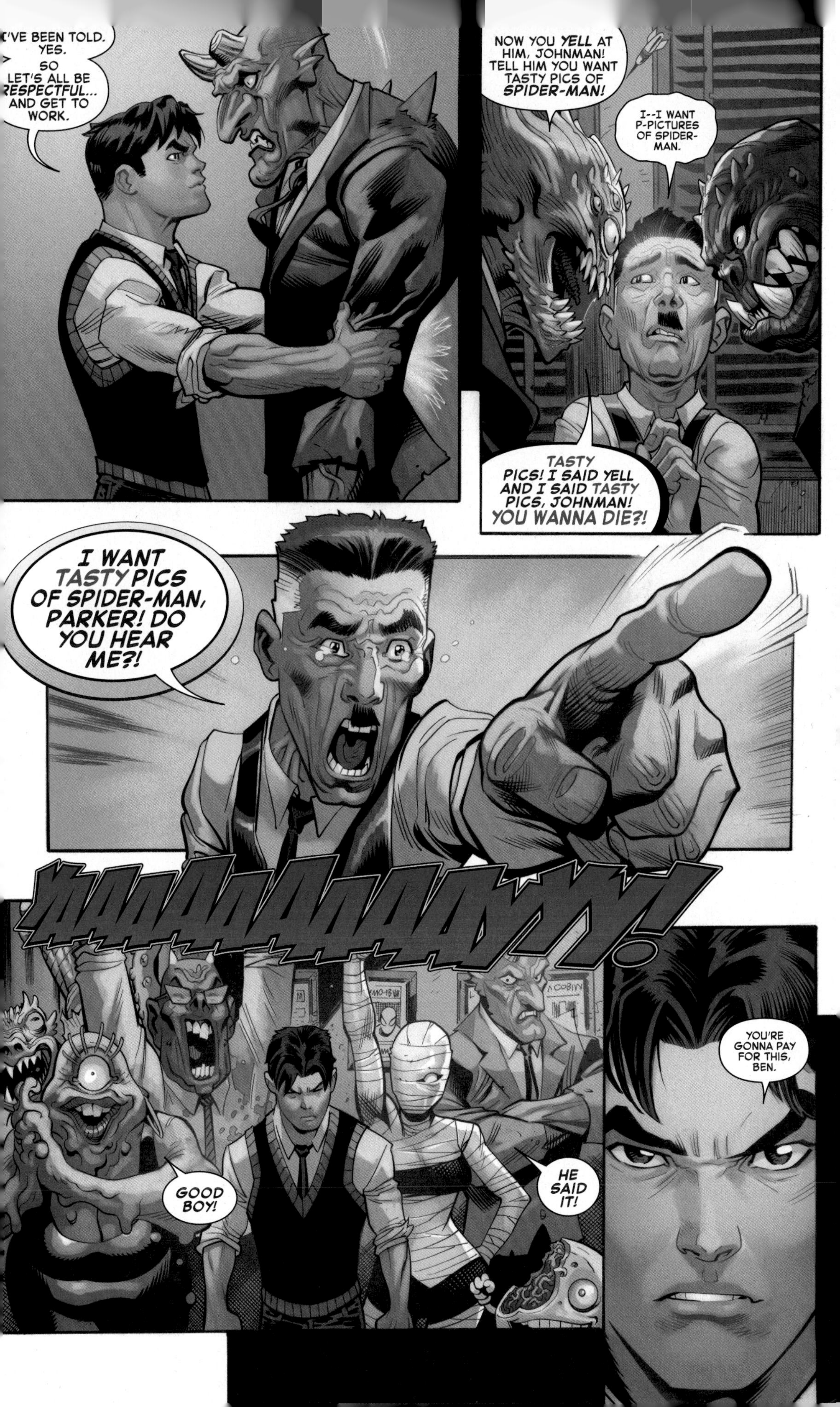
I'VE BEEN TOLD. YES.
SO LET'S ALL BE RESPECTFUL... AND GET TO WORK.
NOW YOU YELL AT HIM, JOHNMAN! TELL HIM YOU WANT TASTY PICS OF SPIDER-MAN!
I--I WANT P-PICTURES OF SPIDER-MAN.
TASTY PICS! I SAID YELL AND I SAID TASTY PICS, JOHNMAN! YOU WANNA DIE?!
I WANT TASTY PICS OF SPIDER-MAN, PARKER! DO YOU HEAR ME?!
WAAAAAAAAAYYY!
GOOD BOY!
HE SAID IT!
YOU'RE GONNA PAY FOR THIS, BEN.

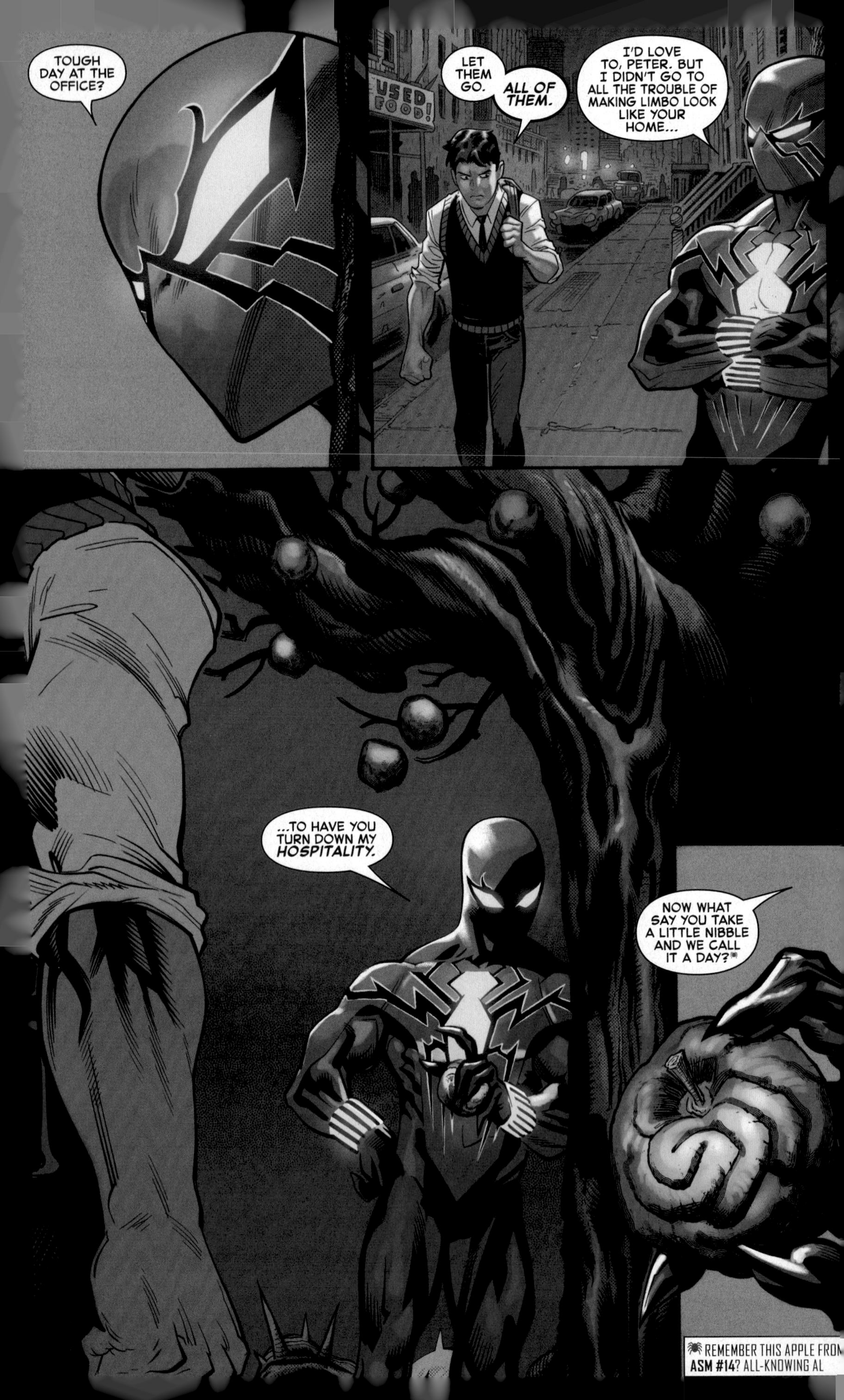
TOUGH DAY AT THE OFFICE?
USED FOOD!
LET THEM GO. ALL OF THEM.
I'D LOVE TO, PETER. BUT I DIDN'T GO TO ALL THE TROUBLE OF MAKING LIMBO LOOK LIKE YOUR HOME...
...TO HAVE YOU TURN DOWN MY HOSPITALITY.
NOW WHAT SAY YOU TAKE A LITTLE NIBBLE AND WE CALL IT A DAY?*
*REMEMBER THIS APPLE FROM ASM #14? ALL-KNOWING AL

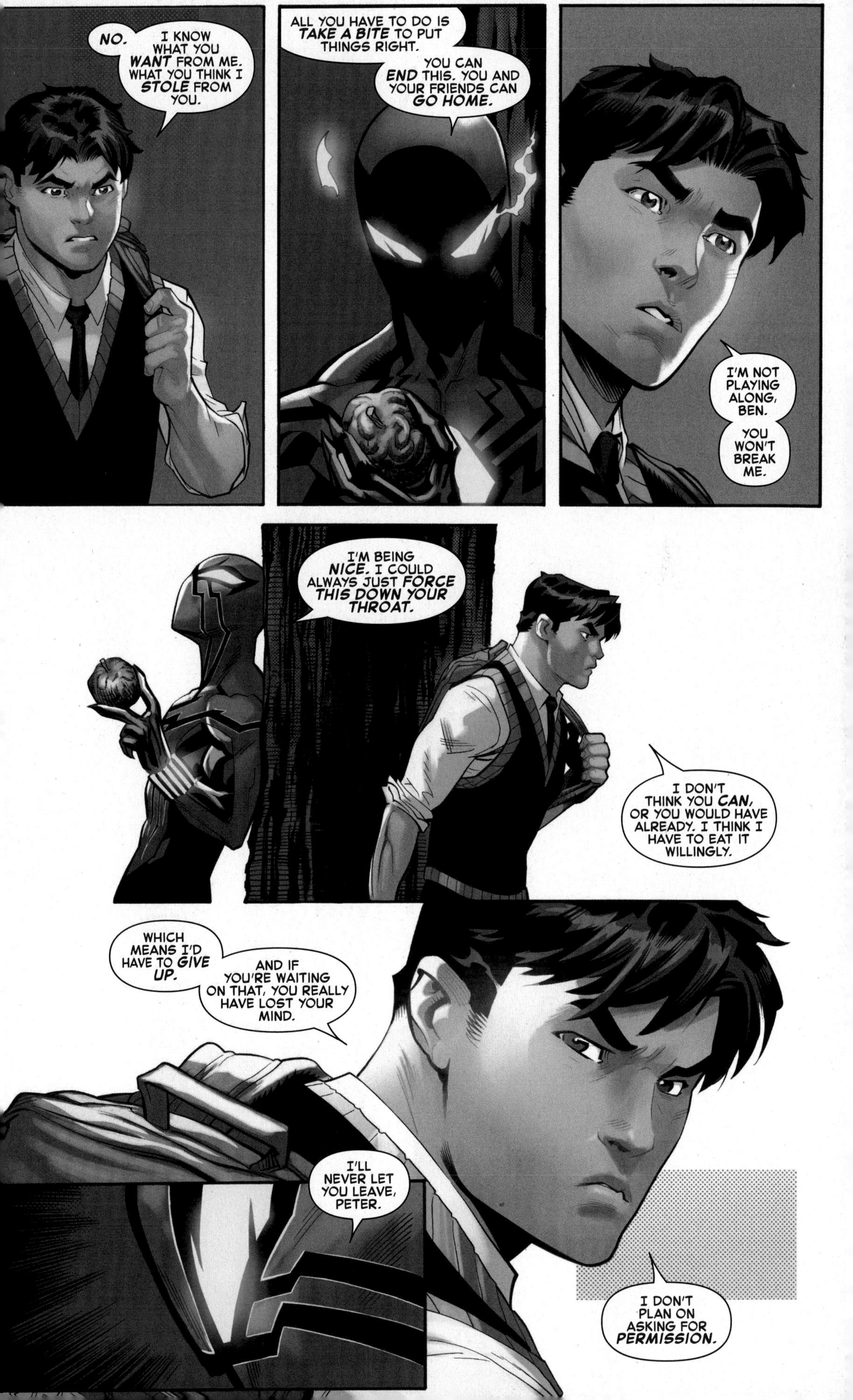
NO.
I KNOW WHAT YOU WANT FROM ME. WHAT YOU THINK I STOLE FROM YOU.
ALL YOU HAVE TO DO IS TAKE A BITE TO PUT THINGS RIGHT.
YOU CAN END THIS. YOU AND YOUR FRIENDS CAN GO HOME.
I'M NOT PLAYING ALONG, BEN.
YOU WON'T BREAK ME.
I'M BEING NICE. I COULD ALWAYS JUST FORCE THIS DOWN YOUR THROAT.
I DON'T THINK YOU CAN, OR YOU WOULD HAVE ALREADY. I THINK I HAVE TO EAT IT WILLINGLY.
WHICH MEANS I'D HAVE TO GIVE UP.
AND IF YOU'RE WAITING ON THAT, YOU REALLY HAVE LOST YOUR MIND.
I'LL NEVER LET YOU LEAVE, PETER.
I DON'T PLAN ON ASKING FOR PERMISSION.

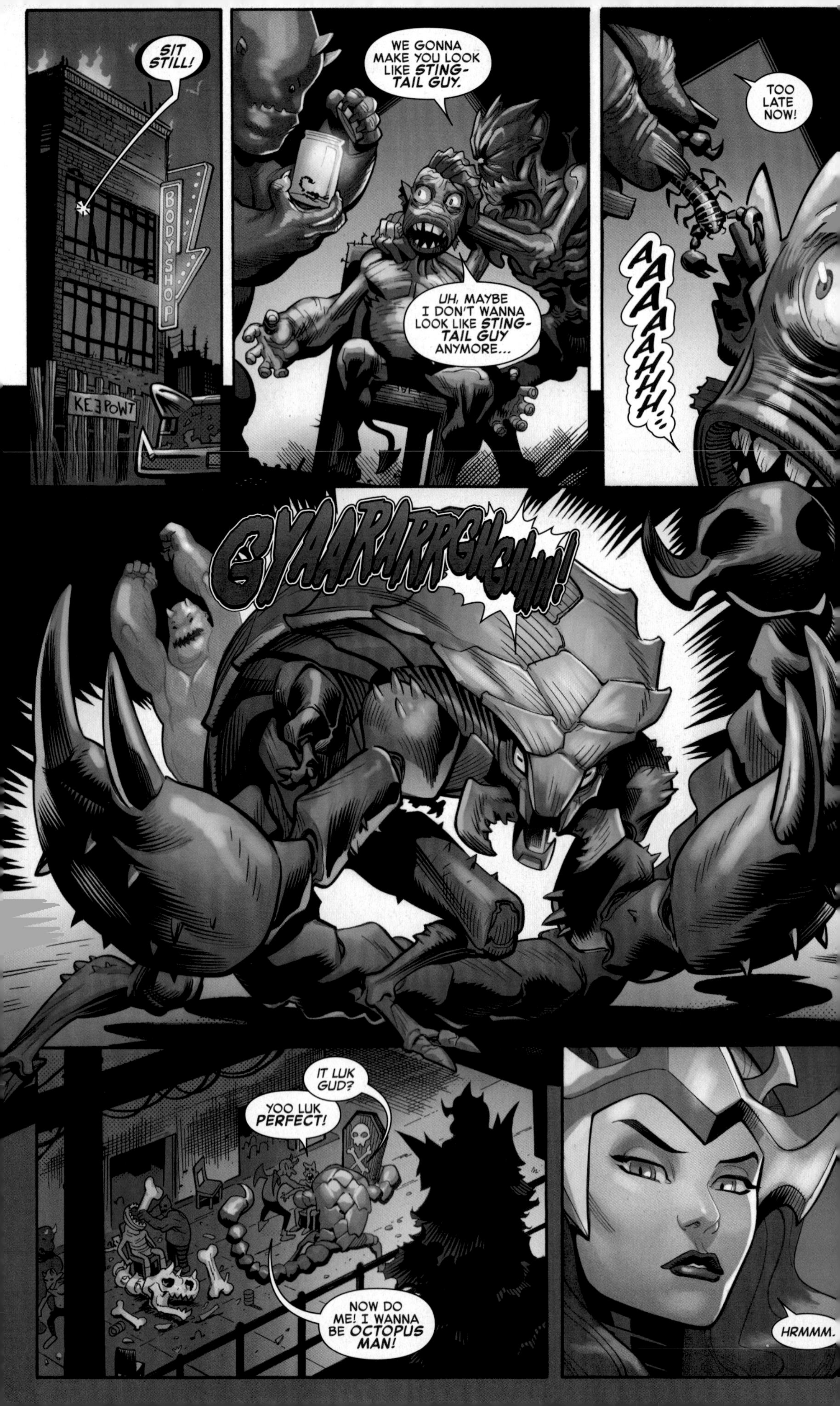
SIT STILL!
BODY SHOP
KEEPOWT
WE GONNA MAKE YOU LOOK LIKE STING-TAIL GUY.
UH, MAYBE I DON'T WANNA LOOK LIKE STING-TAIL GUY ANYMORE...
TOO LATE NOW!
AAAAAHHH...
GYAAARARRGHGHHH!
IT LUK GUD?
YOO LUK PERFECT!
NOW DO ME! I WANNA BE OCTOPUS MAN!
HRMMM.

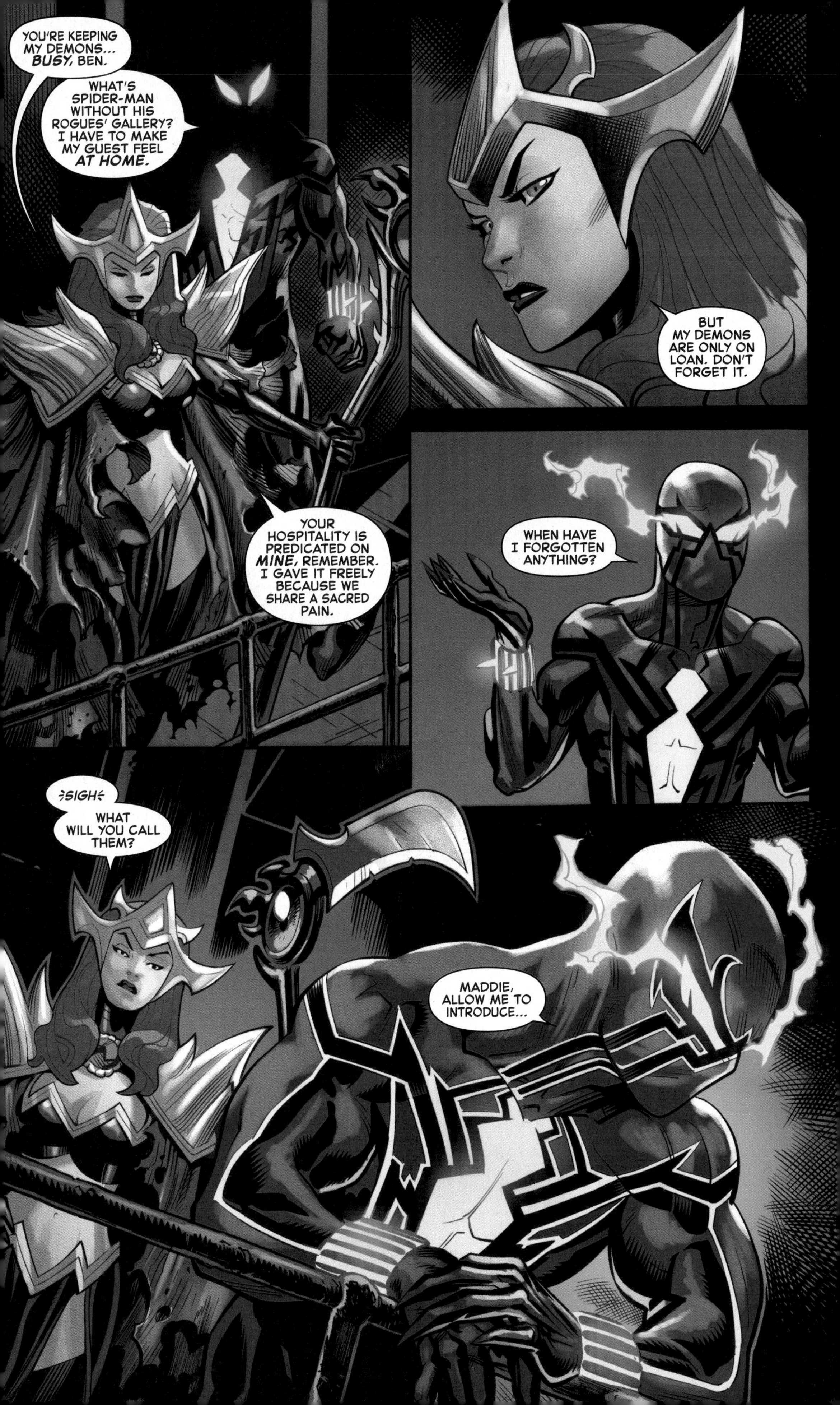

YOU'RE KEEPING MY DEMONS... BUSY, BEN.
WHAT'S SPIDER-MAN WITHOUT HIS ROGUES' GALLERY? I HAVE TO MAKE MY GUEST FEEL AT HOME.
BUT MY DEMONS ARE ONLY ON LOAN. DON'T FORGET IT.
YOUR HOSPITALITY IS PREDICATED ON MINE, REMEMBER. I GAVE IT FREELY BECAUSE WE SHARE A SACRED PAIN.
WHEN HAVE I FORGOTTEN ANYTHING?
>SIGH<
WHAT WILL YOU CALL THEM?
MADDIE, ALLOW ME TO INTRODUCE...

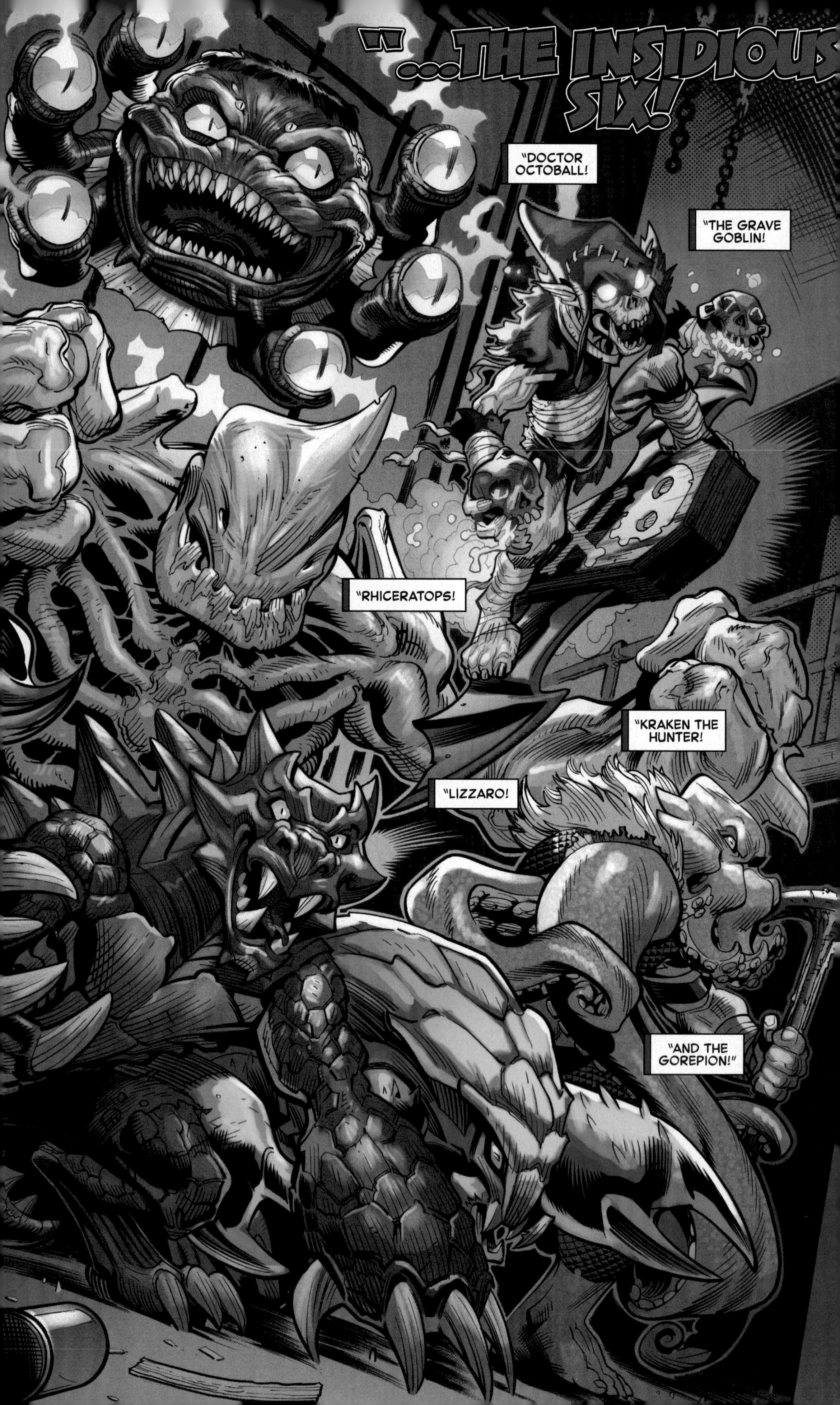

"...THE INSIDIOUS SIX!
"DOCTOR OCTOBALL!
"THE GRAVE GOBLIN!
"RHICERATOPS!
"KRAKEN THE HUNTER!
"LIZZARO!
"AND THE GOREPION!"

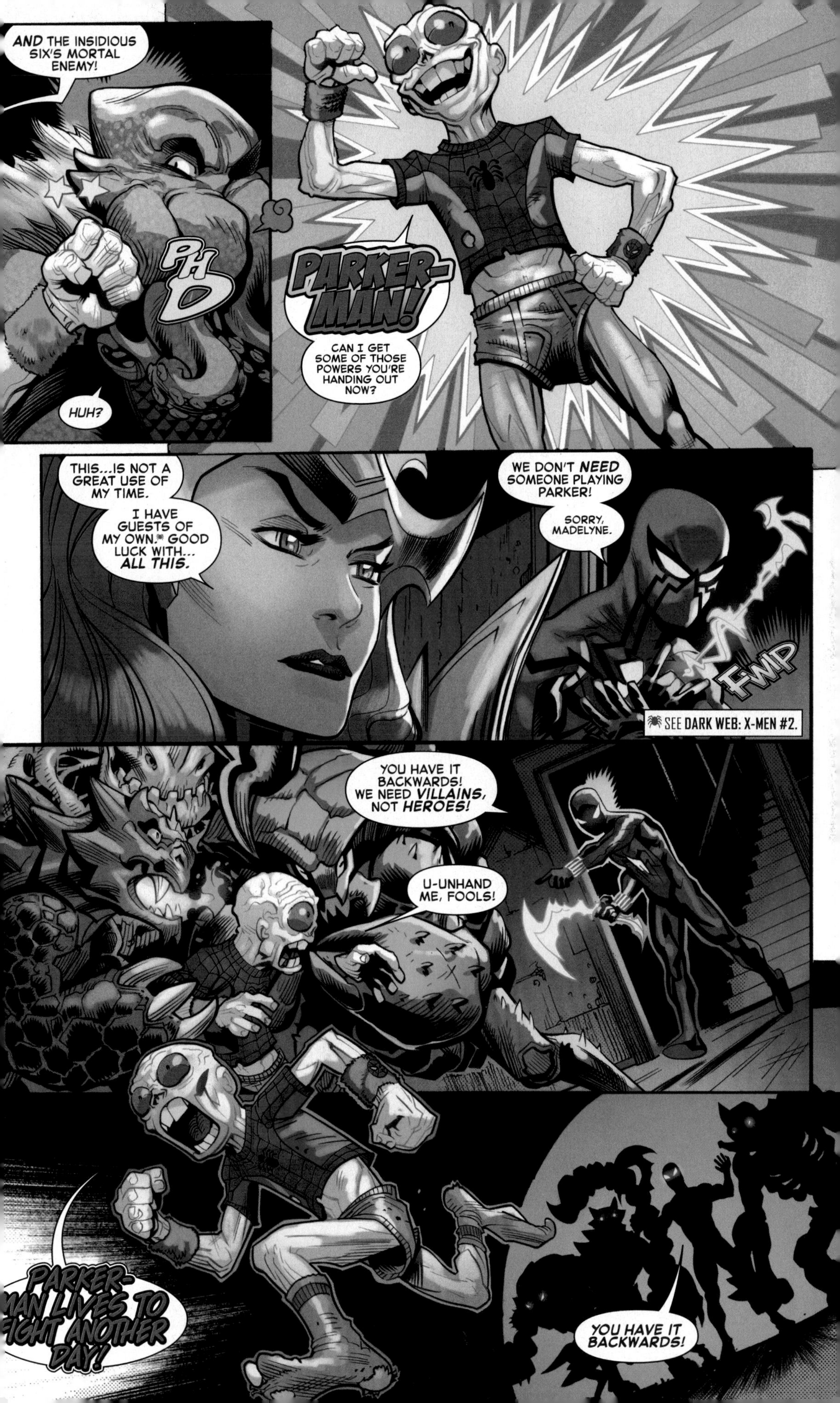

AND THE INSIDIOUS SIX'S MORTAL ENEMY!
PH D
PARKER-MAN!
CAN I GET SOME OF THOSE POWERS YOU'RE HANDING OUT NOW?
HUH?
THIS...IS NOT A GREAT USE OF MY TIME.
I HAVE GUESTS OF MY OWN. GOOD LUCK WITH... ALL THIS.
WE DON'T NEED SOMEONE PLAYING PARKER!
SORRY, MADELYNE.
FWIP
SEE DARK WEB: X-MEN #2.
YOU HAVE IT BACKWARDS! WE NEED VILLAINS, NOT HEROES!
U-UNHAND ME, FOOLS!
PARKER-MAN LIVES TO FIGHT ANOTHER DAY!
YOU HAVE IT BACKWARDS!

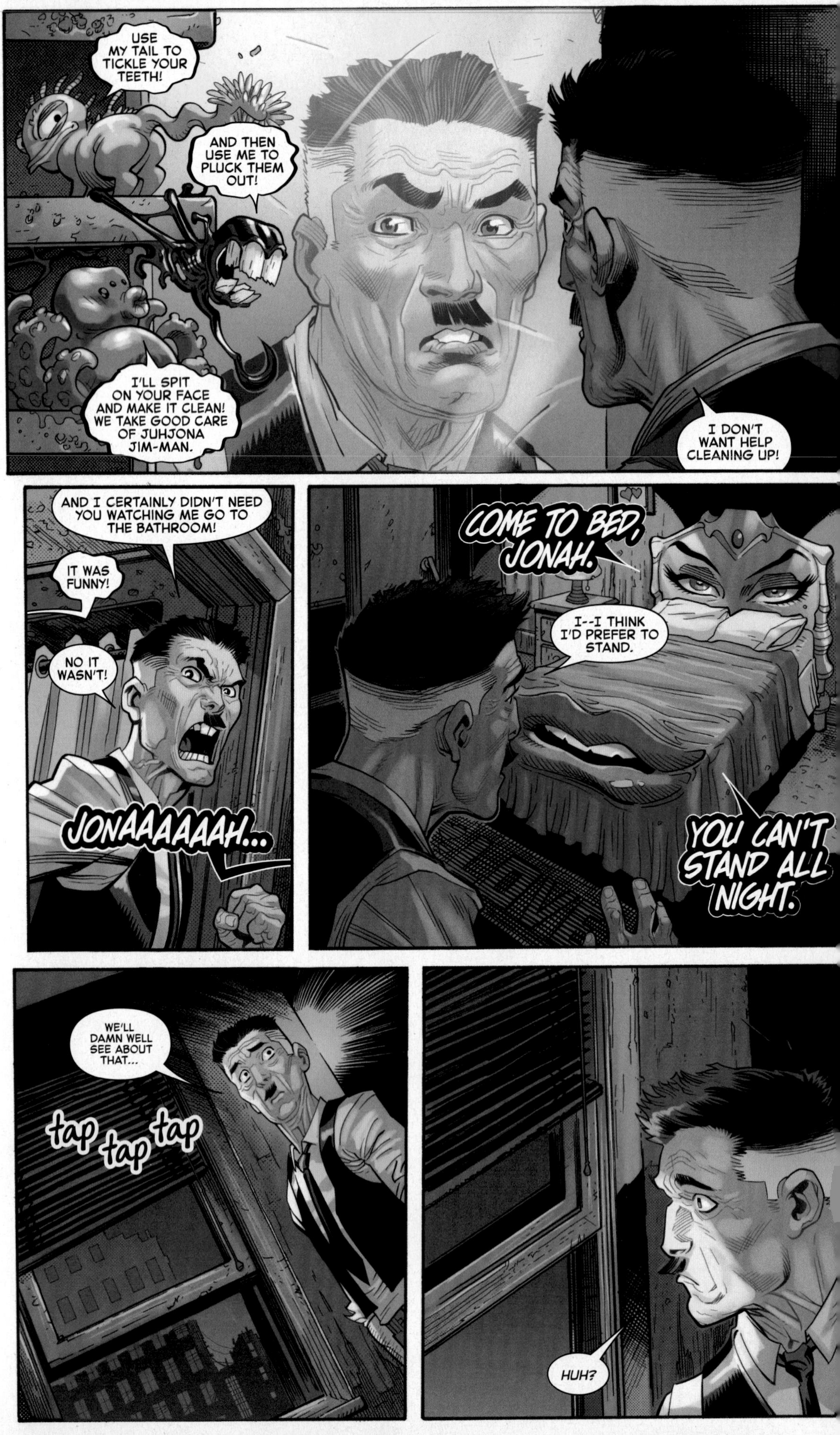
USE MY TAIL TO TICKLE YOUR TEETH!
AND THEN USE ME TO PLUCK THEM OUT!
I'LL SPIT ON YOUR FACE AND MAKE IT CLEAN! WE TAKE GOOD CARE OF JUHJONA JIM-MAN.
I DON'T WANT HELP CLEANING UP!
AND I CERTAINLY DIDN'T NEED YOU WATCHING ME GO TO THE BATHROOM!
IT WAS FUNNY!
NO IT WASN'T!
JONAAAAAAH...
COME TO BED, JONAH.
I--I THINK I'D PREFER TO STAND.
YOU CAN'T STAND ALL NIGHT.
WE'LL DAMN WELL SEE ABOUT THAT...
tap tap tap
HUH?

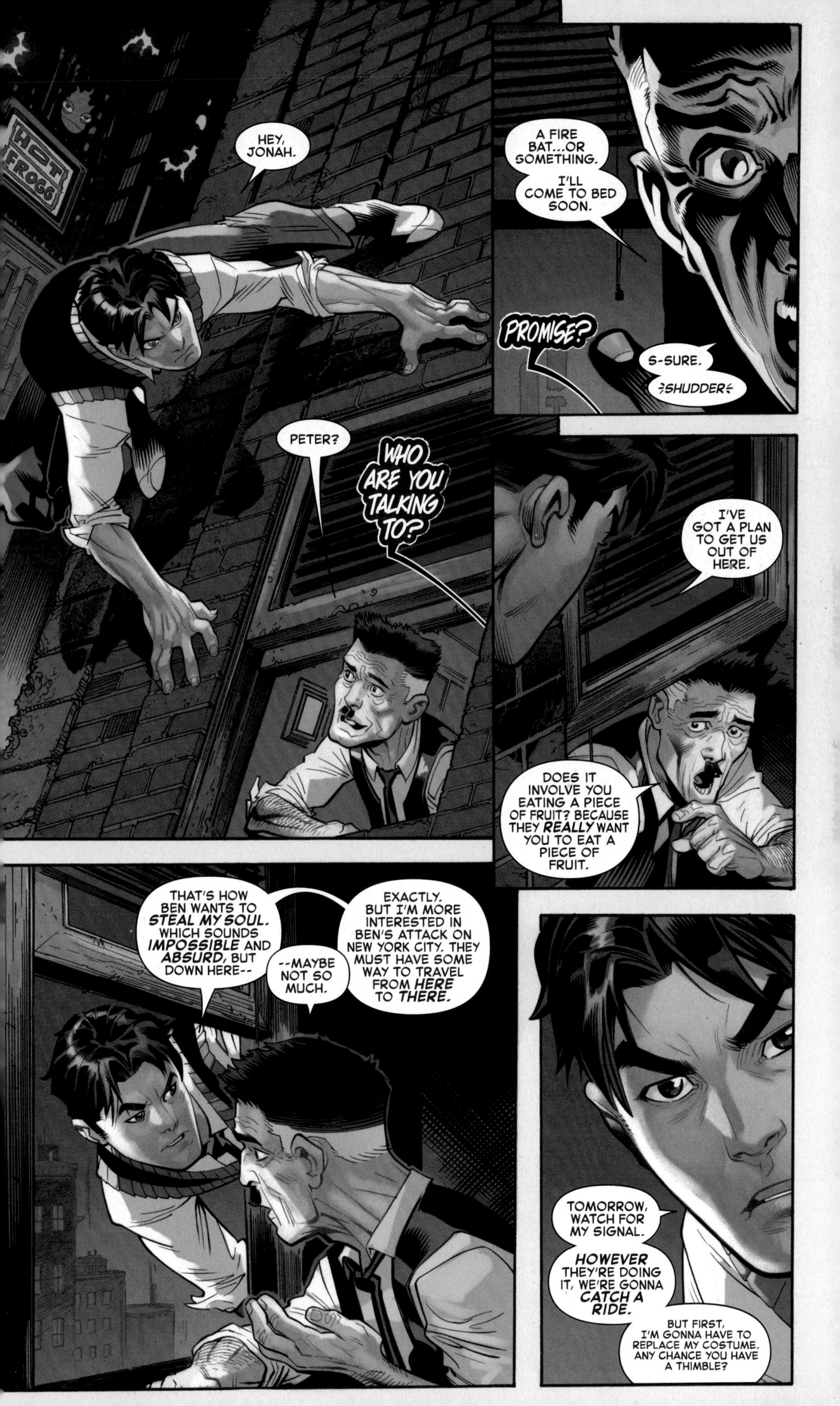

HOT FROGG
HEY, JONAH.
A FIRE BAT...OR SOMETHING.
I'LL COME TO BED SOON.
PROMISE?
S-SURE.
SHUDDER
PETER?
WHO ARE YOU TALKING TO?
I'VE GOT A PLAN TO GET US OUT OF HERE.
DOES IT INVOLVE YOU EATING A PIECE OF FRUIT? BECAUSE THEY REALLY WANT YOU TO EAT A PIECE OF FRUIT.
THAT'S HOW BEN WANTS TO STEAL MY SOUL. WHICH SOUNDS IMPOSSIBLE AND ABSURD, BUT DOWN HERE--
--MAYBE NOT SO MUCH.
EXACTLY. BUT I'M MORE INTERESTED IN BEN'S ATTACK ON NEW YORK CITY. THEY MUST HAVE SOME WAY TO TRAVEL FROM HERE TO THERE.
TOMORROW, WATCH FOR MY SIGNAL.
HOWEVER THEY'RE DOING IT, WE'RE GONNA CATCH A RIDE.
BUT FIRST, I'M GONNA HAVE TO REPLACE MY COSTUME. ANY CHANCE YOU HAVE A THIMBLE?

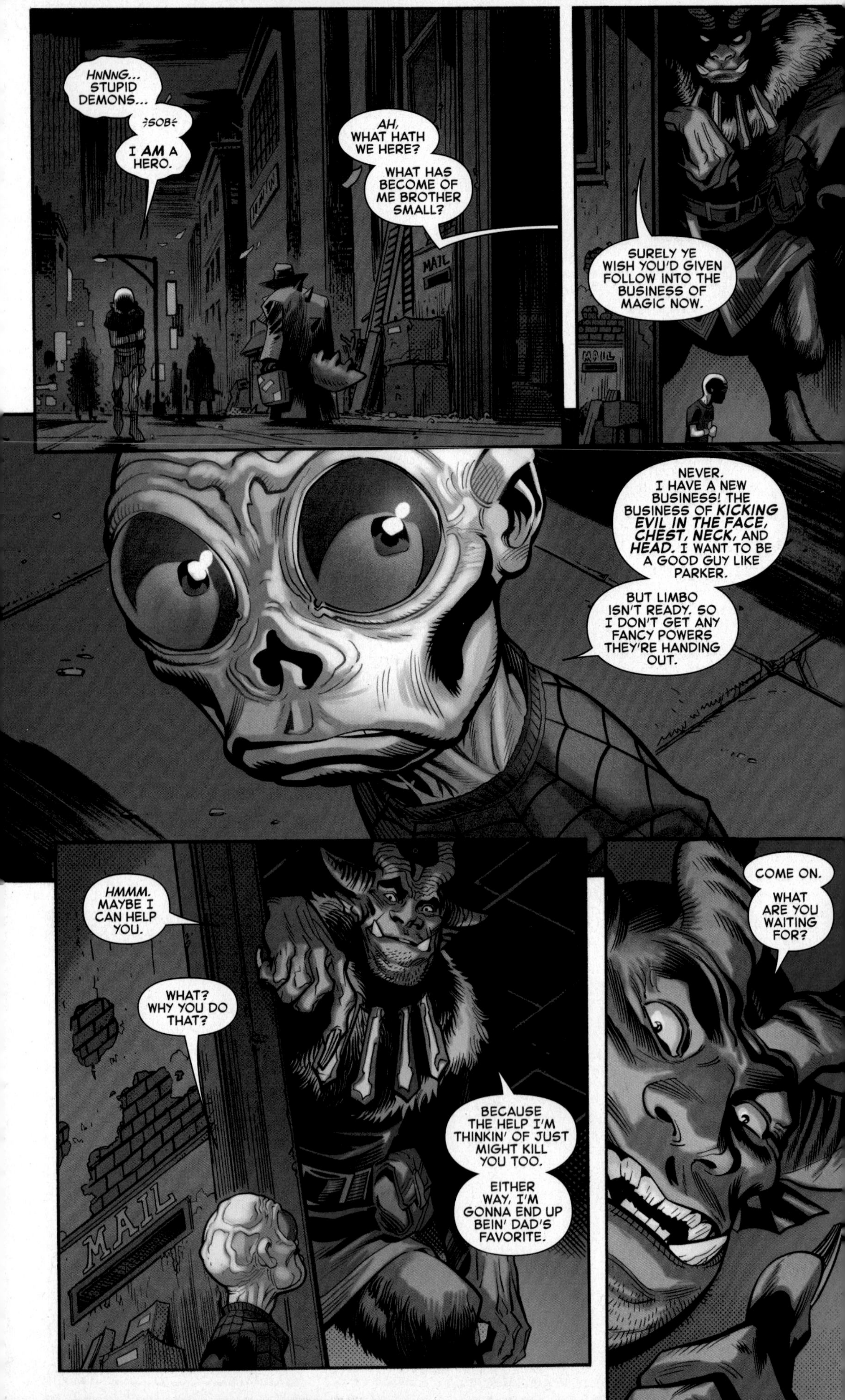
HNNNG... STUPID DEMONS...
SOB
I AM A HERO.
AH, WHAT HATH WE HERE?
WHAT HAS BECOME OF ME BROTHER SMALL?
MAIL
SURELY YE WISH YOU'D GIVEN FOLLOW INTO THE BUSINESS OF MAGIC NOW.
MAIL
NEVER. I HAVE A NEW BUSINESS! THE BUSINESS OF KICKING EVIL IN THE FACE, CHEST, NECK, AND HEAD. I WANT TO BE A GOOD GUY LIKE PARKER.
BUT LIMBO ISN'T READY. SO I DON'T GET ANY FANCY POWERS THEY'RE HANDING OUT.
HMMM. MAYBE I CAN HELP YOU.
WHAT? WHY YOU DO THAT?
BECAUSE THE HELP I'M THINKIN' OF JUST MIGHT KILL YOU TOO.
EITHER WAY, I'M GONNA END UP BEIN' DAD'S FAVORITE.
MAIL
COME ON.
WHAT ARE YOU WAITING FOR?

I HATH HAD TO MAKE YE SMALL BECAUSE ME SHARE OF THE *SUBSTANCE* IS MEAGER![※]

IT FEELS LIKE ONE OF YOUR JOKES, IS ALL I'M SAYING.

REST YER DIM LITTLE HEAD. I'LL MAKE YE BIG AGAIN ONCE ME MAGIC TAKES HOLD.

※ REMEMBER THIS GUY FROM VENOM #13? --EIDETIC AL

FPMᚦ ᛘᚾᚠᛋᚠ� ᛗᛘᚾᚱᚺ IPᛋᛟ!

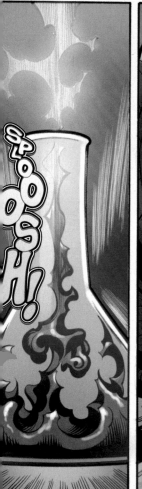

SPOOSH!

WHAT YOU *DO?!* I SUPPOSED TO PUT CLOTHES ON! NOT CLOTHES PUT *ME* ON!

YOU GOT IT *BACKWARDS!* YOU--

HA HA HA HA HA!

LISTEN UP!

I'VE GOT A HOT LEAD ON A STORY! RED-HOT!

ARE WE THE TYPE OF CREW THAT GETS SCOOPED ON A RED-HOT STORY?!

NO!

GIVE US THE LEAD, JAY JAYMAN!

NOT US!

OKAY. THIS IS DEADLY SERIOUS.

APPARENTLY, *SOME* DEMONS HAVE BEEN ALLOWED TO GO TO THE *REAL* NEW YORK CITY.

gasp!

I KNOW. INSTEAD OF DRESSING IN A SUIT AND TIE EVERY MORNING THEY'RE OUT HUNTING HUMANS MAKING THEM SCREAM. MAKING THEM CRY.

WORD IS, THAT'S ALL THESE HUMANS DO SCREAM AND CR AND BLEED. GOO THING THAT'S NO APPEALING TO ANY OF *US.*

NO. NOT... US.

YEAH, WHO WOULD WANT TO DO...*THAT?*

NOT ME...

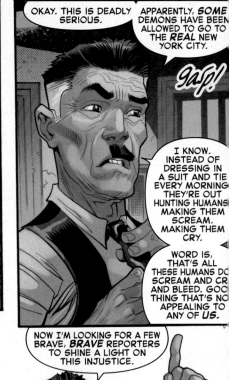

NOW I'M LOOKING FOR A FEW BRAVE, *BRAVE* REPORTERS TO SHINE A LIGHT ON THIS INJUSTICE.

REPORTERS WHO WILL SLEUTH AND INVESTIGATE, BUT NEVER JOIN IN ON THES HEINOUS ACTIONS, WHIC WE'VE ALL AGREED WOULD BE NO FUN AT ALL.

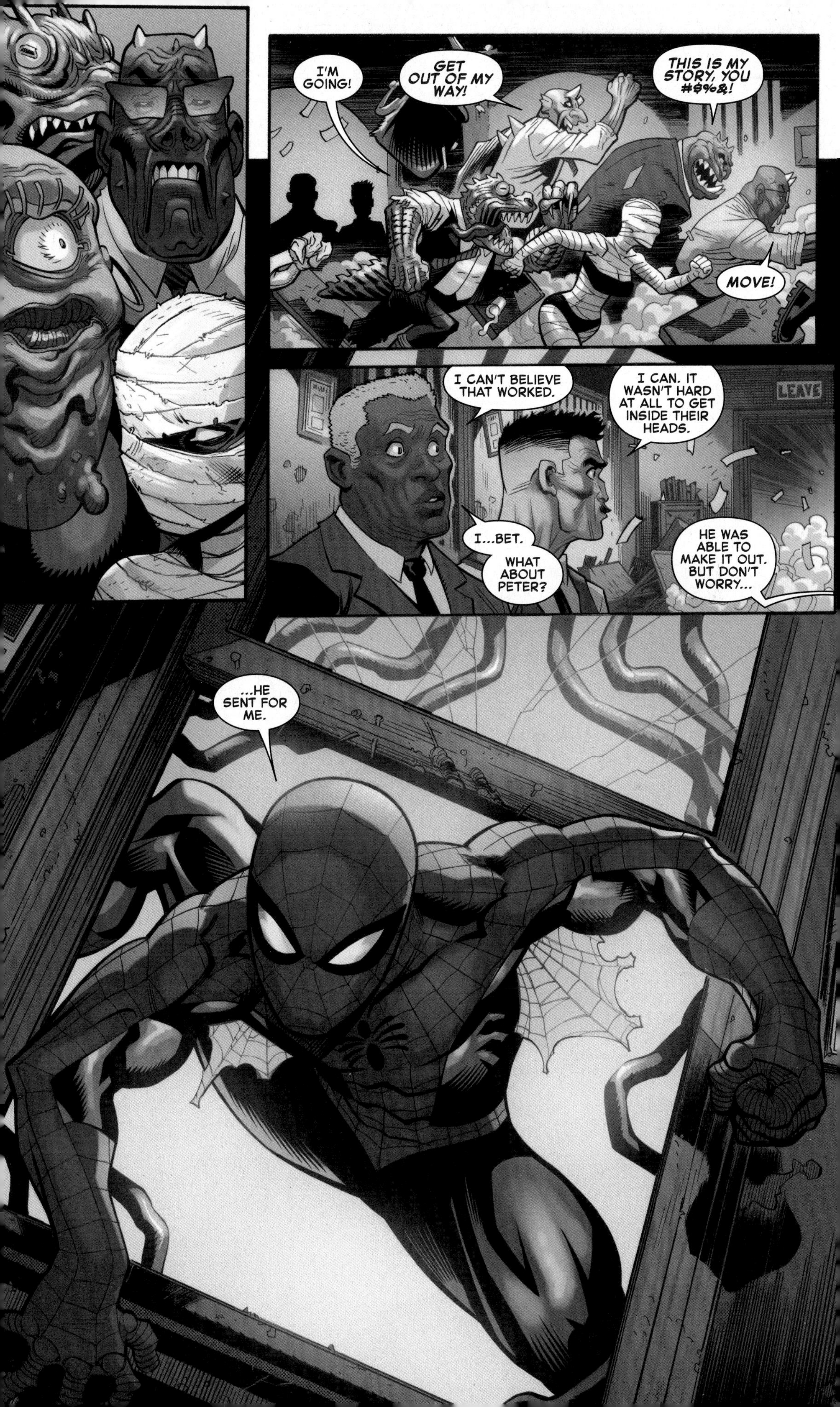
I'M GOING!
GET OUT OF MY WAY!
THIS IS MY STORY, YOU #$%&!
MOVE!
I CAN'T BELIEVE THAT WORKED.
I CAN. IT WASN'T HARD AT ALL TO GET INSIDE THEIR HEADS.
LEAVE
I...BET.
WHAT ABOUT PETER?
HE WAS ABLE TO MAKE IT OUT. BUT DON'T WORRY...
...HE SENT FOR ME.

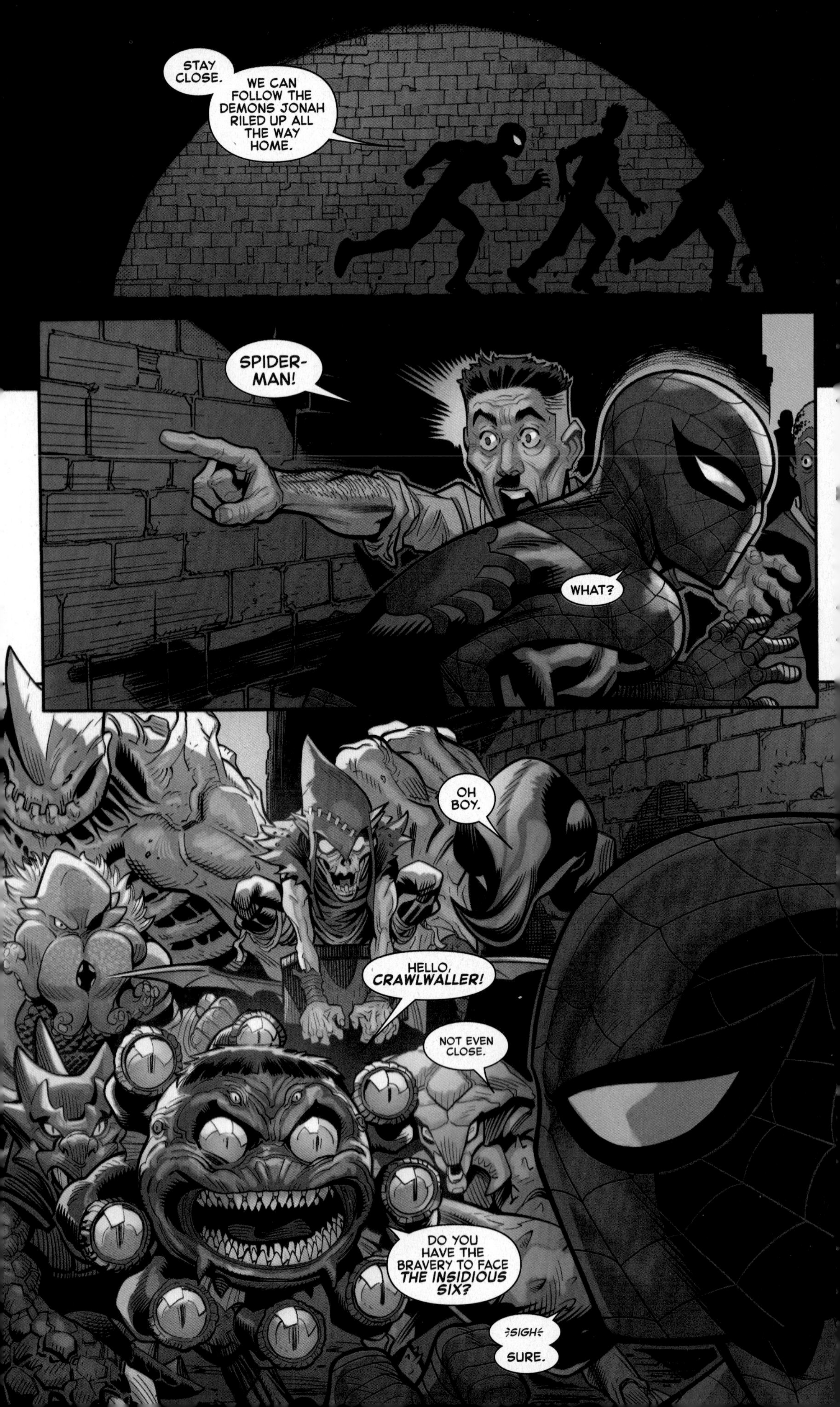
STAY CLOSE.
WE CAN FOLLOW THE DEMONS JONAH RILED UP ALL THE WAY HOME.
SPIDER-MAN!
WHAT?
OH BOY.
HELLO, CRAWLWALLER!
NOT EVEN CLOSE.
DO YOU HAVE THE BRAVERY TO FACE THE INSIDIOUS SIX?
SIGH
SURE.

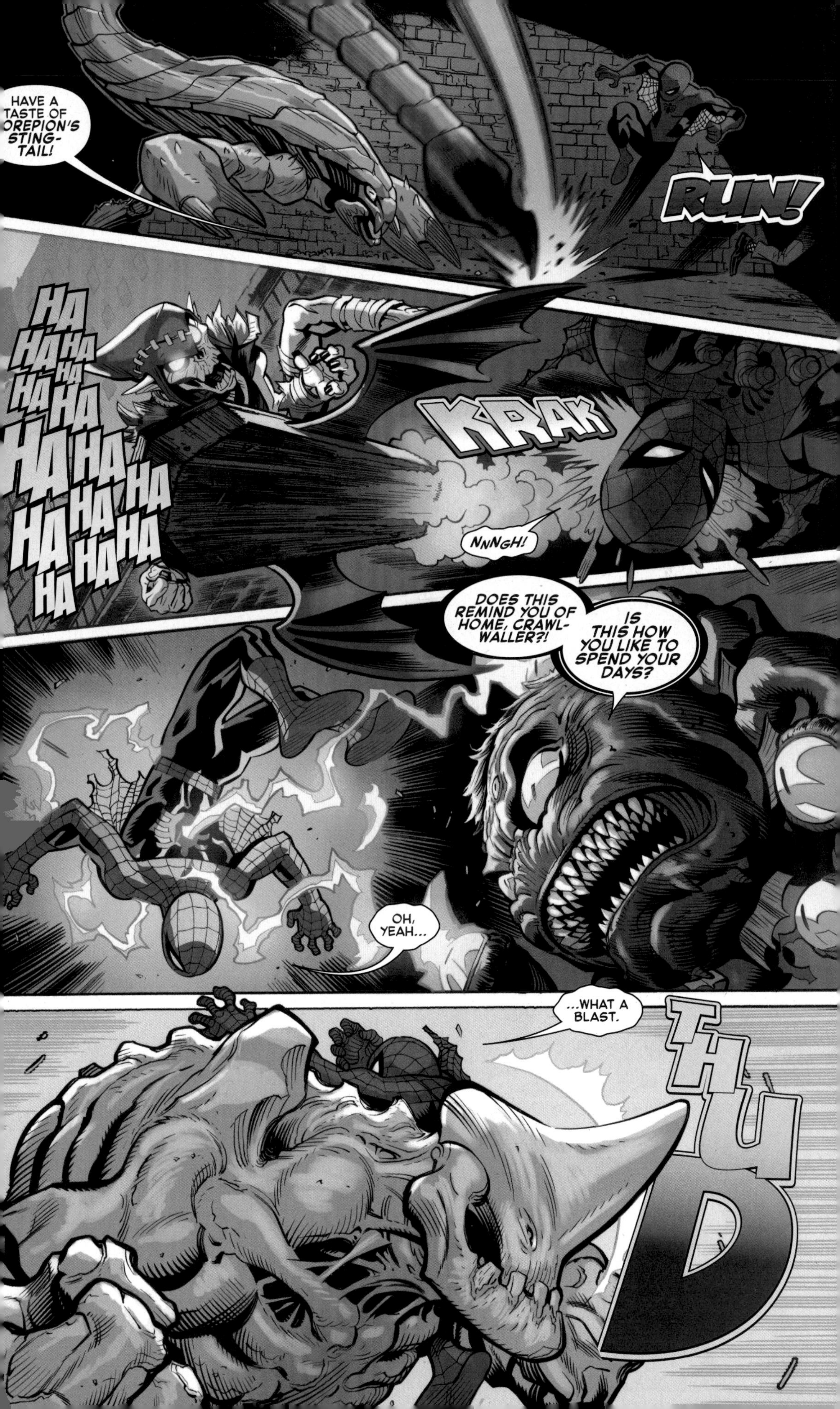
HAVE A TASTE OF OREPION'S STING-TAIL!
RUN!
HA HA HA HA HA HA HA HA HA HA HA HA HA HA HA HA
KRAK
NNNGH!
DOES THIS REMIND YOU OF HOME, CRAWL-WALLER?!
IS THIS HOW YOU LIKE TO SPEND YOUR DAYS?
OH, YEAH...
...WHAT A BLAST.
THUD

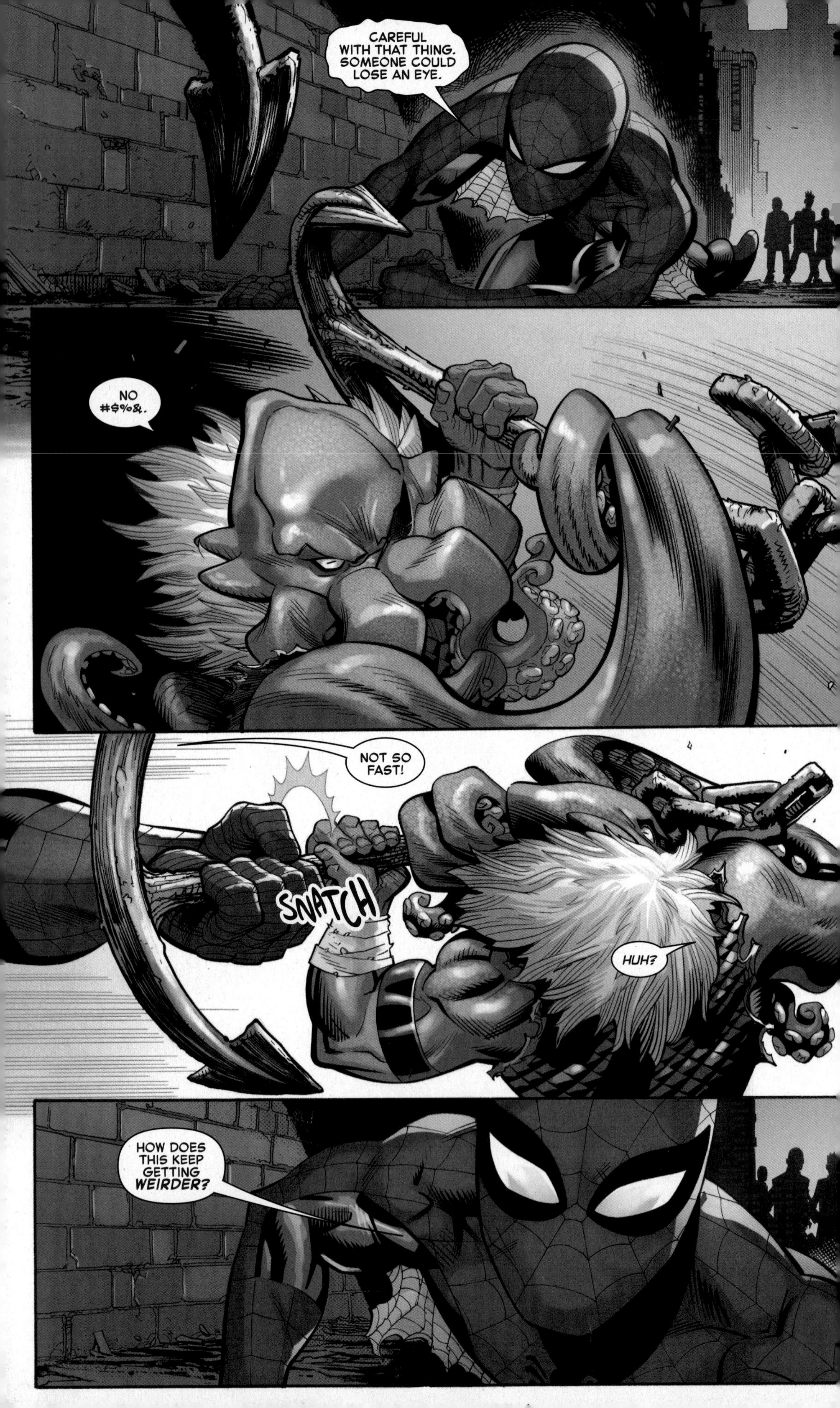
CAREFUL WITH THAT THING. SOMEONE COULD LOSE AN EYE.
NO #$%&.
NOT SO FAST!
SNATCH
HUH?
HOW DOES THIS KEEP GETTING WEIRDER?

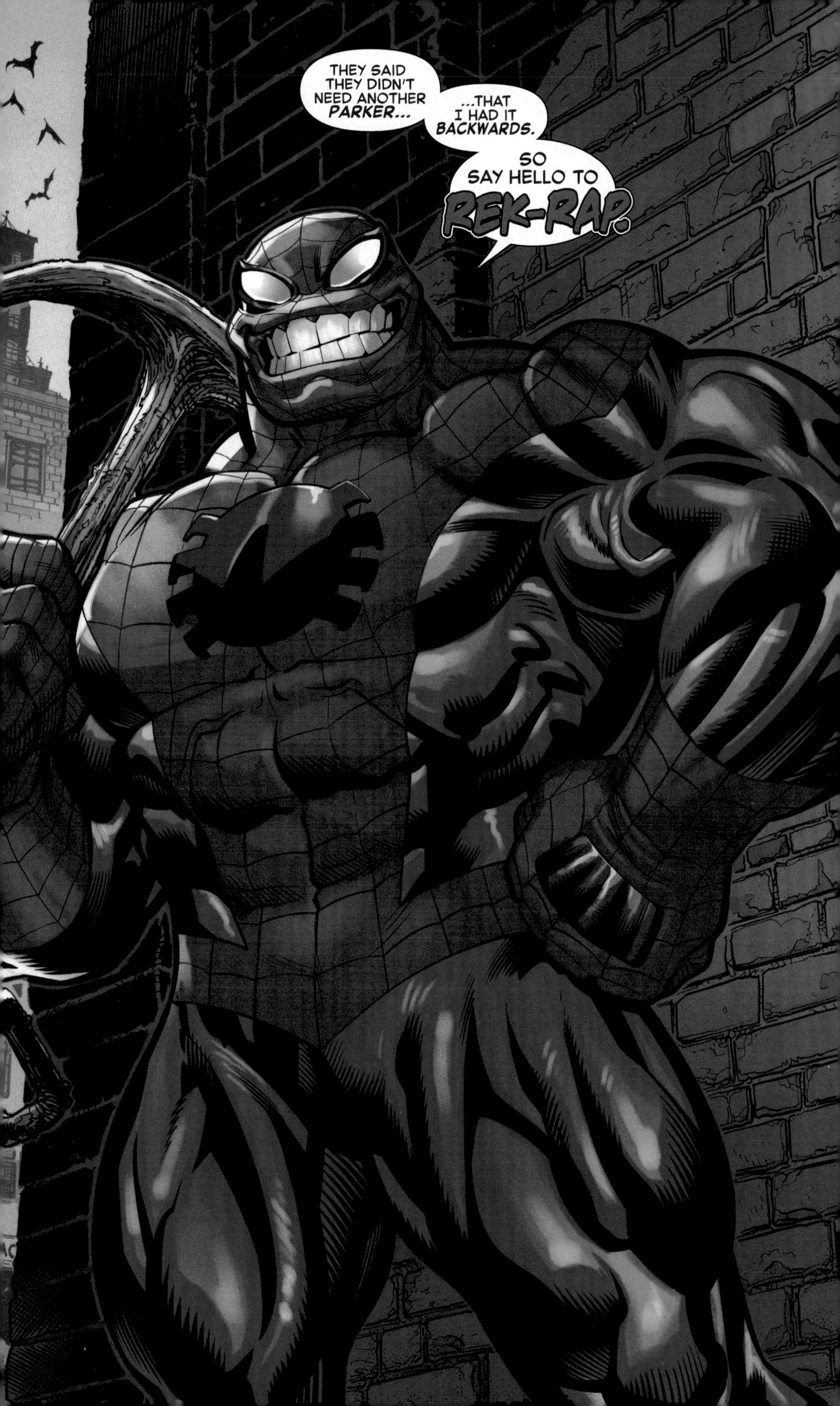

THEY SAID THEY DIDN'T NEED ANOTHER *PARKER...*
...THAT I HAD IT *BACKWARDS.*
SO SAY HELLO TO
REK-RAP.

AMAZING SPIDER-MAN #18

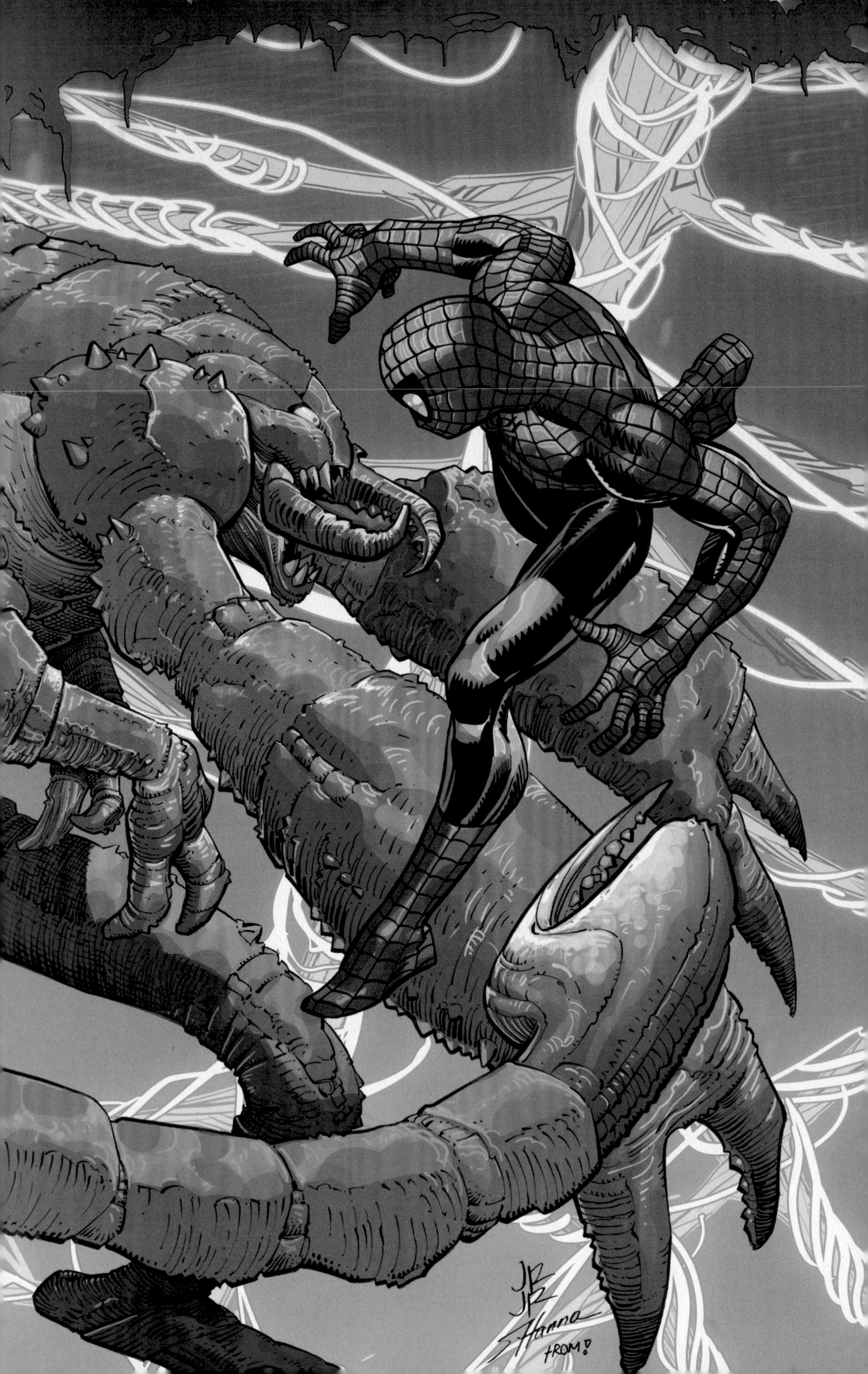

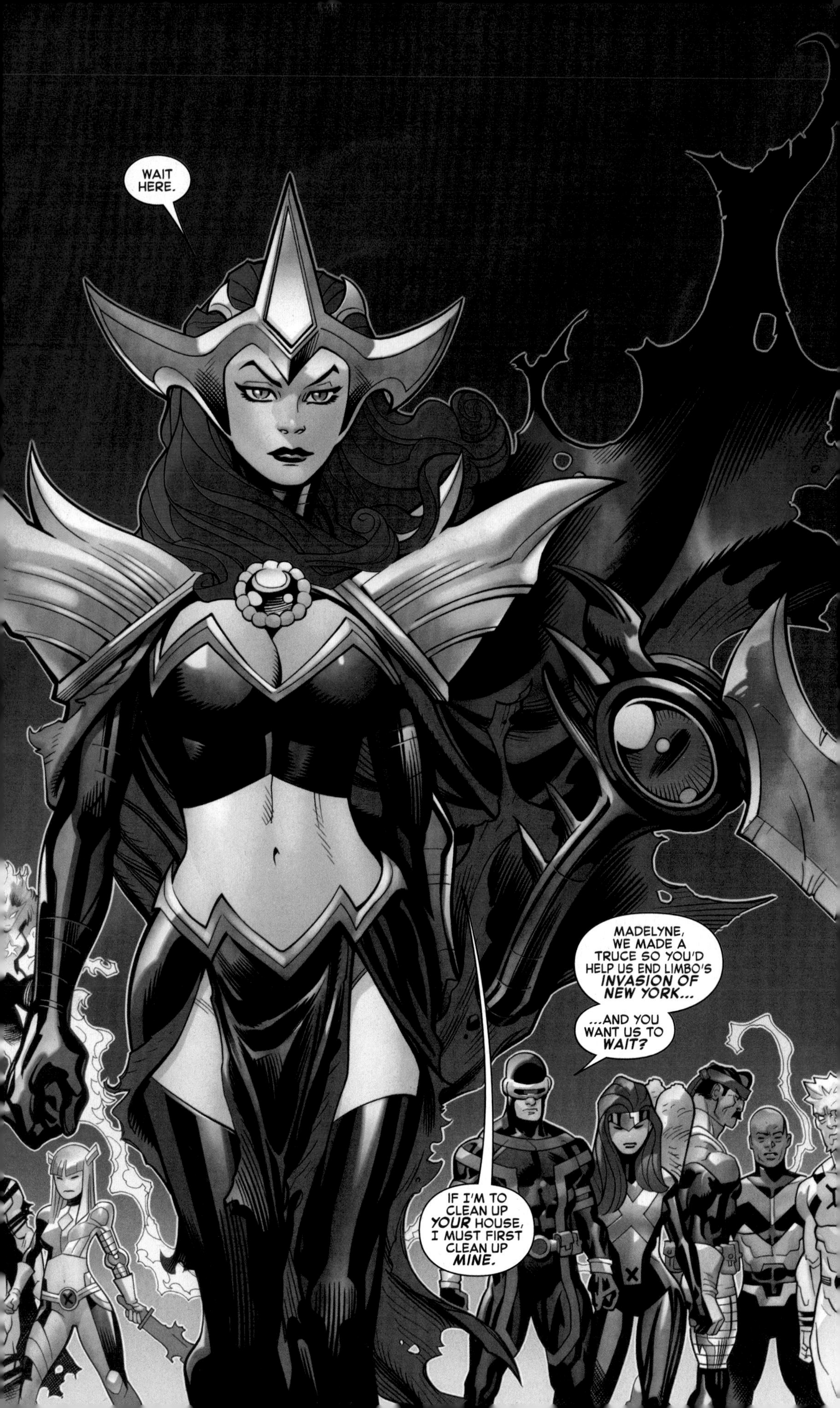
WAIT HERE.
MADELYNE, WE MADE A TRUCE SO YOU'D HELP US END LIMBO'S INVASION OF NEW YORK...
...AND YOU WANT US TO WAIT?
IF I'M TO CLEAN UP YOUR HOUSE, I MUST FIRST CLEAN UP MINE.

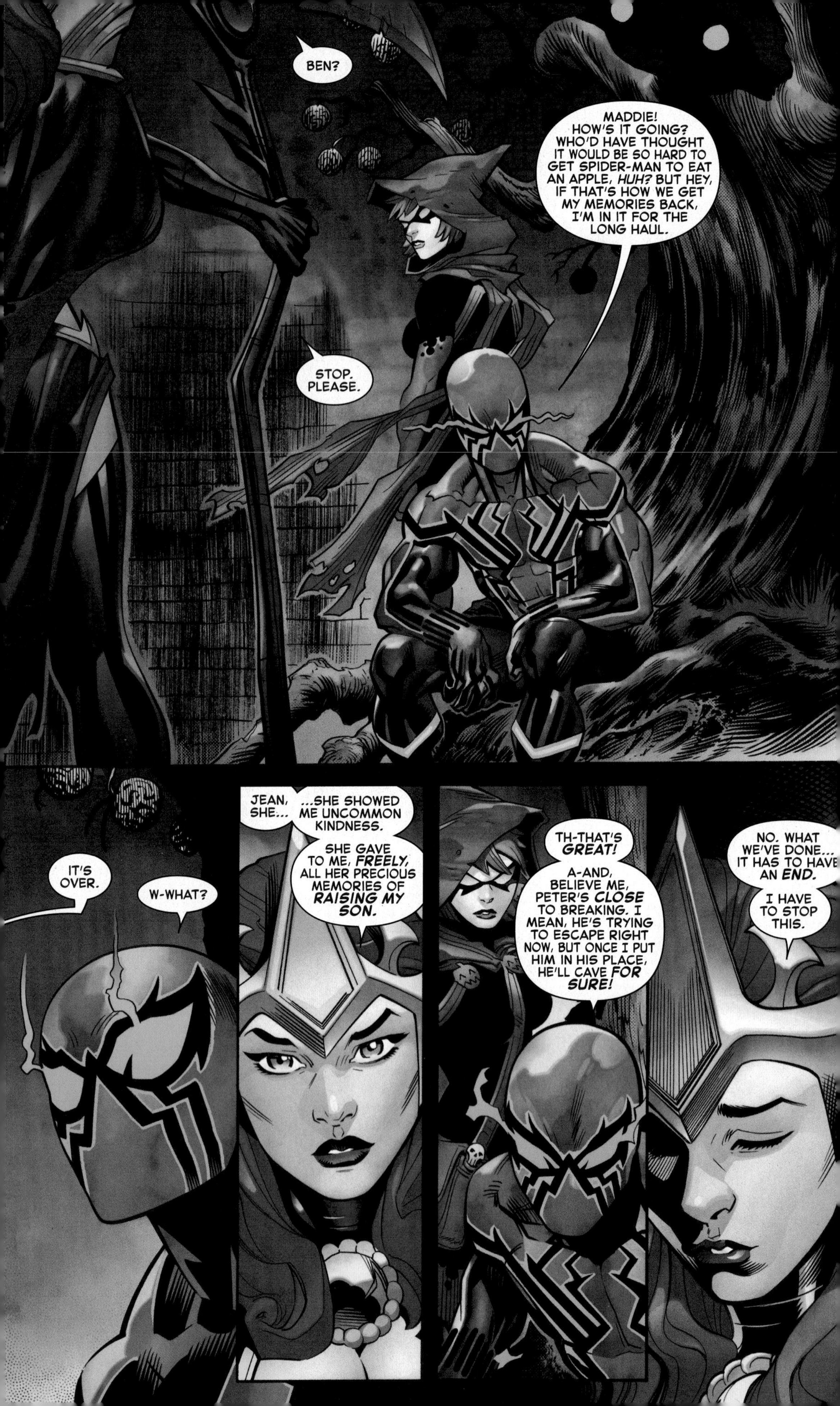

BEN?
MADDIE! HOW'S IT GOING? WHO'D HAVE THOUGHT IT WOULD BE SO HARD TO GET SPIDER-MAN TO EAT AN APPLE, HUH? BUT HEY, IF THAT'S HOW WE GET MY MEMORIES BACK, I'M IN IT FOR THE LONG HAUL.
STOP. PLEASE.
IT'S OVER.
W-WHAT?
JEAN, SHE...
...SHE SHOWED ME UNCOMMON KINDNESS.
SHE GAVE TO ME, FREELY, ALL HER PRECIOUS MEMORIES OF RAISING MY SON.
TH-THAT'S GREAT!
A-AND, BELIEVE ME, PETER'S CLOSE TO BREAKING. I MEAN, HE'S TRYING TO ESCAPE RIGHT NOW, BUT ONCE I PUT HIM IN HIS PLACE, HE'LL CAVE FOR SURE!
NO. WHAT WE'VE DONE... IT HAS TO HAVE AN END.
I HAVE TO STOP THIS.

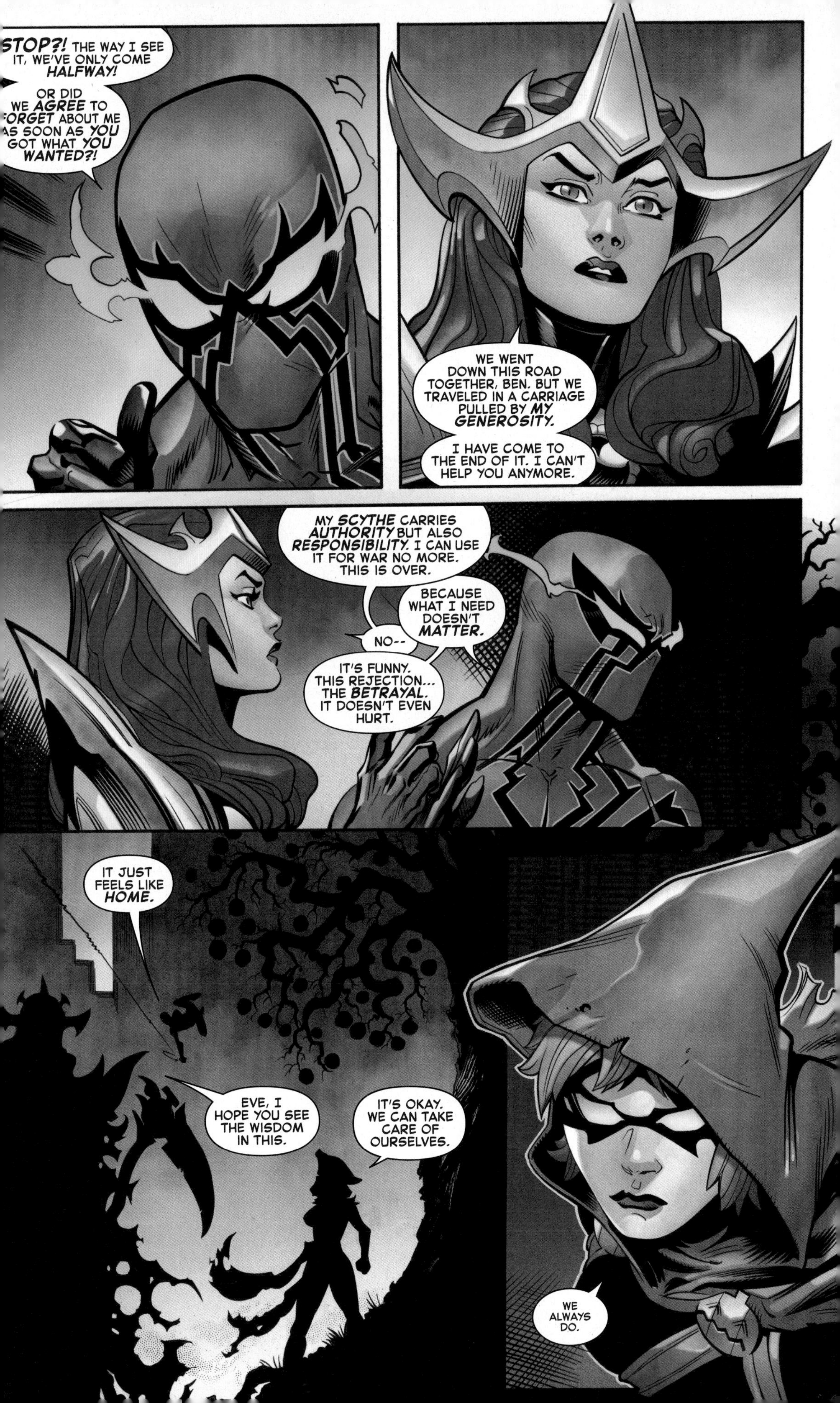
STOP?! THE WAY I SEE IT, WE'VE ONLY COME HALFWAY!
OR DID WE AGREE TO FORGET ABOUT ME AS SOON AS YOU GOT WHAT YOU WANTED?!
WE WENT DOWN THIS ROAD TOGETHER, BEN. BUT WE TRAVELED IN A CARRIAGE PULLED BY MY GENEROSITY.
I HAVE COME TO THE END OF IT. I CAN'T HELP YOU ANYMORE.
MY SCYTHE CARRIES AUTHORITY BUT ALSO RESPONSIBILITY. I CAN USE IT FOR WAR NO MORE. THIS IS OVER.
BECAUSE WHAT I NEED DOESN'T MATTER.
NO--
IT'S FUNNY. THIS REJECTION... THE BETRAYAL. IT DOESN'T EVEN HURT.
IT JUST FEELS LIKE HOME.
EVE, I HOPE YOU SEE THE WISDOM IN THIS.
IT'S OKAY. WE CAN TAKE CARE OF OURSELVES.
WE ALWAYS DO.

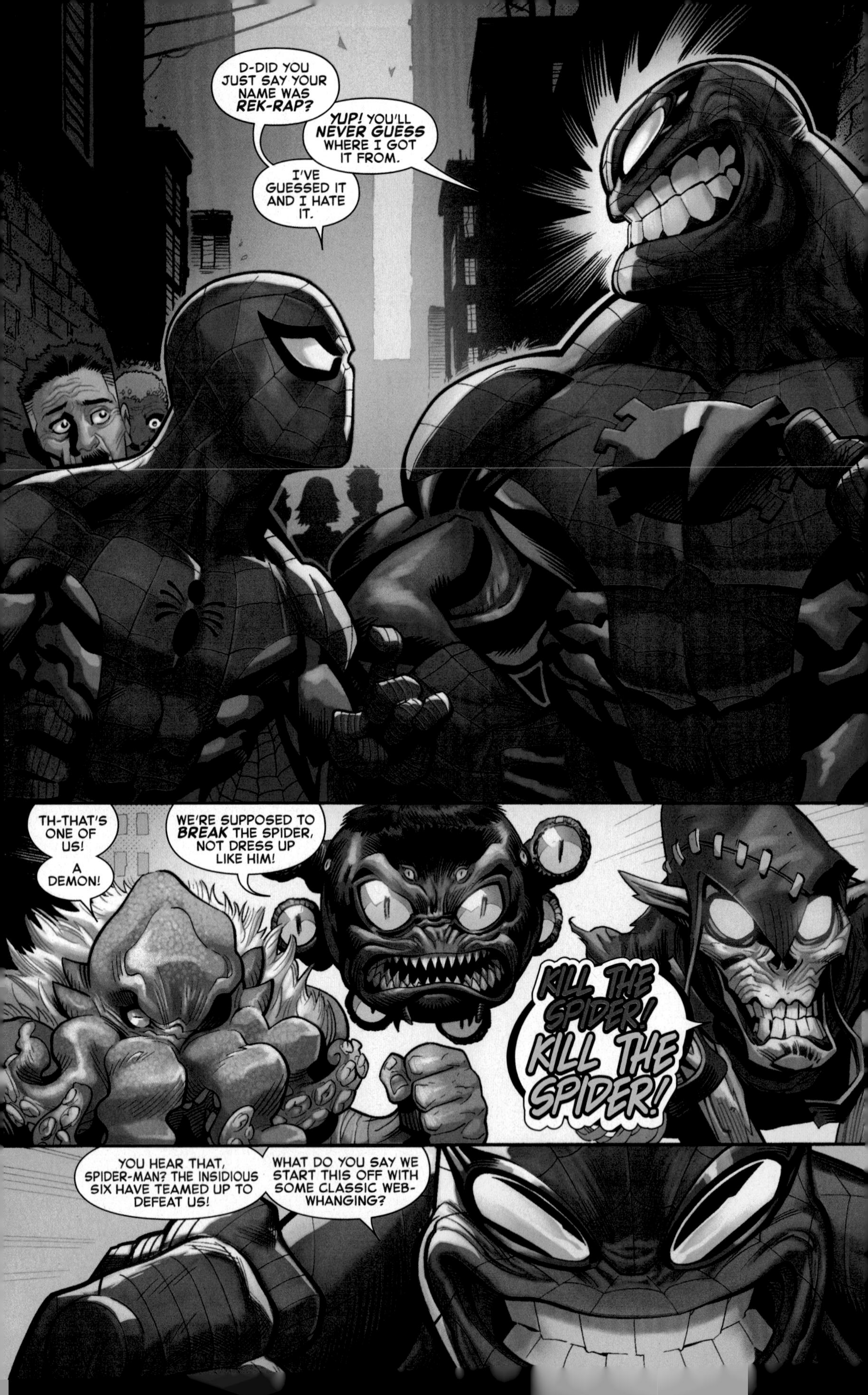
D-DID YOU JUST SAY YOUR NAME WAS REK-RAP?
YUP! YOU'LL NEVER GUESS WHERE I GOT IT FROM.
I'VE GUESSED IT AND I HATE IT.
TH-THAT'S ONE OF US!
A DEMON!
WE'RE SUPPOSED TO BREAK THE SPIDER, NOT DRESS UP LIKE HIM!
KILL THE SPIDER! KILL THE SPIDER!
YOU HEAR THAT, SPIDER-MAN? THE INSIDIOUS SIX HAVE TEAMED UP TO DEFEAT US!
WHAT DO YOU SAY WE START THIS OFF WITH SOME CLASSIC WEB-WHANGING?

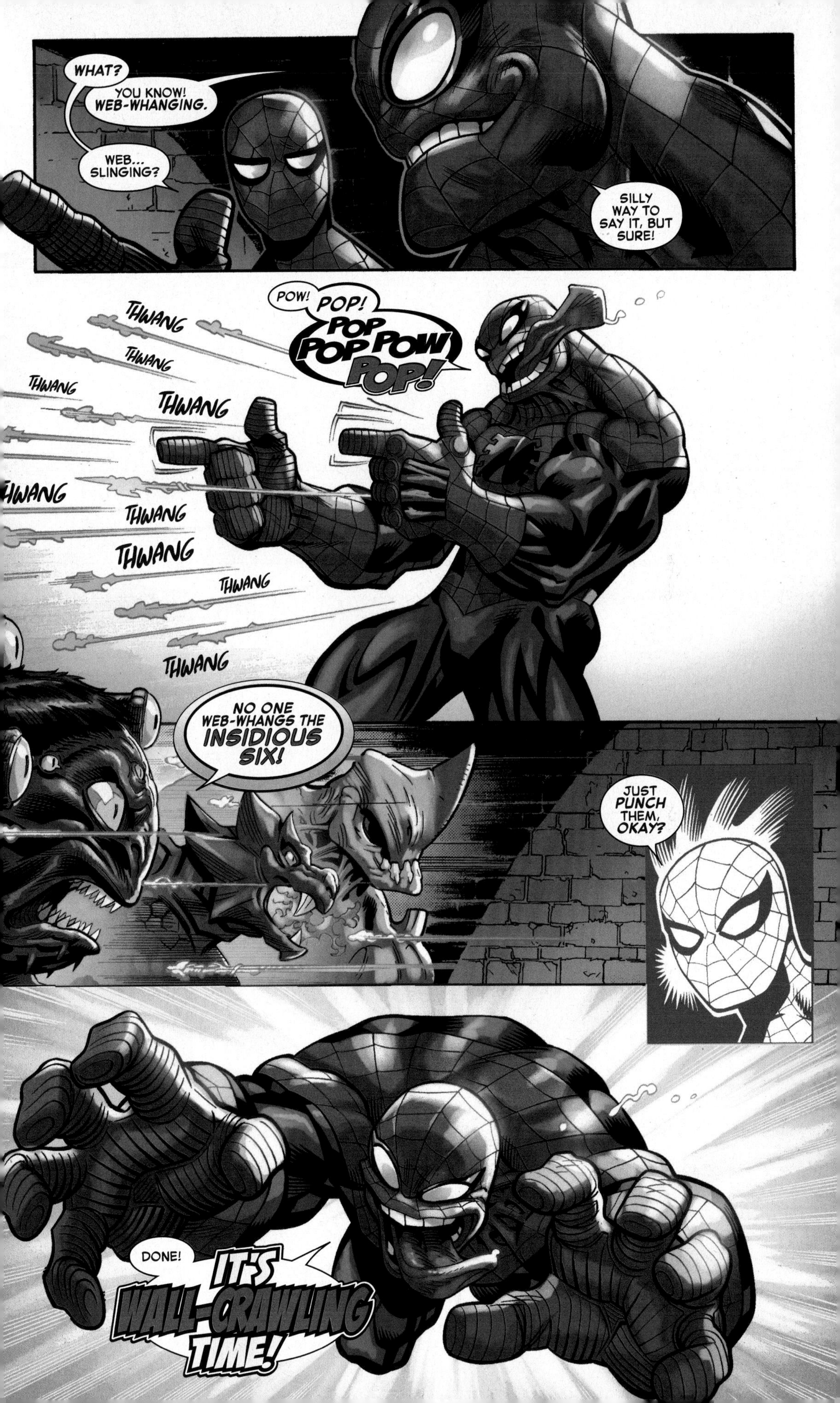

WHAT?
YOU KNOW! WEB-WHANGING.
WEB... SLINGING?
SILLY WAY TO SAY IT, BUT SURE!
POW! POP! POP POP POW POP!
THWANG
THWANG
THWANG
THWANG
THWANG
THWANG
THWANG
THWANG
THWANG
NO ONE WEB-WHANGS THE INSIDIOUS SIX!
JUST PUNCH THEM, OKAY?
DONE!
IT'S WALL-CRAWLING TIME!

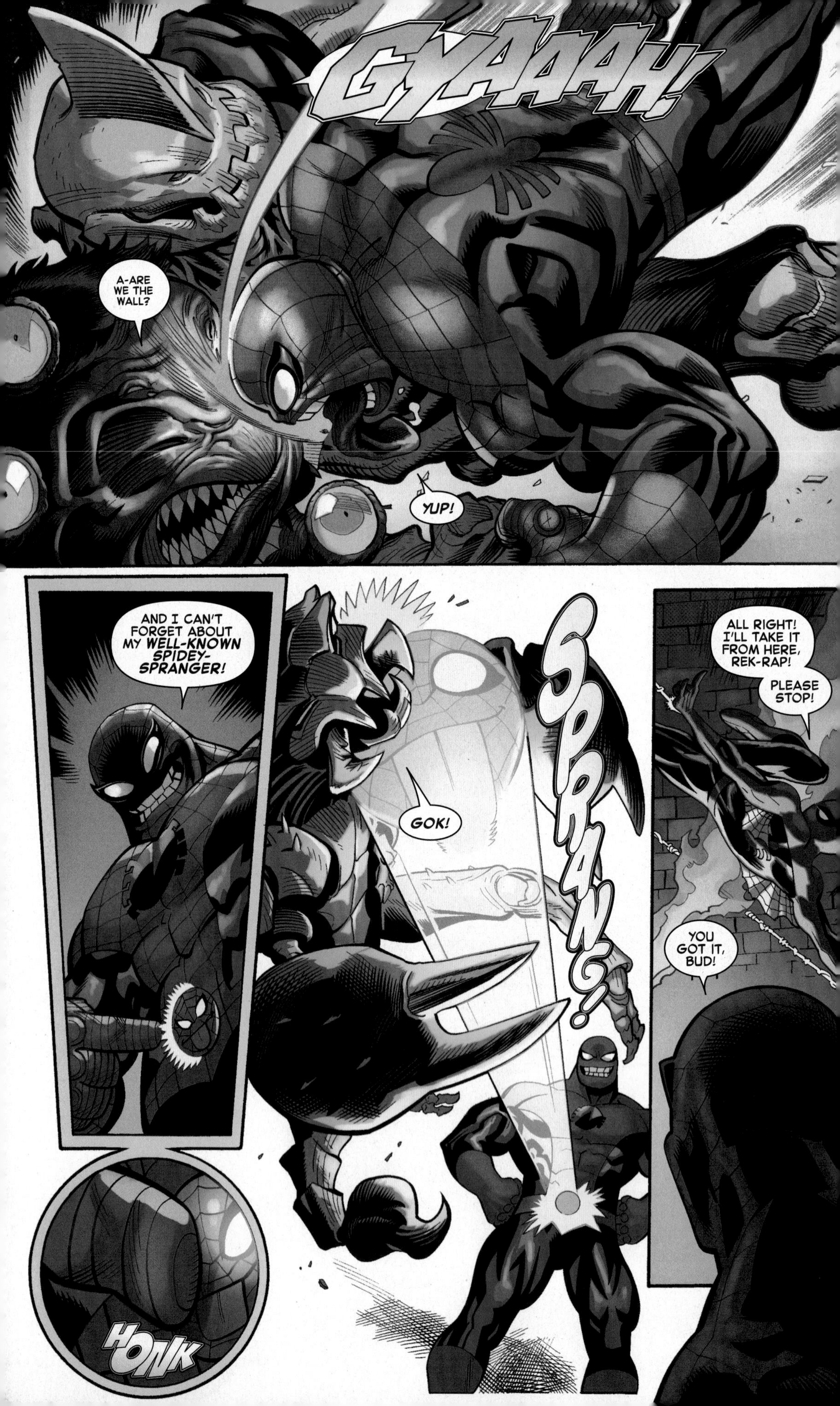

GYAAAH!
A-ARE WE THE WALL?
YUP!
AND I CAN'T FORGET ABOUT MY WELL-KNOWN SPIDEY-SPRANGER!
GOK!
SPRANG!
ALL RIGHT! I'LL TAKE IT FROM HERE, REK-RAP!
PLEASE STOP!
YOU GOT IT, BUD!
HONK

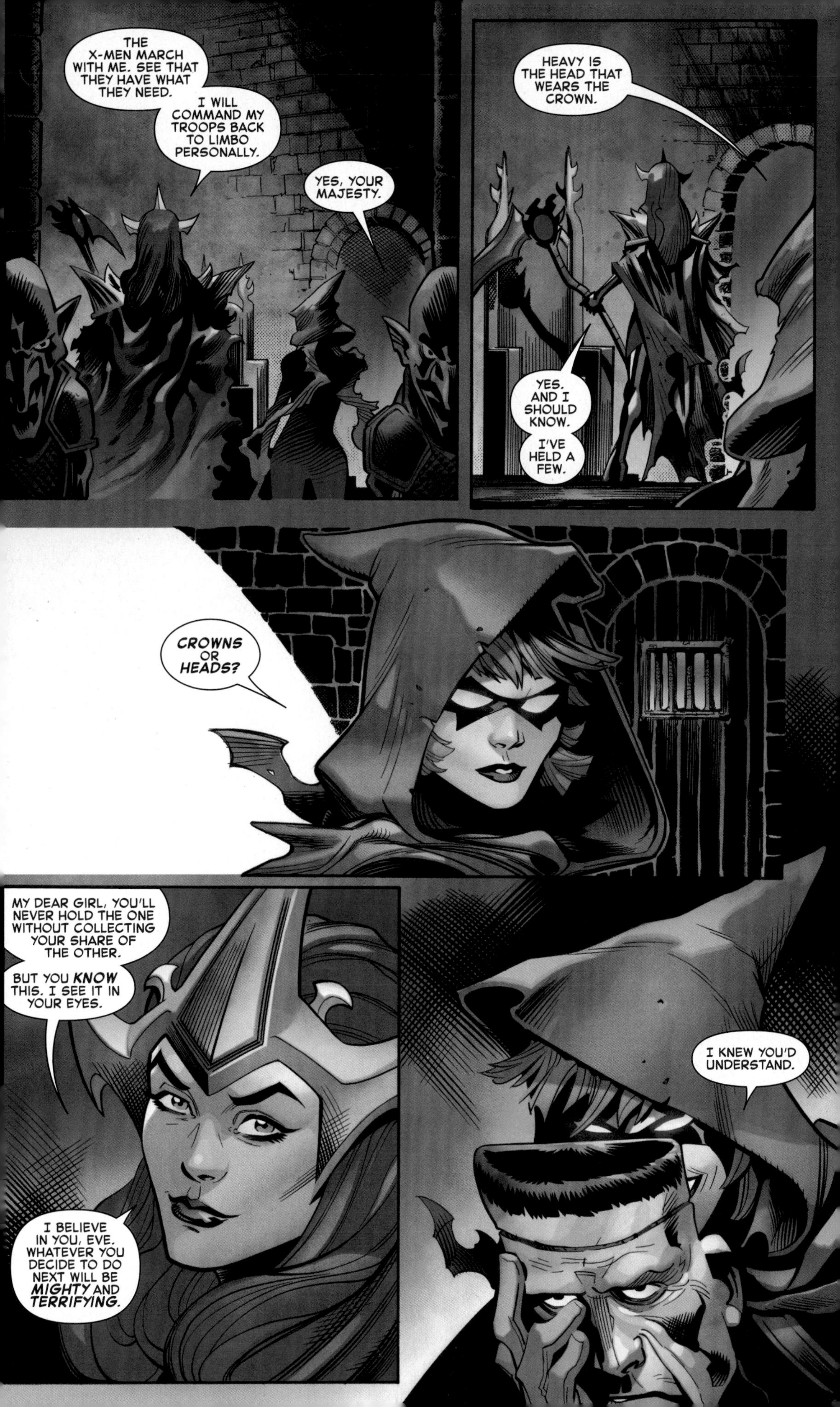
THE X-MEN MARCH WITH ME. SEE THAT THEY HAVE WHAT THEY NEED.
I WILL COMMAND MY TROOPS BACK TO LIMBO PERSONALLY.
YES, YOUR MAJESTY.
HEAVY IS THE HEAD THAT WEARS THE CROWN.
YES. AND I SHOULD KNOW.
I'VE HELD A FEW.
CROWNS OR *HEADS?*
MY DEAR GIRL, YOU'LL NEVER HOLD THE ONE WITHOUT COLLECTING YOUR SHARE OF THE OTHER.
BUT YOU *KNOW* THIS. I SEE IT IN YOUR EYES.
I BELIEVE IN YOU, EVE. WHATEVER YOU DECIDE TO DO NEXT WILL BE *MIGHTY* AND *TERRIFYING*.
I KNEW YOU'D UNDERSTAND.

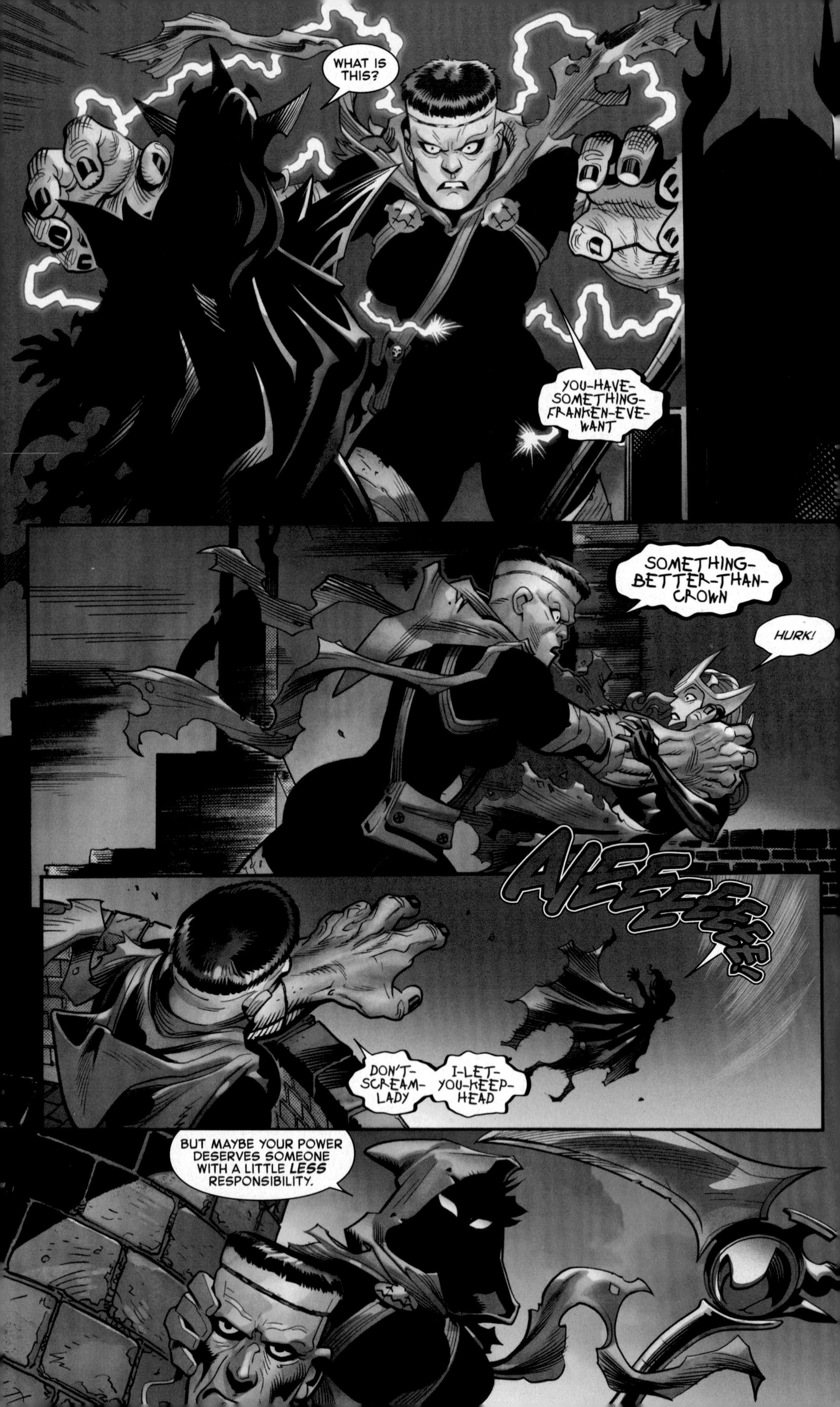
WHAT IS THIS?
YOU-HAVE-SOMETHING-FRANKEN-EVE-WANT
SOMETHING-BETTER-THAN-CROWN
HURK!
AIEEEEEEEE!
DON'T-SCREAM-LADY
I-LET-YOU-KEEP-HEAD
BUT MAYBE YOUR POWER DESERVES SOMEONE WITH A LITTLE LESS RESPONSIBILITY.

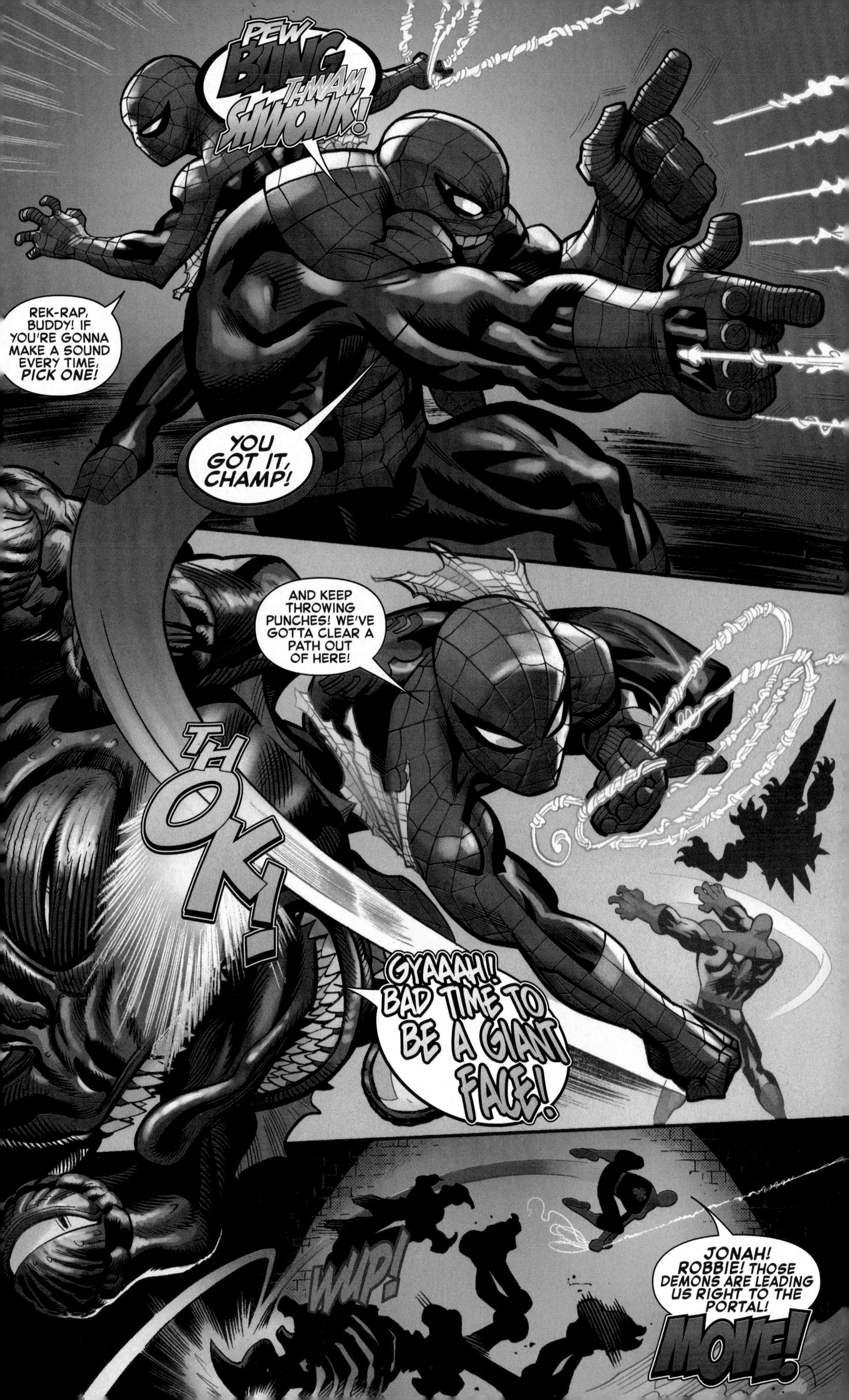
PEW BANG THWAM SHWONK!
REK-RAP, BUDDY! IF YOU'RE GONNA MAKE A SOUND EVERY TIME, PICK ONE!
YOU GOT IT, CHAMP!
AND KEEP THROWING PUNCHES! WE'VE GOTTA CLEAR A PATH OUT OF HERE!
THOK!
GYAAAH! BAD TIME TO BE A GIANT FACE!
WUP!
JONAH! ROBBIE! THOSE DEMONS ARE LEADING US RIGHT TO THE PORTAL! MOVE!

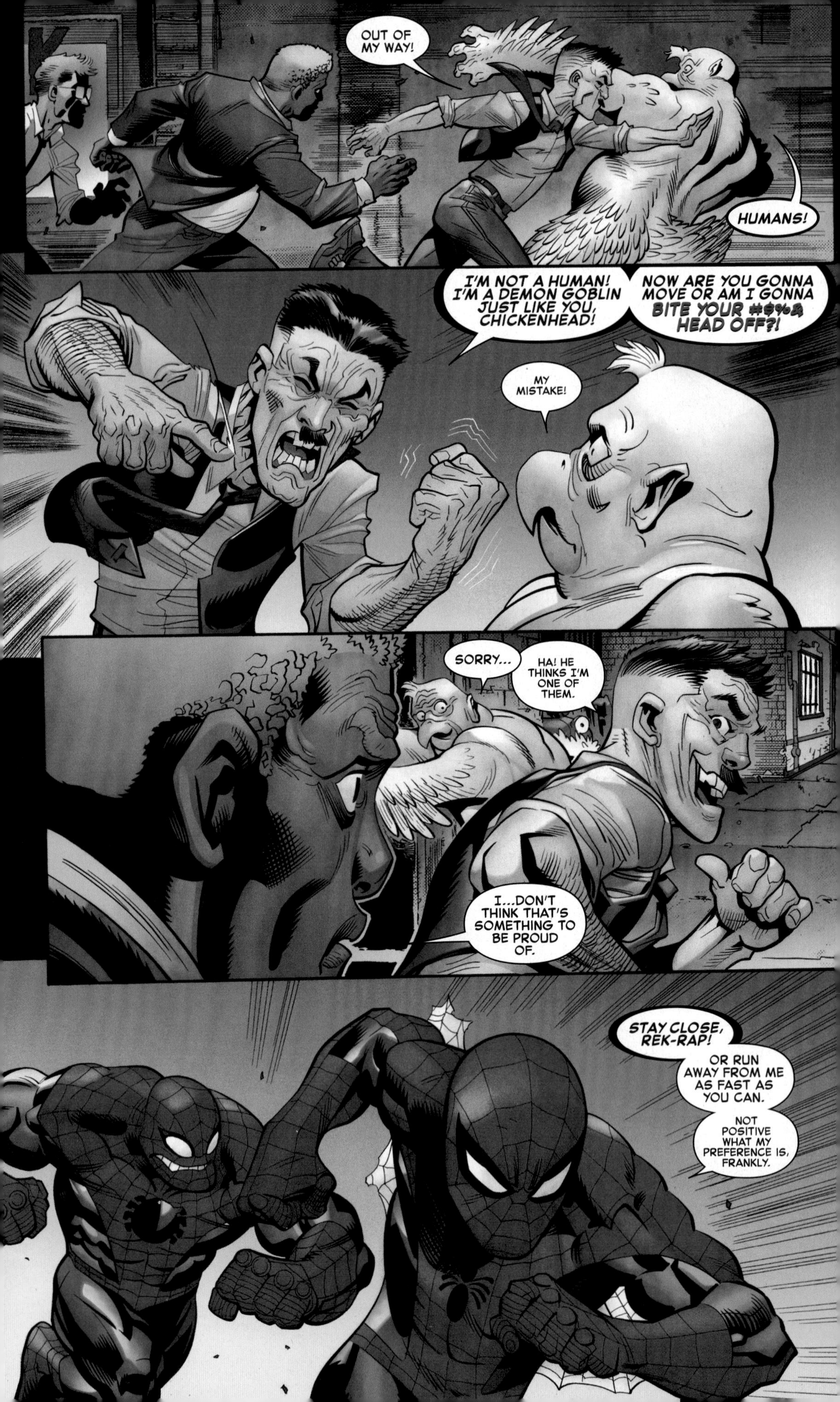
OUT OF MY WAY!
HUMANS!
I'M NOT A HUMAN! I'M A DEMON GOBLIN JUST LIKE YOU, CHICKENHEAD!
NOW ARE YOU GONNA MOVE OR AM I GONNA BITE YOUR #$%& HEAD OFF?!
MY MISTAKE!
SORRY...
HA! HE THINKS I'M ONE OF THEM.
I...DON'T THINK THAT'S SOMETHING TO BE PROUD OF.
STAY CLOSE, REK-RAP!
OR RUN AWAY FROM ME AS FAST AS YOU CAN.
NOT POSITIVE WHAT MY PREFERENCE IS, FRANKLY.

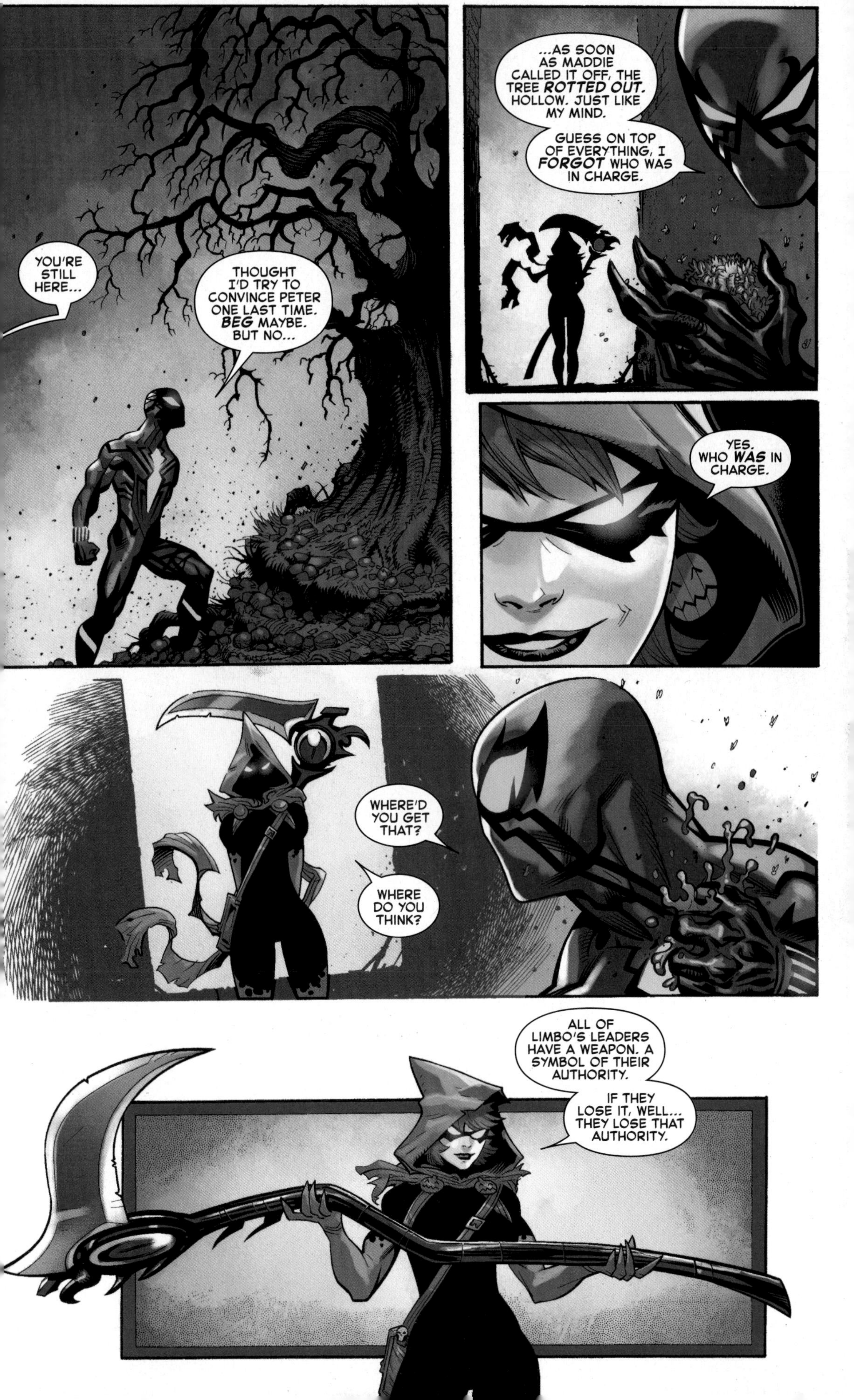

YOU'RE STILL HERE...
THOUGHT I'D TRY TO CONVINCE PETER ONE LAST TIME. BEG MAYBE. BUT NO...
...AS SOON AS MADDIE CALLED IT OFF, THE TREE ROTTED OUT. HOLLOW. JUST LIKE MY MIND.
GUESS ON TOP OF EVERYTHING, I FORGOT WHO WAS IN CHARGE.
YES. WHO WAS IN CHARGE.
WHERE'D YOU GET THAT?
WHERE DO YOU THINK?
ALL OF LIMBO'S LEADERS HAVE A WEAPON. A SYMBOL OF THEIR AUTHORITY.
IF THEY LOSE IT, WELL... THEY LOSE THAT AUTHORITY.

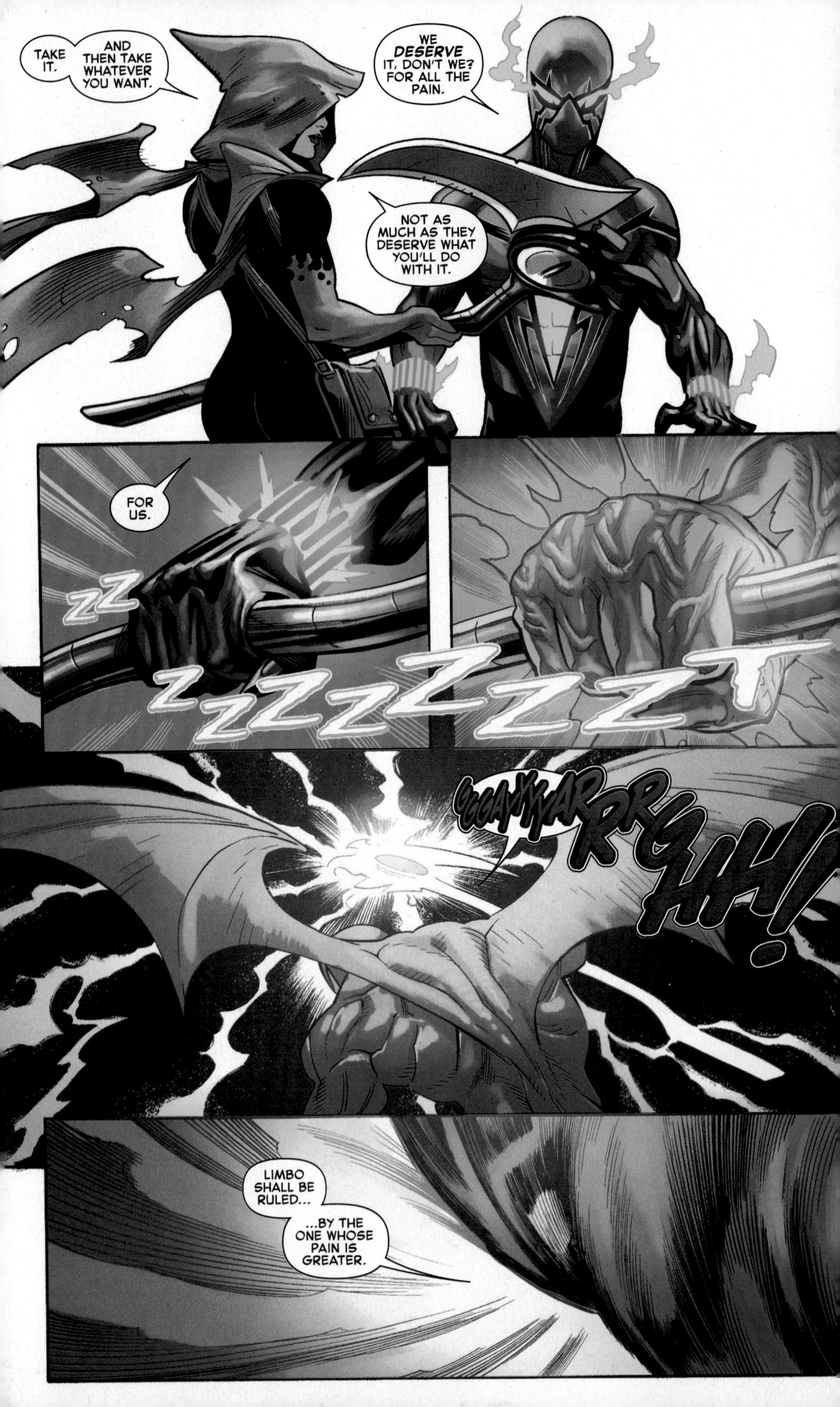
TAKE IT.
AND THEN TAKE WHATEVER YOU WANT.
WE DESERVE IT, DON'T WE? FOR ALL THE PAIN.
NOT AS MUCH AS THEY DESERVE WHAT YOU'LL DO WITH IT.
FOR US.
ZZ
ZZZZZZZZZT
RRGHH!
LIMBO SHALL BE RULED...
...BY THE ONE WHOSE PAIN IS GREATER.

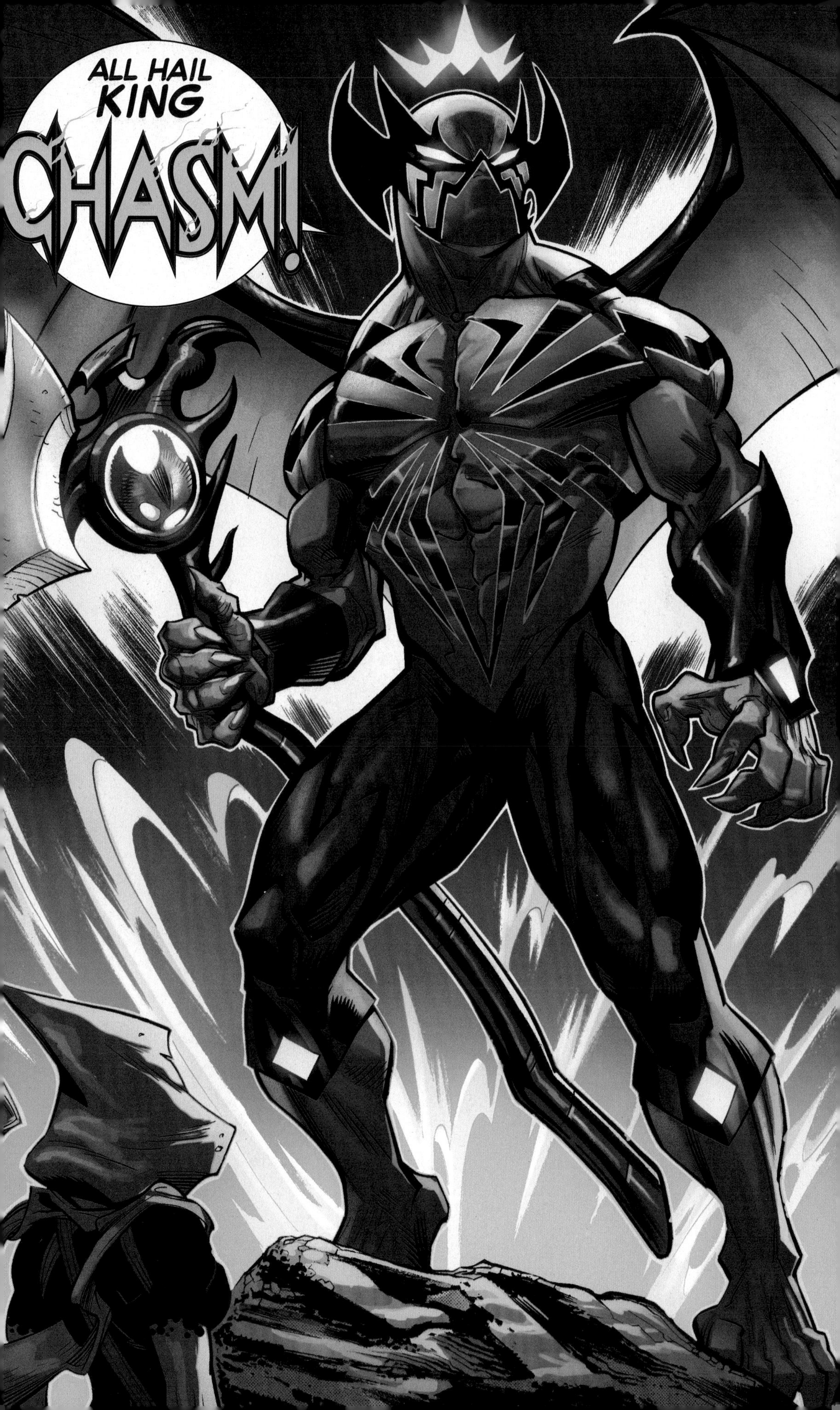
ALL HAIL KING CHASM!

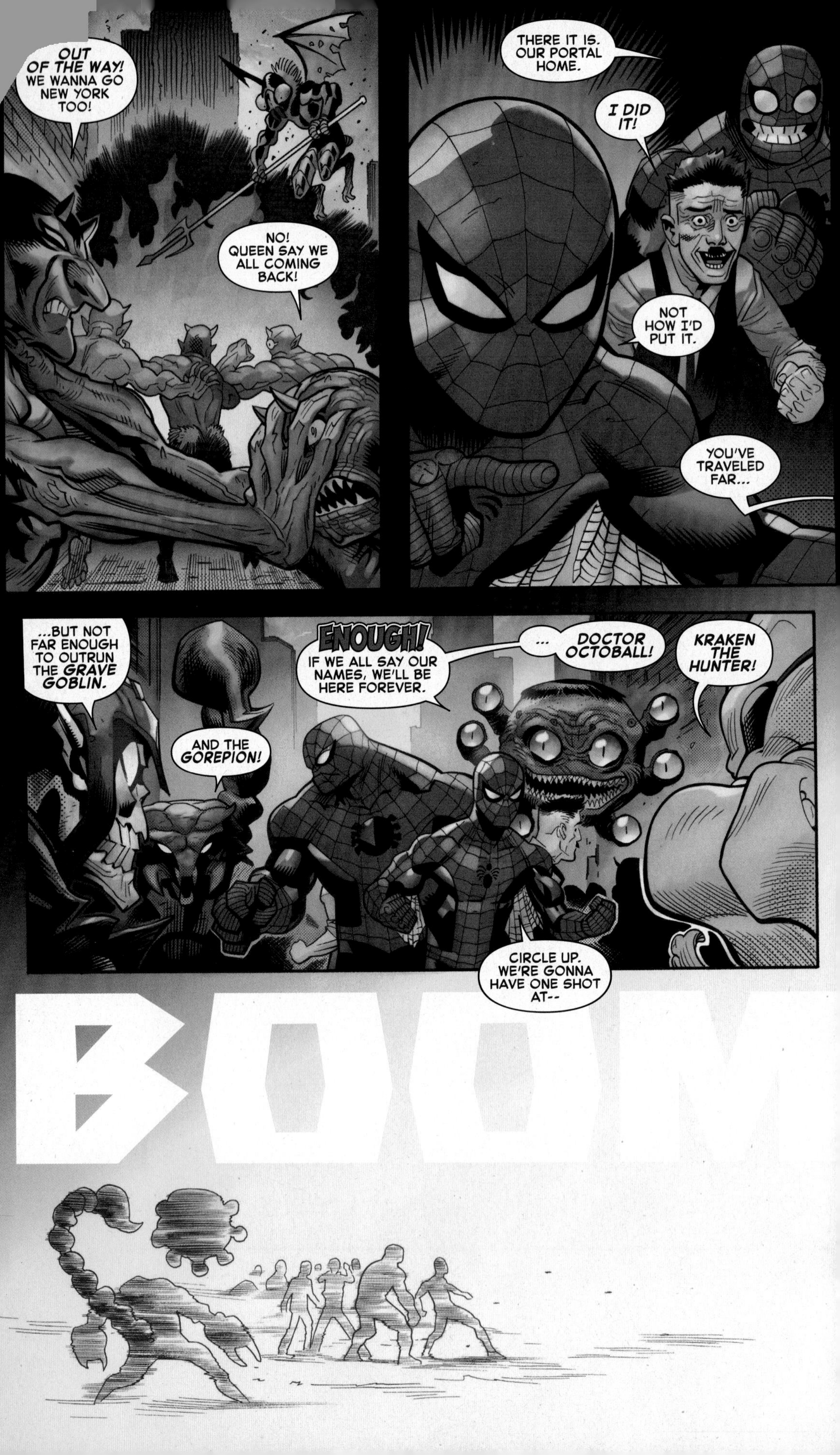

OUT OF THE WAY! WE WANNA GO NEW YORK TOO!
NO! QUEEN SAY WE ALL COMING BACK!
THERE IT IS. OUR PORTAL HOME.
I DID IT!
NOT HOW I'D PUT IT.
YOU'VE TRAVELED FAR...
...BUT NOT FAR ENOUGH TO OUTRUN THE GRAVE GOBLIN.
AND THE GOREPION!
ENOUGH! IF WE ALL SAY OUR NAMES, WE'LL BE HERE FOREVER.
... DOCTOR OCTOBALL!
KRAKEN THE HUNTER!
CIRCLE UP. WE'RE GONNA HAVE ONE SHOT AT--
BOOM

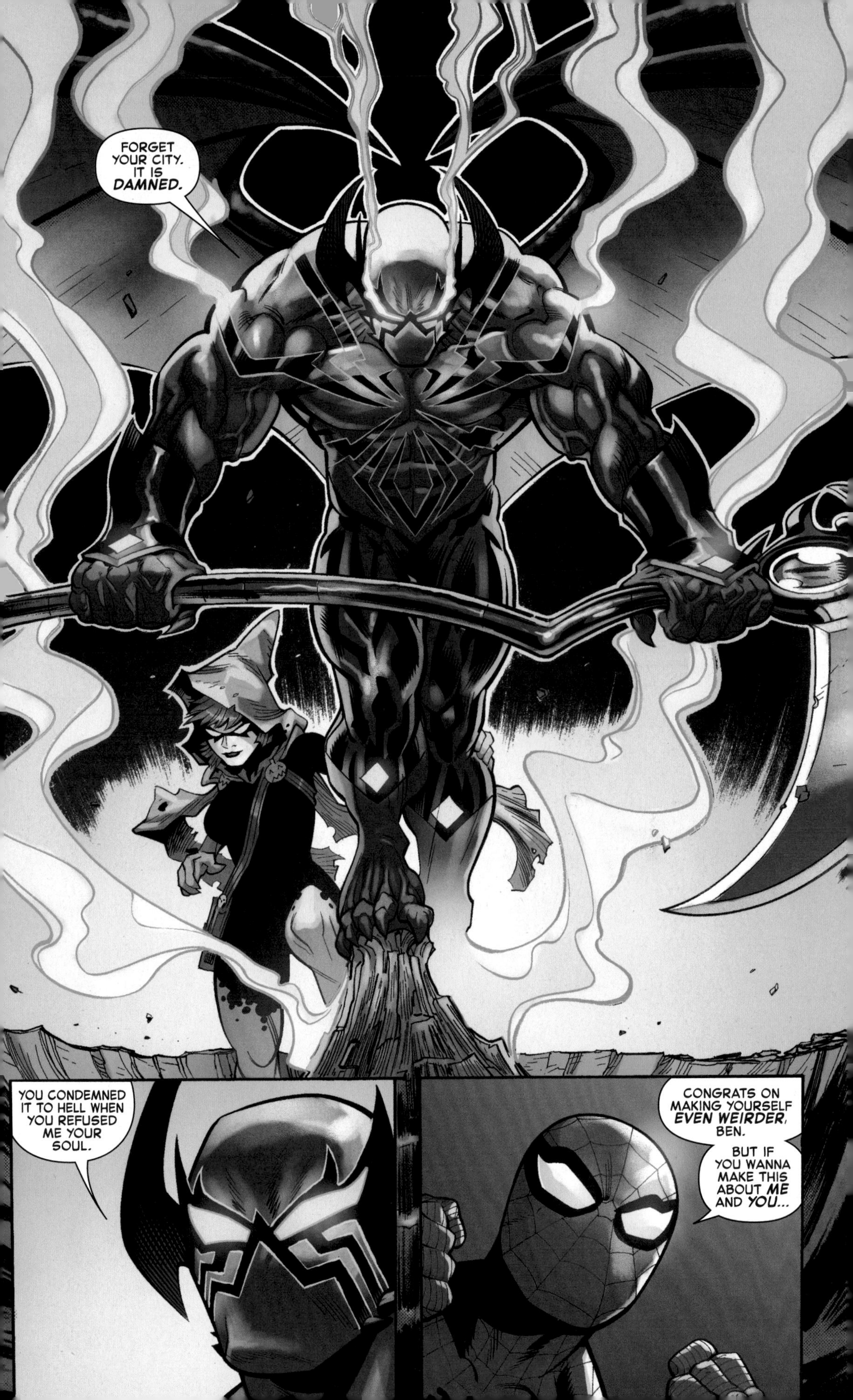
FORGET YOUR CITY. IT IS *DAMNED.*
YOU CONDEMNED IT TO HELL WHEN YOU REFUSED ME YOUR SOUL.
CONGRATS ON MAKING YOURSELF *EVEN WEIRDER*, BEN.
BUT IF YOU WANNA MAKE THIS ABOUT *ME* AND *YOU*...

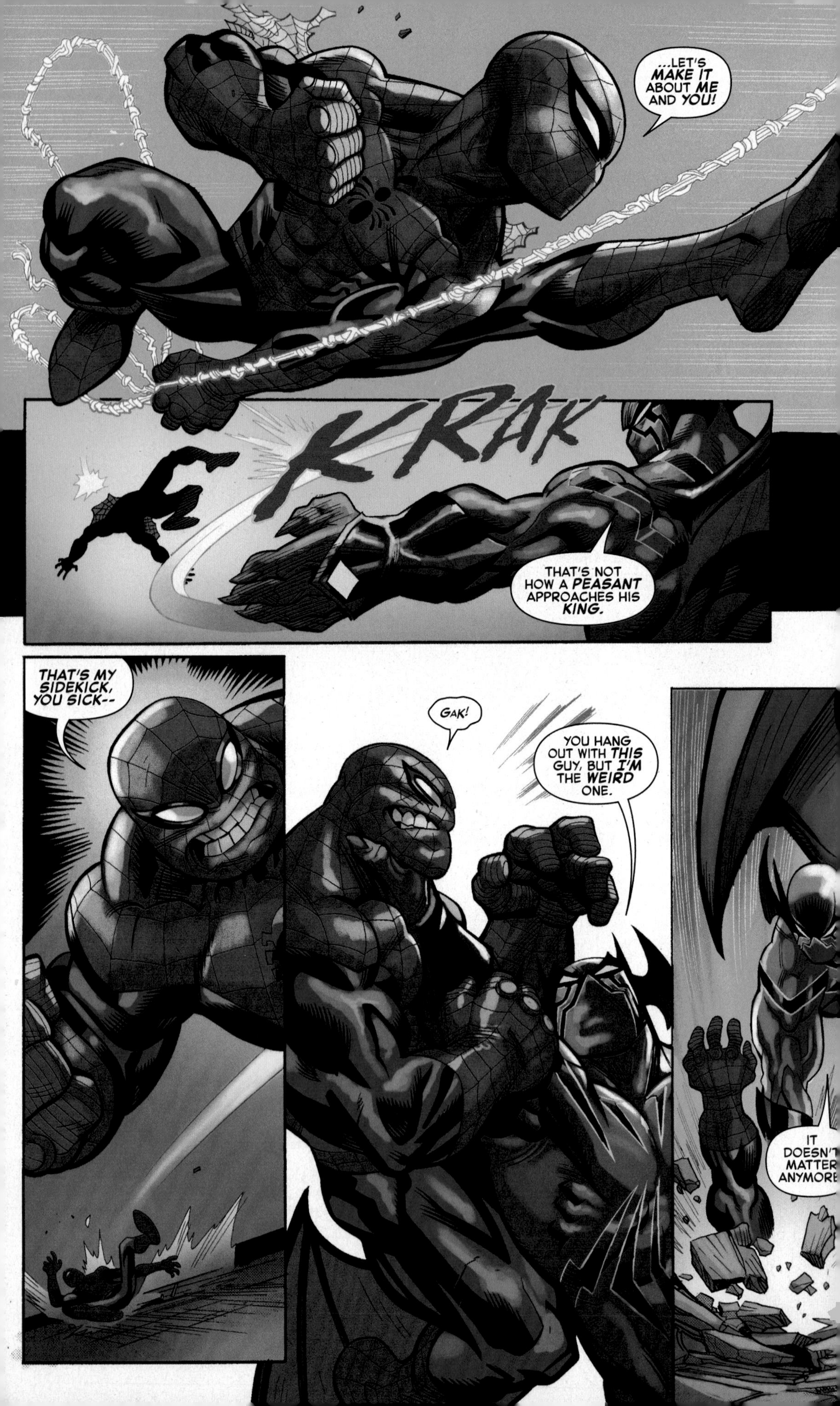
...LET'S MAKE IT ABOUT ME AND YOU!
KRAK
THAT'S NOT HOW A PEASANT APPROACHES HIS KING.
THAT'S MY SIDEKICK, YOU SICK--
GAK!
YOU HANG OUT WITH THIS GUY, BUT I'M THE WEIRD ONE.
IT DOESN'T MATTER ANYMORE

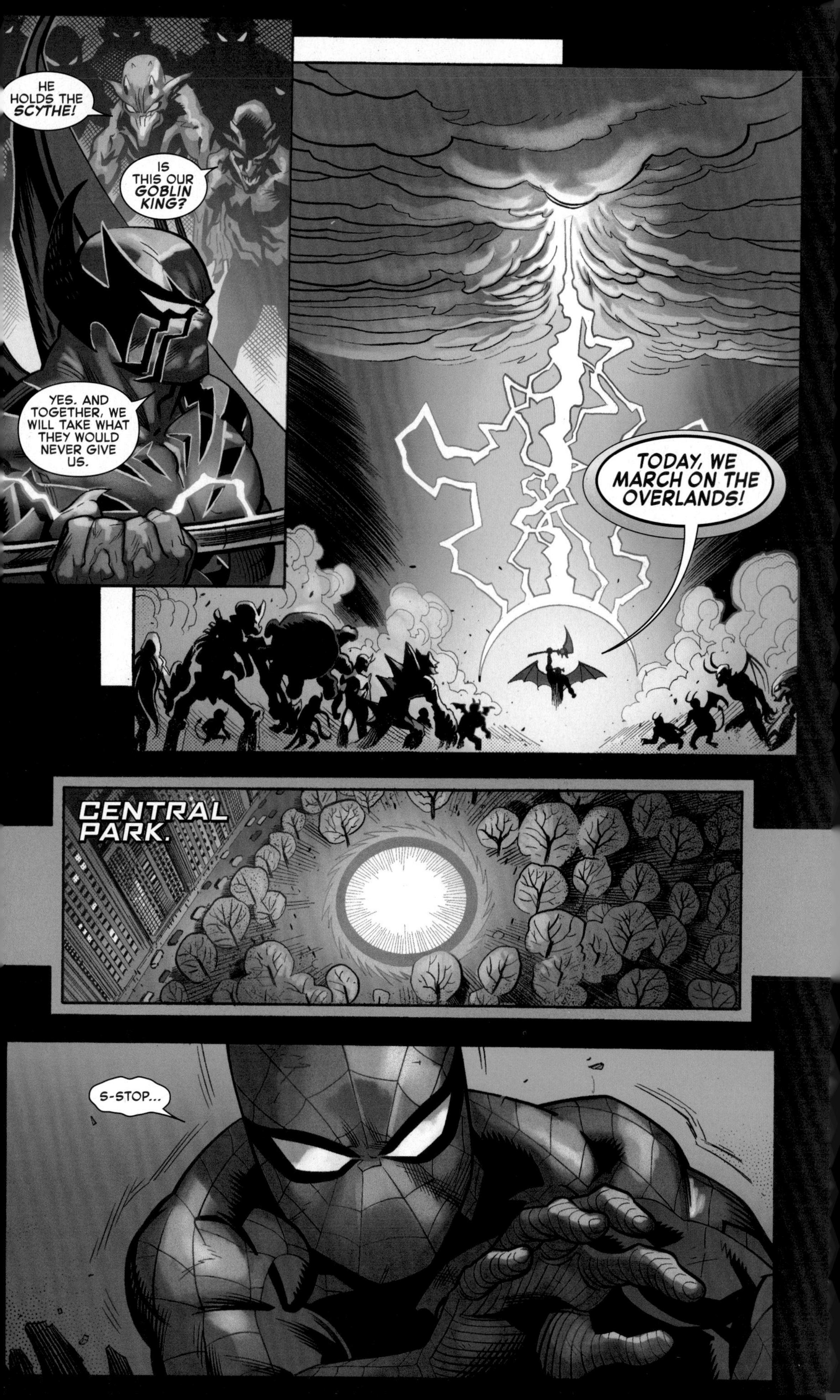
HE HOLDS THE SCYTHE!
IS THIS OUR GOBLIN KING?
YES. AND TOGETHER, WE WILL TAKE WHAT THEY WOULD NEVER GIVE US.
TODAY, WE MARCH ON THE OVERLANDS!
CENTRAL PARK.
S-STOP...

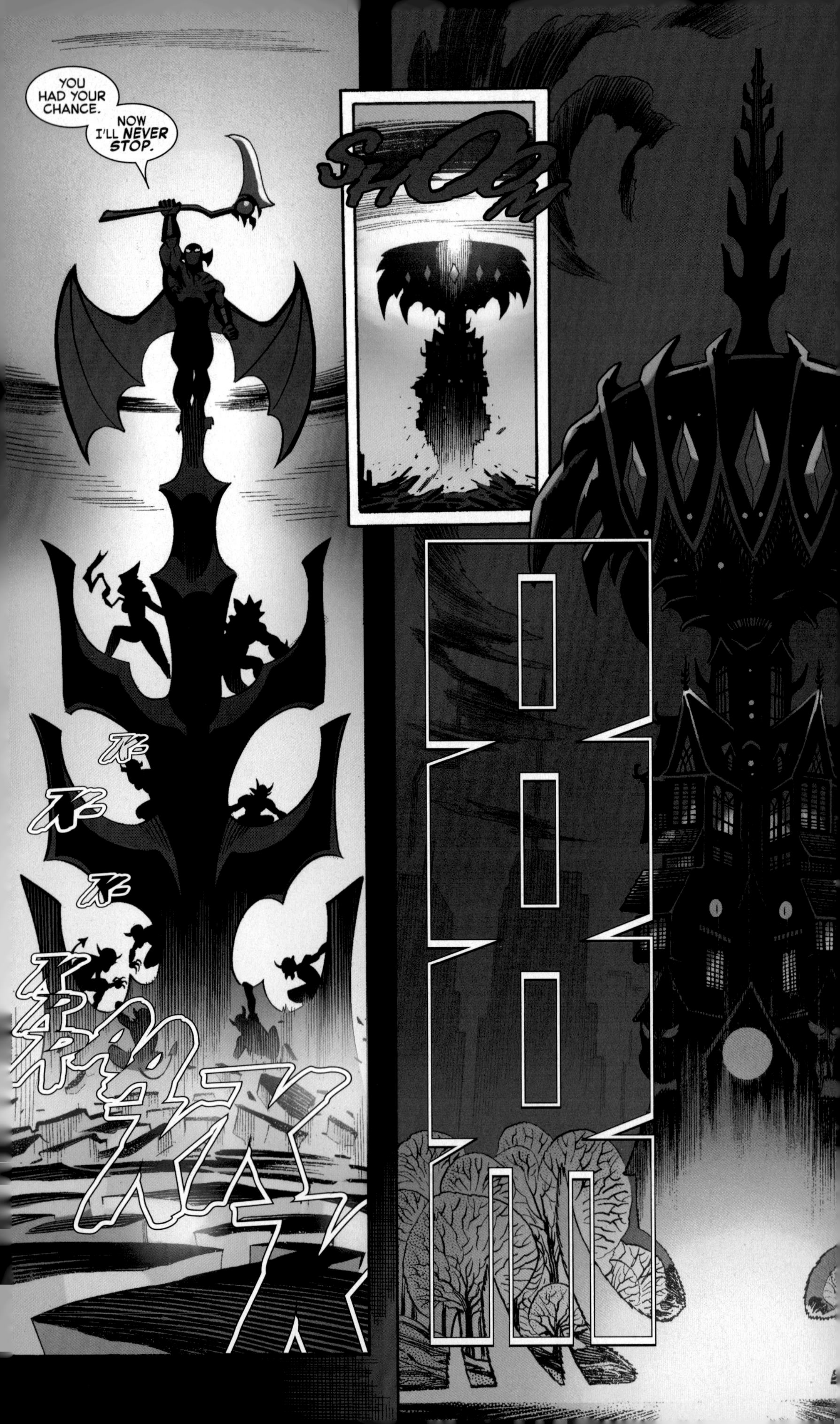
YOU HAD YOUR CHANCE.
NOW I'LL NEVER STOP.

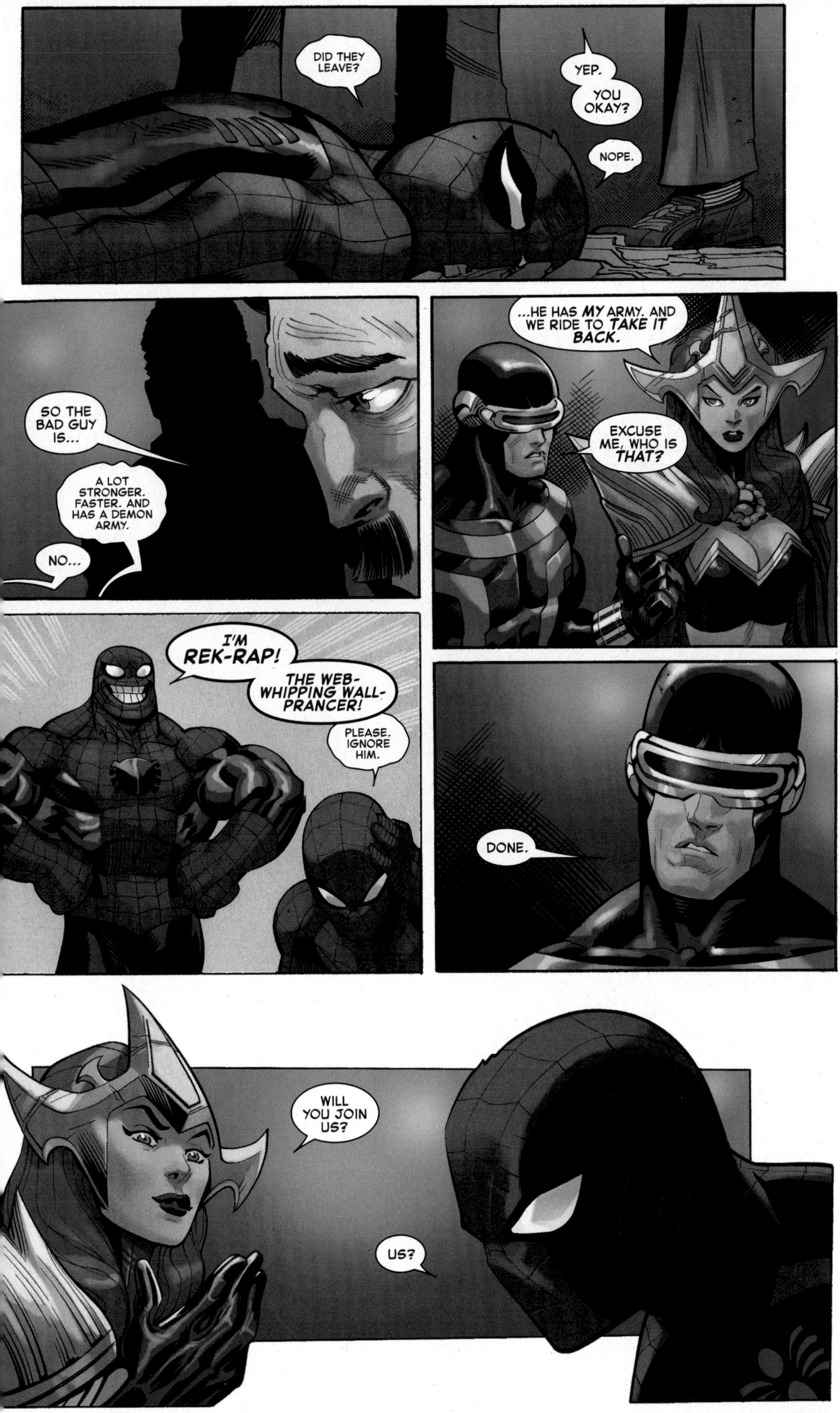
DID THEY LEAVE?
YEP.
YOU OKAY?
NOPE.
...HE HAS MY ARMY. AND WE RIDE TO TAKE IT BACK.
SO THE BAD GUY IS...
A LOT STRONGER. FASTER. AND HAS A DEMON ARMY.
NO...
EXCUSE ME, WHO IS THAT?
I'M REK-RAP!
THE WEB-WHIPPING WALL-PRANCER!
PLEASE. IGNORE HIM.
DONE.
WILL YOU JOIN US?
US?

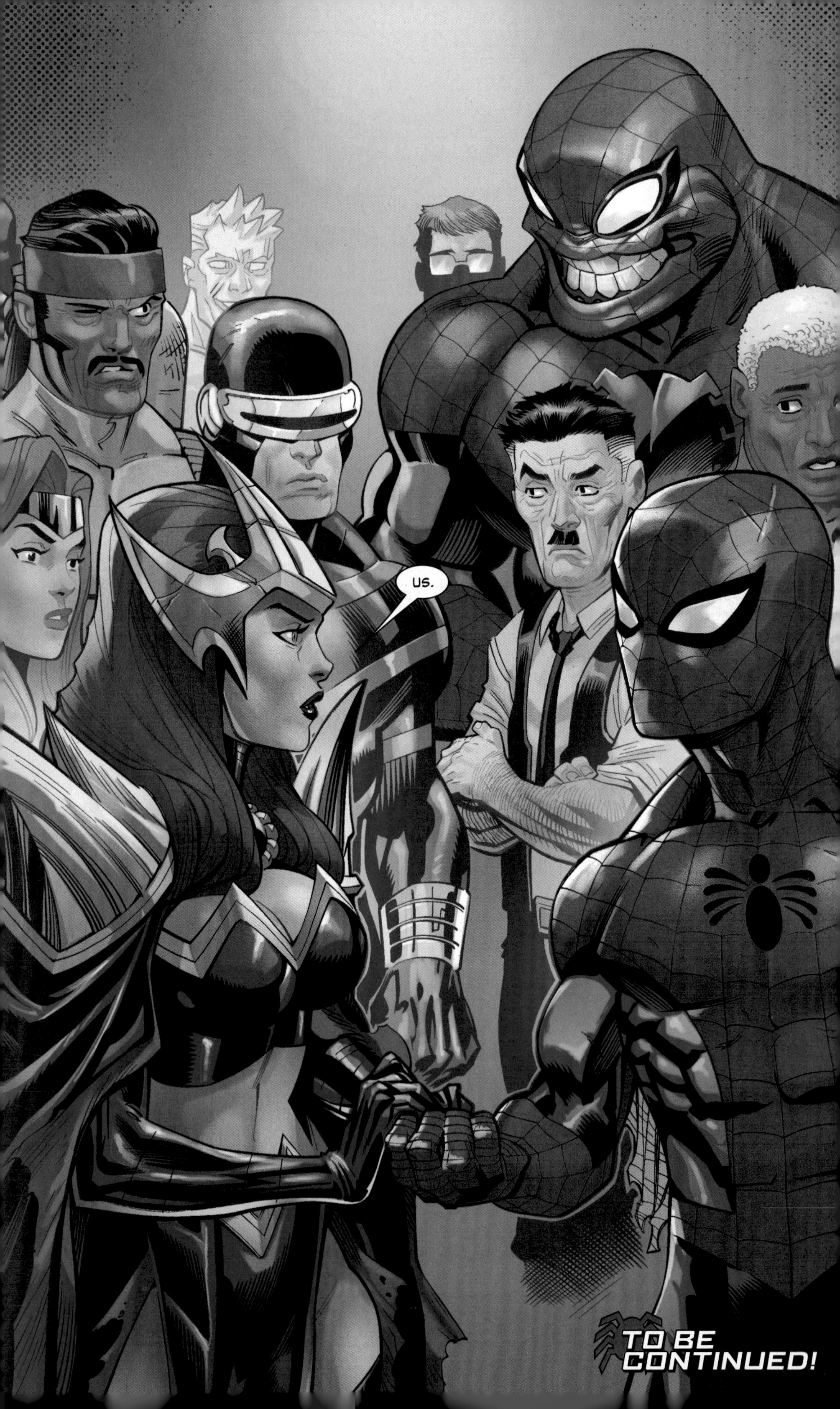

US.
TO BE CONTINUED!

VENOM #14

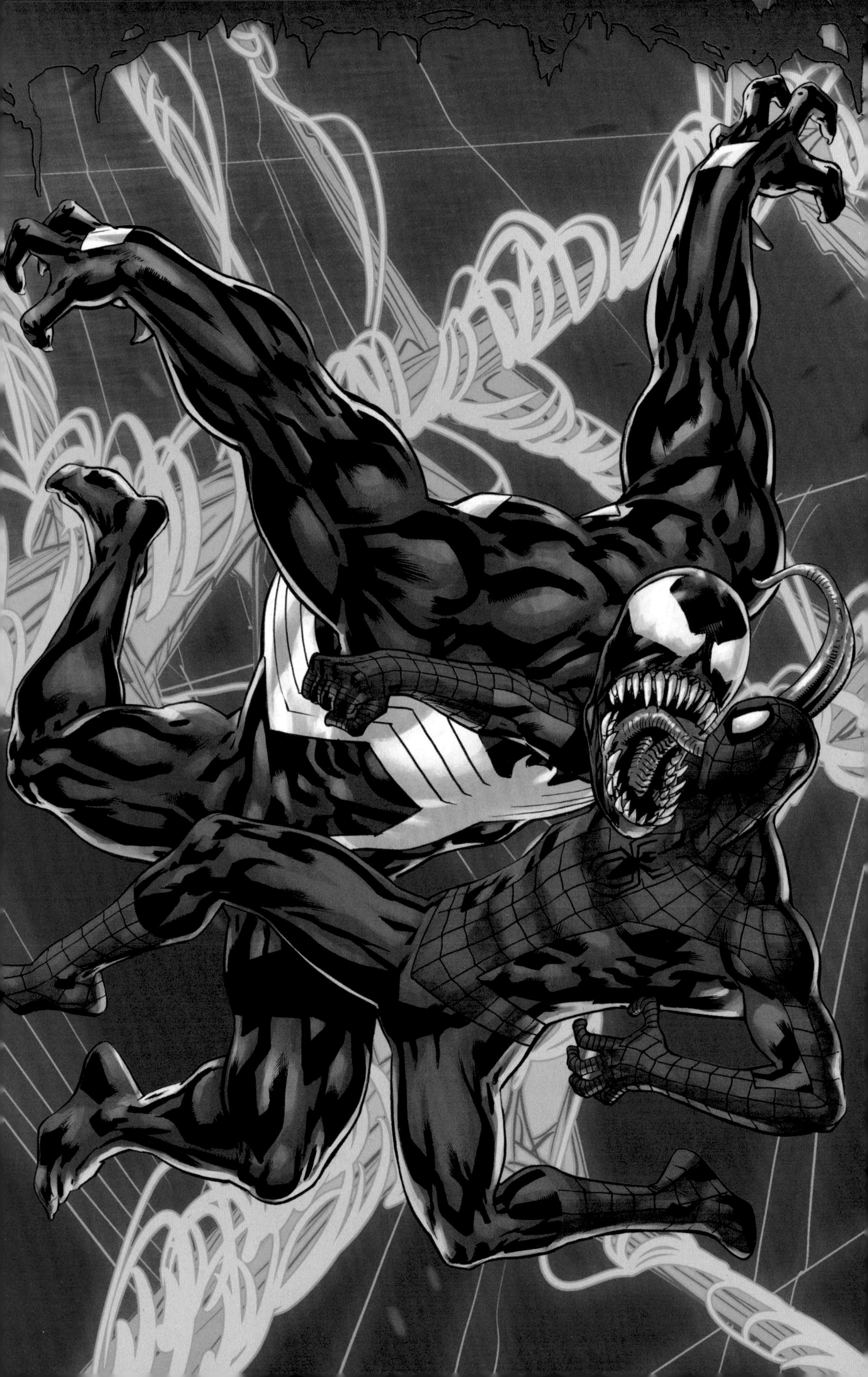

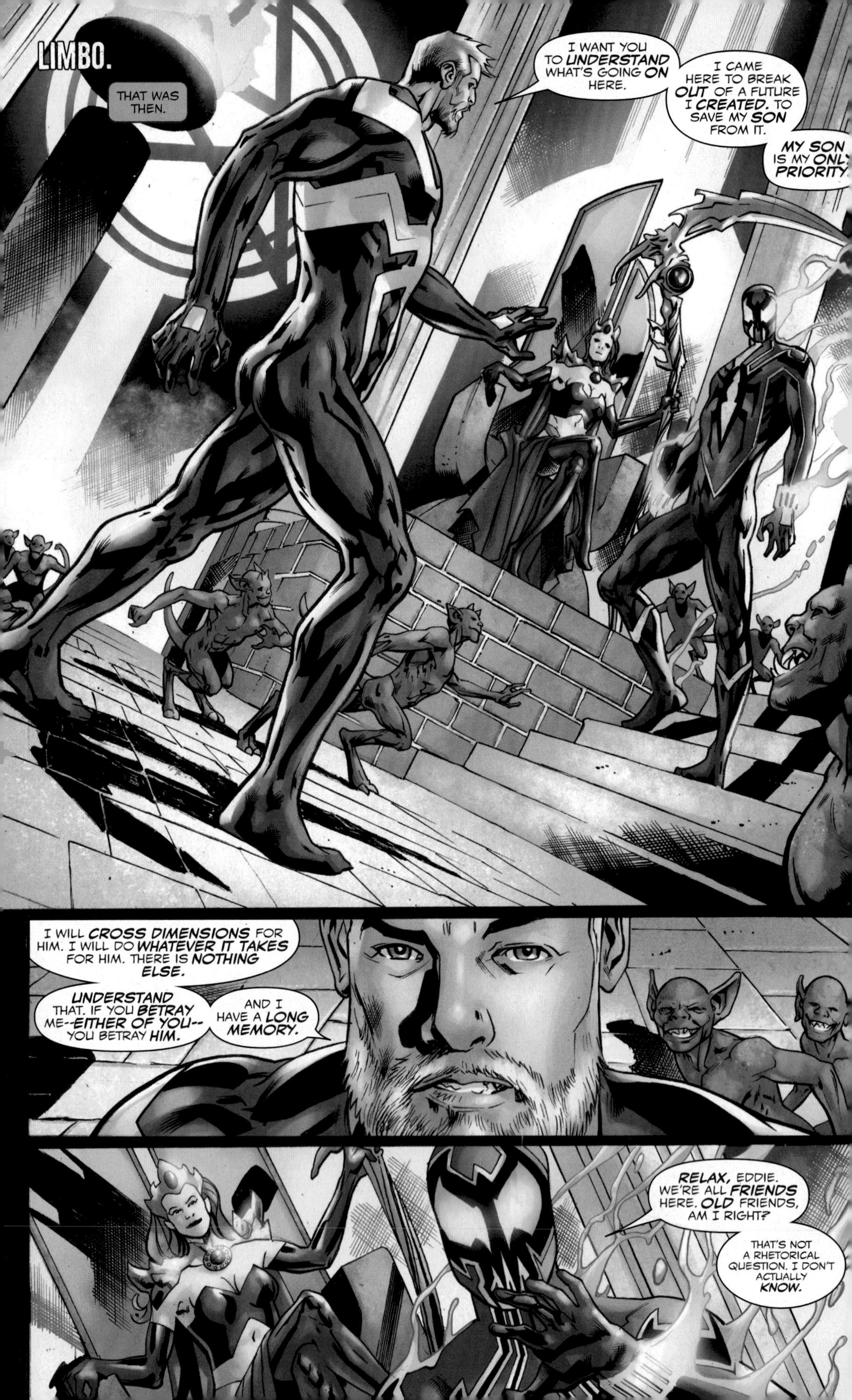
LIMBO.
THAT WAS THEN.
I WANT YOU TO UNDERSTAND WHAT'S GOING ON HERE.
I CAME HERE TO BREAK OUT OF A FUTURE I CREATED. TO SAVE MY SON FROM IT.
MY SON IS MY ONLY PRIORITY.
I WILL CROSS DIMENSIONS FOR HIM. I WILL DO WHATEVER IT TAKES FOR HIM. THERE IS NOTHING ELSE.
UNDERSTAND THAT. IF YOU BETRAY ME--EITHER OF YOU--YOU BETRAY HIM.
AND I HAVE A LONG MEMORY.
RELAX, EDDIE. WE'RE ALL FRIENDS HERE. OLD FRIENDS, AM I RIGHT?
THAT'S NOT A RHETORICAL QUESTION. I DON'T ACTUALLY KNOW.

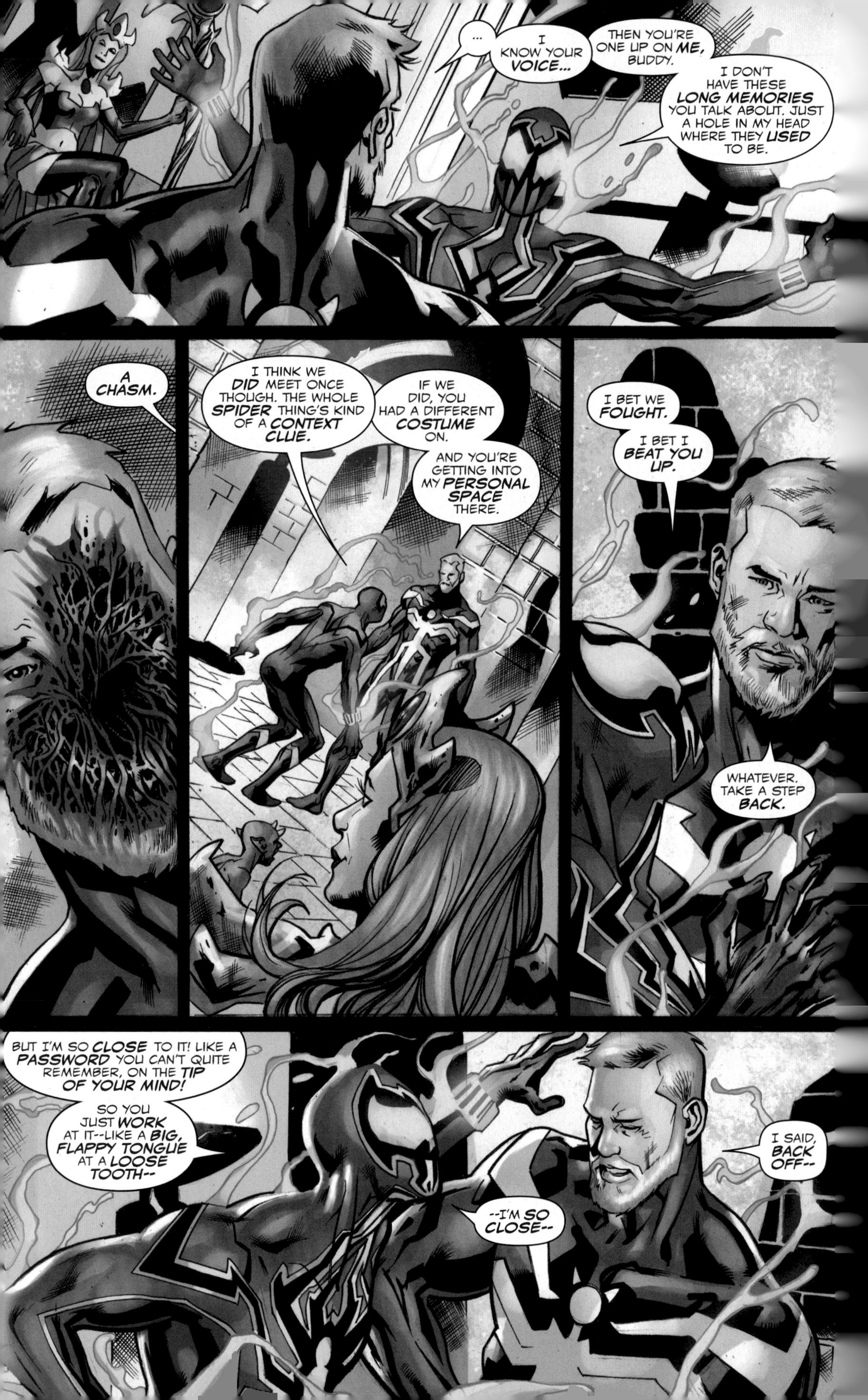
...
I KNOW YOUR VOICE...
THEN YOU'RE ONE UP ON ME, BUDDY.
I DON'T HAVE THESE LONG MEMORIES YOU TALK ABOUT. JUST A HOLE IN MY HEAD WHERE THEY USED TO BE.
A CHASM.
I THINK WE DID MEET ONCE THOUGH. THE WHOLE SPIDER THING'S KIND OF A CONTEXT CLUE.
IF WE DID, YOU HAD A DIFFERENT COSTUME ON.
AND YOU'RE GETTING INTO MY PERSONAL SPACE THERE.
I BET WE FOUGHT.
I BET I BEAT YOU UP.
WHATEVER. TAKE A STEP BACK.
BUT I'M SO CLOSE TO IT! LIKE A PASSWORD YOU CAN'T QUITE REMEMBER, ON THE TIP OF YOUR MIND!
SO YOU JUST WORK AT IT--LIKE A BIG, FLAPPY TONGUE AT A LOOSE TOOTH--
I SAID, BACK OFF--
--I'M SO CLOSE--

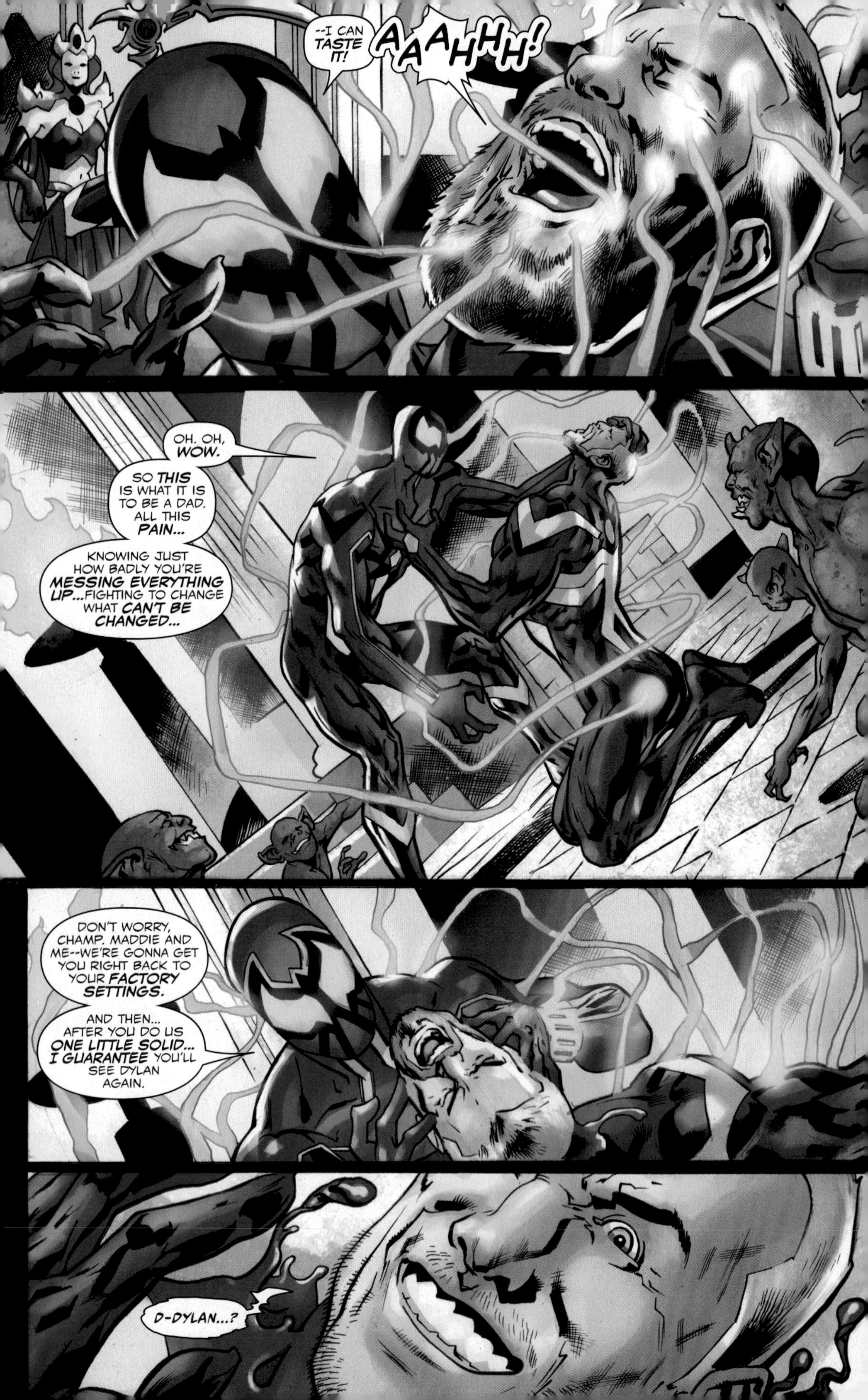
--I CAN TASTE IT!
AAAHHH!
OH. OH, WOW.
SO THIS IS WHAT IT IS TO BE A DAD. ALL THIS PAIN...
KNOWING JUST HOW BADLY YOU'RE MESSING EVERYTHING UP...FIGHTING TO CHANGE WHAT CAN'T BE CHANGED...
DON'T WORRY, CHAMP. MADDIE AND ME--WE'RE GONNA GET YOU RIGHT BACK TO YOUR FACTORY SETTINGS.
AND THEN... AFTER YOU DO US ONE LITTLE SOLID... I GUARANTEE YOU'LL SEE DYLAN AGAIN.
D-DYLAN...?

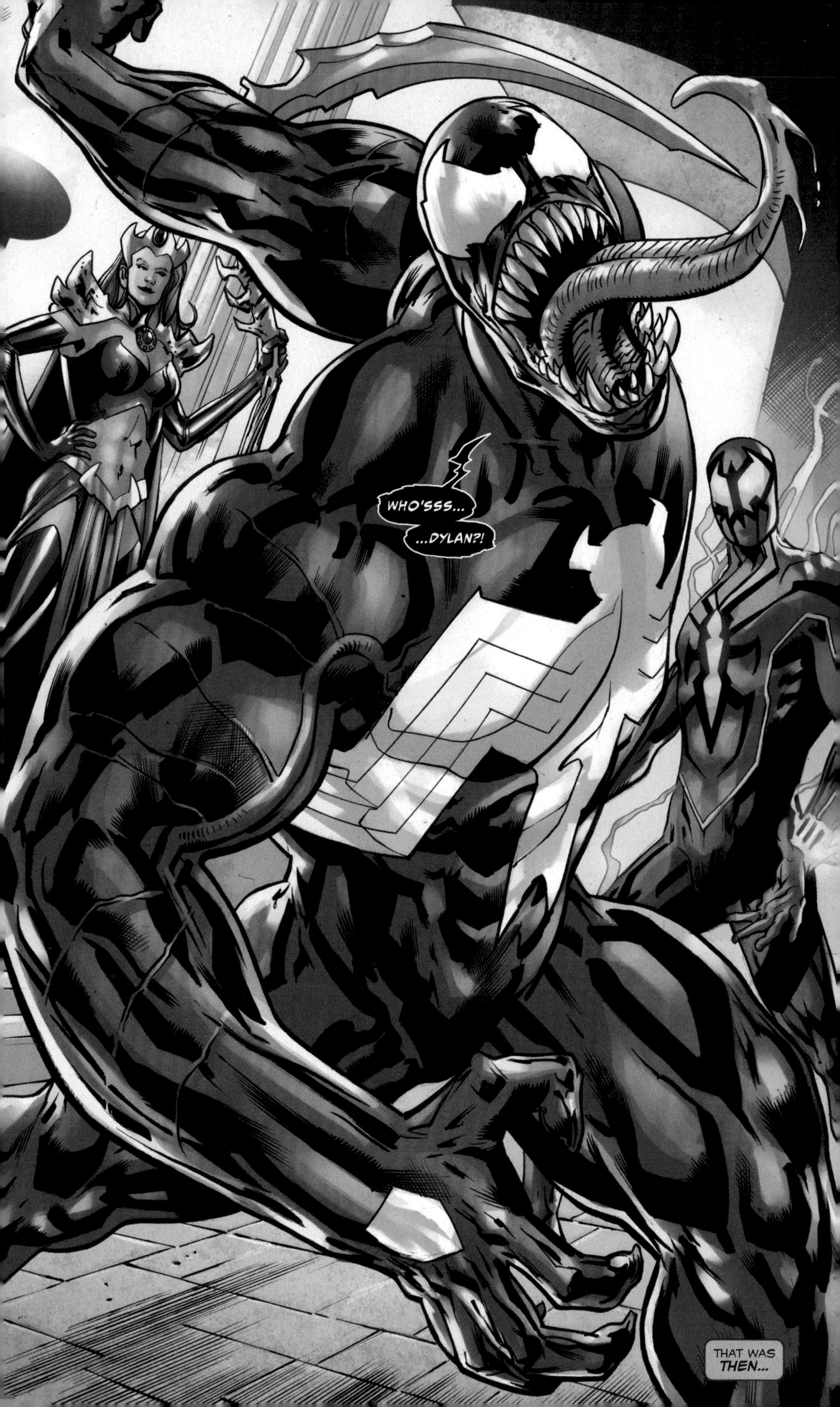

WHO'SSS...
...DYLAN?!
THAT WAS THEN...

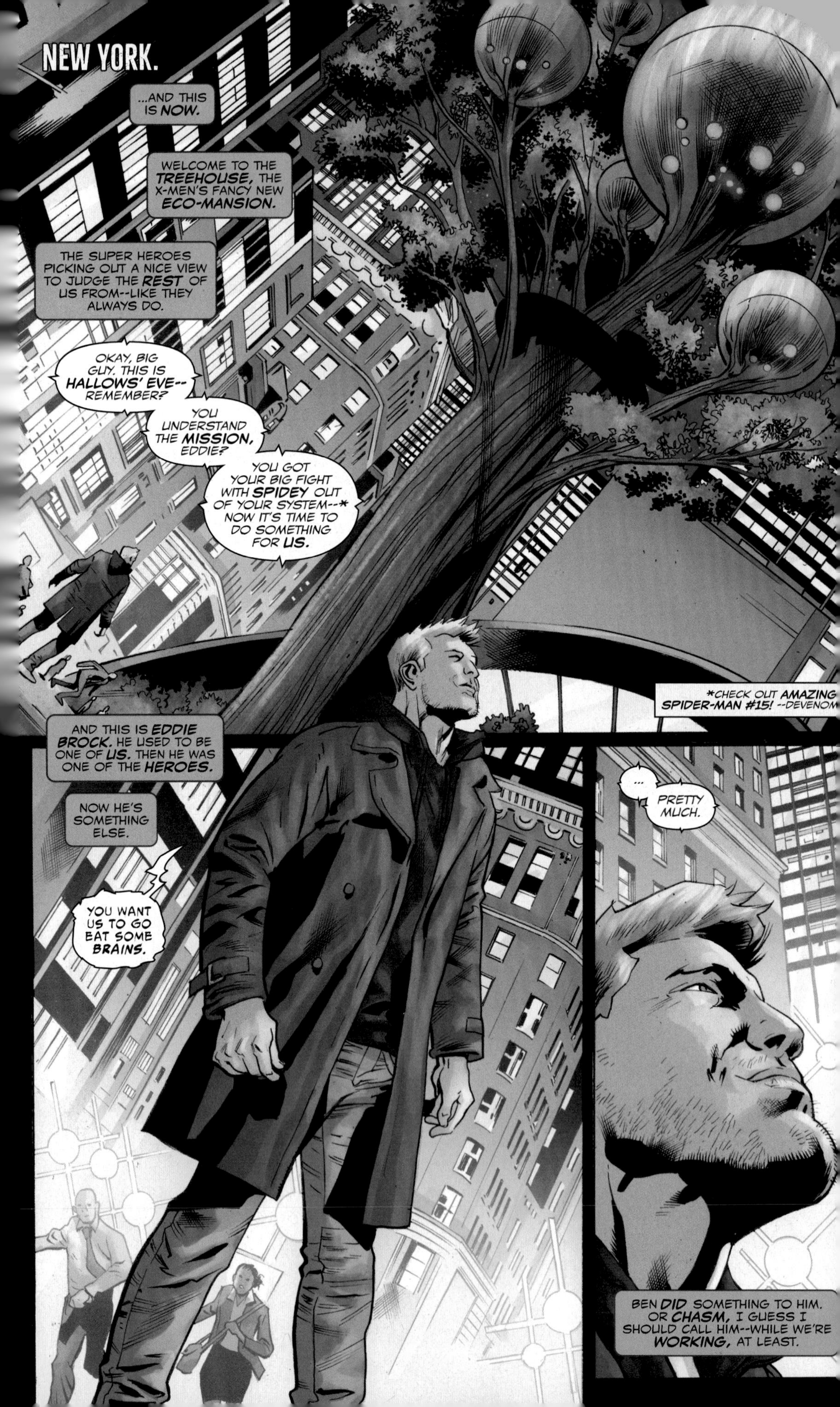
NEW YORK.
...AND THIS IS NOW.
WELCOME TO THE TREEHOUSE, THE X-MEN'S FANCY NEW ECO-MANSION.
THE SUPER HEROES PICKING OUT A NICE VIEW TO JUDGE THE REST OF US FROM--LIKE THEY ALWAYS DO.
OKAY, BIG GUY. THIS IS HALLOWS' EVE--REMEMBER?
YOU UNDERSTAND THE MISSION, EDDIE?
YOU GOT YOUR BIG FIGHT WITH SPIDEY OUT OF YOUR SYSTEM--* NOW IT'S TIME TO DO SOMETHING FOR US.
*CHECK OUT AMAZING SPIDER-MAN #15! --DEVENOM
AND THIS IS EDDIE BROCK. HE USED TO BE ONE OF US. THEN HE WAS ONE OF THE HEROES.
NOW HE'S SOMETHING ELSE.
YOU WANT US TO GO EAT SOME BRAINS.
...
PRETTY MUCH.
BEN DID SOMETHING TO HIM. OR CHASM, I GUESS I SHOULD CALL HIM--WHILE WE'RE WORKING, AT LEAST.

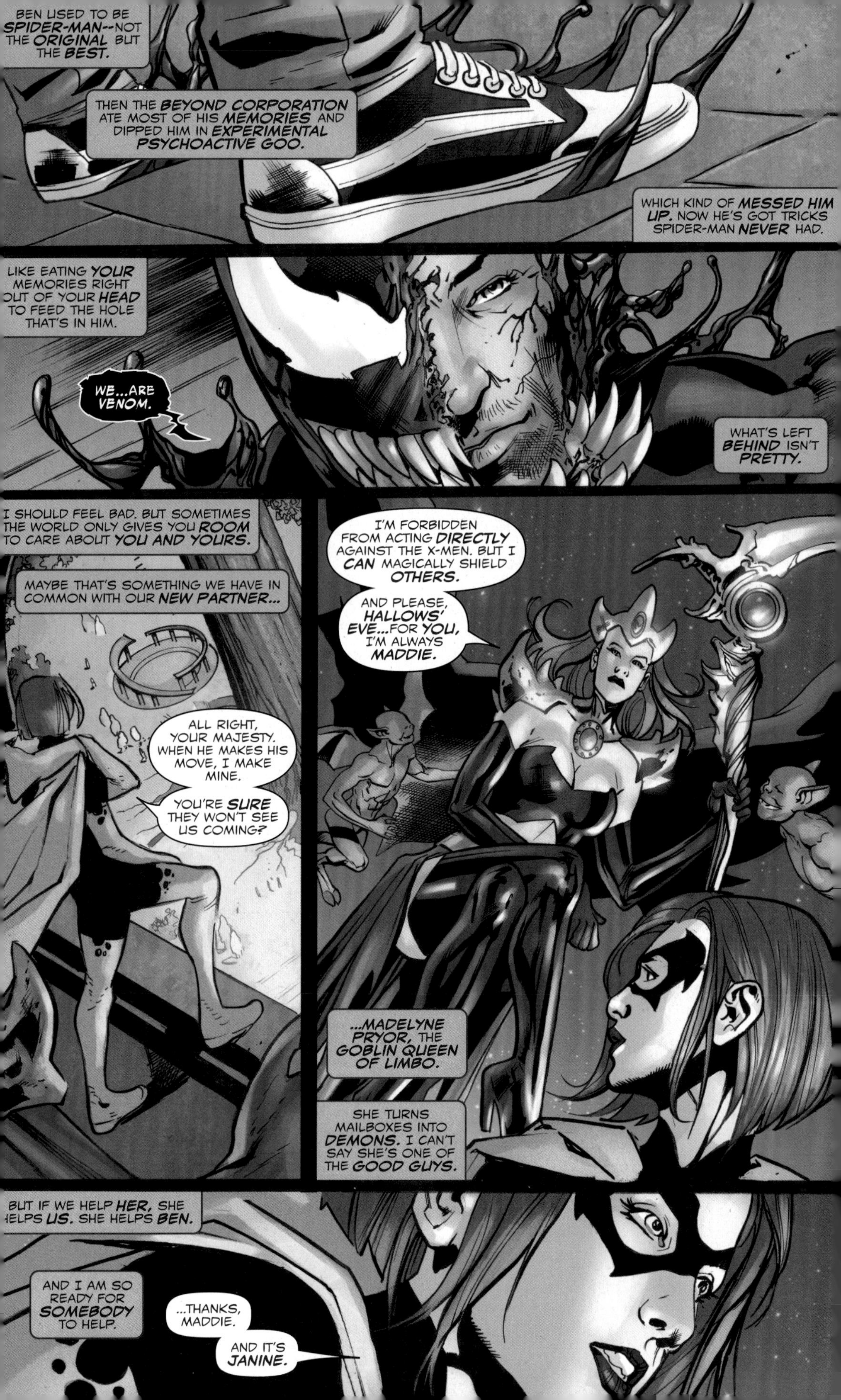

BEN USED TO BE SPIDER-MAN--NOT THE ORIGINAL BUT THE BEST.
THEN THE BEYOND CORPORATION ATE MOST OF HIS MEMORIES AND DIPPED HIM IN EXPERIMENTAL PSYCHOACTIVE GOO.
WHICH KIND OF MESSED HIM UP. NOW HE'S GOT TRICKS SPIDER-MAN NEVER HAD.
LIKE EATING YOUR MEMORIES RIGHT OUT OF YOUR HEAD TO FEED THE HOLE THAT'S IN HIM.
WE...ARE VENOM.
WHAT'S LEFT BEHIND ISN'T PRETTY.
I SHOULD FEEL BAD. BUT SOMETIMES THE WORLD ONLY GIVES YOU ROOM TO CARE ABOUT YOU AND YOURS.
MAYBE THAT'S SOMETHING WE HAVE IN COMMON WITH OUR NEW PARTNER...
I'M FORBIDDEN FROM ACTING DIRECTLY AGAINST THE X-MEN. BUT I CAN MAGICALLY SHIELD OTHERS.
AND PLEASE, HALLOWS' EVE...FOR YOU, I'M ALWAYS MADDIE.
ALL RIGHT, YOUR MAJESTY. WHEN HE MAKES HIS MOVE, I MAKE MINE.
YOU'RE SURE THEY WON'T SEE US COMING?
...MADELYNE PRYOR, THE GOBLIN QUEEN OF LIMBO.
SHE TURNS MAILBOXES INTO DEMONS. I CAN'T SAY SHE'S ONE OF THE GOOD GUYS.
BUT IF WE HELP HER, SHE HELPS US. SHE HELPS BEN.
AND I AM SO READY FOR SOMEBODY TO HELP.
...THANKS, MADDIE.
AND IT'S JANINE.

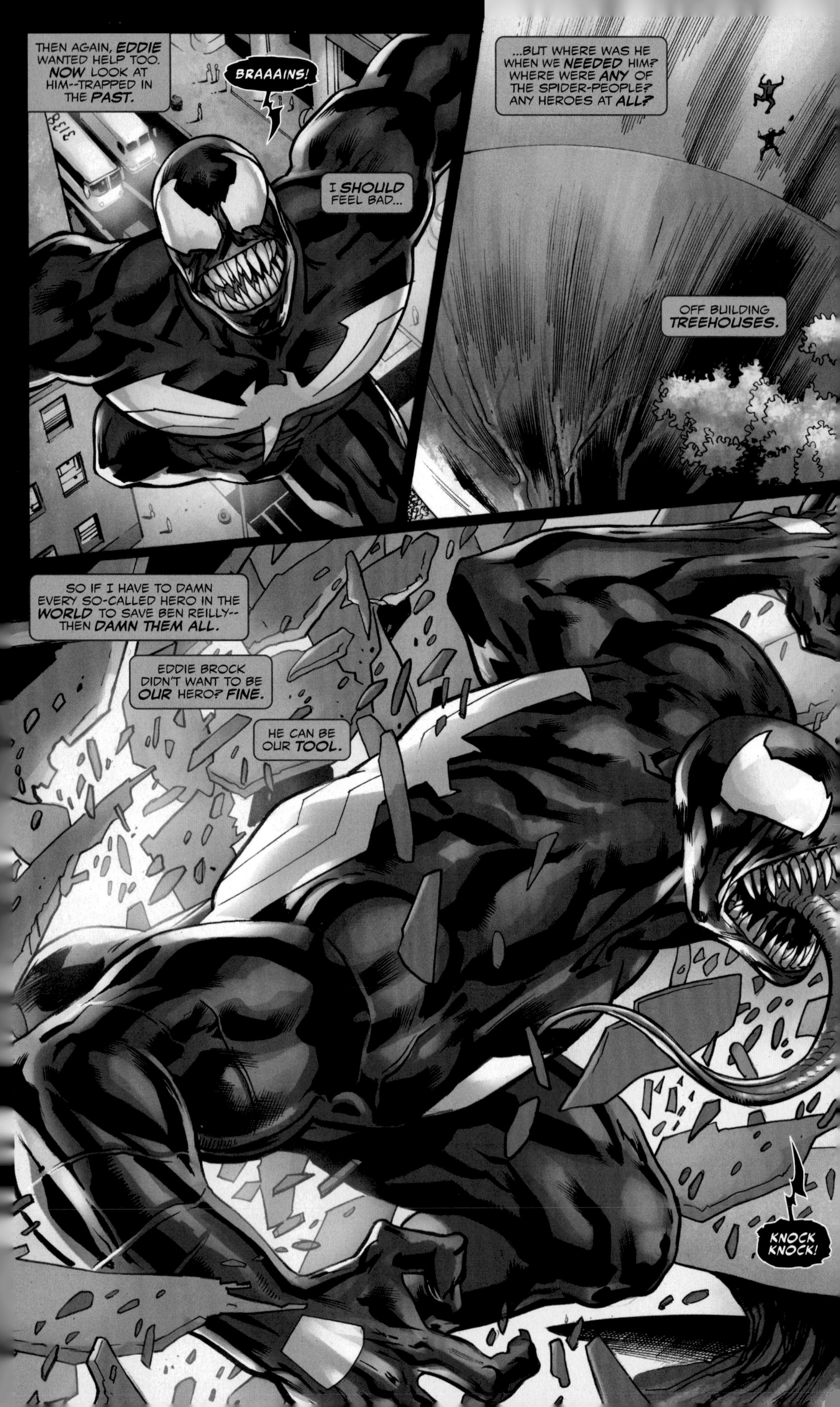
THEN AGAIN, EDDIE WANTED HELP TOO. NOW LOOK AT HIM--TRAPPED IN THE PAST.
BRAAAINS!
I SHOULD FEEL BAD...
...BUT WHERE WAS HE WHEN WE NEEDED HIM? WHERE WERE ANY OF THE SPIDER-PEOPLE? ANY HEROES AT ALL?
OFF BUILDING TREEHOUSES.
SO IF I HAVE TO DAMN EVERY SO-CALLED HERO IN THE WORLD TO SAVE BEN REILLY-- THEN DAMN THEM ALL.
EDDIE BROCK DIDN'T WANT TO BE OUR HERO? FINE.
HE CAN BE OUR TOOL.
KNOCK KNOCK!

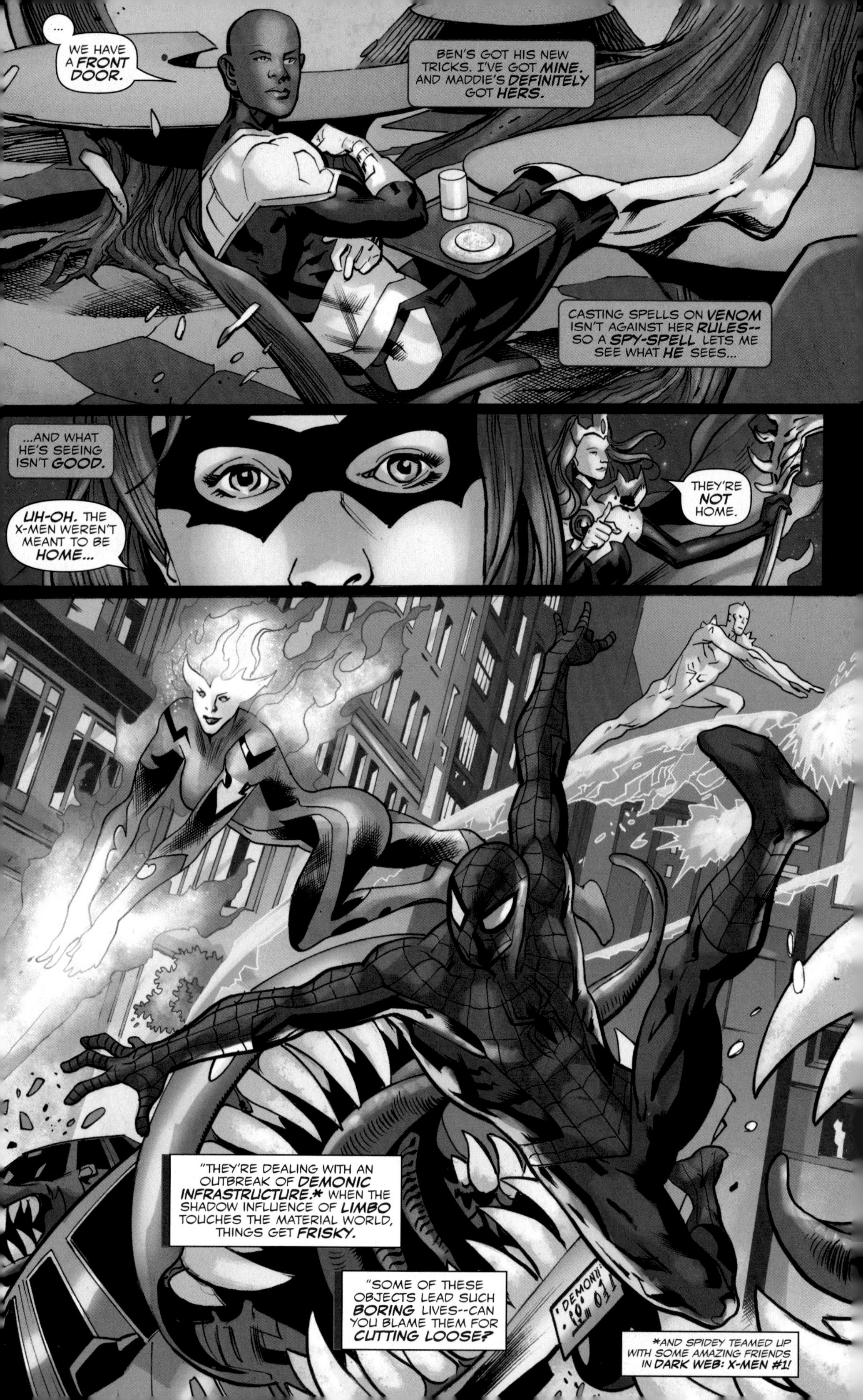
...
WE HAVE A FRONT DOOR.
BEN'S GOT HIS NEW TRICKS. I'VE GOT MINE. AND MADDIE'S DEFINITELY GOT HERS.
CASTING SPELLS ON VENOM ISN'T AGAINST HER RULES-- SO A SPY-SPELL LETS ME SEE WHAT HE SEES...
...AND WHAT HE'S SEEING ISN'T GOOD.
UH-OH. THE X-MEN WEREN'T MEANT TO BE HOME...
THEY'RE NOT HOME.
"THEY'RE DEALING WITH AN OUTBREAK OF DEMONIC INFRASTRUCTURE.* WHEN THE SHADOW INFLUENCE OF LIMBO TOUCHES THE MATERIAL WORLD, THINGS GET FRISKY.
"SOME OF THESE OBJECTS LEAD SUCH BORING LIVES--CAN YOU BLAME THEM FOR CUTTING LOOSE?
*AND SPIDEY TEAMED UP WITH SOME AMAZING FRIENDS IN DARK WEB: X-MEN #1!

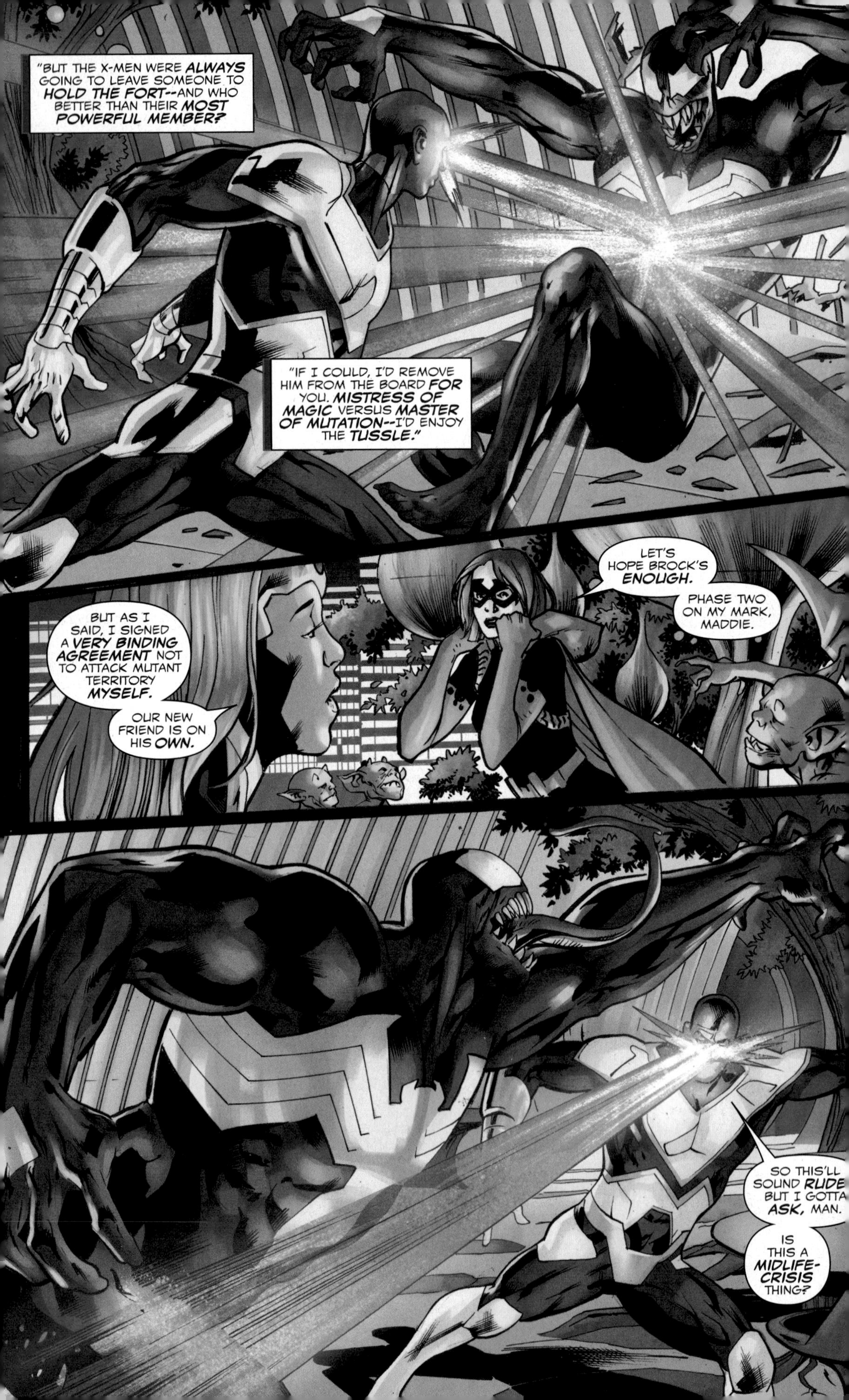
"BUT THE X-MEN WERE ALWAYS GOING TO LEAVE SOMEONE TO HOLD THE FORT--AND WHO BETTER THAN THEIR MOST POWERFUL MEMBER?
"IF I COULD, I'D REMOVE HIM FROM THE BOARD FOR YOU. MISTRESS OF MAGIC VERSUS MASTER OF MUTATION--I'D ENJOY THE TUSSLE."
BUT AS I SAID, I SIGNED A VERY BINDING AGREEMENT NOT TO ATTACK MUTANT TERRITORY MYSELF.
OUR NEW FRIEND IS ON HIS OWN.
LET'S HOPE BROCK'S ENOUGH.
PHASE TWO ON MY MARK, MADDIE.
SO THIS'LL SOUND RUDE BUT I GOTTA ASK, MAN.
IS THIS A MIDLIFE-CRISIS THING?

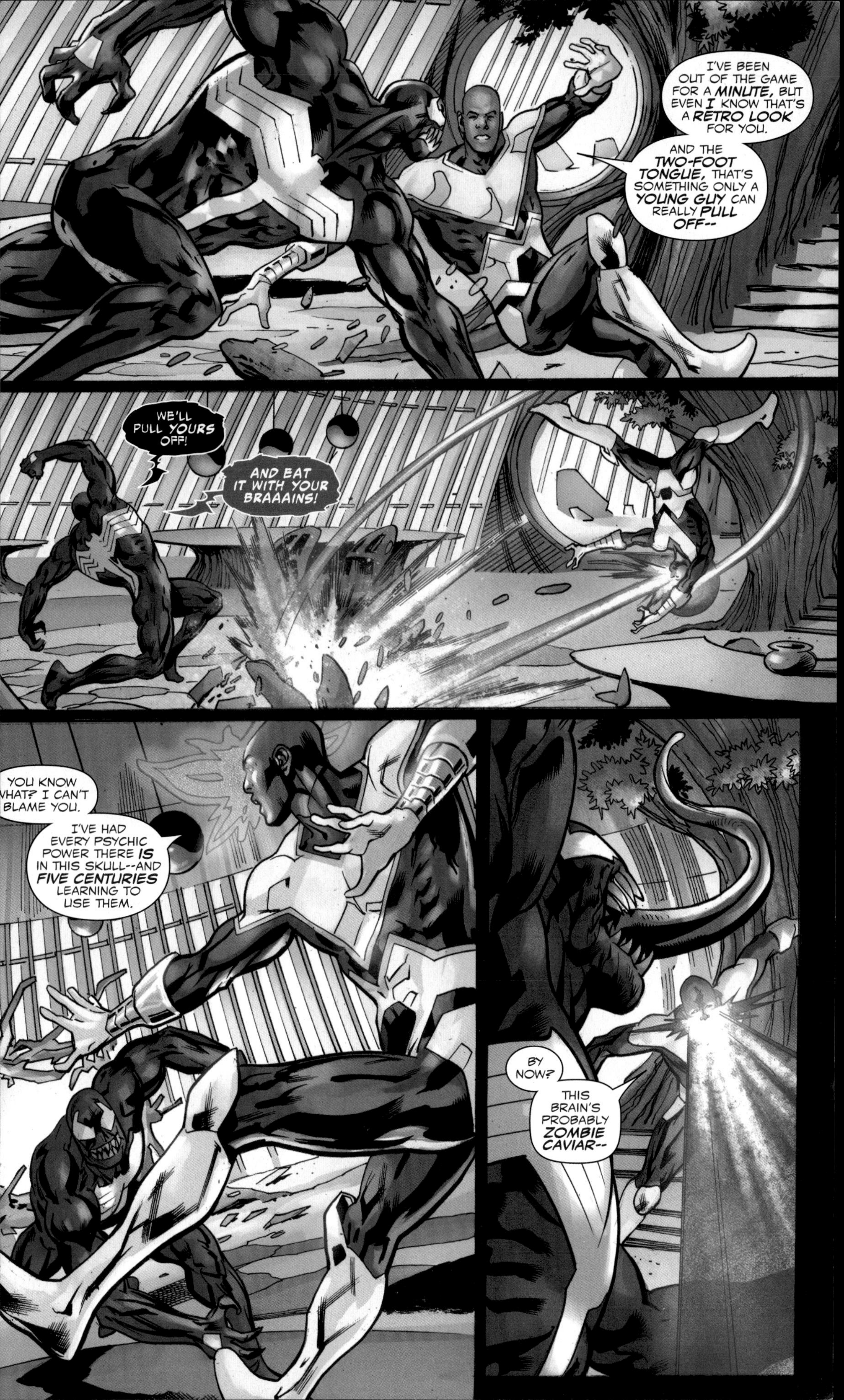
I'VE BEEN OUT OF THE GAME FOR A MINUTE, BUT EVEN I KNOW THAT'S A RETRO LOOK FOR YOU.
AND THE TWO-FOOT TONGUE, THAT'S SOMETHING ONLY A YOUNG GUY CAN REALLY PULL OFF--
WE'LL PULL YOURS OFF!
AND EAT IT WITH YOUR BRAAAINS!
YOU KNOW WHAT? I CAN'T BLAME YOU.
I'VE HAD EVERY PSYCHIC POWER THERE IS IN THIS SKULL--AND FIVE CENTURIES LEARNING TO USE THEM.
BY NOW?
THIS BRAIN'S PROBABLY ZOMBIE CAVIAR--

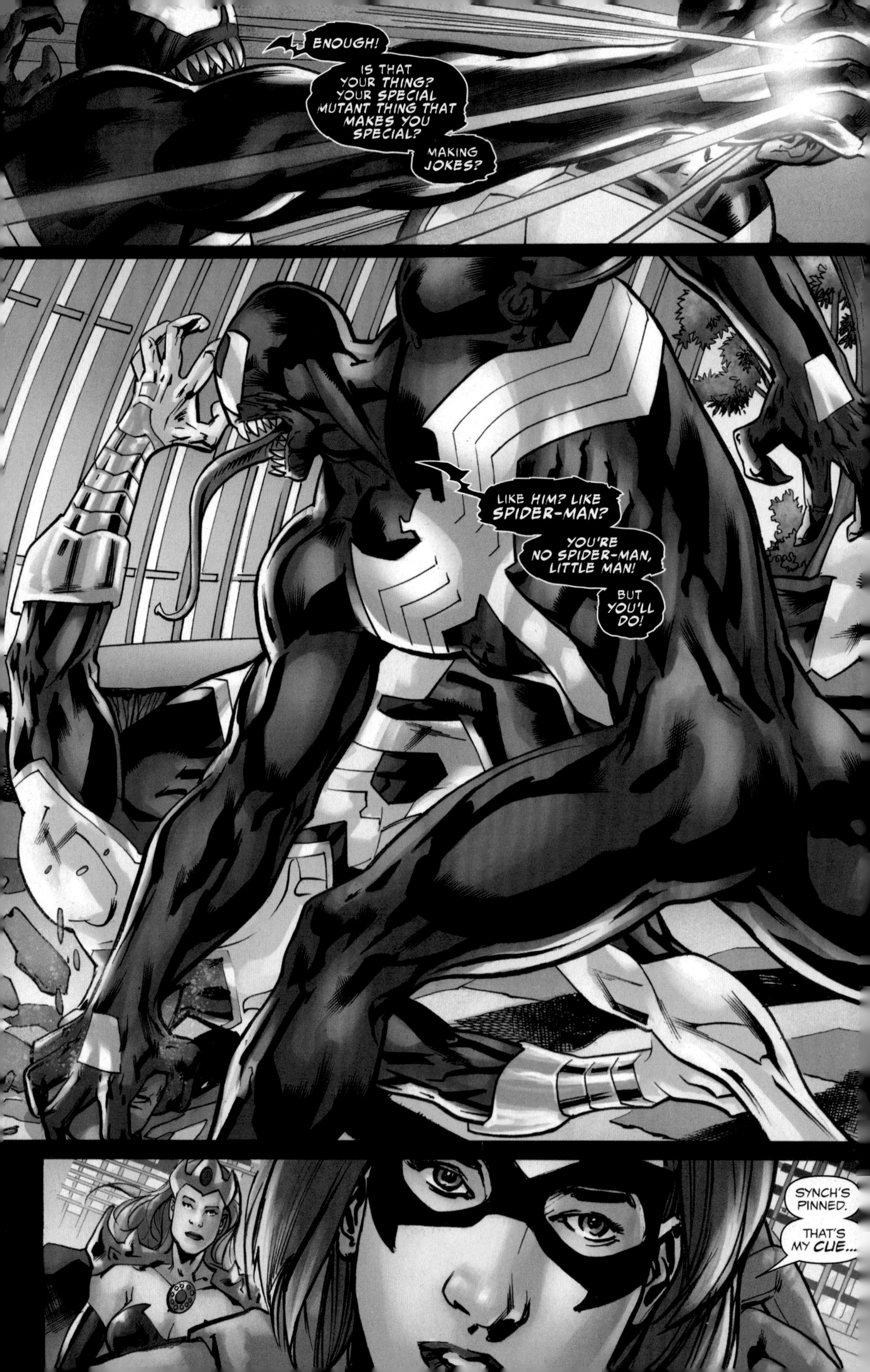
ENOUGH!
IS THAT YOUR THING? YOUR SPECIAL MUTANT THING THAT MAKES YOU SPECIAL?
MAKING JOKES?
LIKE HIM? LIKE SPIDER-MAN?
YOU'RE NO SPIDER-MAN, LITTLE MAN!
BUT YOU'LL DO!
SYNCH'S PINNED.
THAT'S MY CUE...

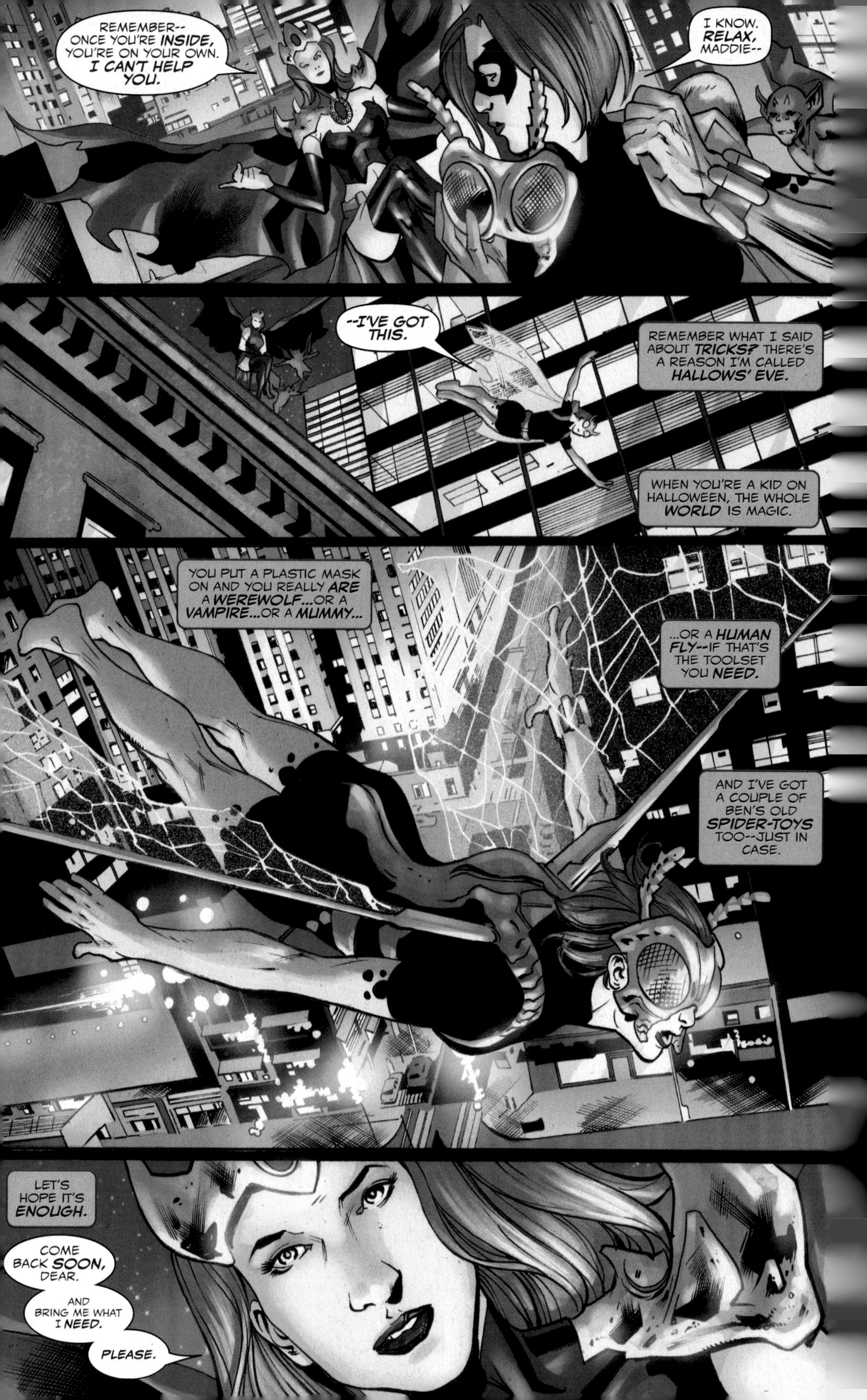
REMEMBER-- ONCE YOU'RE INSIDE, YOU'RE ON YOUR OWN. I CAN'T HELP YOU.
I KNOW. RELAX, MADDIE--
--I'VE GOT THIS.
REMEMBER WHAT I SAID ABOUT TRICKS? THERE'S A REASON I'M CALLED HALLOWS' EVE.
WHEN YOU'RE A KID ON HALLOWEEN, THE WHOLE WORLD IS MAGIC.
YOU PUT A PLASTIC MASK ON AND YOU REALLY ARE A WEREWOLF...OR A VAMPIRE...OR A MUMMY...
...OR A HUMAN FLY--IF THAT'S THE TOOLSET YOU NEED.
AND I'VE GOT A COUPLE OF BEN'S OLD SPIDER-TOYS TOO--JUST IN CASE.
LET'S HOPE IT'S ENOUGH.
COME BACK SOON, DEAR.
AND BRING ME WHAT I NEED.
PLEASE.

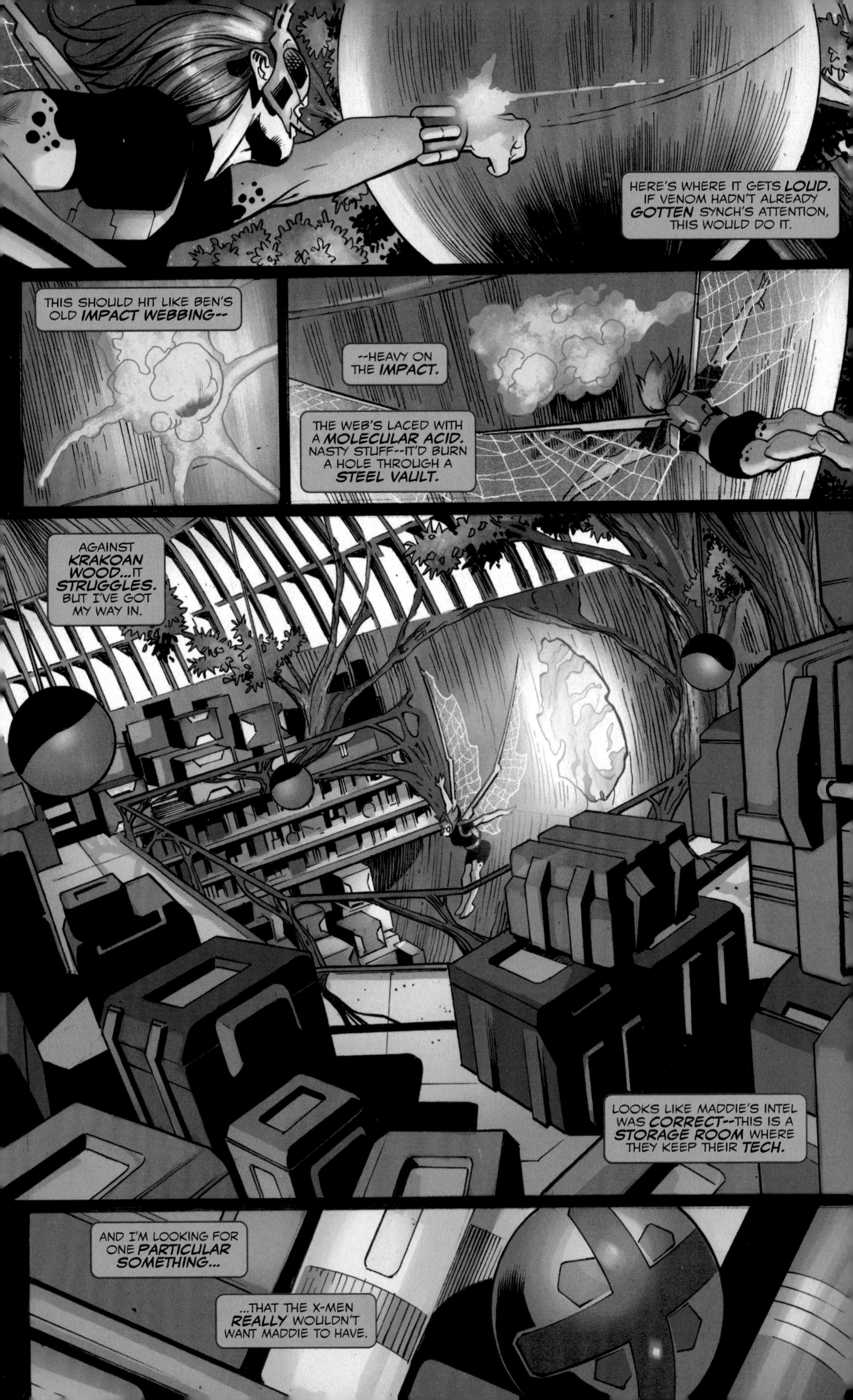
HERE'S WHERE IT GETS LOUD. IF VENOM HADN'T ALREADY GOTTEN SYNCH'S ATTENTION, THIS WOULD DO IT.
THIS SHOULD HIT LIKE BEN'S OLD IMPACT WEBBING--
--HEAVY ON THE IMPACT.
THE WEB'S LACED WITH A MOLECULAR ACID. NASTY STUFF--IT'D BURN A HOLE THROUGH A STEEL VAULT.
AGAINST KRAKOAN WOOD...IT STRUGGLES. BUT I'VE GOT MY WAY IN.
LOOKS LIKE MADDIE'S INTEL WAS CORRECT--THIS IS A STORAGE ROOM WHERE THEY KEEP THEIR TECH.
AND I'M LOOKING FOR ONE PARTICULAR SOMETHING...
...THAT THE X-MEN REALLY WOULDN'T WANT MADDIE TO HAVE.

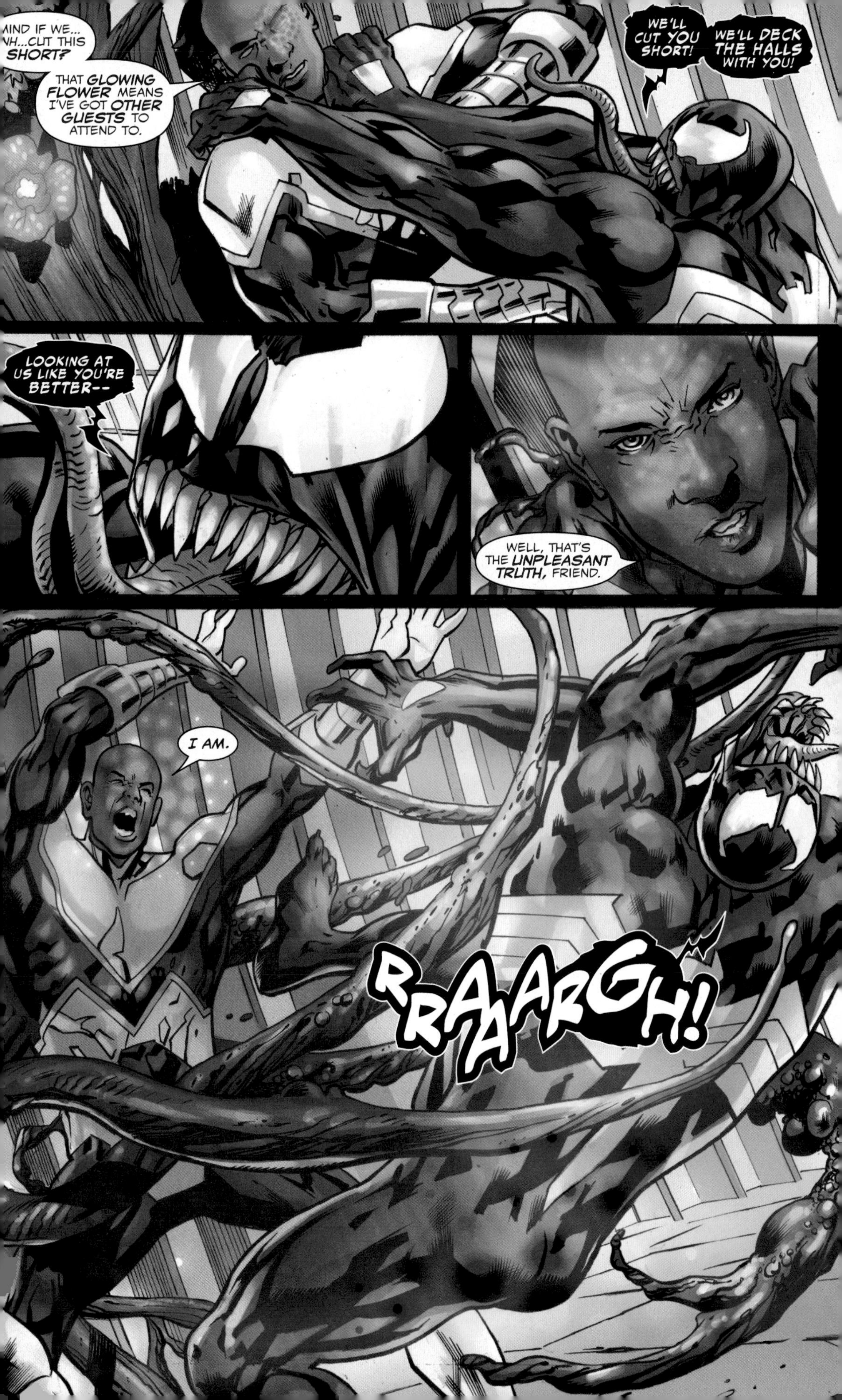
MIND IF WE... UH...CUT THIS SHORT?
THAT GLOWING FLOWER MEANS I'VE GOT OTHER GUESTS TO ATTEND TO.
WE'LL CUT YOU SHORT!
WE'LL DECK THE HALLS WITH YOU!
LOOKING AT US LIKE YOU'RE BETTER--
WELL, THAT'S THE UNPLEASANT TRUTH, FRIEND.
I AM.
RRAAARGH!

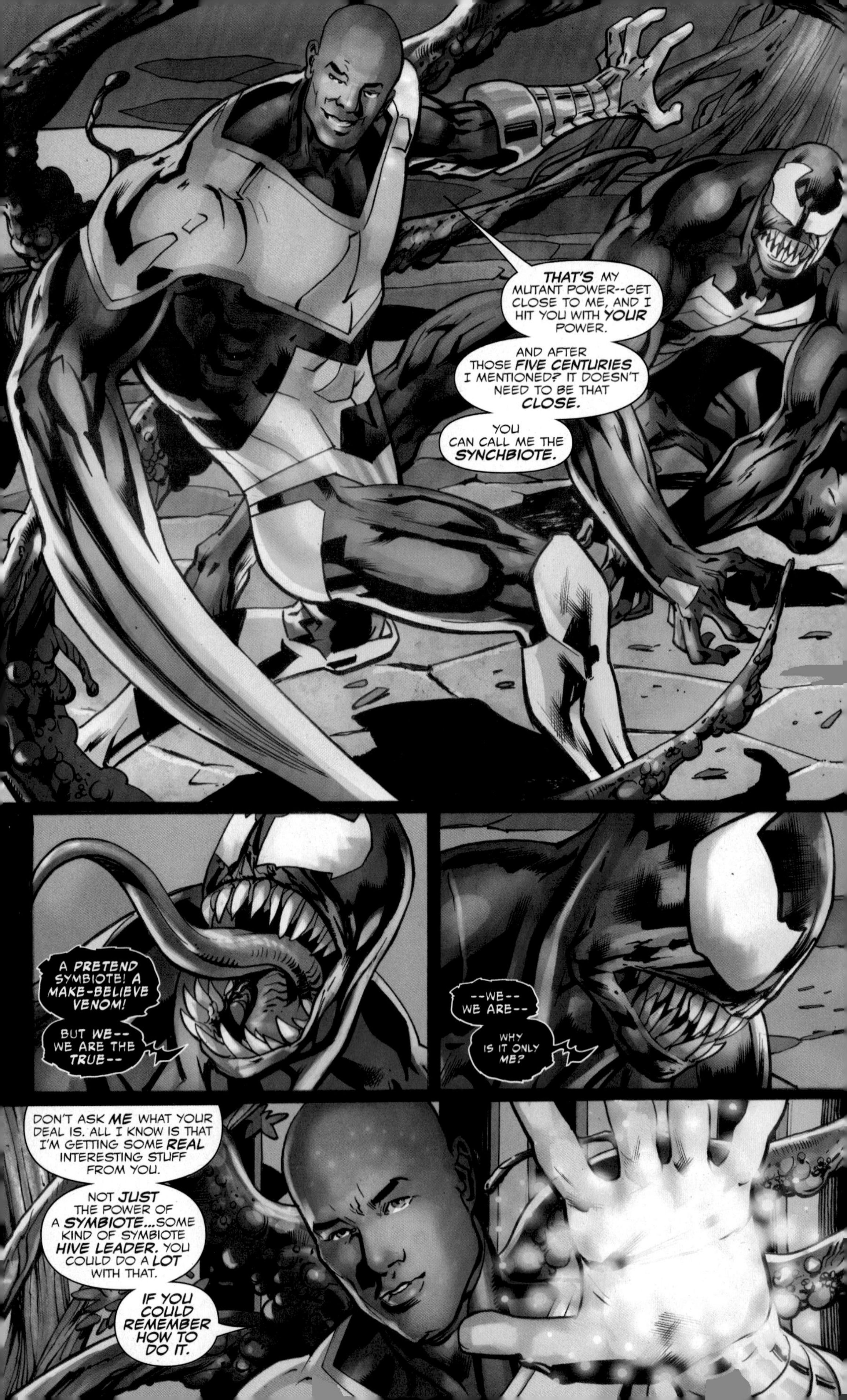
THAT'S MY MUTANT POWER--GET CLOSE TO ME, AND I HIT YOU WITH YOUR POWER.
AND AFTER THOSE FIVE CENTURIES I MENTIONED? IT DOESN'T NEED TO BE THAT CLOSE.
YOU CAN CALL ME THE SYNCHBIOTE.
A PRETEND SYMBIOTE! A MAKE-BELIEVE VENOM!
BUT WE-- WE ARE THE TRUE--
--WE-- WE ARE--
WHY IS IT ONLY ME?
DON'T ASK ME WHAT YOUR DEAL IS. ALL I KNOW IS THAT I'M GETTING SOME REAL INTERESTING STUFF FROM YOU.
NOT JUST THE POWER OF A SYMBIOTE...SOME KIND OF SYMBIOTE HIVE LEADER. YOU COULD DO A LOT WITH THAT.
IF YOU COULD REMEMBER HOW TO DO IT.

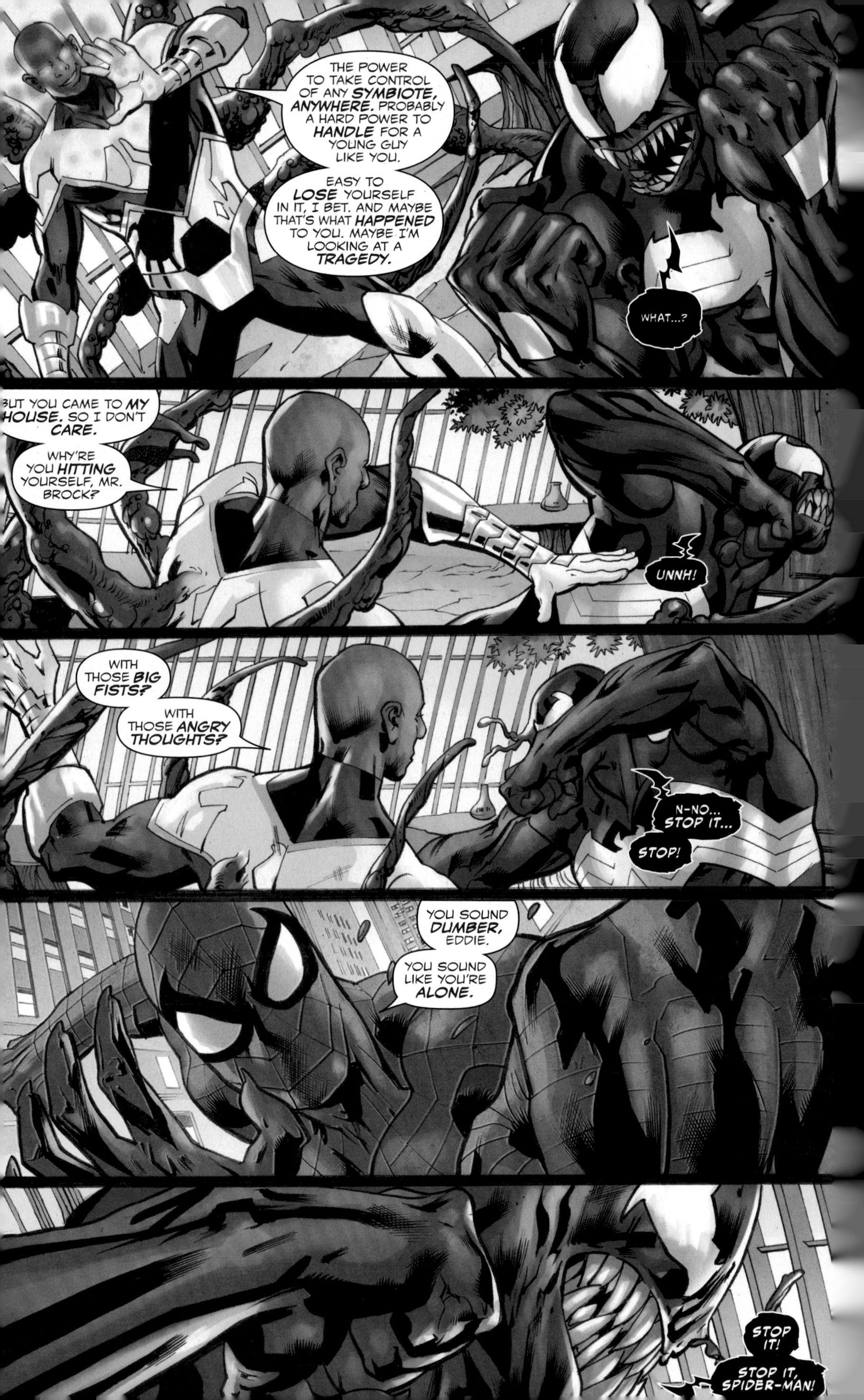
THE POWER TO TAKE CONTROL OF ANY SYMBIOTE, ANYWHERE. PROBABLY A HARD POWER TO HANDLE FOR A YOUNG GUY LIKE YOU.
EASY TO LOSE YOURSELF IN IT, I BET. AND MAYBE THAT'S WHAT HAPPENED TO YOU. MAYBE I'M LOOKING AT A TRAGEDY.
WHAT...?
BUT YOU CAME TO MY HOUSE. SO I DON'T CARE.
WHY'RE YOU HITTING YOURSELF, MR. BROCK?
UNNH!
WITH THOSE BIG FISTS?
WITH THOSE ANGRY THOUGHTS?
N-NO... STOP IT...
STOP!
YOU SOUND DUMBER, EDDIE.
YOU SOUND LIKE YOU'RE ALONE.
STOP IT!
STOP IT, SPIDER-MAN!

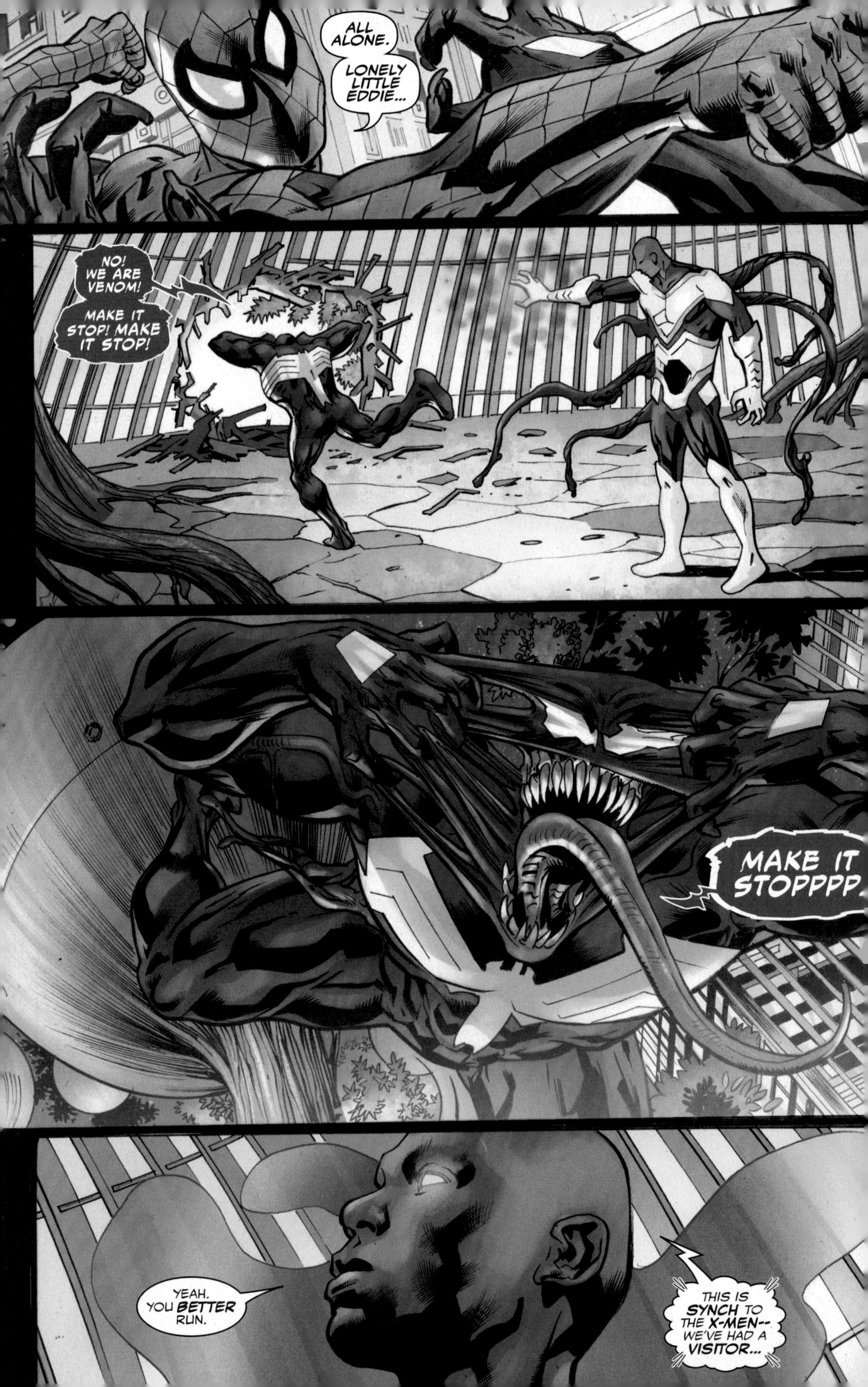
ALL ALONE.
LONELY LITTLE EDDIE...
NO! WE ARE VENOM!
MAKE IT STOP! MAKE IT STOP!
MAKE IT STOPPPP.
YEAH. YOU BETTER RUN.
THIS IS SYNCH TO THE X-MEN-- WE'VE HAD A VISITOR...

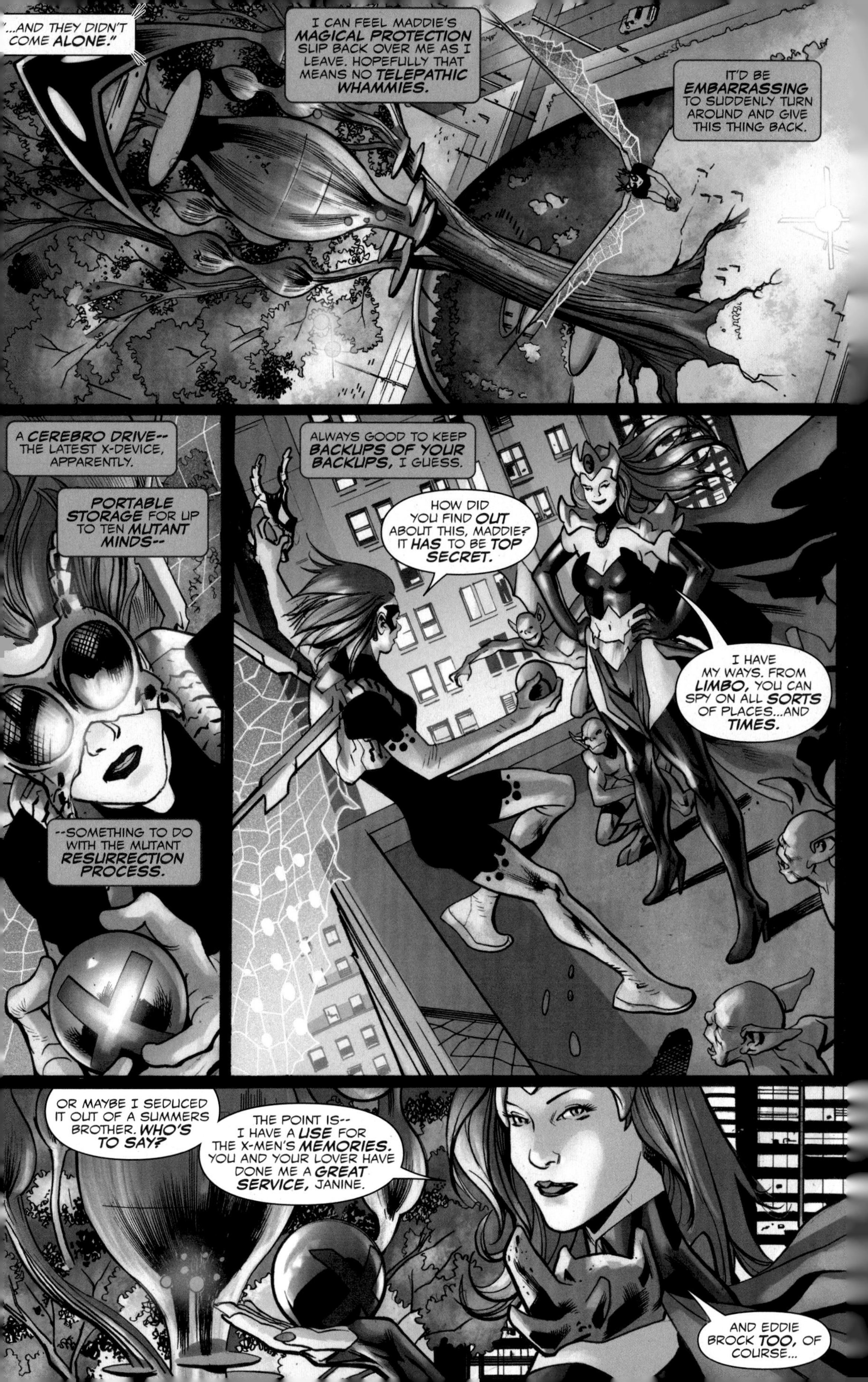
"...AND THEY DIDN'T COME ALONE."
I CAN FEEL MADDIE'S MAGICAL PROTECTION SLIP BACK OVER ME AS I LEAVE. HOPEFULLY THAT MEANS NO TELEPATHIC WHAMMIES.
IT'D BE EMBARRASSING TO SUDDENLY TURN AROUND AND GIVE THIS THING BACK.
A CEREBRO DRIVE-- THE LATEST X-DEVICE, APPARENTLY.
PORTABLE STORAGE FOR UP TO TEN MUTANT MINDS--
--SOMETHING TO DO WITH THE MUTANT RESURRECTION PROCESS.
ALWAYS GOOD TO KEEP BACKUPS OF YOUR BACKUPS, I GUESS.
HOW DID YOU FIND OUT ABOUT THIS, MADDIE? IT HAS TO BE TOP SECRET.
I HAVE MY WAYS. FROM LIMBO, YOU CAN SPY ON ALL SORTS OF PLACES...AND TIMES.
OR MAYBE I SEDUCED IT OUT OF A SUMMERS BROTHER. WHO'S TO SAY?
THE POINT IS-- I HAVE A USE FOR THE X-MEN'S MEMORIES. YOU AND YOUR LOVER HAVE DONE ME A GREAT SERVICE, JANINE.
AND EDDIE BROCK TOO, OF COURSE...

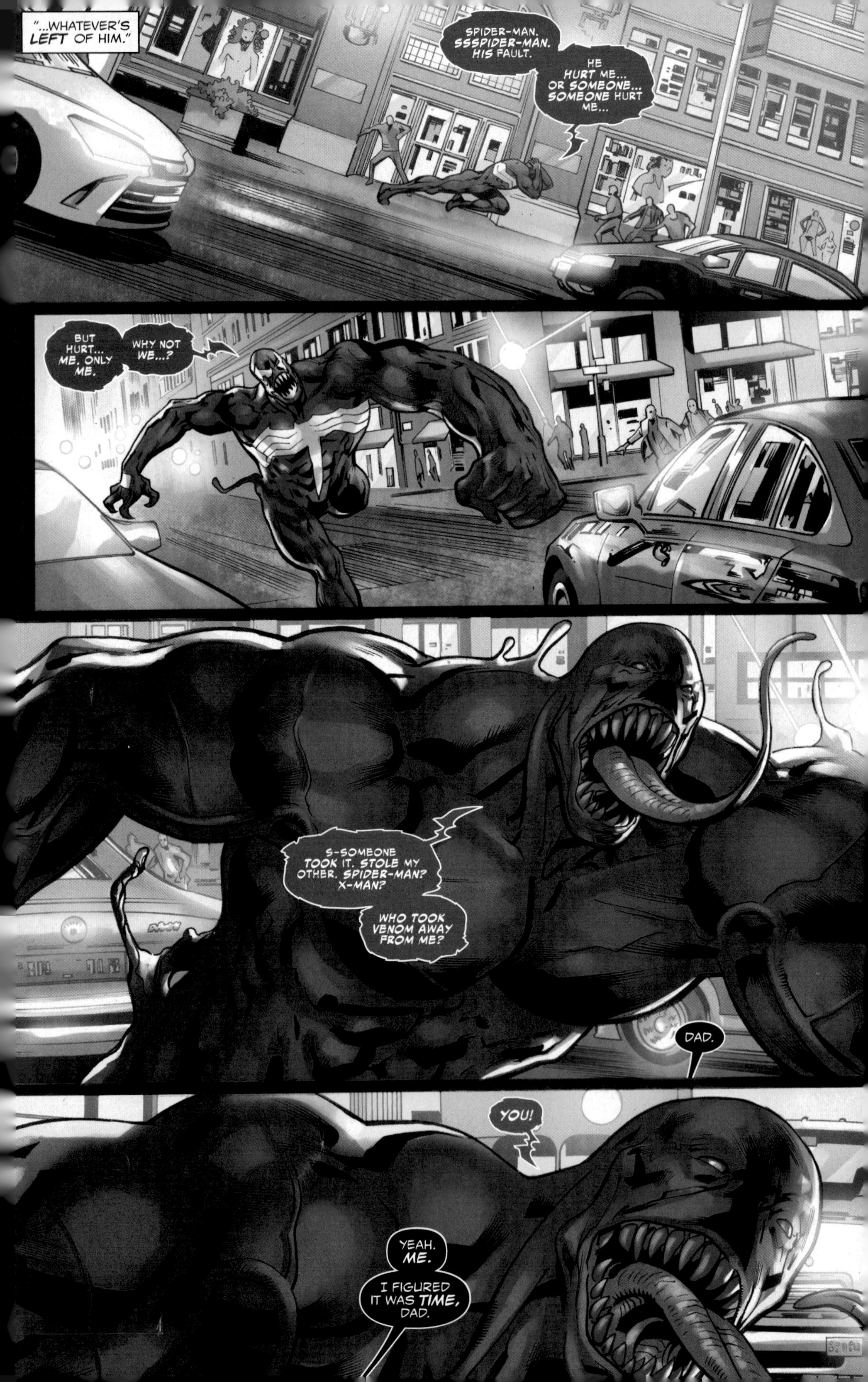
"...WHATEVER'S LEFT OF HIM."
SPIDER-MAN. SSSPIDER-MAN. HIS FAULT.
HE HURT ME... OR SOMEONE... SOMEONE HURT ME...
BUT HURT... ME. ONLY ME.
WHY NOT WE...?
S-SOMEONE TOOK IT. STOLE MY OTHER. SPIDER-MAN? X-MAN?
WHO TOOK VENOM AWAY FROM ME?
DAD.
YOU!
YEAH. ME.
I FIGURED IT WAS TIME, DAD.

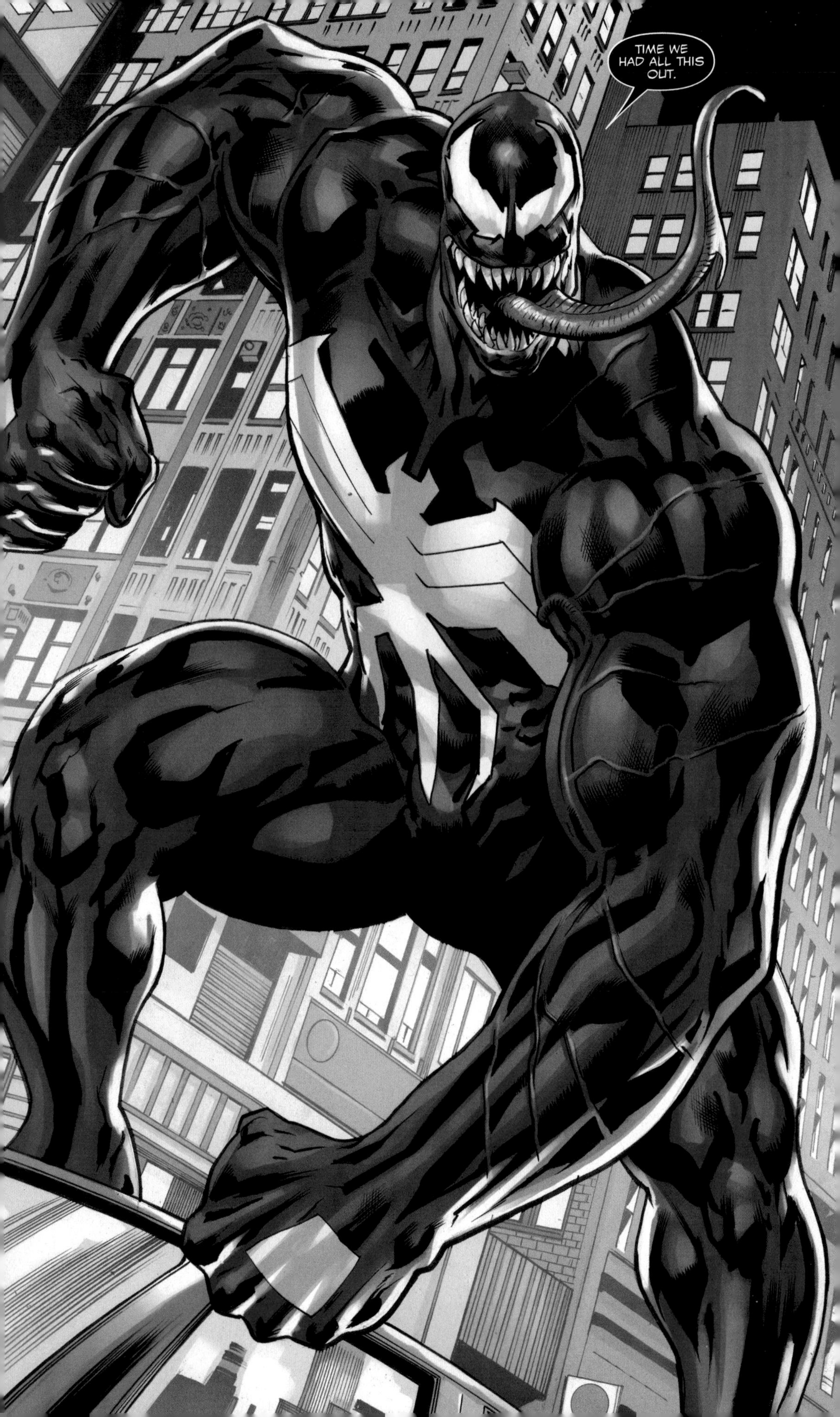
TIME WE HAD ALL THIS OUT.

VENOM #15

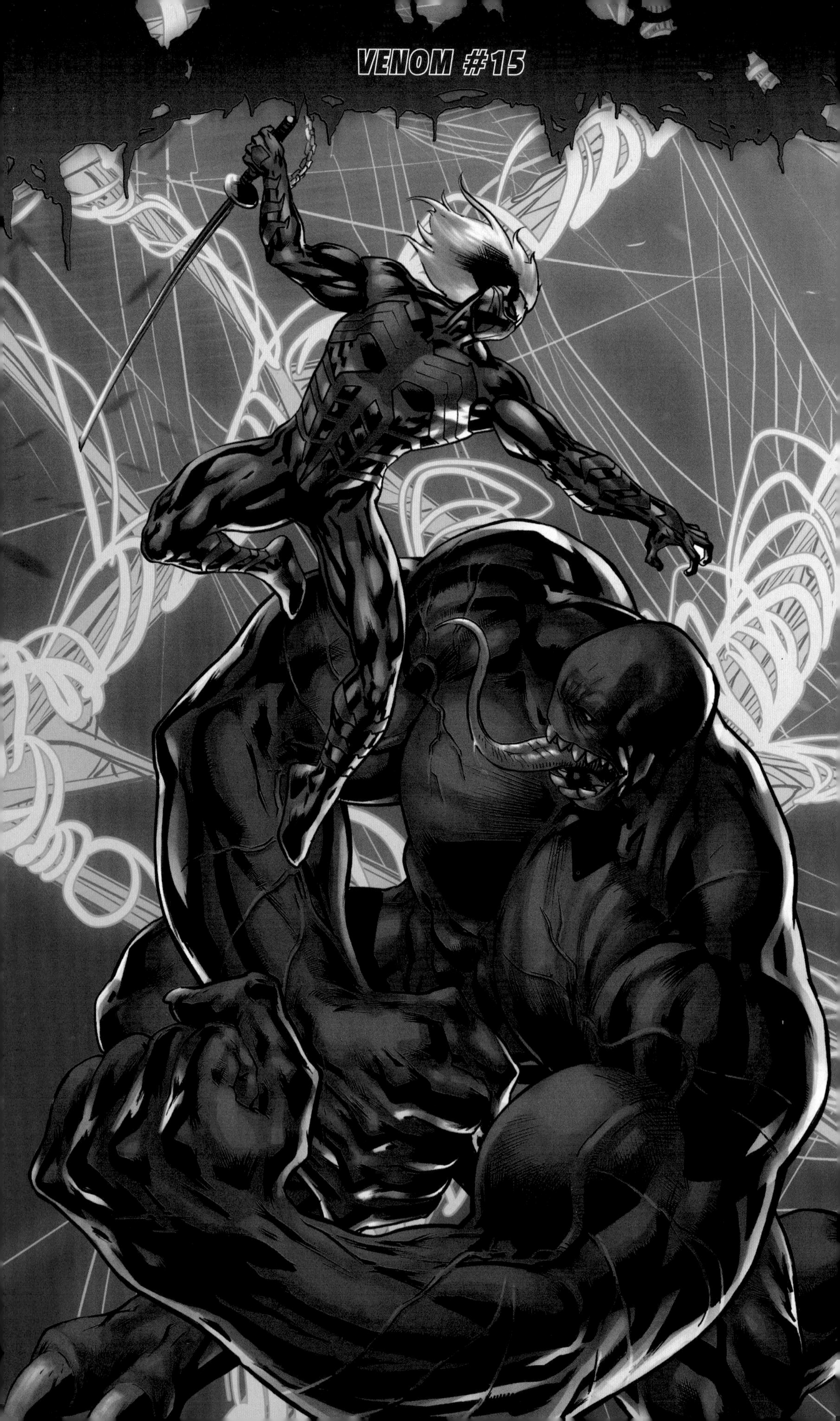

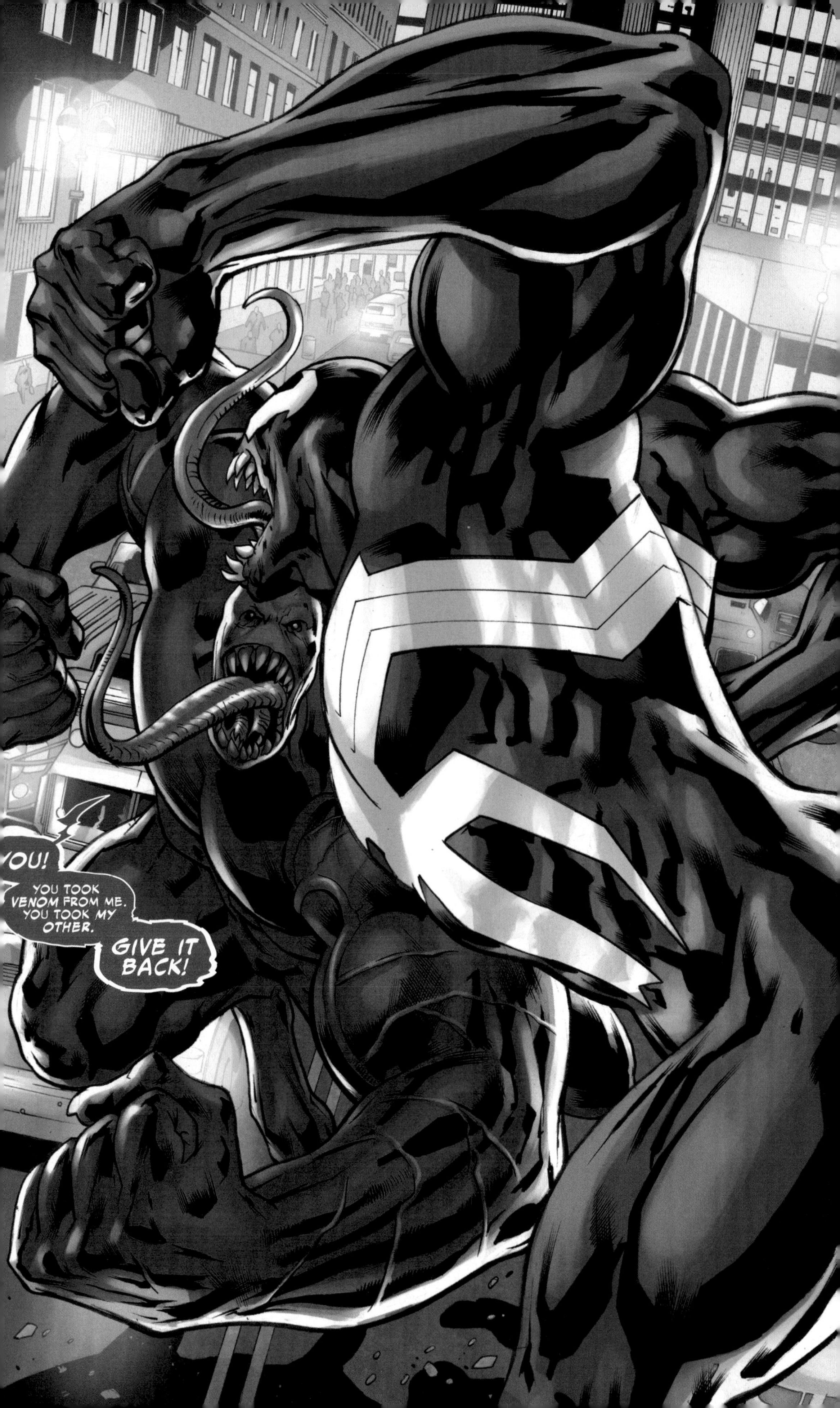

YOU!
YOU TOOK VENOM FROM ME. YOU TOOK MY OTHER.
GIVE IT BACK!

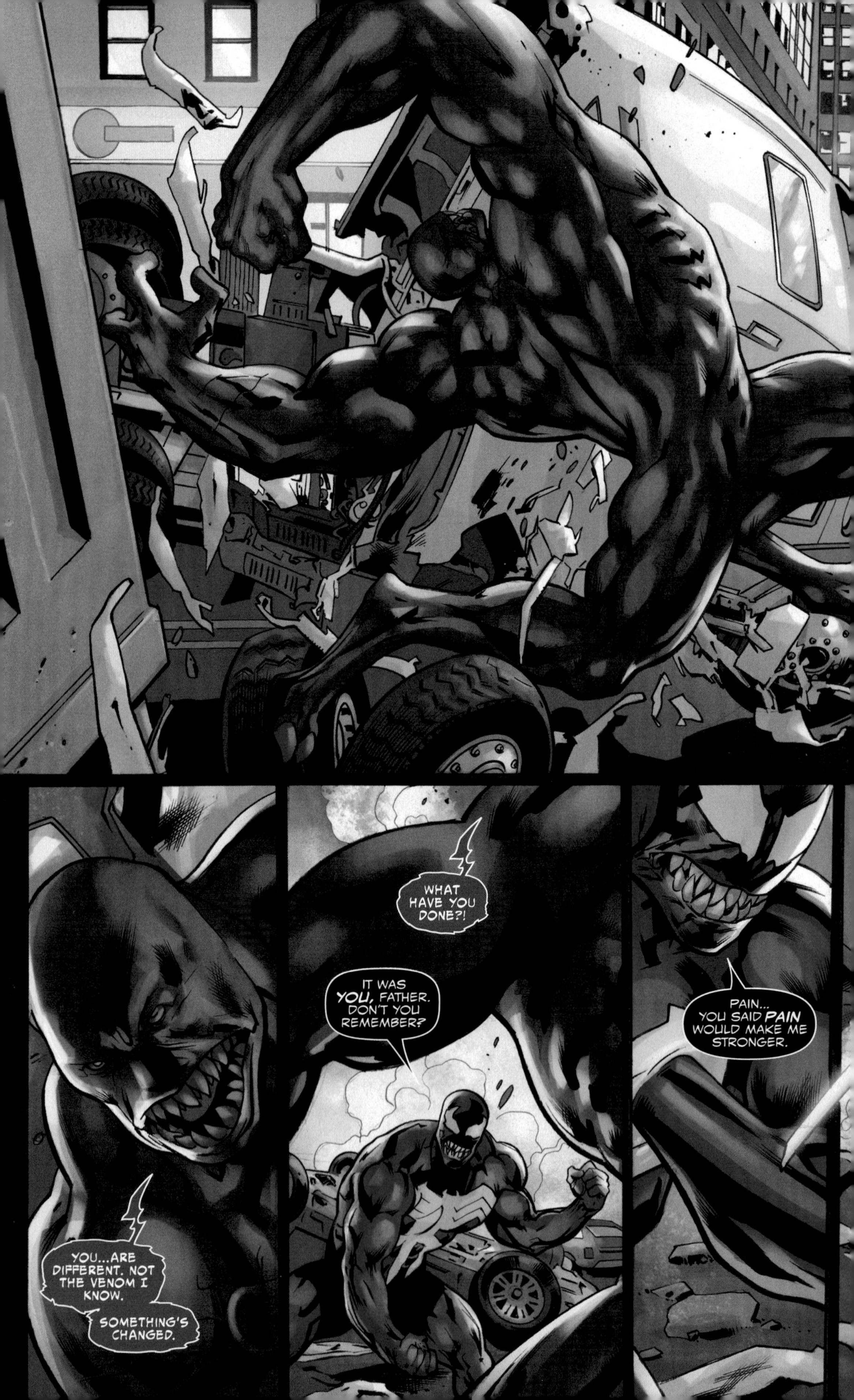
YOU...ARE DIFFERENT. NOT THE VENOM I KNOW.
SOMETHING'S CHANGED.
WHAT HAVE YOU DONE?!
IT WAS YOU, FATHER. DON'T YOU REMEMBER?
PAIN... YOU SAID PAIN WOULD MAKE ME STRONGER.

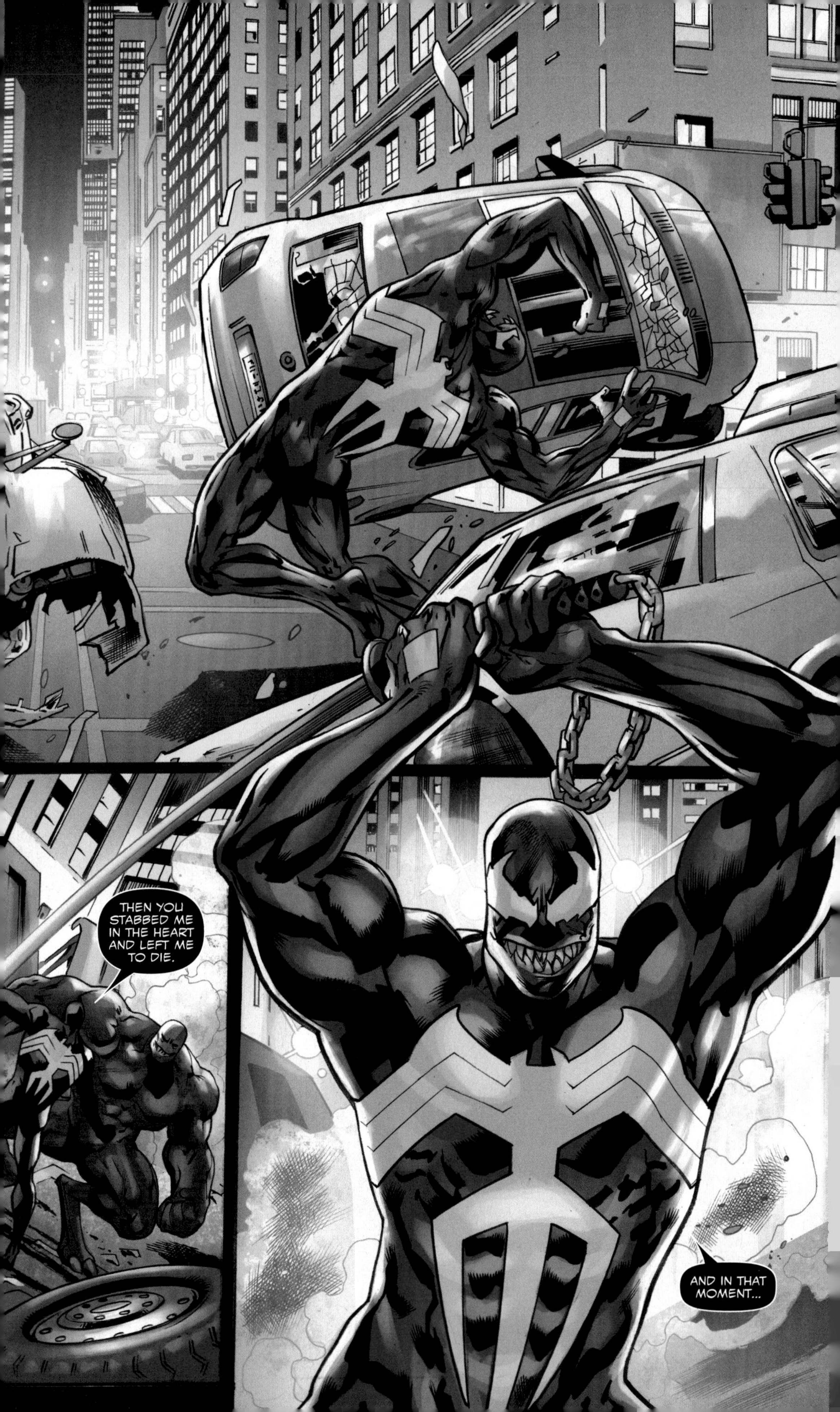
THEN YOU STABBED ME IN THE HEART AND LEFT ME TO DIE.
AND IN THAT MOMENT...

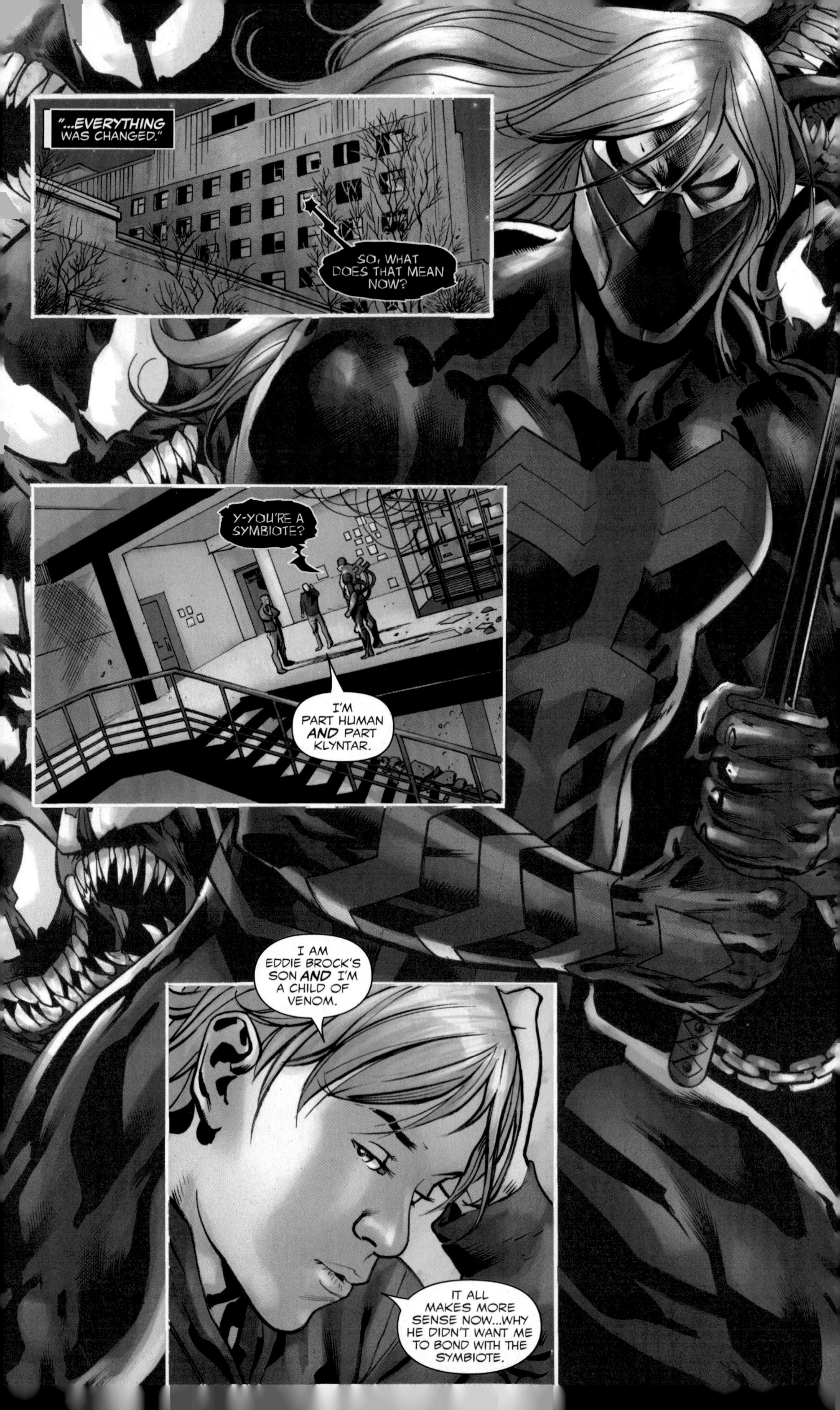
"...EVERYTHING WAS CHANGED."
SO, WHAT DOES THAT MEAN NOW?
Y-YOU'RE A SYMBIOTE?
I'M PART HUMAN AND PART KLYNTAR.
I AM EDDIE BROCK'S SON AND I'M A CHILD OF VENOM.
IT ALL MAKES MORE SENSE NOW...WHY HE DIDN'T WANT ME TO BOND WITH THE SYMBIOTE.

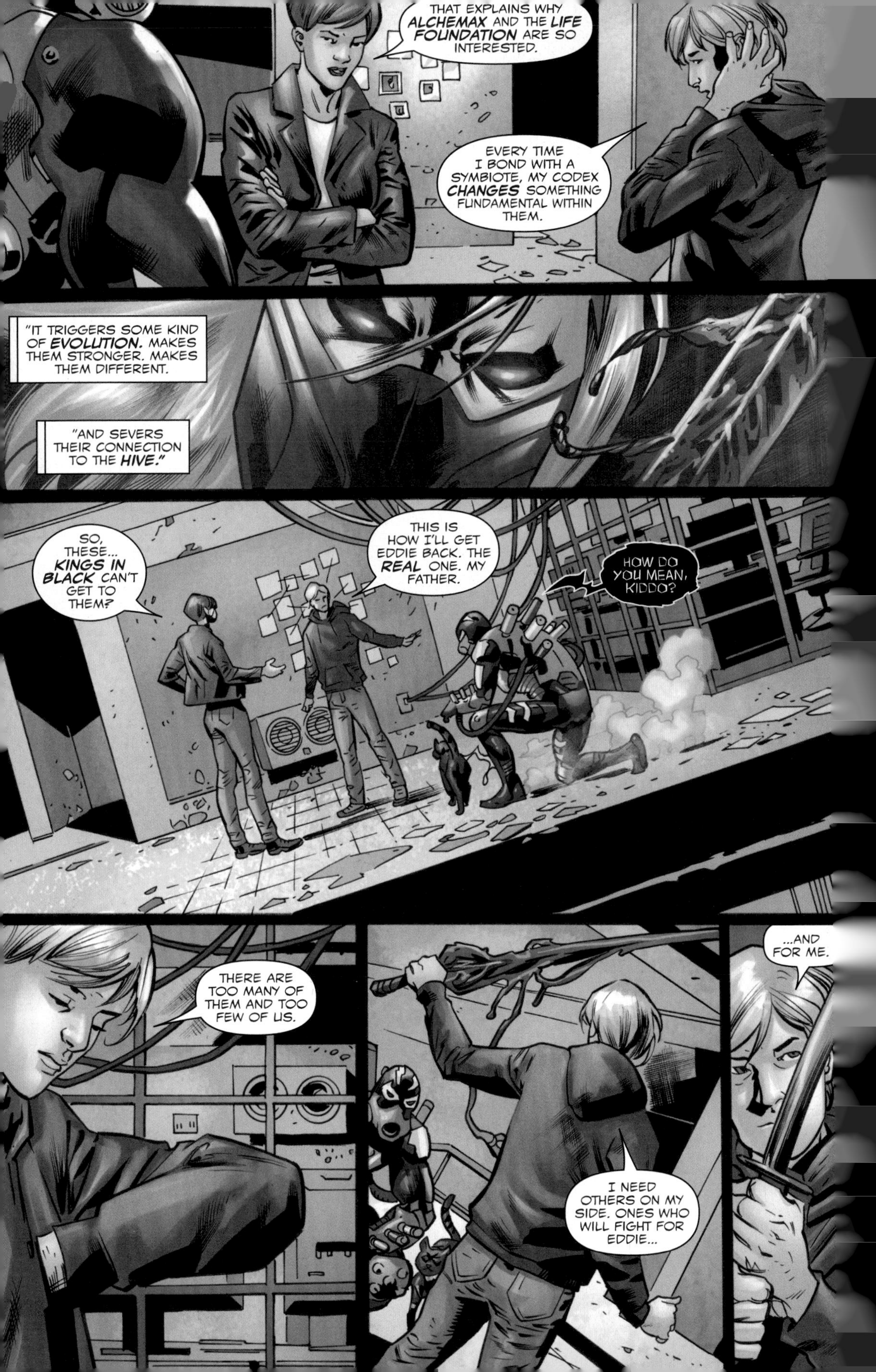
THAT EXPLAINS WHY ALCHEMAX AND THE LIFE FOUNDATION ARE SO INTERESTED.
EVERY TIME I BOND WITH A SYMBIOTE, MY CODEX CHANGES SOMETHING FUNDAMENTAL WITHIN THEM.
"IT TRIGGERS SOME KIND OF EVOLUTION. MAKES THEM STRONGER. MAKES THEM DIFFERENT.
"AND SEVERS THEIR CONNECTION TO THE HIVE."
SO, THESE... KINGS IN BLACK CAN'T GET TO THEM?
THIS IS HOW I'LL GET EDDIE BACK. THE REAL ONE. MY FATHER.
HOW DO YOU MEAN, KIDDO?
THERE ARE TOO MANY OF THEM AND TOO FEW OF US.
I NEED OTHERS ON MY SIDE. ONES WHO WILL FIGHT FOR EDDIE...
...AND FOR ME.

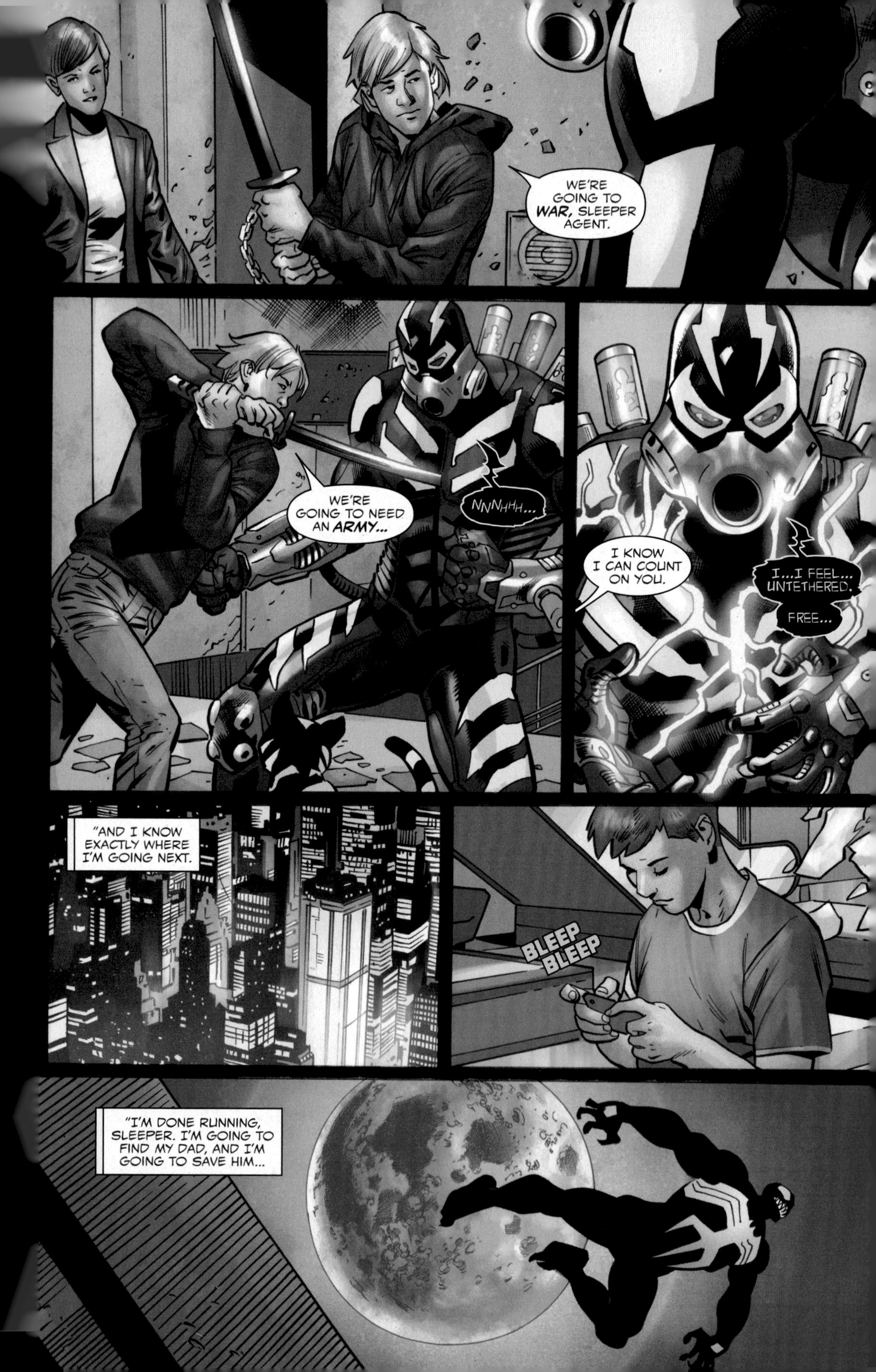
WE'RE GOING TO WAR, SLEEPER AGENT.
WE'RE GOING TO NEED AN ARMY...
NNNHHH...
I KNOW I CAN COUNT ON YOU.
I...I FEEL... UNTETHERED.
FREE...
"AND I KNOW EXACTLY WHERE I'M GOING NEXT.
BLEEP BLEEP
"I'M DONE RUNNING, SLEEPER. I'M GOING TO FIND MY DAD, AND I'M GOING TO SAVE HIM...

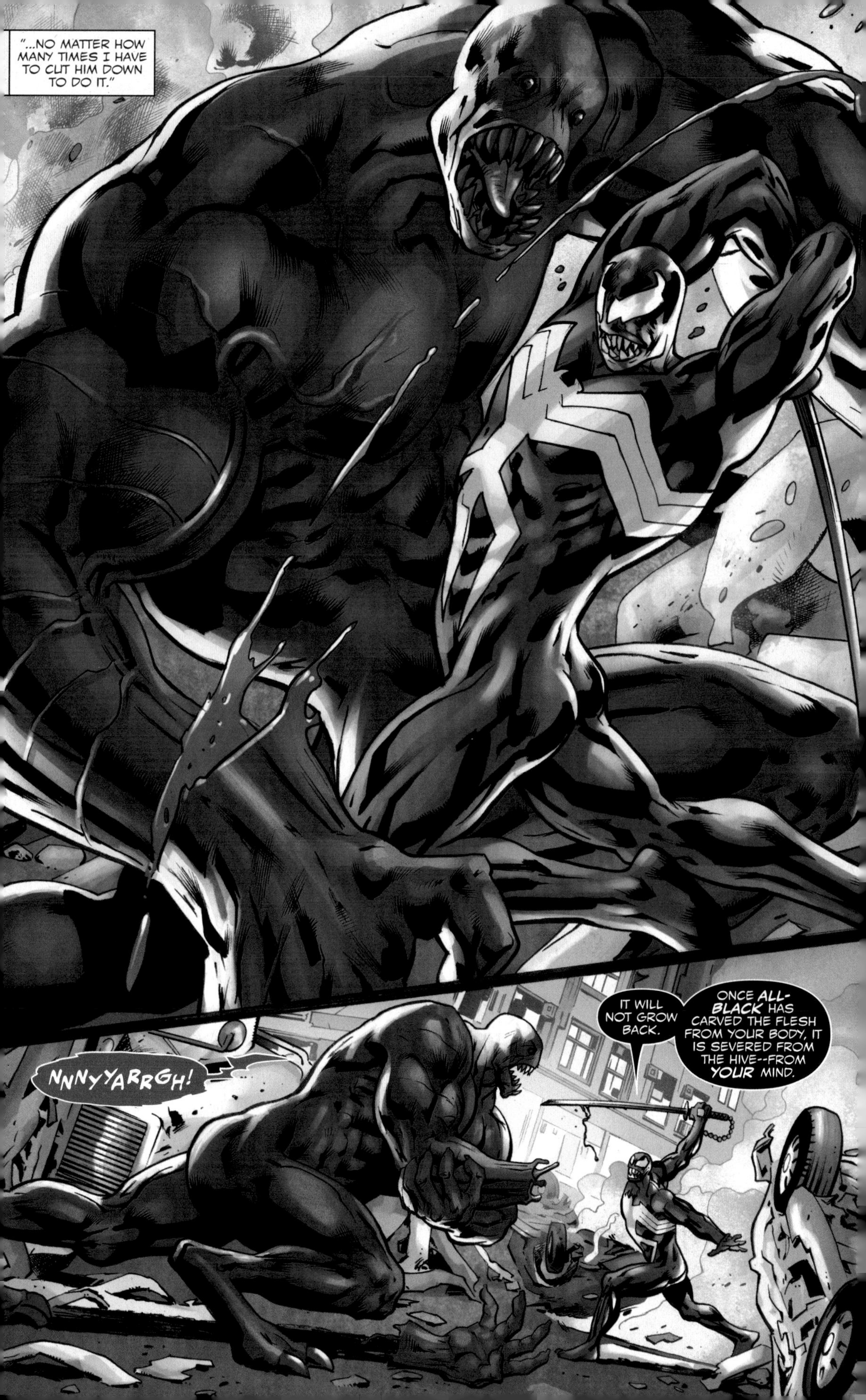
"...NO MATTER HOW MANY TIMES I HAVE TO CUT HIM DOWN TO DO IT."
NNNYYARRGH!
IT WILL NOT GROW BACK.
ONCE ALL-BLACK HAS CARVED THE FLESH FROM YOUR BODY, IT IS SEVERED FROM THE HIVE--FROM YOUR MIND.

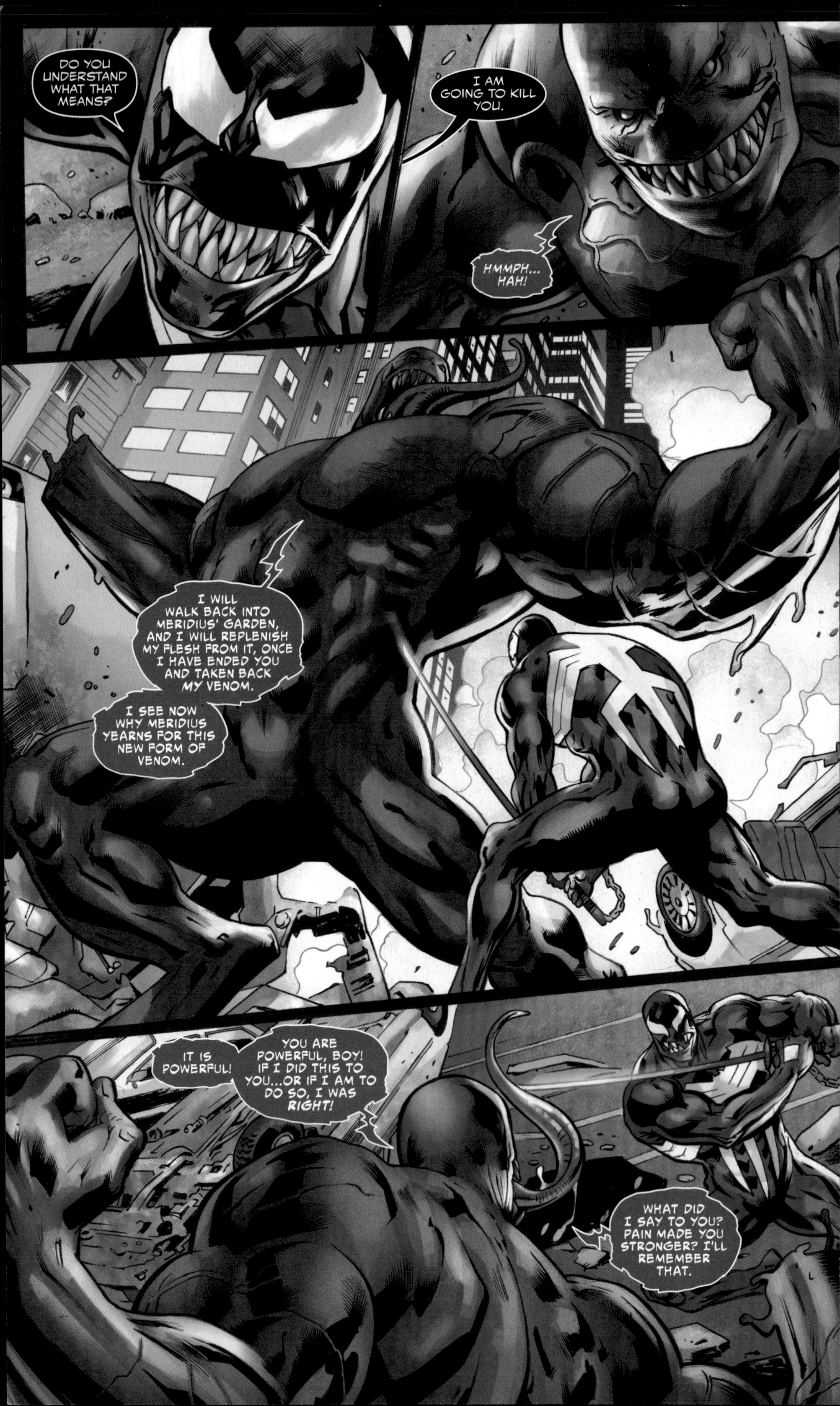

DO YOU UNDERSTAND WHAT THAT MEANS?
I AM GOING TO KILL YOU.
HMMPH... HAH!
I WILL WALK BACK INTO MERIDIUS' GARDEN, AND I WILL REPLENISH MY FLESH FROM IT, ONCE I HAVE ENDED YOU AND TAKEN BACK MY VENOM.
I SEE NOW WHY MERIDIUS YEARNS FOR THIS NEW FORM OF VENOM.
IT IS POWERFUL!
YOU ARE POWERFUL, BOY! IF I DID THIS TO YOU...OR IF I AM TO DO SO, I WAS RIGHT!
WHAT DID I SAY TO YOU? PAIN MADE YOU STRONGER? I'LL REMEMBER THAT.

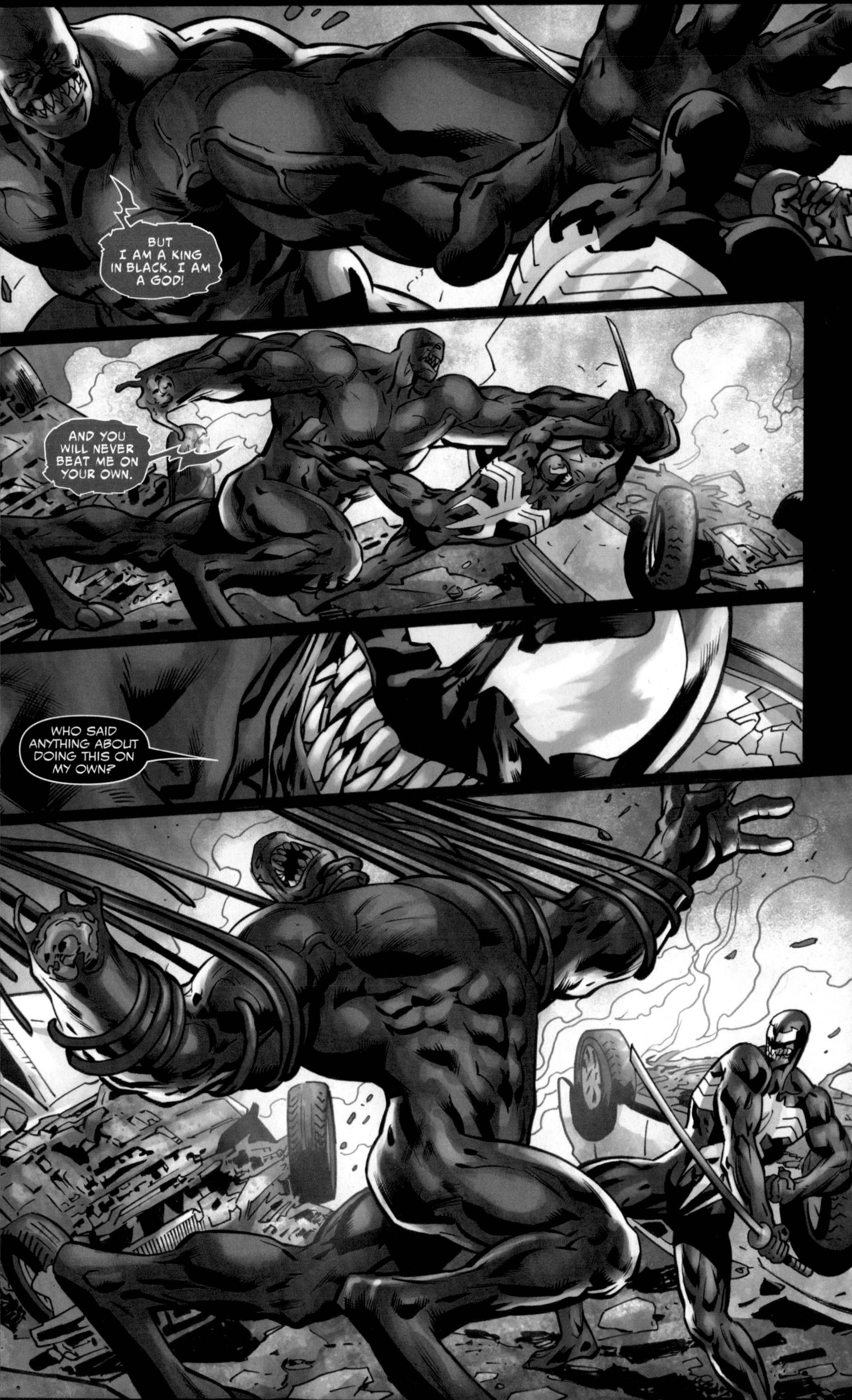

BUT I AM A KING IN BLACK. I AM A GOD!
AND YOU WILL NEVER BEAT ME ON YOUR OWN.
WHO SAID ANYTHING ABOUT DOING THIS ON MY OWN?

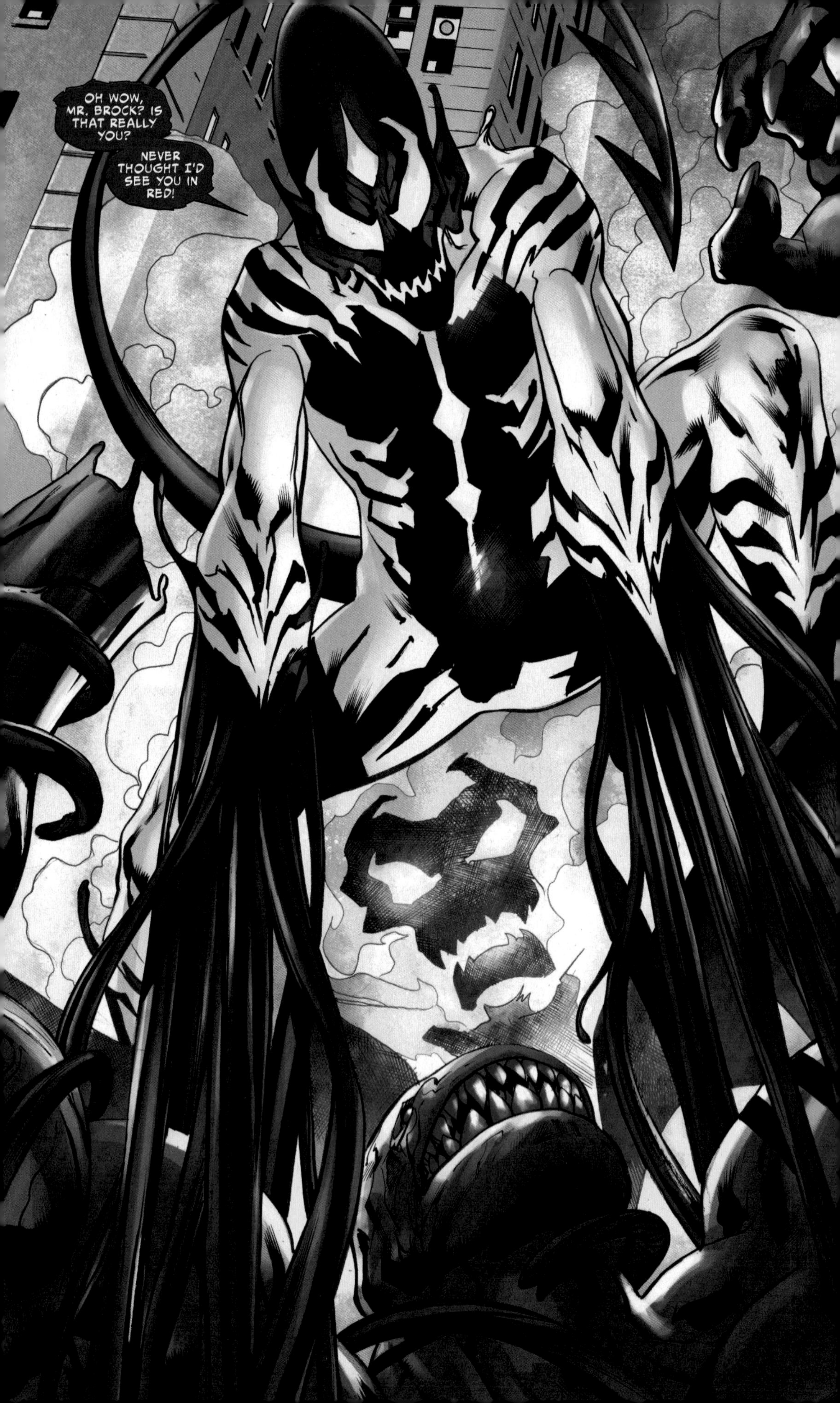
OH WOW, MR. BROCK? IS THAT REALLY YOU?
NEVER THOUGHT I'D SEE YOU IN RED!

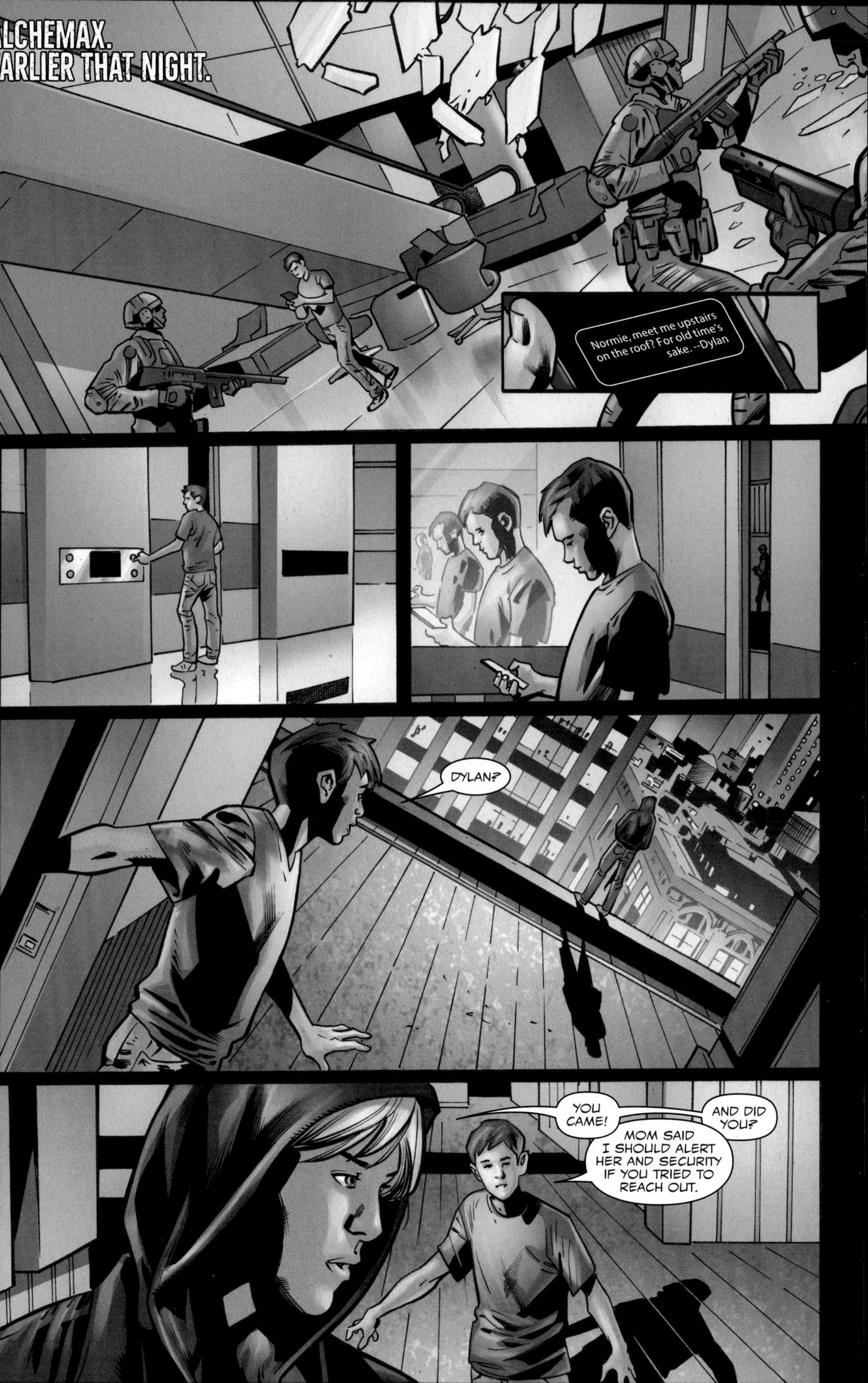
ALCHEMAX.
EARLIER THAT NIGHT.
Normie, meet me upstairs on the roof? For old time's sake. --Dylan
DYLAN?
YOU CAME!
AND DID YOU?
MOM SAID I SHOULD ALERT HER AND SECURITY IF YOU TRIED TO REACH OUT.

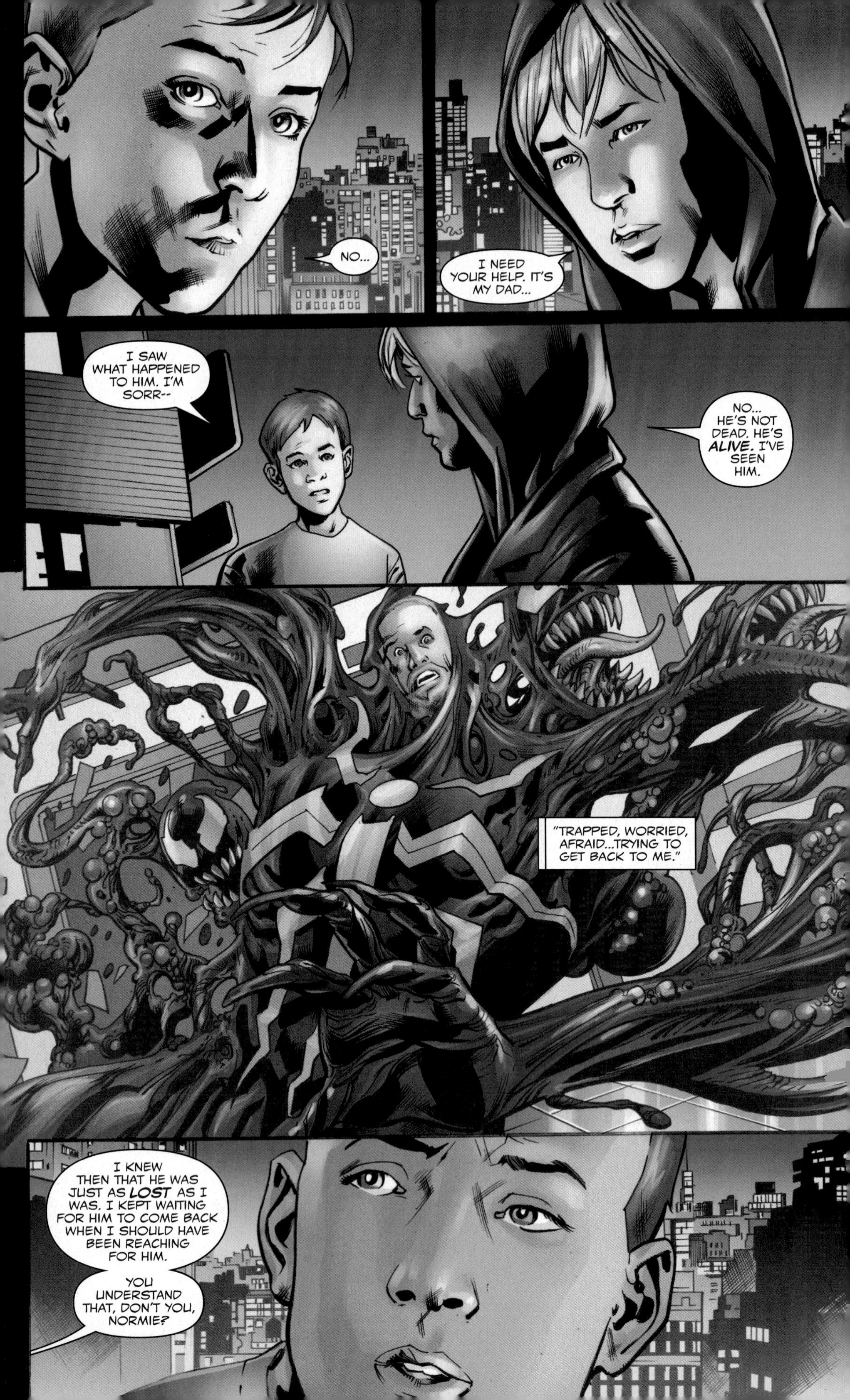
NO...
I NEED YOUR HELP. IT'S MY DAD...
I SAW WHAT HAPPENED TO HIM. I'M SORR--
NO... HE'S NOT DEAD. HE'S ALIVE. I'VE SEEN HIM.
"TRAPPED, WORRIED, AFRAID...TRYING TO GET BACK TO ME."
I KNEW THEN THAT HE WAS JUST AS LOST AS I WAS. I KEPT WAITING FOR HIM TO COME BACK WHEN I SHOULD HAVE BEEN REACHING FOR HIM.
YOU UNDERSTAND THAT, DON'T YOU, NORMIE?

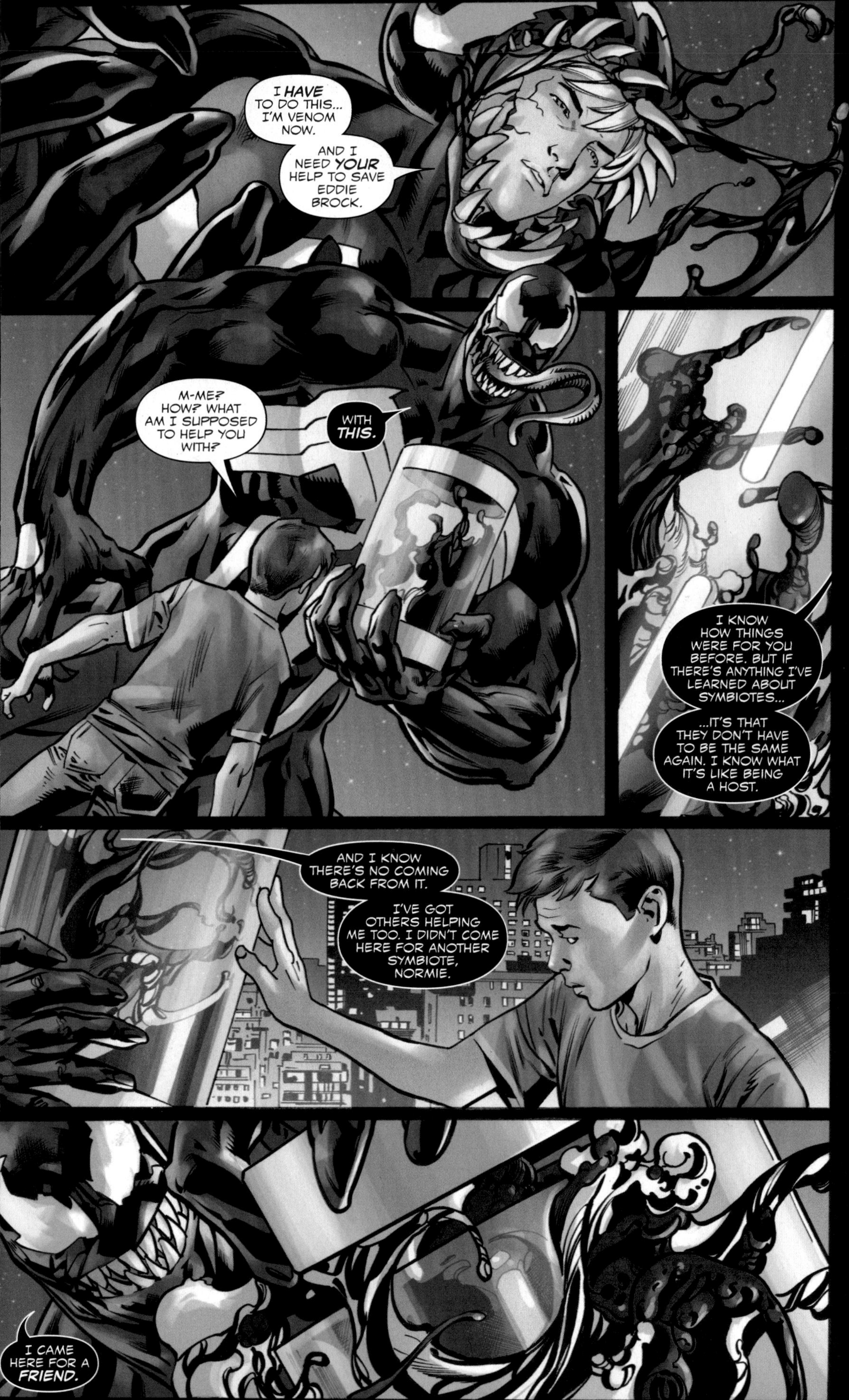
I HAVE TO DO THIS... I'M VENOM NOW.
AND I NEED YOUR HELP TO SAVE EDDIE BROCK.
M-ME? HOW? WHAT AM I SUPPOSED TO HELP YOU WITH?
WITH THIS.
I KNOW HOW THINGS WERE FOR YOU BEFORE. BUT IF THERE'S ANYTHING I'VE LEARNED ABOUT SYMBIOTES...
...IT'S THAT THEY DON'T HAVE TO BE THE SAME AGAIN. I KNOW WHAT IT'S LIKE BEING A HOST.
AND I KNOW THERE'S NO COMING BACK FROM IT.
I'VE GOT OTHERS HELPING ME TOO. I DIDN'T COME HERE FOR ANOTHER SYMBIOTE, NORMIE.
I CAME HERE FOR A FRIEND.

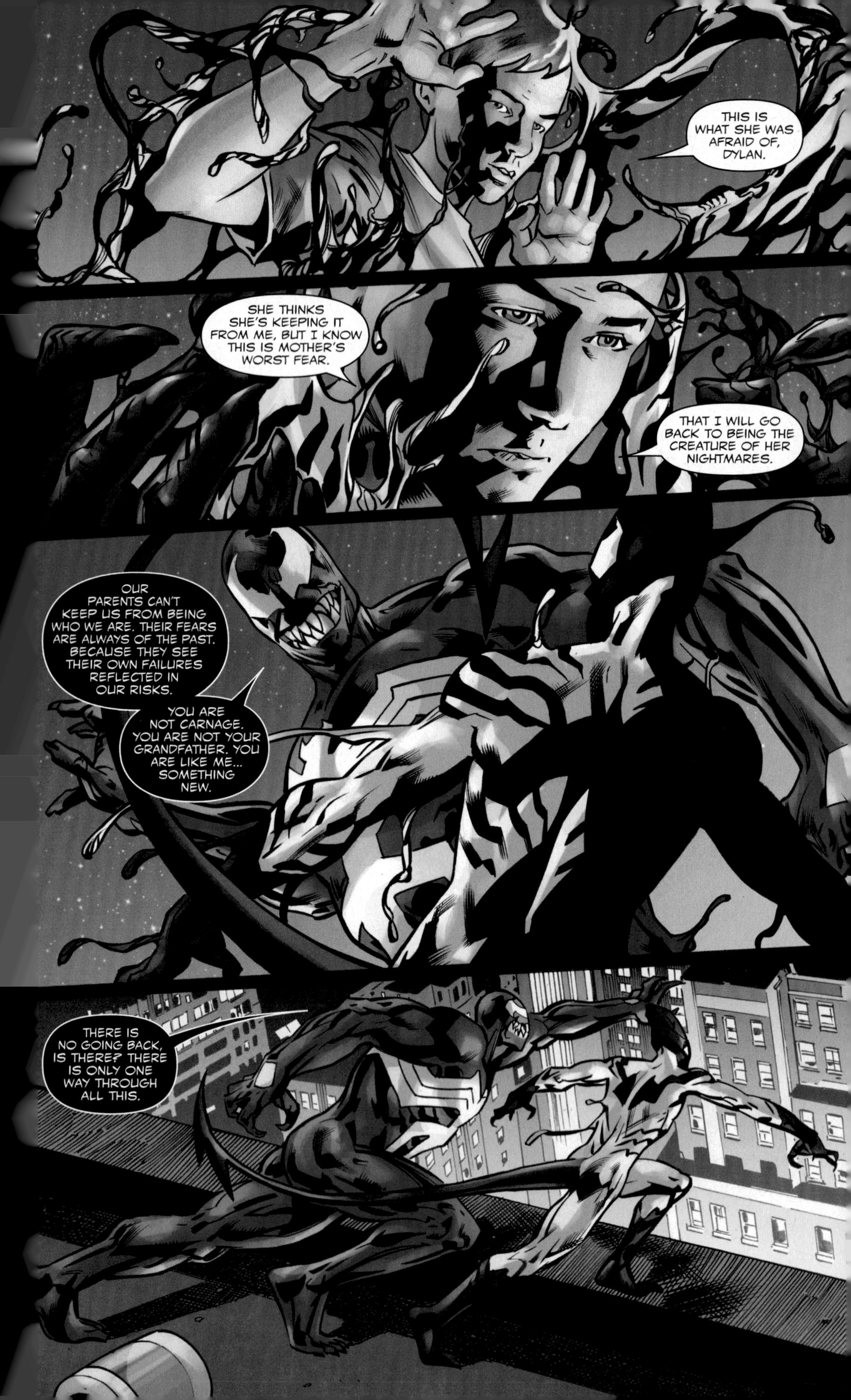
THIS IS WHAT SHE WAS AFRAID OF, DYLAN.
SHE THINKS SHE'S KEEPING IT FROM ME, BUT I KNOW THIS IS MOTHER'S WORST FEAR.
THAT I WILL GO BACK TO BEING THE CREATURE OF HER NIGHTMARES.
OUR PARENTS CAN'T KEEP US FROM BEING WHO WE ARE. THEIR FEARS ARE ALWAYS OF THE PAST. BECAUSE THEY SEE THEIR OWN FAILURES REFLECTED IN OUR RISKS.
YOU ARE NOT CARNAGE. YOU ARE NOT YOUR GRANDFATHER. YOU ARE LIKE ME... SOMETHING NEW.
THERE IS NO GOING BACK, IS THERE? THERE IS ONLY ONE WAY THROUGH ALL THIS.

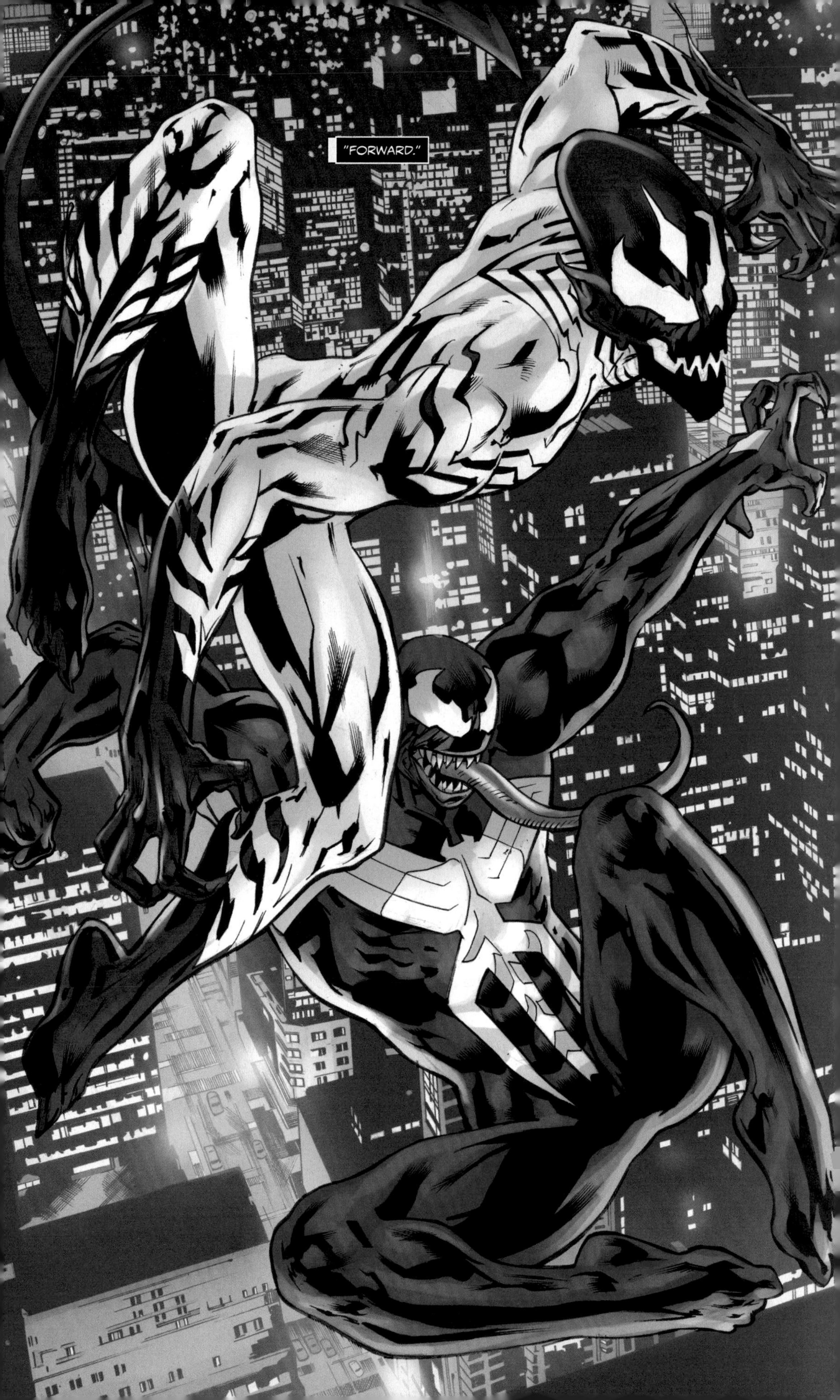
"FORWARD."

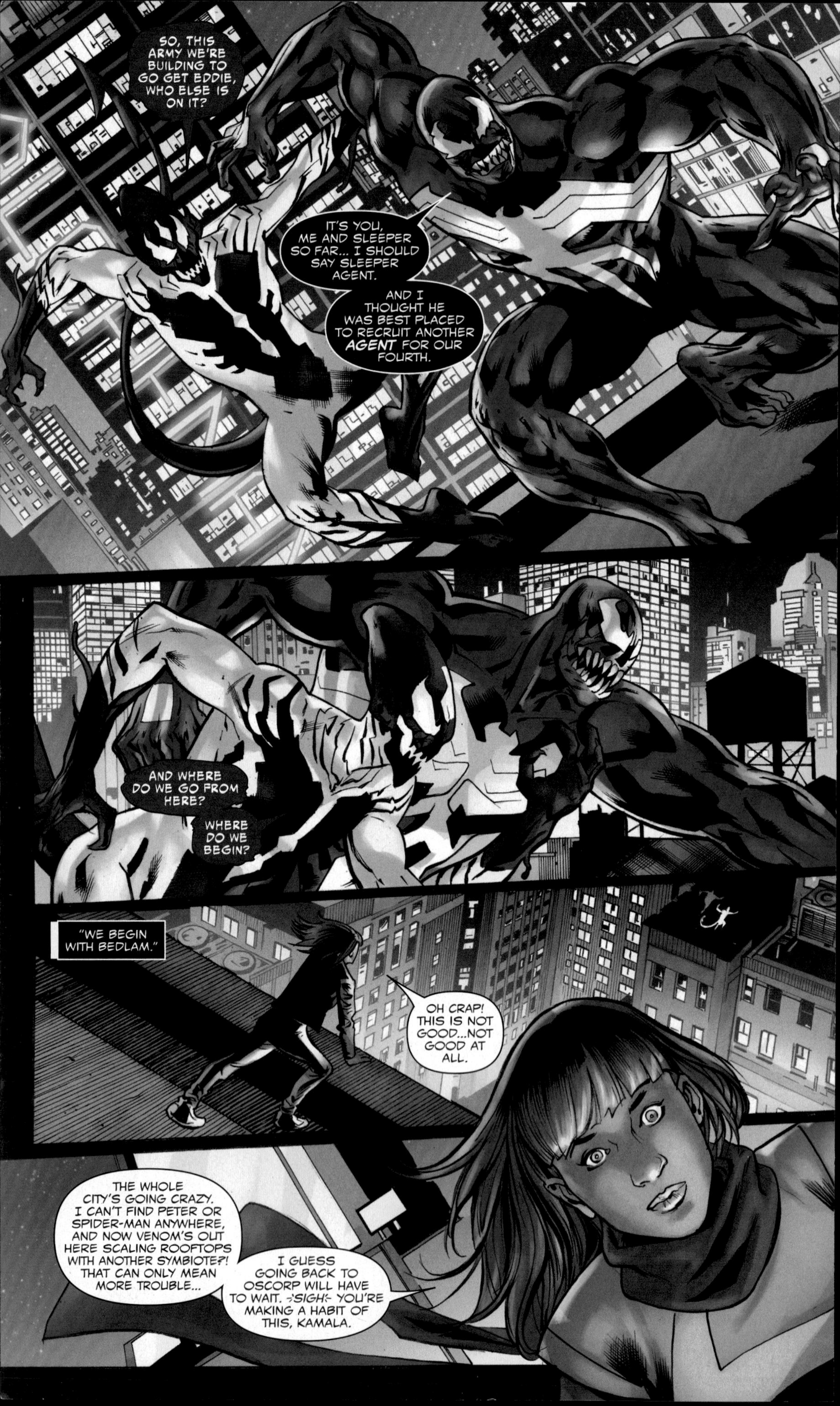
SO, THIS ARMY WE'RE BUILDING TO GO GET EDDIE, WHO ELSE IS ON IT?
IT'S YOU, ME AND SLEEPER SO FAR... I SHOULD SAY SLEEPER AGENT.
AND I THOUGHT HE WAS BEST PLACED TO RECRUIT ANOTHER AGENT FOR OUR FOURTH.
AND WHERE DO WE GO FROM HERE?
WHERE DO WE BEGIN?
"WE BEGIN WITH BEDLAM."
OH CRAP! THIS IS NOT GOOD...NOT GOOD AT ALL.
THE WHOLE CITY'S GOING CRAZY. I CAN'T FIND PETER OR SPIDER-MAN ANYWHERE, AND NOW VENOM'S OUT HERE SCALING ROOFTOPS WITH ANOTHER SYMBIOTE?! THAT CAN ONLY MEAN MORE TROUBLE...
I GUESS GOING BACK TO OSCORP WILL HAVE TO WAIT. -SIGH- YOU'RE MAKING A HABIT OF THIS, KAMALA.

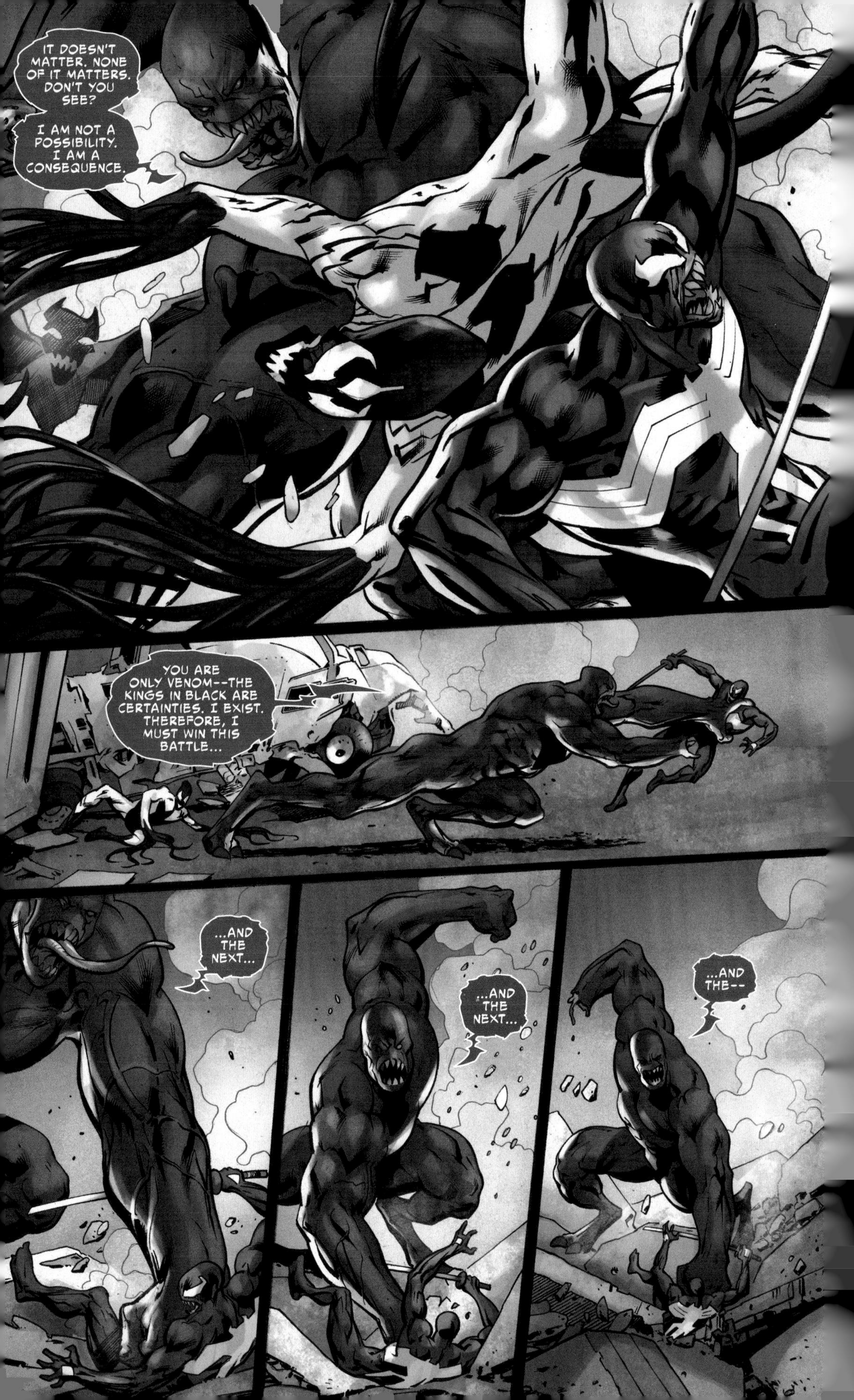
IT DOESN'T MATTER. NONE OF IT MATTERS. DON'T YOU SEE?
I AM NOT A POSSIBILITY. I AM A CONSEQUENCE.
YOU ARE ONLY VENOM--THE KINGS IN BLACK ARE CERTAINTIES. I EXIST. THEREFORE, I MUST WIN THIS BATTLE...
...AND THE NEXT...
...AND THE NEXT...
...AND THE--

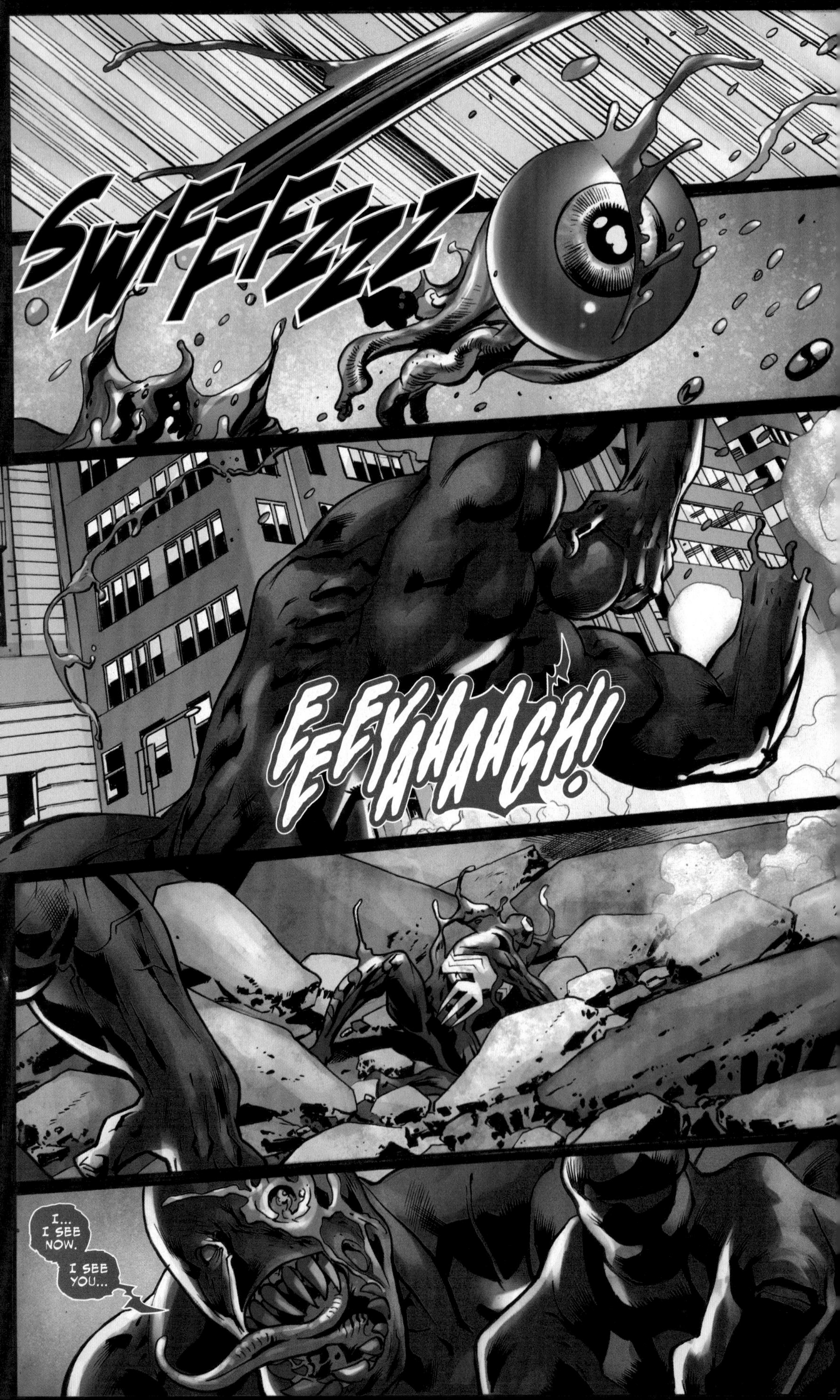
SWIFFFZZZ
EEEYAAAAGH!
I... I SEE NOW.
I SEE YOU...

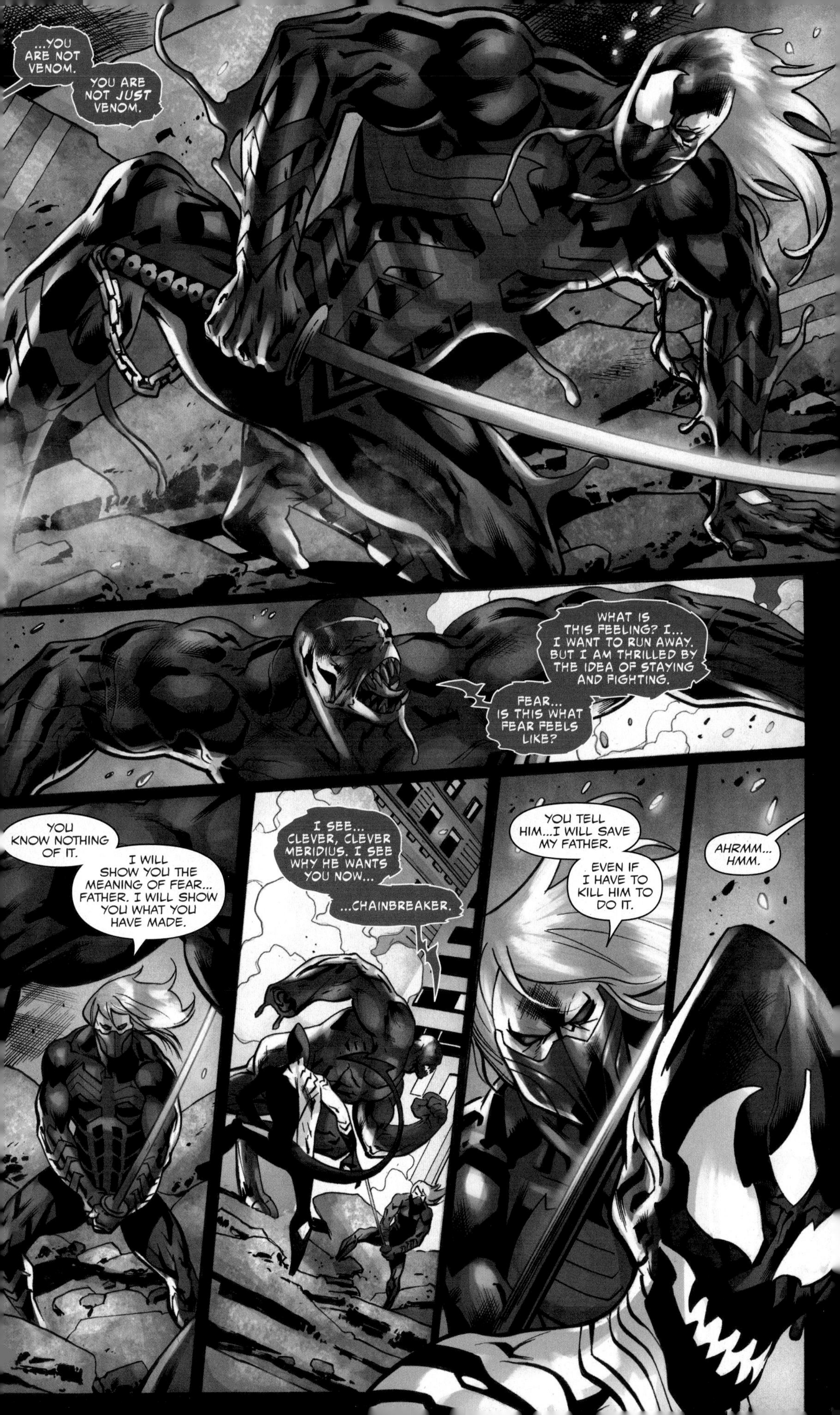
...YOU ARE NOT VENOM.
YOU ARE NOT JUST VENOM.
WHAT IS THIS FEELING? I... I WANT TO RUN AWAY. BUT I AM THRILLED BY THE IDEA OF STAYING AND FIGHTING.
FEAR... IS THIS WHAT FEAR FEELS LIKE?
YOU KNOW NOTHING OF IT.
I WILL SHOW YOU THE MEANING OF FEAR... FATHER. I WILL SHOW YOU WHAT YOU HAVE MADE.
I SEE... CLEVER, CLEVER MERIDIUS. I SEE WHY HE WANTS YOU NOW...
...CHAINBREAKER.
YOU TELL HIM...I WILL SAVE MY FATHER.
EVEN IF I HAVE TO KILL HIM TO DO IT.
AHRMM... HMM.

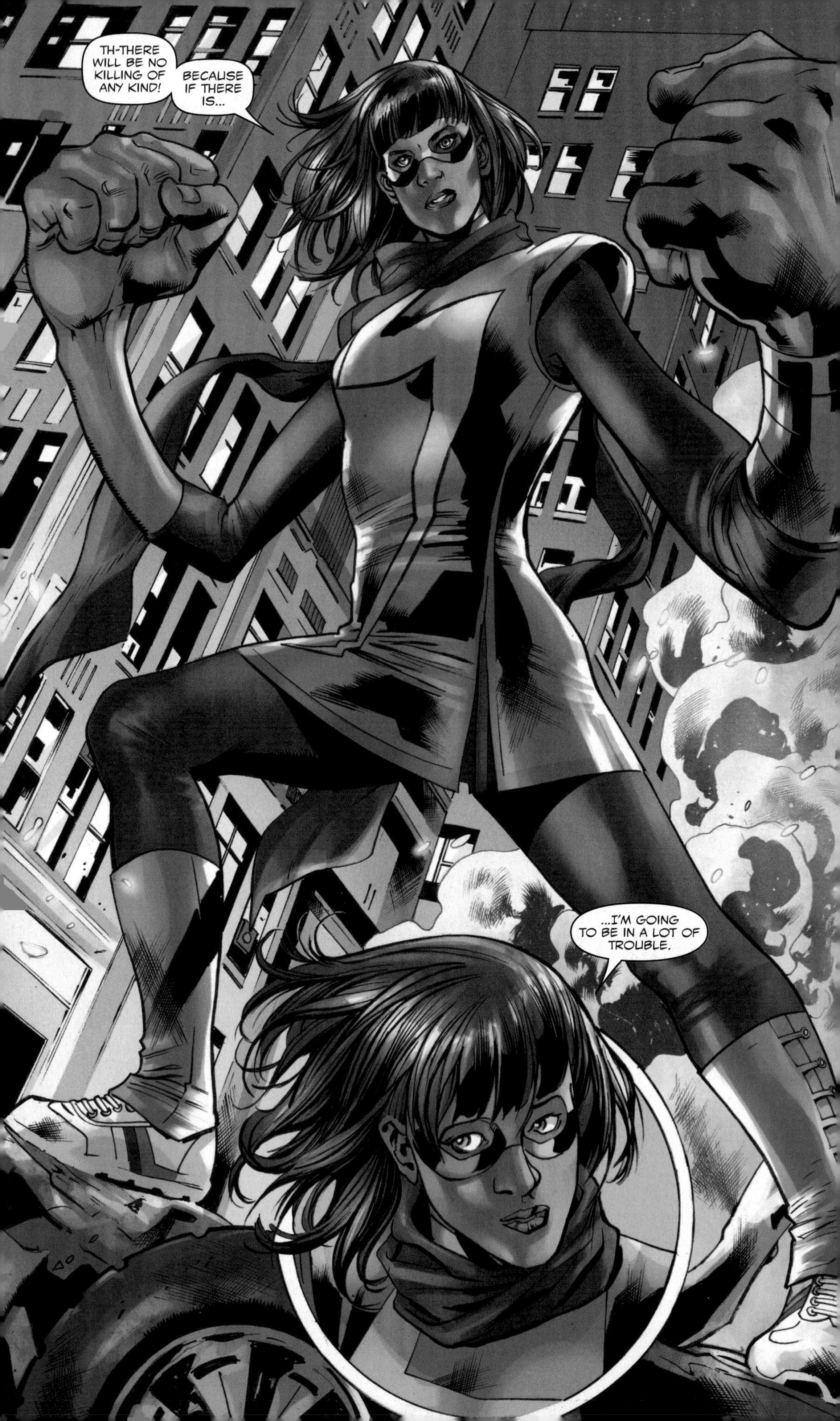
TH-THERE WILL BE NO KILLING OF ANY KIND!
BECAUSE IF THERE IS...
...I'M GOING TO BE IN A LOT OF TROUBLE.

VENOM #16

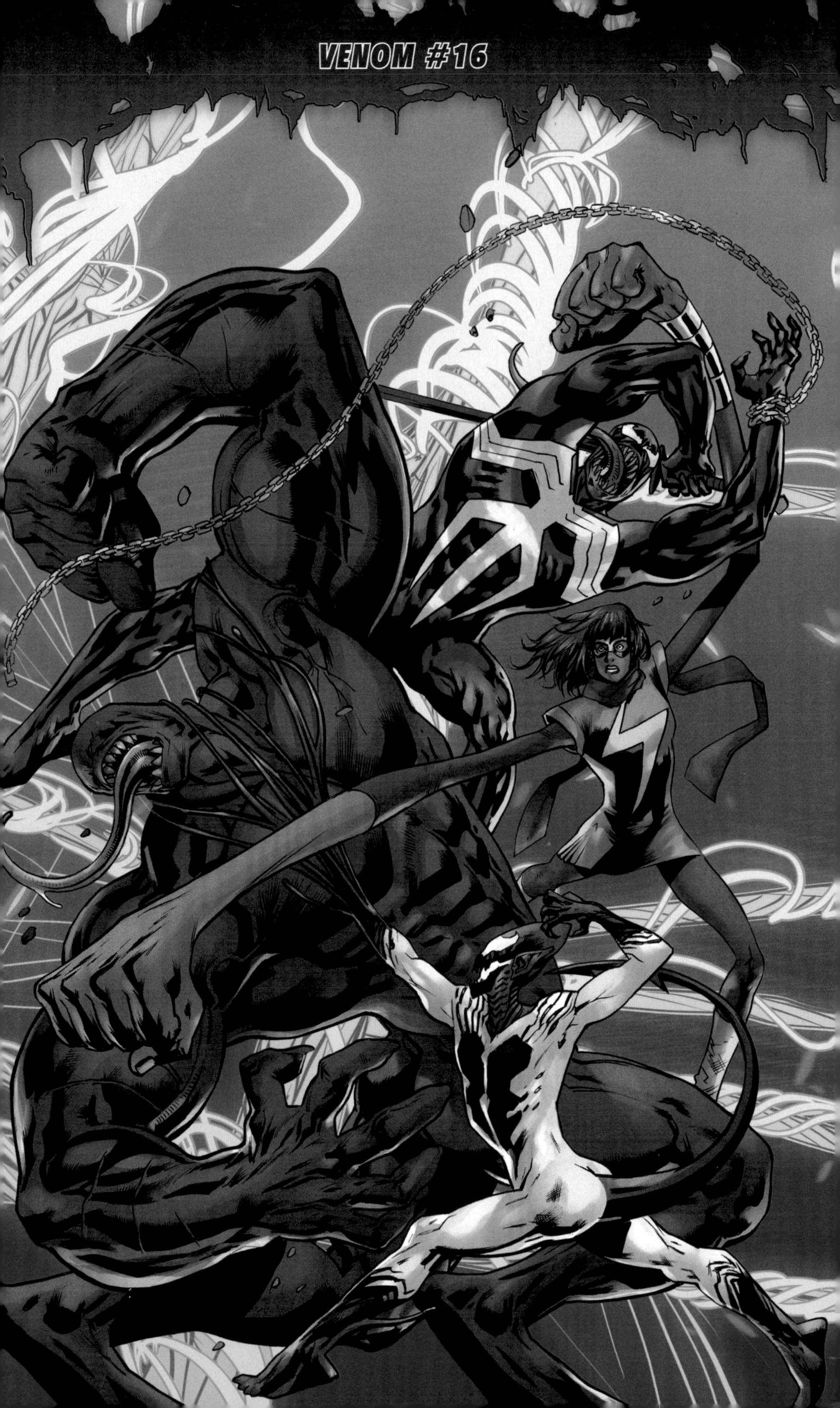

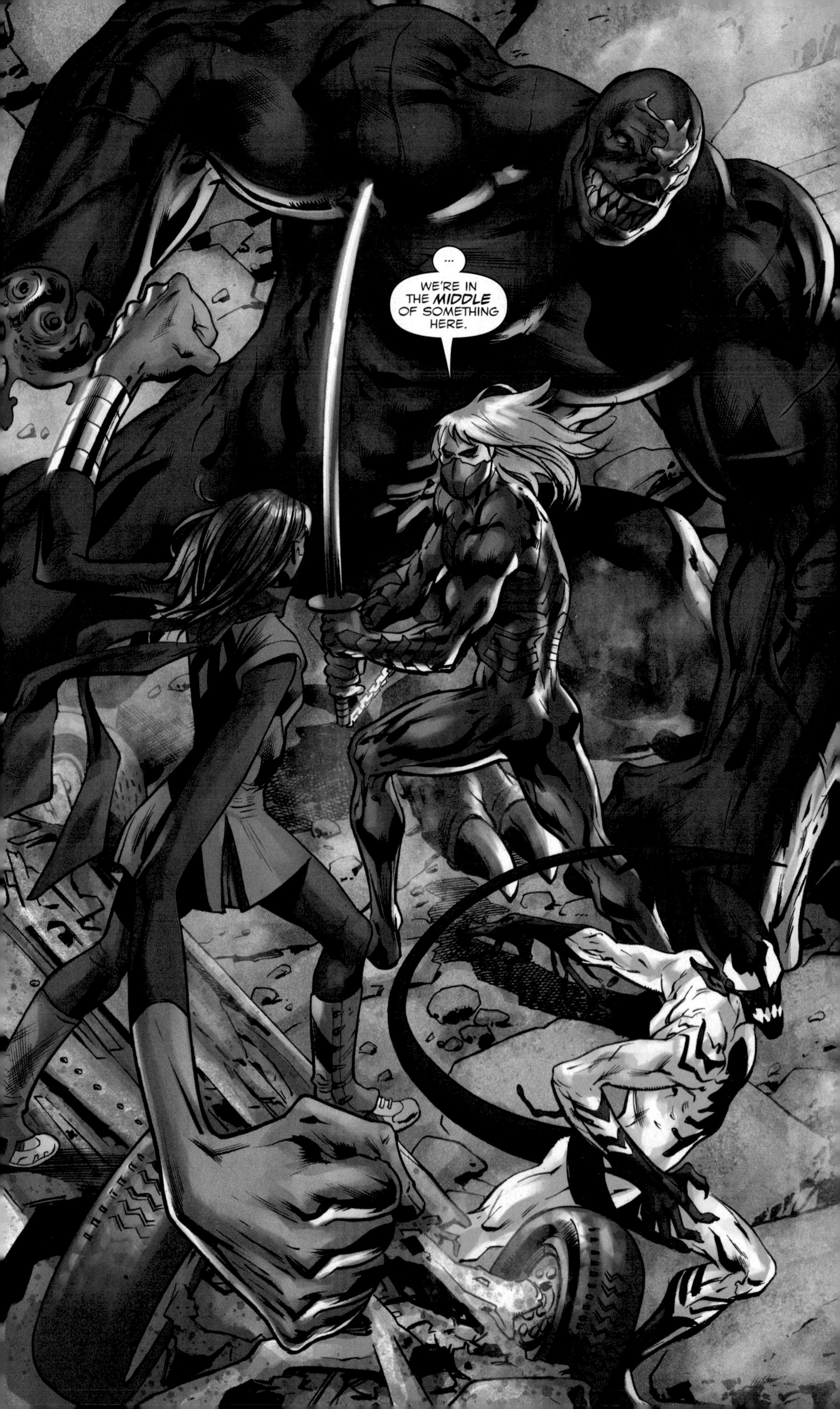
...
WE'RE IN THE MIDDLE OF SOMETHING HERE.

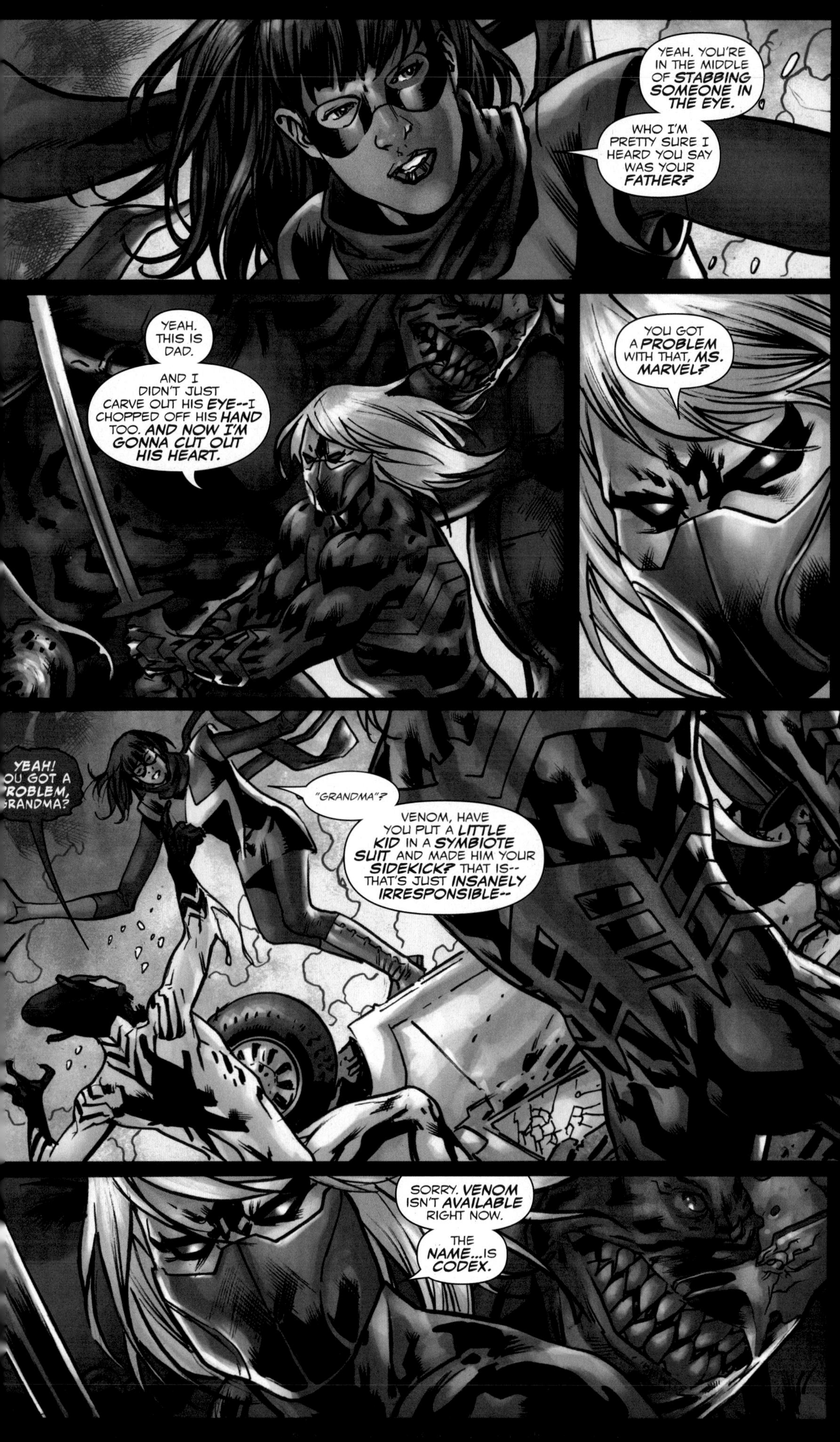
YEAH. YOU'RE IN THE MIDDLE OF STABBING SOMEONE IN THE EYE.
WHO I'M PRETTY SURE I HEARD YOU SAY WAS YOUR FATHER?
YEAH. THIS IS DAD.
AND I DIDN'T JUST CARVE OUT HIS EYE--I CHOPPED OFF HIS HAND TOO. AND NOW I'M GONNA CUT OUT HIS HEART.
YOU GOT A PROBLEM WITH THAT, MS. MARVEL?
YEAH! OU GOT A ROBLEM, RANDMA?
"GRANDMA"?
VENOM, HAVE YOU PUT A LITTLE KID IN A SYMBIOTE SUIT AND MADE HIM YOUR SIDEKICK? THAT IS-- THAT'S JUST INSANELY IRRESPONSIBLE--
SORRY. VENOM ISN'T AVAILABLE RIGHT NOW.
THE NAME...IS CODEX.

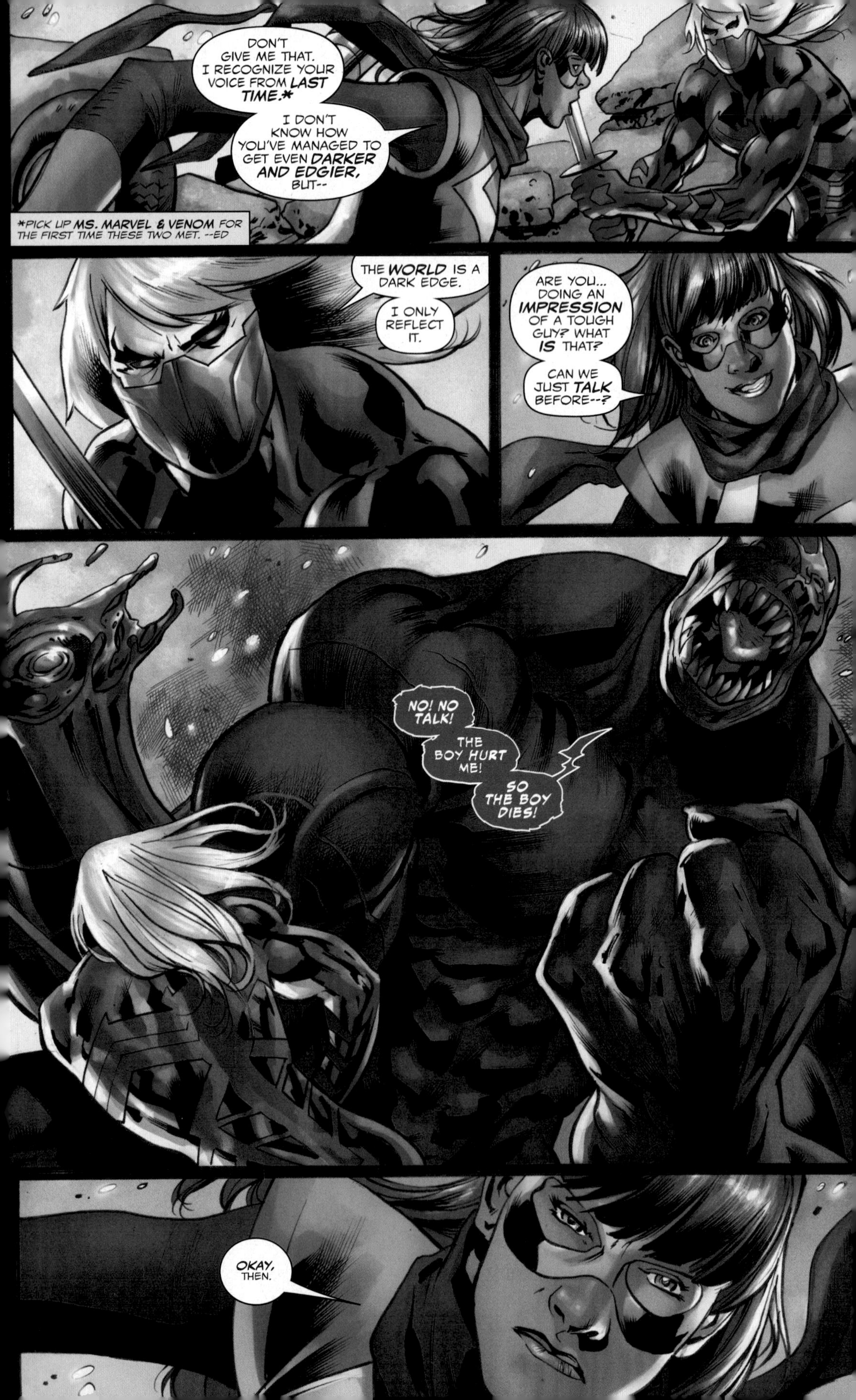
DON'T GIVE ME THAT. I RECOGNIZE YOUR VOICE FROM LAST TIME.*
I DON'T KNOW HOW YOU'VE MANAGED TO GET EVEN DARKER AND EDGIER, BUT--
*PICK UP MS. MARVEL & VENOM FOR THE FIRST TIME THESE TWO MET. --ED
THE WORLD IS A DARK EDGE.
I ONLY REFLECT IT.
ARE YOU... DOING AN IMPRESSION OF A TOUGH GUY? WHAT IS THAT?
CAN WE JUST TALK BEFORE--?
NO! NO TALK!
THE BOY HURT ME!
SO THE BOY DIES!
OKAY, THEN.

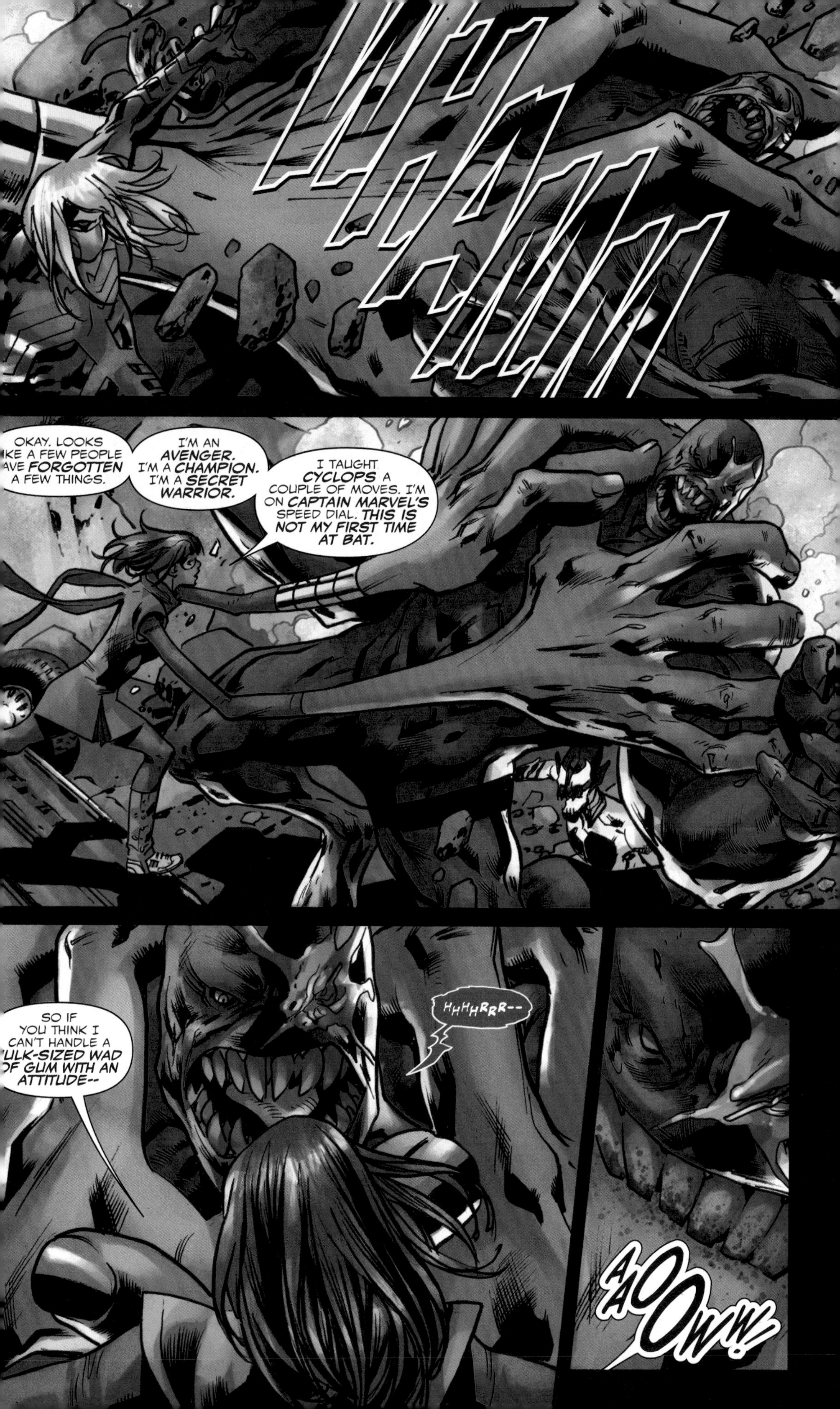

OKAY. LOOKS
IKE A FEW PEOPLE
AVE FORGOTTEN
A FEW THINGS.
I'M AN AVENGER. I'M A CHAMPION. I'M A SECRET WARRIOR.
I TAUGHT CYCLOPS A COUPLE OF MOVES. I'M ON CAPTAIN MARVEL'S SPEED DIAL. THIS IS NOT MY FIRST TIME AT BAT.
SO IF YOU THINK I CAN'T HANDLE A
ULK-SIZED WAD
OF GUM WITH AN ATTITUDE--
HHHHRRR--
AAOOWW!!

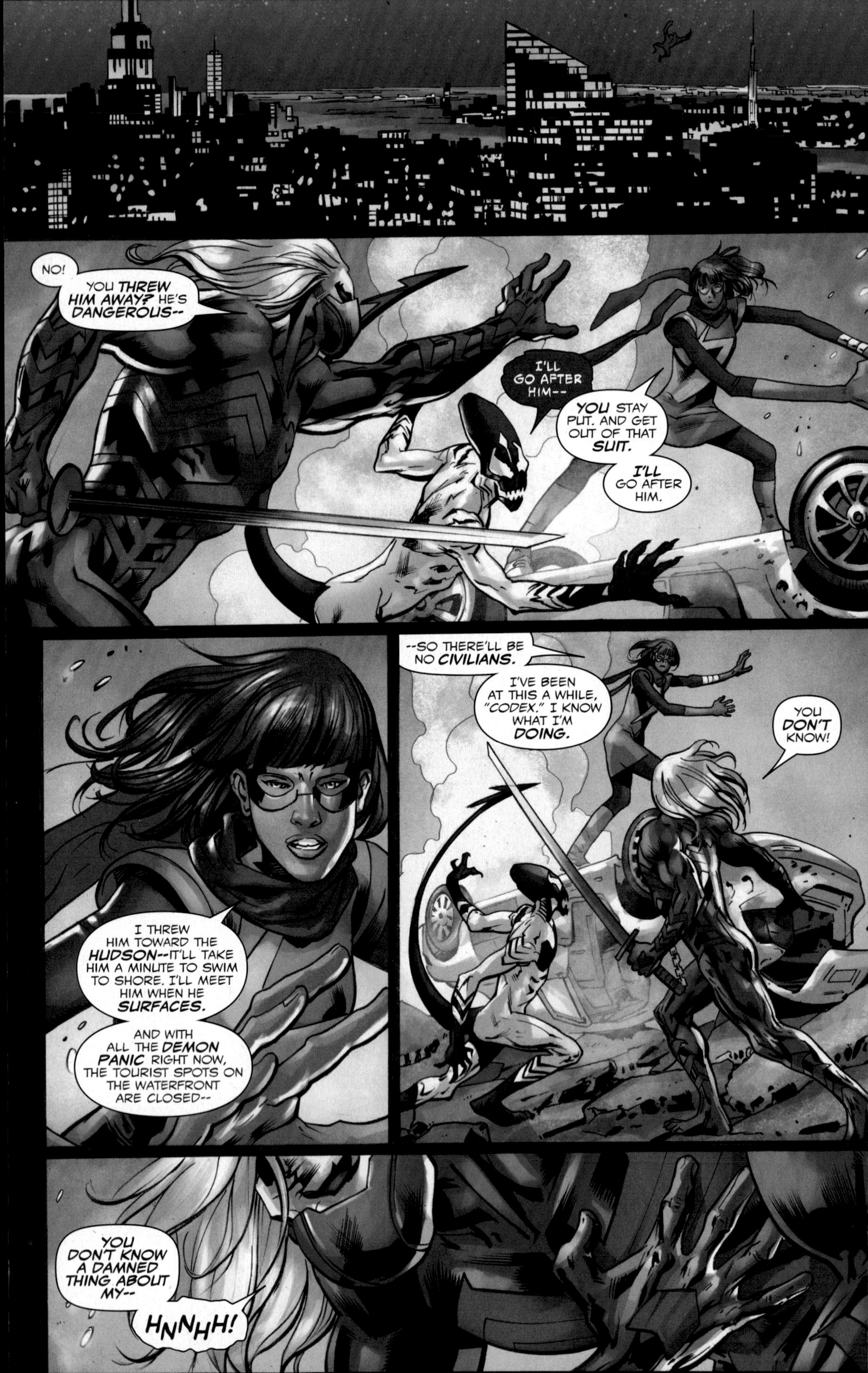
NO!
YOU THREW HIM AWAY? HE'S DANGEROUS--
I'LL GO AFTER HIM--
YOU STAY PUT. AND GET OUT OF THAT SUIT.
I'LL GO AFTER HIM.
I THREW HIM TOWARD THE HUDSON--IT'LL TAKE HIM A MINUTE TO SWIM TO SHORE. I'LL MEET HIM WHEN HE SURFACES.
AND WITH ALL THE DEMON PANIC RIGHT NOW, THE TOURIST SPOTS ON THE WATERFRONT ARE CLOSED--
--SO THERE'LL BE NO CIVILIANS.
I'VE BEEN AT THIS A WHILE, "CODEX." I KNOW WHAT I'M DOING.
YOU DON'T KNOW!
YOU DON'T KNOW A DAMNED THING ABOUT MY--
HNNHH!

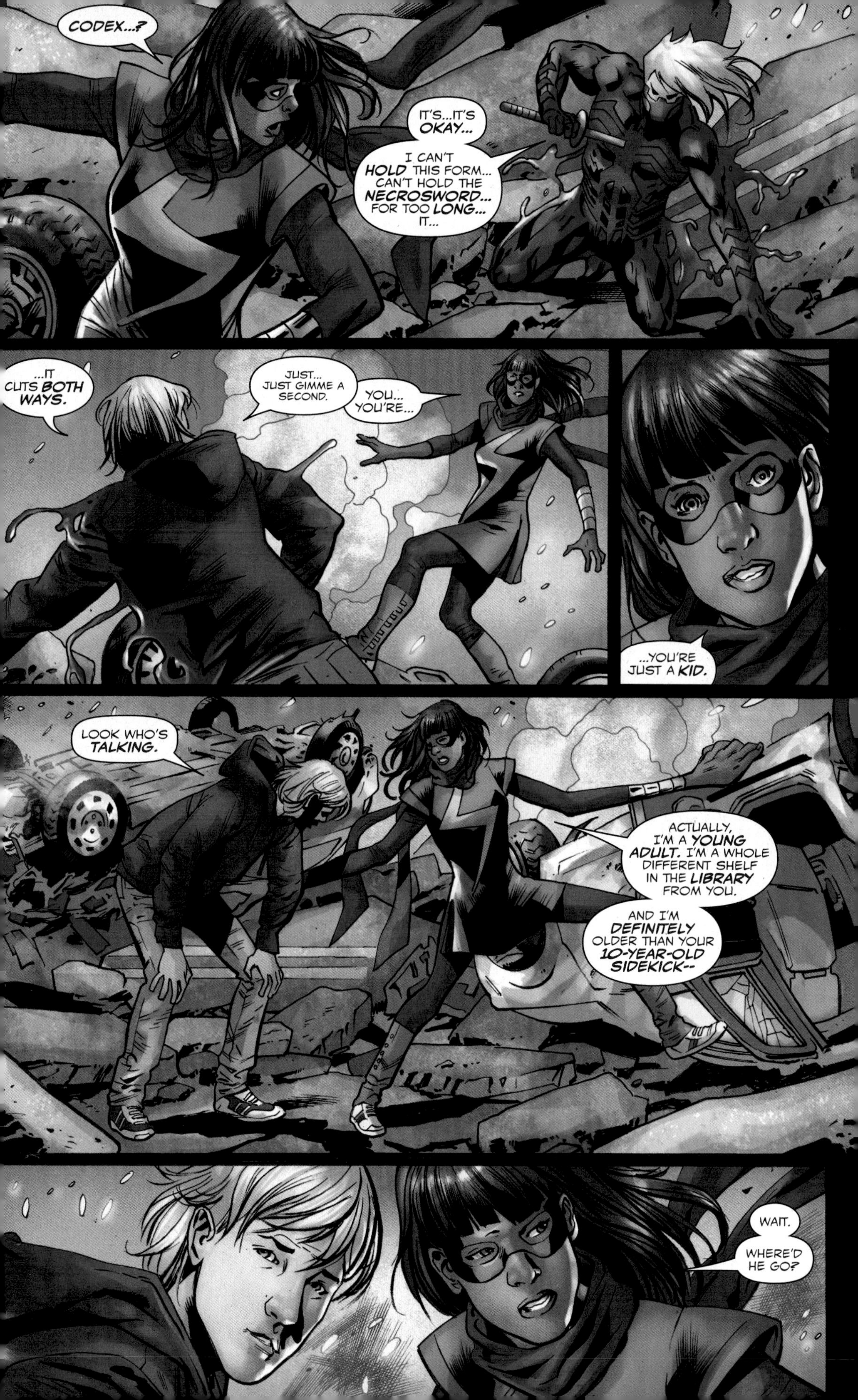
CODEX...?
IT'S...IT'S OKAY...
I CAN'T HOLD THIS FORM... CAN'T HOLD THE NECROSWORD... FOR TOO LONG... IT...
...IT CUTS BOTH WAYS.
JUST... JUST GIMME A SECOND.
YOU... YOU'RE...
...YOU'RE JUST A KID.
LOOK WHO'S TALKING.
ACTUALLY, I'M A YOUNG ADULT. I'M A WHOLE DIFFERENT SHELF IN THE LIBRARY FROM YOU.
AND I'M DEFINITELY OLDER THAN YOUR 10-YEAR-OLD SIDEKICK--
WAIT.
WHERE'D HE GO?

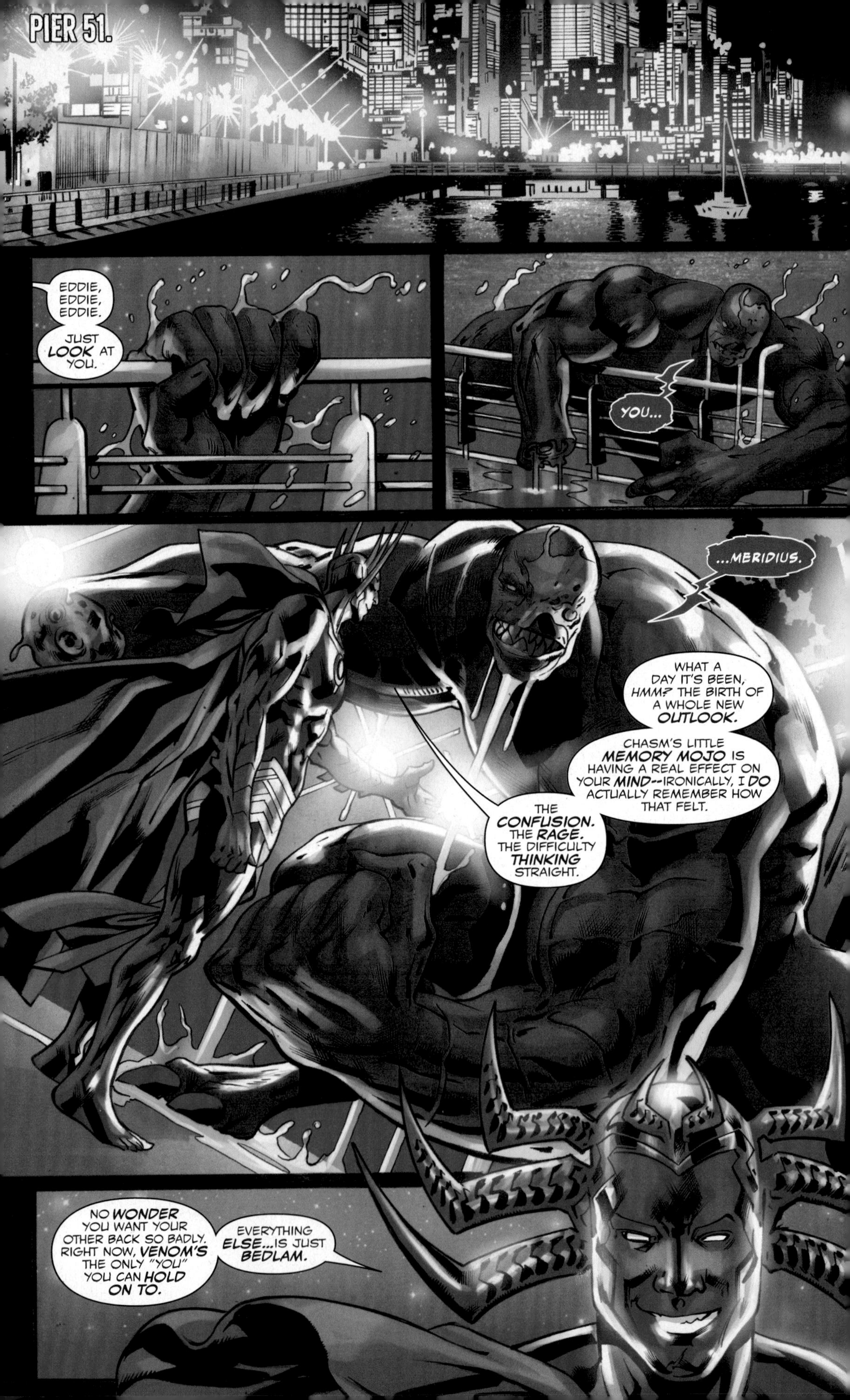
PIER 51.
EDDIE, EDDIE, EDDIE.
JUST LOOK AT YOU.
YOU...
...MERIDIUS.
WHAT A DAY IT'S BEEN, HMM? THE BIRTH OF A WHOLE NEW OUTLOOK.
CHASM'S LITTLE MEMORY MOJO IS HAVING A REAL EFFECT ON YOUR MIND--IRONICALLY, I DO ACTUALLY REMEMBER HOW THAT FELT.
THE CONFUSION. THE RAGE. THE DIFFICULTY THINKING STRAIGHT.
NO WONDER YOU WANT YOUR OTHER BACK SO BADLY. RIGHT NOW, VENOM'S THE ONLY "YOU" YOU CAN HOLD ON TO.
EVERYTHING ELSE...IS JUST BEDLAM.

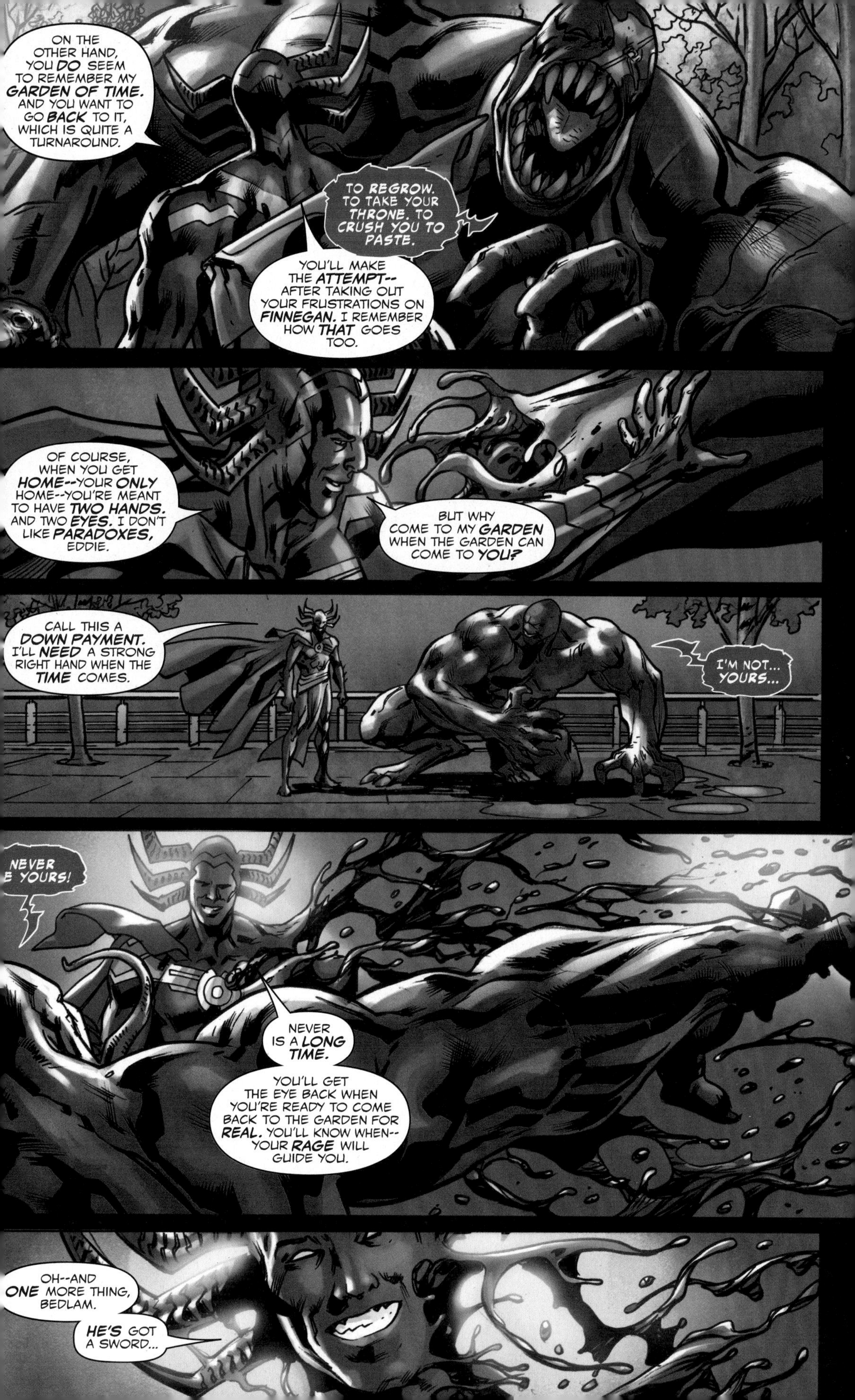
ON THE OTHER HAND, YOU DO SEEM TO REMEMBER MY GARDEN OF TIME. AND YOU WANT TO GO BACK TO IT, WHICH IS QUITE A TURNAROUND.
TO REGROW. TO TAKE YOUR THRONE. TO CRUSH YOU TO PASTE.
YOU'LL MAKE THE ATTEMPT-- AFTER TAKING OUT YOUR FRUSTRATIONS ON FINNEGAN. I REMEMBER HOW THAT GOES TOO.
OF COURSE, WHEN YOU GET HOME--YOUR ONLY HOME--YOU'RE MEANT TO HAVE TWO HANDS. AND TWO EYES. I DON'T LIKE PARADOXES, EDDIE.
BUT WHY COME TO MY GARDEN WHEN THE GARDEN CAN COME TO YOU?
CALL THIS A DOWN PAYMENT. I'LL NEED A STRONG RIGHT HAND WHEN THE TIME COMES.
I'M NOT... YOURS...
NEVER
E YOURS!
NEVER IS A LONG TIME.
YOU'LL GET THE EYE BACK WHEN YOU'RE READY TO COME BACK TO THE GARDEN FOR REAL. YOU'LL KNOW WHEN-- YOUR RAGE WILL GUIDE YOU.
OH--AND ONE MORE THING, BEDLAM.
HE'S GOT A SWORD...

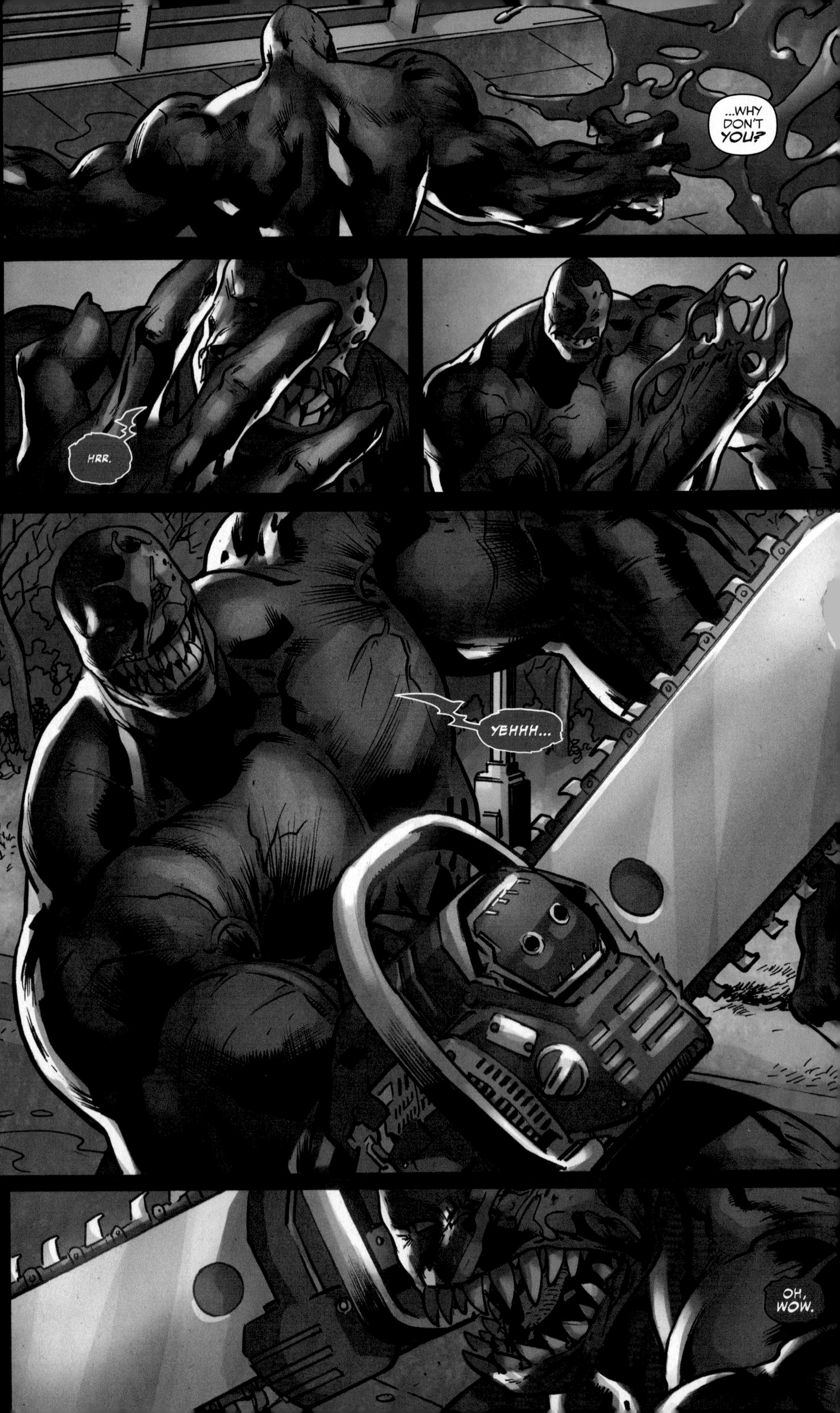
...WHY DON'T YOU?
HRR.
YEHHH...
OH, WOW.

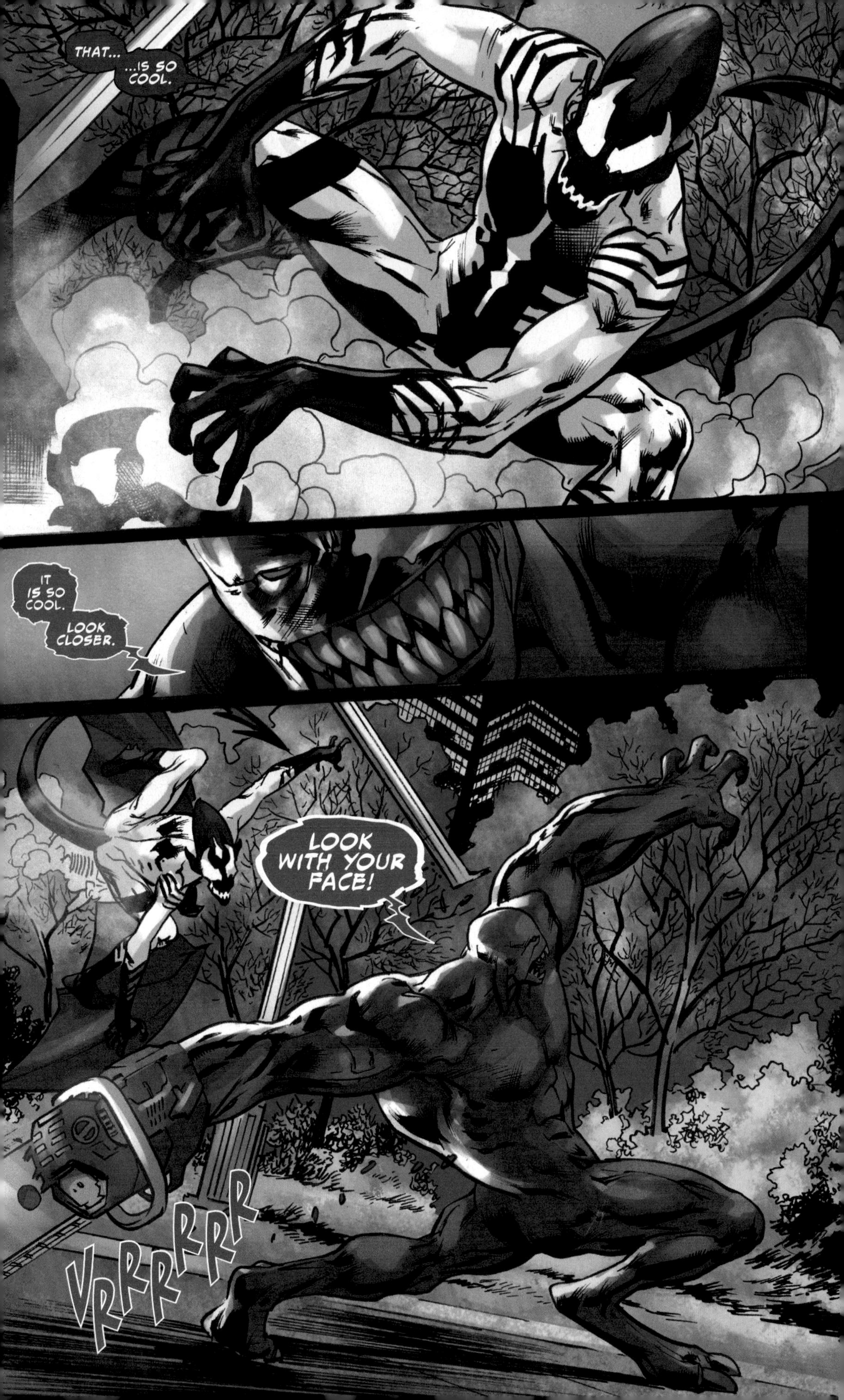
THAT...
...IS SO COOL.
IT IS SO COOL.
LOOK CLOSER.
IT IS SO COOL.
LOOK WITH YOUR FACE!
VRRRRRR

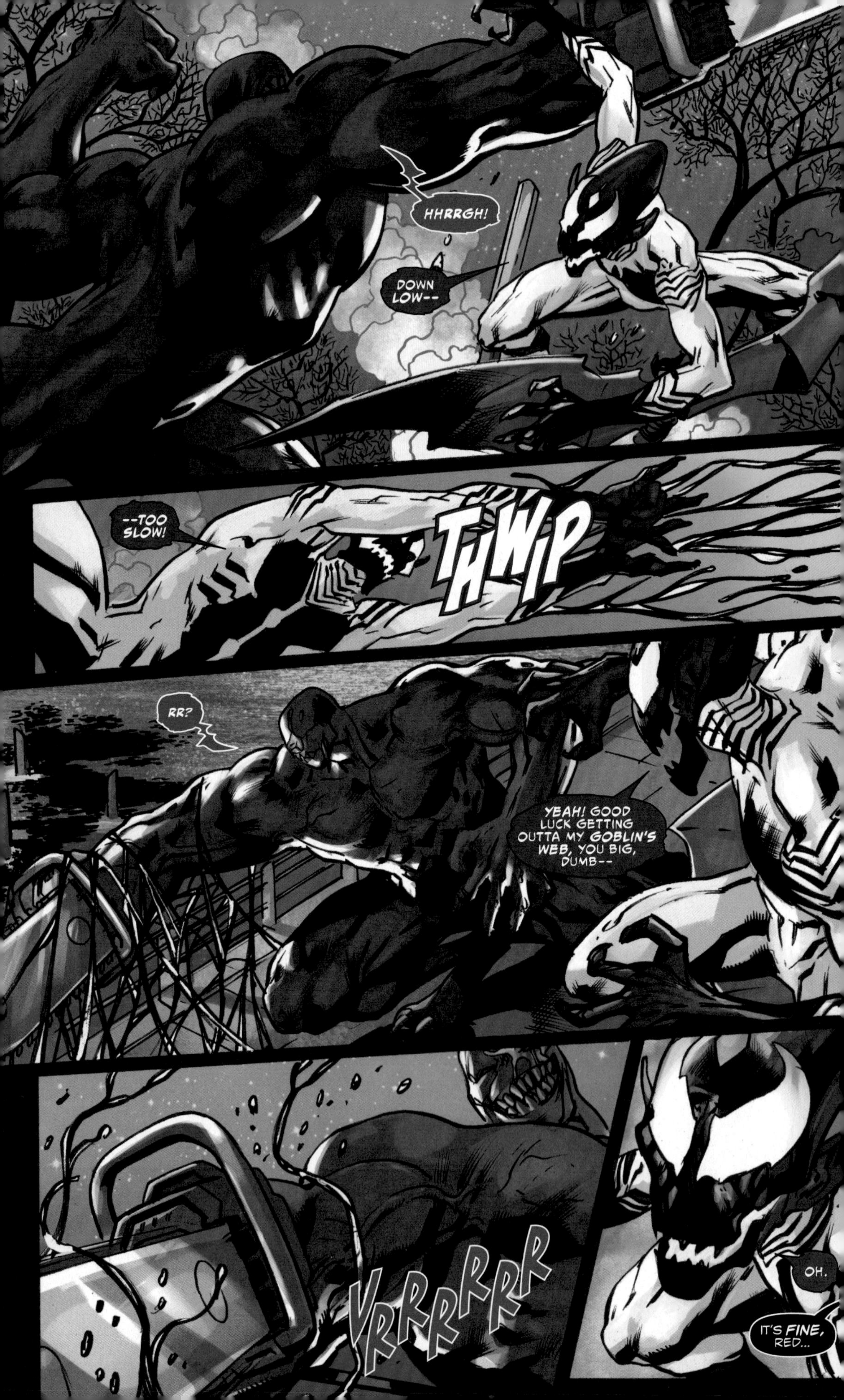
HHRRGH!
DOWN LOW--
--TOO SLOW!
THWIP
RR?
YEAH! GOOD LUCK GETTING OUTTA MY GOBLIN'S WEB, YOU BIG, DUMB--
VRRRRRR
OH.
IT'S FINE, RED...

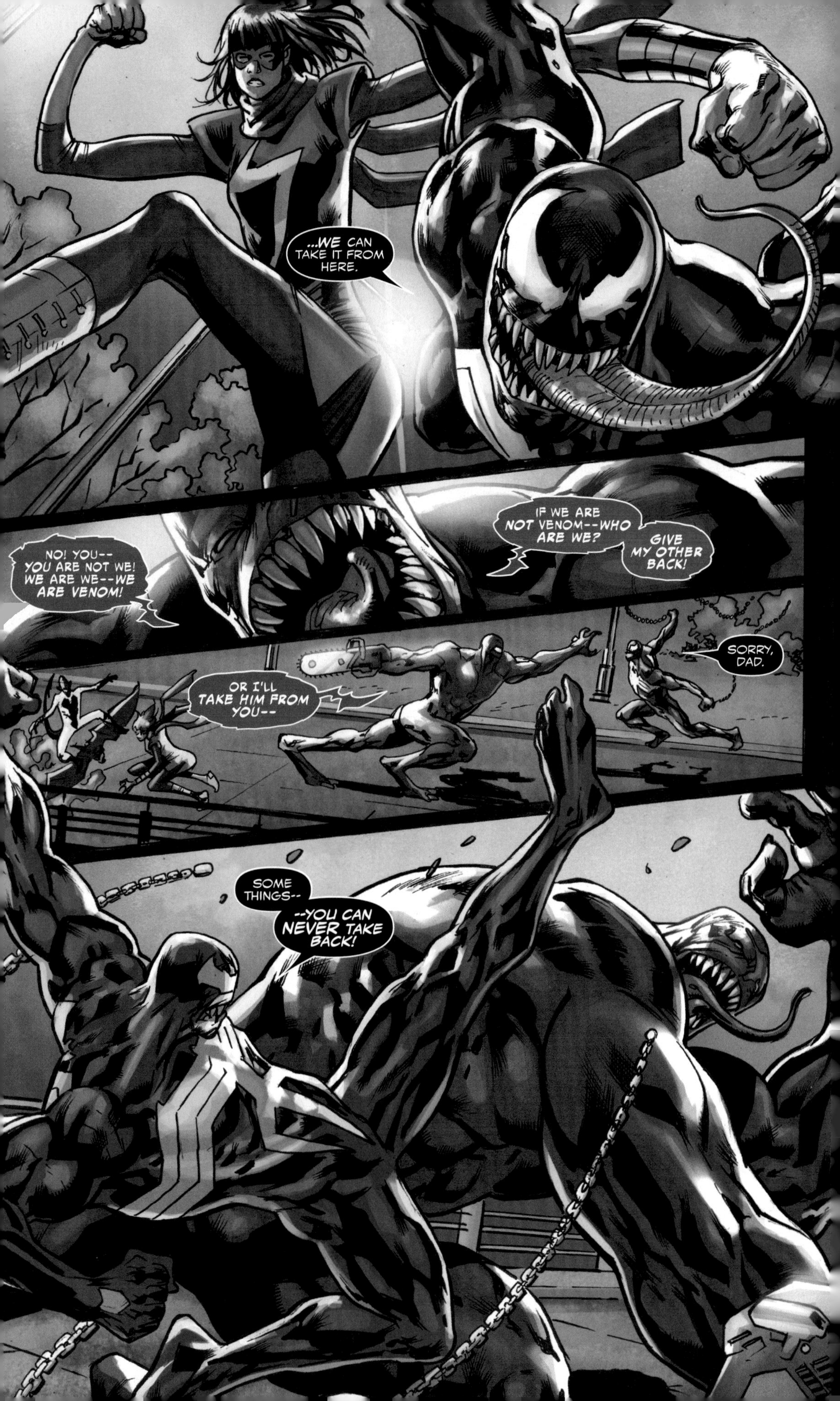
...WE CAN TAKE IT FROM HERE.
NO! YOU-- YOU ARE NOT WE! WE ARE WE--WE ARE VENOM!
IF WE ARE NOT VENOM--WHO ARE WE?
GIVE MY OTHER BACK!
OR I'LL TAKE HIM FROM YOU--
SORRY, DAD.
SOME THINGS--
--YOU CAN NEVER TAKE BACK!

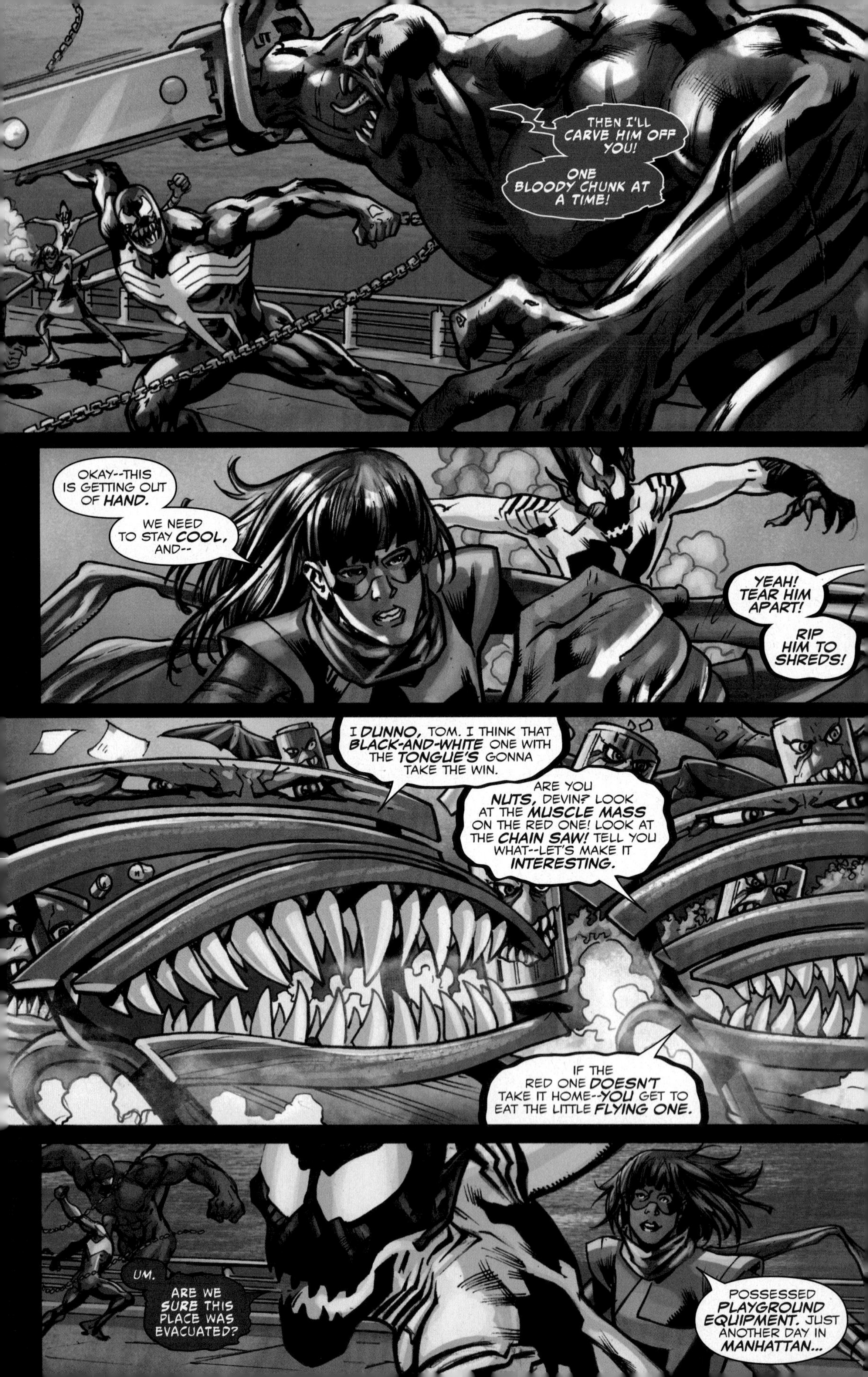
THEN I'LL CARVE HIM OFF YOU!
ONE BLOODY CHUNK AT A TIME!
OKAY--THIS IS GETTING OUT OF HAND.
WE NEED TO STAY COOL, AND--
YEAH! TEAR HIM APART!
RIP HIM TO SHREDS!
I DUNNO, TOM. I THINK THAT BLACK-AND-WHITE ONE WITH THE TONGUE'S GONNA TAKE THE WIN.
ARE YOU NUTS, DEVIN? LOOK AT THE MUSCLE MASS ON THE RED ONE! LOOK AT THE CHAIN SAW! TELL YOU WHAT--LET'S MAKE IT INTERESTING.
IF THE RED ONE DOESN'T TAKE IT HOME--YOU GET TO EAT THE LITTLE FLYING ONE.
UM.
ARE WE SURE THIS PLACE WAS EVACUATED?
POSSESSED PLAYGROUND EQUIPMENT. JUST ANOTHER DAY IN MANHATTAN...

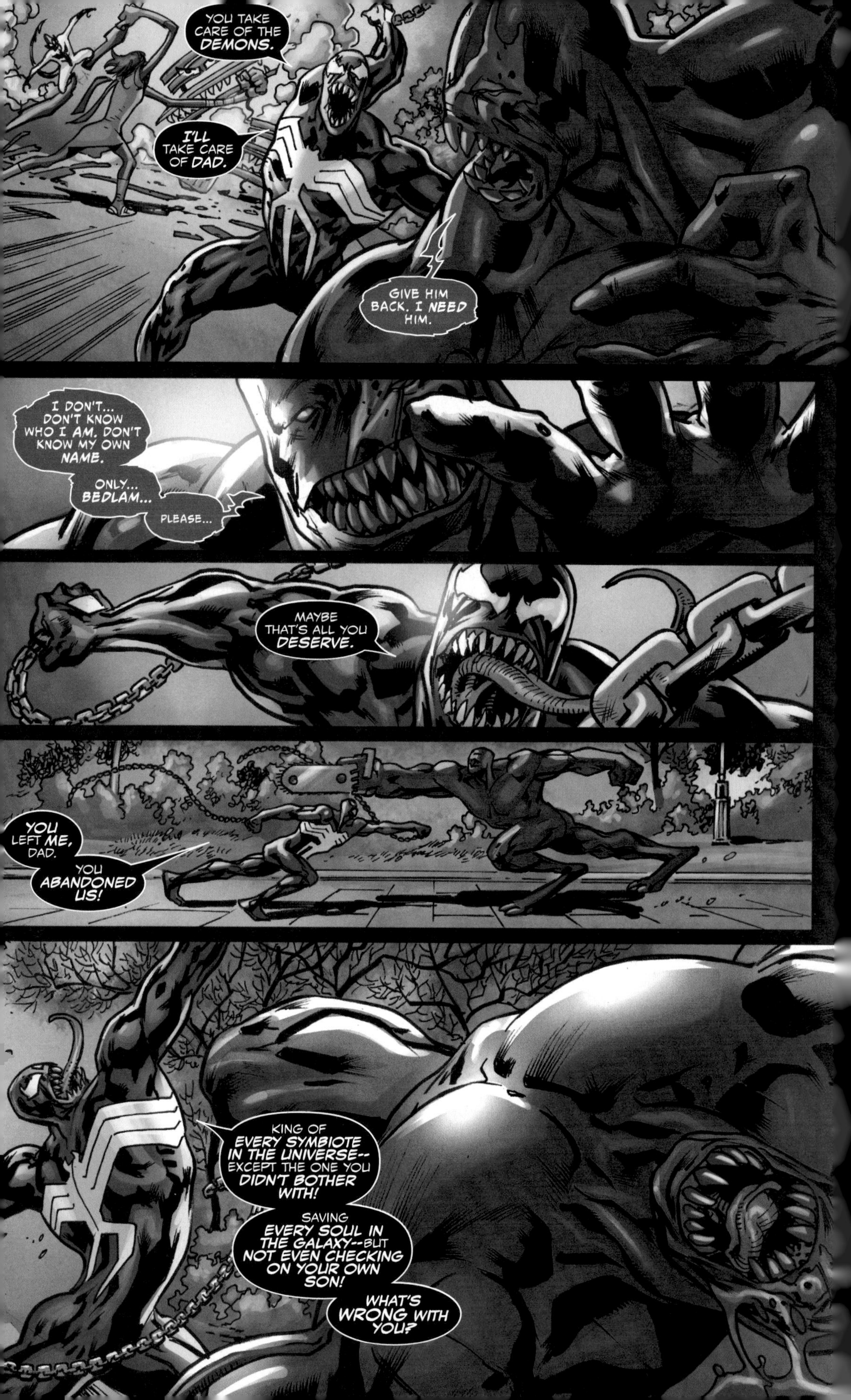
YOU TAKE CARE OF THE DEMONS.
I'LL TAKE CARE OF DAD.
GIVE HIM BACK. I NEED HIM.
I DON'T... DON'T KNOW WHO I AM. DON'T KNOW MY OWN NAME.
ONLY... BEDLAM...
PLEASE...
MAYBE THAT'S ALL YOU DESERVE.
YOU LEFT ME, DAD.
YOU ABANDONED US!
KING OF EVERY SYMBIOTE IN THE UNIVERSE-- EXCEPT THE ONE YOU DIDN'T BOTHER WITH!
SAVING EVERY SOUL IN THE GALAXY--BUT NOT EVEN CHECKING ON YOUR OWN SON!
WHAT'S WRONG WITH YOU?

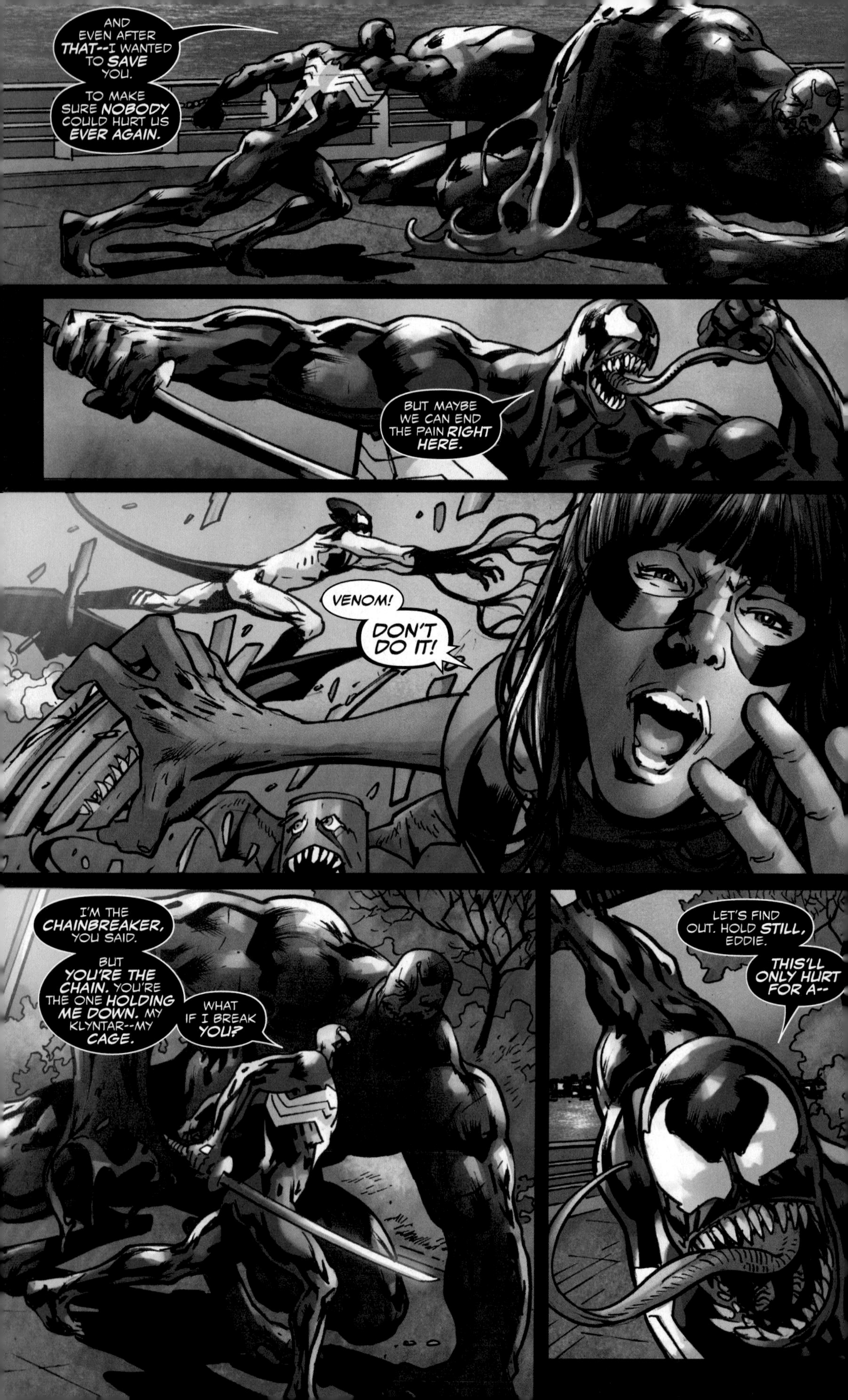
AND EVEN AFTER THAT--I WANTED TO SAVE YOU.
TO MAKE SURE NOBODY COULD HURT US EVER AGAIN.
BUT MAYBE WE CAN END THE PAIN RIGHT HERE.
VENOM!
DON'T DO IT!
I'M THE CHAINBREAKER, YOU SAID.
BUT YOU'RE THE CHAIN. YOU'RE THE ONE HOLDING ME DOWN. MY KLYNTAR--MY CAGE.
WHAT IF I BREAK YOU?
LET'S FIND OUT. HOLD STILL, EDDIE.
THIS'LL ONLY HURT FOR A--

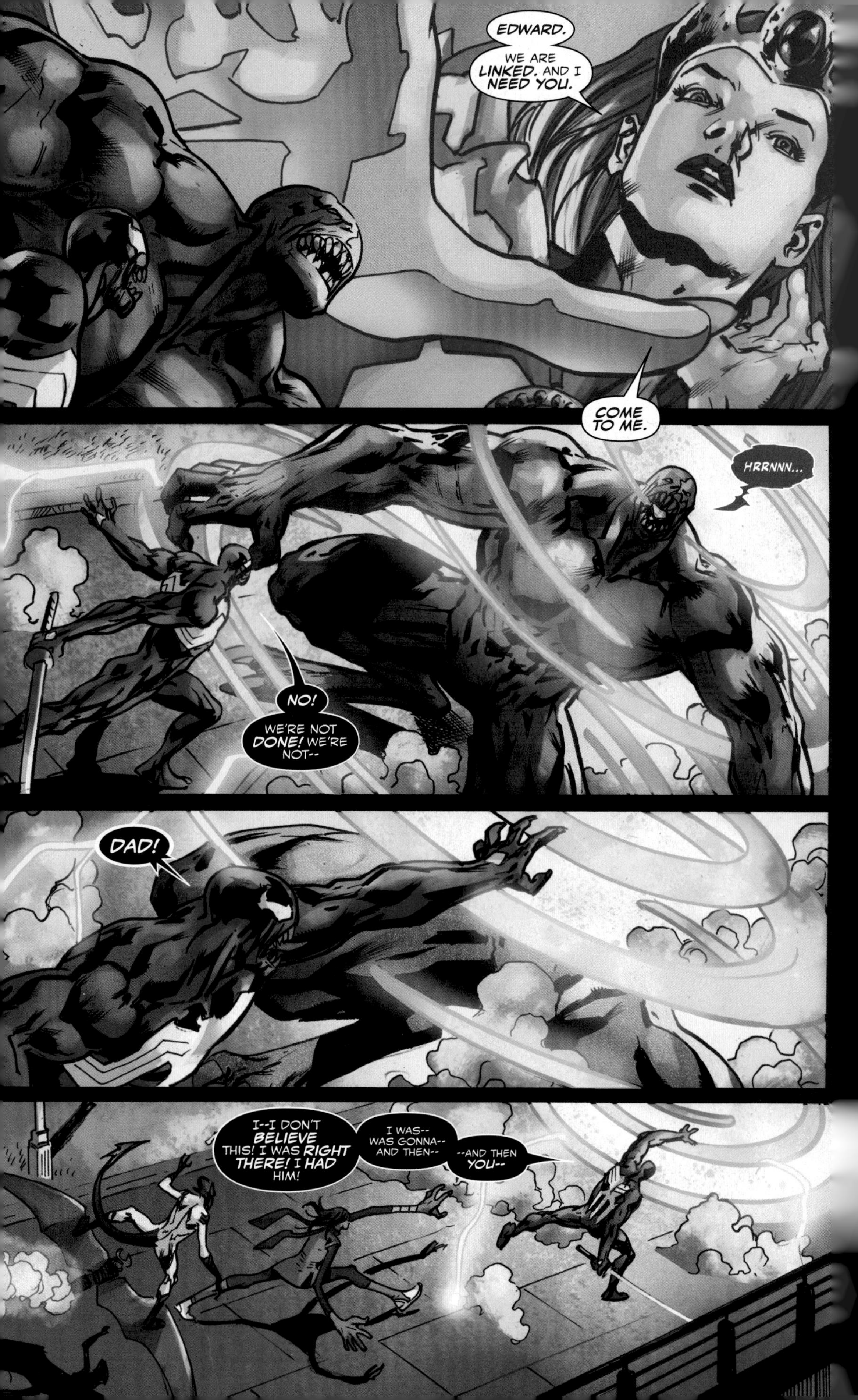
EDWARD.
WE ARE LINKED. AND I NEED YOU.
COME TO ME.
HRRNNN...
NO!
WE'RE NOT DONE! WE'RE NOT--
DAD!
I--I DON'T BELIEVE THIS! I WAS RIGHT THERE! I HAD HIM!
I WAS-- WAS GONNA-- AND THEN--
--AND THEN YOU--

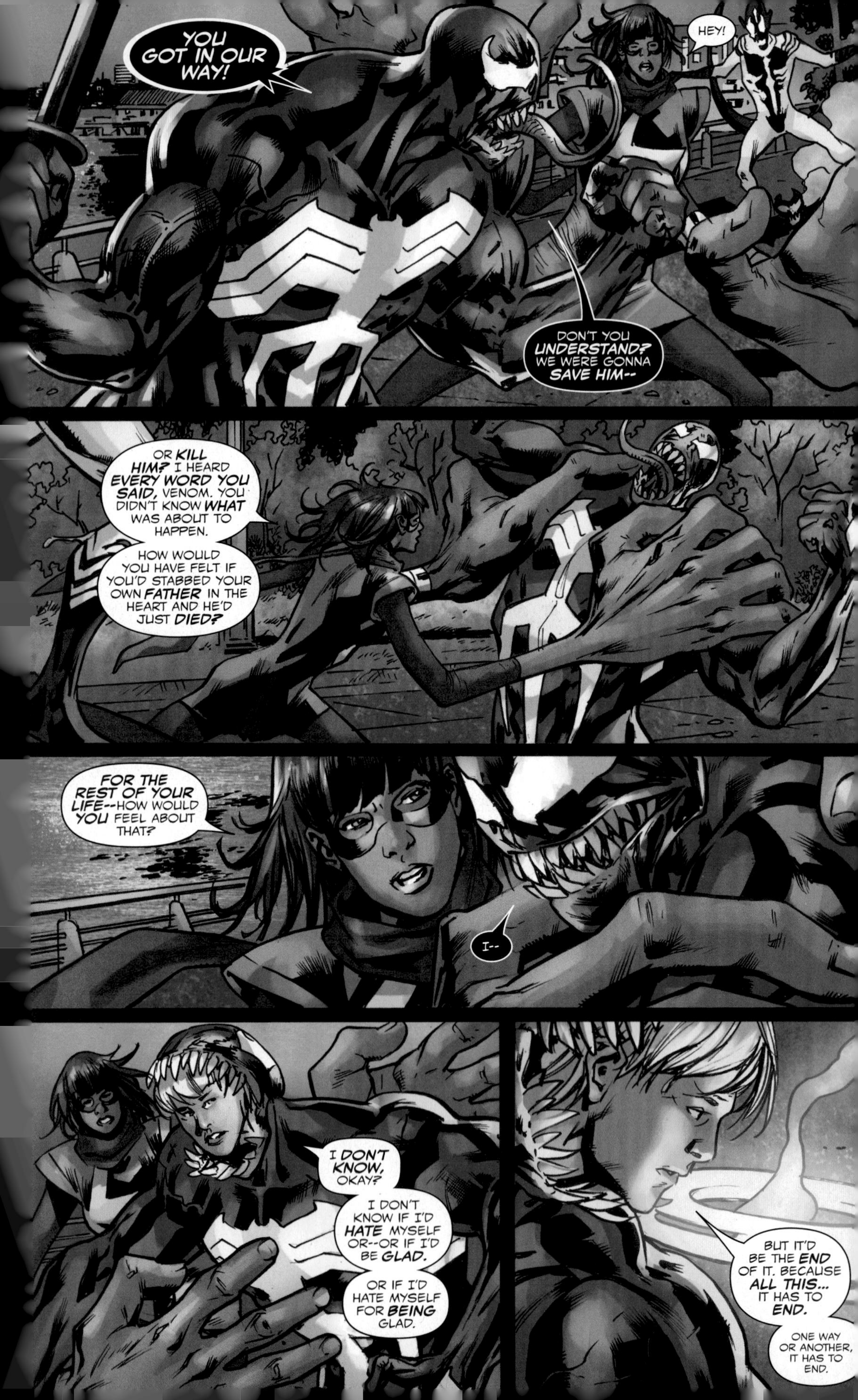
YOU GOT IN OUR WAY!
HEY!
DON'T YOU UNDERSTAND? WE WERE GONNA SAVE HIM--
OR KILL HIM? I HEARD EVERY WORD YOU SAID, VENOM. YOU DIDN'T KNOW WHAT WAS ABOUT TO HAPPEN.
HOW WOULD YOU HAVE FELT IF YOU'D STABBED YOUR OWN FATHER IN THE HEART AND HE'D JUST DIED?
FOR THE REST OF YOUR LIFE--HOW WOULD YOU FEEL ABOUT THAT?
I--
I DON'T KNOW, OKAY?
I DON'T KNOW IF I'D HATE MYSELF OR--OR IF I'D BE GLAD.
OR IF I'D HATE MYSELF FOR BEING GLAD.
BUT IT'D BE THE END OF IT. BECAUSE ALL THIS... IT HAS TO END.
ONE WAY OR ANOTHER, IT HAS TO END.

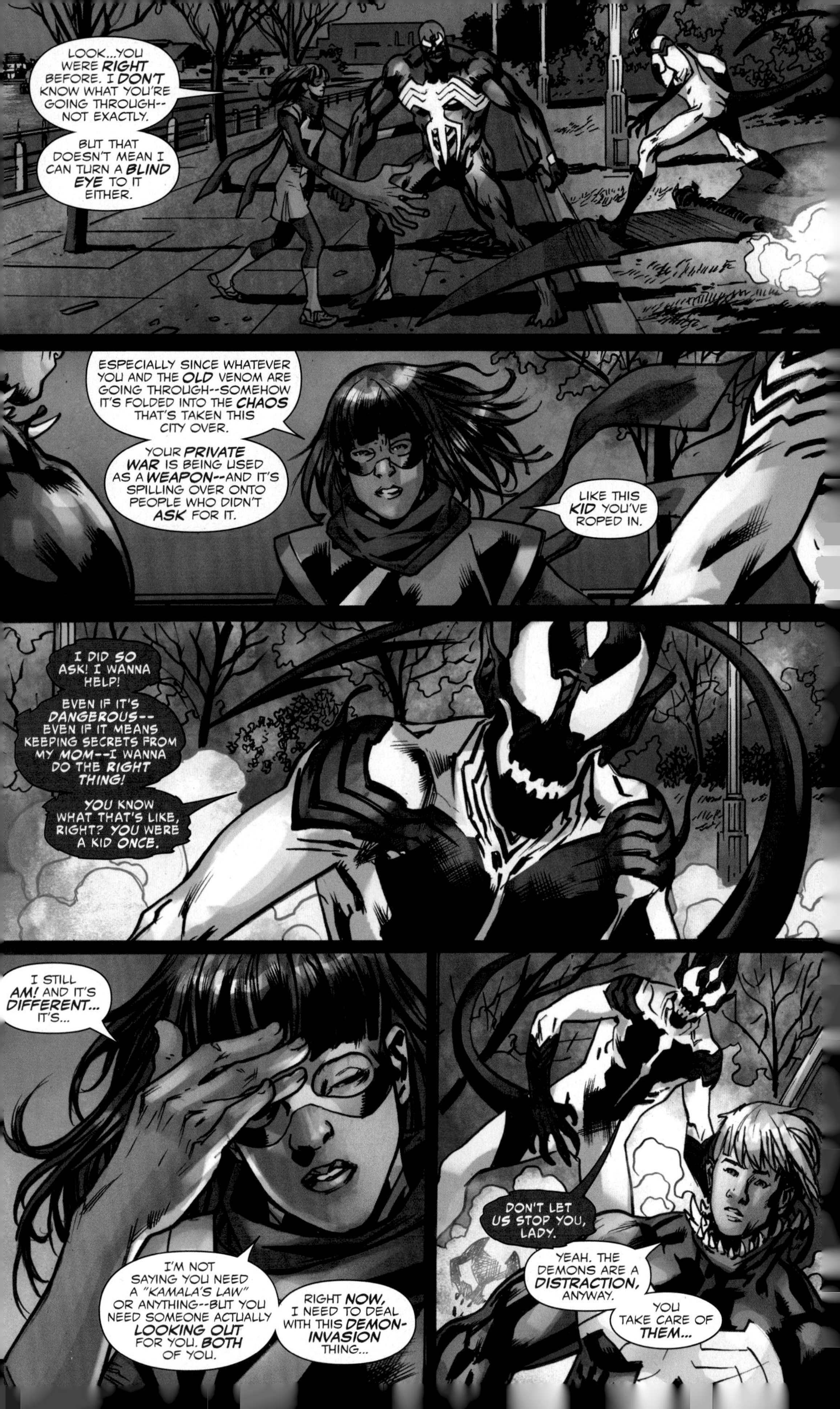
LOOK...YOU WERE RIGHT BEFORE. I DON'T KNOW WHAT YOU'RE GOING THROUGH--NOT EXACTLY.
BUT THAT DOESN'T MEAN I CAN TURN A BLIND EYE TO IT EITHER.
ESPECIALLY SINCE WHATEVER YOU AND THE OLD VENOM ARE GOING THROUGH--SOMEHOW IT'S FOLDED INTO THE CHAOS THAT'S TAKEN THIS CITY OVER.
YOUR PRIVATE WAR IS BEING USED AS A WEAPON--AND IT'S SPILLING OVER ONTO PEOPLE WHO DIDN'T ASK FOR IT.
LIKE THIS KID YOU'VE ROPED IN.
I DID SO ASK! I WANNA HELP!
EVEN IF IT'S DANGEROUS--EVEN IF IT MEANS KEEPING SECRETS FROM MY MOM--I WANNA DO THE RIGHT THING!
YOU KNOW WHAT THAT'S LIKE, RIGHT? YOU WERE A KID ONCE.
I STILL AM! AND IT'S DIFFERENT... IT'S...
I'M NOT SAYING YOU NEED A "KAMALA'S LAW" OR ANYTHING--BUT YOU NEED SOMEONE ACTUALLY LOOKING OUT FOR YOU. BOTH OF YOU.
RIGHT NOW, I NEED TO DEAL WITH THIS DEMON-INVASION THING...
DON'T LET US STOP YOU, LADY.
YEAH. THE DEMONS ARE A DISTRACTION, ANYWAY.
YOU TAKE CARE OF THEM...

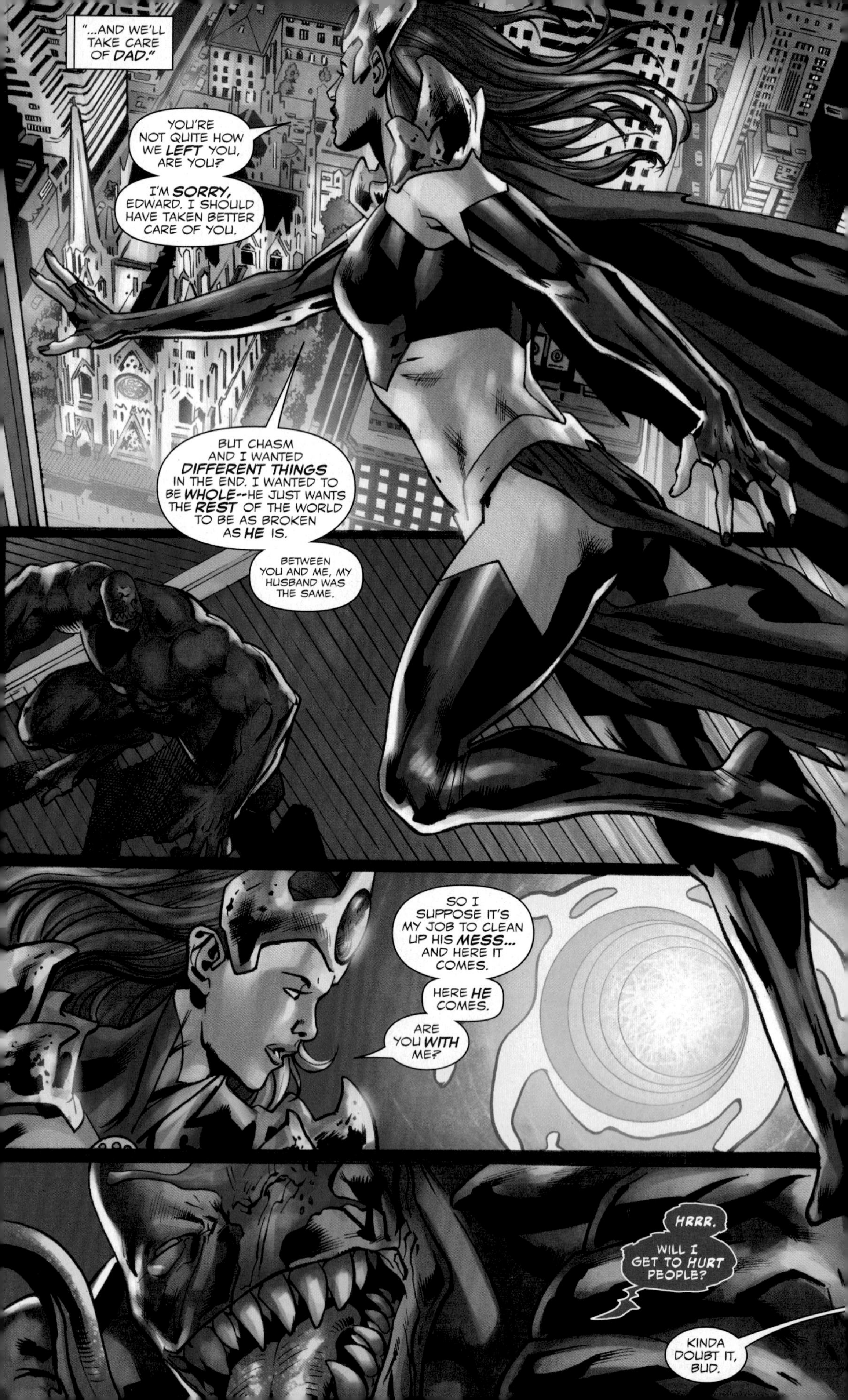
"...AND WE'LL TAKE CARE OF DAD."
YOU'RE NOT QUITE HOW WE LEFT YOU, ARE YOU?
I'M SORRY, EDWARD. I SHOULD HAVE TAKEN BETTER CARE OF YOU.
BUT CHASM AND I WANTED DIFFERENT THINGS IN THE END. I WANTED TO BE WHOLE--HE JUST WANTS THE REST OF THE WORLD TO BE AS BROKEN AS HE IS.
BETWEEN YOU AND ME, MY HUSBAND WAS THE SAME.
SO I SUPPOSE IT'S MY JOB TO CLEAN UP HIS MESS... AND HERE IT COMES.
HERE HE COMES.
ARE YOU WITH ME?
HRRR.
WILL I GET TO HURT PEOPLE?
KINDA DOUBT IT, BUD.

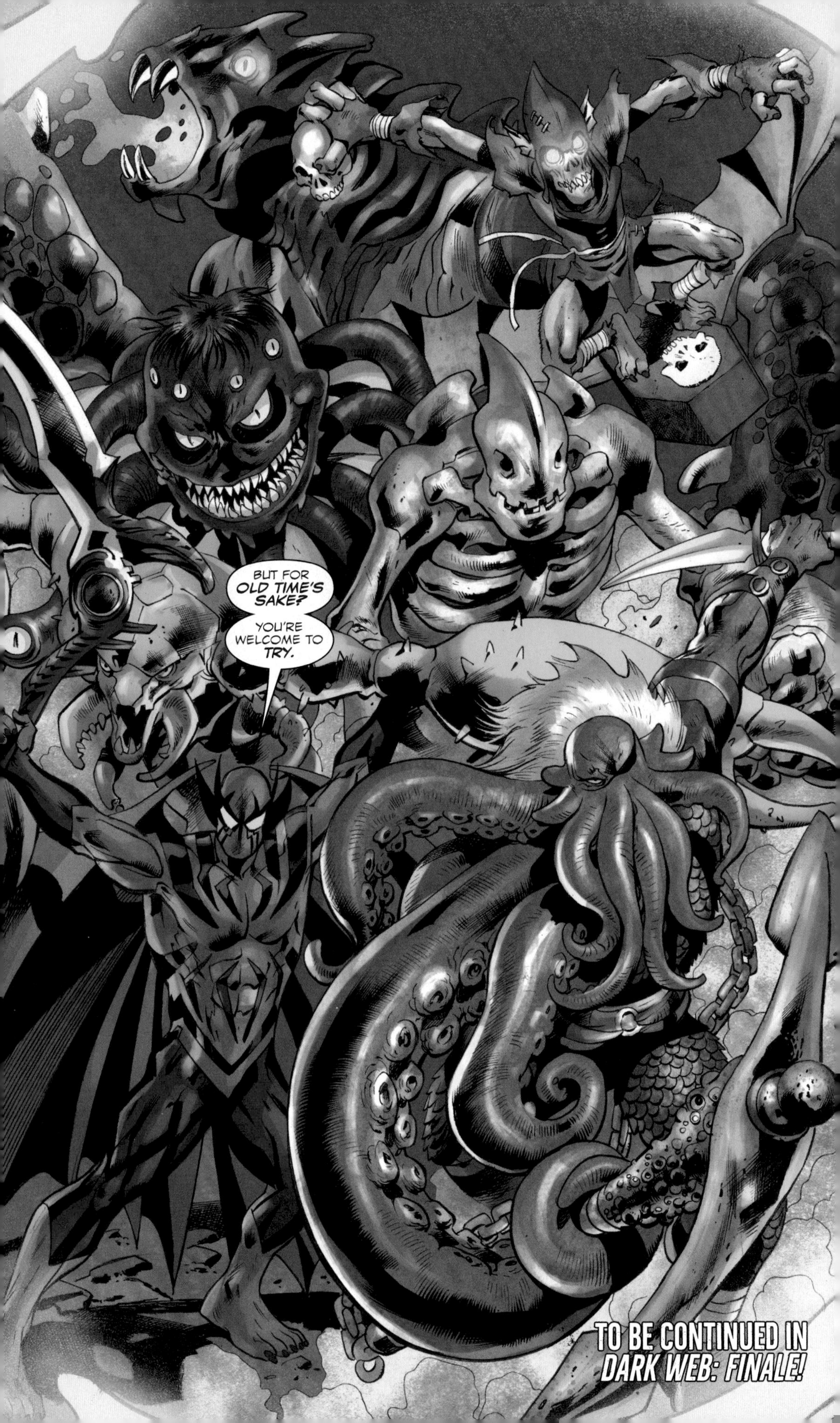
BUT FOR OLD TIME'S SAKE?
YOU'RE WELCOME TO TRY.
TO BE CONTINUED IN DARK WEB: FINALE!

DARK WEB: X-MEN #1

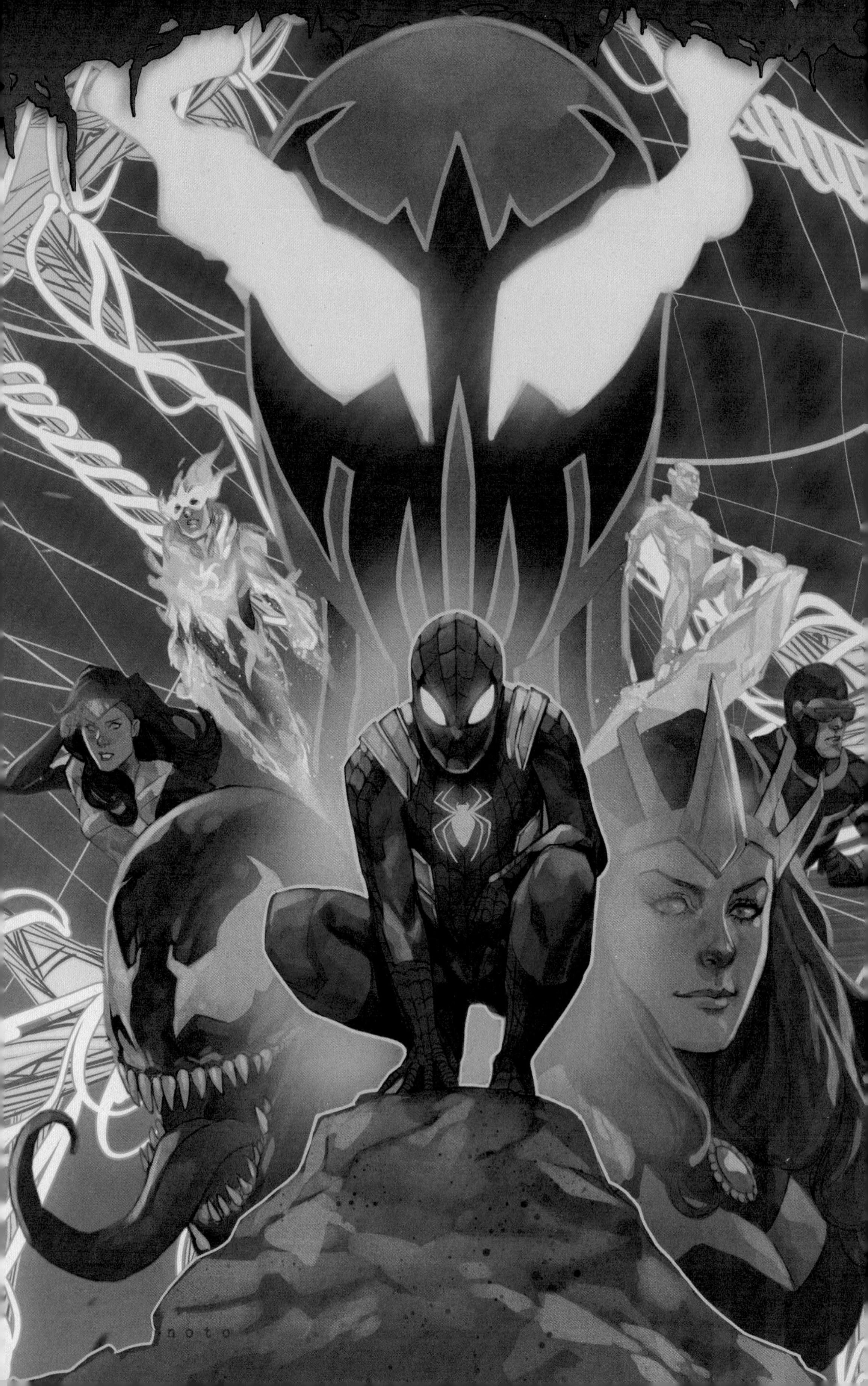
noto

[darkweb...[0.1]
[x_men.....[0.1]

"The holidays are magic, and that's bad news this year."

-- J. JONAH JAMESON

[darkweb...[0.1]
[x_men.....[0.1]

[darkweb_xmen_01]

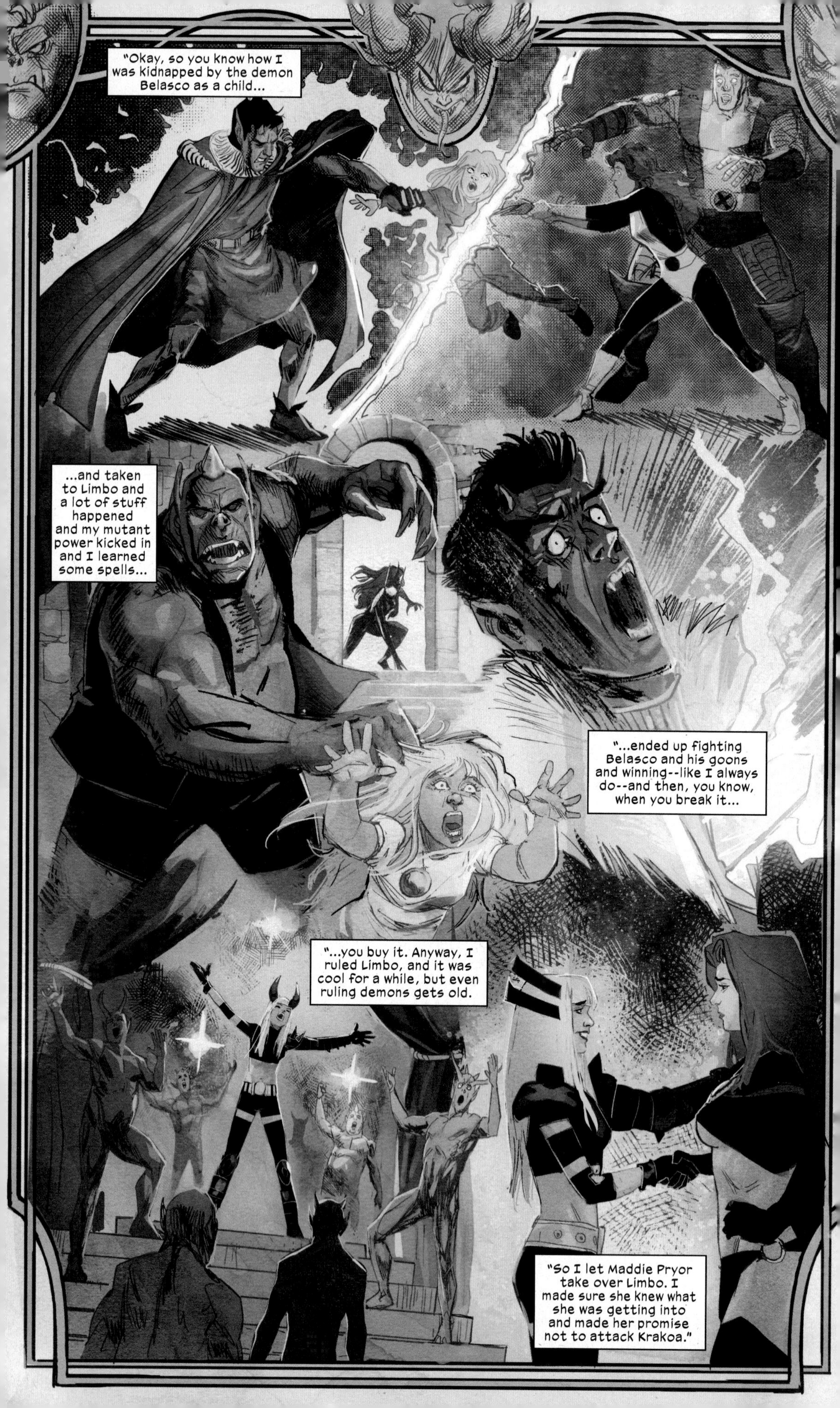
"Okay, so you know how I was kidnapped by the demon Belasco as a child...
...and taken to Limbo and a lot of stuff happened and my mutant power kicked in and I learned some spells...
"...ended up fighting Belasco and his goons and winning--like I always do--and then, you know, when you break it...
"...you buy it. Anyway, I ruled Limbo, and it was cool for a while, but even ruling demons gets old.
"So I let Maddie Pryor take over Limbo. I made sure she knew what she was getting into and made her promise not to attack Krakoa."

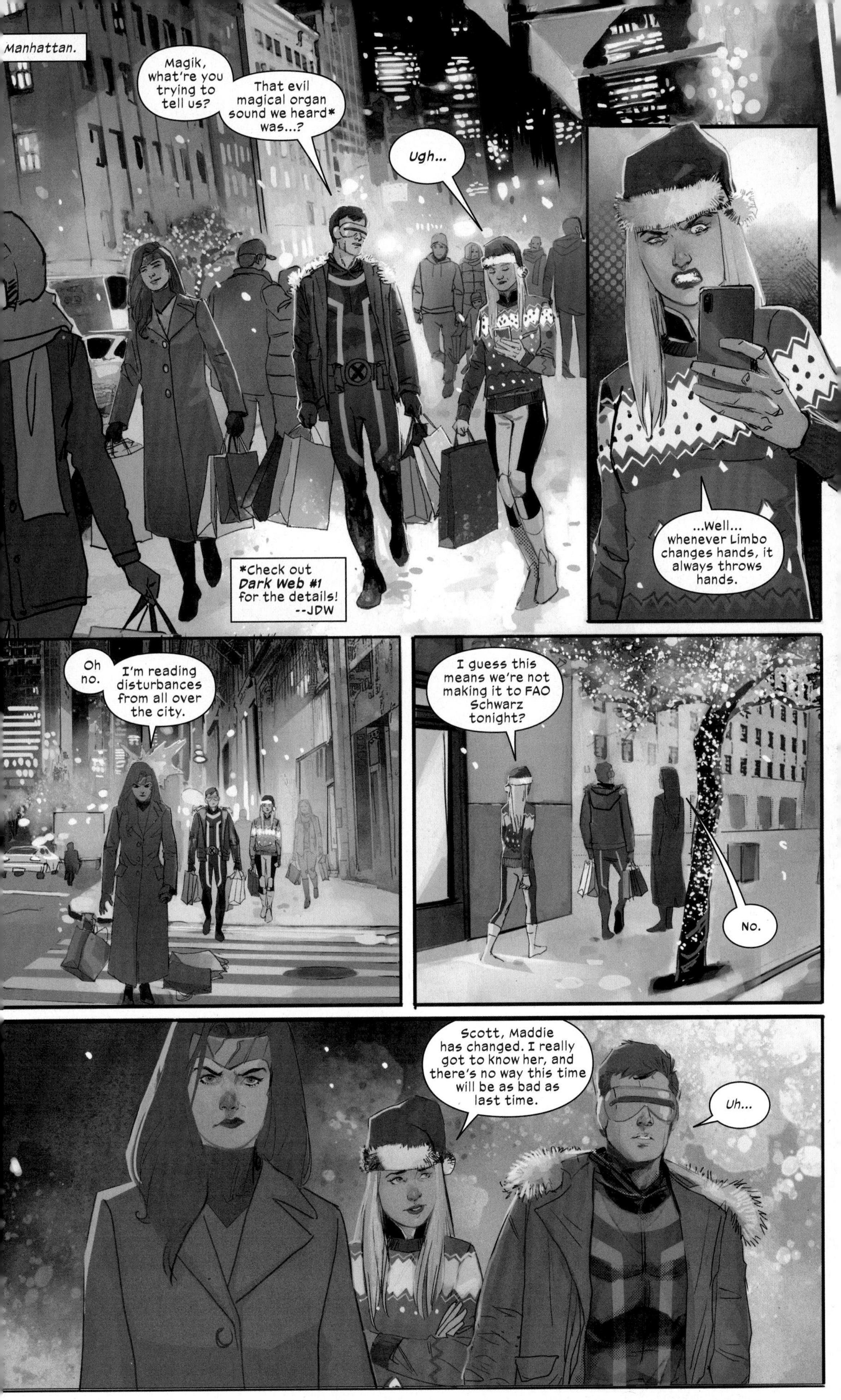
Manhattan.
Magik, what're you trying to tell us?
That evil magical organ sound we heard* was...?
Ugh...
*Check out Dark Web #1 for the details! --JDW
...Well... whenever Limbo changes hands, it always throws hands.
Oh no.
I'm reading disturbances from all over the city.
I guess this means we're not making it to FAO Schwarz tonight?
No.
Scott, Maddie has changed. I really got to know her, and there's no way this time will be as bad as last time.
Uh...

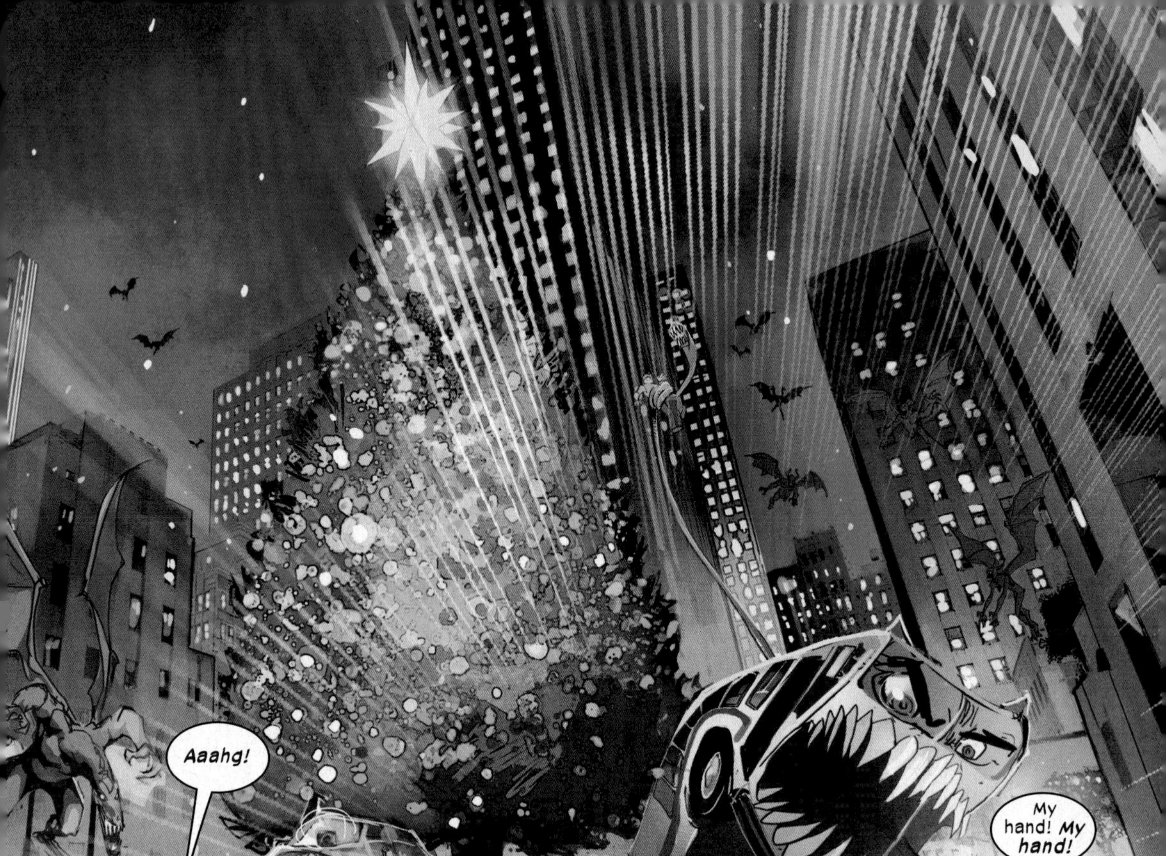
Aaahg!
My hand! My hand!
Run for your life!

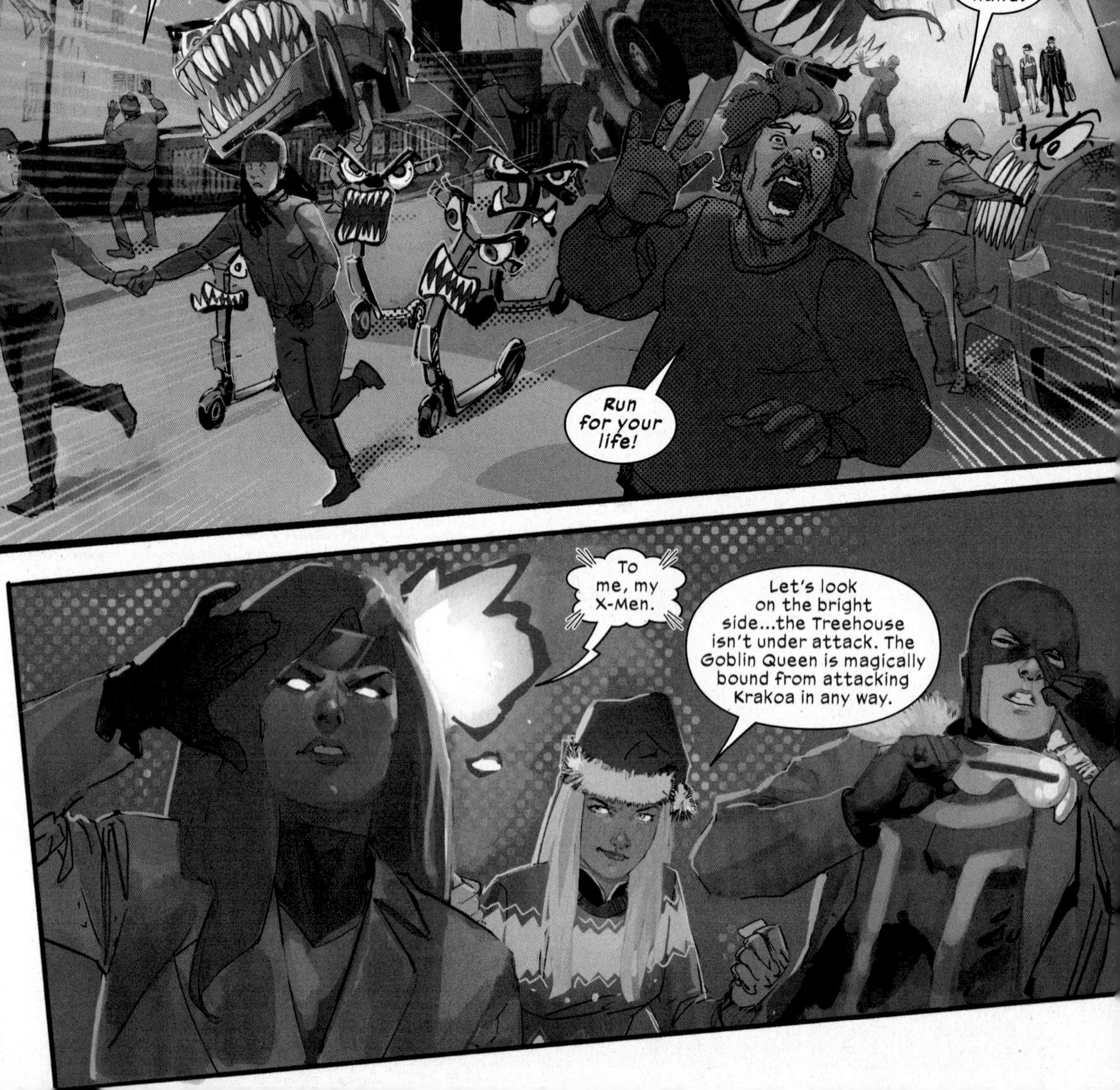
To me, my X-Men.
Let's look on the bright side...the Treehouse isn't under attack. The Goblin Queen is magically bound from attacking Krakoa in any way.

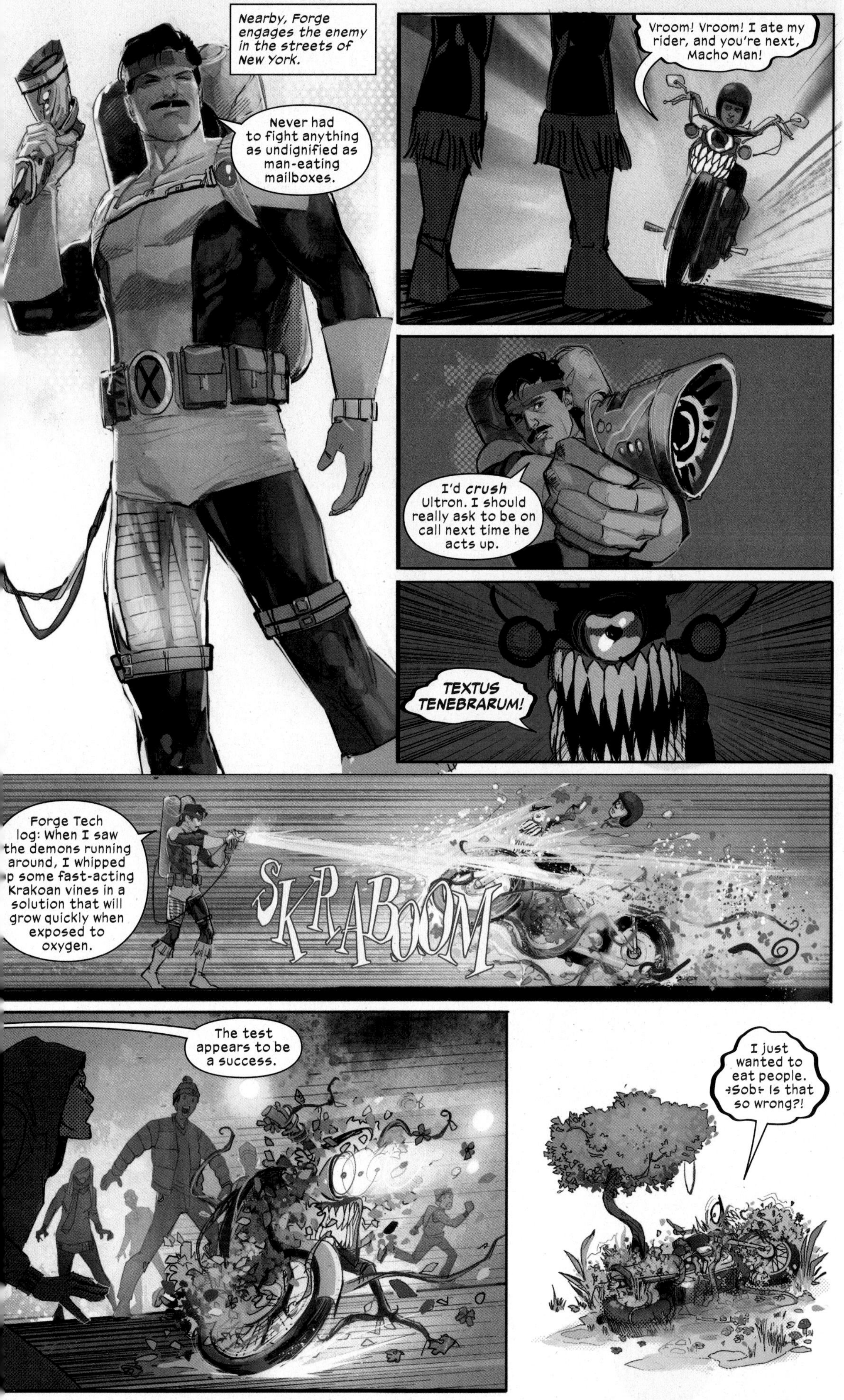
Nearby, Forge engages the enemy in the streets of New York.
Never had to fight anything as undignified as man-eating mailboxes.
Vroom! Vroom! I ate my rider, and you're next, Macho Man!
I'd *crush* Ultron. I should really ask to be on call next time he acts up.
TEXTUS TENEBRARUM!
Forge Tech log: When I saw the demons running around, I whipped up some fast-acting Krakoan vines in a solution that will grow quickly when exposed to oxygen.
SKRABOOM
The test appears to be a success.
I just wanted to eat people. ⸗Sob⸗ Is that so wrong?!

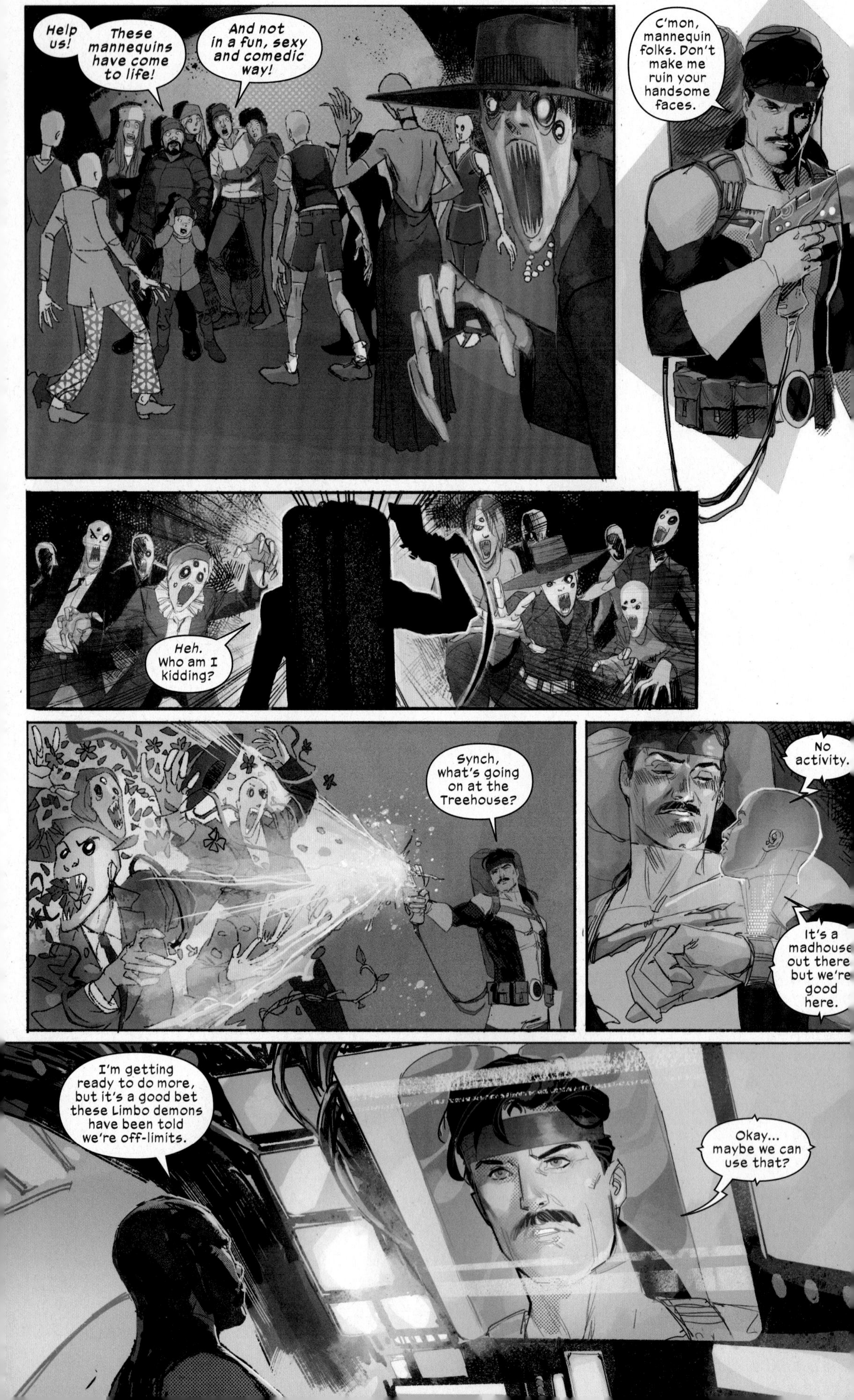
Help us!
These mannequins have come to life!
And not in a fun, sexy and comedic way!
C'mon, mannequin folks. Don't make me ruin your handsome faces.
Heh. Who am I kidding?
Synch, what's going on at the Treehouse?
No activity.
It's a madhouse out there but we're good here.
I'm getting ready to do more, but it's a good bet these Limbo demons have been told we're off-limits.
Okay... maybe we can use that?

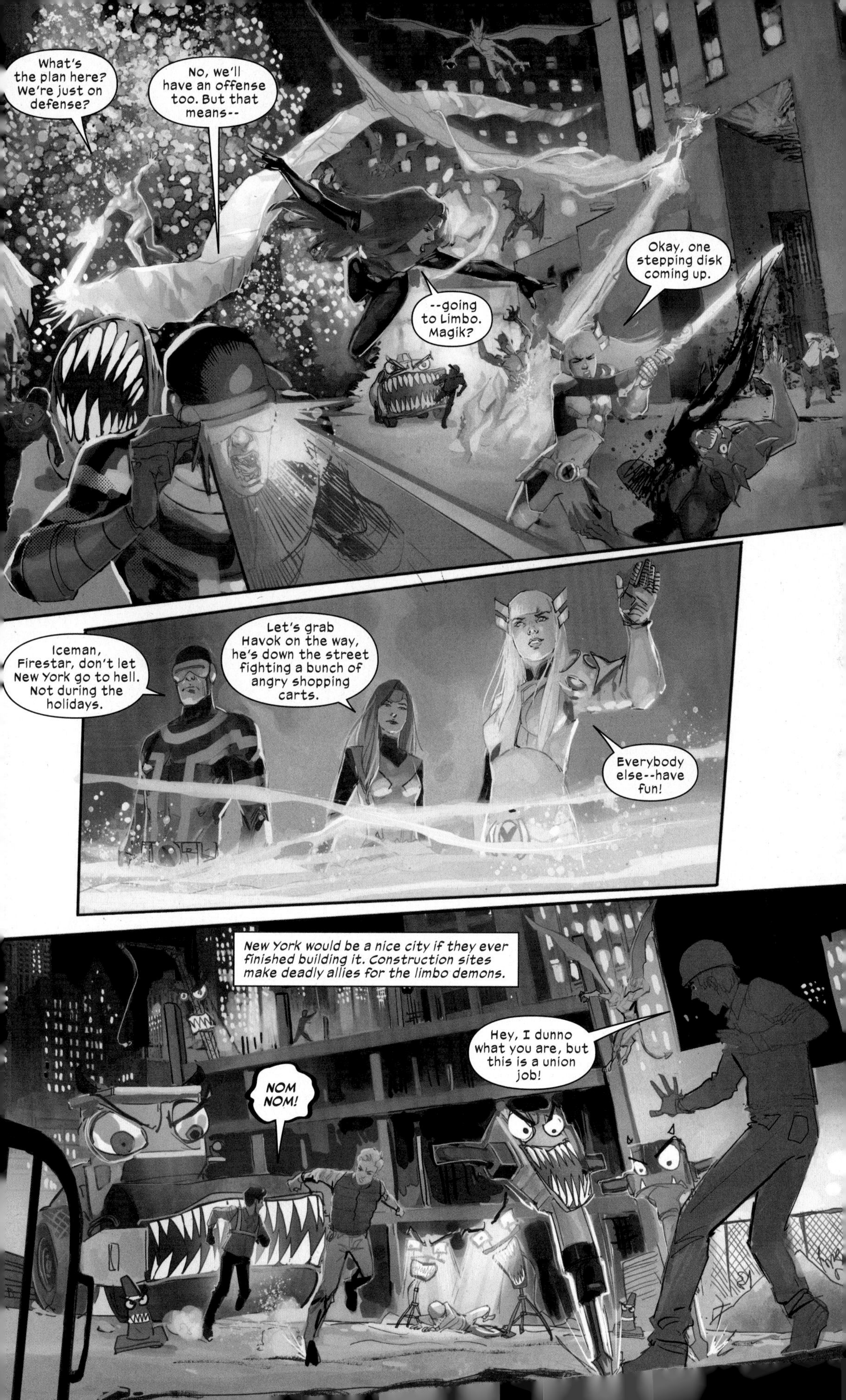

What's the plan here? We're just on defense?
No, we'll have an offense too. But that means--
--going to Limbo. Magik?
Okay, one stepping disk coming up.
Iceman, Firestar, don't let New York go to hell. Not during the holidays.
Let's grab Havok on the way, he's down the street fighting a bunch of angry shopping carts.
Everybody else--have fun!
New York would be a nice city if they ever finished building it. Construction sites make deadly allies for the limbo demons.
NOM NOM!
Hey, I dunno what you are, but this is a union job!

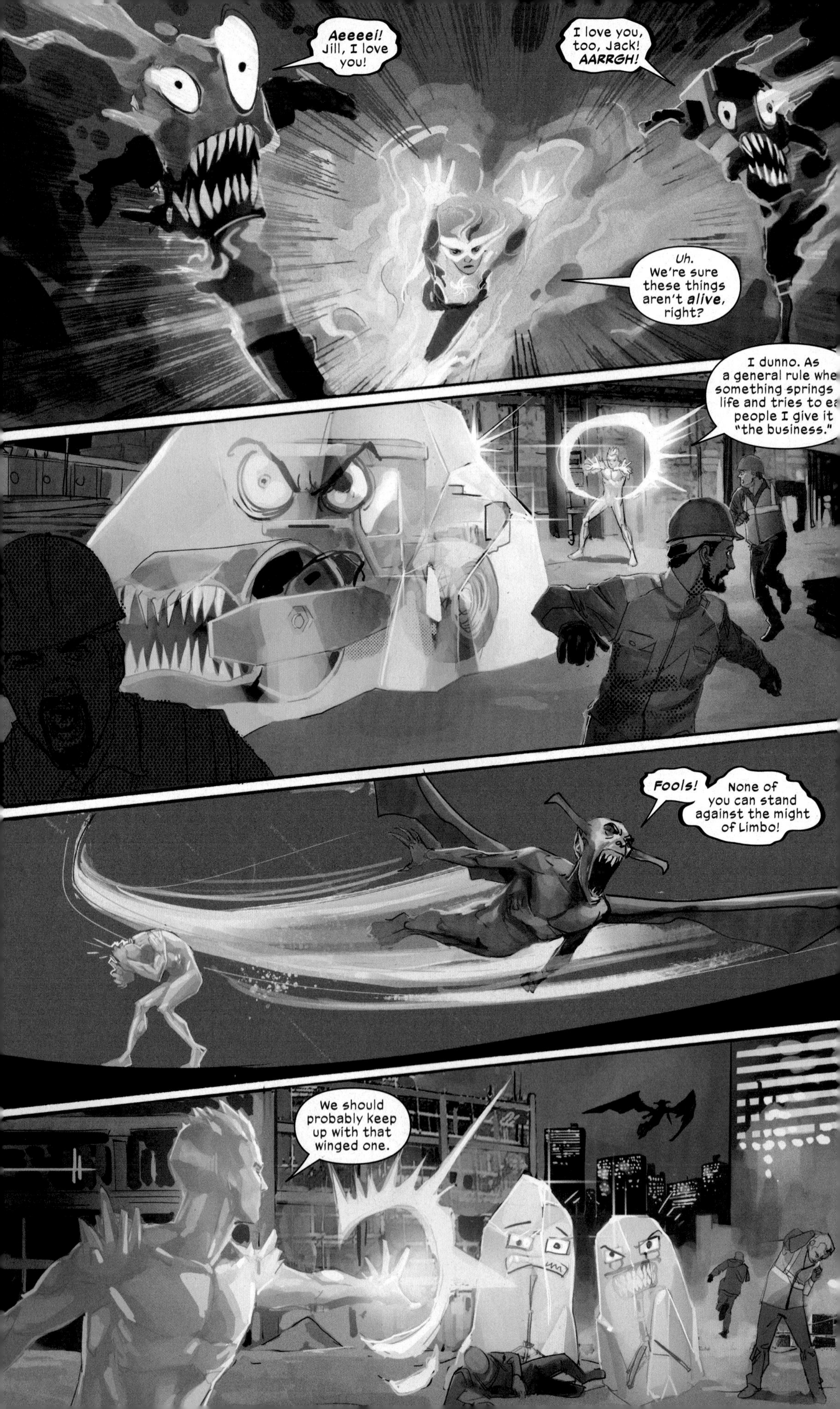

Aeeeei! Jill, I love you!
I love you, too, Jack! AARRGH!
Uh. We're sure these things aren't alive, right?
I dunno. As a general rule whe something springs life and tries to ea people I give it "the business."
Fools!
None of you can stand against the might of Limbo!
We should probably keep up with that winged one.

The holidays are fragile.

They can be ruined by a careless utterance of a family secret.

Or a drunk uncle.

FOOP!

But nothing ruins the holidays like a demon from Limbo relieving itself in a famous landmark Christmas tree...and infecting it with dark magic.

Did that thing just make a boom-boom in the tree?

Ew, gross! This city sucks!

Something's happening!

He-he...

Ho-ho...

...ho-ho-holy $%#@, time to die!

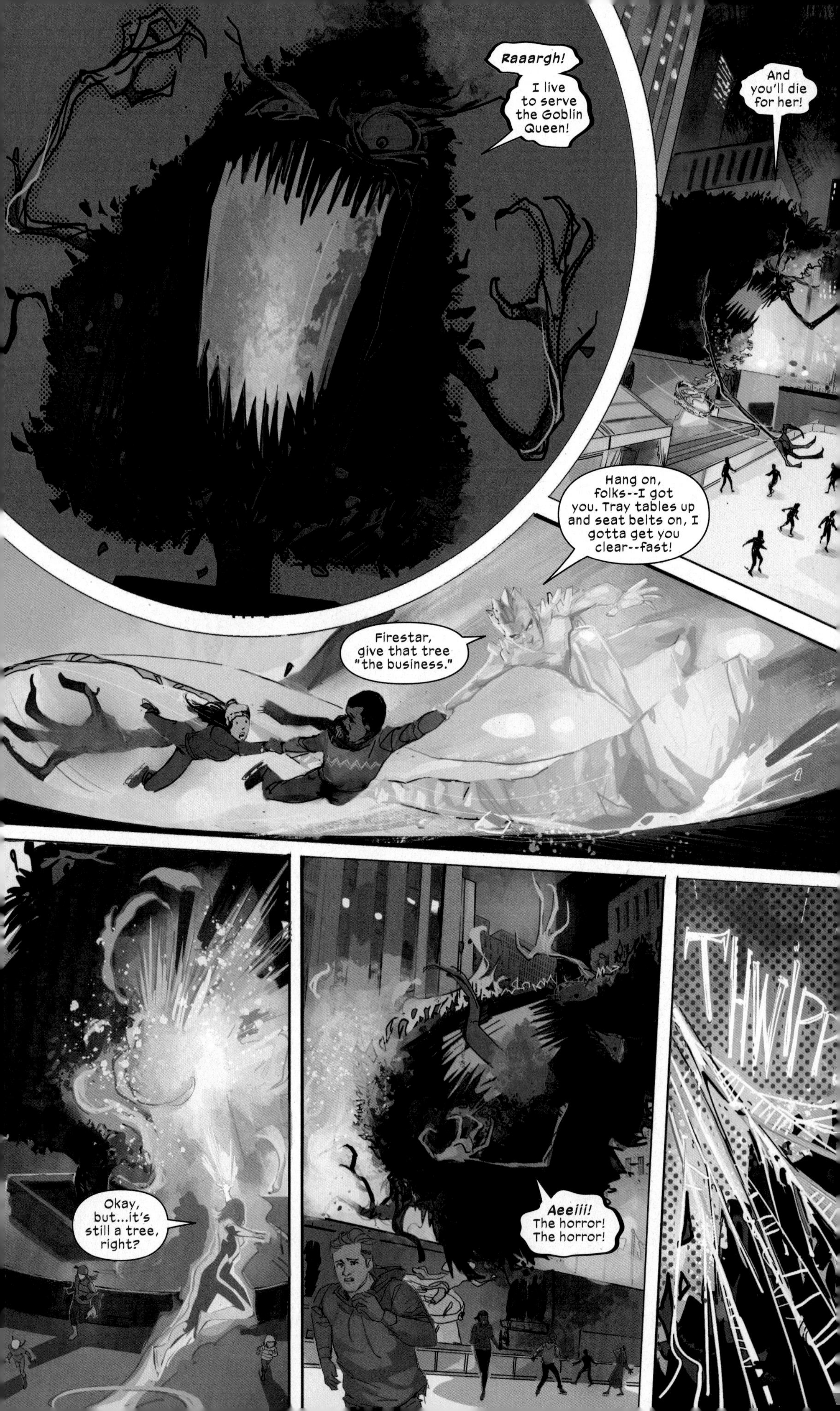
Raaargh!
I live to serve the Goblin Queen!
And you'll die for her!
Hang on, folks--I got you. Tray tables up and seat belts on, I gotta get you clear--fast!
Firestar, give that tree "the business."
Okay, but...it's still a tree, right?
Aeeiii! The horror! The horror!
THWIPP

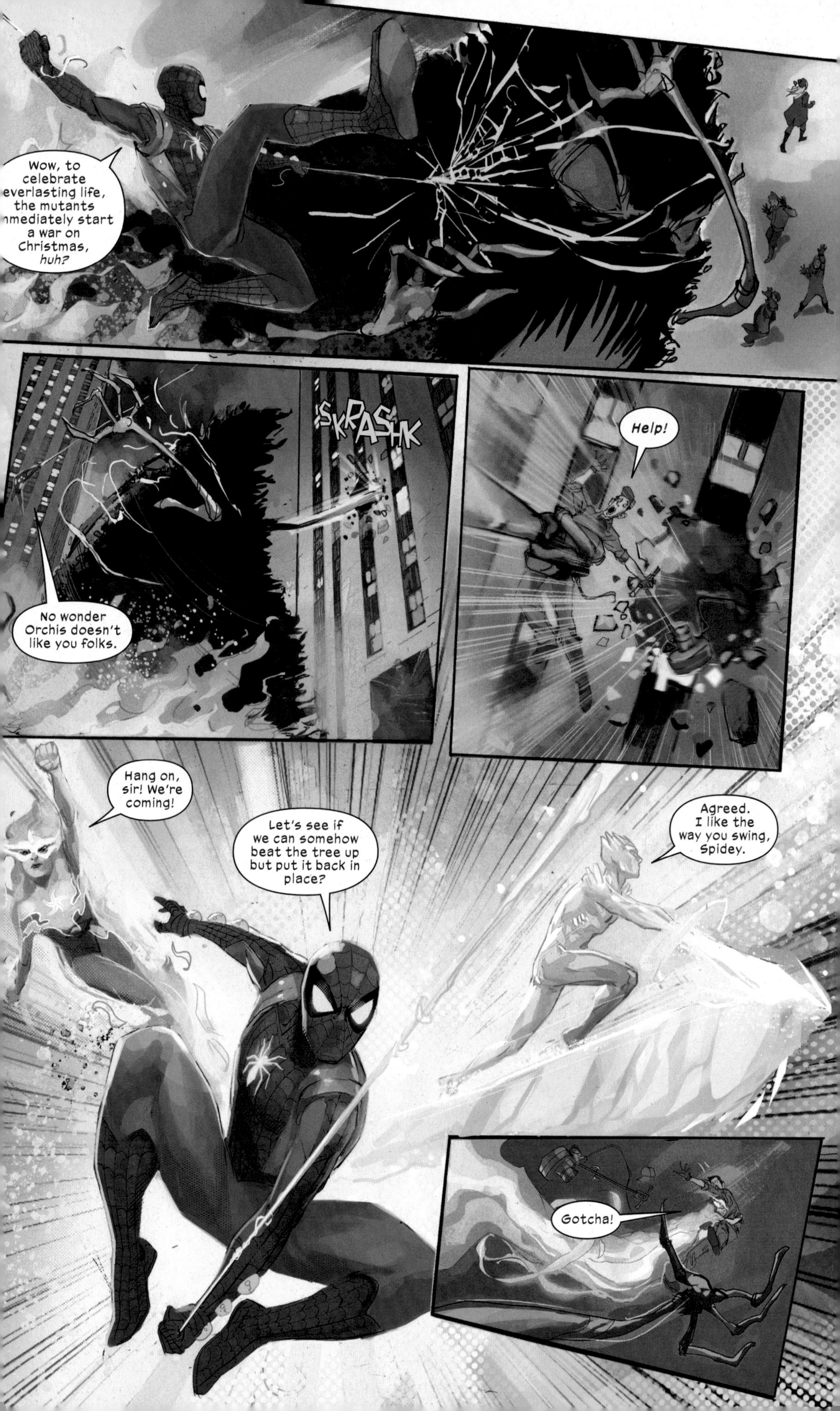
Wow, to celebrate everlasting life, the mutants mmediately start a war on Christmas, *huh?*
SKRASHK
No wonder Orchis doesn't like you folks.
Help!
Hang on, sir! We're coming!
Let's see if we can somehow beat the tree up but put it back in place?
Agreed. I like the way you swing, Spidey.
Gotcha!

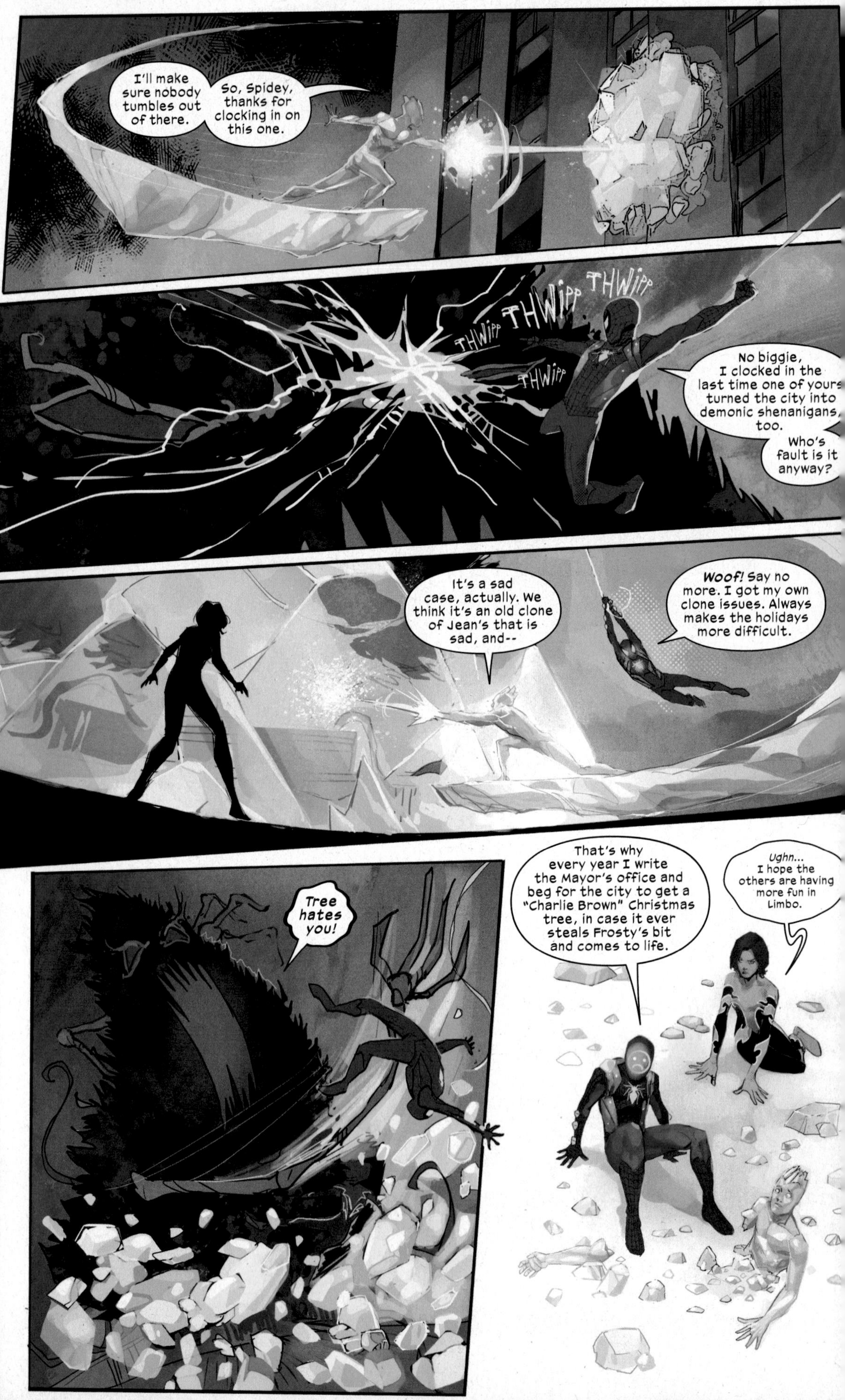
I'll make sure nobody tumbles out of there.
So, Spidey, thanks for clocking in on this one.
THWIPP THWIPP THWIPP THWIPP THWIPP
No biggie, I clocked in the last time one of yours turned the city into demonic shenanigans, too.
Who's fault is it anyway?
It's a sad case, actually. We think it's an old clone of Jean's that is sad, and--
Woof! Say no more. I got my own clone issues. Always makes the holidays more difficult.
Tree hates you!
That's why every year I write the Mayor's office and beg for the city to get a "Charlie Brown" Christmas tree, in case it ever steals Frosty's bit and comes to life.
Ughn... I hope the others are having more fun in Limbo.

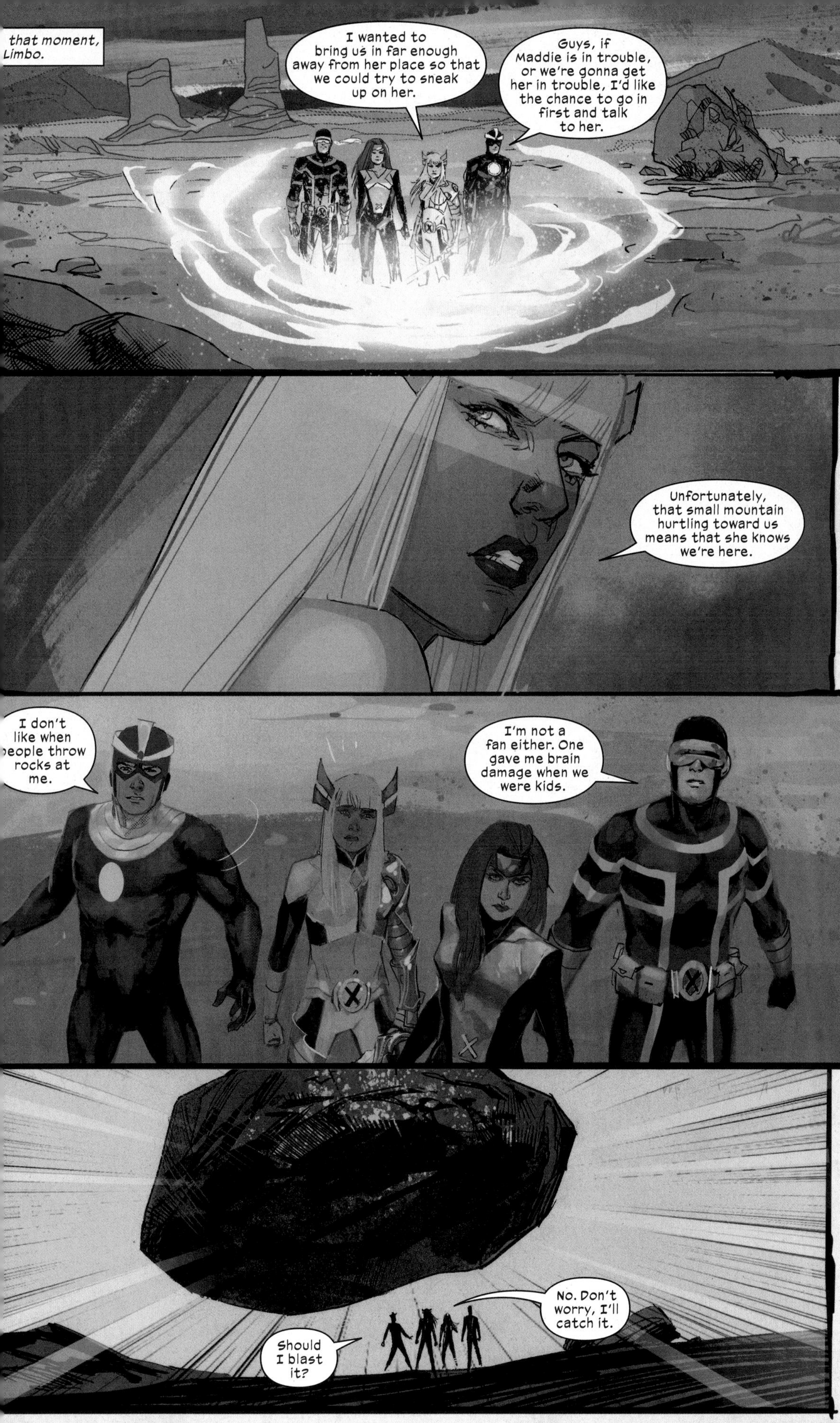

that moment,
Limbo.
I wanted to bring us in far enough away from her place so that we could try to sneak up on her.
Guys, if Maddie is in trouble, or we're gonna get her in trouble, I'd like the chance to go in first and talk to her.
Unfortunately, that small mountain hurtling toward us means that she knows we're here.
I don't like when people throw rocks at me.
I'm not a fan either. One gave me brain damage when we were kids.
Should I blast it?
No. Don't worry, I'll catch it.

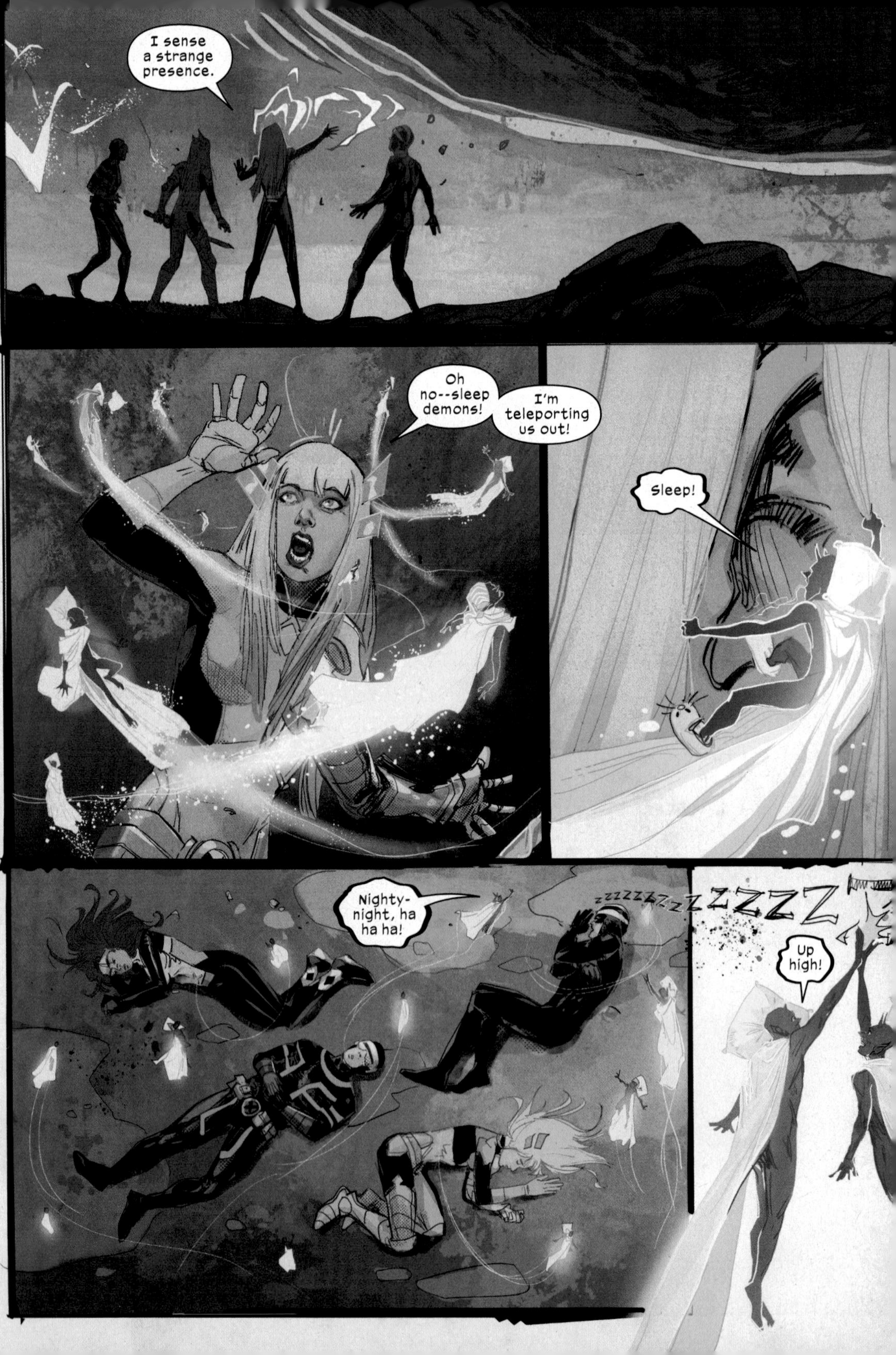

I sense a strange presence.
Oh no--sleep demons!
I'm teleporting us out!
Sleep!
Nighty-night, ha ha ha!
zzzzzzzzZZZZZ
Up high!

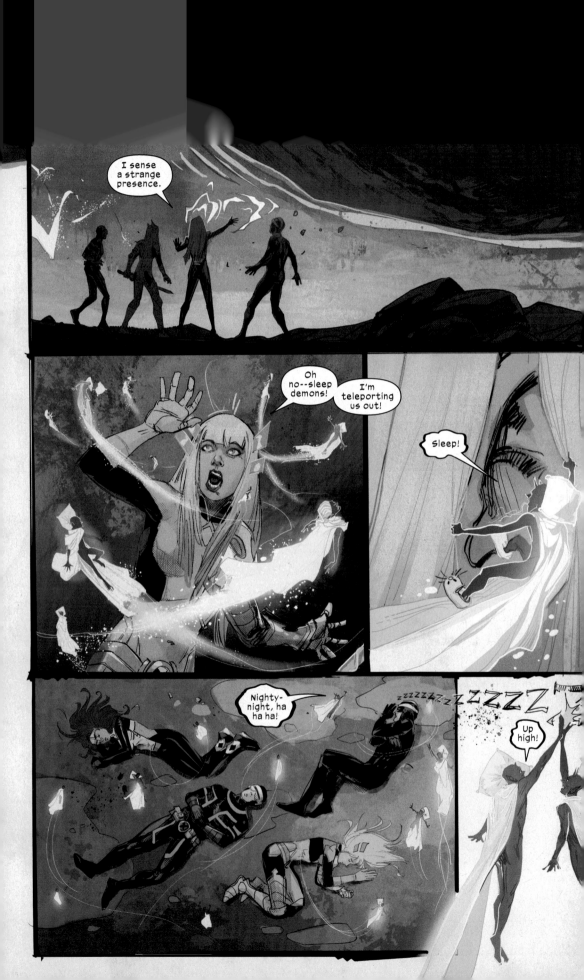

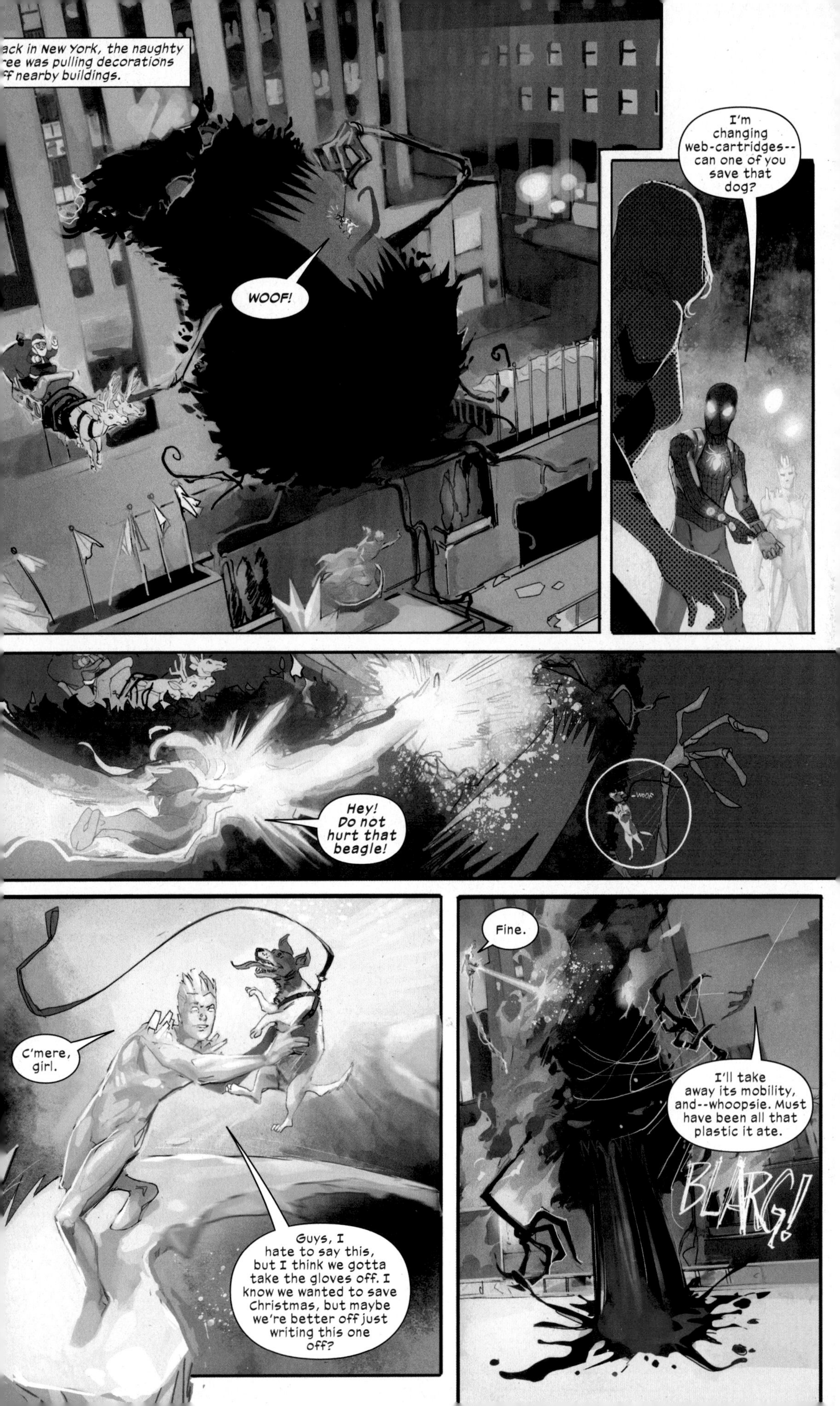
ack in New York, the naughty ree was pulling decorations f nearby buildings.
WOOF!
I'm changing web-cartridges--can one of you save that dog?
Hey! Do not hurt that beagle!
-WOOF
C'mere, girl.
Guys, I hate to say this, but I think we gotta take the gloves off. I know we wanted to save Christmas, but maybe we're better off just writing this one off?
Fine.
I'll take away its mobility, and--whoopsie. Must have been all that plastic it ate.
BLARG!

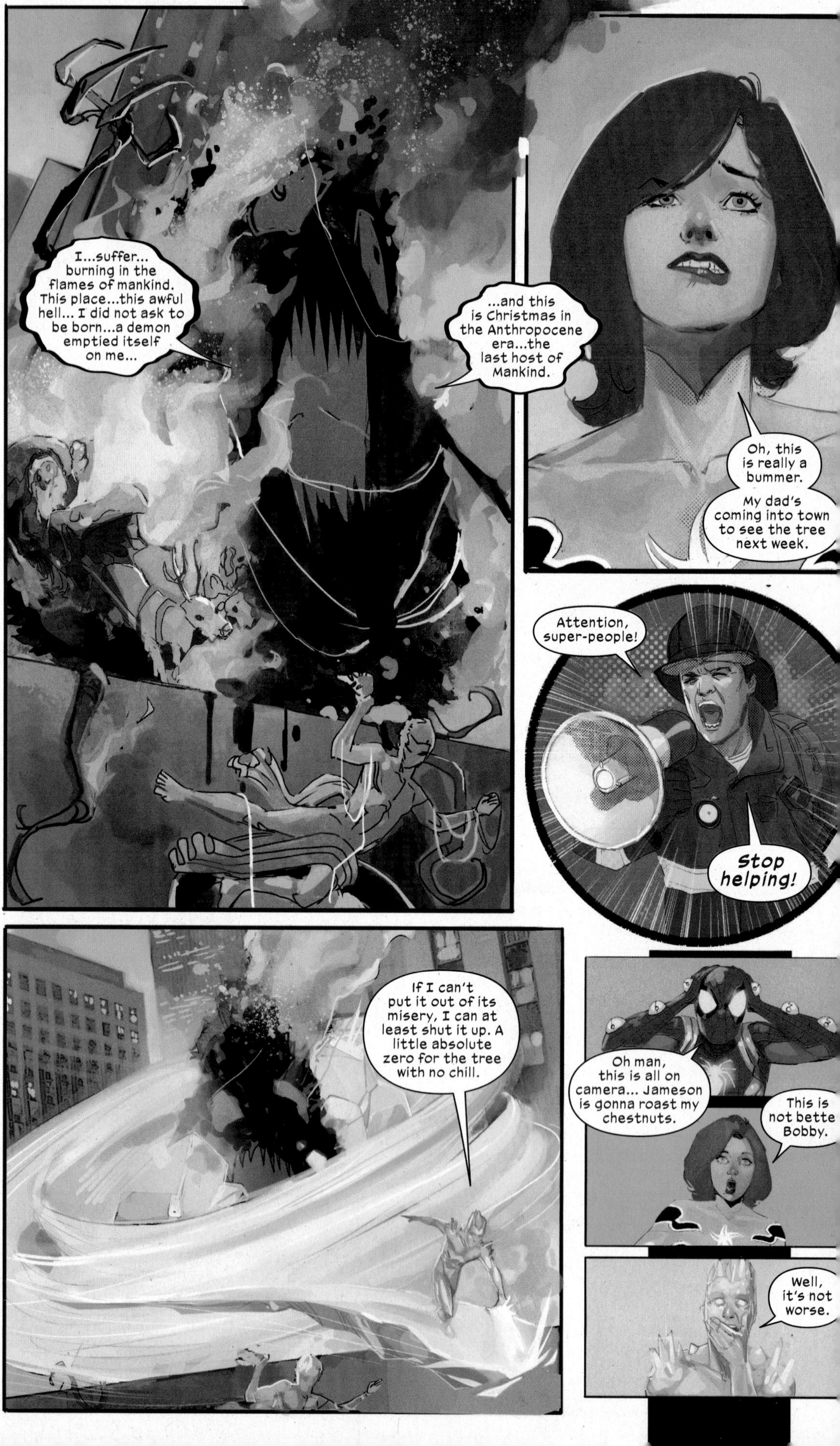
I...suffer... burning in the flames of mankind. This place...this awful hell... I did not ask to be born...a demon emptied itself on me...
...and this is Christmas in the Anthropocene era...the last host of Mankind.
Oh, this is really a bummer.
My dad's coming into town to see the tree next week.
Attention, super-people!
Stop helping!
If I can't put it out of its misery, I can at least shut it up. A little absolute zero for the tree with no chill.
Oh man, this is all on camera... Jameson is gonna roast my chestnuts.
This is not bette Bobby.
Well, it's not worse.

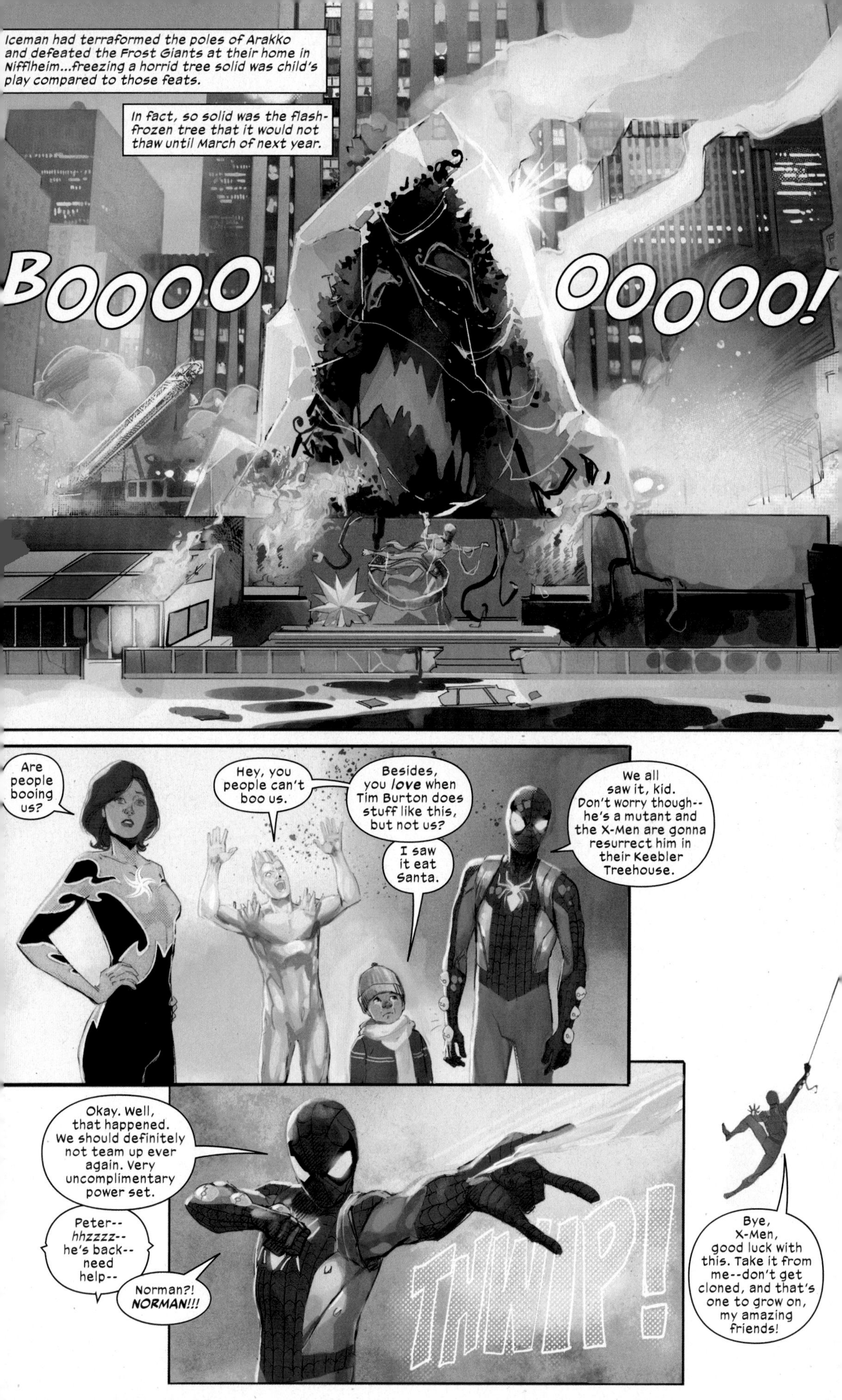

Iceman had terraformed the poles of Arakko and defeated the Frost Giants at their home in Nifflheim...freezing a horrid tree solid was child's play compared to those feats.
In fact, so solid was the flash-frozen tree that it would not thaw until March of next year.
BOOOO OOOOOO!
Are people booing us?
Hey, you people can't boo us.
Besides, you love when Tim Burton does stuff like this, but not us?
I saw it eat Santa.
We all saw it, kid. Don't worry though-- he's a mutant and the X-Men are gonna resurrect him in their Keebler Treehouse.
Okay. Well, that happened. We should definitely not team up ever again. Very uncomplimentary power set.
Peter-- hhzzzz-- he's back-- need help--
Norman?! NORMAN!!!
THWIP!
Bye, X-Men, good luck with this. Take it from me--don't get cloned, and that's one to grow on, my amazing friends!

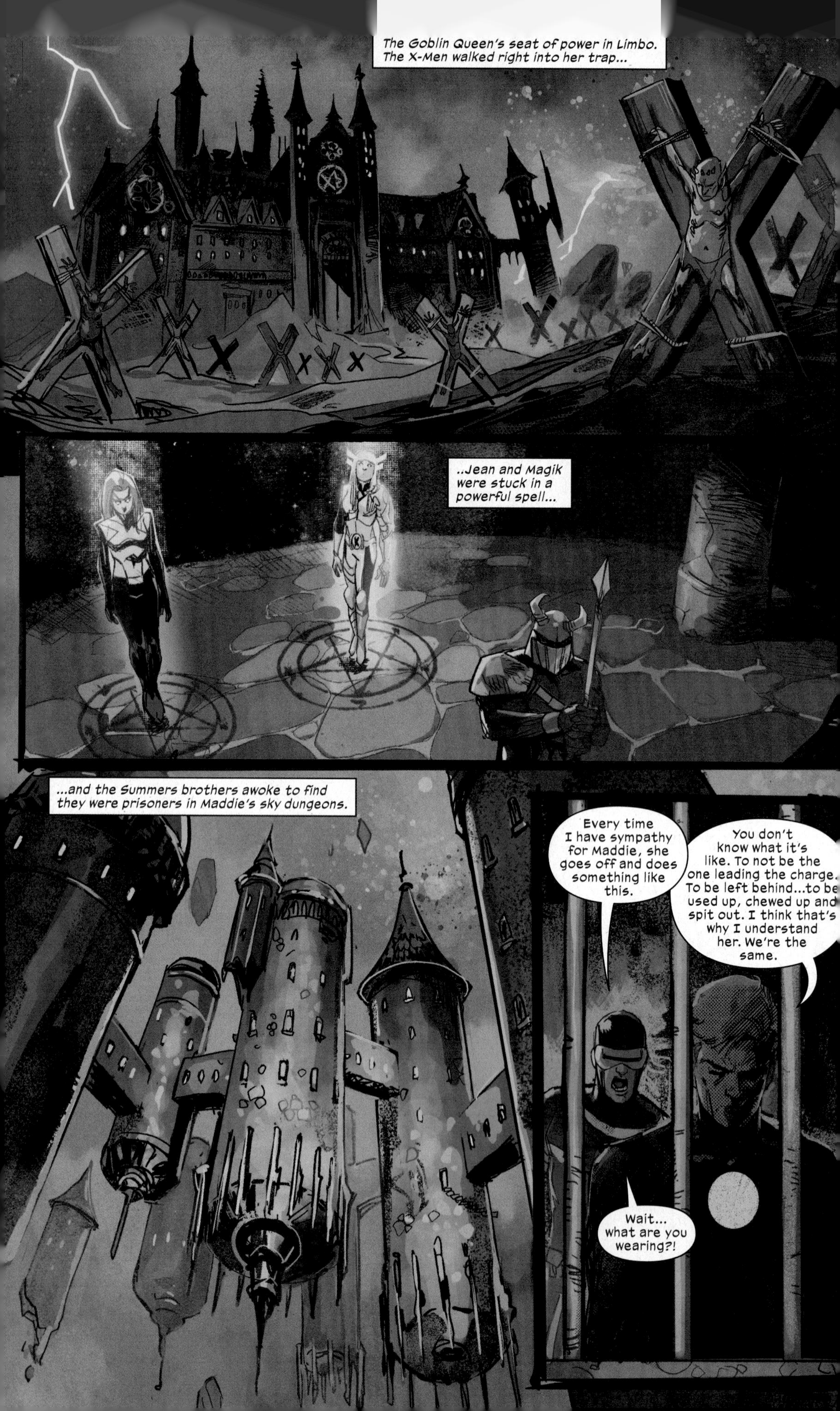

The Goblin Queen's seat of power in Limbo. The X-Men walked right into her trap...
..Jean and Magik were stuck in a powerful spell...
...and the Summers brothers awoke to find they were prisoners in Maddie's sky dungeons.
Every time I have sympathy for Maddie, she goes off and does something like this.
You don't know what it's like. To not be the one leading the charge. To be left behind...to be used up, chewed up and spit out. I think that's why I understand her. We're the same.
Wait... what are you wearing?!

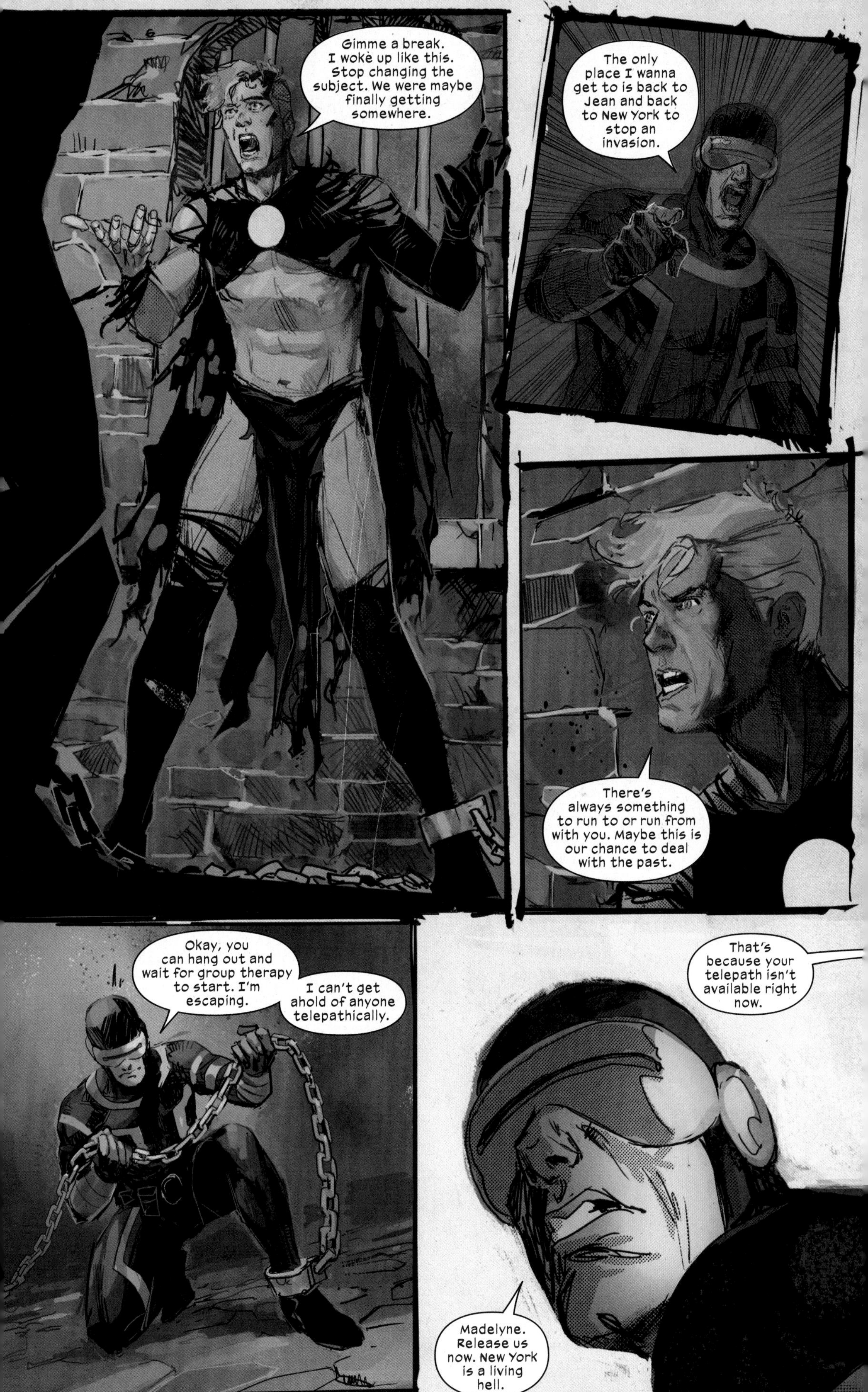
Gimme a break. I woke up like this. Stop changing the subject. We were maybe finally getting somewhere.
The only place I wanna get to is back to Jean and back to New York to stop an invasion.
There's always something to run to or run from with you. Maybe this is our chance to deal with the past.
Okay, you can hang out and wait for group therapy to start. I'm escaping.
I can't get ahold of anyone telepathically.
That's because your telepath isn't available right now.
Madelyne. Release us now. New York is a living hell.

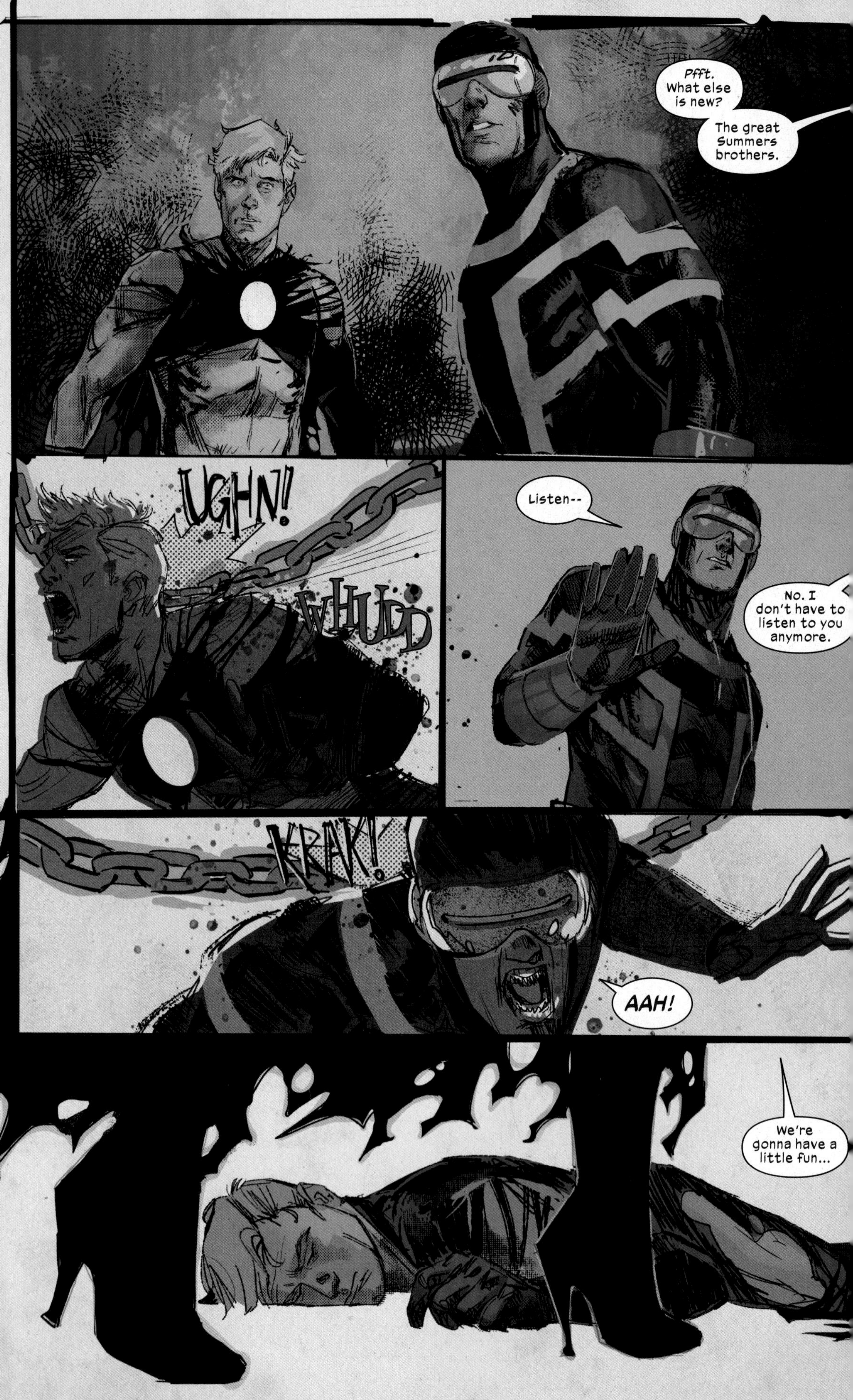

Pfft. What else is new?
The great Summers brothers.
UGHN!
WHUDD
Listen--
No. I don't have to listen to you anymore.
KRAK!
AAH!
We're gonna have a little fun...

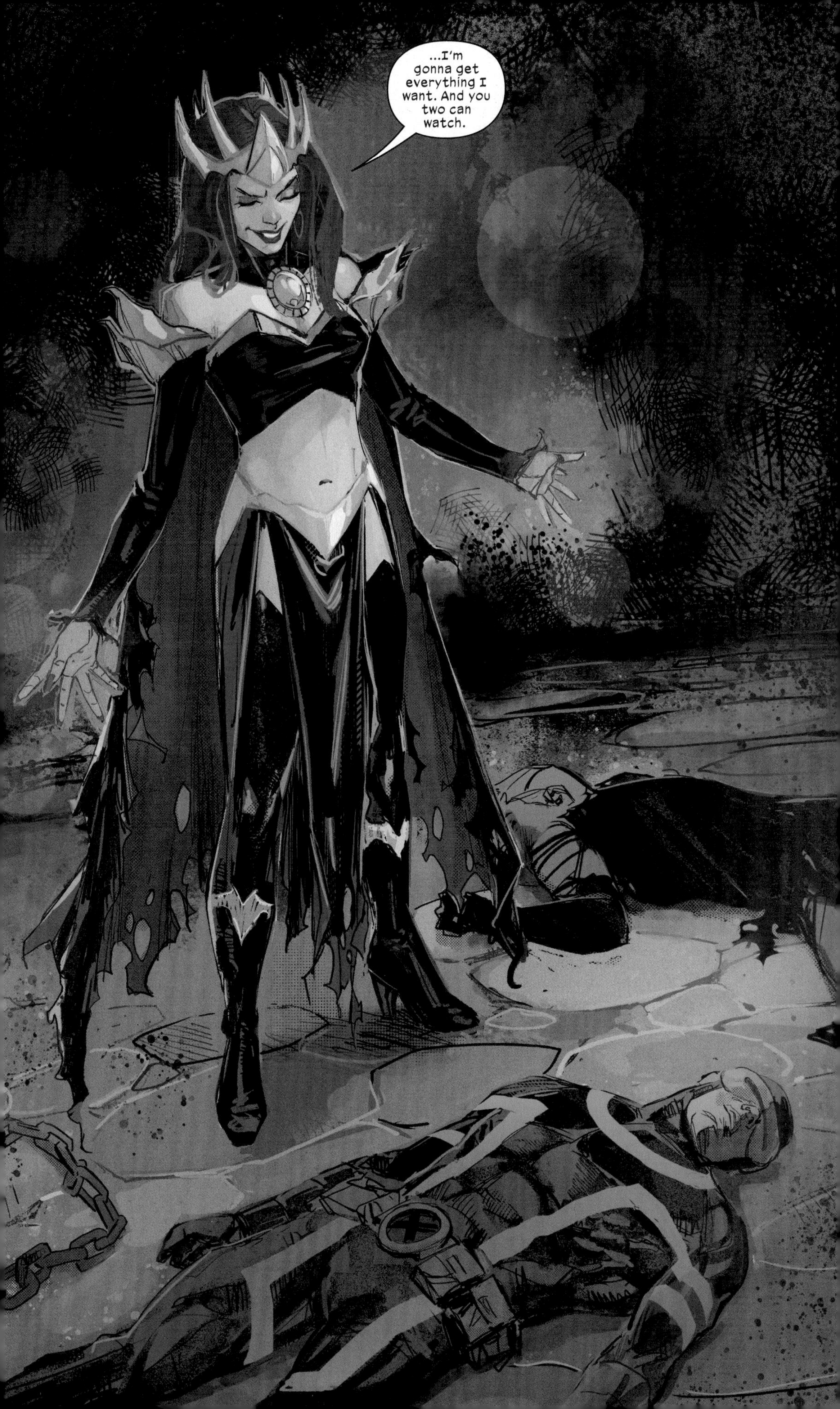
...I'm gonna get everything I want. And you two can watch.

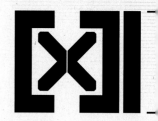

THE X OF GIFTS

The X-Men's white elephant gift exchange.

The parameters:
Gifts should be less than fifty U.S. dollars if purchased, but making the gift was encouraged.

Gifts could only be stolen once per round.

Numbers were selected telepathically and the gift-selecting order was determined:

Jean Grey, Synch, Havok, Forge, Firestar, Magik, Iceman and then Cyclops.

After a few rounds of thievery and at least one accusation of telepathic shenanigans, this is how it all sorted:

Jean Grey went home with Synch's gift, a limited-edition single-cask whiskey from Japan. It will be opened and shared on New Year's Eve.

When the fun ended, **Synch** was holding onto a really interesting art piece made of carbon and diamonds. It's in his window at the Treehouse. When the light shines through, it looks like a nebula. Firestar created it by using her mutant gift at full power along the edge of a volcano. Everyone agreed it was the coolest gift, and it was stolen the most times.

Havok didn't love the look of his teammates' choices and finagled to get his own gift of a year-round "Coffees of the World" gift delivery.

Forge took home a knock-off hoodie sold by the street vendors outside the Treehouse. It has Iceman's handsome face on it, and you only get one guess as to who gifted it.

Firestar ended up with Forge's gift. A living clock that displayed the full date that was made with nothing more than flowers from Krakoa. A truly one-of-a-kind item.

Magik received Jean Grey's gift, a lovely bit of asteroid plucked from high orbit around our planet. Jean noticed it while saving the world when the Eternals attacked.

Iceman left the White Elephant with a wrapped Teddy Bear that was obviously the handiwork of Magik, but the surprise when it was unwrapped was the discovery that it had the old mummified heart of a rhyming demon formerly of Limbo. Iceman is not quite sure where the appropriate place to keep it is.

Cyclops was happy to end up with his own gift, a BAND OF BROTHERS 4K set of Blu-ray discs autographed by Tom Hanks.

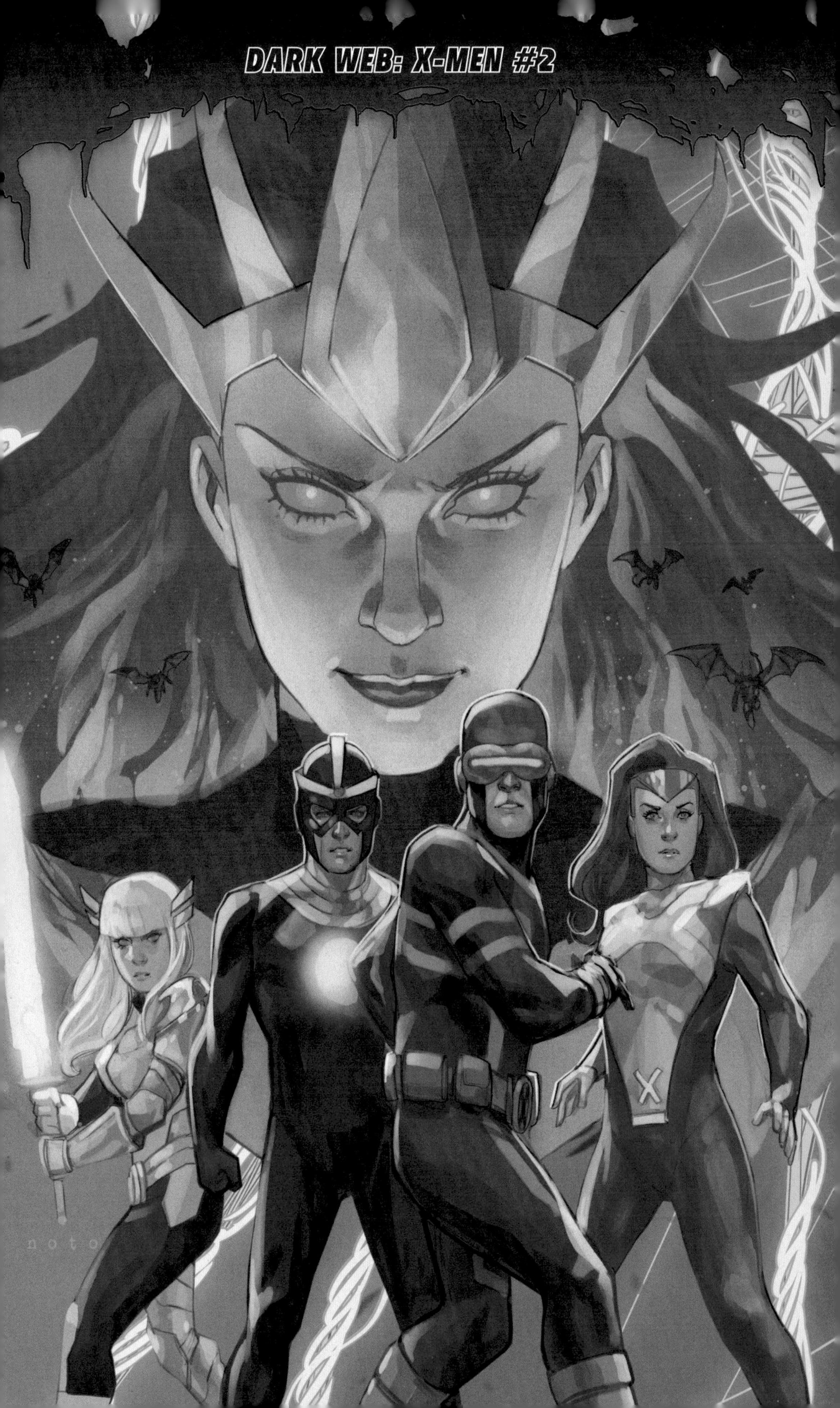
DARK WEB: X-MEN #2
noto

"The Summers are their own worst enemies. I'll see to it that it's true."

-- MR. SINISTER

[darkweb_xmen_02]

Madelyne Pryor's dreams always start so happily.

They are happy days that never came to be.

Taking her son, Nathan, to the zoo or the beach...

In these dreams, he is happy...

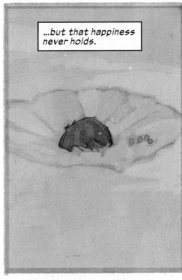

...but that happiness never holds.

Even in her dreams, she loses him.

And when she wakes, she still has her waking nightmare to look forward to.

It's no wonder she holds a grudge against Scott. Against Jean. Against the world.

She was born to breed and then be cast aside.

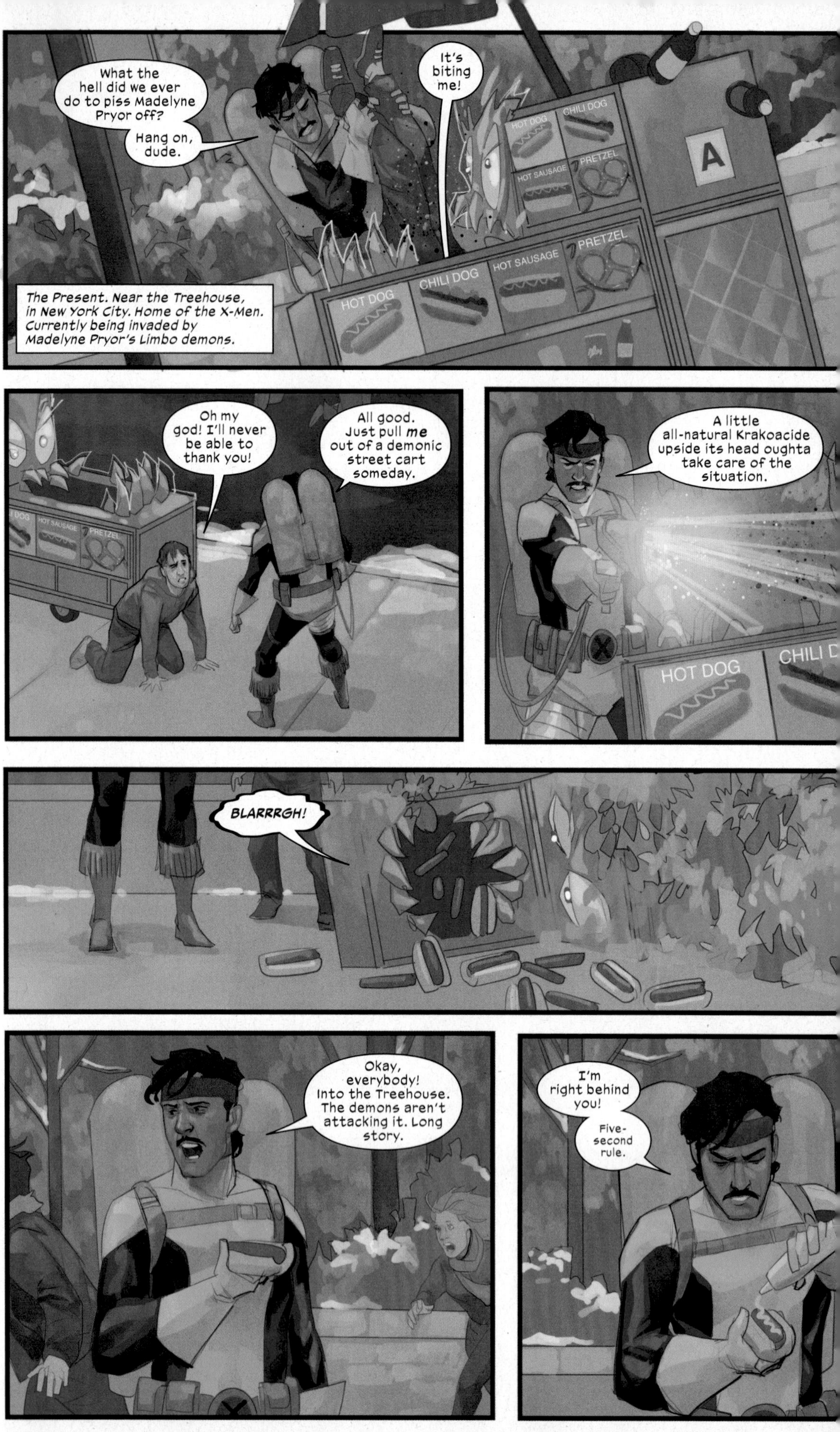
What the hell did we ever do to piss Madelyne Pryor off?
Hang on, dude.
It's biting me!
HOT DOG
CHILI DOG
HOT SAUSAGE
PRETZEL
A
The Present. Near the Treehouse, in New York City. Home of the X-Men. Currently being invaded by Madelyne Pryor's Limbo demons.
Oh my god! I'll never be able to thank you!
All good. Just pull *me* out of a demonic street cart someday.
A little all-natural Krakoacide upside its head oughta take care of the situation.
BLARRRGH!
Okay, everybody! Into the Treehouse. The demons aren't attacking it. Long story.
I'm right behind you!
Five-second rule.

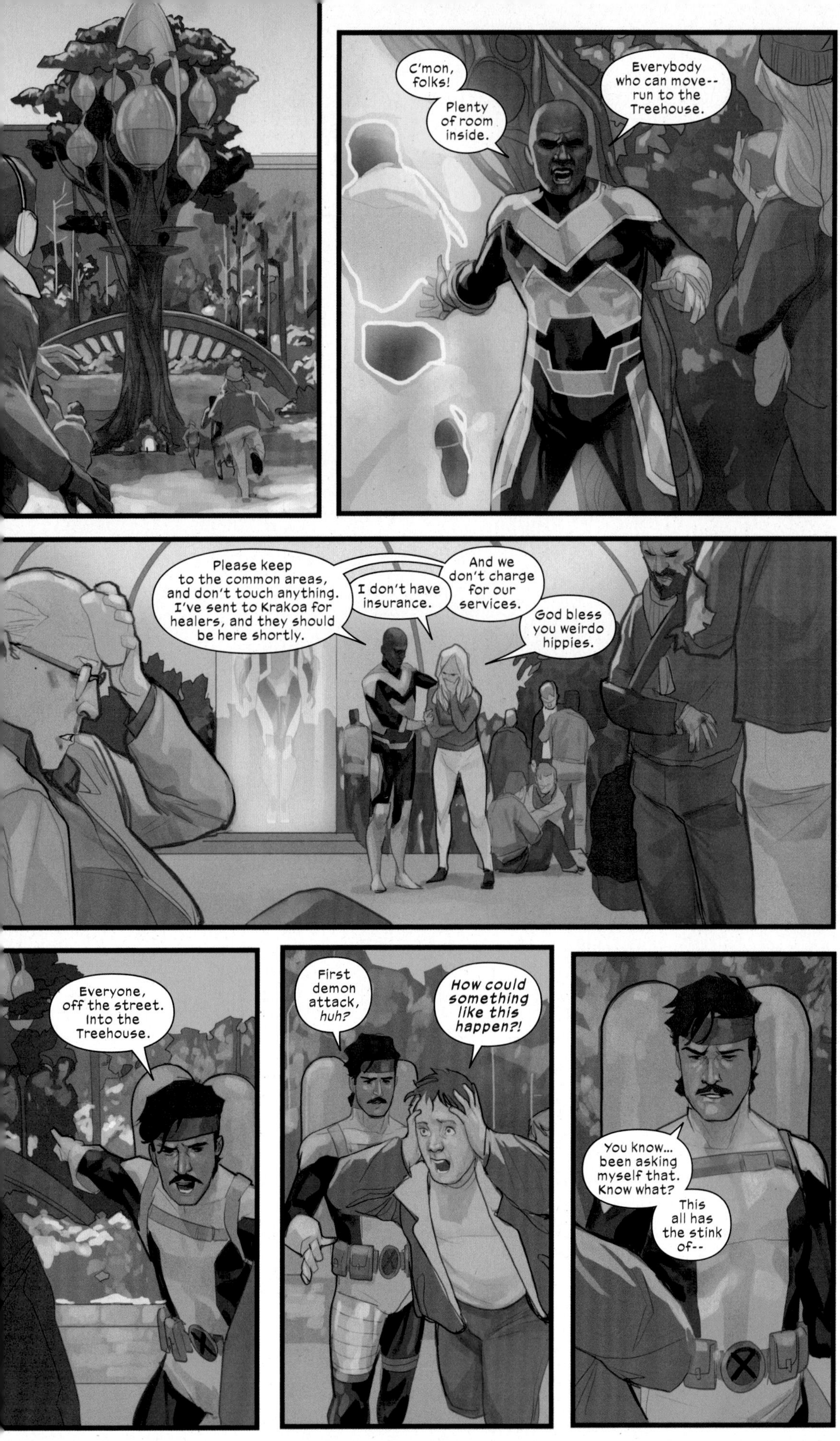
C'mon, folks!
Plenty of room inside.
Everybody who can move-- run to the Treehouse.
Please keep to the common areas, and don't touch anything. I've sent to Krakoa for healers, and they should be here shortly.
I don't have insurance.
And we don't charge for our services.
God bless you weirdo hippies.
Everyone, off the street. Into the Treehouse.
First demon attack, *huh?*
How could something like this happen?!
You know... been asking myself that. Know what?
This all has the stink of--

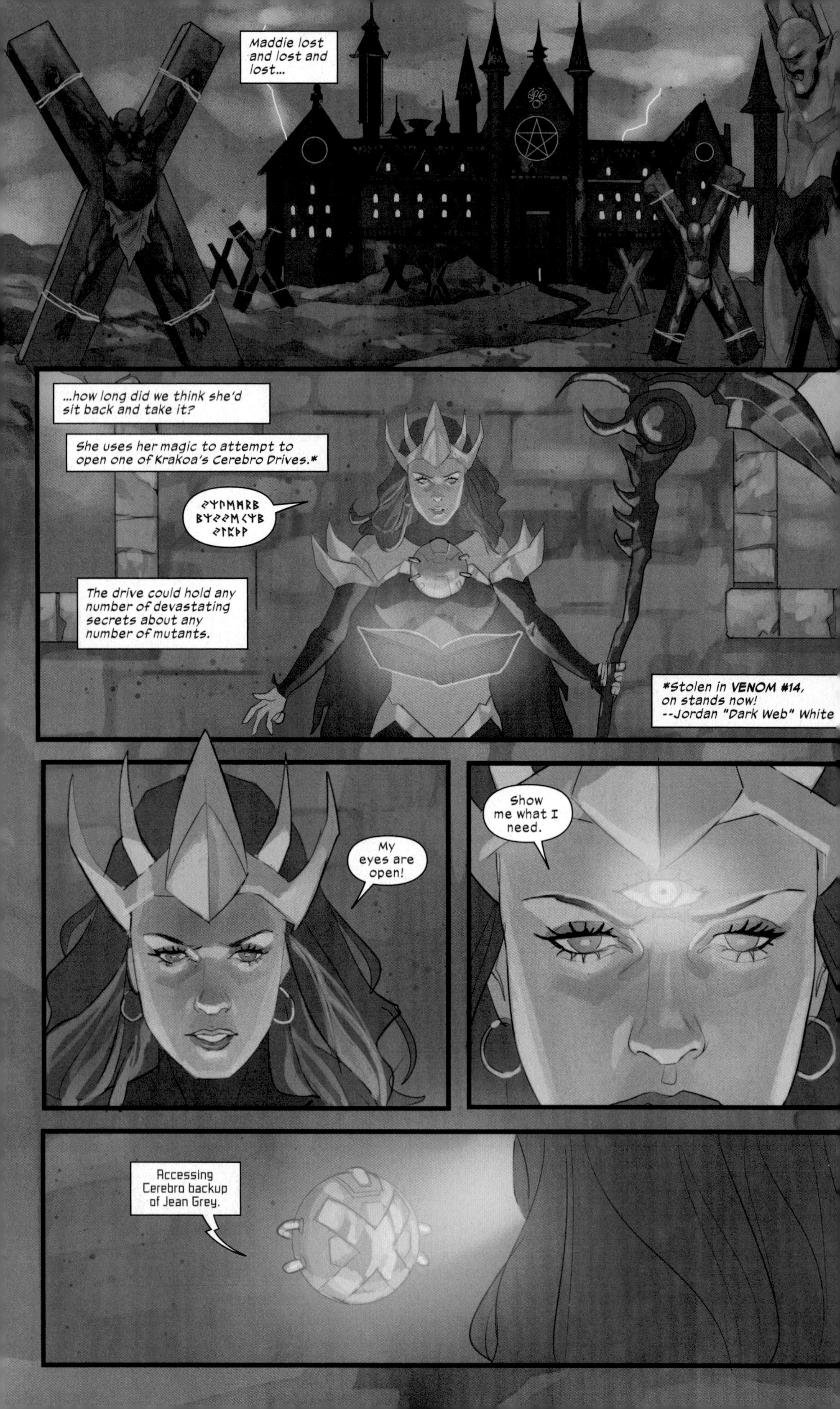

Maddie lost and lost and lost...
...how long did we think she'd sit back and take it?
She uses her magic to attempt to open one of Krakoa's Cerebro Drives.*
The drive could hold any number of devastating secrets about any number of mutants.
*Stolen in VENOM #14, on stands now! --Jordan "Dark Web" White
My eyes are open!
Show me what I need.
Accessing Cerebro backup of Jean Grey.

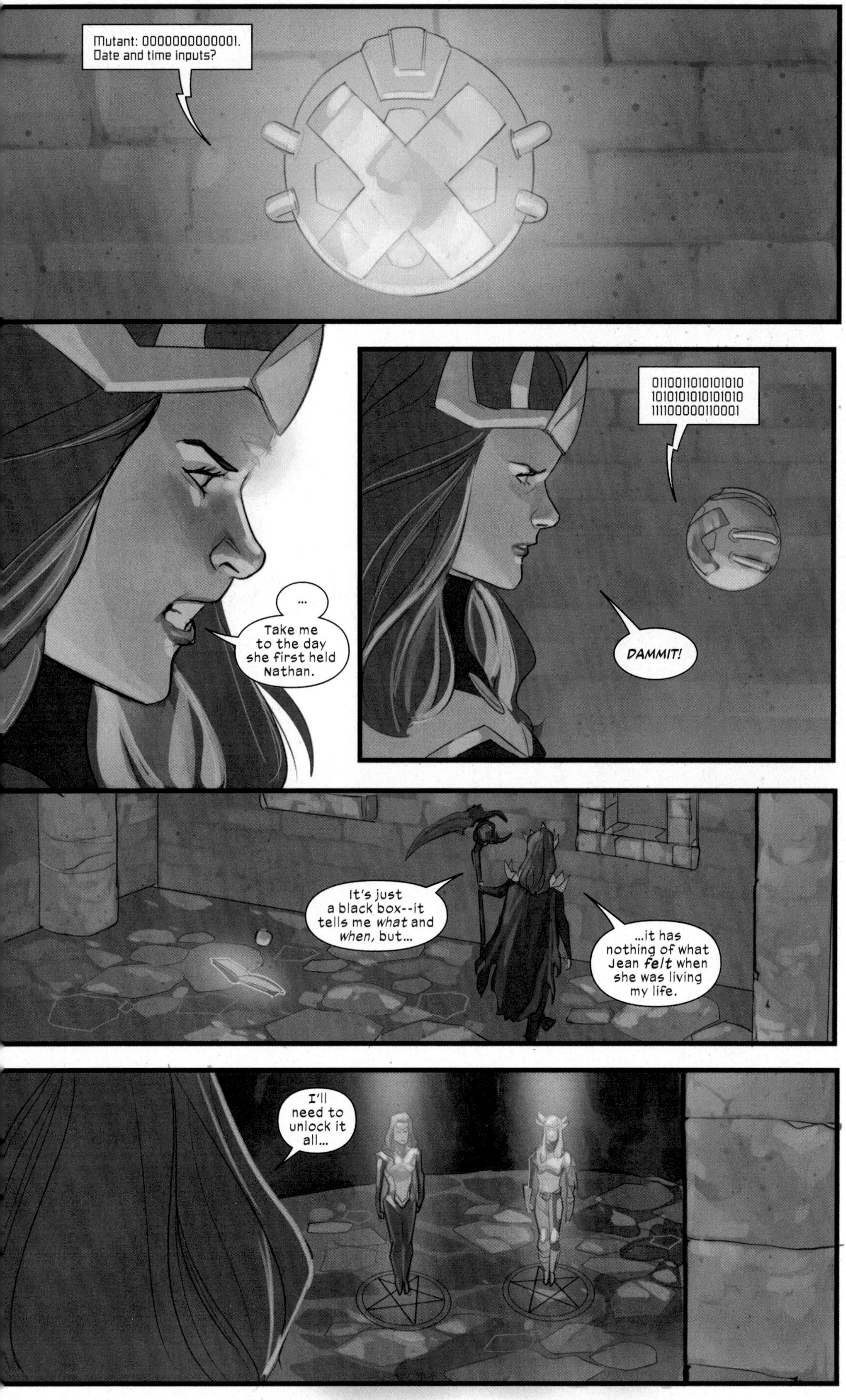
Mutant: 0000000000001.
Date and time inputs?
...
Take me to the day she first held Nathan.
0110011010101010
1010101010101010
1111000000110001
DAMMIT!
It's just a black box--it tells me *what* and *when*, but...
...it has nothing of what Jean ***felt*** when she was living my life.
I'll need to unlock it all...

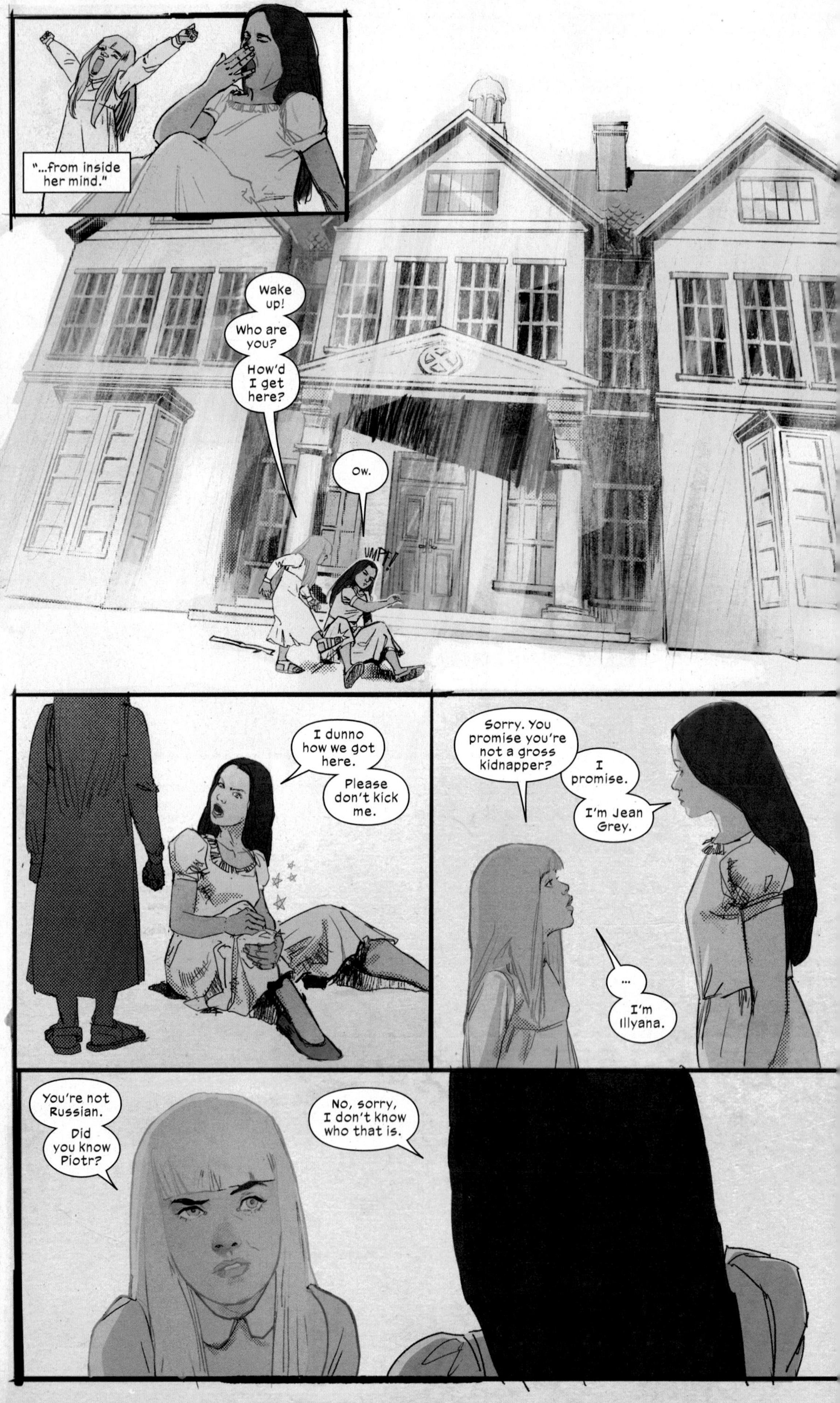
"...from inside her mind."
Wake up!
Who are you?
How'd I get here?
Ow.
UMPF!
I dunno how we got here.
Please don't kick me.
Sorry. You promise you're not a gross kidnapper?
I promise.
I'm Jean Grey.
...
I'm Illyana.
You're not Russian.
Did you know Piotr?
No, sorry, I don't know who that is.

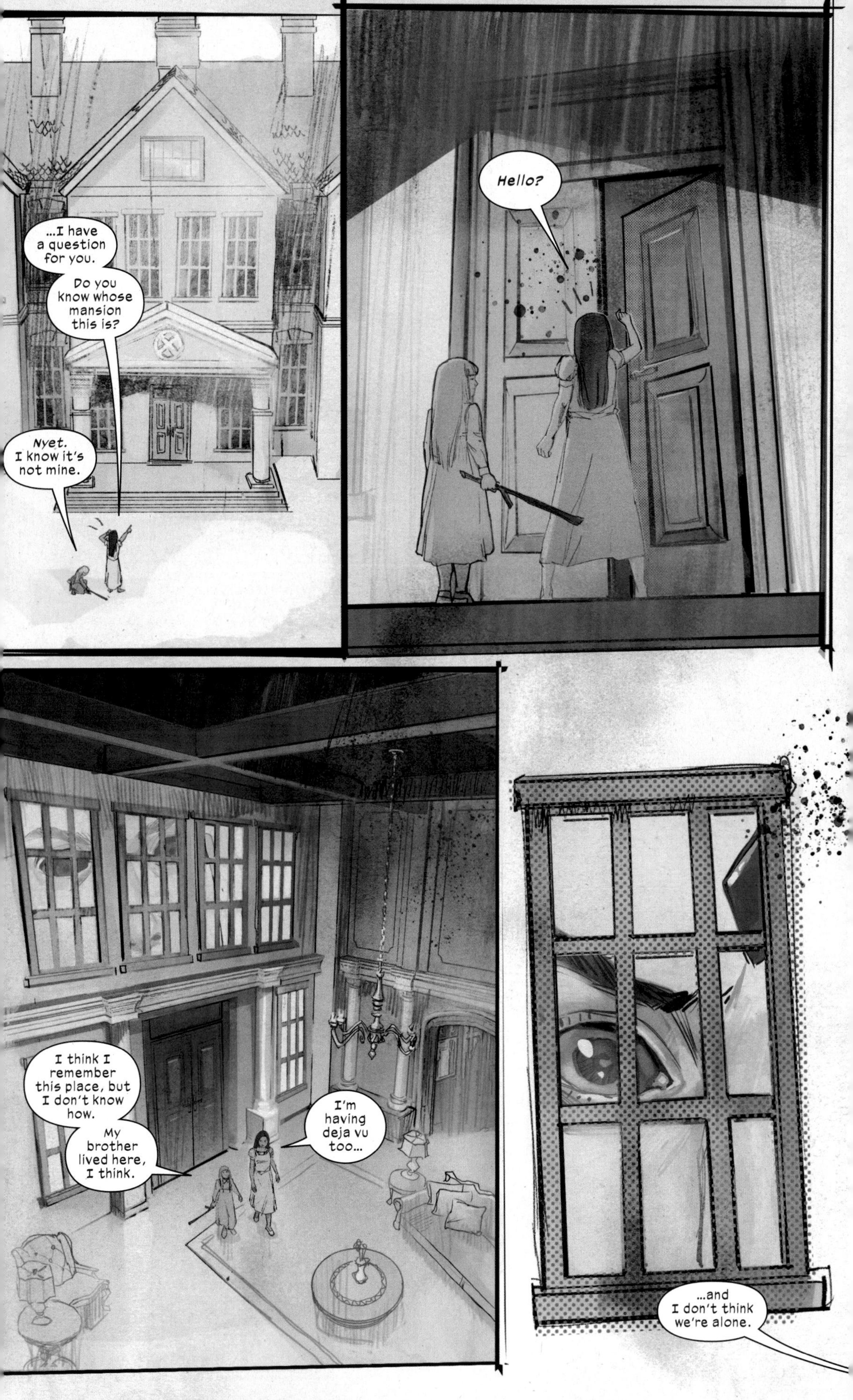
...I have a question for you.
Do you know whose mansion this is?
Nyet. I know it's not mine.
Hello?
I think I remember this place, but I don't know how.
My brother lived here, I think.
I'm having deja vu too...
...and I don't think we're alone.

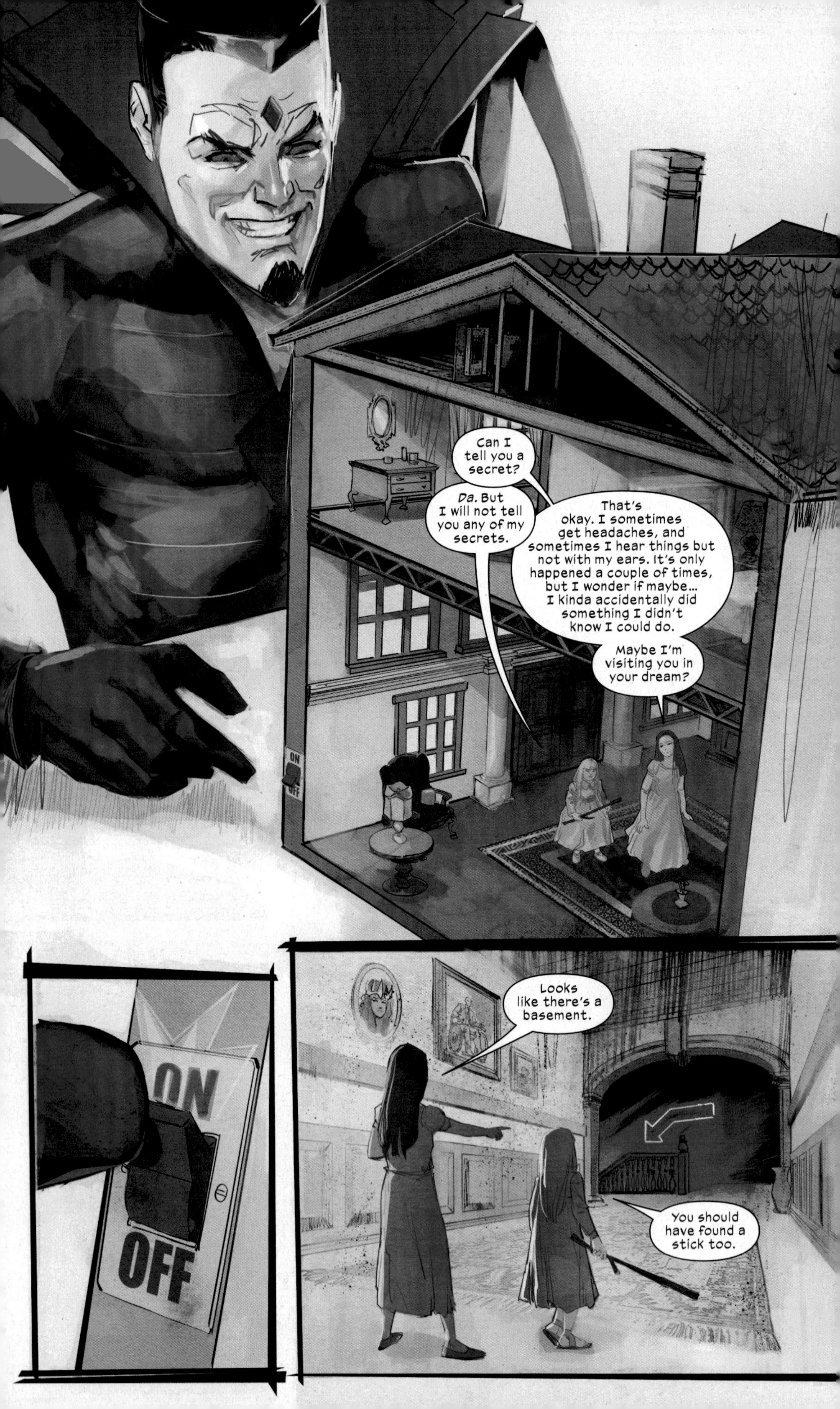
Can I tell you a secret?
Da. But I will not tell you any of my secrets.
That's okay. I sometimes get headaches, and sometimes I hear things but not with my ears. It's only happened a couple of times, but I wonder if maybe... I kinda accidentally did something I didn't know I could do.
Maybe I'm visiting you in your dream?
ON
OFF
ON
OFF
Looks like there's a basement.
You should have found a stick too.

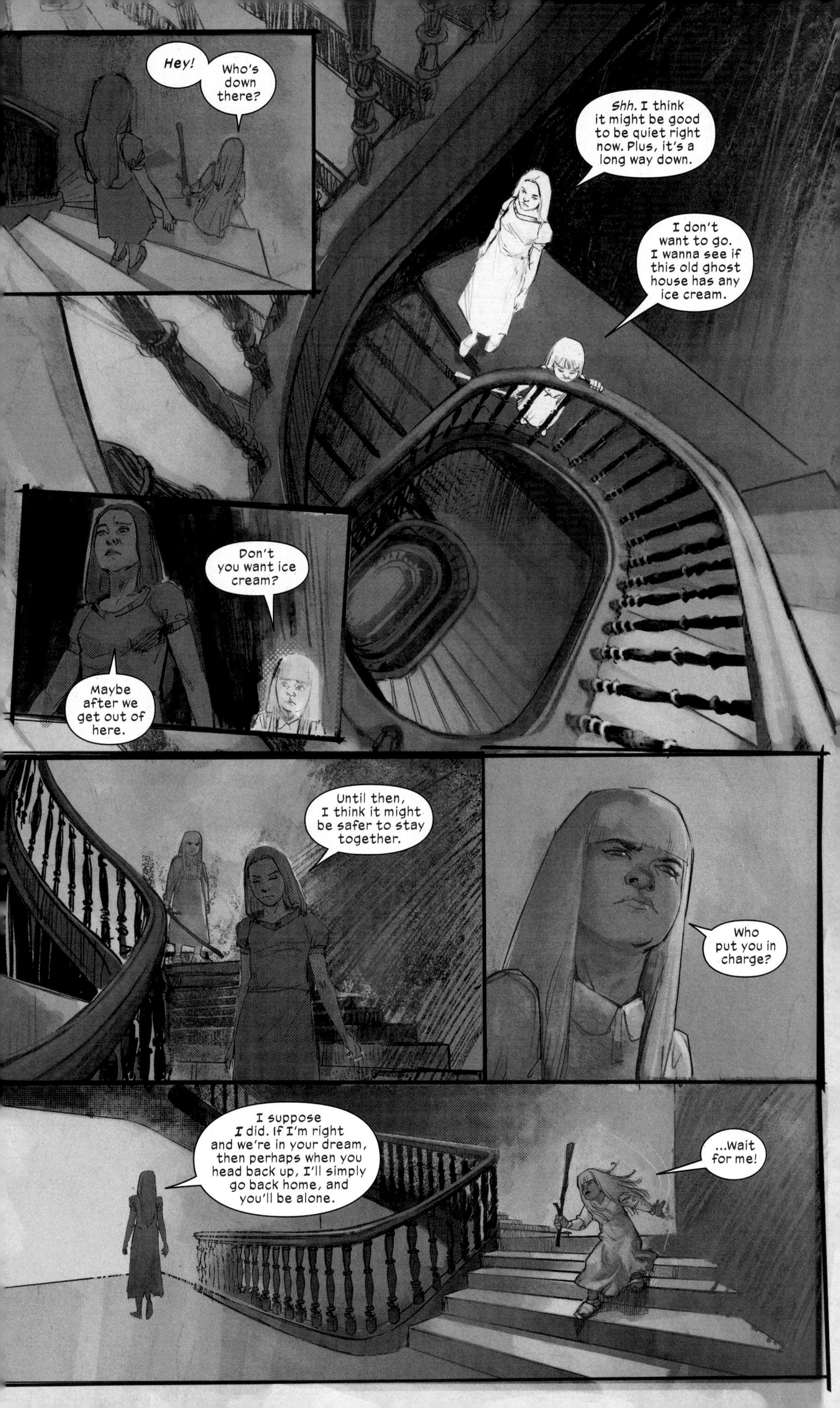
Hey!
Who's down there?
Shh. I think it might be good to be quiet right now. Plus, it's a long way down.
I don't want to go. I wanna see if this old ghost house has any ice cream.
Don't you want ice cream?
Maybe after we get out of here.
Until then, I think it might be safer to stay together.
Who put you in charge?
I suppose I did. If I'm right and we're in your dream, then perhaps when you head back up, I'll simply go back home, and you'll be alone.
...Wait for me!

The Goblin Queen was already a powerful force by nature of her copied mutant powers. Jean Grey is a powerful telepath and telekinetic, and after Magik turned the throne of the demon realm Limbo over to her, she inherited many powerful spells.

Cyclops and Havok were separated from Magik and Jean Grey when they arrived in Limbo and Maddie set about to divide and conquer. She deployed her mutant gifts against the women and her spell books against the men. The outfit that she had Havok placed into is another matter and is probably indicative of her need to make the men feel the same shame she'd felt rightly or wrongly at their hands in the past. Life is messy, and it's messier when you're a clone -- let's leave it at that.

Some of you might be thinking, "Hey, why did Magik entrust Limbo to her anyway?" And that's not an unfair question, but let's see where things end up for Limbo at the end of the story.

Right now, let's see how the Summers brothers are dealing with being magically held in check in Maddie's dungeon.

[Limbo...(DarkWeb)]

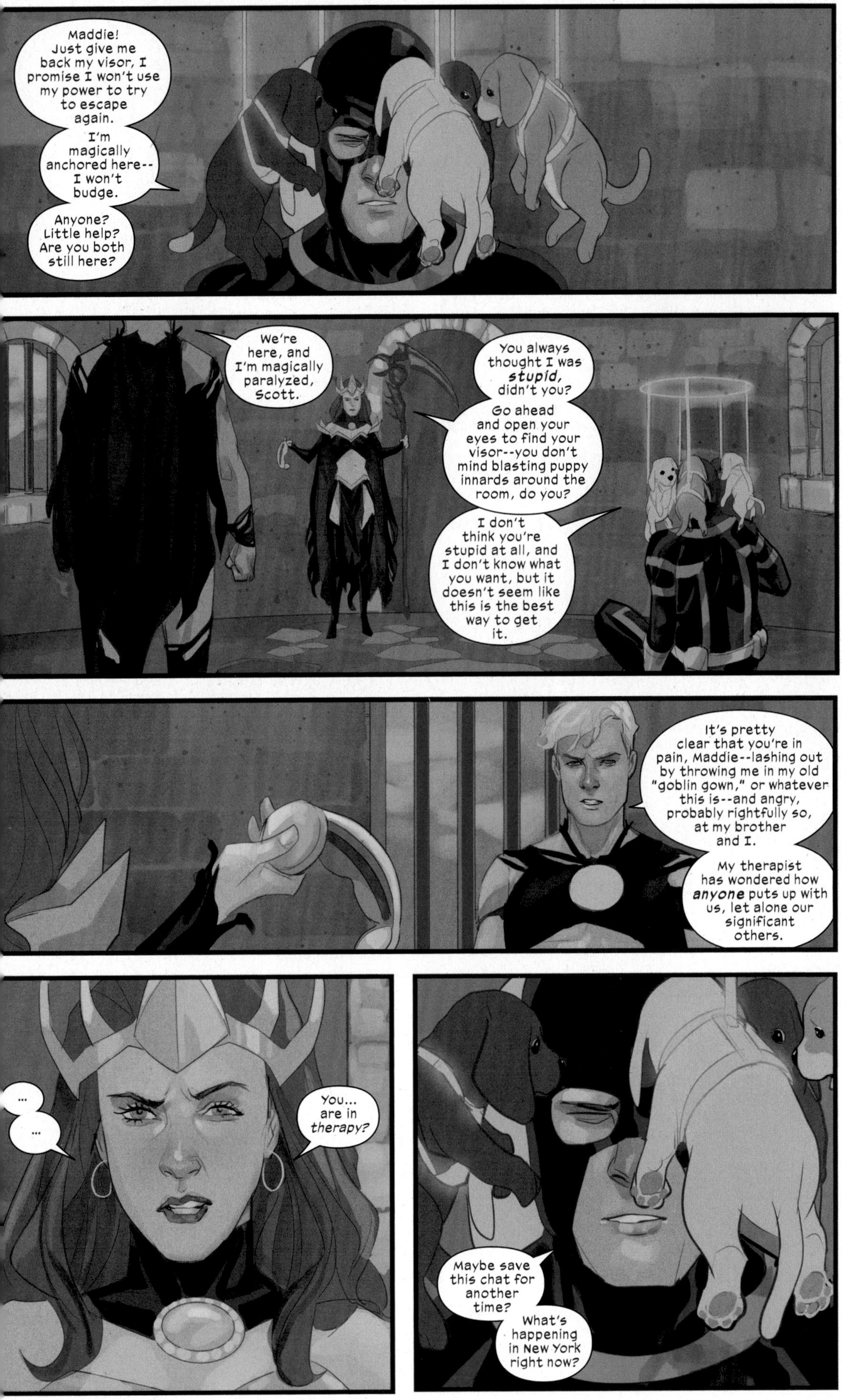
Maddie! Just give me back my visor, I promise I won't use my power to try to escape again.
I'm magically anchored here-- I won't budge.
Anyone? Little help? Are you both still here?
We're here, and I'm magically paralyzed, Scott.
You always thought I was *stupid,* didn't you?
Go ahead and open your eyes to find your visor--you don't mind blasting puppy innards around the room, do you?
I don't think you're stupid at all, and I don't know what you want, but it doesn't seem like this is the best way to get it.
It's pretty clear that you're in pain, Maddie--lashing out by throwing me in my old "goblin gown," or whatever this is--and angry, probably rightfully so, at my brother and I.
My therapist has wondered how **anyone** puts up with us, let alone our significant others.
...
...
You... are in *therapy?*
Maybe save this chat for another time?
What's happening in New York right now?

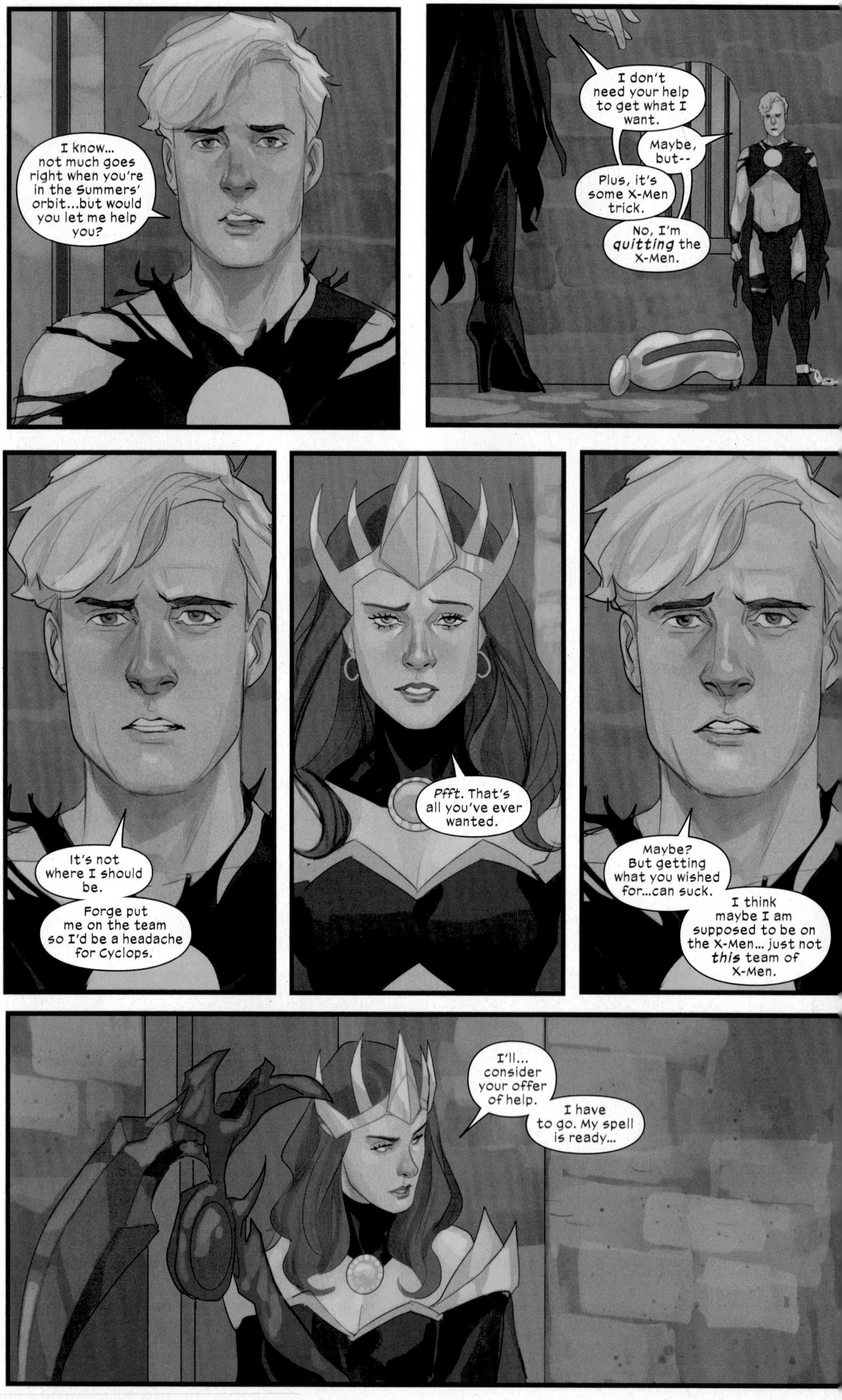

I know... not much goes right when you're in the Summers' orbit...but would you let me help you?
I don't need your help to get what I want.
Maybe, but--
Plus, it's some X-Men trick.
No, I'm *quitting* the X-Men.
It's not where I should be.
Forge put me on the team so I'd be a headache for Cyclops.
Pfft. That's all you've ever wanted.
Maybe? But getting what you wished for...can suck.
I think maybe I am supposed to be on the X-Men... just not *this* team of X-Men.
I'll... consider your offer of help.
I have to go. My spell is ready...

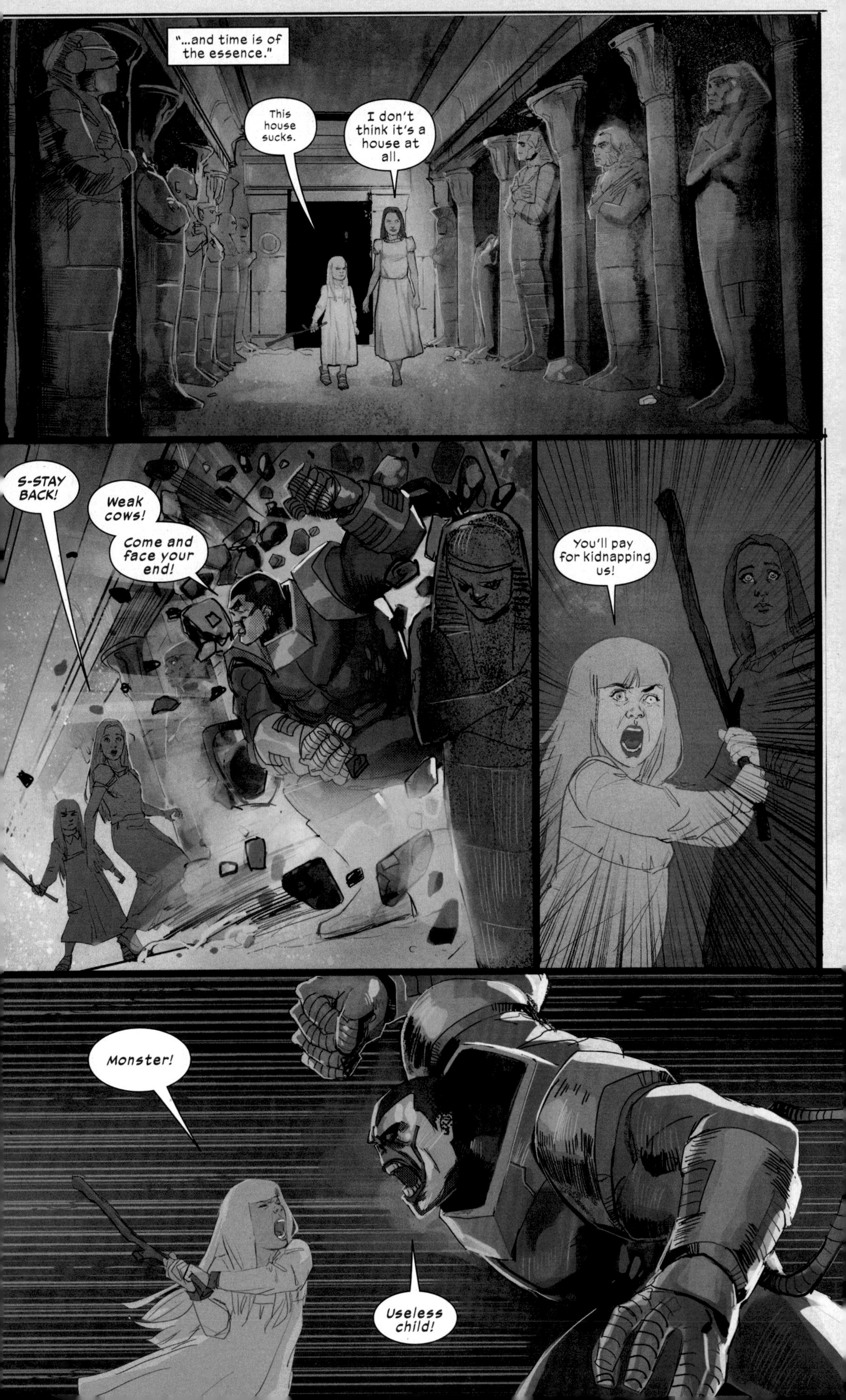
"...and time is of the essence."
This house sucks.
I don't think it's a house at all.
S-STAY BACK!
Weak cows!
Come and face your end!
You'll pay for kidnapping us!
Monster!
Useless child!

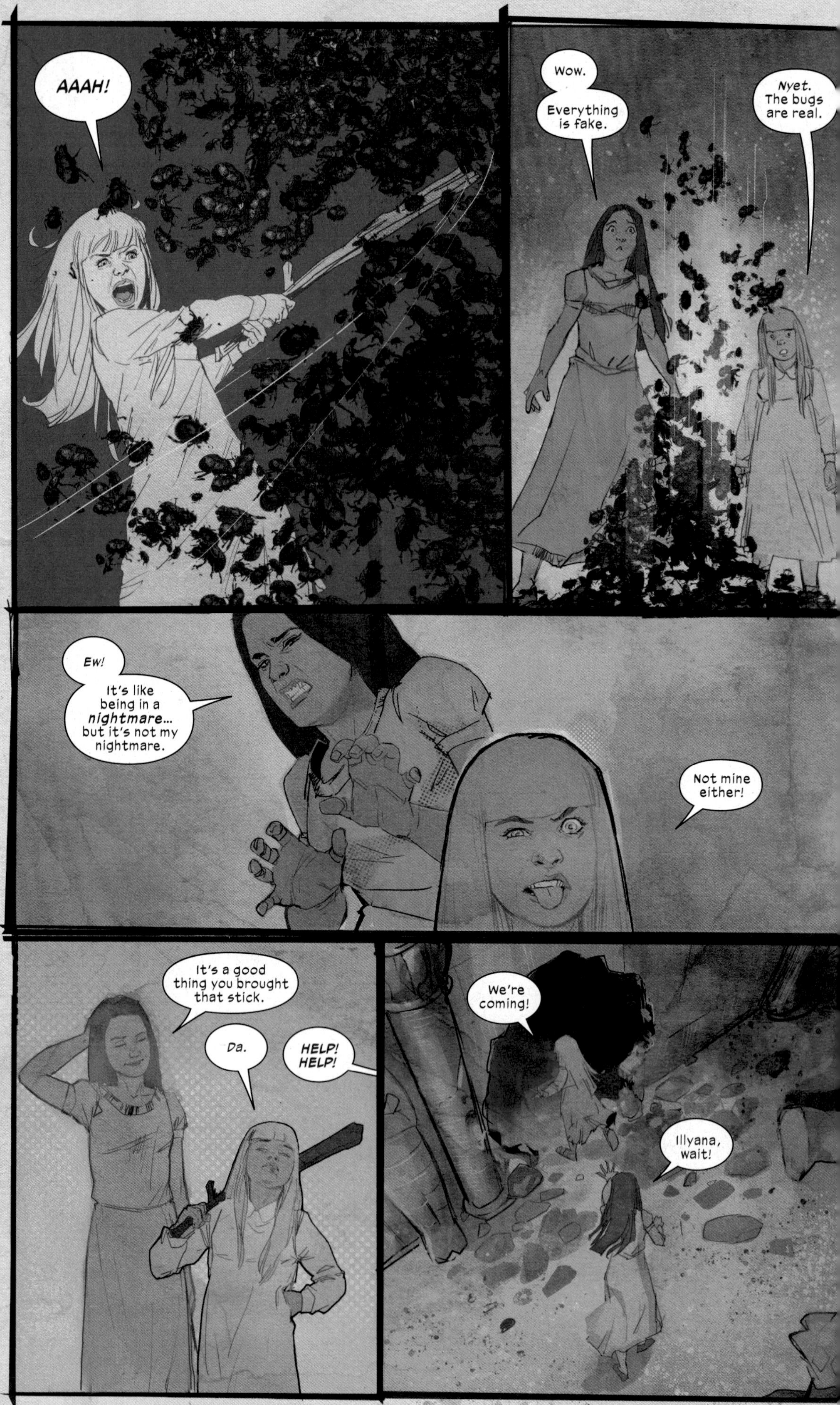
AAAH!
Wow.
Everything is fake.
Nyet. The bugs are real.
Ew!
It's like being in a nightmare... but it's not my nightmare.
Not mine either!
It's a good thing you brought that stick.
Da.
HELP! HELP!
We're coming!
Illyana, wait!

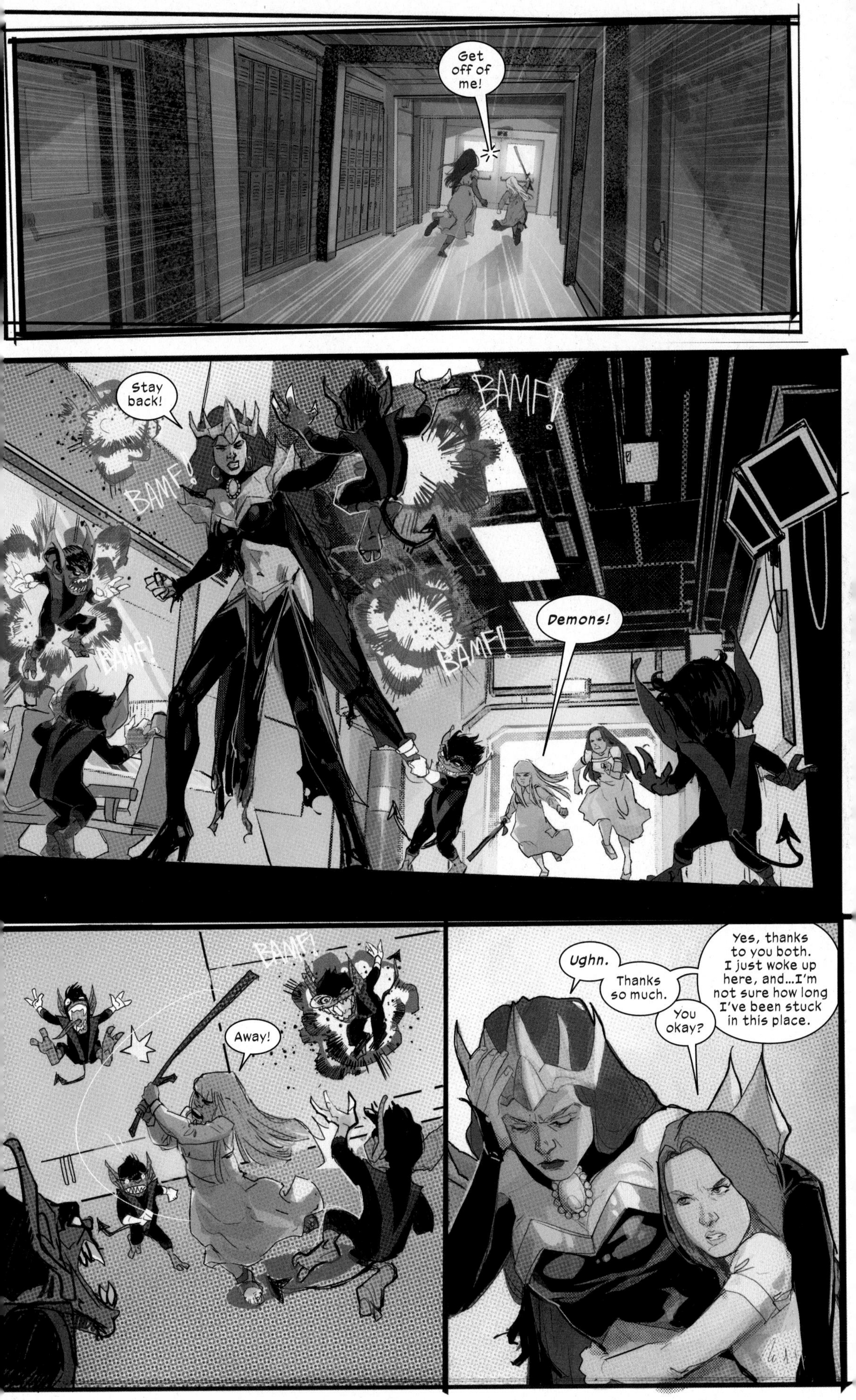
Get off of me!
Stay back!
BAMF!
BAMF!
BAMF!
BAMF!
Demons!
BAMF!
Away!
Ughn.
Thanks so much.
You okay?
Yes, thanks to you both. I just woke up here, and...I'm not sure how long I've been stuck in this place.

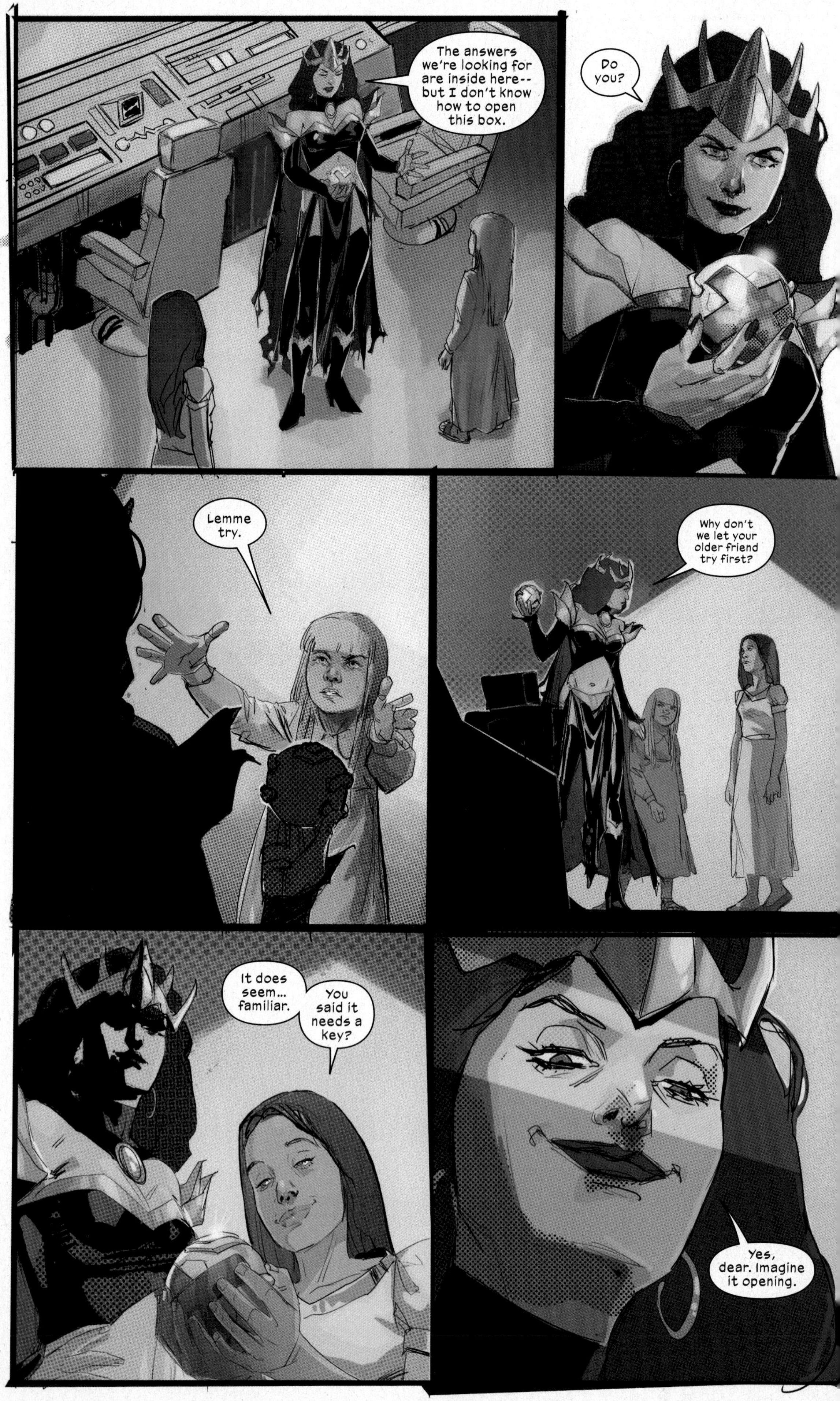
The answers we're looking for are inside here-- but I don't know how to open this box.
Do you?
Lemme try.
Why don't we let your older friend try first?
It does seem... familiar.
You said it needs a key?
Yes, dear. Imagine it opening.

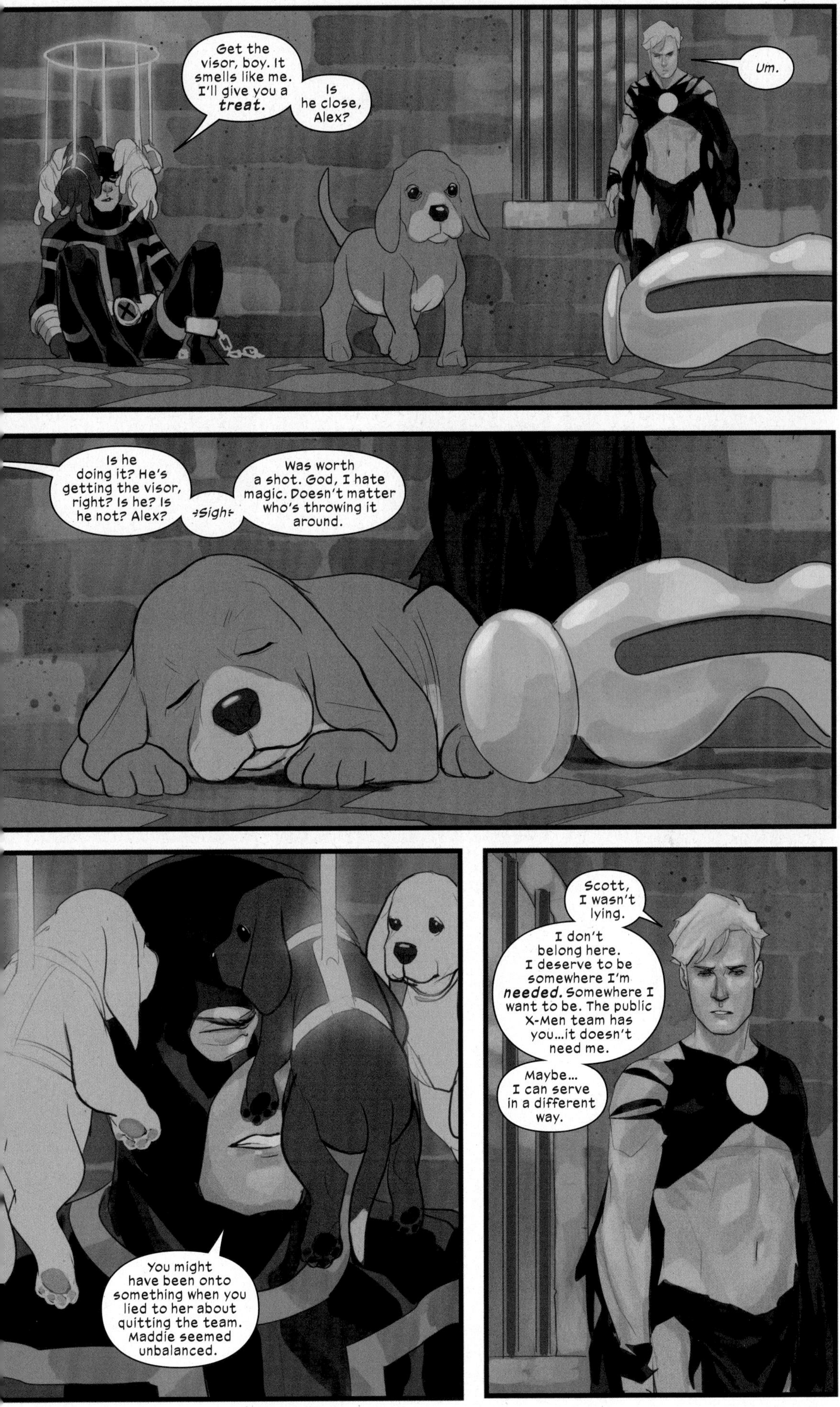

Get the visor, boy. It smells like me. I'll give you a *treat.*
Is he close, Alex?
Um.
Is he doing it? He's getting the visor, right? Is he? Is he not? Alex?
Sigh
Was worth a shot. God, I hate magic. Doesn't matter who's throwing it around.
You might have been onto something when you lied to her about quitting the team. Maddie seemed unbalanced.
Scott, I wasn't lying.
I don't belong here. I deserve to be somewhere I'm *needed.* Somewhere I want to be. The public X-Men team has you...it doesn't need me.
Maybe... I can serve in a different way.

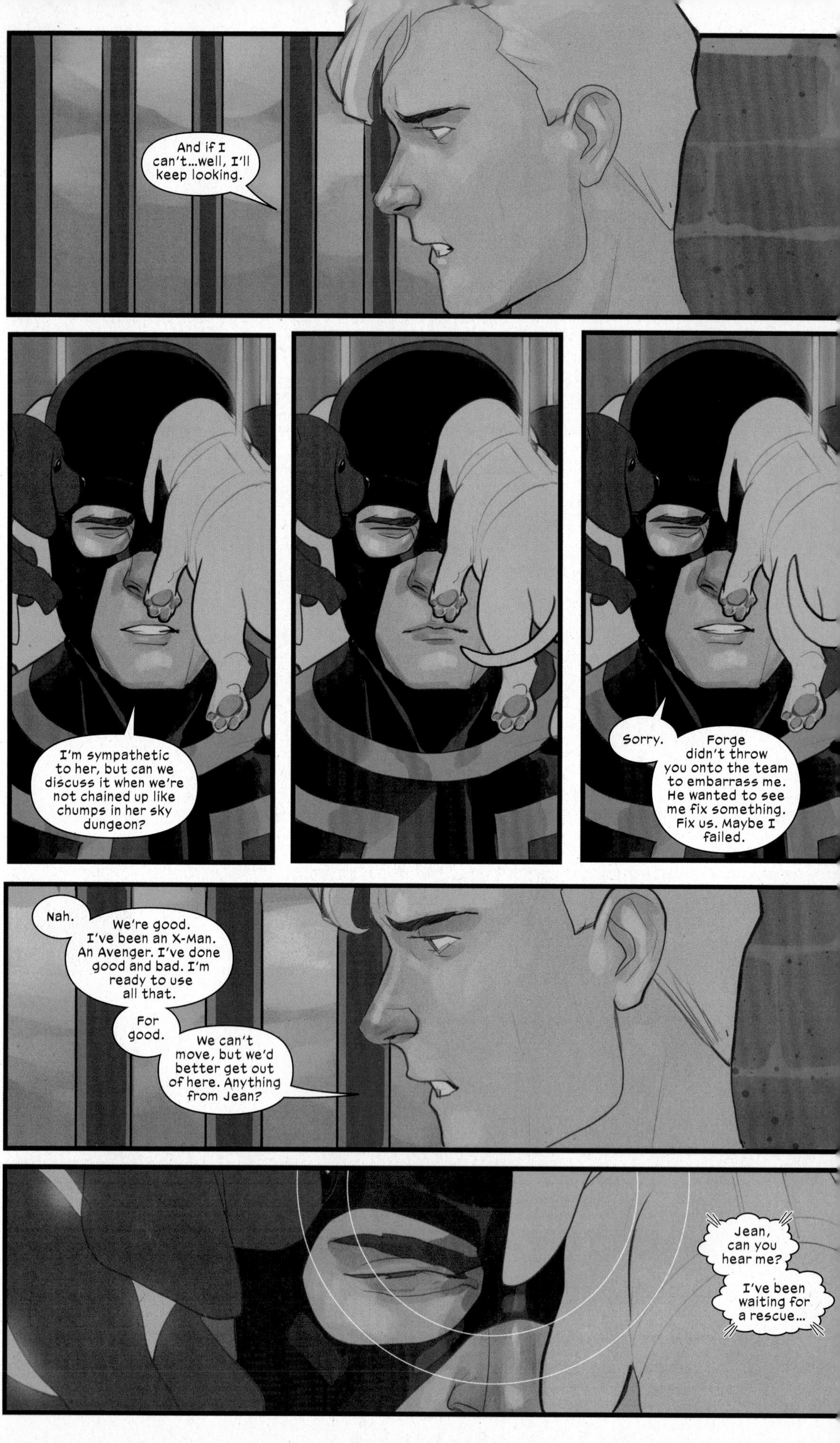
And if I can't...well, I'll keep looking.
I'm sympathetic to her, but can we discuss it when we're not chained up like chumps in her sky dungeon?
Sorry.
Forge didn't throw you onto the team to embarrass me. He wanted to see me fix something. Fix us. Maybe I failed.
Nah.
We're good. I've been an X-Man. An Avenger. I've done good and bad. I'm ready to use all that.
For good.
We can't move, but we'd better get out of here. Anything from Jean?
Jean, can you hear me?
I've been waiting for a rescue...

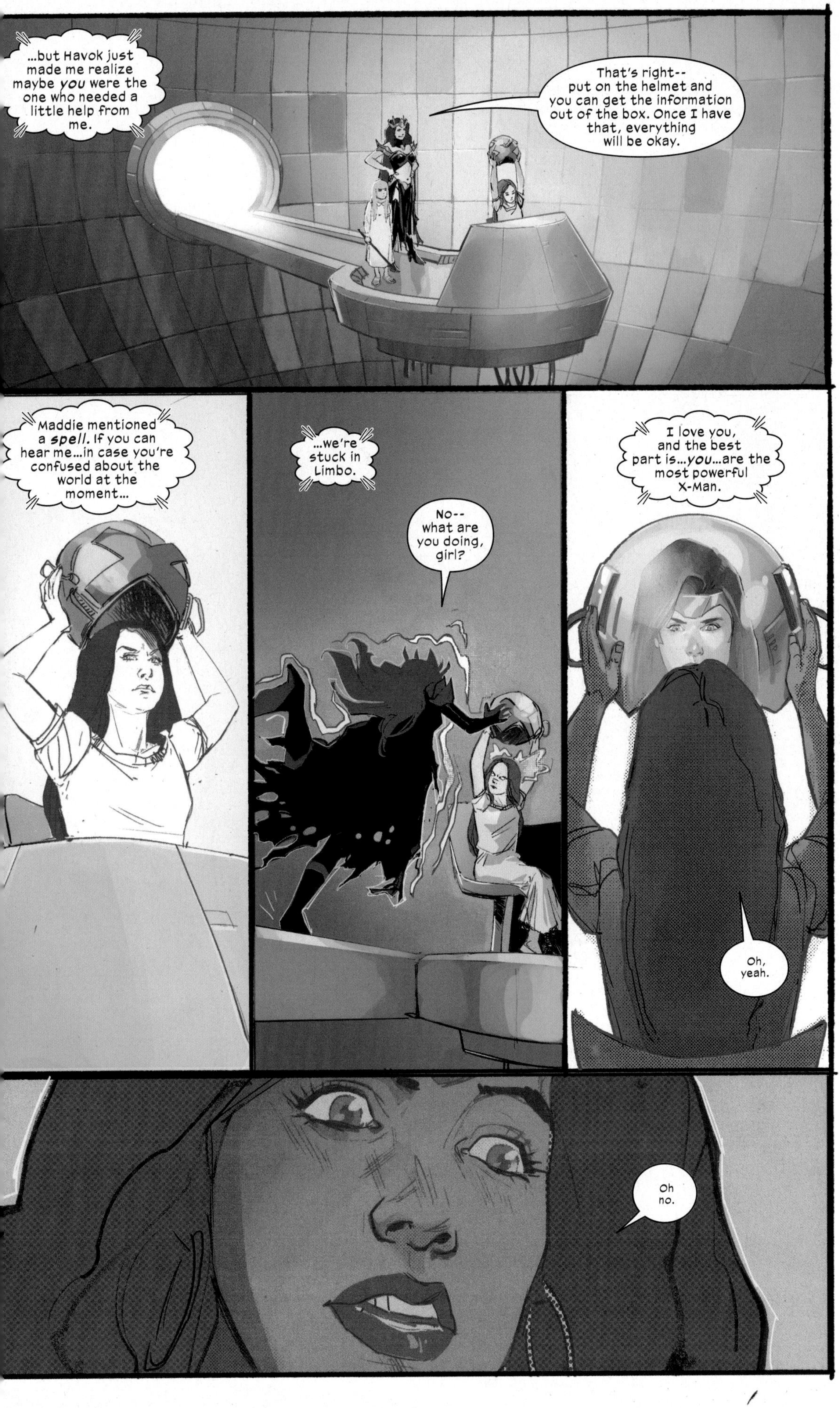

...but Havok just made me realize maybe *you* were the one who needed a little help from me.
That's right-- put on the helmet and you can get the information out of the box. Once I have that, everything will be okay.
Maddie mentioned a *spell*. If you can hear me...in case you're confused about the world at the moment...
...we're stuck in Limbo.
No-- what are you doing, girl?
I love you, and the best part is...*you*...are the most powerful X-Man.
Oh, yeah.
Oh no.

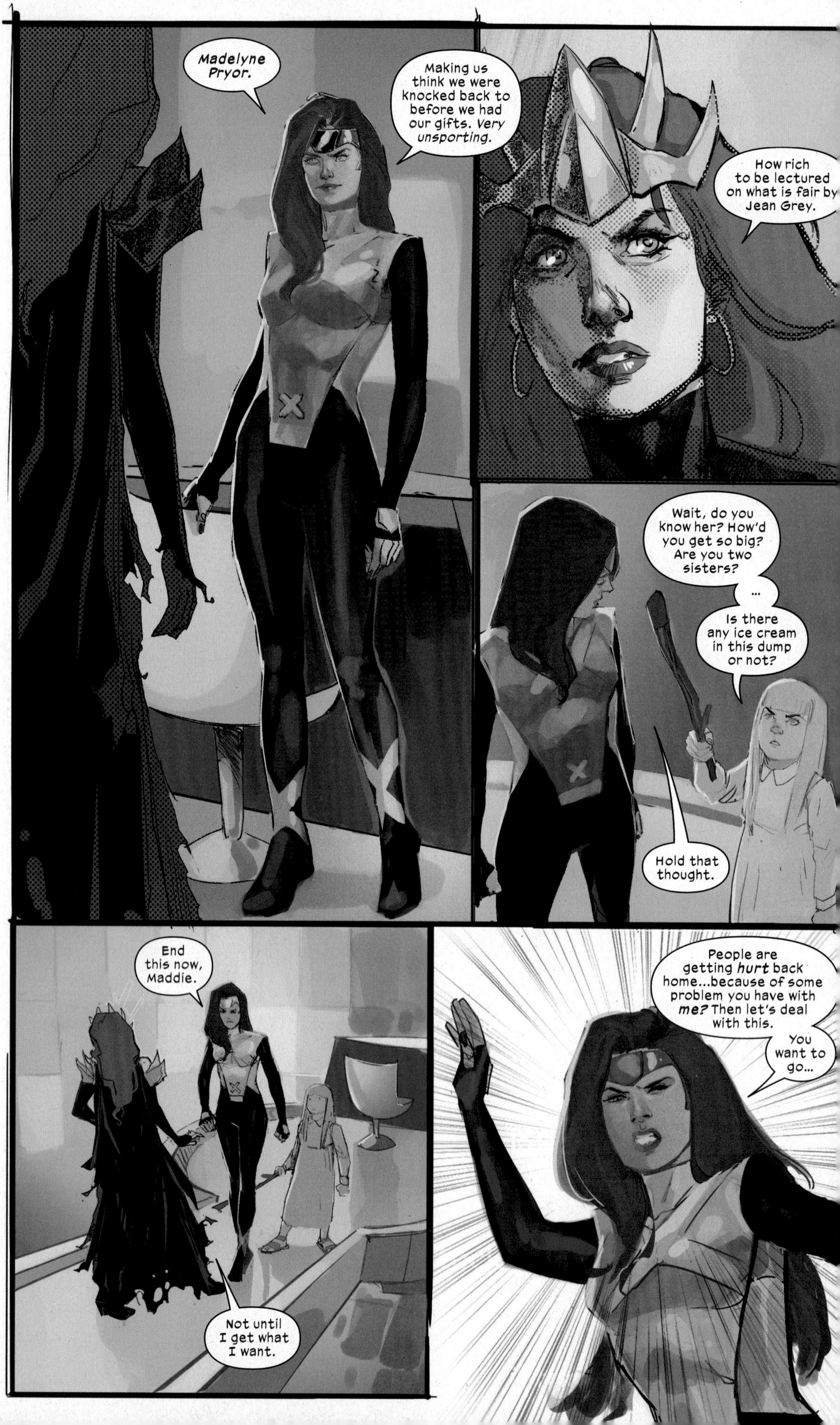

Madelyne Pryor.
Making us think we were knocked back to before we had our gifts. *Very unsporting.*
How rich to be lectured on what is fair by Jean Grey.
Wait, do you know her? How'd you get so big? Are you two sisters?
...
Is there any ice cream in this dump or not?
Hold that thought.
End this now, Maddie.
Not until I get what I want.
People are getting *hurt* back home...because of some problem you have with *me?* Then let's deal with this.
You want to go...

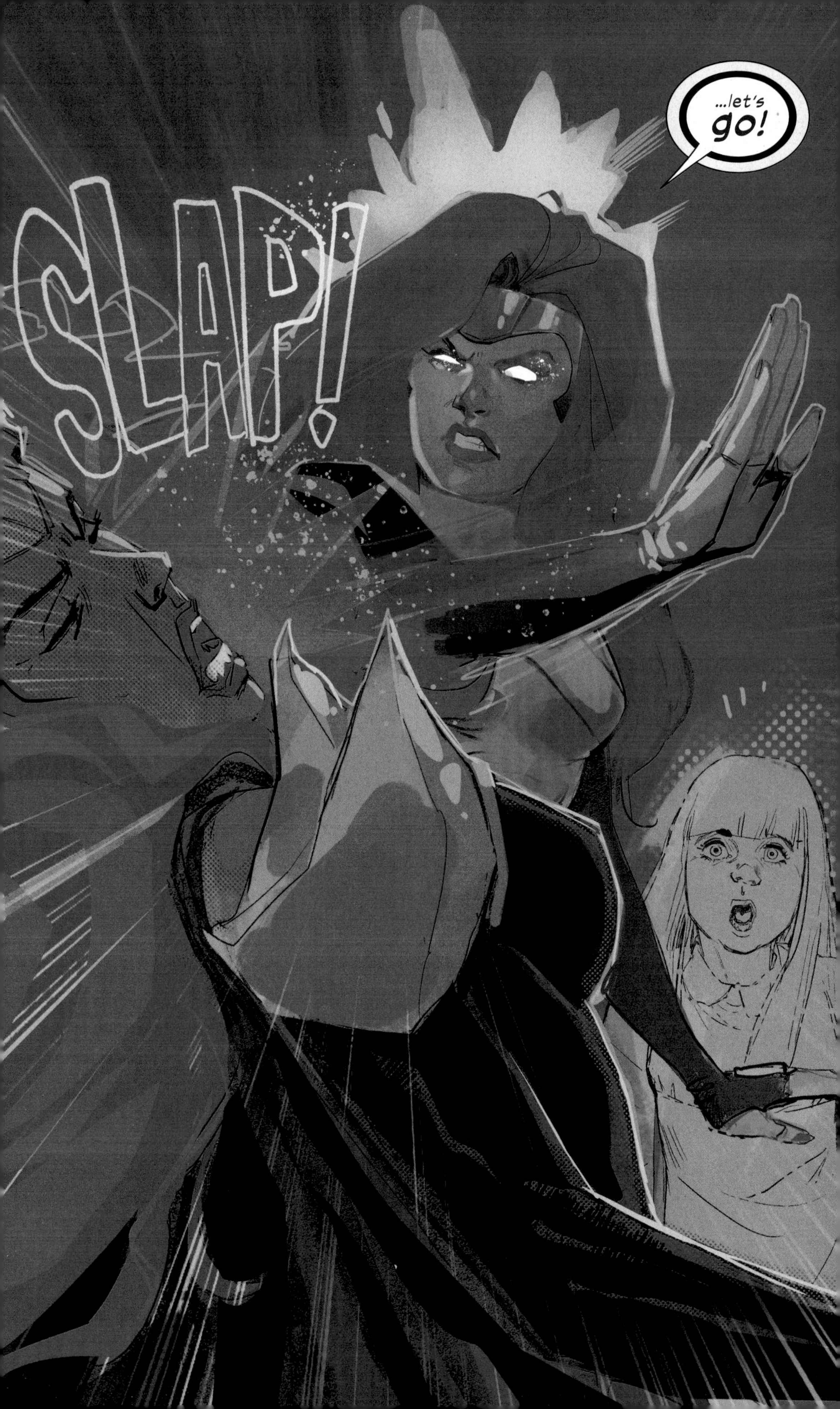
SLAP!
...let's go!

DARK WEB: X-MEN #3

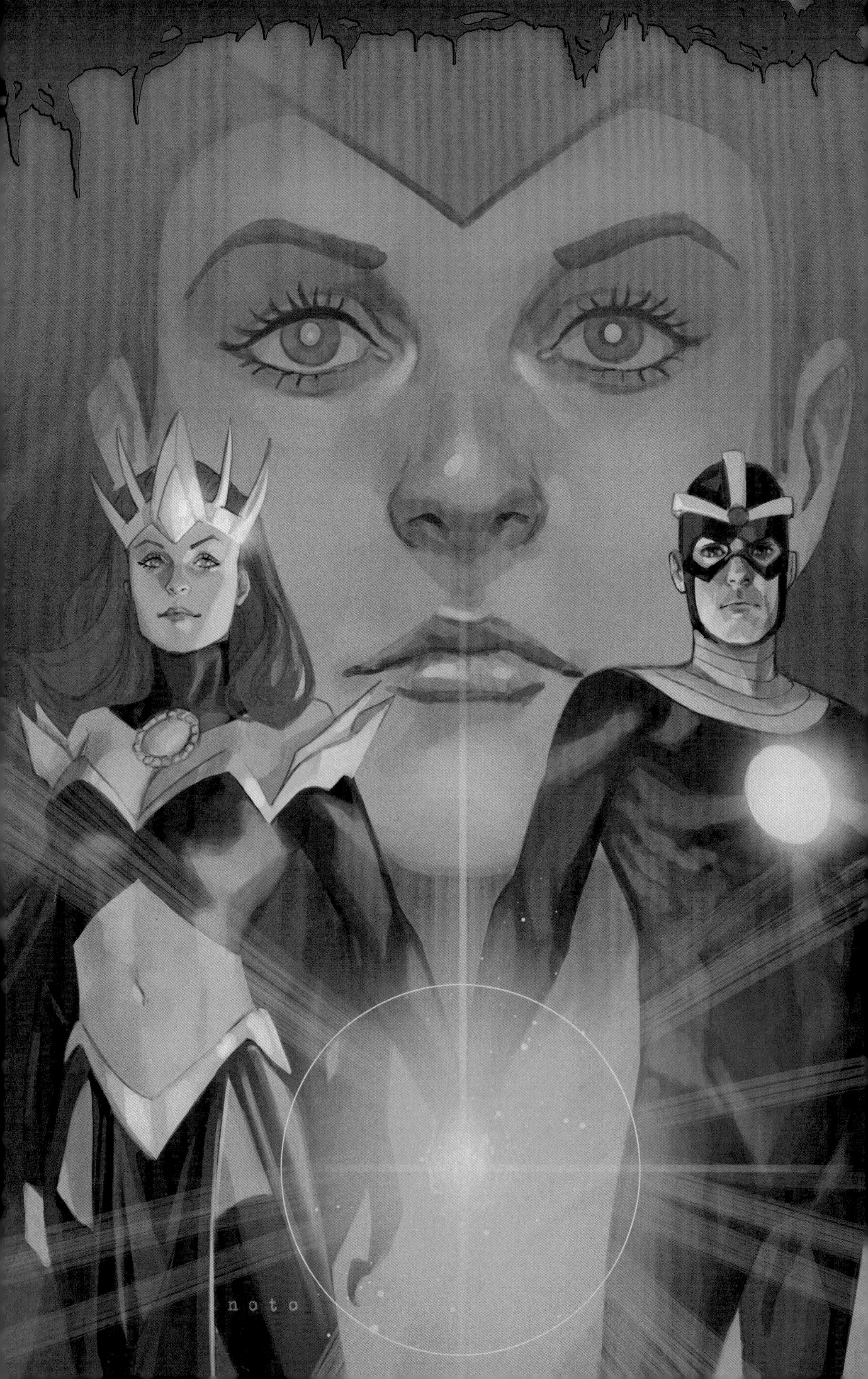
noto

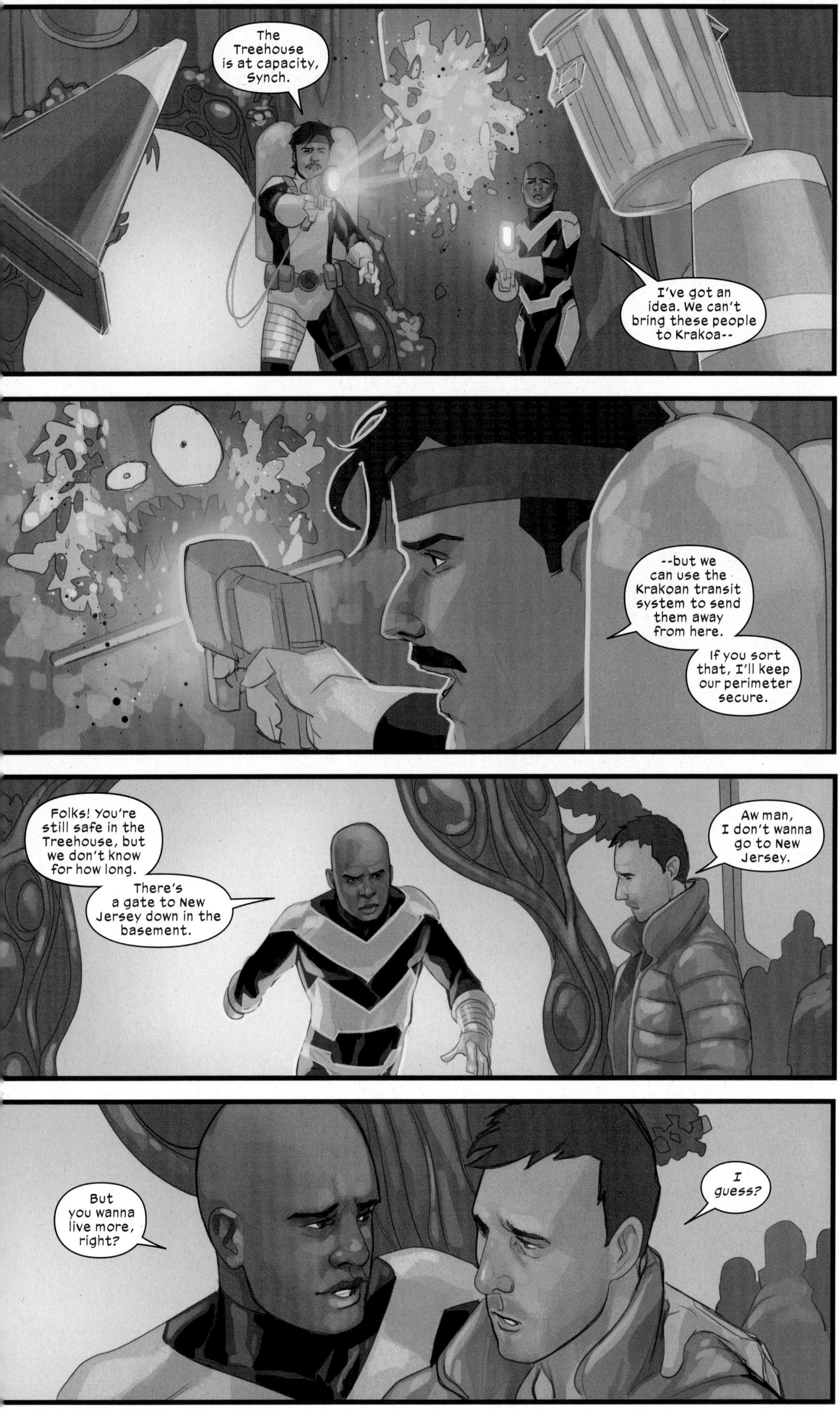

The Treehouse is at capacity, Synch.
I've got an idea. We can't bring these people to Krakoa--
--but we can use the Krakoan transit system to send them away from here.
If you sort that, I'll keep our perimeter secure.
Folks! You're still safe in the Treehouse, but we don't know for how long.
There's a gate to New Jersey down in the basement.
Aw man, I don't wanna go to New Jersey.
But you wanna live more, right?
I guess?

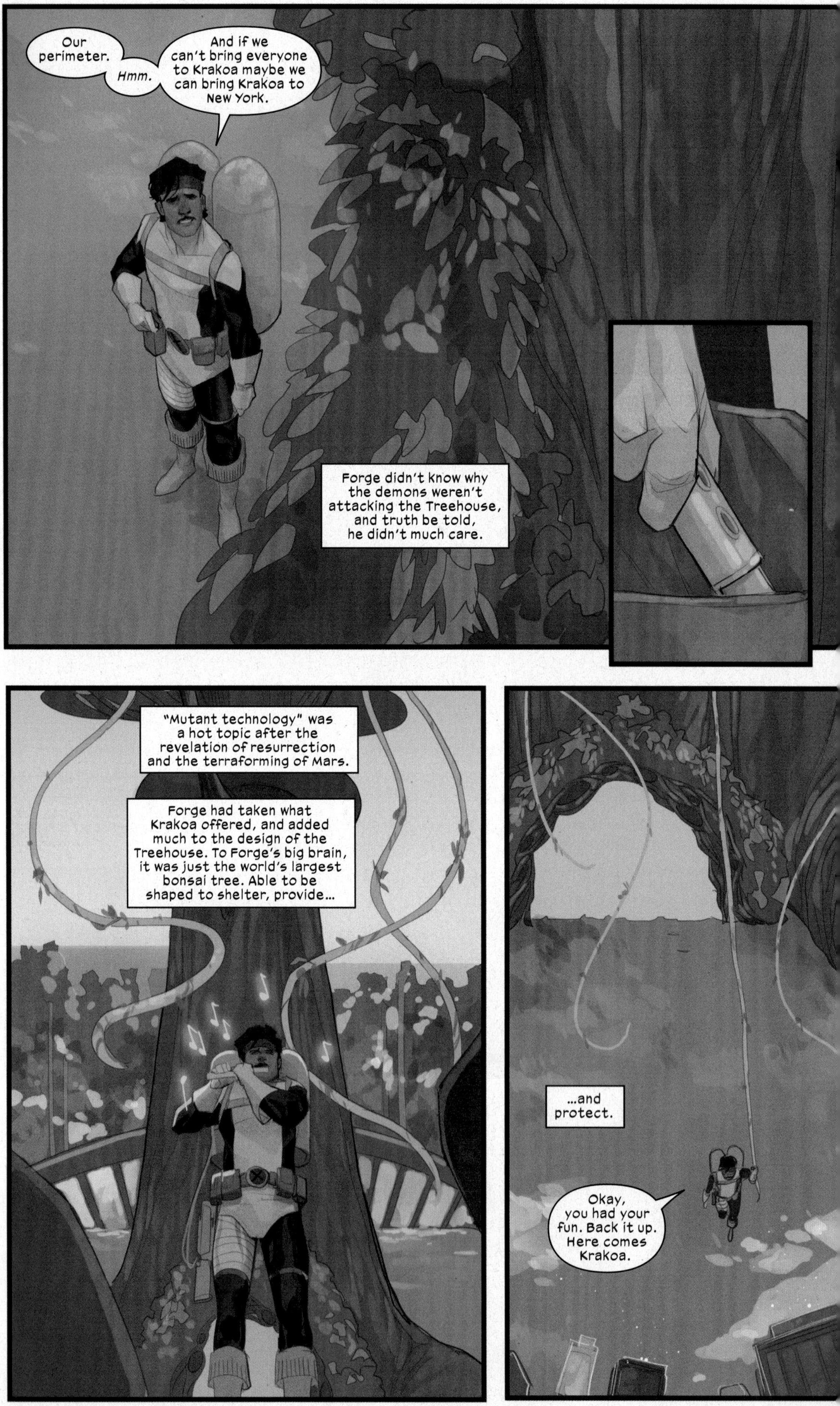
Our perimeter.
Hmm.
And if we can't bring everyone to Krakoa maybe we can bring Krakoa to New York.
Forge didn't know why the demons weren't attacking the Treehouse, and truth be told, he didn't much care.
"Mutant technology" was a hot topic after the revelation of resurrection and the terraforming of Mars.
Forge had taken what Krakoa offered, and added much to the design of the Treehouse. To Forge's big brain, it was just the world's largest bonsai tree. Able to be shaped to shelter, provide...
...and protect.
Okay, you had your fun. Back it up. Here comes Krakoa.

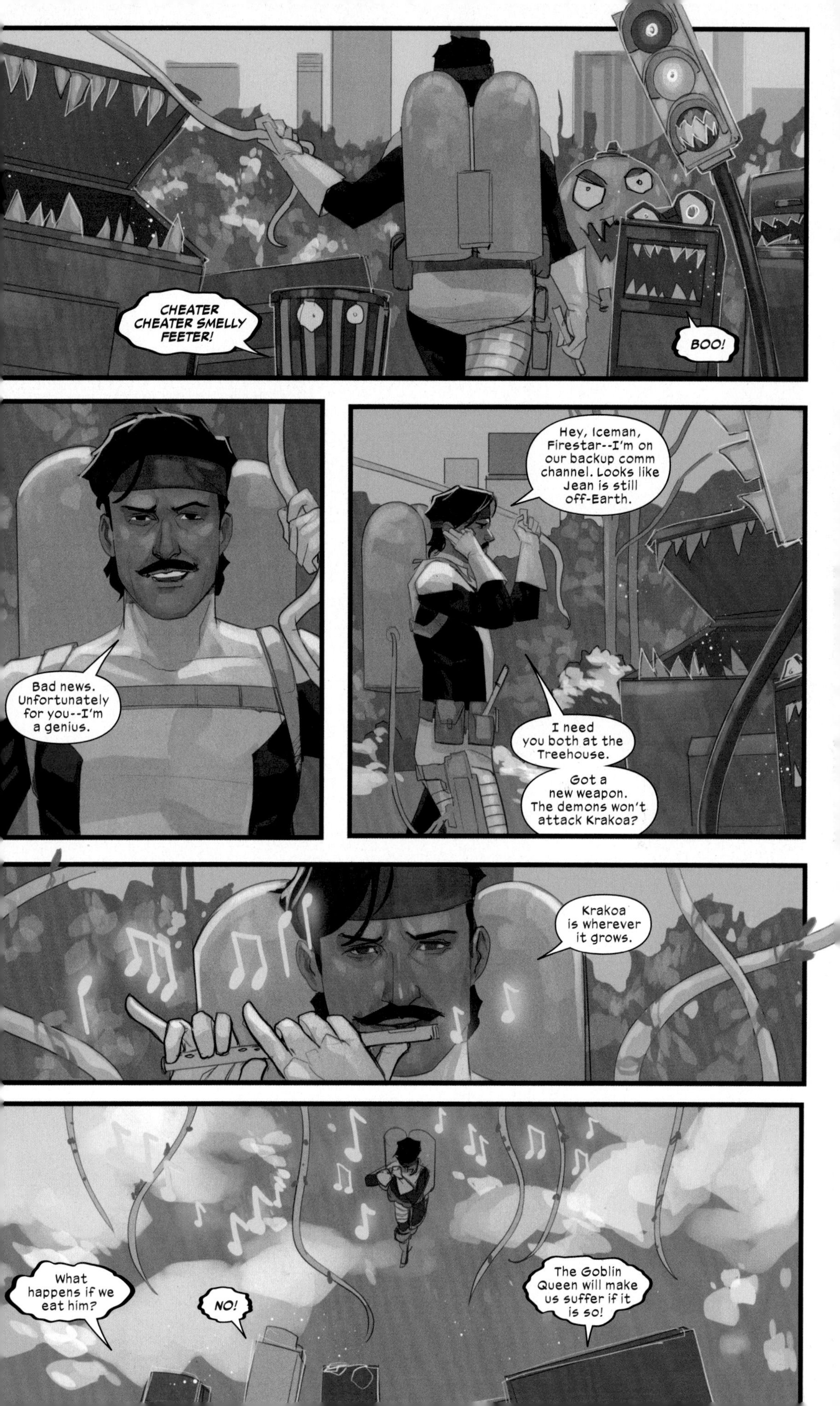
CHEATER CHEATER SMELLY FEETER!
BOO!
Bad news. Unfortunately for you--I'm a genius.
Hey, Iceman, Firestar--I'm on our backup comm channel. Looks like Jean is still off-Earth.
I need you both at the Treehouse.
Got a new weapon. The demons won't attack Krakoa?
Krakoa is wherever it grows.
What happens if we eat him?
NO!
The Goblin Queen will make us suffer if it is so!

"Being at peace with yourself can sometimes be difficult, even more so when you've been cloned."

-- JEAN GREY

[darkweb...[0.3]
[x_men.....[0.3]

[darkweb_xmen_03]

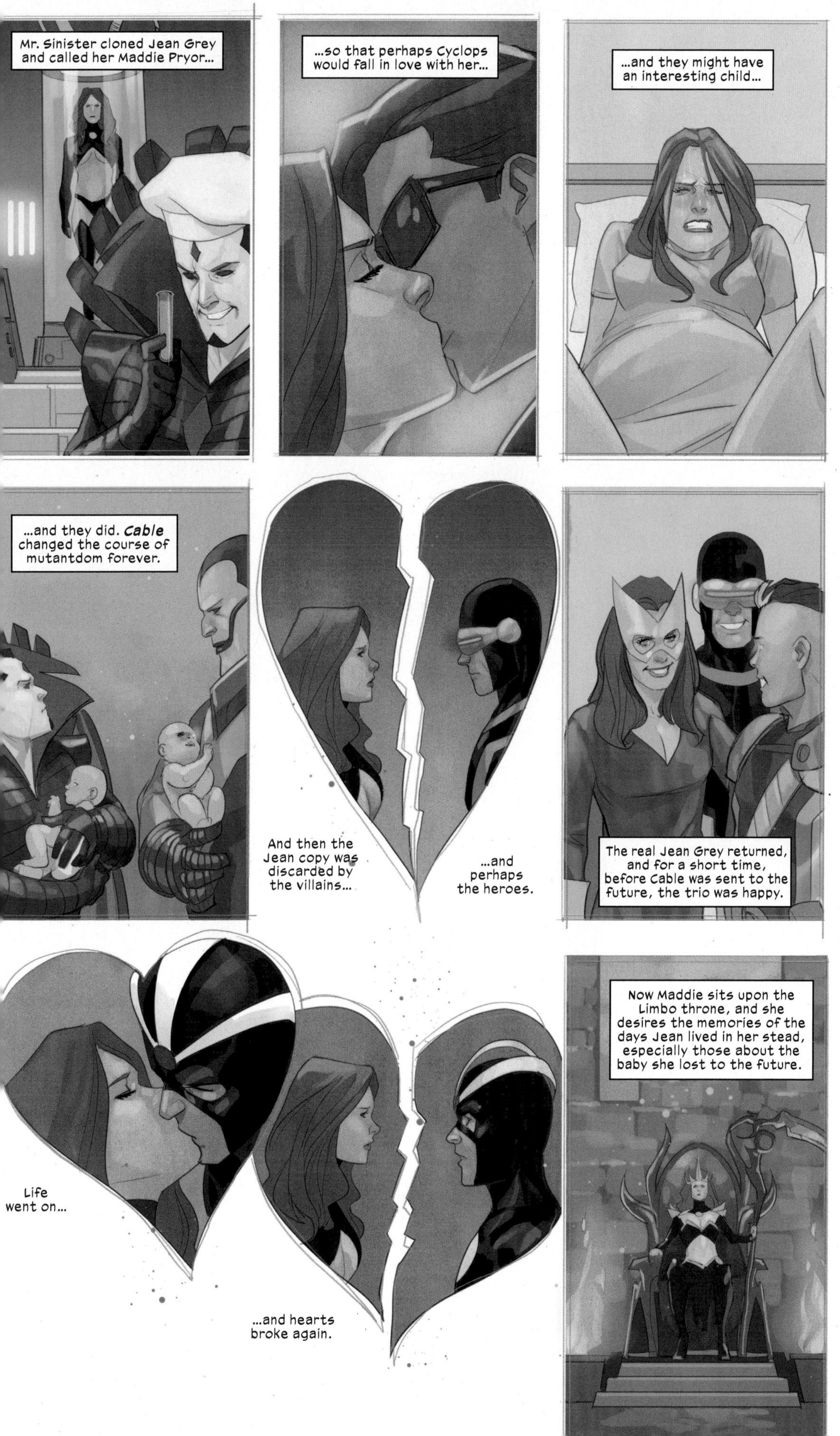
Mr. Sinister cloned Jean Grey and called her Maddie Pryor...
...so that perhaps Cyclops would fall in love with her...
...and they might have an interesting child...
...and they did. *Cable* changed the course of mutantdom forever.
And then the Jean copy was discarded by the villains...
...and perhaps the heroes.
The real Jean Grey returned, and for a short time, before Cable was sent to the future, the trio was happy.
Life went on...
...and hearts broke again.
Now Maddie sits upon the Limbo throne, and she desires the memories of the days Jean lived in her stead, especially those about the baby she lost to the future.

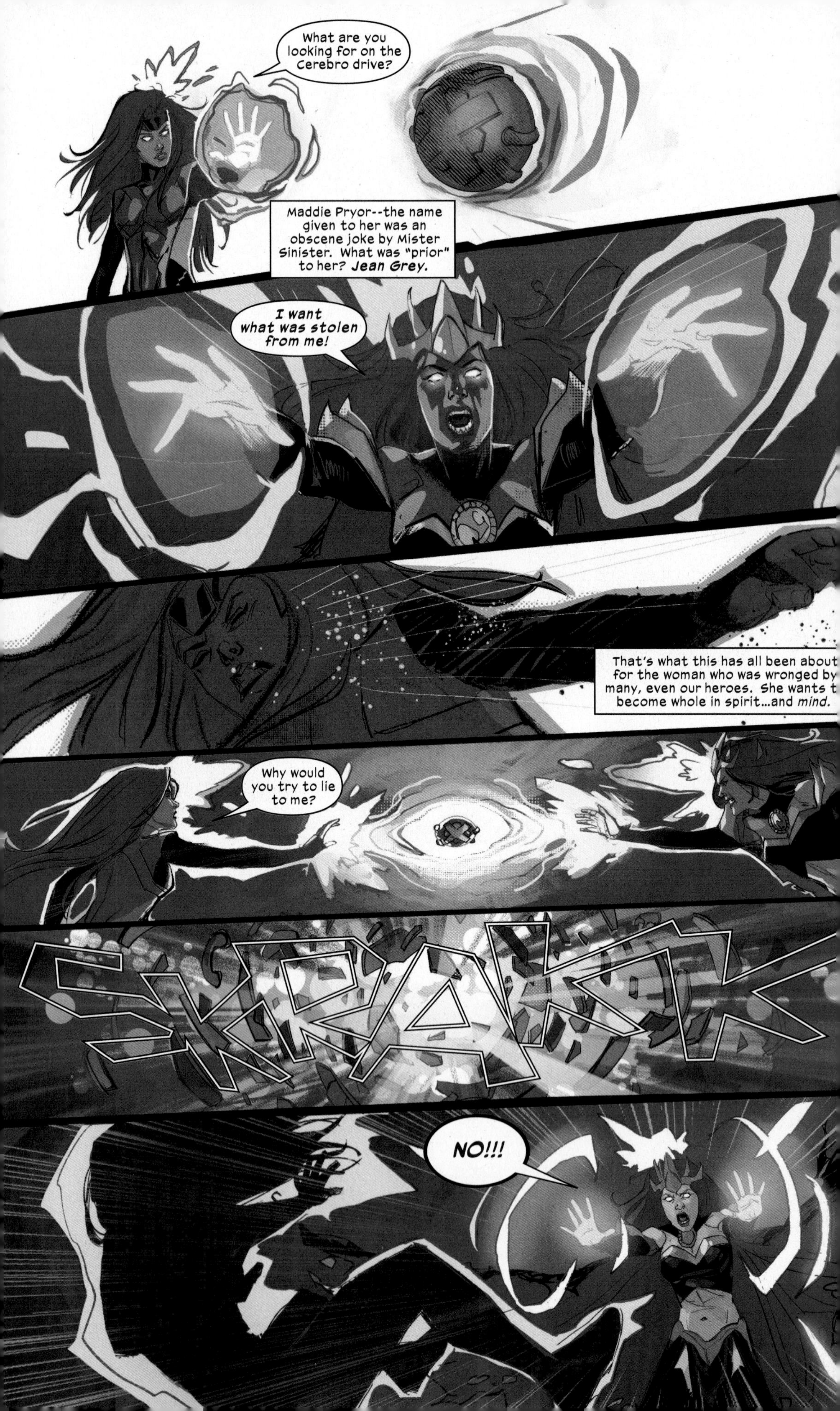

What are you looking for on the Cerebro drive?
Maddie Pryor--the name given to her was an obscene joke by Mister Sinister. What was "prior" to her? Jean Grey.
I want what was stolen from me!
That's what this has all been about for the woman who was wronged by many, even our heroes. She wants t become whole in spirit...and mind.
Why would you try to lie to me?
SKRAKK
NO!!!

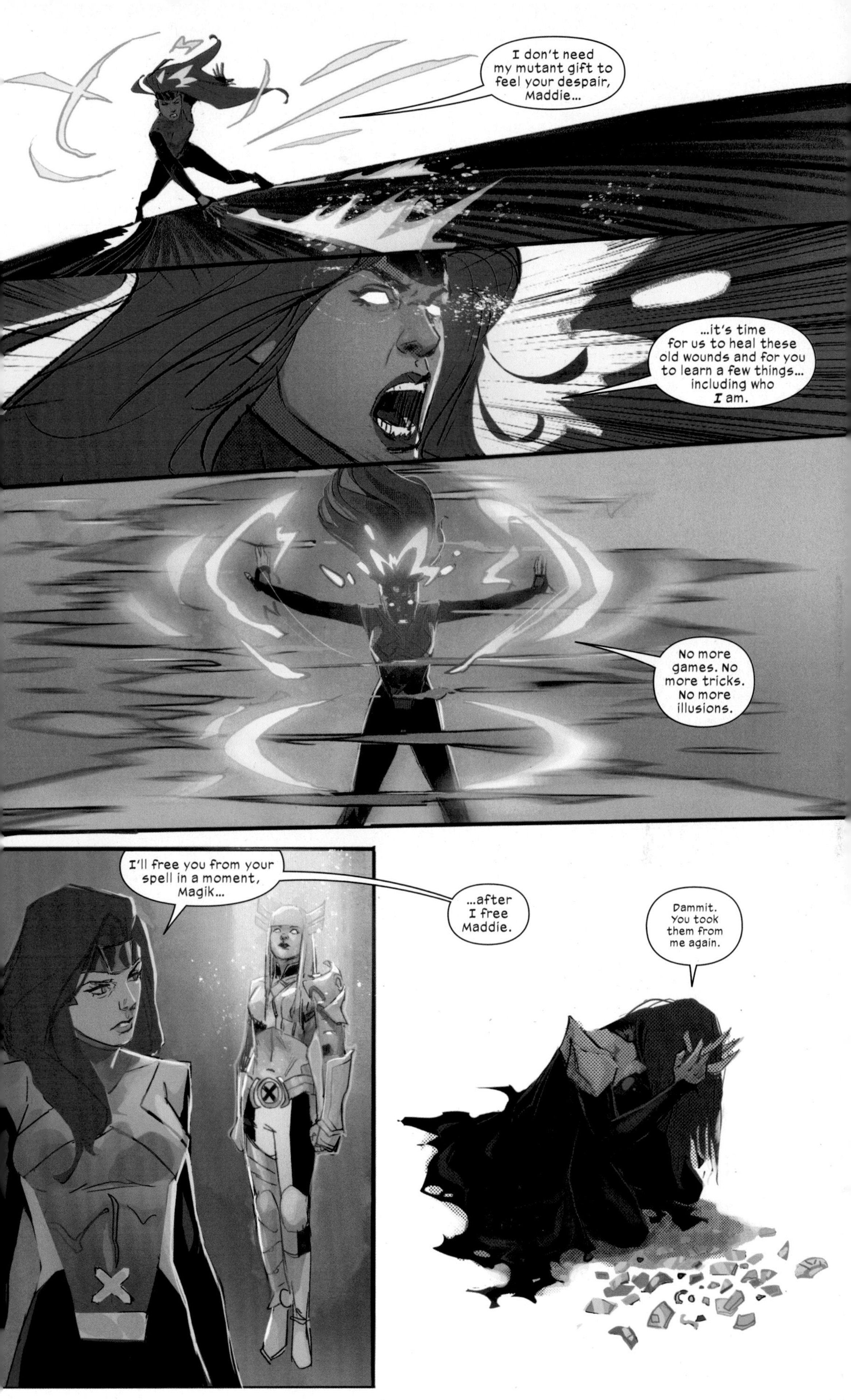
I don't need my mutant gift to feel your despair, Maddie...
...it's time for us to heal these old wounds and for you to learn a few things... including who I am.
No more games. No more tricks. No more illusions.
I'll free you from your spell in a moment, Magik...
...after I free Maddie.
Dammit. You took them from me again.

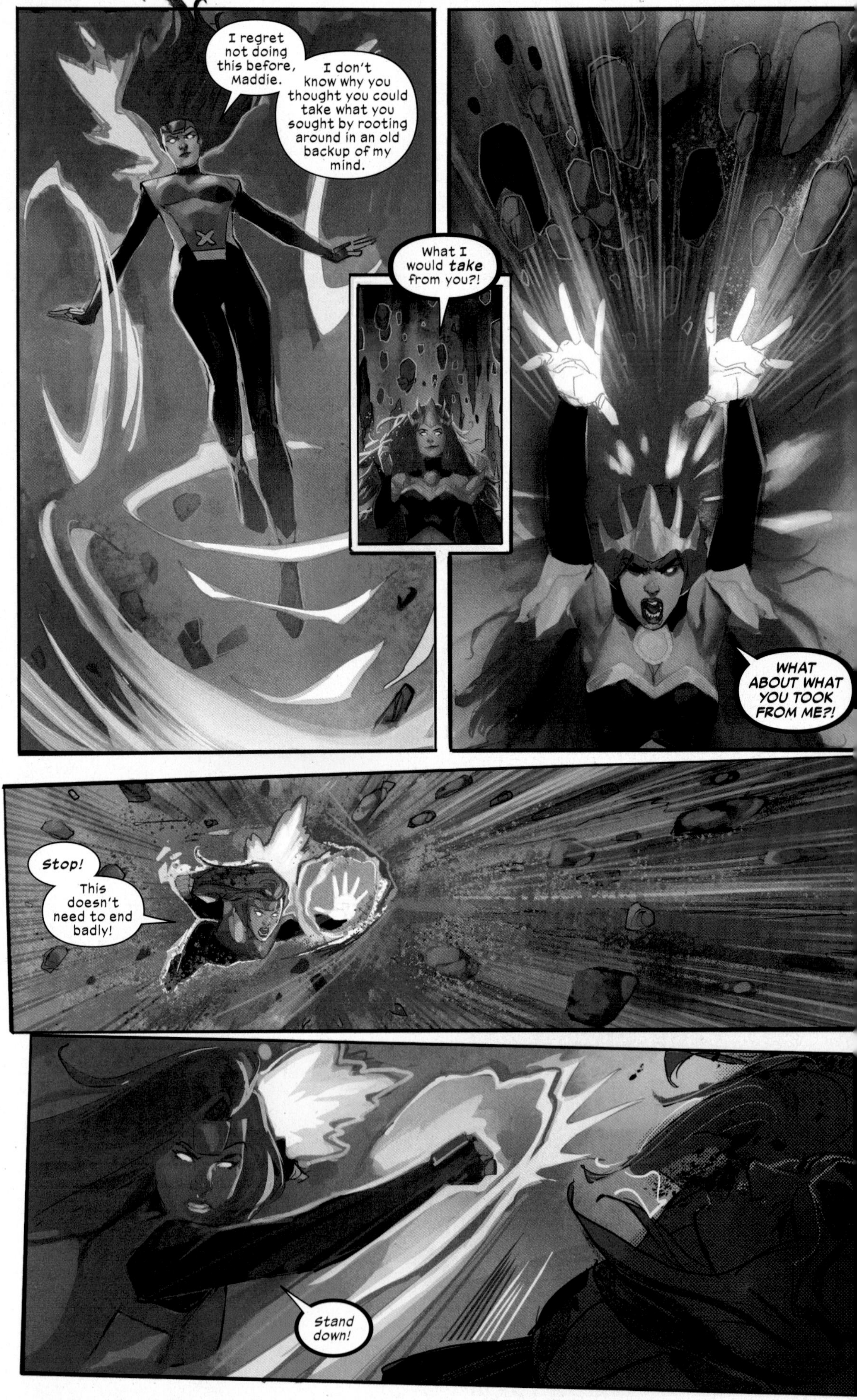
I regret not doing this before, Maddie.
I don't know why you thought you could take what you sought by rooting around in an old backup of my mind.
What I would *take* from you?!
WHAT ABOUT WHAT YOU TOOK FROM ME?!
Stop!
This doesn't need to end badly!
Stand down!

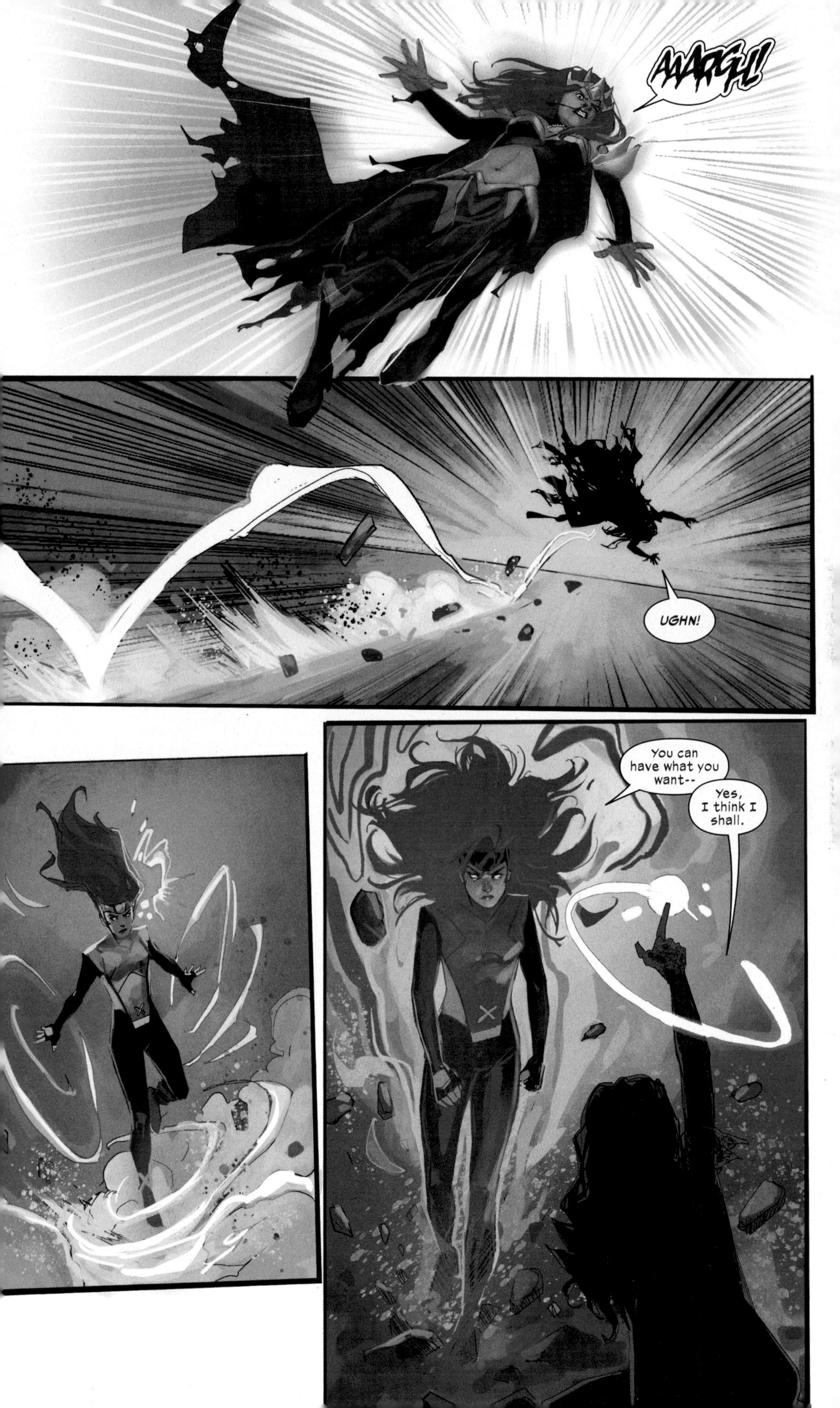

AAARGH!!
UGHN!
You can have what you want--
Yes, I think I shall.

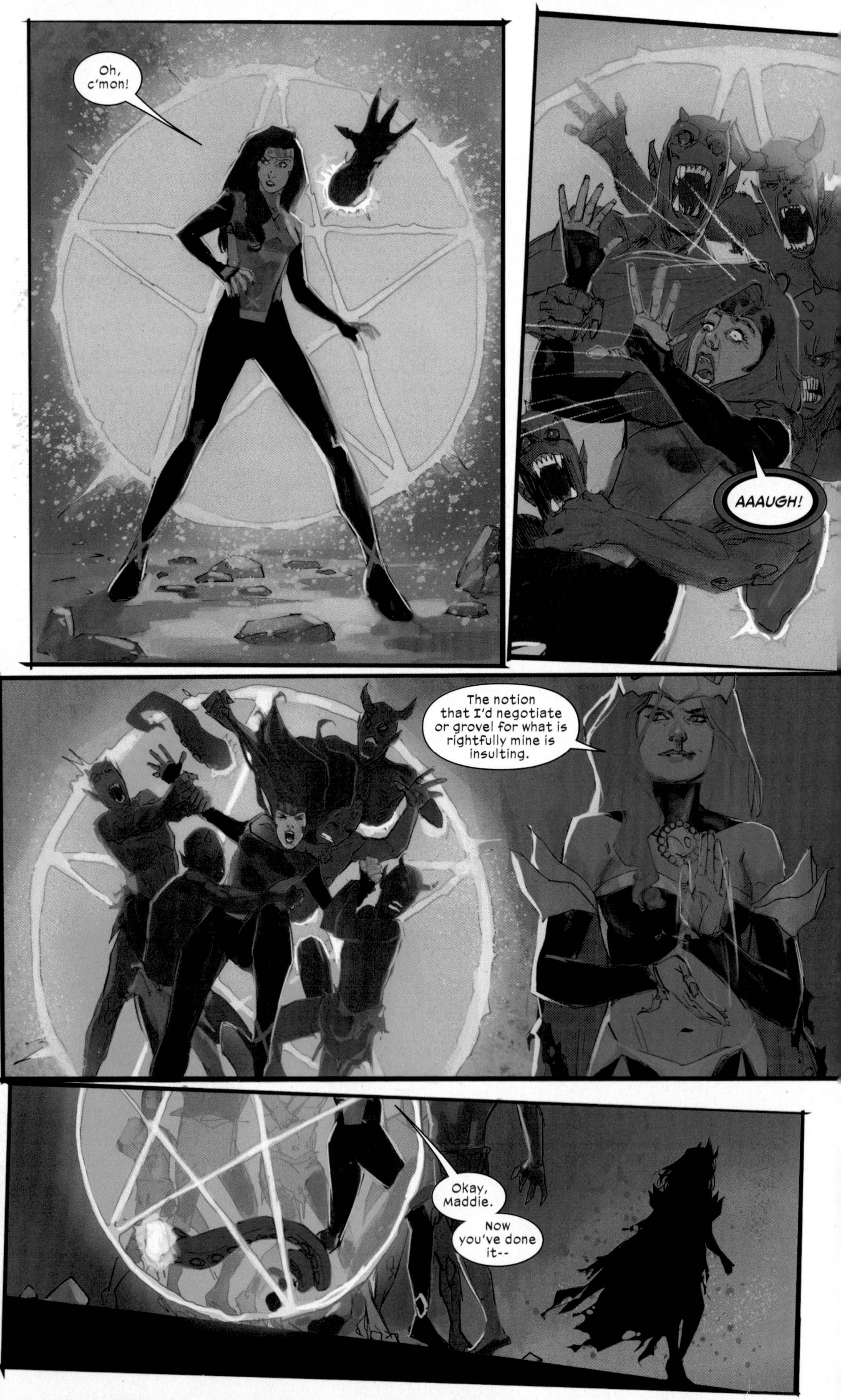

Oh, c'mon!
AAAUGH!
The notion that I'd negotiate or grovel for what is rightfully mine is insulting.
Okay, Maddie.
Now you've done it--

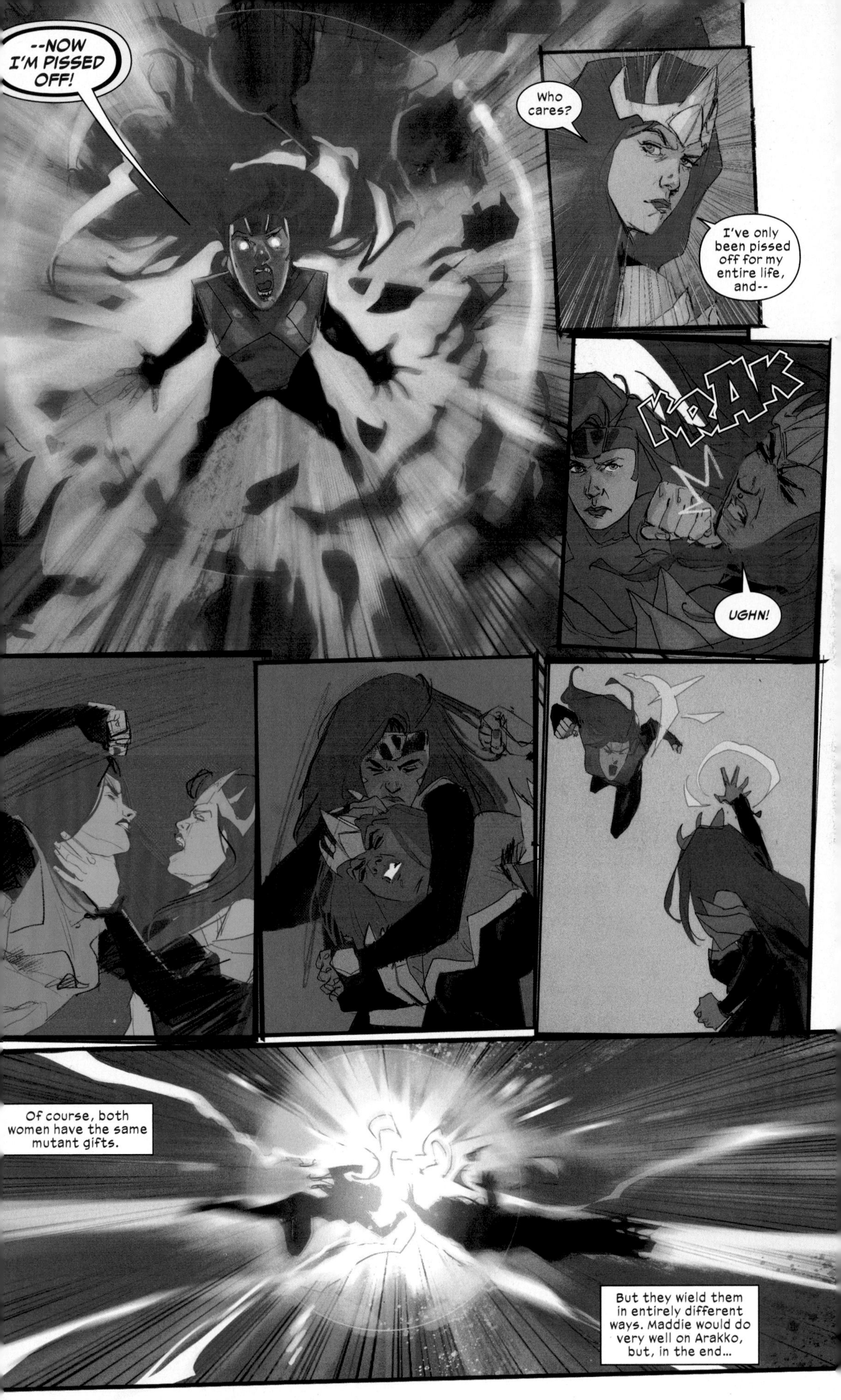

--NOW I'M PISSED OFF!
Who cares?
I've only been pissed off for my entire life, and--
UGHN!
Of course, both women have the same mutant gifts.
But they wield them in entirely different ways. Maddie would do very well on Arakko, but, in the end...

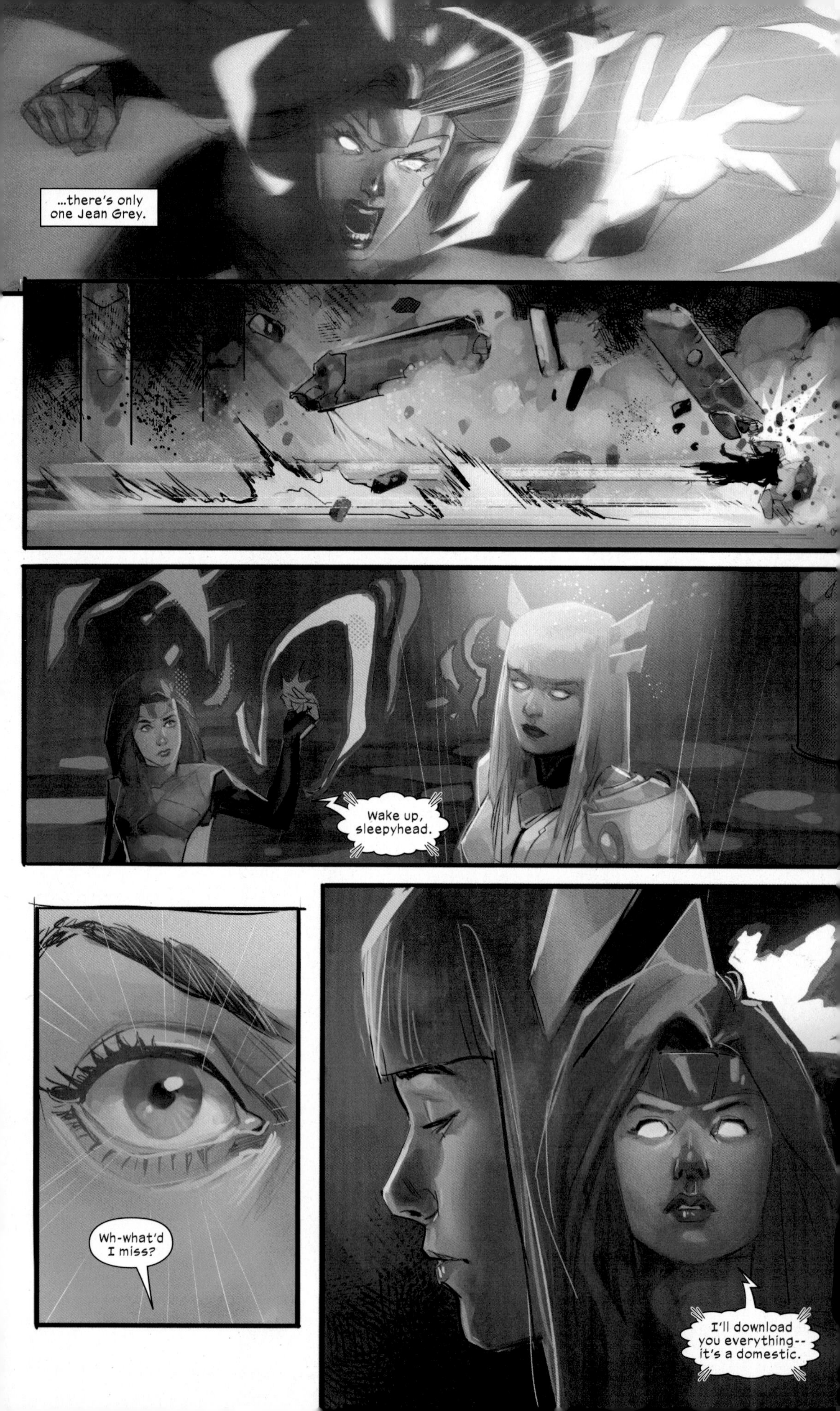
...there's only one Jean Grey.
Wake up, sleepyhead.
Wh-what'd I miss?
I'll download you everything-- it's a domestic.

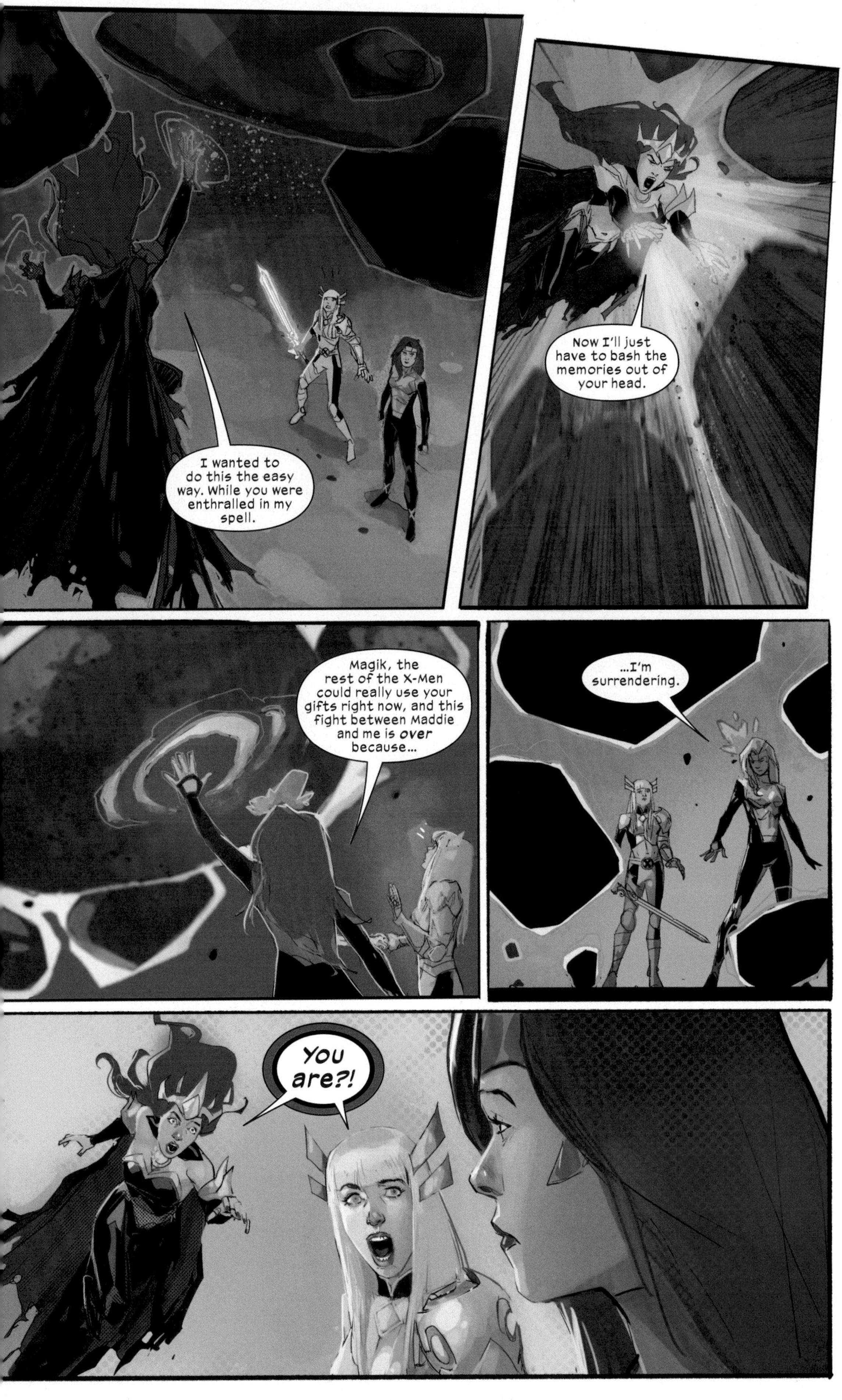
I wanted to do this the easy way. While you were enthralled in my spell.
Now I'll just have to bash the memories out of your head.
Magik, the rest of the X-Men could really use your gifts right now, and this fight between Maddie and me is *over* because...
...I'm surrendering.
You are?!

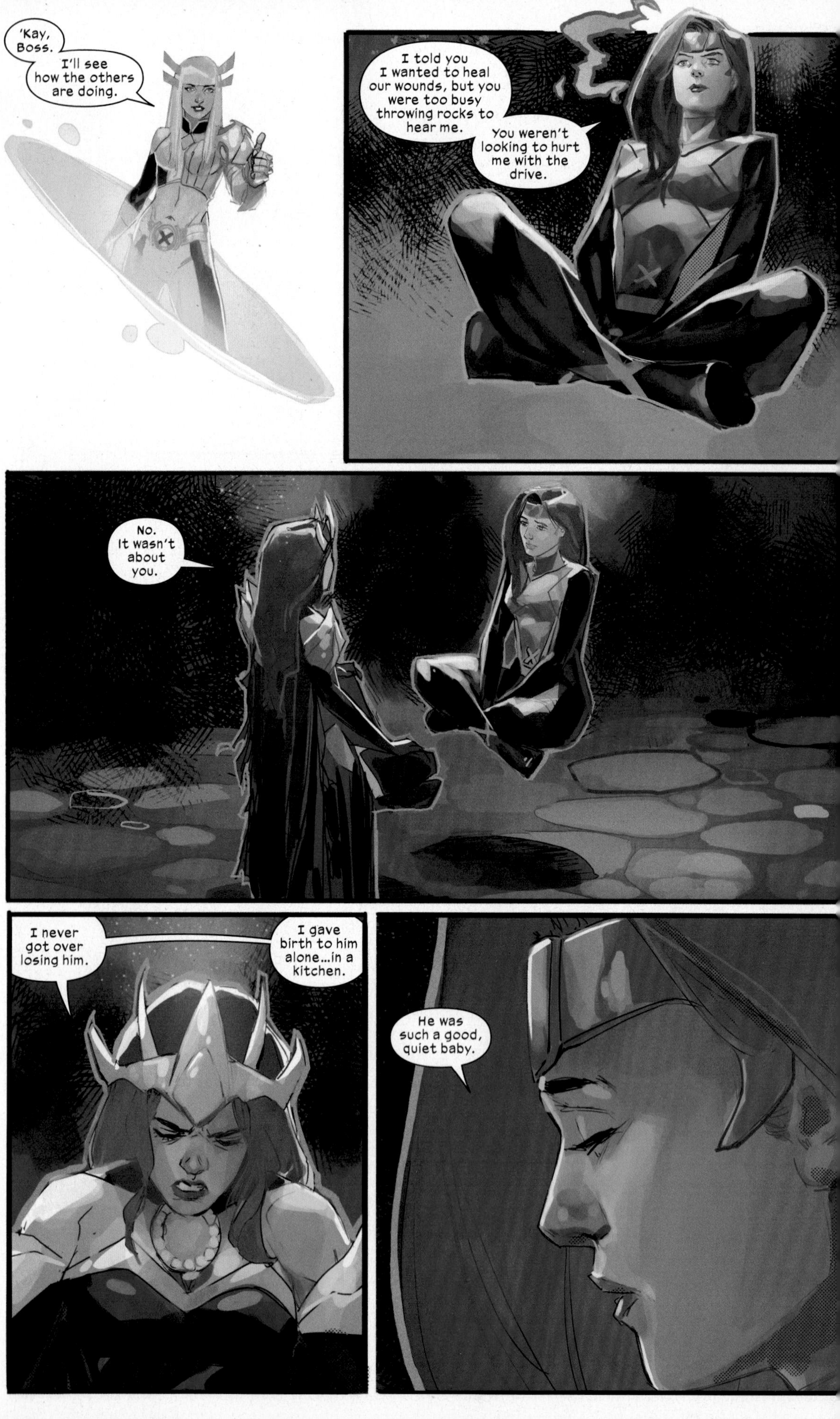
'Kay, Boss.
I'll see how the others are doing.
I told you I wanted to heal our wounds, but you were too busy throwing rocks to hear me.
You weren't looking to hurt me with the drive.
No. It wasn't about you.
I never got over losing him.
I gave birth to him alone...in a kitchen.
He was such a good, quiet baby.

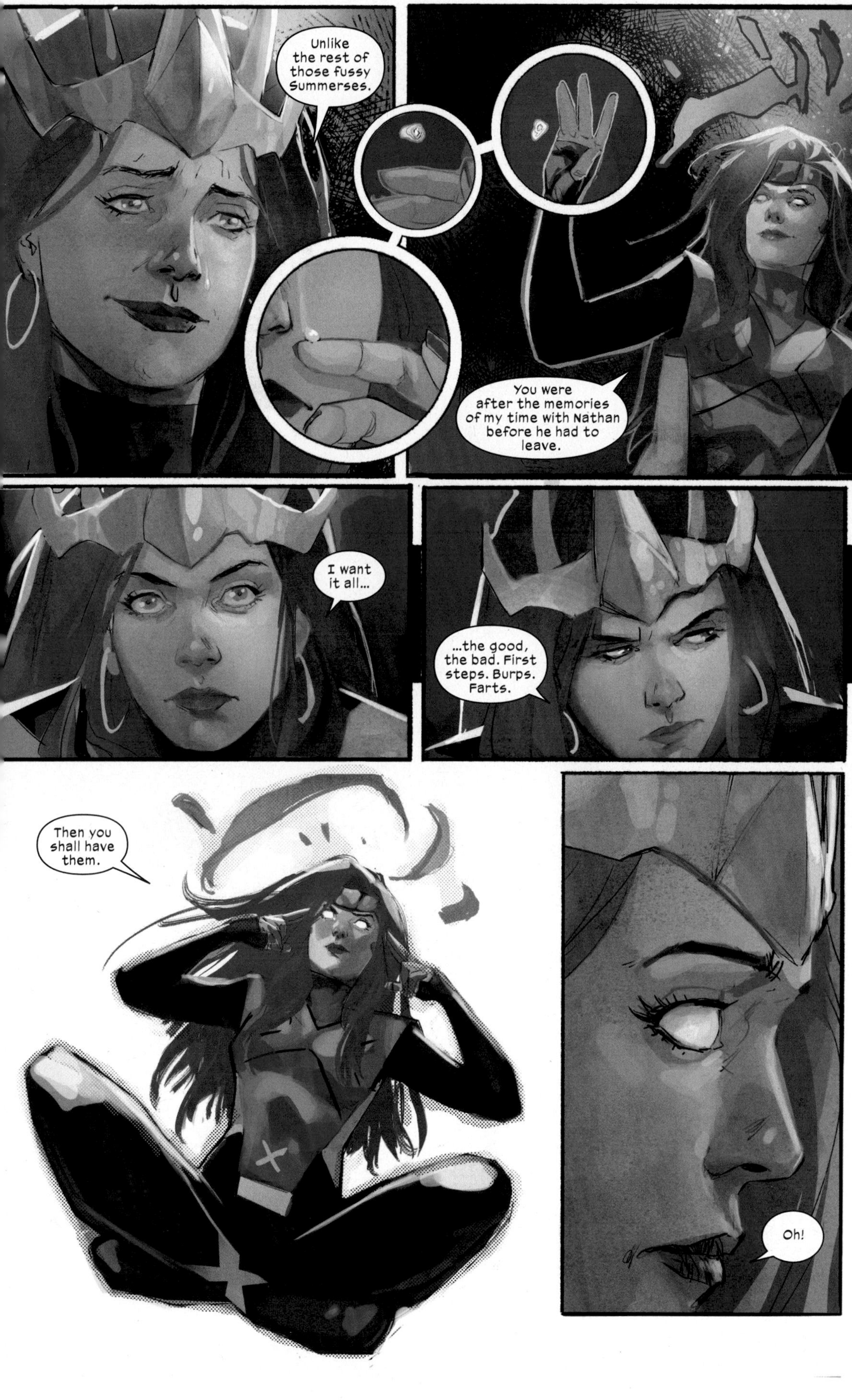
Unlike the rest of those fussy Summerses.
You were after the memories of my time with Nathan before he had to leave.
I want it all...
...the good, the bad. First steps. Burps. Farts.
Then you shall have them.
Oh!

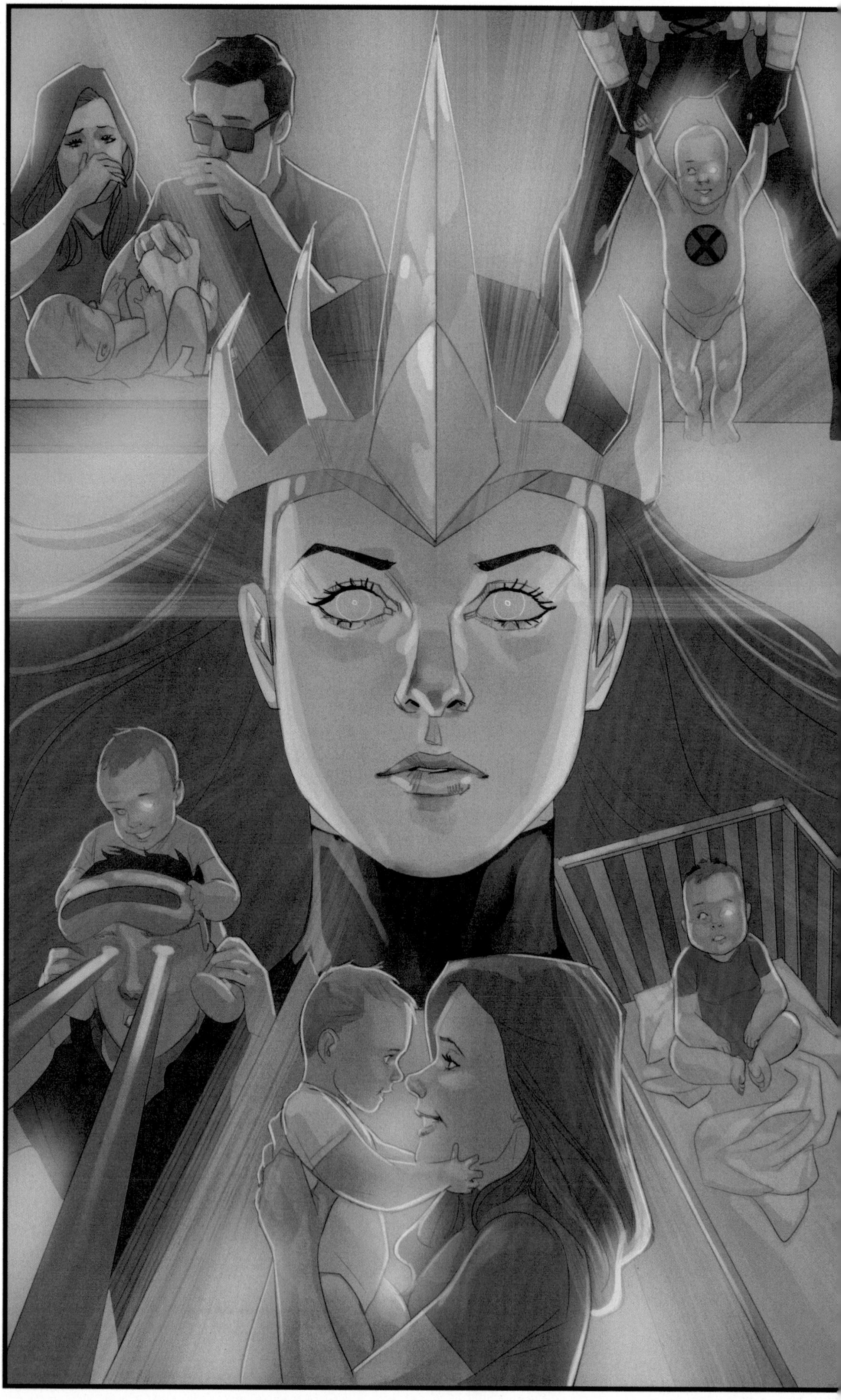

JEAN GREY NOTES:

A few of the cherished memories Jean shared with Maddie:

Nathan only left behind one baby tooth before heading into the future and it later went missing. Even though there was no evidence of this, everyone just assumed it was Mr. Sinister. What a creep!

Maddie was also interested in her own funeral. Her body was cremated and a very small service was held. Aside from the priest, the only attendees were the original X-Men and Baby Nathan.

Having a funeral for the Goblin Queen presided over by a priest was perhaps a weird decision, but it was the thought that counted, and Maddie was glad to have a look into it.

The truth is, none of the memories shared were minute-by-minute, blow-by-blow accounts. What Maddie inherited from Jean were the emotional cores of those days, the highs and lows of being a mutant, a mother and, at that time, a member of X-Factor.

Maddie's heart broke for Jean when she and Scott gave the baby to the future to save him from the Techno-Organic Virus. Jean also gave Maddie more recent memories of Cable. His young teen self was an important piece of the formation of Krakoa, and while he's already moved on, they had so many big adventures and small meals together, and Maddie was invited to enjoy them all... How this light will affect her darker impulses is, well, a story for another day.

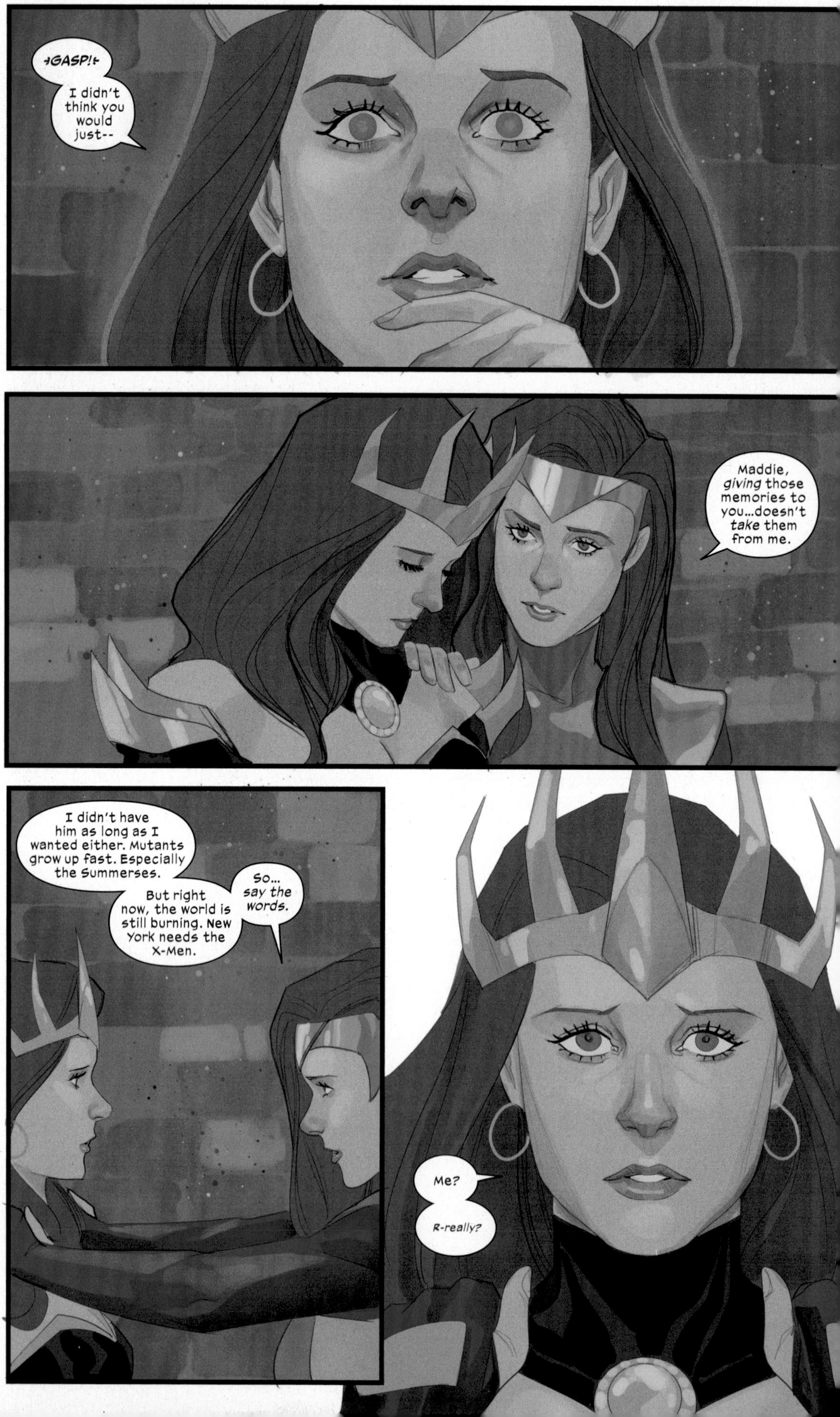

GASP!
I didn't think you would just--
Maddie, giving those memories to you...doesn't take them from me.
I didn't have him as long as I wanted either. Mutants grow up fast. Especially the Summerses.
But right now, the world is still burning. New York needs the X-Men.
So... say the words.
Me?
R-really?

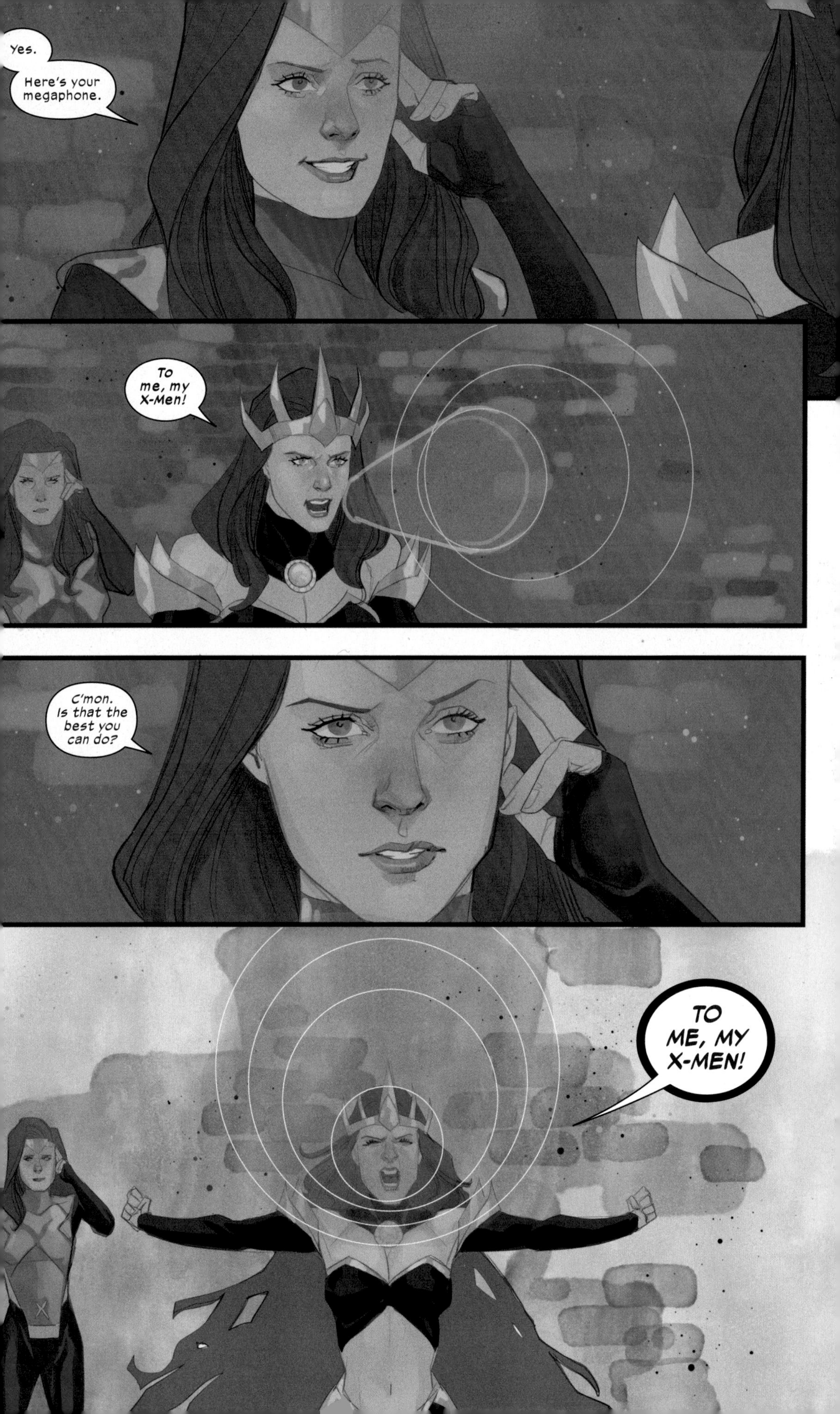
Yes.
Here's your megaphone.
To me, my X-Men!
C'mon. Is that the best you can do?
TO ME, MY X-MEN!

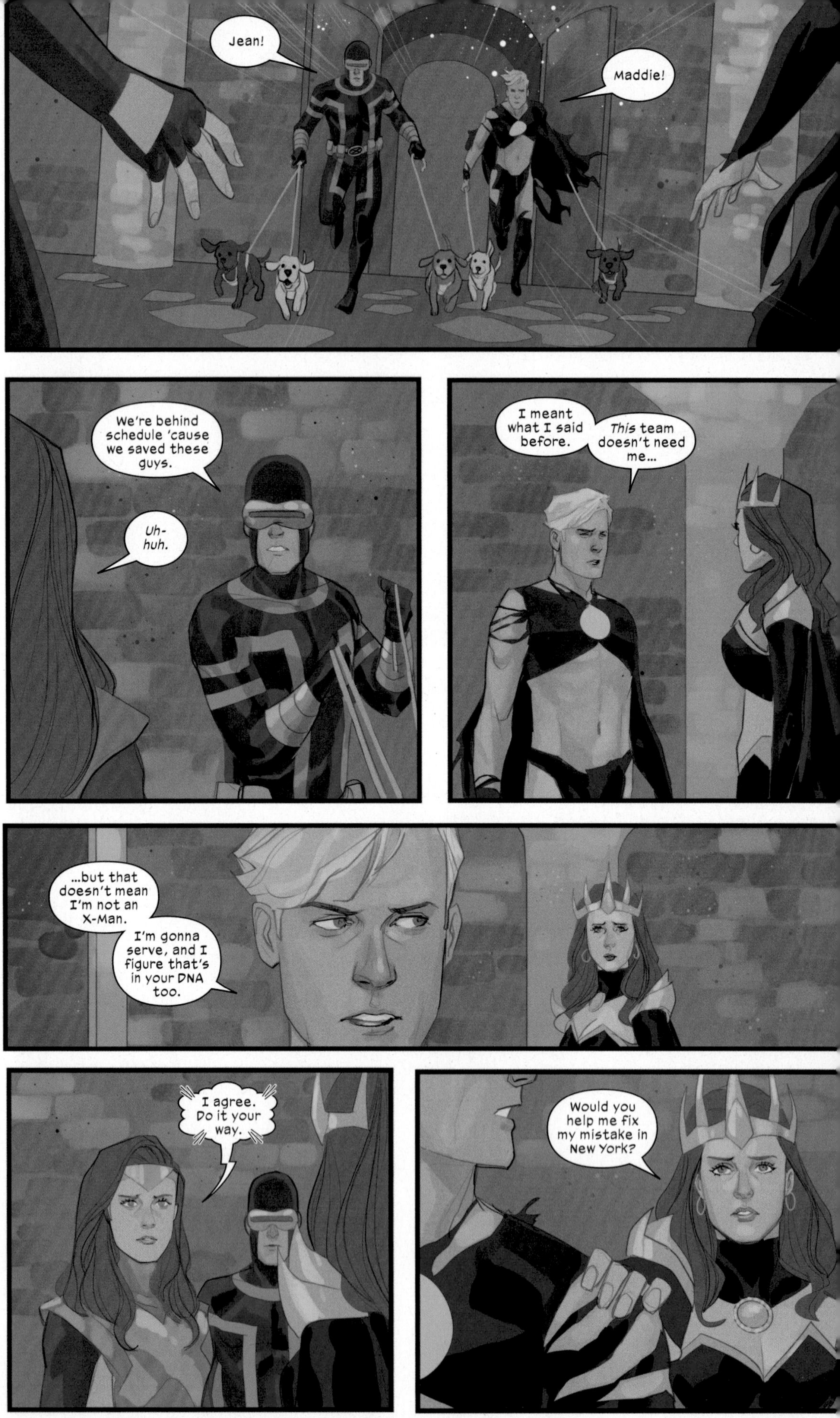
Jean!
Maddie!
We're behind schedule 'cause we saved these guys.
Uh-huh.
I meant what I said before.
This team doesn't need me...
...but that doesn't mean I'm not an X-Man.
I'm gonna serve, and I figure that's in your DNA too.
I agree. Do it your way.
Would you help me fix my mistake in New York?

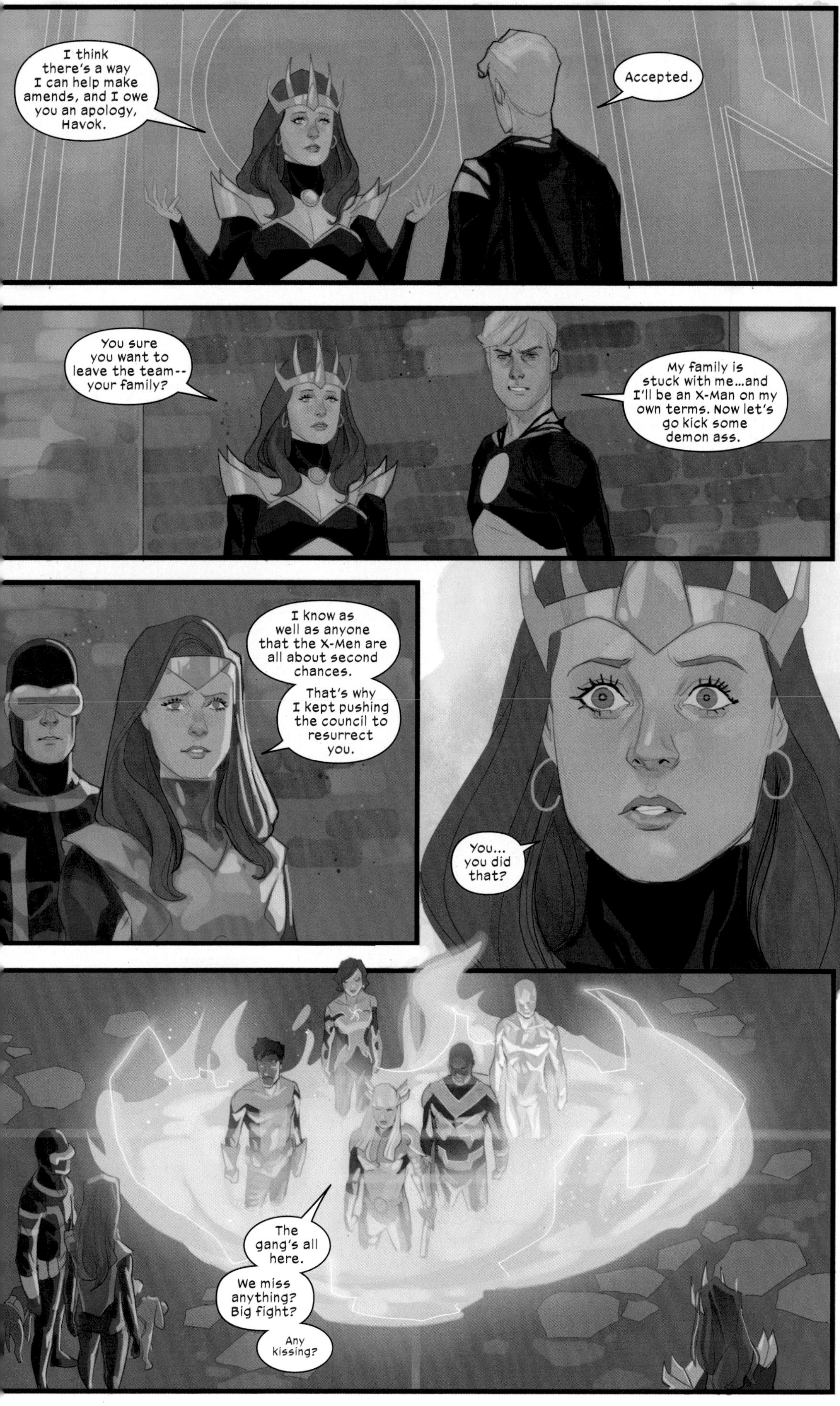
I think there's a way I can help make amends, and I owe you an apology, Havok.
Accepted.
You sure you want to leave the team--your family?
My family is stuck with me...and I'll be an X-Man on my own terms. Now let's go kick some demon ass.
I know as well as anyone that the X-Men are all about second chances.
That's why I kept pushing the council to resurrect you.
You... you did that?
The gang's all here.
We miss anything? Big fight?
Any kissing?

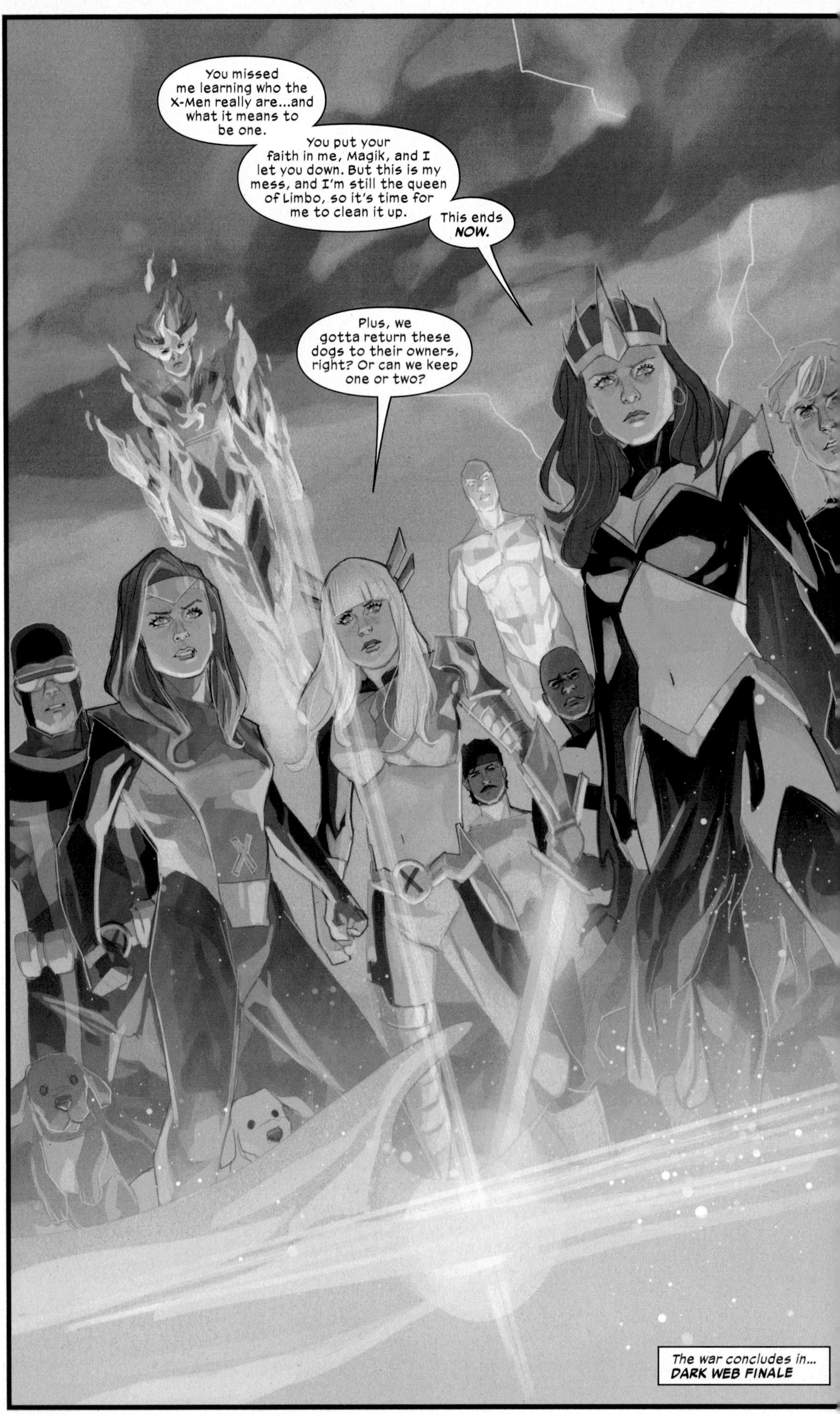
You missed me learning who the X-Men really are...and what it means to be one.
You put your faith in me, Magik, and I let you down. But this is my mess, and I'm still the queen of Limbo, so it's time for me to clean it up.
This ends **NOW.**
Plus, we gotta return these dogs to their owners, right? Or can we keep one or two?
The war concludes in... ***DARK WEB FINALE***

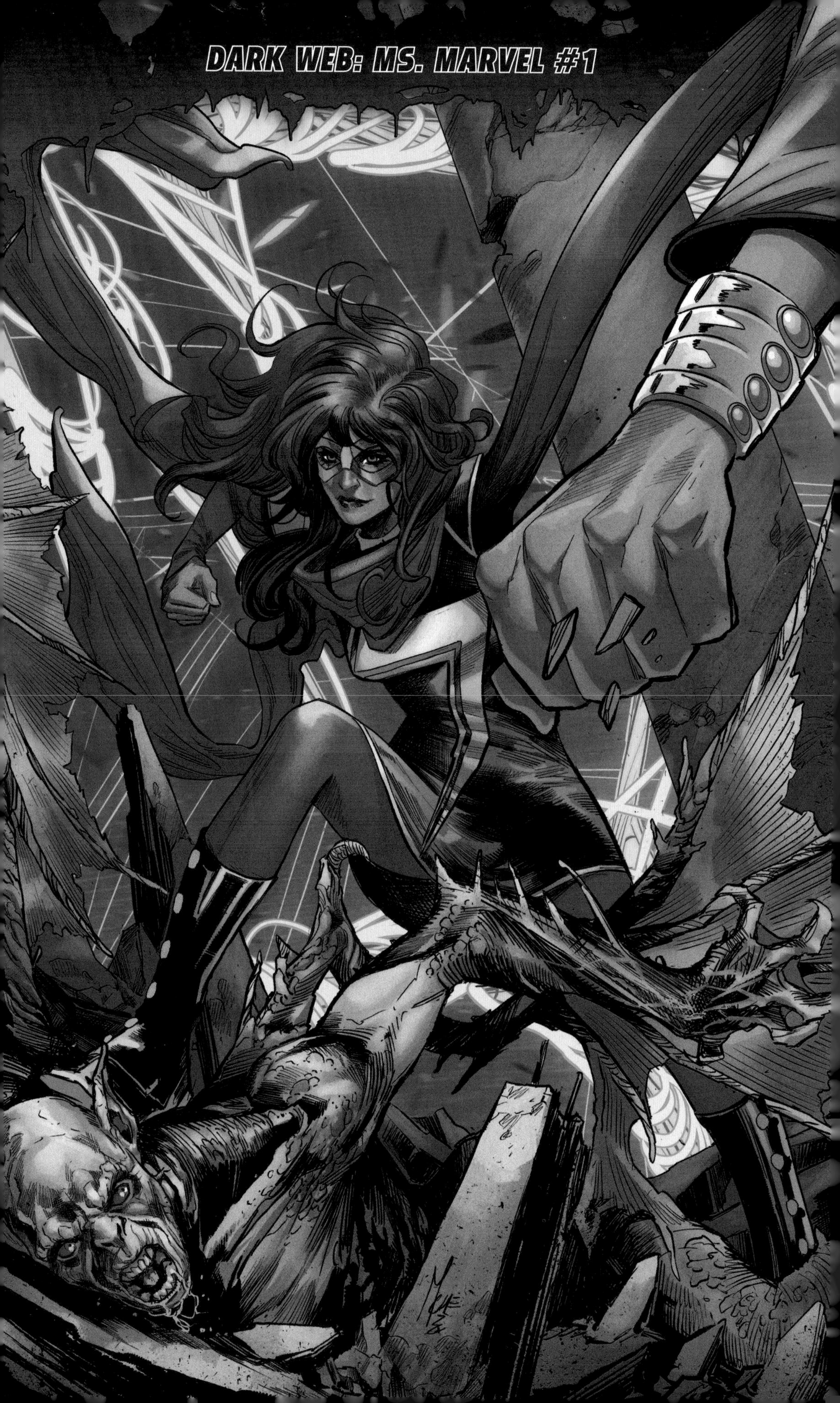
DARK WEB: MS. MARVEL #1

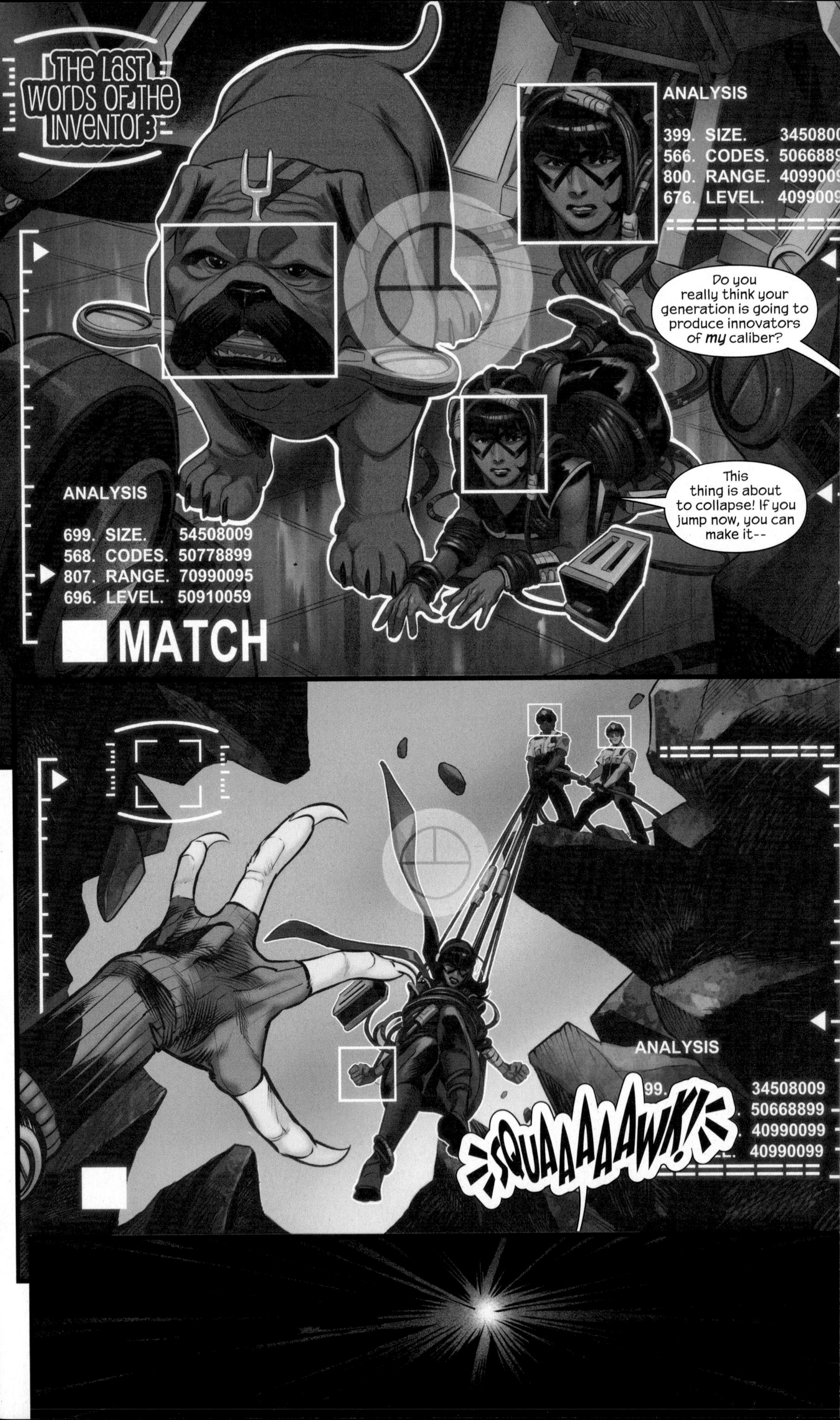

THE LAST WORDS OF THE INVENTOR:
ANALYSIS
399. SIZE. 3450800
566. CODES. 5066889
800. RANGE. 4099009
676. LEVEL. 4099009
Do you really think your generation is going to produce innovators of *my* caliber?
This thing is about to collapse! If you jump now, you can make it--
ANALYSIS
699. SIZE. 54508009
568. CODES. 50778899
807. RANGE. 70990095
696. LEVEL. 50910059
MATCH
ANALYSIS
99. 34508009
50668899
40990099
40990099
SQUAAAAAWK!

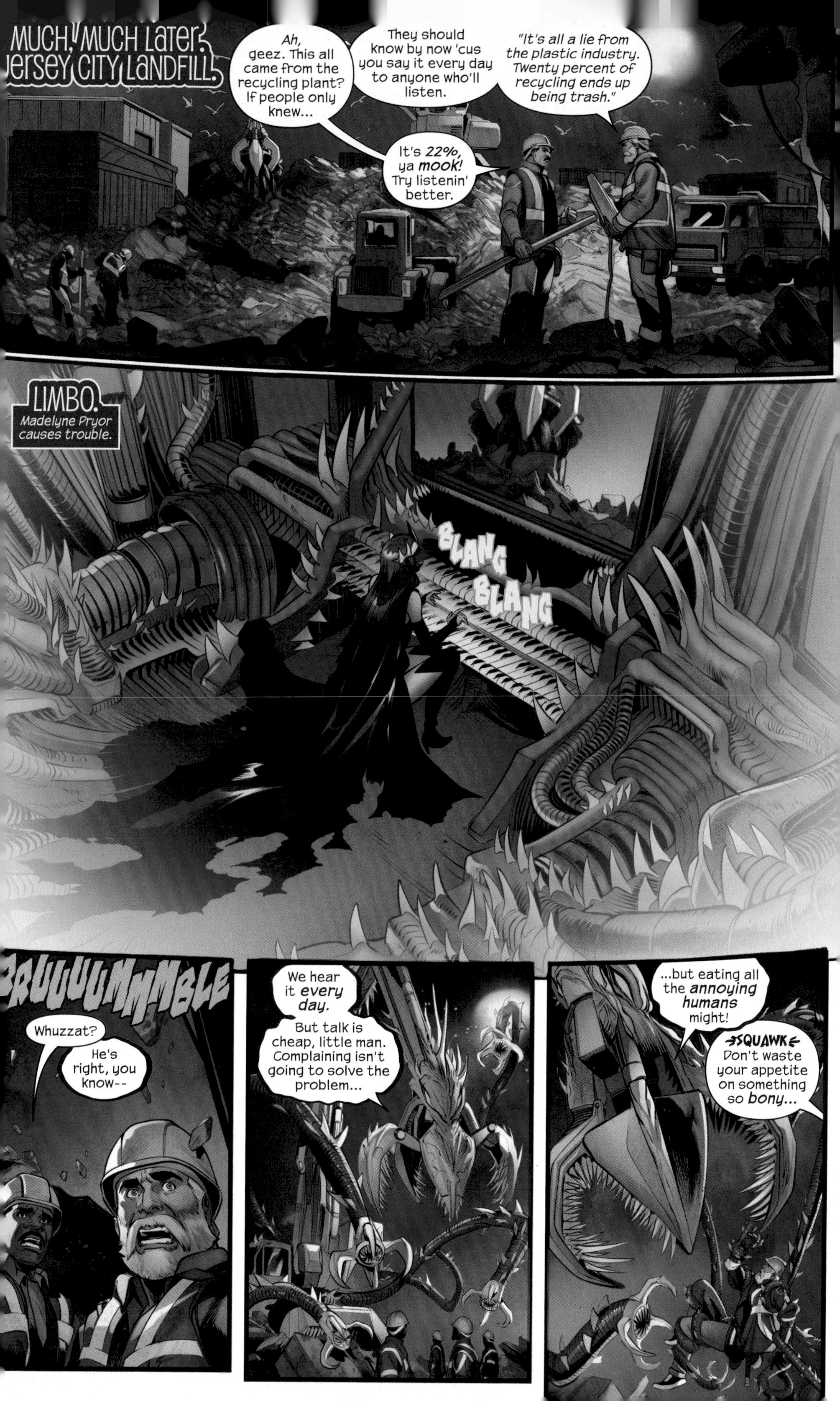
MUCH, MUCH LATER. JERSEY CITY LANDFILL.
Ah, geez. This all came from the recycling plant? If people only knew...
They should know by now 'cus you say it every day to anyone who'll listen.
"It's all a lie from the plastic industry. Twenty percent of recycling ends up being trash."
It's 22%, ya mook! Try listenin' better.
LIMBO.
Madelyne Pryor causes trouble.
BLANG BLANG
RUUUUMMMBLE
Whuzzat?
He's right, you know--
We hear it every day.
But talk is cheap, little man. Complaining isn't going to solve the problem...
...but eating all the annoying humans might!
SQUAWK
Don't waste your appetite on something so bony...

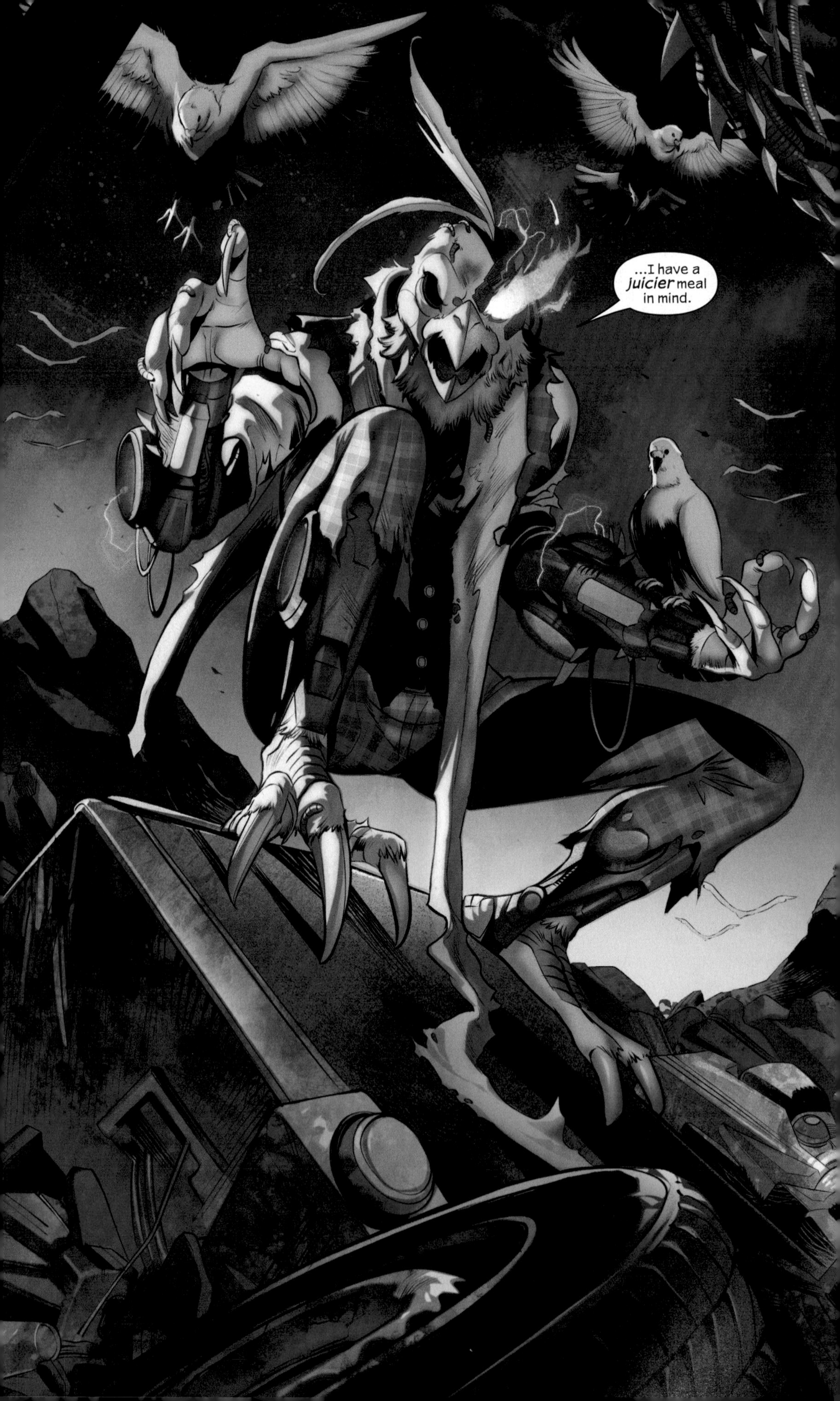
...I have a *juicier* meal in mind.

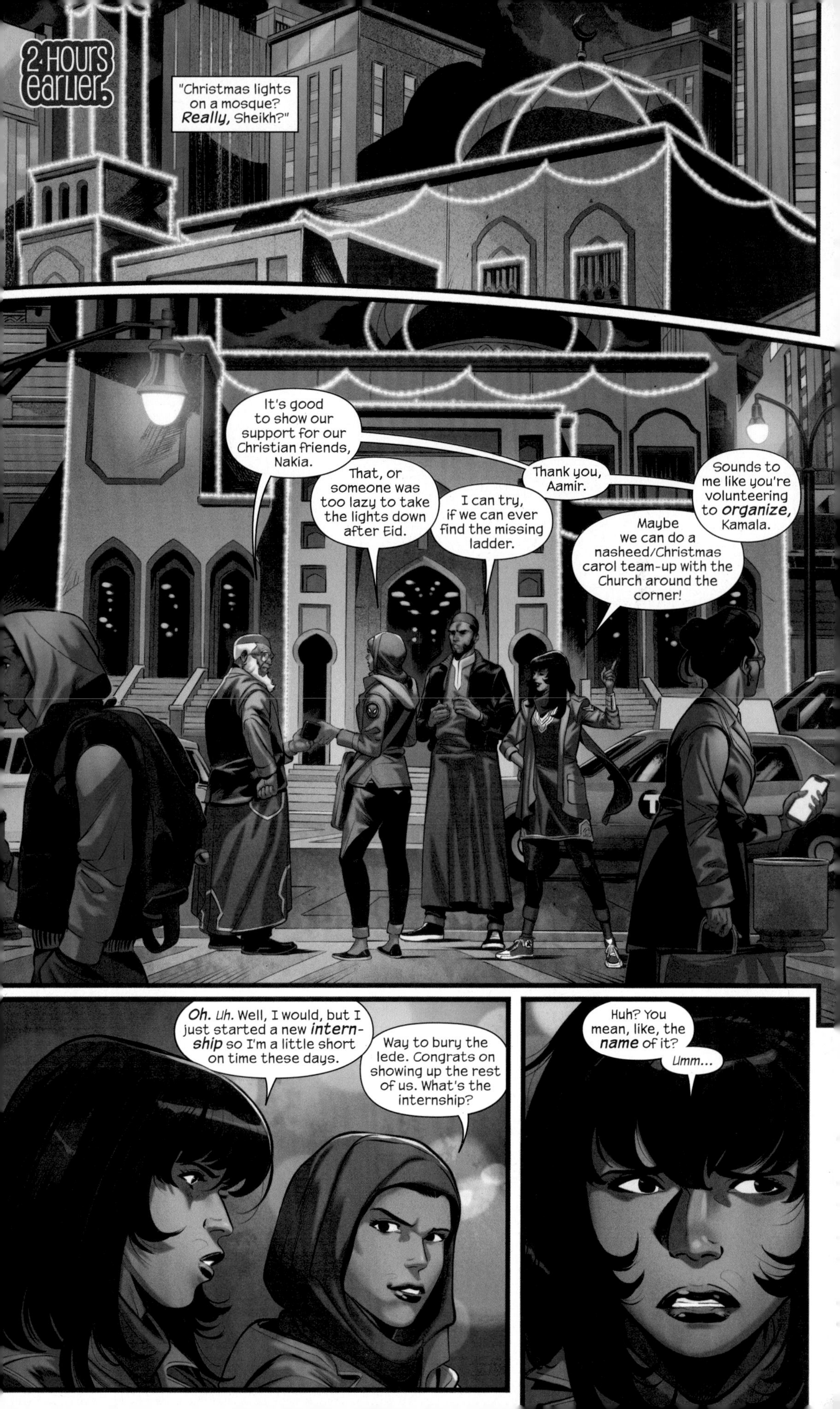
2 HOURS EARLIER.
"Christmas lights on a mosque? *Really,* Sheikh?"
It's good to show our support for our Christian friends, Nakia.
That, or someone was too lazy to take the lights down after Eid.
Thank you, Aamir.
I can try, if we can ever find the missing ladder.
Sounds to me like you're volunteering to *organize,* Kamala.
Maybe we can do a nasheed/Christmas carol team-up with the Church around the corner!
Oh. Uh. Well, I would, but I just started a new *internship* so I'm a little short on time these days.
Way to bury the lede. Congrats on showing up the rest of us. What's the internship?
Huh? You mean, like, the *name* of it?
Umm...

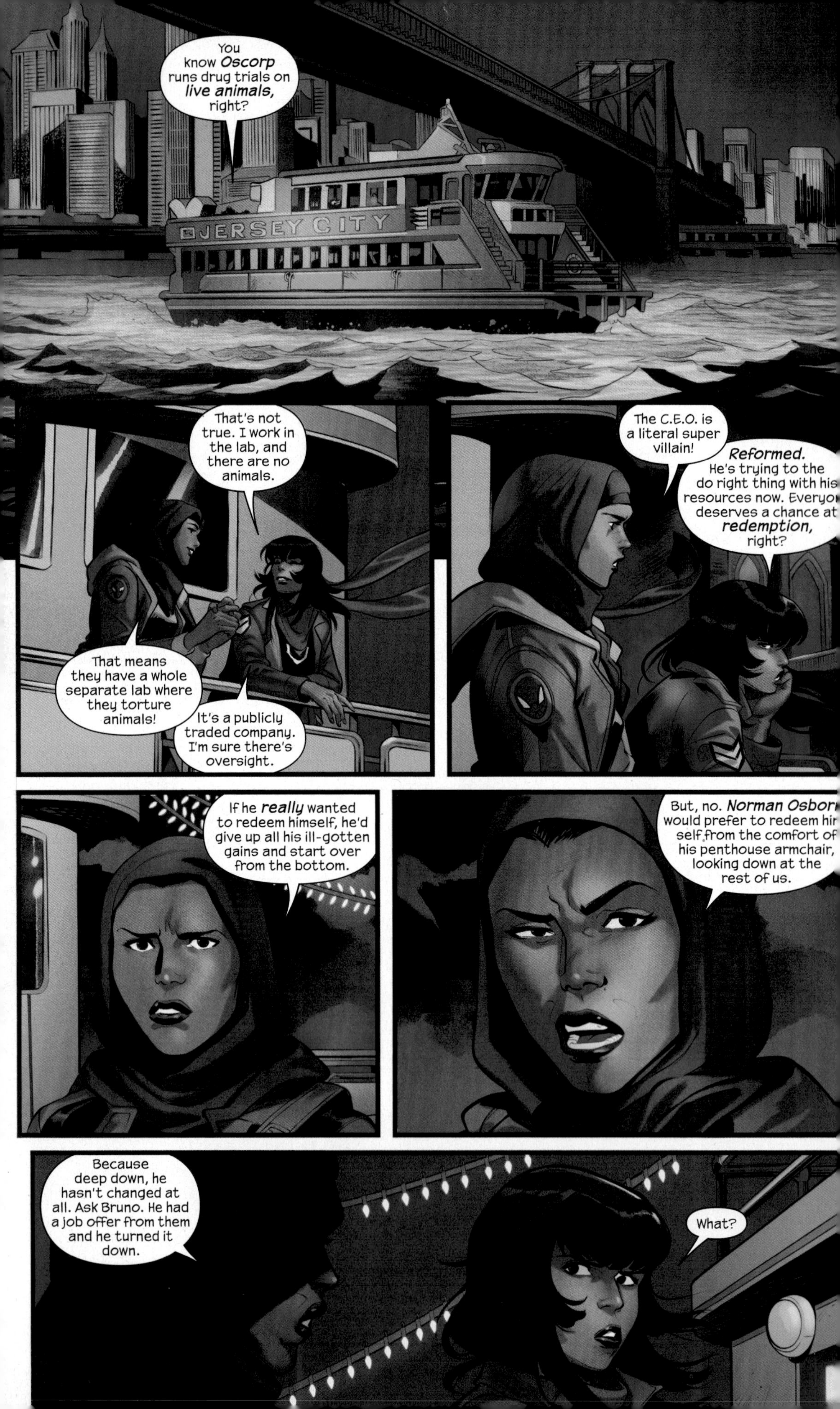

JERSEY CITY
You know Oscorp runs drug trials on live animals, right?
That's not true. I work in the lab, and there are no animals.
That means they have a whole separate lab where they torture animals!
It's a publicly traded company. I'm sure there's oversight.
The C.E.O. is a literal super villain!
Reformed. He's trying to the do right thing with his resources now. Everyo deserves a chance at redemption, right?
If he really wanted to redeem himself, he'd give up all his ill-gotten gains and start over from the bottom.
But, no. Norman Osbor would prefer to redeem hir self from the comfort of his penthouse armchair, looking down at the rest of us.
Because deep down, he hasn't changed at all. Ask Bruno. He had a job offer from them and he turned it down.
What?

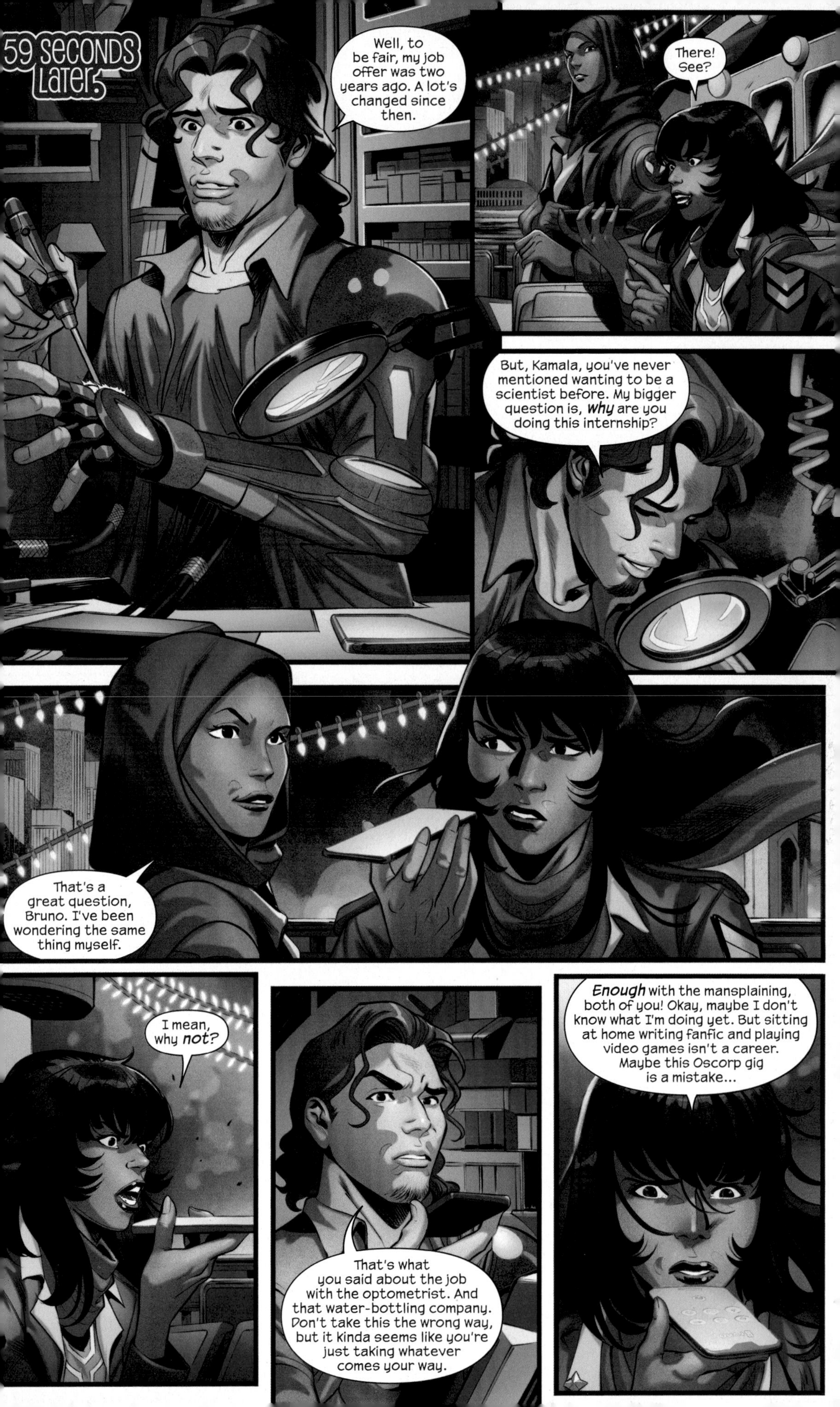
59 SECONDS LATER.
Well, to be fair, my job offer was two years ago. A lot's changed since then.
There! See?
But, Kamala, you've never mentioned wanting to be a scientist before. My bigger question is, *why* are you doing this internship?
That's a great question, Bruno. I've been wondering the same thing myself.
I mean, why *not*?
That's what you said about the job with the optometrist. And that water-bottling company. Don't take this the wrong way, but it kinda seems like you're just taking whatever comes your way.
Enough with the mansplaining, both of you! Okay, maybe I don't know what I'm doing yet. But sitting at home writing fanfic and playing video games isn't a career. Maybe this Oscorp gig is a mistake...

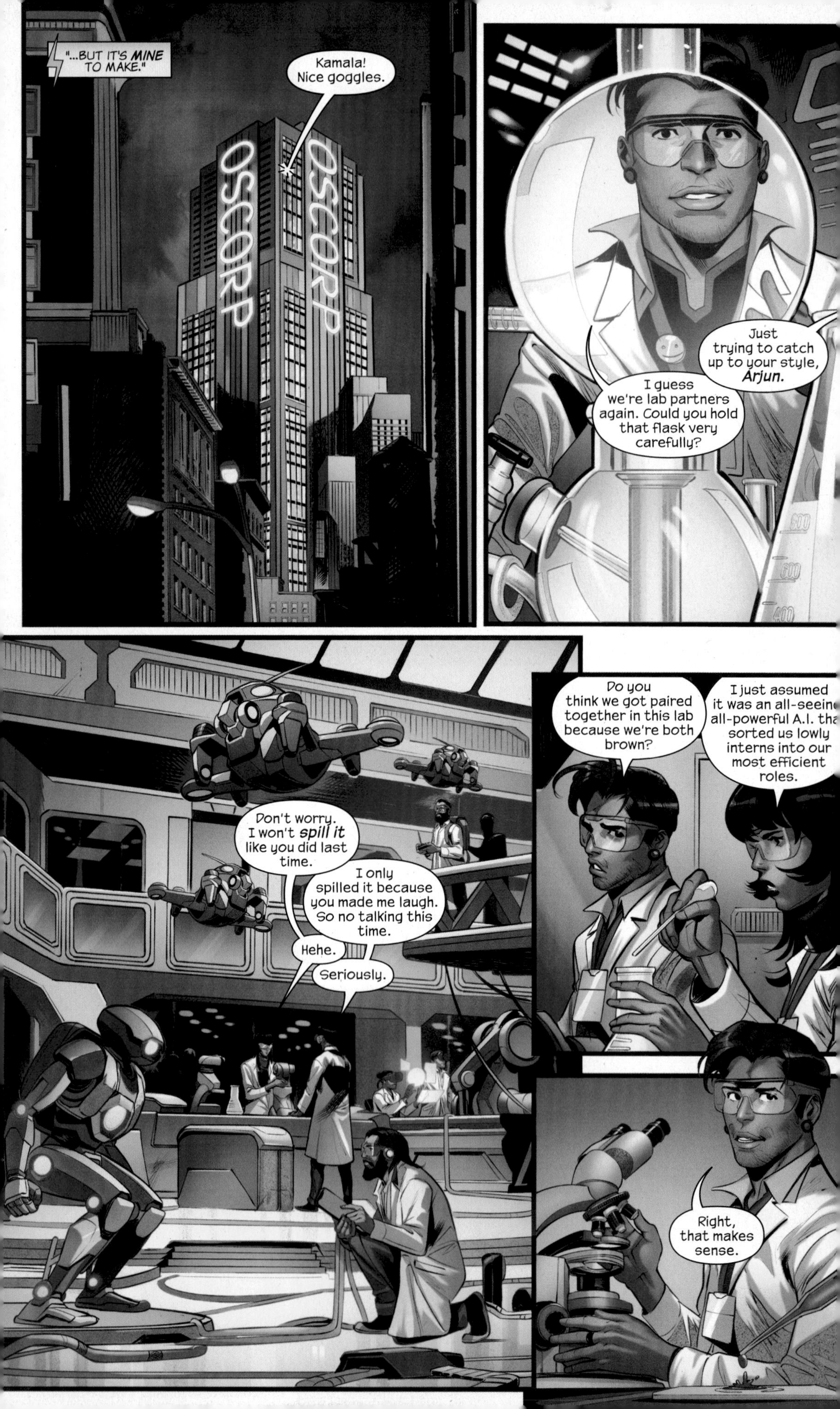

"...BUT IT'S MINE TO MAKE."
Kamala! Nice goggles.
OSCORP
OSCORP
I guess we're lab partners again. Could you hold that flask very carefully?
Just trying to catch up to your style, Arjun.
Don't worry. I won't spill it like you did last time.
I only spilled it because you made me laugh. So no talking this time.
Hehe.
Seriously.
Do you think we got paired together in this lab because we're both brown?
I just assumed it was an all-seein all-powerful A.I. tha sorted us lowly interns into our most efficient roles.
Right, that makes sense.

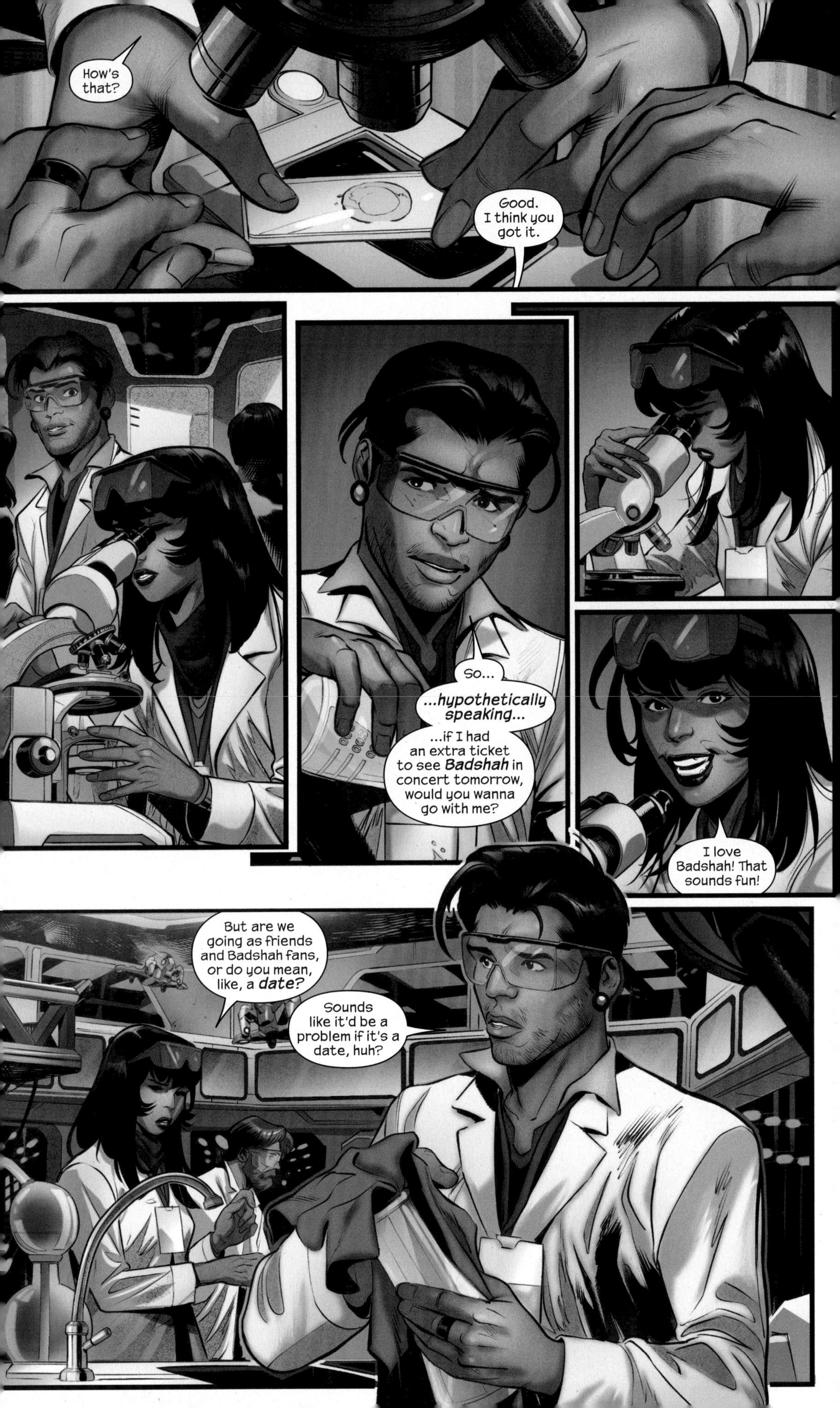
How's that?
Good. I think you got it.
So...
...hypothetically speaking...
...if I had an extra ticket to see Badshah in concert tomorrow, would you wanna go with me?
I love Badshah! That sounds fun!
But are we going as friends and Badshah fans, or do you mean, like, a date?
Sounds like it'd be a problem if it's a date, huh?

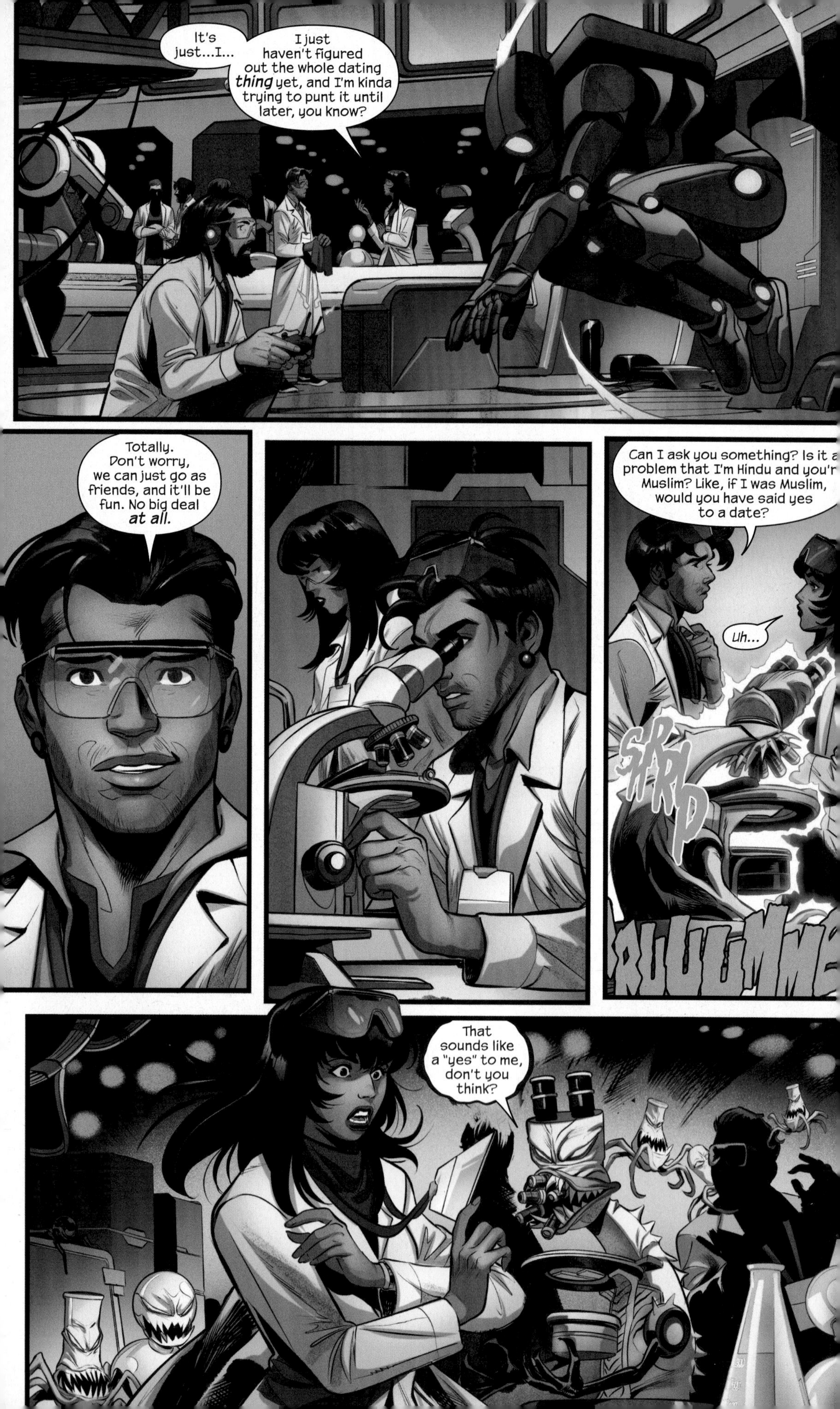
It's just...I...
I just haven't figured out the whole dating *thing* yet, and I'm kinda trying to punt it until later, you know?
Totally. Don't worry, we can just go as friends, and it'll be fun. No big deal *at all.*
Can I ask you something? Is it a problem that I'm Hindu and you'r Muslim? Like, if I was Muslim, would you have said yes to a date?
Uh...
SHRIP
RUUUMMB
That sounds like a "yes" to me, don't you think?

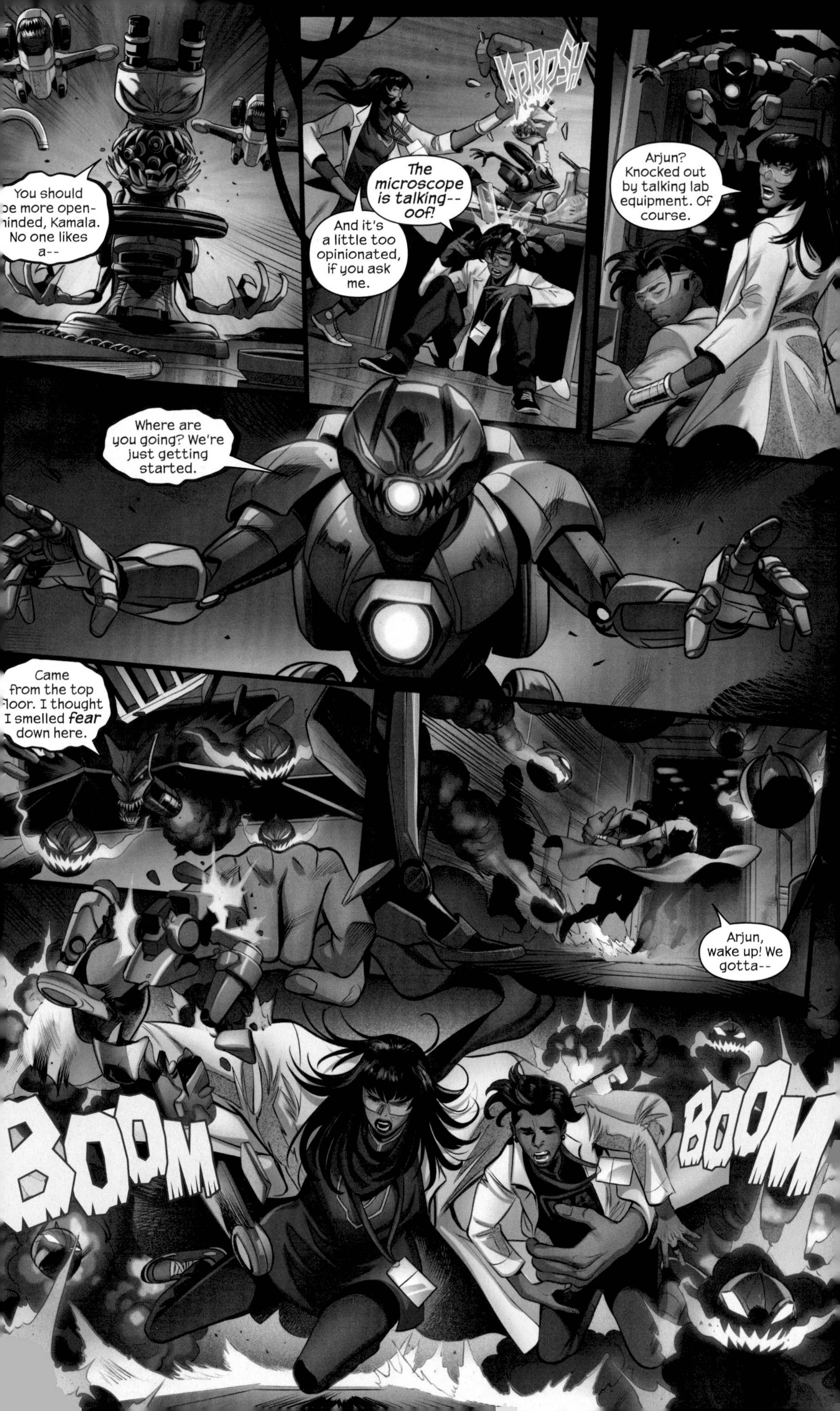
You should be more open-minded, Kamala. No one likes a--
KRRSH!
The microscope is talking-- oof!
And it's a little too opinionated, if you ask me.
Arjun? Knocked out by talking lab equipment. Of course.
Where are you going? We're just getting started.
Came from the top floor. I thought I smelled fear down here.
Arjun, wake up! We gotta--
BOOM
BOOM

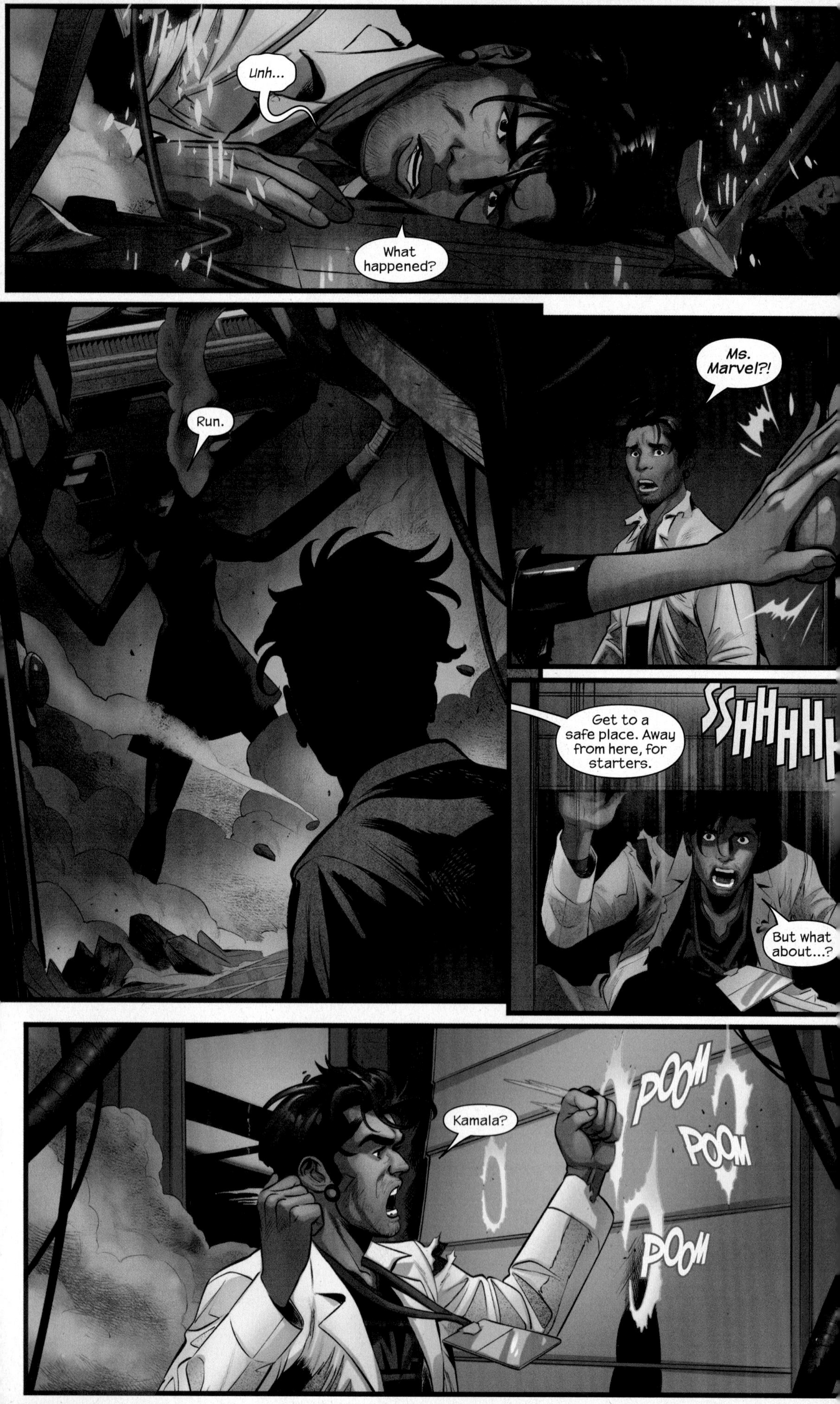

Unh...
What happened?
Run.
Ms. Marvel?!
Get to a safe place. Away from here, for starters.
SSHHHH
But what about...?
Kamala?
POOM
POOM
POOM

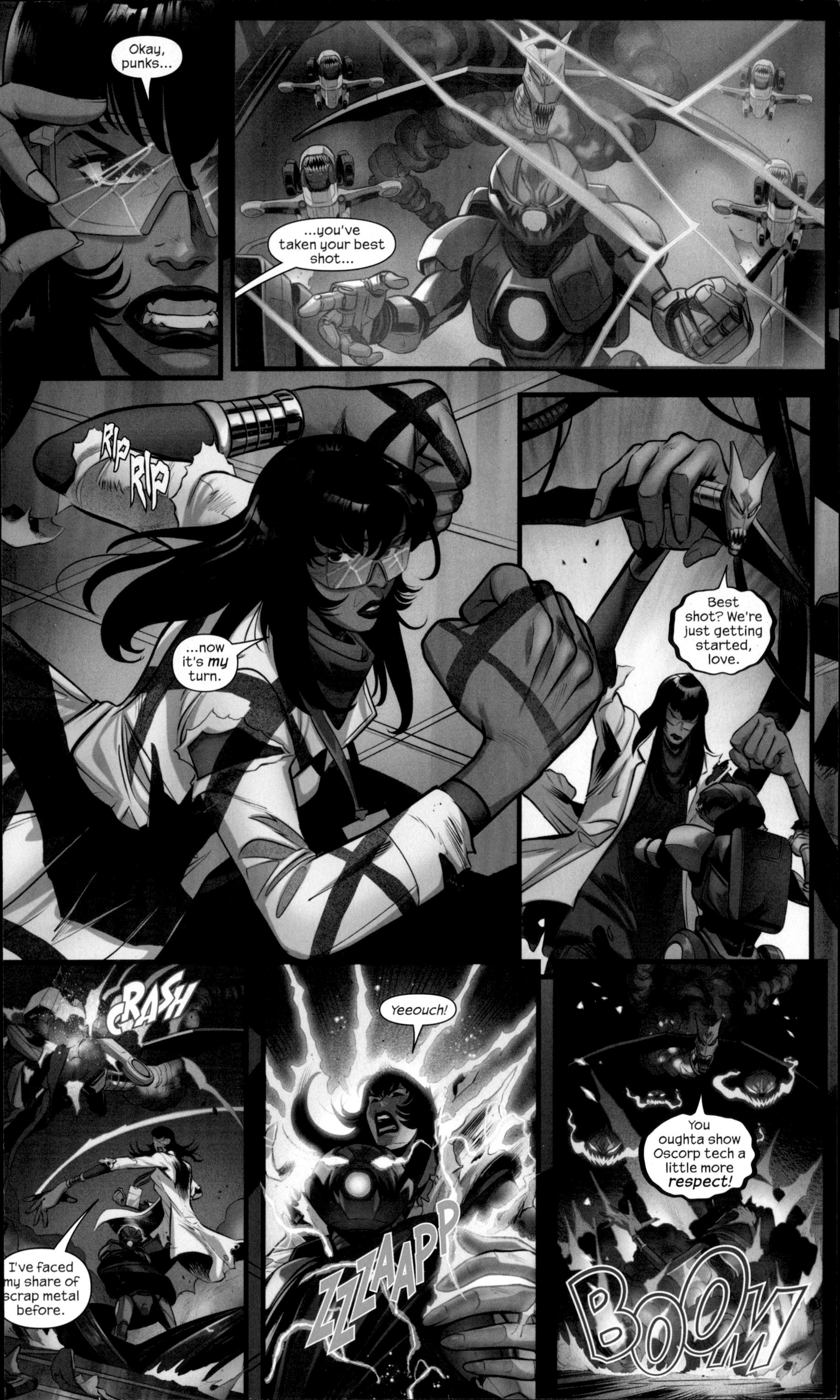

Okay, punks...
...you've taken your best shot...
RIP RIP
...now it's *my* turn.
Best shot? We're just getting started, love.
CRASH
I've faced my share of scrap metal before.
Yeeouch!
ZZZAAPP
You oughta show Oscorp tech a little more *respect!*
BOOOM

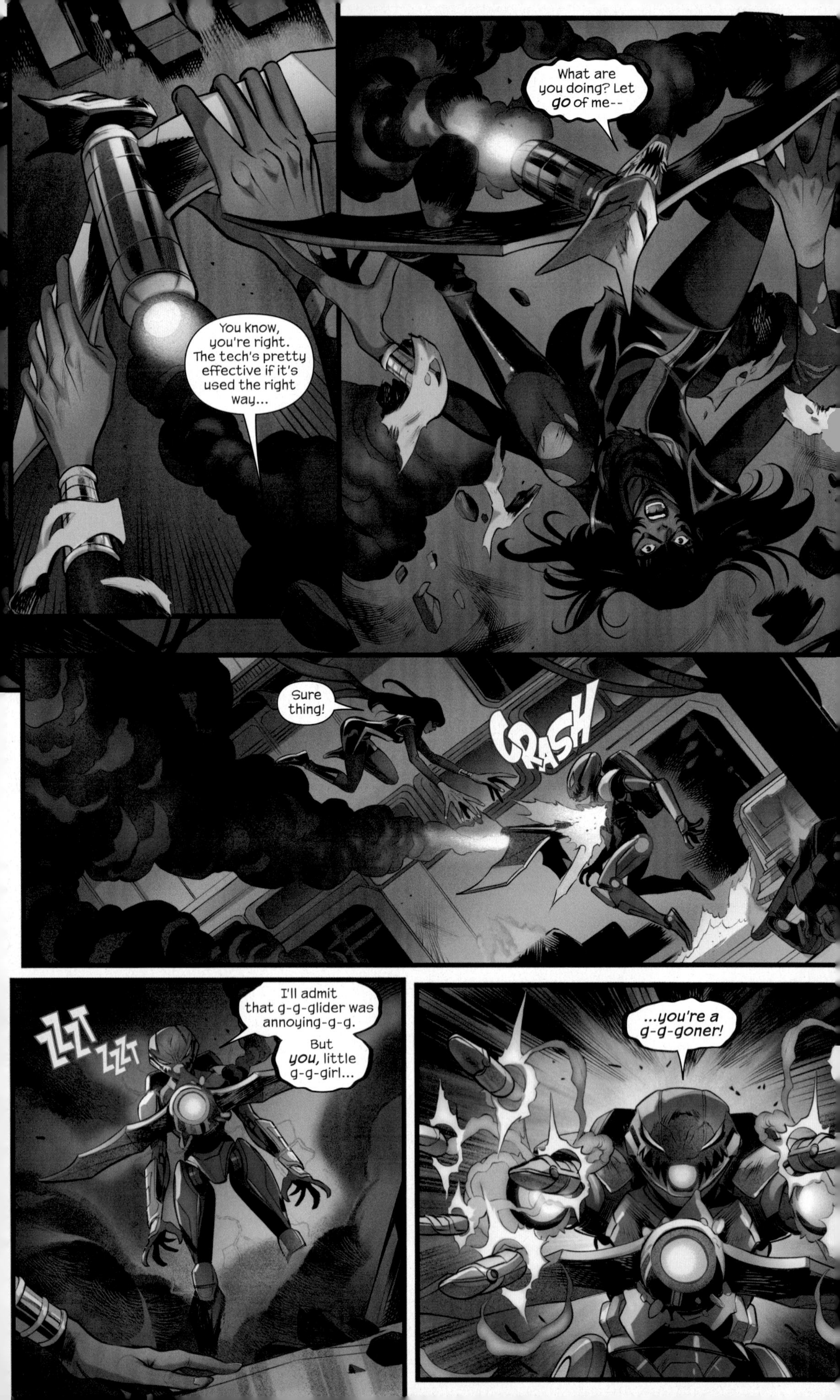
You know, you're right. The tech's pretty effective if it's used the right way...
What are you doing? Let go of me--
Sure thing!
CRASH
ZZZT ZZZT
I'll admit that g-g-glider was annoying-g-g.
But you, little g-g-girl...
...you're a g-g-goner!

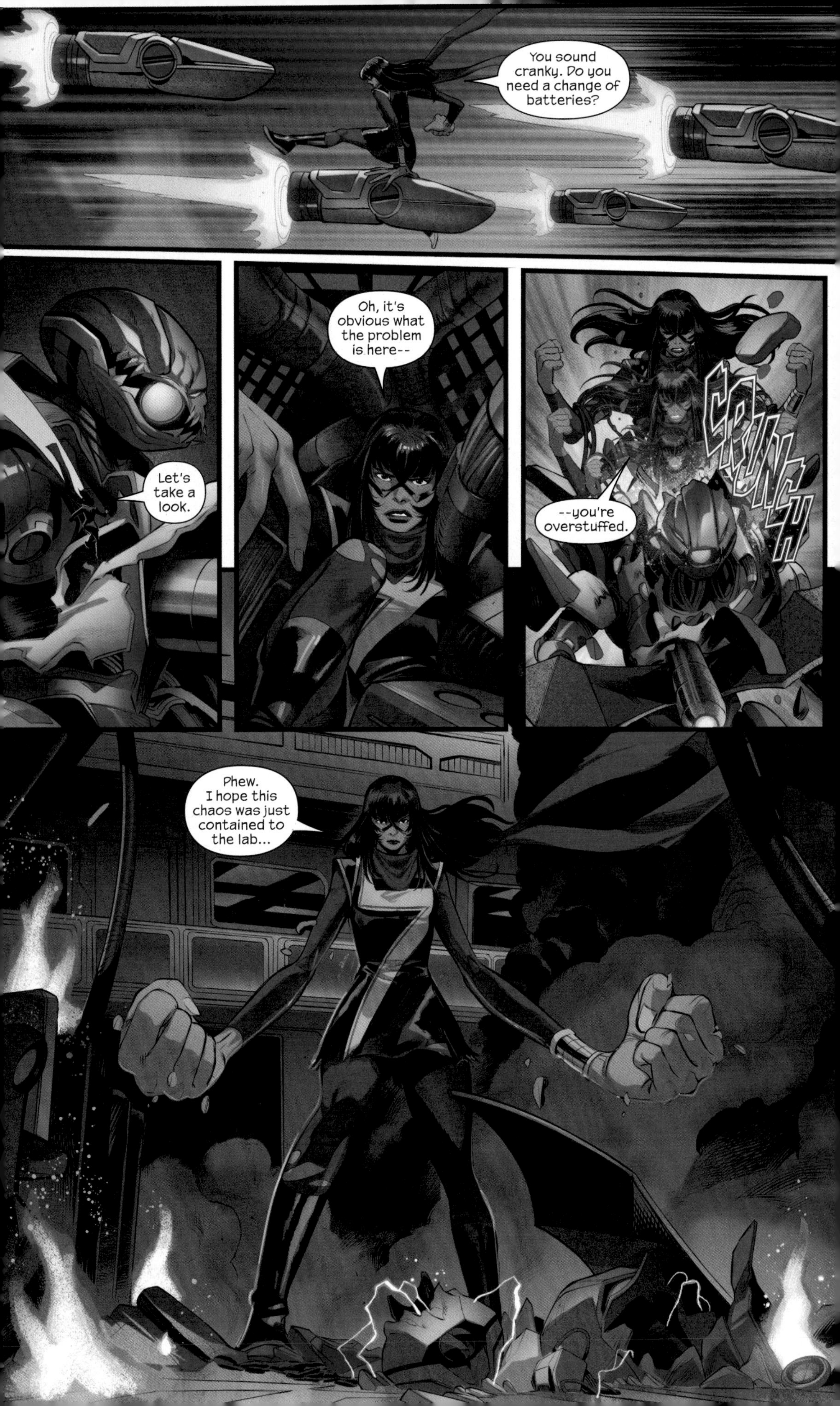

You sound cranky. Do you need a change of batteries?
Let's take a look.
Oh, it's obvious what the problem is here--
CRUNCH
--you're overstuffed.
Phew. I hope this chaos was just contained to the lab...

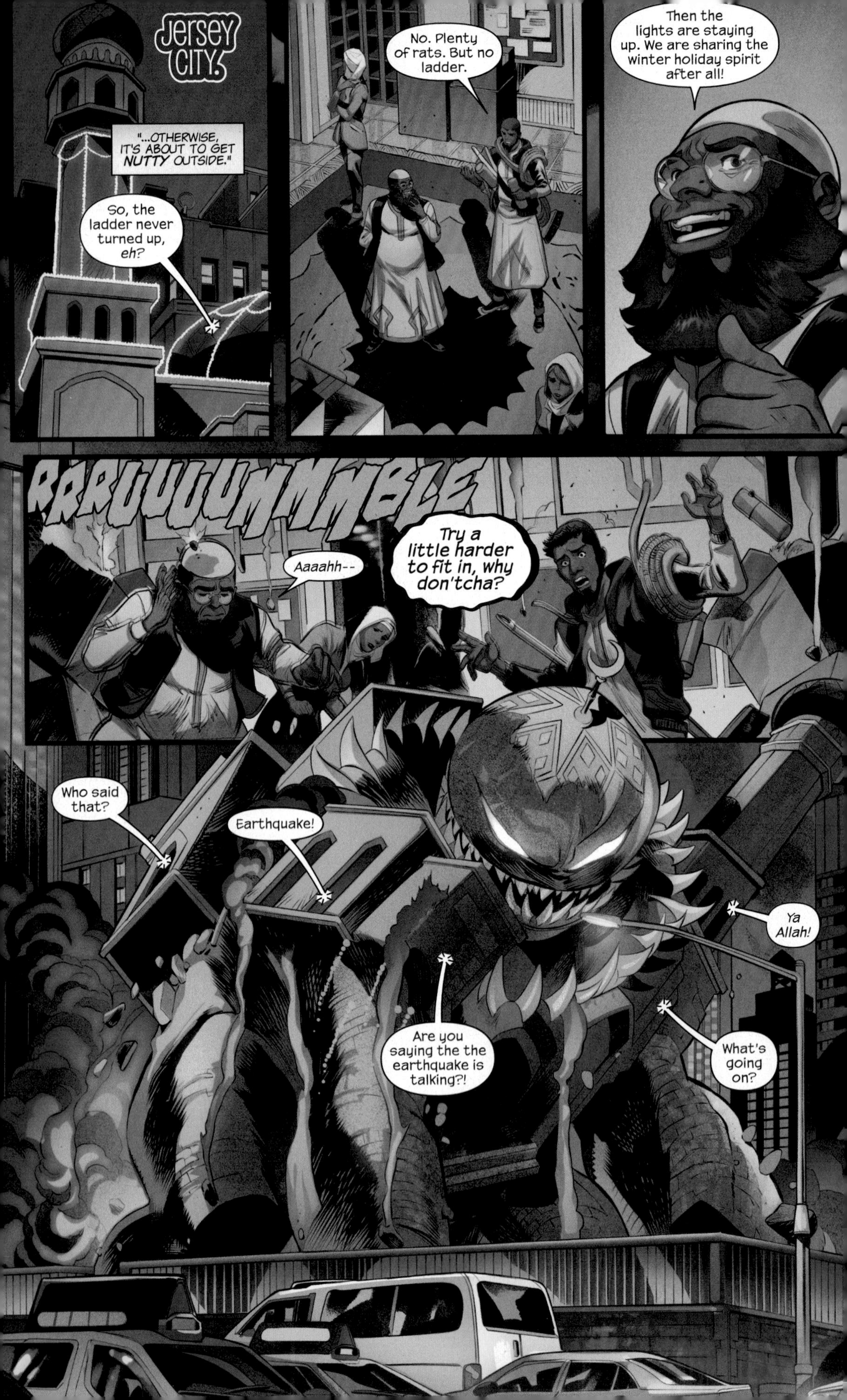
JERSEY CITY.
"...OTHERWISE, IT'S ABOUT TO GET NUTTY OUTSIDE."
So, the ladder never turned up, eh?
No. Plenty of rats. But no ladder.
Then the lights are staying up. We are sharing the winter holiday spirit after all!
RRRUUUUMMMBLE
Aaaahh--
Try a little harder to fit in, why don'tcha?
Who said that?
Earthquake!
Ya Allah!
Are you saying the the earthquake is talking?!
What's going on?

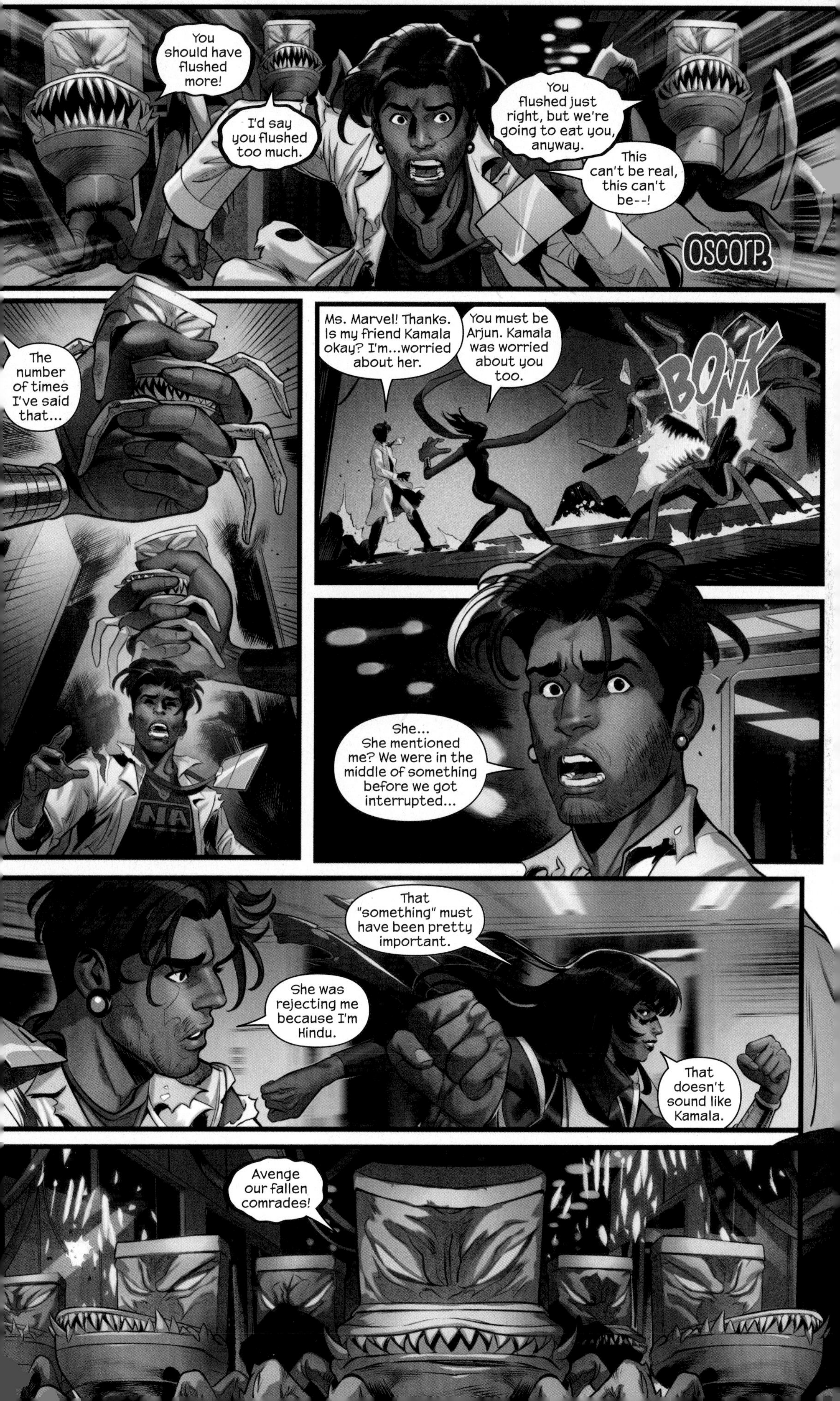

You should have flushed more!
I'd say you flushed too much.
You flushed just right, but we're going to eat you, anyway.
This can't be real, this can't be--!
OSCORP.
The number of times I've said that...
Ms. Marvel! Thanks. Is my friend Kamala okay? I'm...worried about her.
You must be Arjun. Kamala was worried about you too.
BONK
She... She mentioned me? We were in the middle of something before we got interrupted...
That "something" must have been pretty important.
She was rejecting me because I'm Hindu.
That doesn't sound like Kamala.
Avenge our fallen comrades!

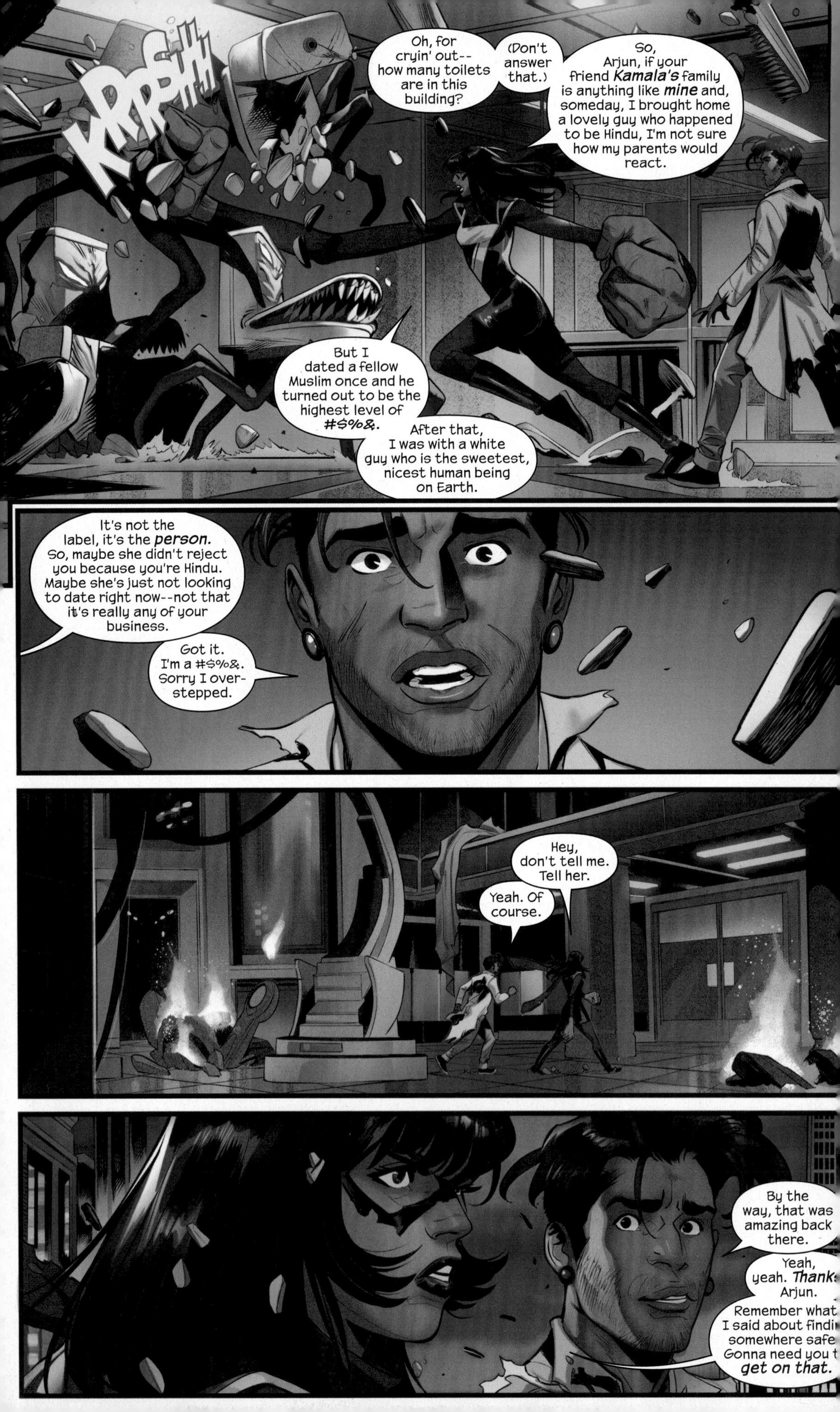

KRRSHH
Oh, for cryin' out-- how many toilets are in this building?
(Don't answer that.)
So, Arjun, if your friend Kamala's family is anything like mine and, someday, I brought home a lovely guy who happened to be Hindu, I'm not sure how my parents would react.
But I dated a fellow Muslim once and he turned out to be the highest level of #$%&.
After that, I was with a white guy who is the sweetest, nicest human being on Earth.
It's not the label, it's the person. So, maybe she didn't reject you because you're Hindu. Maybe she's just not looking to date right now--not that it's really any of your business.
Got it. I'm a #$%&. Sorry I over-stepped.
Hey, don't tell me. Tell her.
Yeah. Of course.
By the way, that was amazing back there.
Yeah, yeah. Thank Arjun.
Remember what I said about findi somewhere safe Gonna need you t get on that.

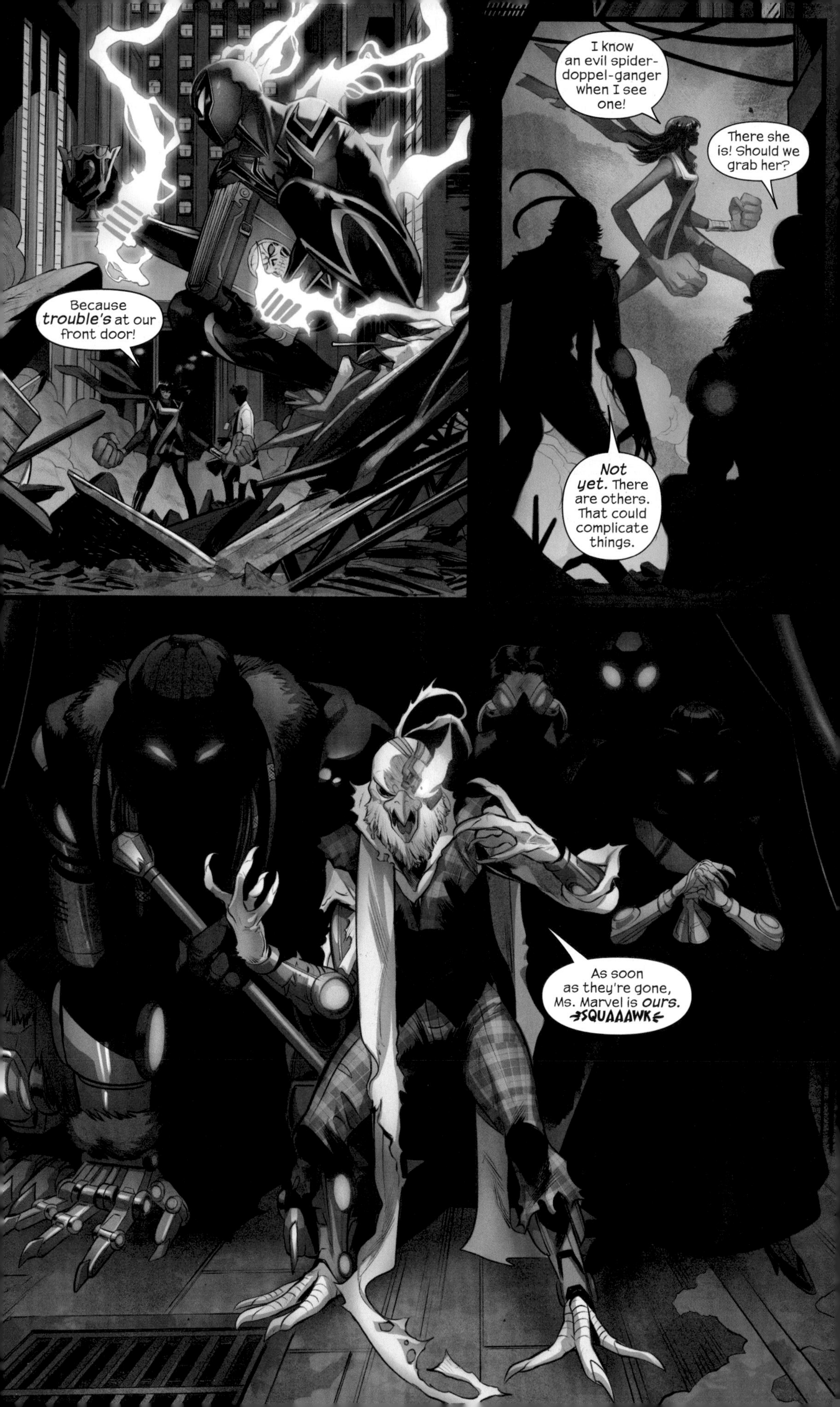

Because *trouble's* at our front door!
I know an evil spider-doppel-ganger when I see one!
There she is! Should we grab her?
Not yet. There are others. That could complicate things.
As soon as they're gone, Ms. Marvel is *ours.*
SQUAAAWK

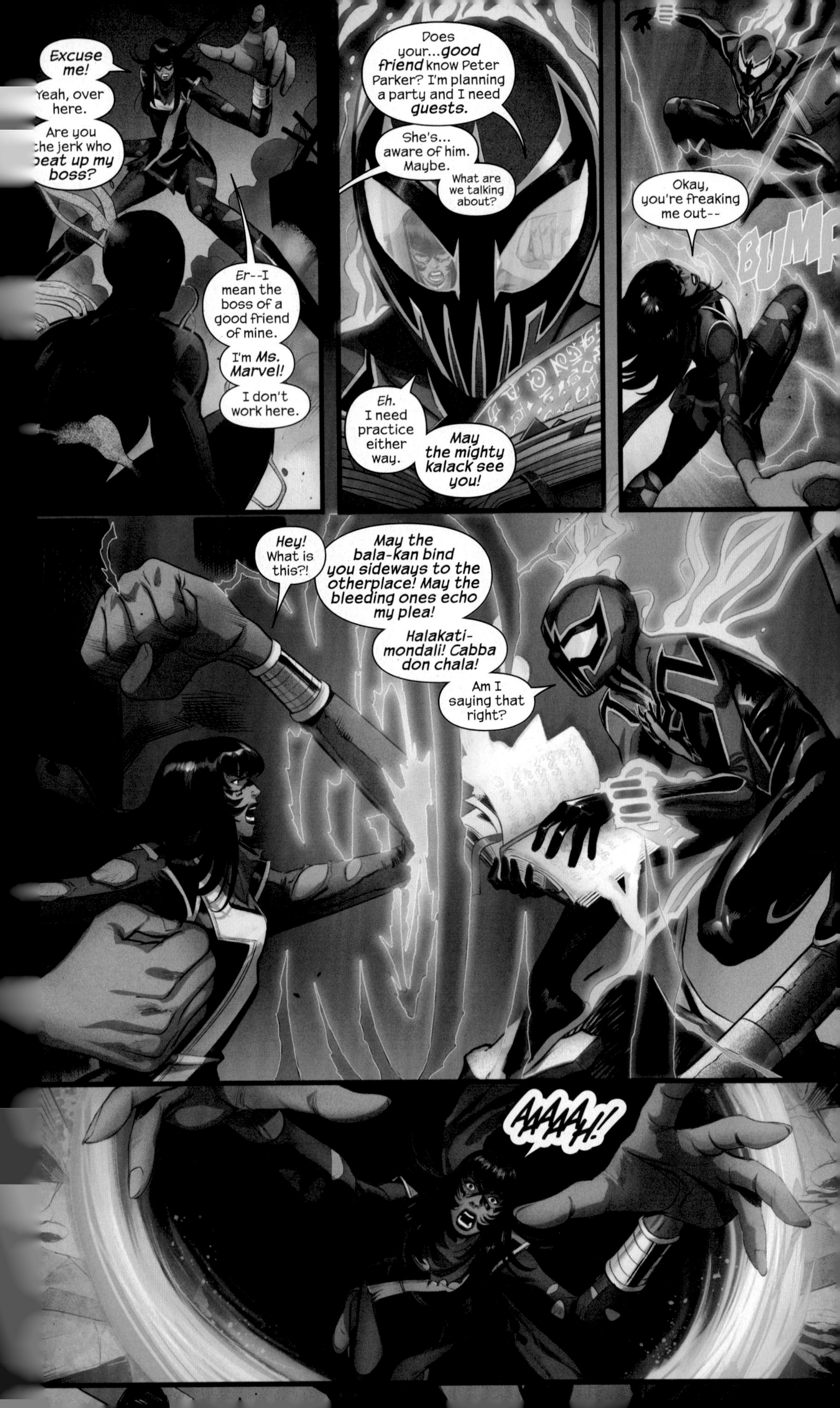

Excuse me!
Yeah, over here.
Are you the jerk who beat up my boss?
Er--I mean the boss of a good friend of mine.
I'm Ms. Marvel!
I don't work here.
Does your...good friend know Peter Parker? I'm planning a party and I need guests.
She's... aware of him. Maybe.
What are we talking about?
Eh. I need practice either way.
May the mighty kalack see you!
Okay, you're freaking me out--
BUMP
Hey! What is this?!
May the bala-kan bind you sideways to the otherplace! May the bleeding ones echo my plea!
Halakati-mondali! Cabba don chala!
Am I saying that right?
AAAAAH!!

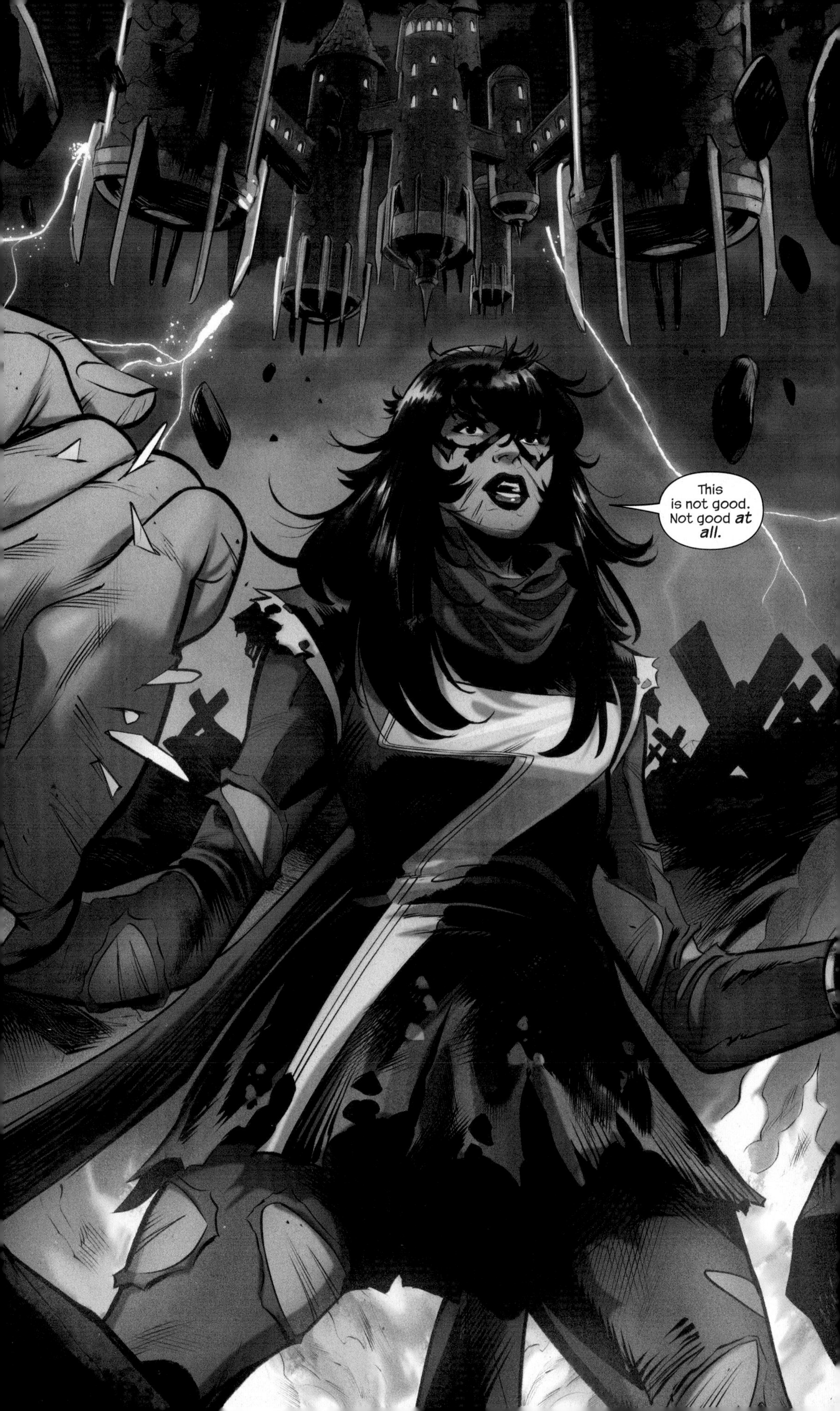
This is not good. Not good *at all.*

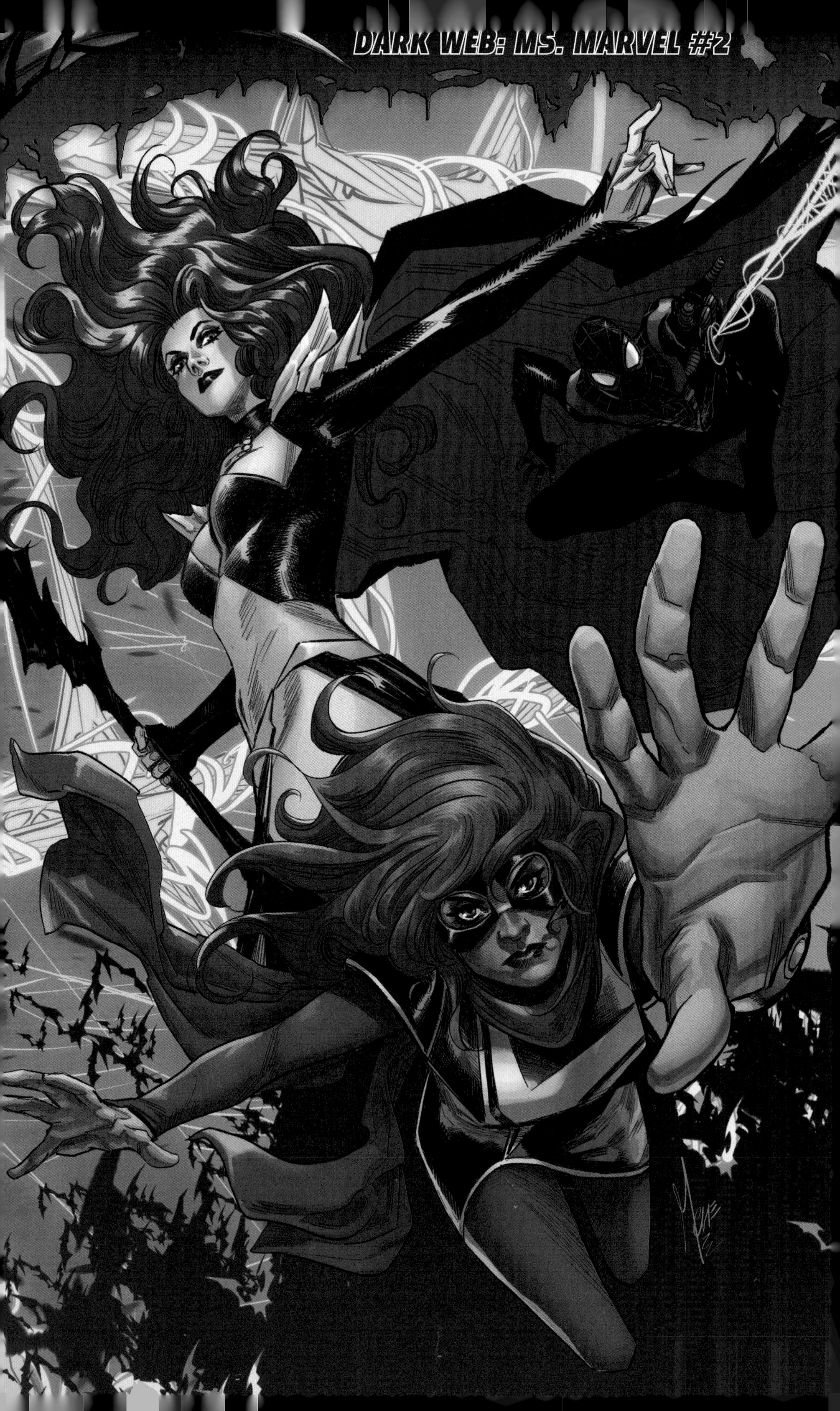
DARK WEB: MS. MARVEL #2

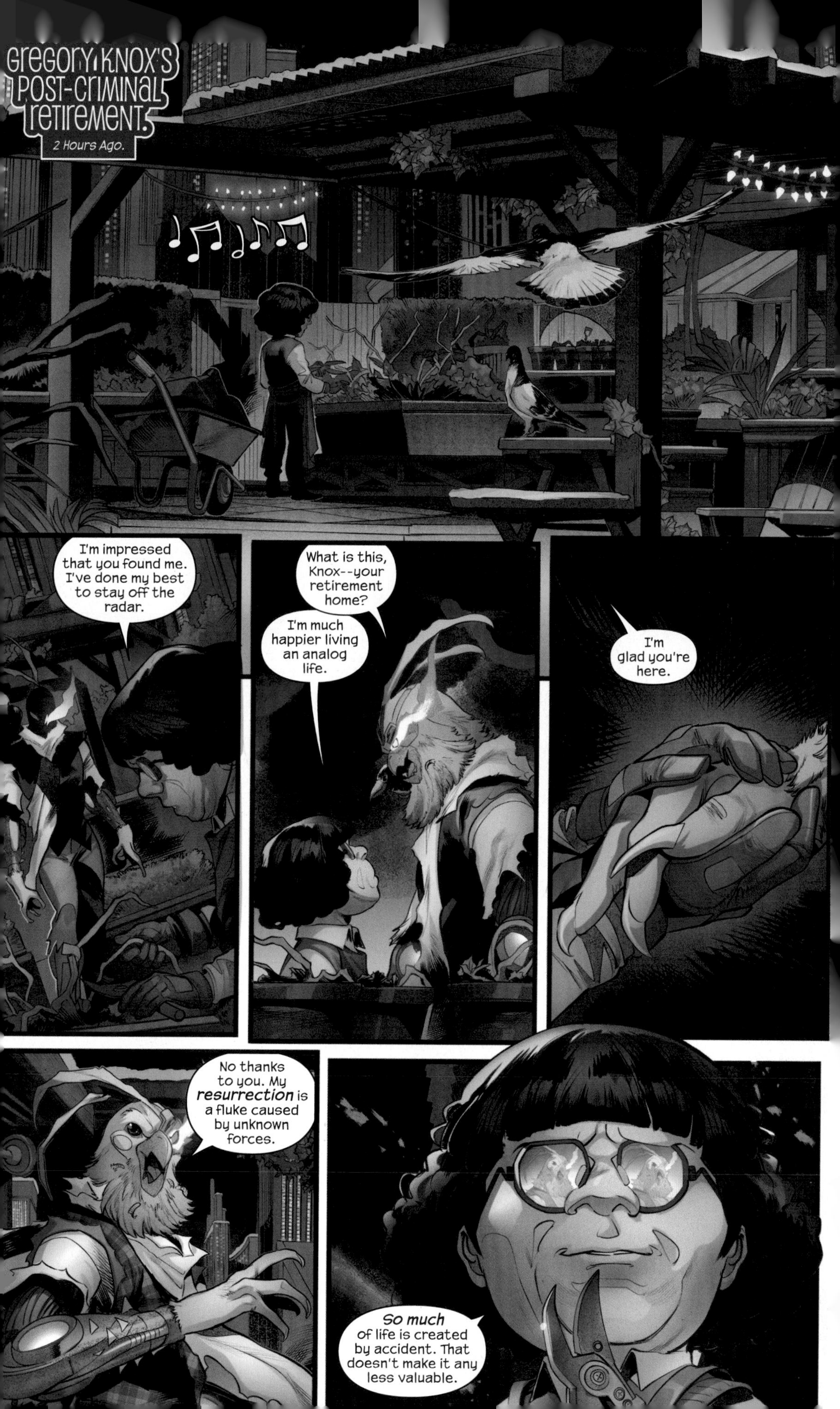

GREGORY KNOX'S POST-CRIMINAL RETIREMENT.
2 Hours Ago.
I'm impressed that you found me. I've done my best to stay off the radar.
What is this, Knox--your retirement home?
I'm much happier living an analog life.
I'm glad you're here.
No thanks to you. My *resurrection* is a fluke caused by unknown forces.
So much of life is created by accident. That doesn't make it any less valuable.

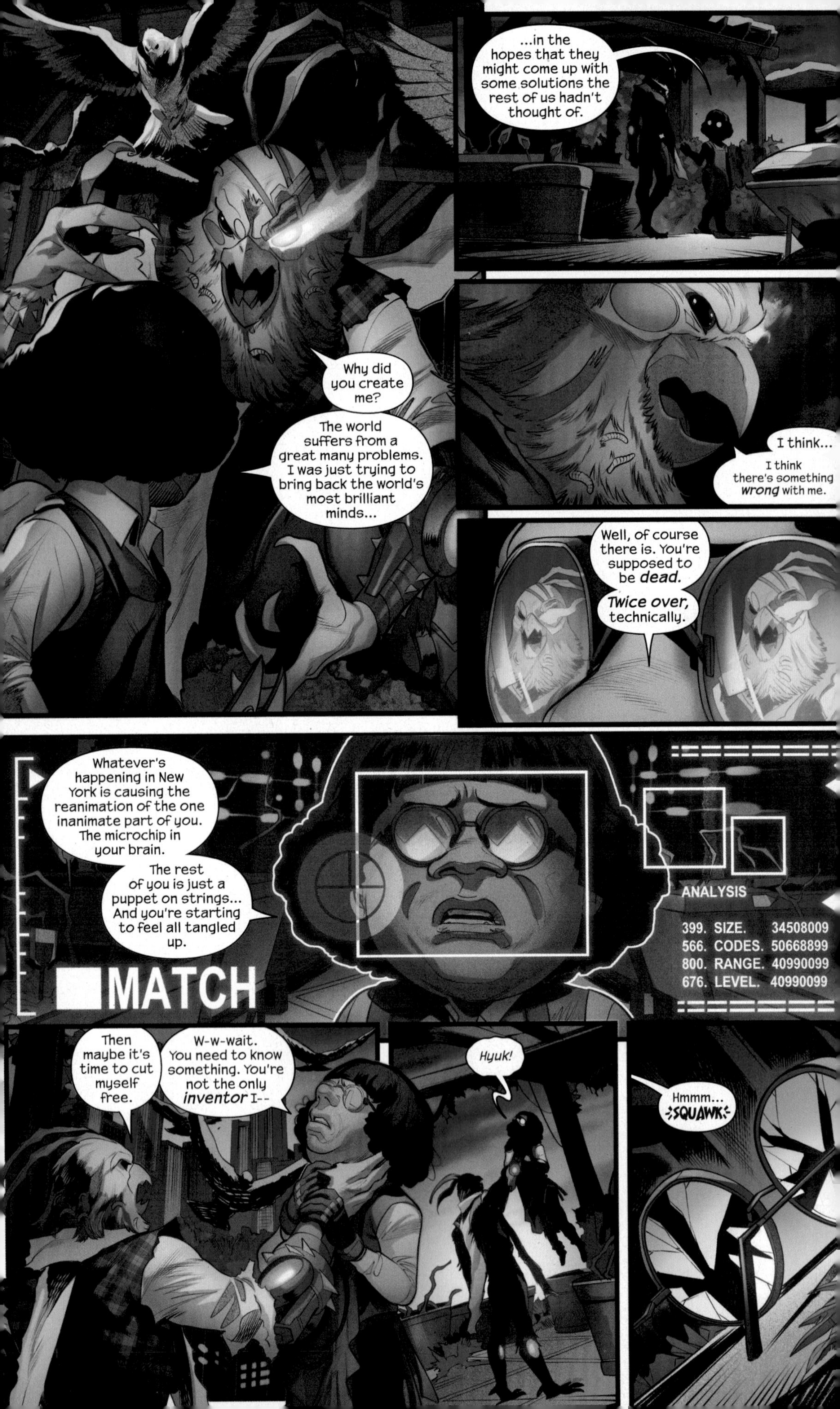

...in the hopes that they might come up with some solutions the rest of us hadn't thought of.
Why did you create me?
The world suffers from a great many problems. I was just trying to bring back the world's most brilliant minds...
I think...
I think there's something *wrong* with me.
Well, of course there is. You're supposed to be *dead.*
Twice over, technically.
Whatever's happening in New York is causing the reanimation of the one inanimate part of you. The microchip in your brain.
The rest of you is just a puppet on strings... And you're starting to feel all tangled up.
MATCH
ANALYSIS
399. SIZE. 34508009
566. CODES. 50668899
800. RANGE. 40990099
676. LEVEL. 40990099
Then maybe it's time to cut myself free.
W-w-wait. You need to know something. You're not the only *inventor* I--
Hyuk!
Hmmm...
SQUAWK

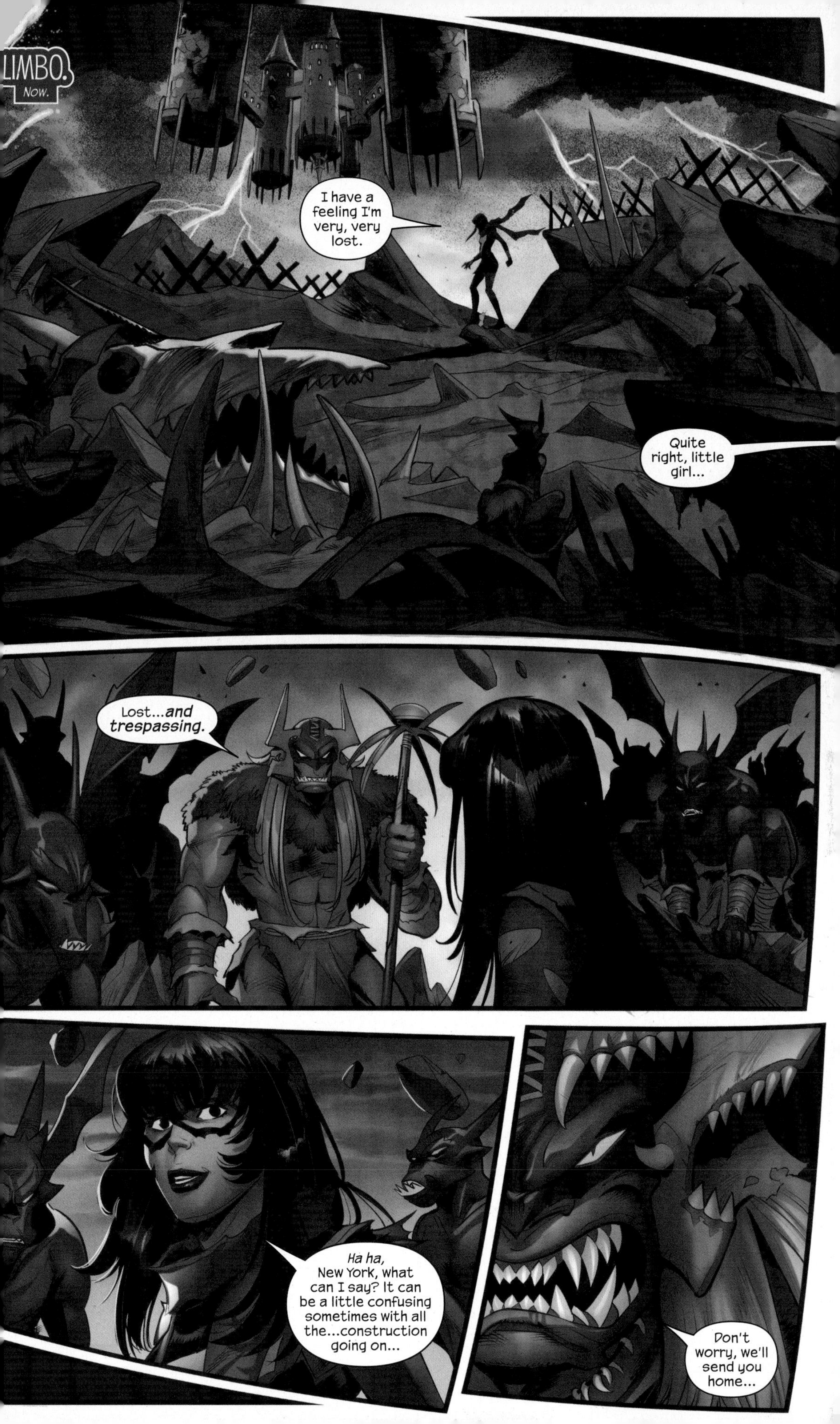
LIMBO.
Now.
I have a feeling I'm very, very lost.
Quite right, little girl...
Lost...*and trespassing.*
Ha ha, New York, what can I say? It can be a little confusing sometimes with all the...construction going on...
Don't worry, we'll send you home...

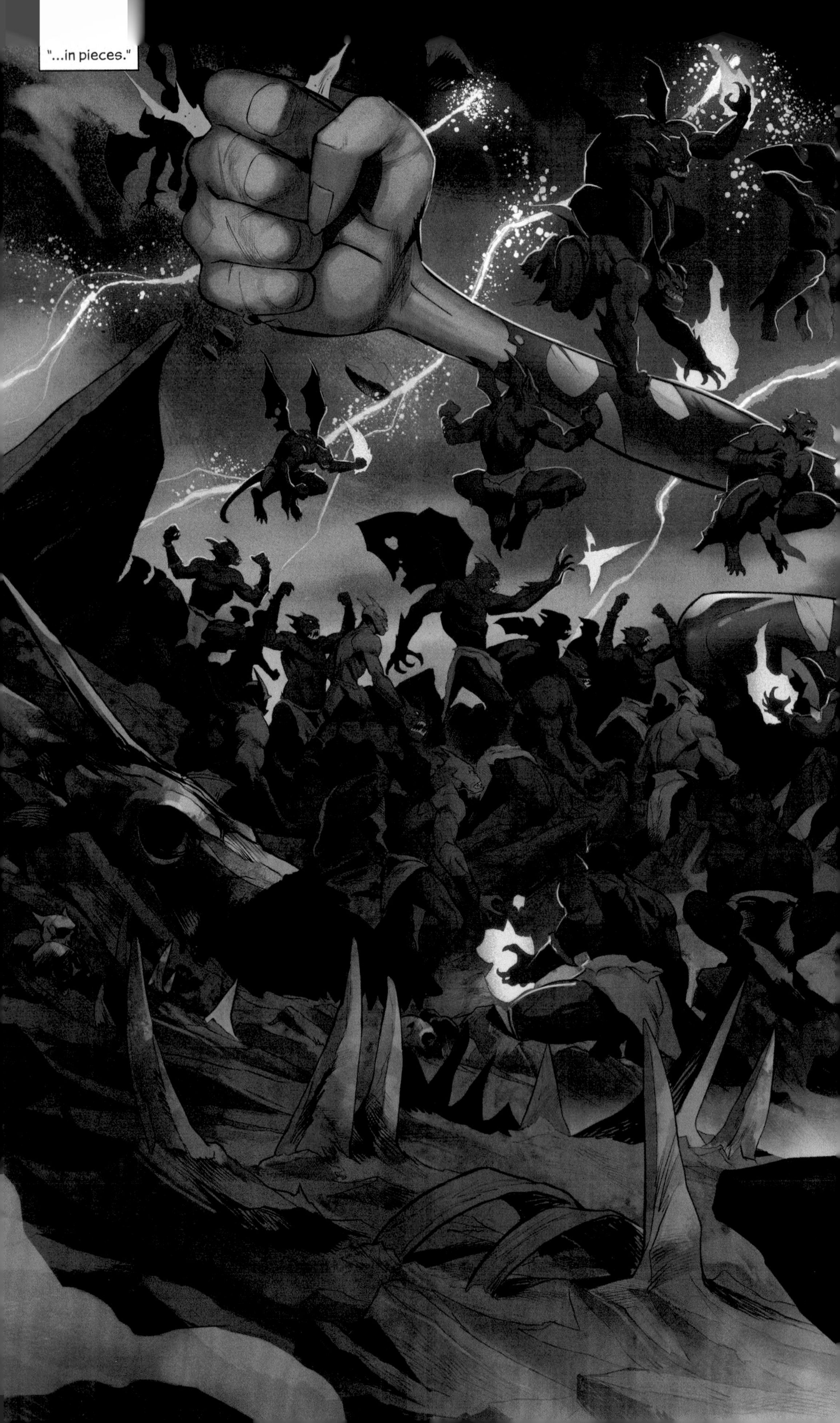
"...in pieces."

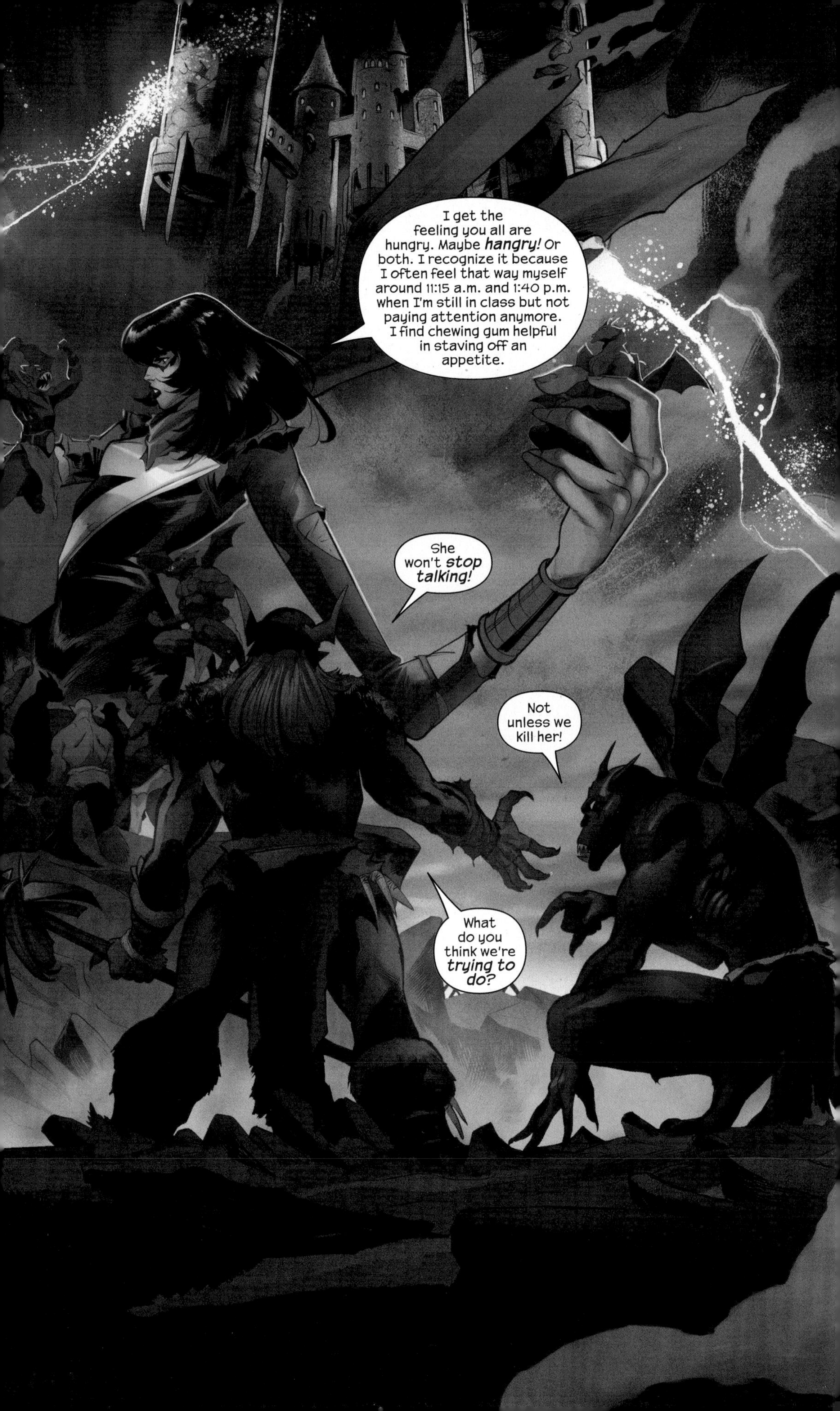
I get the feeling you all are hungry. Maybe *hangry!* Or both. I recognize it because I often feel that way myself around 11:15 a.m. and 1:40 p.m. when I'm still in class but not paying attention anymore. I find chewing gum helpful in staving off an appetite.
She won't *stop talking!*
Not unless we kill her!
What do you think we're *trying to do?*

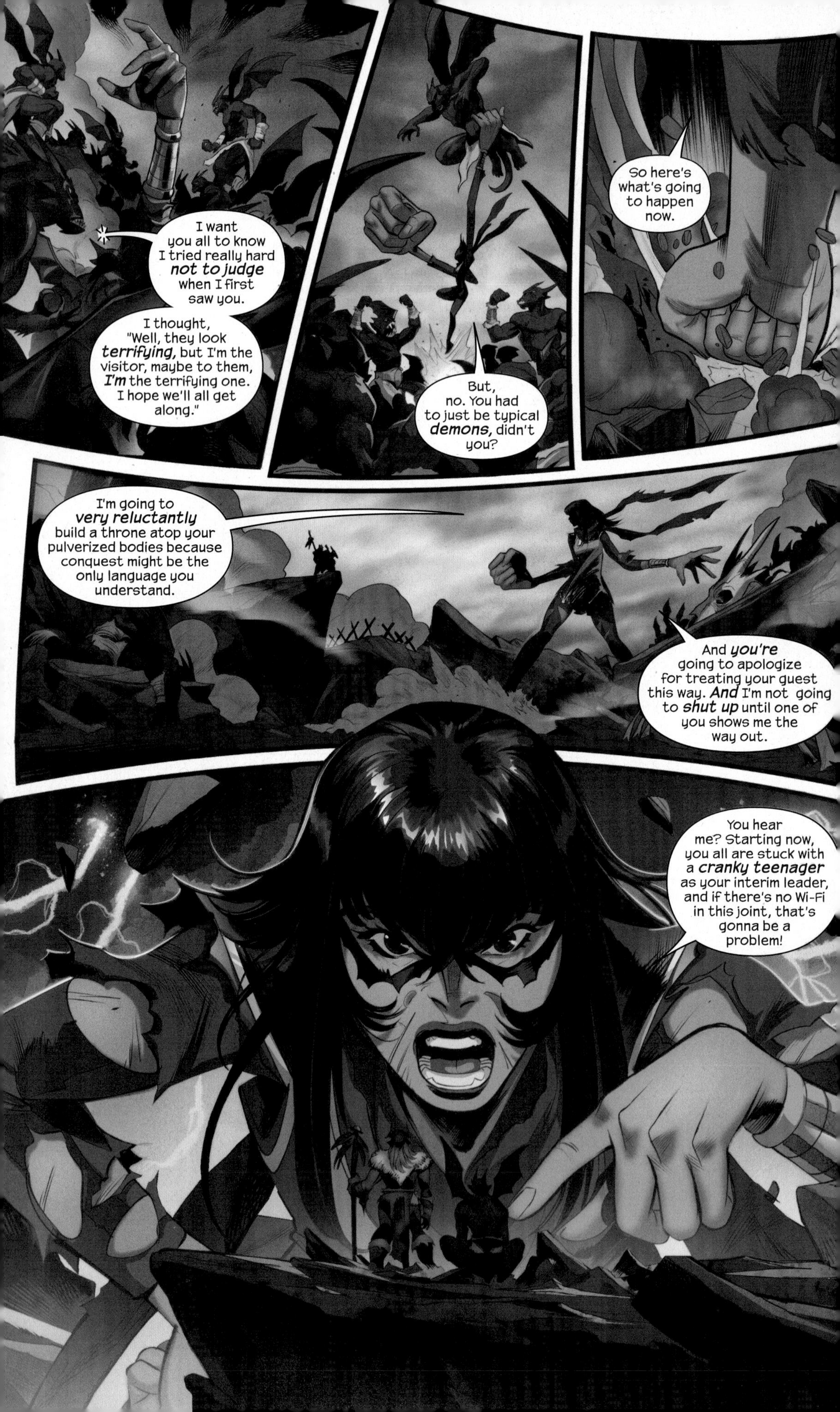
I want you all to know I tried really hard not to judge when I first saw you.
I thought, "Well, they look terrifying, but I'm the visitor, maybe to them, I'm the terrifying one. I hope we'll all get along."
But, no. You had to just be typical demons, didn't you?
So here's what's going to happen now.
I'm going to very reluctantly build a throne atop your pulverized bodies because conquest might be the only language you understand.
And you're going to apologize for treating your guest this way. And I'm not going to shut up until one of you shows me the way out.
You hear me? Starting now, you all are stuck with a cranky teenager as your interim leader, and if there's no Wi-Fi in this joint, that's gonna be a problem!

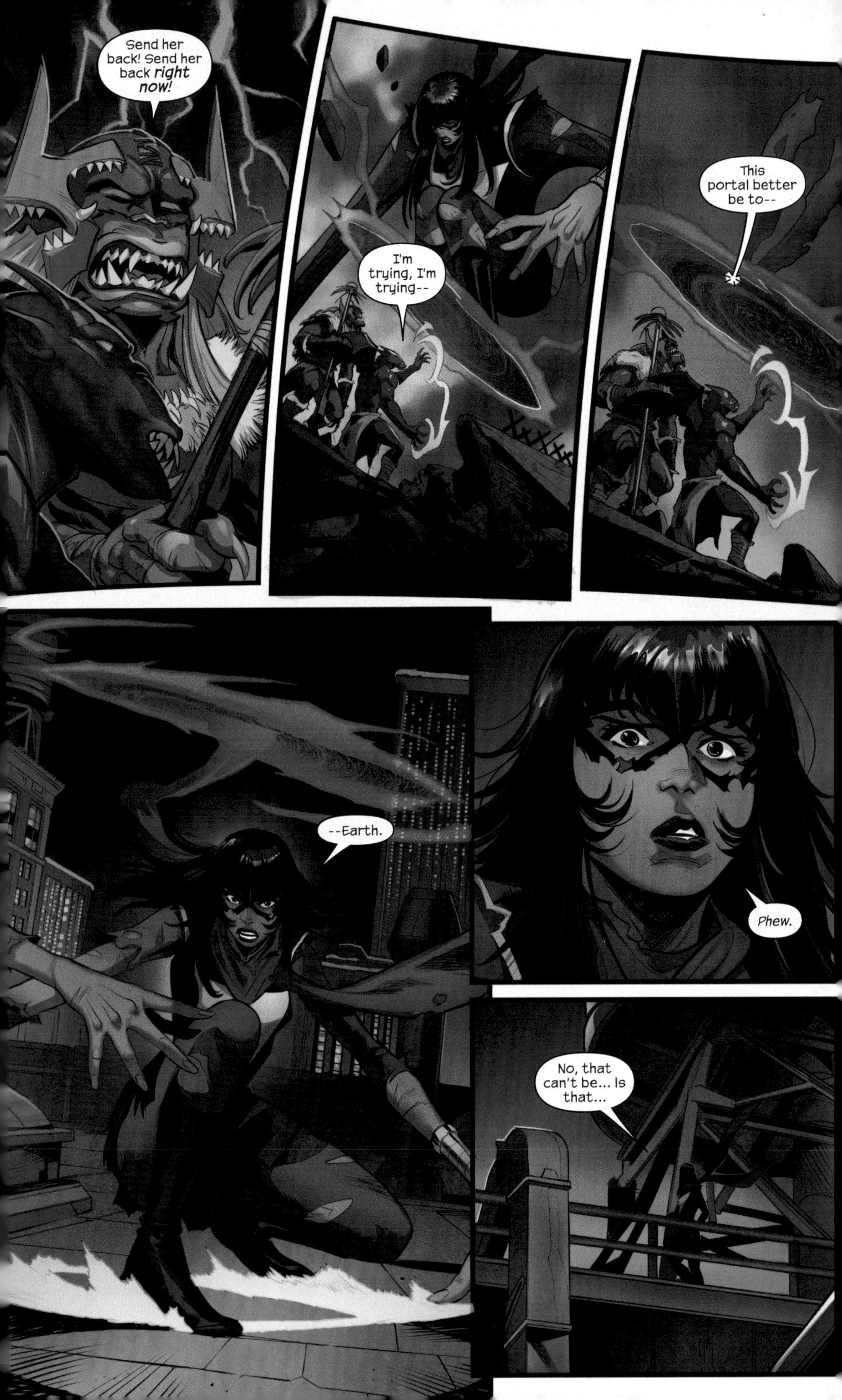
Send her back! Send her back **right now!**
I'm trying, I'm trying--
This portal better be to--
--Earth.
Phew.
No, that can't be... Is that...

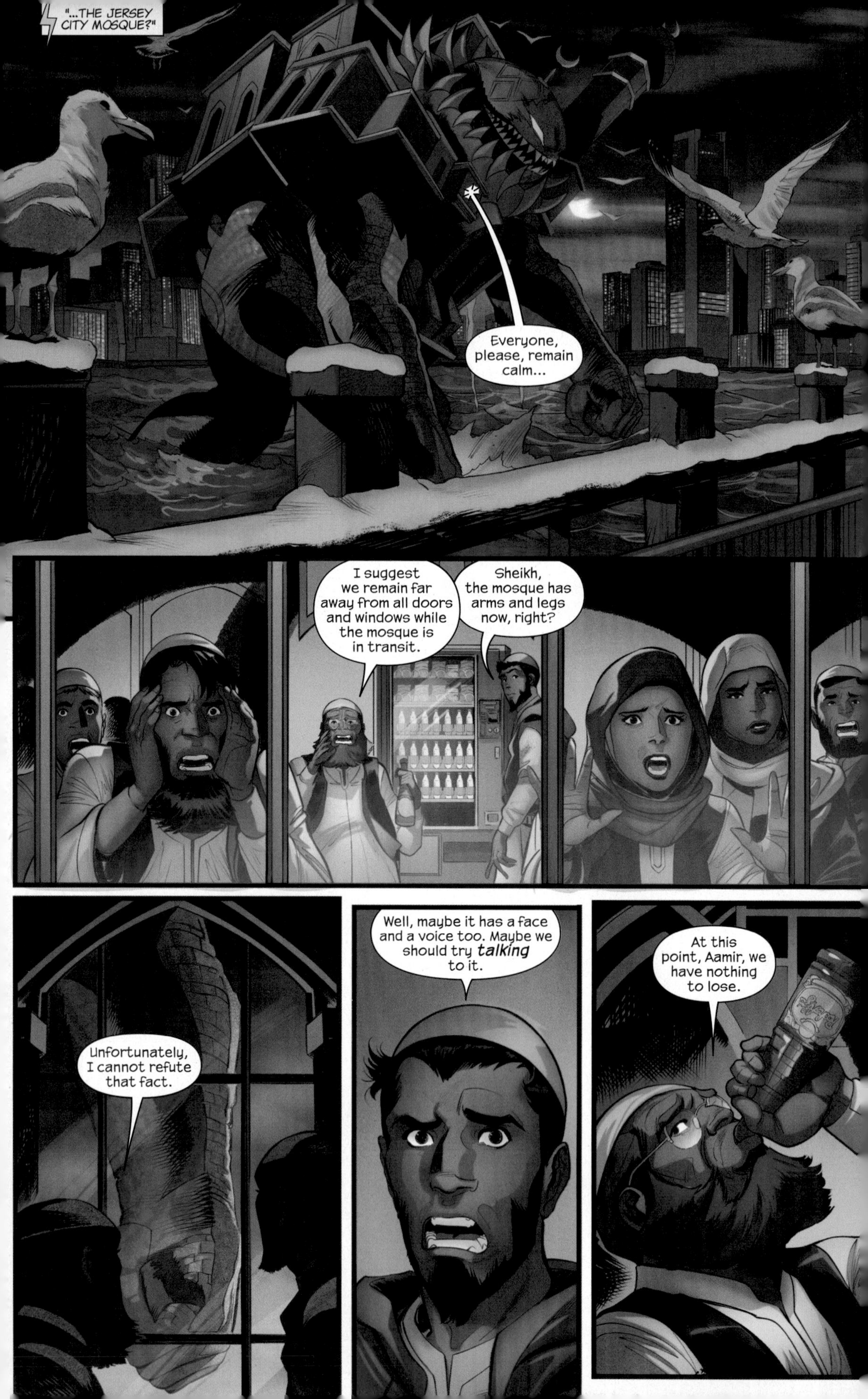
"...THE JERSEY CITY MOSQUE?"
Everyone, please, remain calm...
I suggest we remain far away from all doors and windows while the mosque is in transit.
Sheikh, the mosque has arms and legs now, right?
Unfortunately, I cannot refute that fact.
Well, maybe it has a face and a voice too. Maybe we should try *talking* to it.
At this point, Aamir, we have nothing to lose.

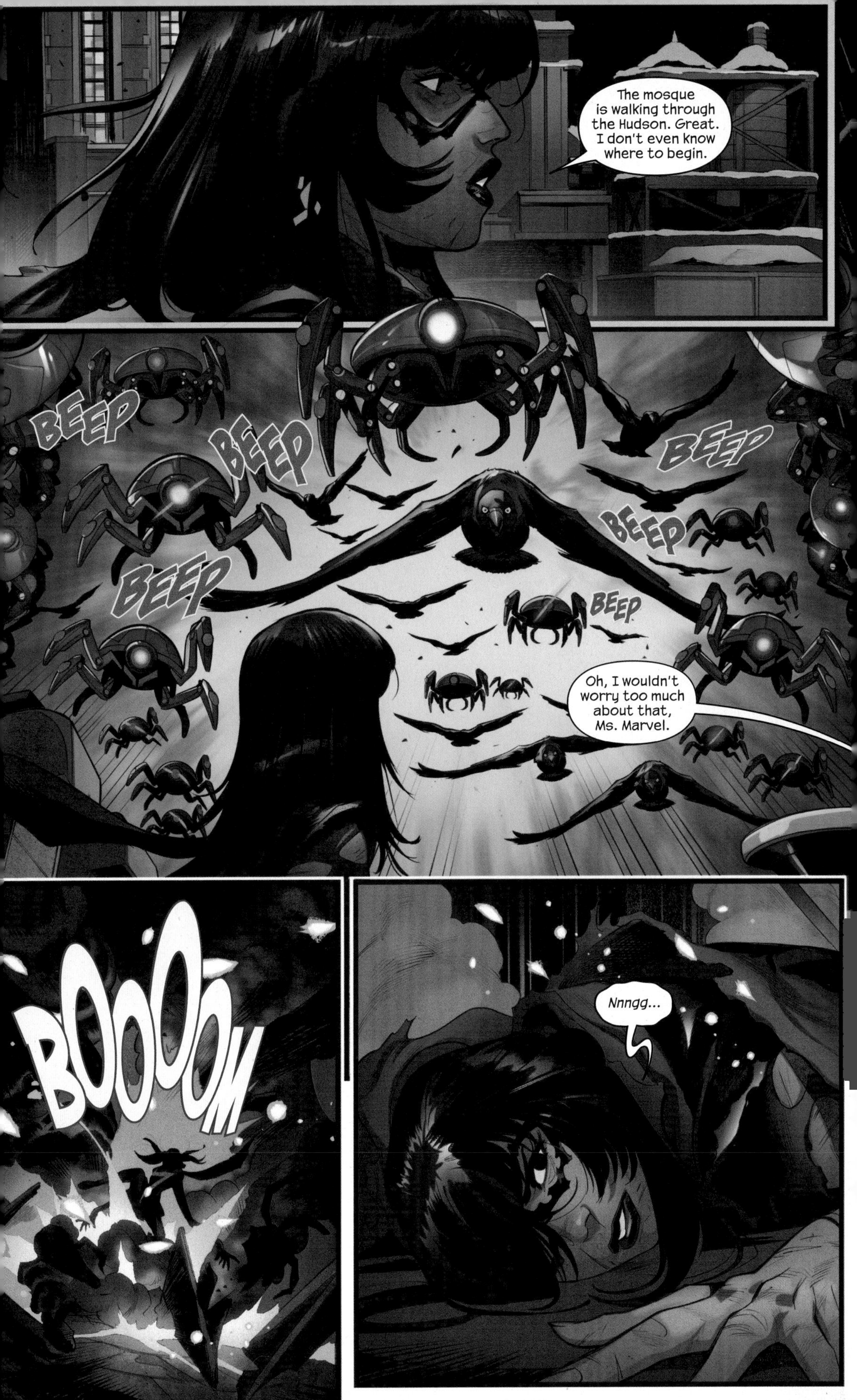

The mosque is walking through the Hudson. Great. I don't even know where to begin.
BEEP
BEEP
BEEP
BEEP
BEEP
BEEP
Oh, I wouldn't worry too much about that, Ms. Marvel.
BOOOOOM
Nnngg...

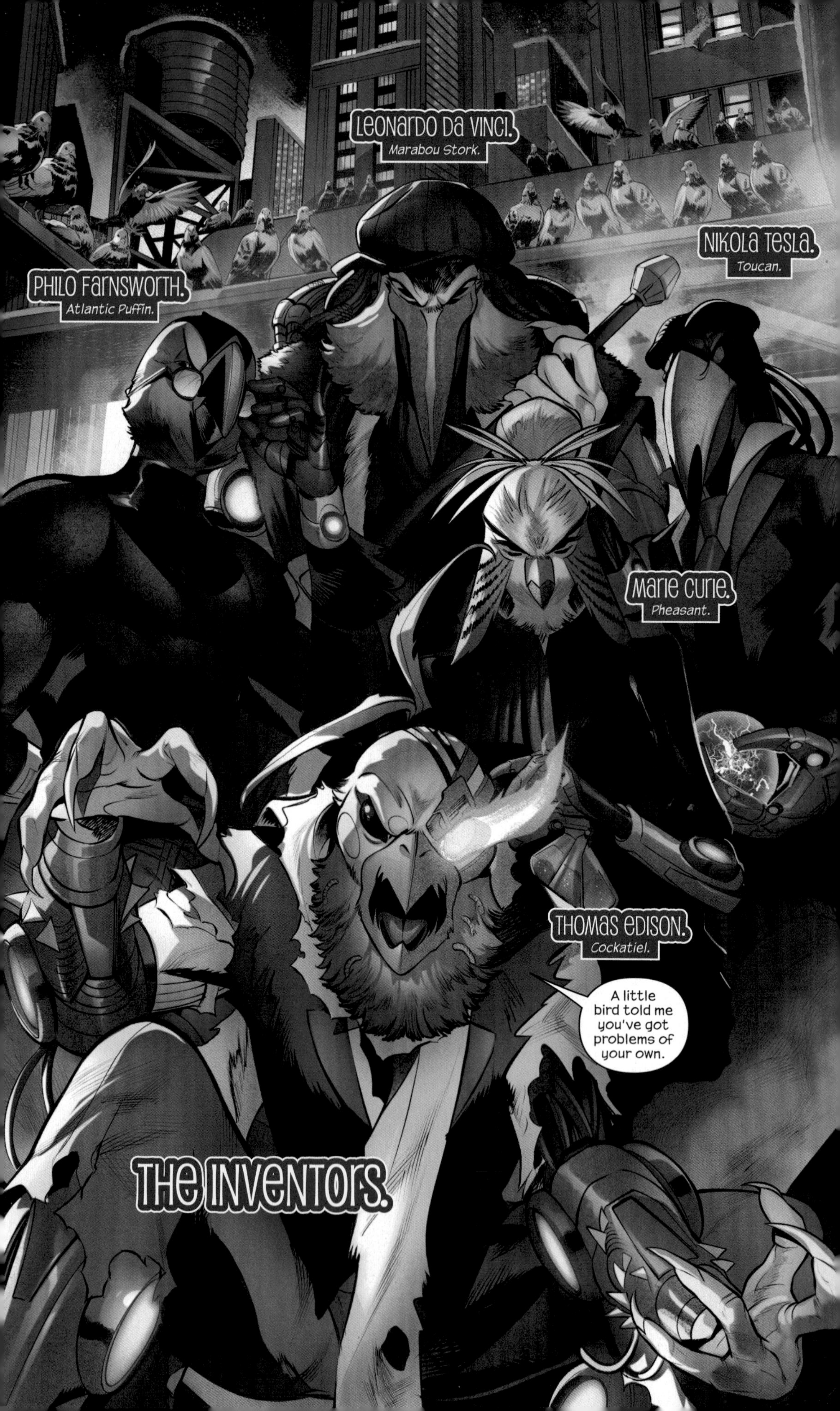
LEONARDO DA VINCI.
Marabou Stork.
NIKOLA TESLA.
Toucan.
PHILO FARNSWORTH.
Atlantic Puffin.
MARIE CURIE.
Pheasant.
THOMAS EDISON.
Cockatiel.
A little bird told me you've got problems of your own.
THE INVENTORS.

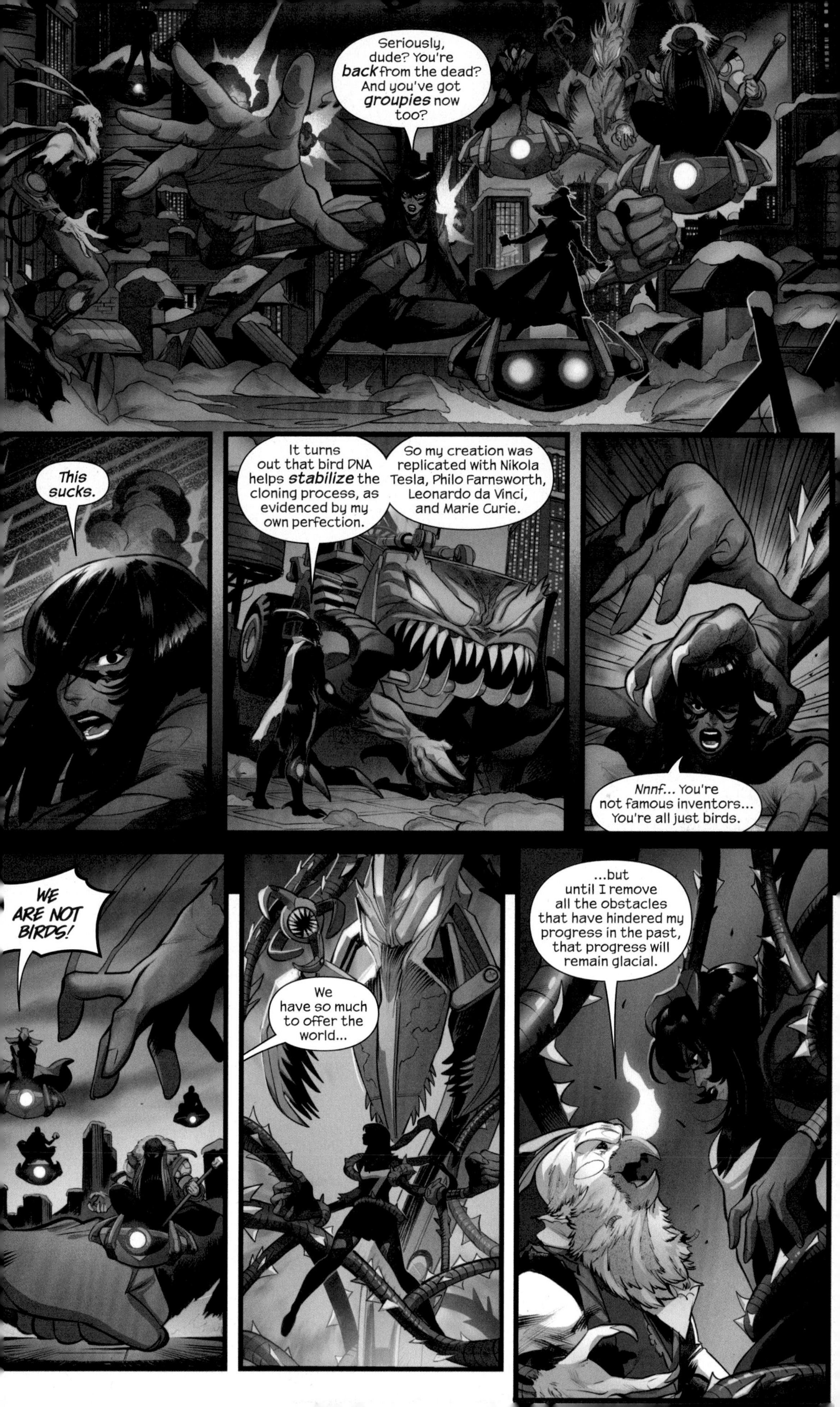
Seriously, dude? You're back from the dead? And you've got groupies now too?
This sucks.
It turns out that bird DNA helps stabilize the cloning process, as evidenced by my own perfection.
So my creation was replicated with Nikola Tesla, Philo Farnsworth, Leonardo da Vinci, and Marie Curie.
Nnnf... You're not famous inventors... You're all just birds.
WE ARE NOT BIRDS!
We have so much to offer the world...
...but until I remove all the obstacles that have hindered my progress in the past, that progress will remain glacial.

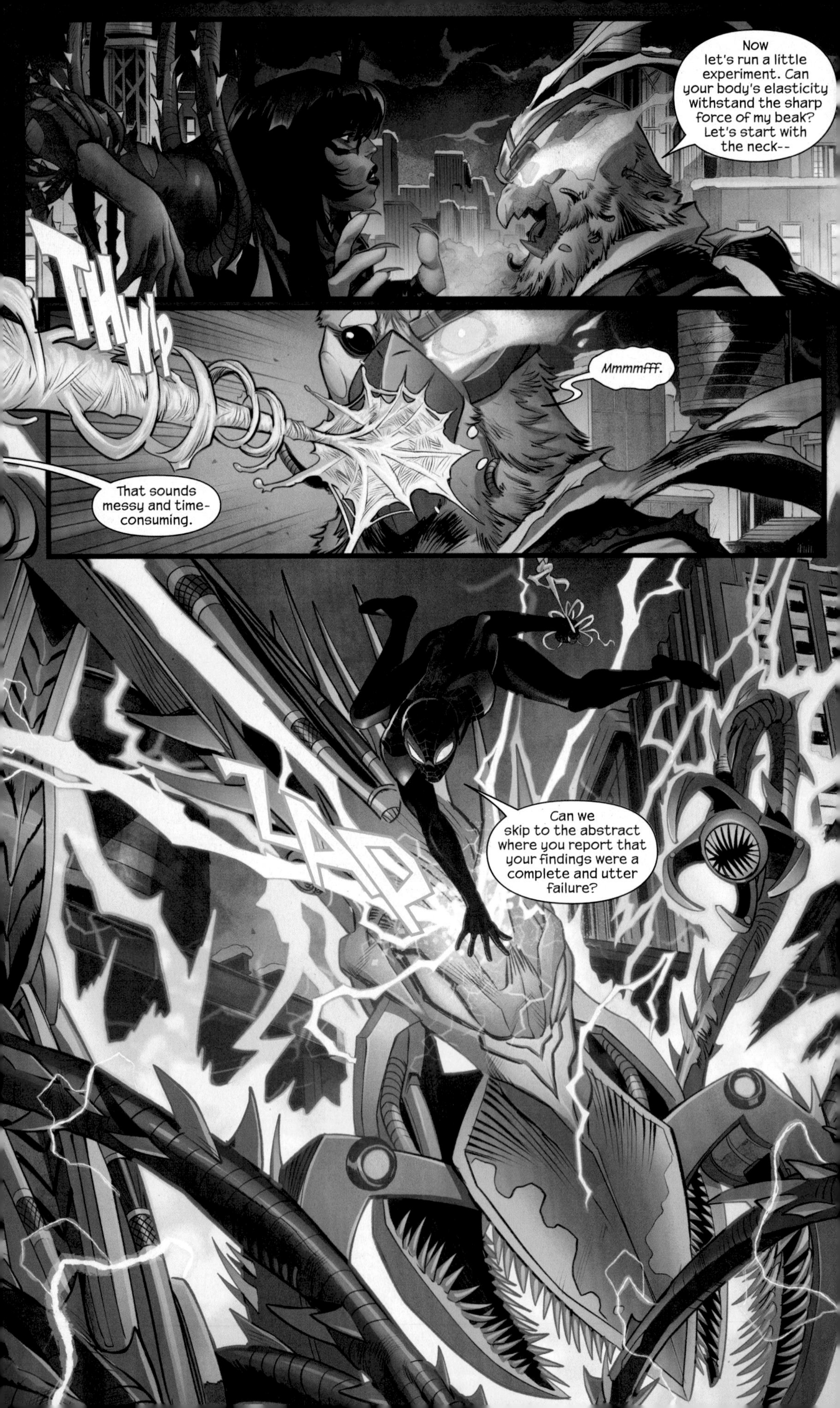
Now let's run a little experiment. Can your body's elasticity withstand the sharp force of my beak? Let's start with the neck--
THWIP
Mmmmfff.
That sounds messy and time-consuming.
ZAP
Can we skip to the abstract where you report that your findings were a complete and utter failure?

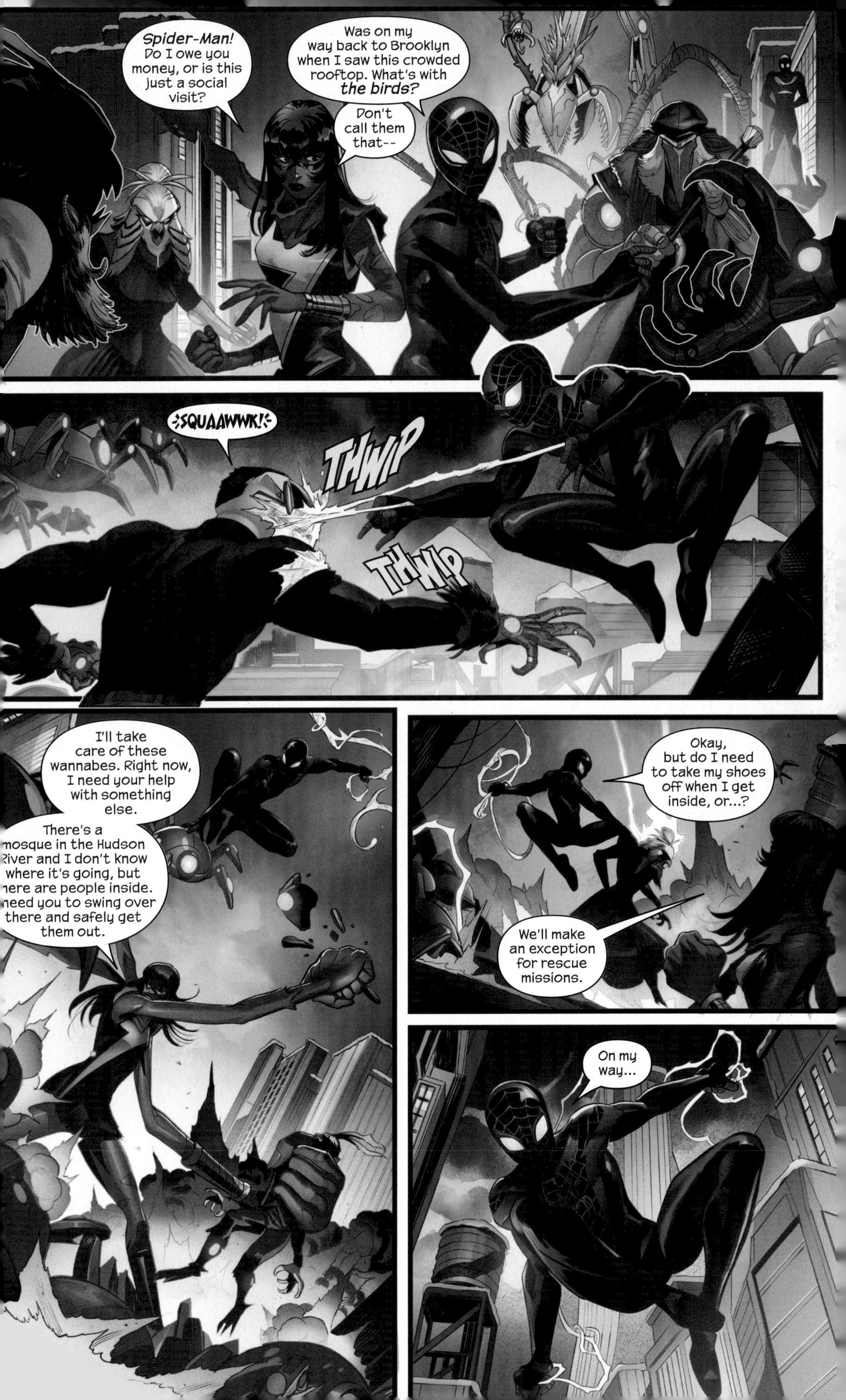
Spider-Man! Do I owe you money, or is this just a social visit?
Was on my way back to Brooklyn when I saw this crowded rooftop. What's with the birds?
Don't call them that--
SQUAAWWK!
THWIP
THWIP
I'll take care of these wannabes. Right now, I need your help with something else.
There's a mosque in the Hudson River and I don't know where it's going, but here are people inside. need you to swing over there and safely get them out.
Okay, but do I need to take my shoes off when I get inside, or...?
We'll make an exception for rescue missions.
On my way...

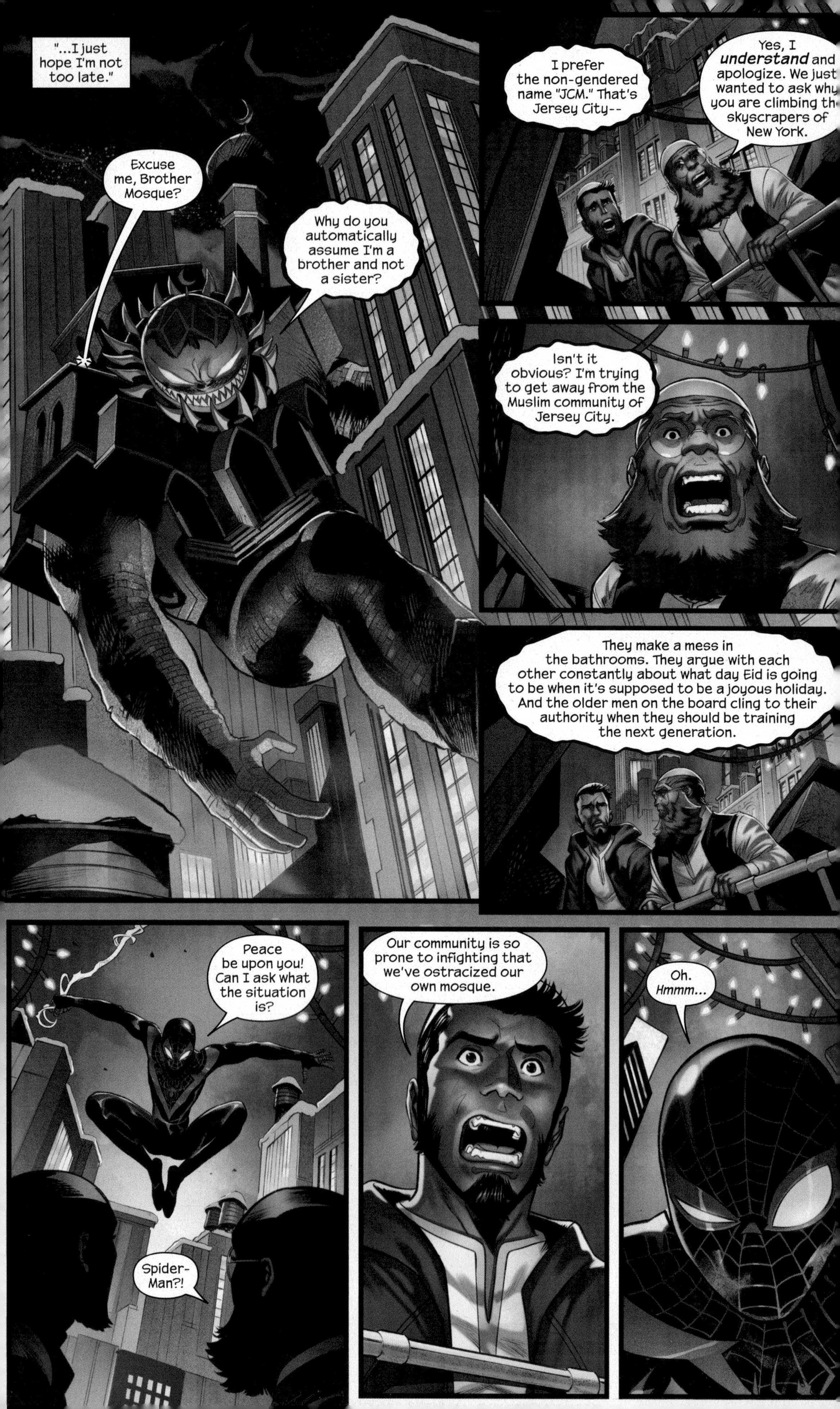
"...I just hope I'm not too late."
Excuse me, Brother Mosque?
Why do you automatically assume I'm a brother and not a sister?
I prefer the non-gendered name "JCM." That's Jersey City--
Yes, I *understand* and apologize. We just wanted to ask why you are climbing the skyscrapers of New York.
Isn't it obvious? I'm trying to get away from the Muslim community of Jersey City.
They make a mess in the bathrooms. They argue with each other constantly about what day Eid is going to be when it's supposed to be a joyous holiday. And the older men on the board cling to their authority when they should be training the next generation.
Peace be upon you! Can I ask what the situation is?
Spider-Man?!
Our community is so prone to infighting that we've ostracized our own mosque.
Oh. Hmmm...

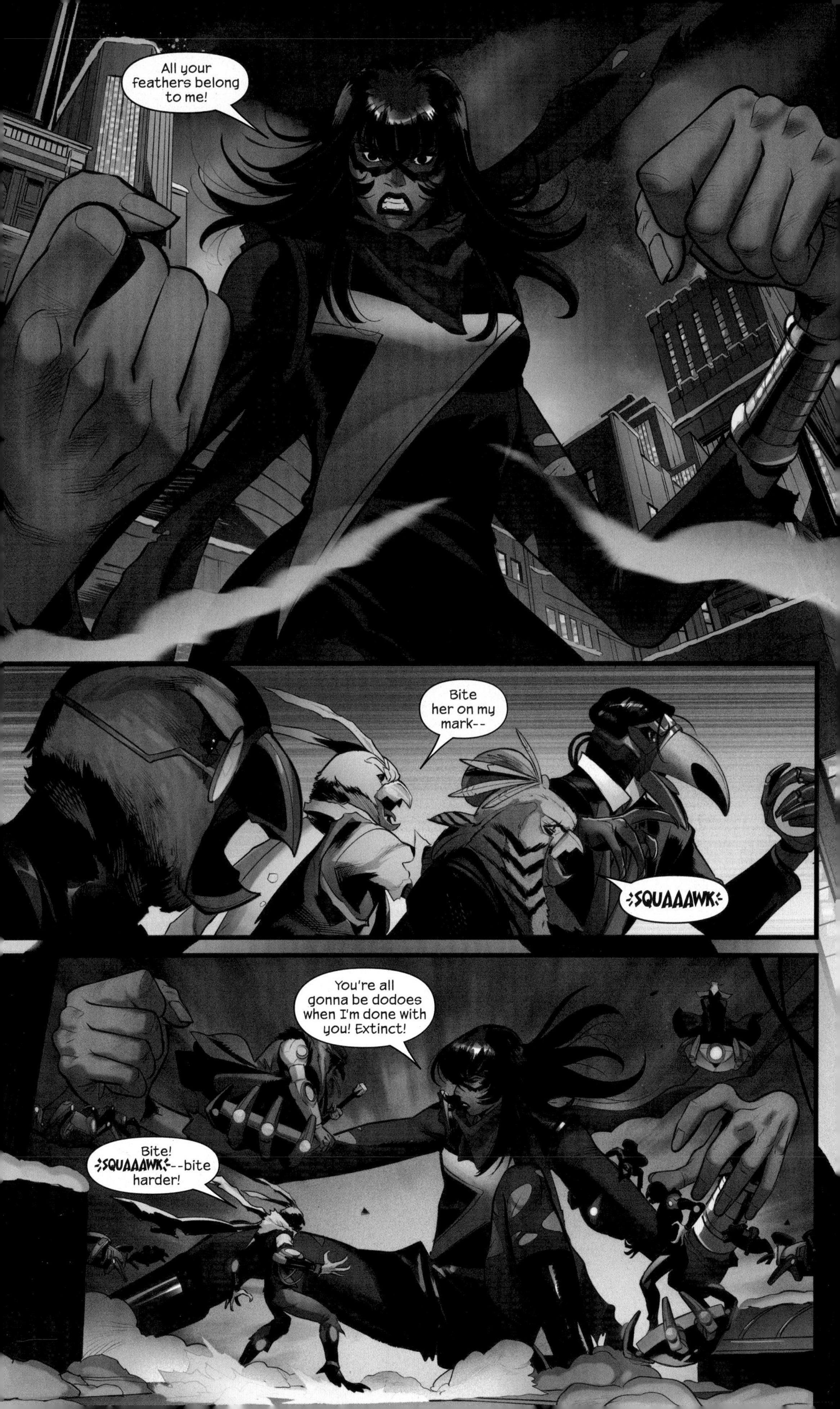
All your feathers belong to me!
Bite her on my mark--
SQUAAAWK
You're all gonna be dodoes when I'm done with you! Extinct!
Bite! SQUAAAWK--bite harder!

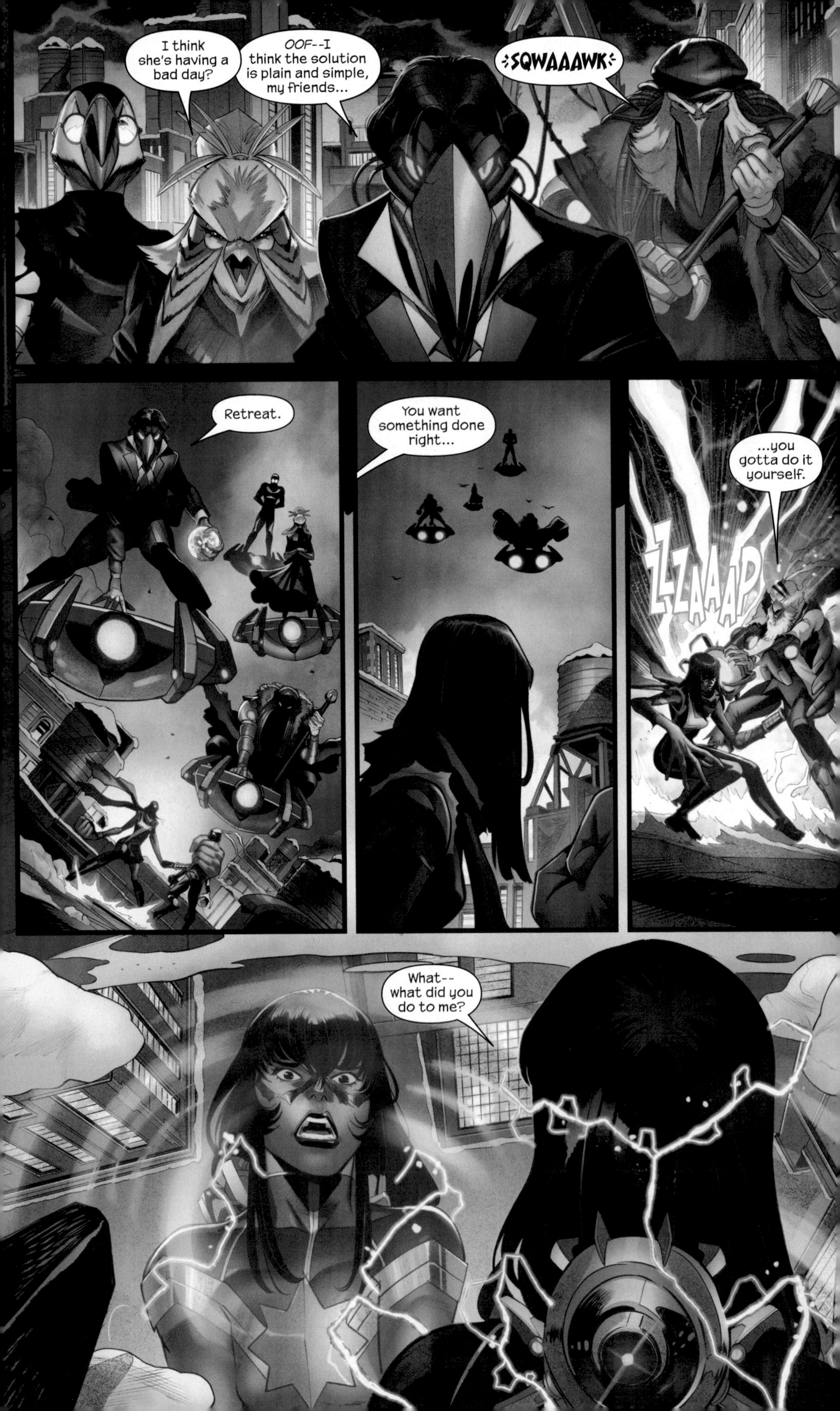
I think she's having a bad day?
OOF--I think the solution is plain and simple, my friends...
SQWAAAWK
Retreat.
You want something done right...
...you gotta do it yourself.
ZZAAAP
What-- what did you do to me?

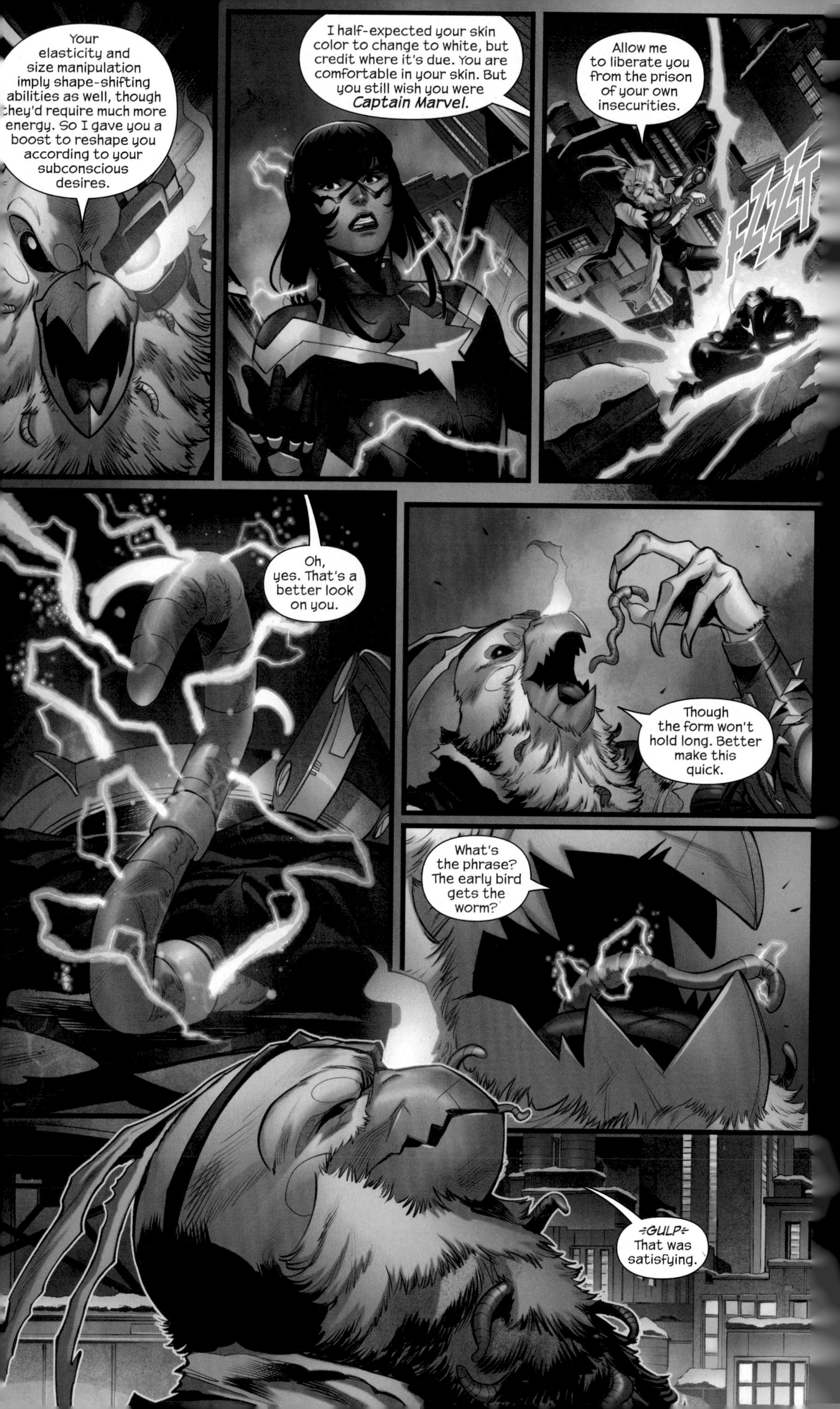

Your elasticity and size manipulation imply shape-shifting abilities as well, though they'd require much more energy. So I gave you a boost to reshape you according to your subconscious desires.
I half-expected your skin color to change to white, but credit where it's due. You are comfortable in your skin. But you still wish you were Captain Marvel.
Allow me to liberate you from the prison of your own insecurities.
FZZZT
Oh, yes. That's a better look on you.
Though the form won't hold long. Better make this quick.
What's the phrase? The early bird gets the worm?
GULP
That was satisfying.

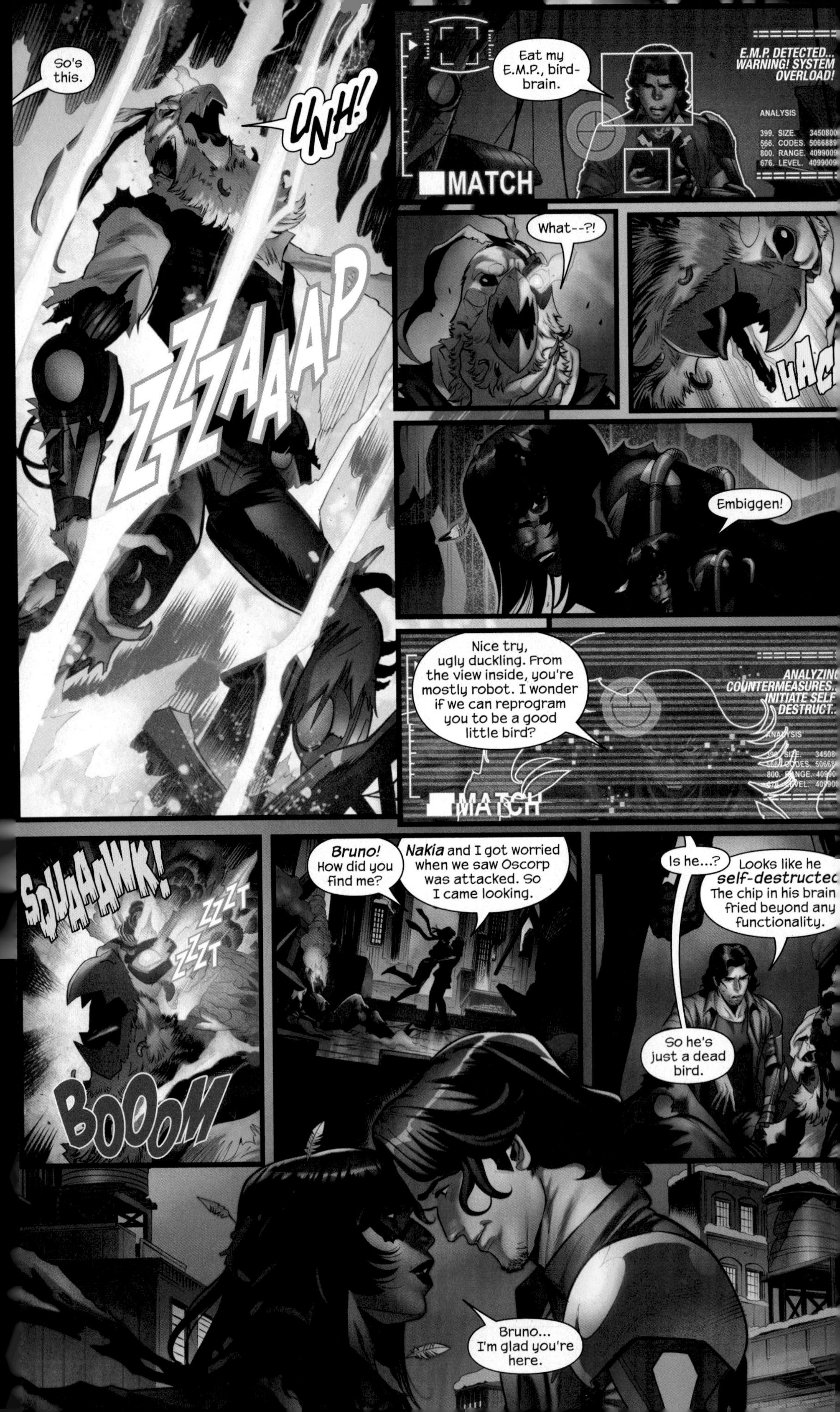

So's this.
UNH!
ZZZAAAP
Eat my E.M.P., bird-brain.
E.M.P. DETECTED... WARNING! SYSTEM OVERLOAD!
ANALYSIS
MATCH
What--?!
Embiggen!
Nice try, ugly duckling. From the view inside, you're mostly robot. I wonder if we can reprogram you to be a good little bird?
COUNTERMEASURES... INITIATE SELF DESTRUCT..
MATCH
SQUAAAWK!
ZZZT
ZZZT
BOOOM
Bruno! How did you find me?
Nakia and I got worried when we saw Oscorp was attacked. So I came looking.
Is he...?
Looks like he self-destructed. The chip in his brain fried beyond any functionality.
So he's just a dead bird.
Bruno... I'm glad you're here.

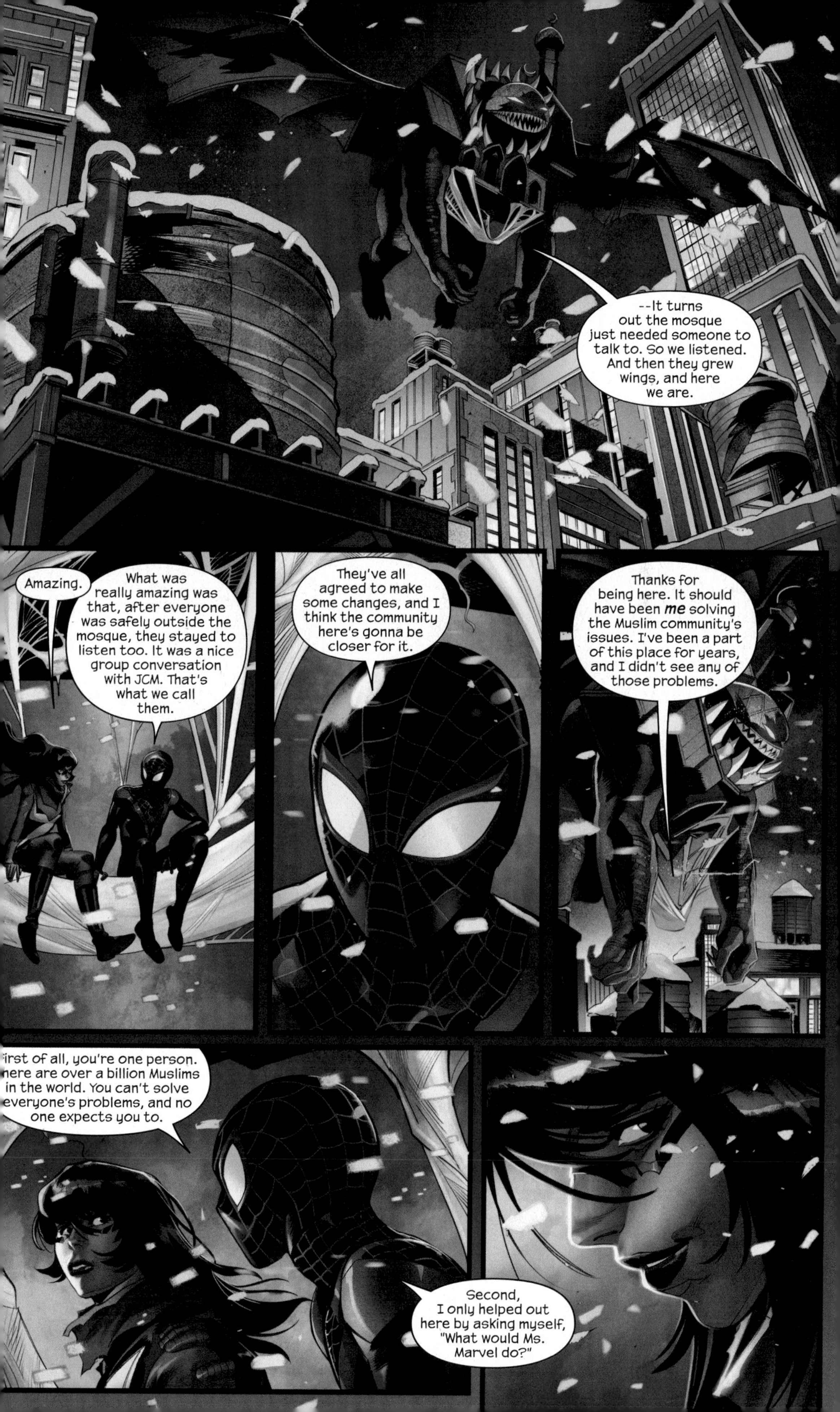
--It turns out the mosque just needed someone to talk to. So we listened. And then they grew wings, and here we are.
Amazing.
What was really amazing was that, after everyone was safely outside the mosque, they stayed to listen too. It was a nice group conversation with JCM. That's what we call them.
They've all agreed to make some changes, and I think the community here's gonna be closer for it.
Thanks for being here. It should have been *me* solving the Muslim community's issues. I've been a part of this place for years, and I didn't see any of those problems.
irst of all, you're one person. here are over a billion Muslims in the world. You can't solve everyone's problems, and no one expects you to.
Second, I only helped out here by asking myself, "What would Ms. Marvel do?"

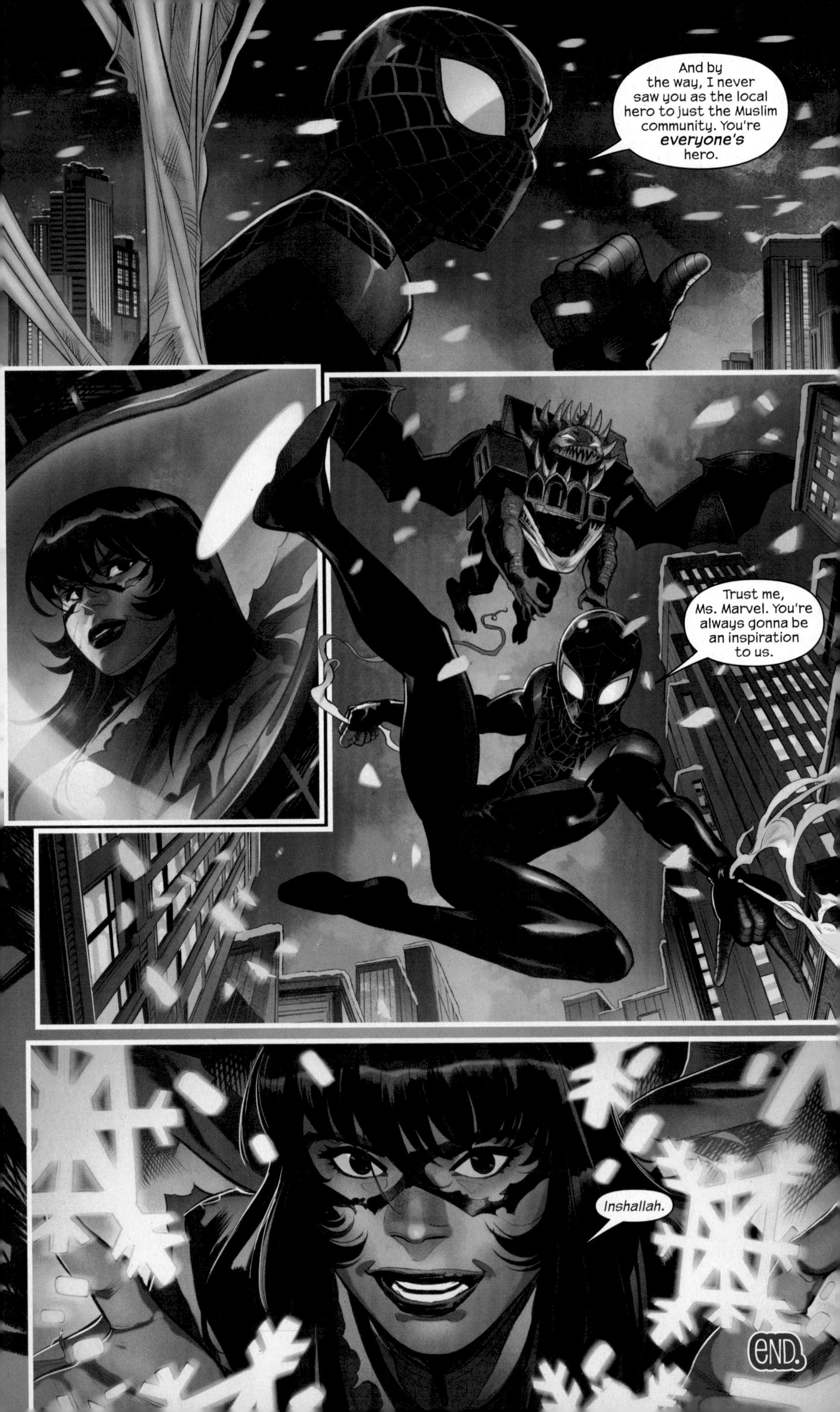
And by the way, I never saw you as the local hero to just the Muslim community. You're *everyone's* hero.
Trust me, Ms. Marvel. You're always gonna be an inspiration to us.
Inshallah.
END.

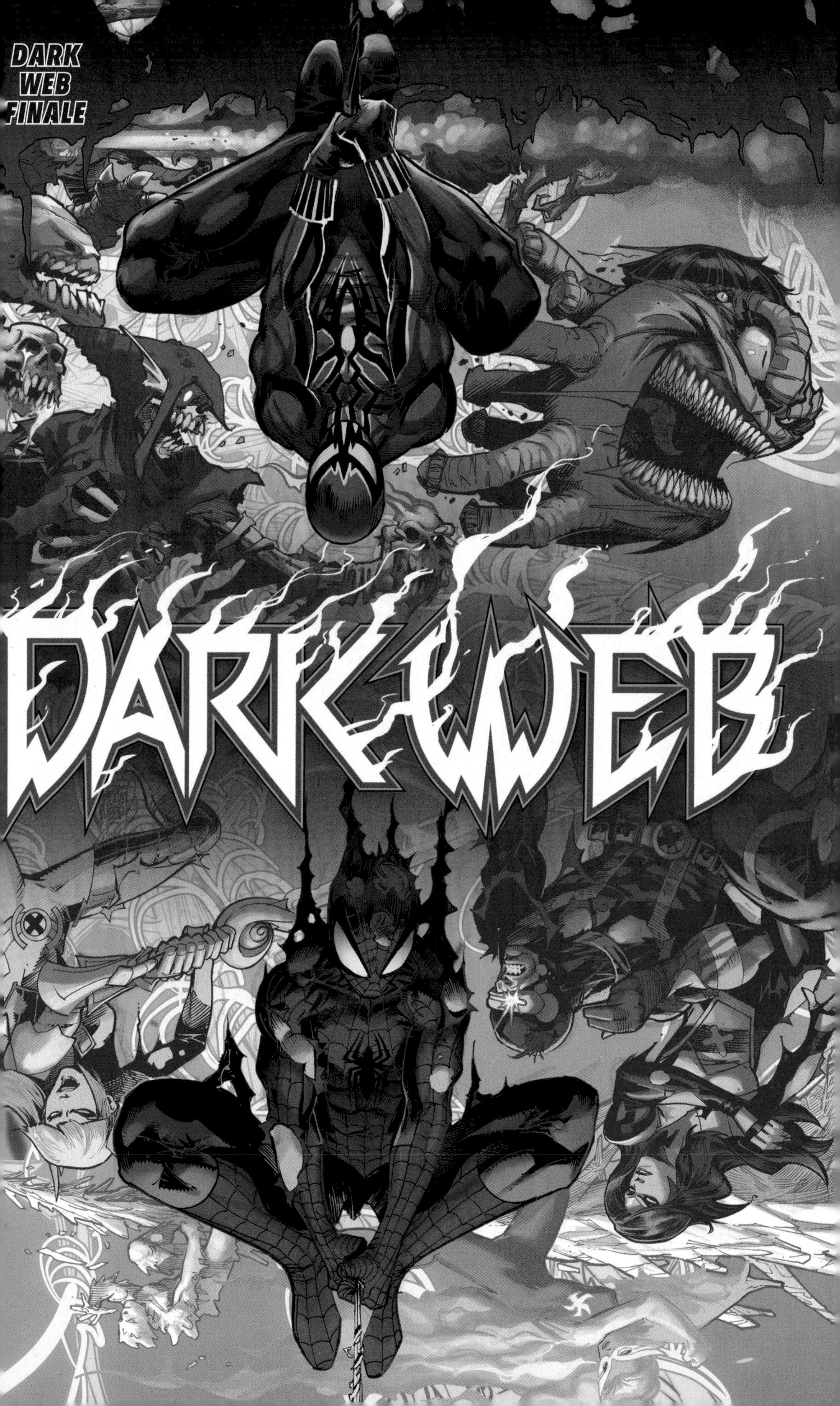
DARK
WEB
FINALE
DARK WEB

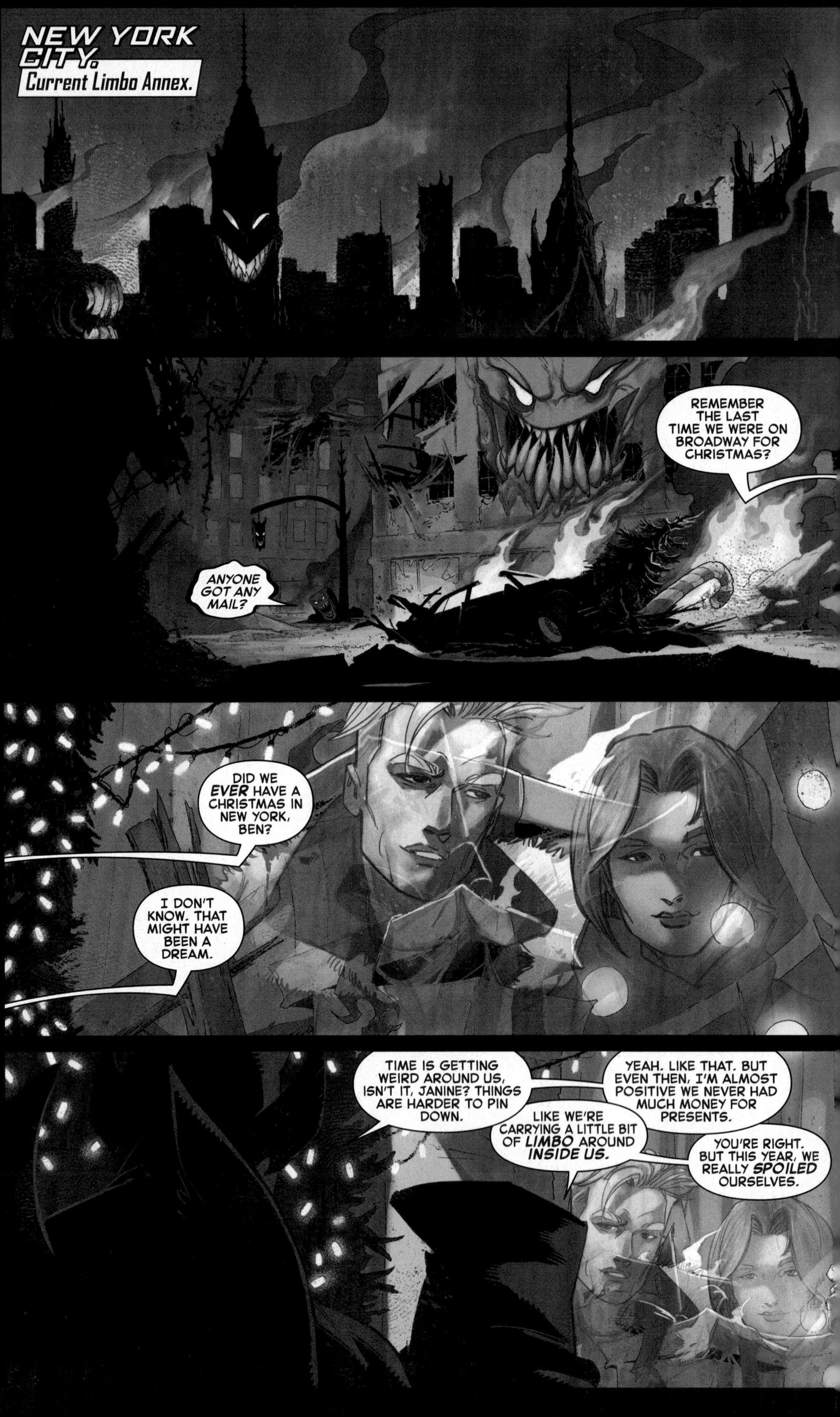
NEW YORK CITY.
Current Limbo Annex.
REMEMBER THE LAST TIME WE WERE ON BROADWAY FOR CHRISTMAS?
ANYONE GOT ANY MAIL?
DID WE EVER HAVE A CHRISTMAS IN NEW YORK, BEN?
I DON'T KNOW. THAT MIGHT HAVE BEEN A DREAM.
TIME IS GETTING WEIRD AROUND US, ISN'T IT, JANINE? THINGS ARE HARDER TO PIN DOWN.
LIKE WE'RE CARRYING A LITTLE BIT OF LIMBO AROUND INSIDE US.
YEAH. LIKE THAT. BUT EVEN THEN, I'M ALMOST POSITIVE WE NEVER HAD MUCH MONEY FOR PRESENTS.
YOU'RE RIGHT. BUT THIS YEAR, WE REALLY SPOILED OURSELVES.

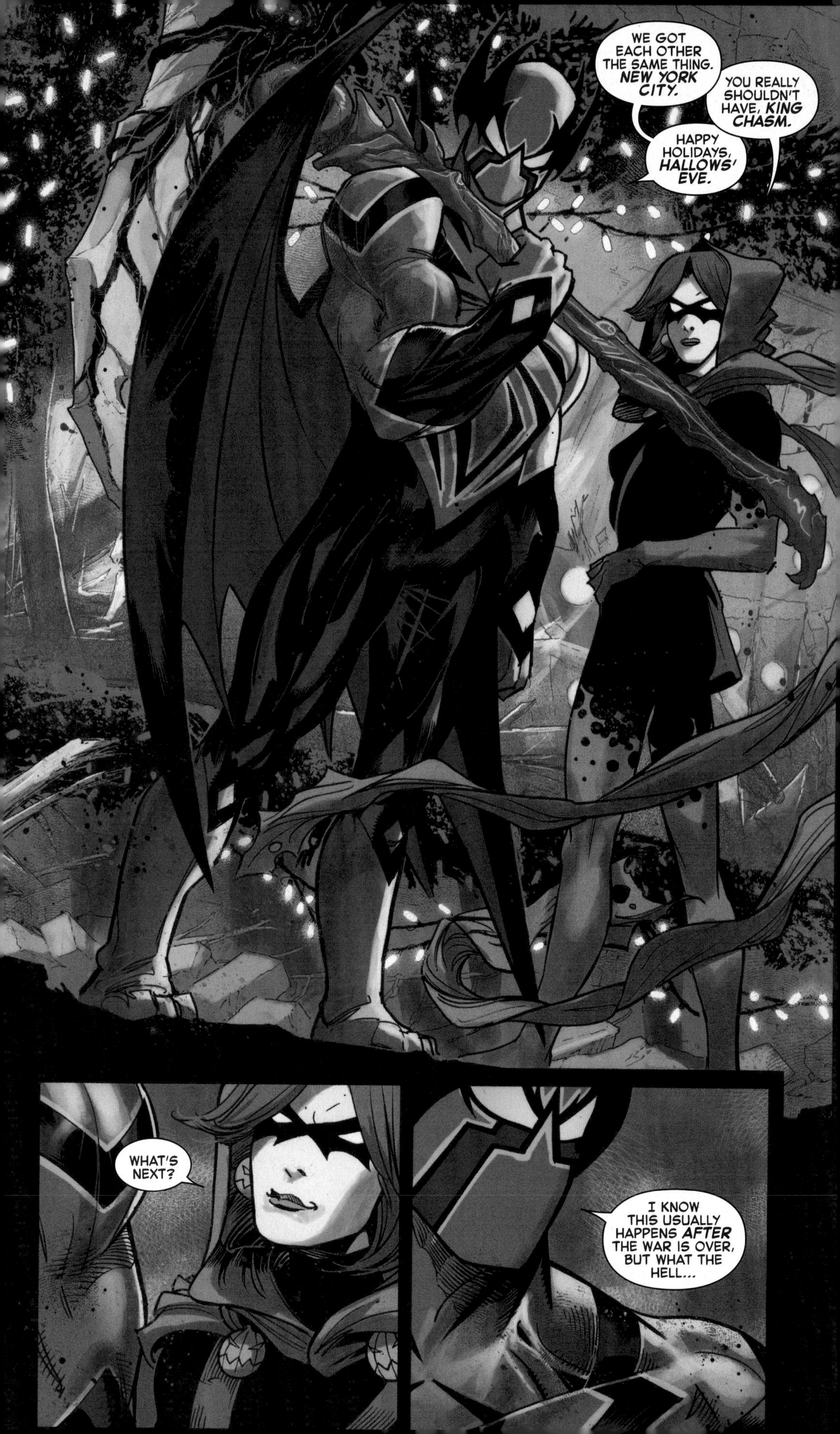
WE GOT EACH OTHER THE SAME THING. NEW YORK CITY.
HAPPY HOLIDAYS, HALLOWS' EVE.
YOU REALLY SHOULDN'T HAVE, KING CHASM.
WHAT'S NEXT?
I KNOW THIS USUALLY HAPPENS AFTER THE WAR IS OVER, BUT WHAT THE HELL...

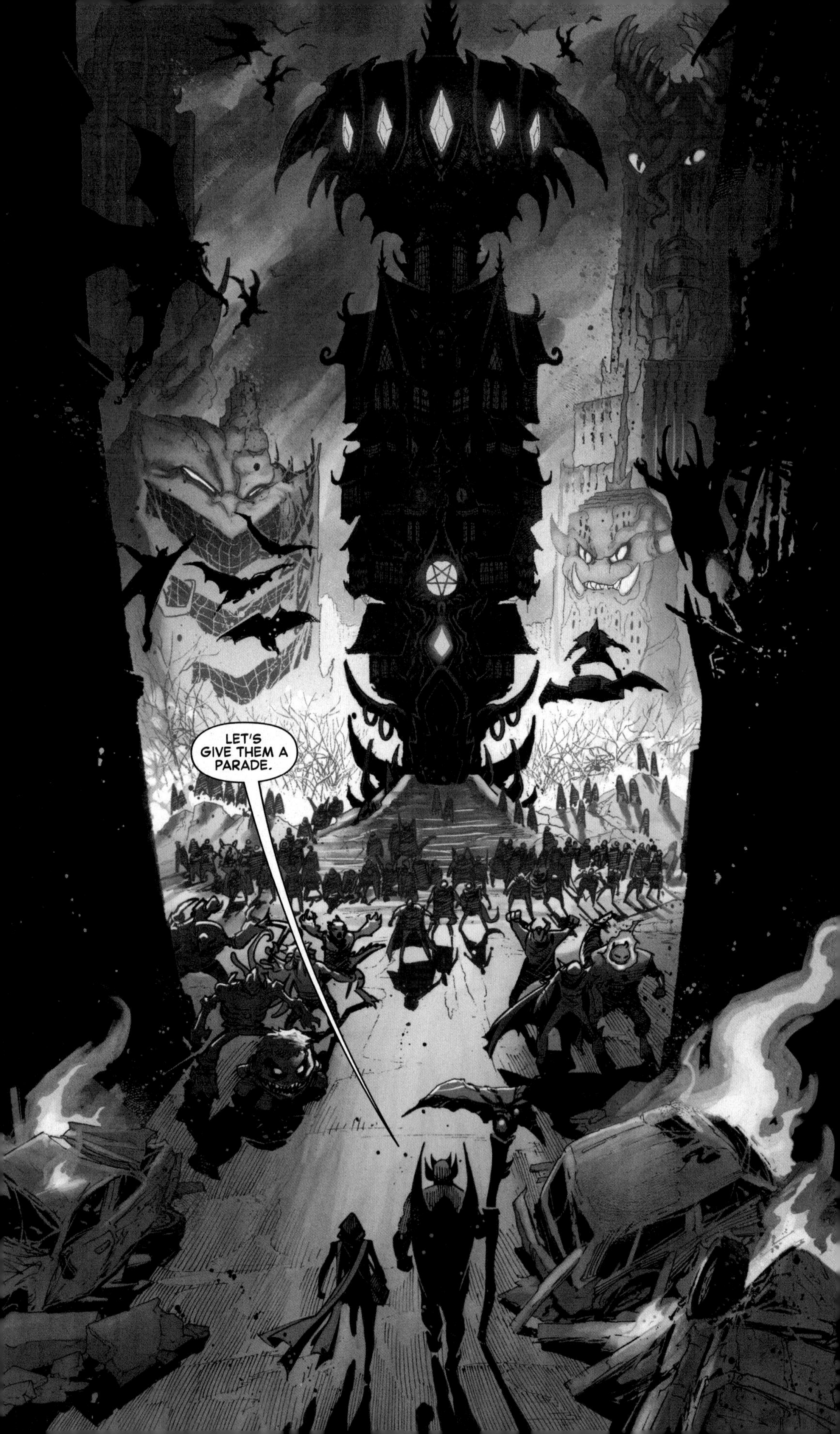
LET'S GIVE THEM A PARADE.

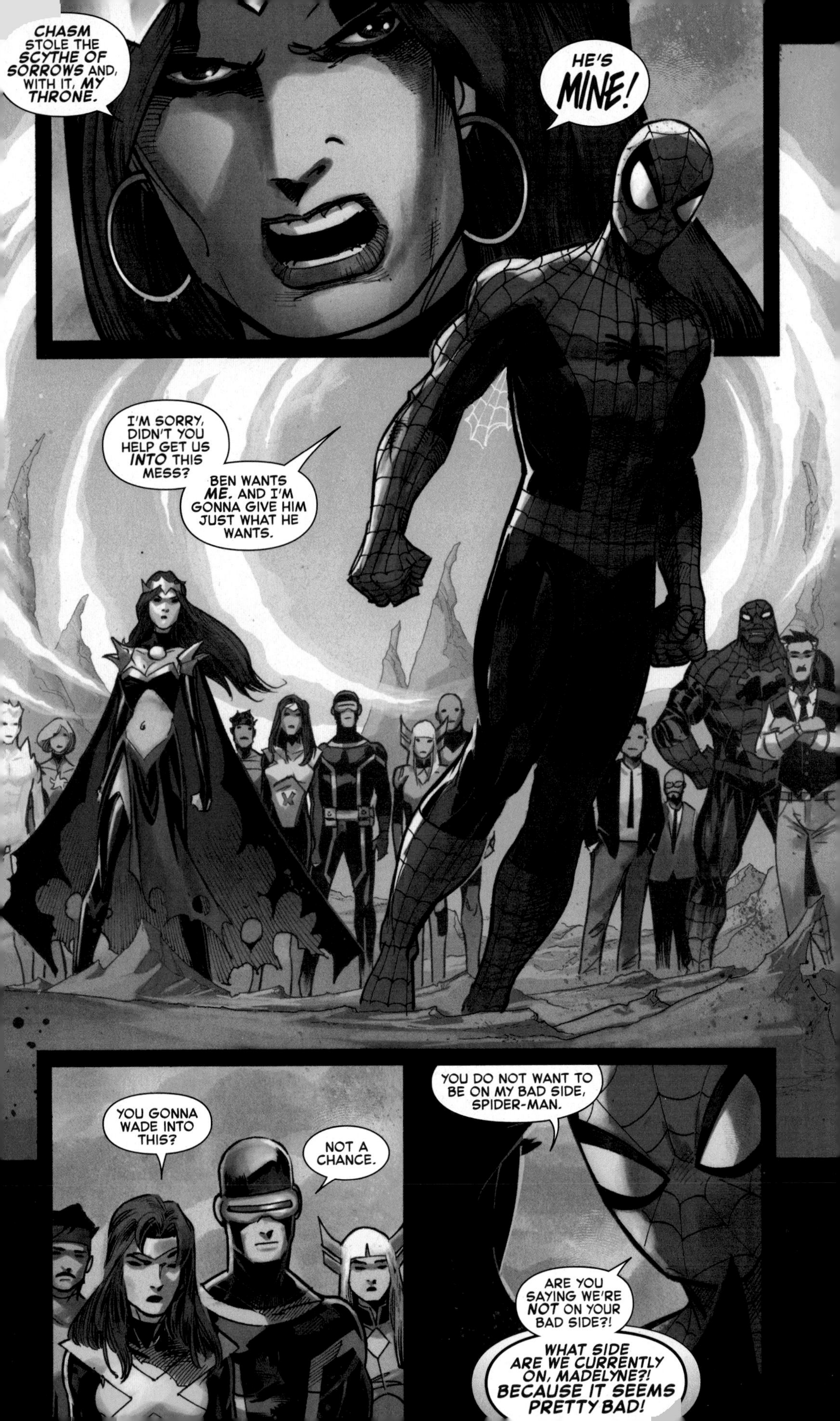
CHASM STOLE THE SCYTHE OF SORROWS AND, WITH IT, MY THRONE.
HE'S MINE!
I'M SORRY, DIDN'T YOU HELP GET US INTO THIS MESS?
BEN WANTS ME. AND I'M GONNA GIVE HIM JUST WHAT HE WANTS.
YOU GONNA WADE INTO THIS?
NOT A CHANCE.
YOU DO NOT WANT TO BE ON MY BAD SIDE, SPIDER-MAN.
ARE YOU SAYING WE'RE NOT ON YOUR BAD SIDE?!
WHAT SIDE ARE WE CURRENTLY ON, MADELYNE?! BECAUSE IT SEEMS PRETTY BAD!

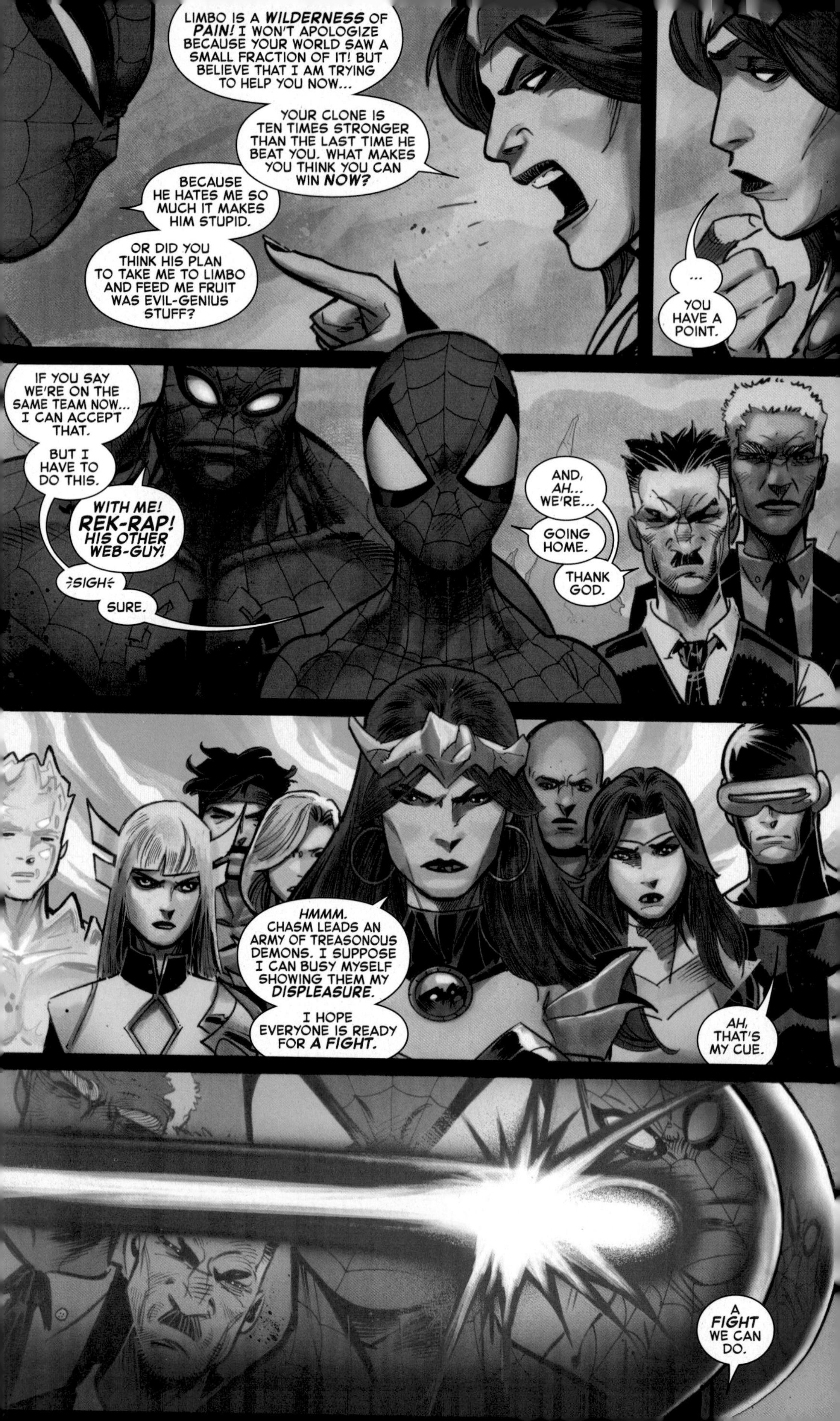

LIMBO IS A WILDERNESS OF PAIN! I WON'T APOLOGIZE BECAUSE YOUR WORLD SAW A SMALL FRACTION OF IT! BUT BELIEVE THAT I AM TRYING TO HELP YOU NOW...
YOUR CLONE IS TEN TIMES STRONGER THAN THE LAST TIME HE BEAT YOU. WHAT MAKES YOU THINK YOU CAN WIN NOW?
BECAUSE HE HATES ME SO MUCH IT MAKES HIM STUPID.
OR DID YOU THINK HIS PLAN TO TAKE ME TO LIMBO AND FEED ME FRUIT WAS EVIL-GENIUS STUFF?
...
YOU HAVE A POINT.
IF YOU SAY WE'RE ON THE SAME TEAM NOW... I CAN ACCEPT THAT.
BUT I HAVE TO DO THIS.
WITH ME! REK-RAP! HIS OTHER WEB-GUY!
⁼SIGH⁼
SURE.
AND, AH... WE'RE...
GOING HOME.
THANK GOD.
HMMM. CHASM LEADS AN ARMY OF TREASONOUS DEMONS. I SUPPOSE I CAN BUSY MYSELF SHOWING THEM MY DISPLEASURE.
I HOPE EVERYONE IS READY FOR A FIGHT.
AH, THAT'S MY CUE.
A FIGHT WE CAN DO.

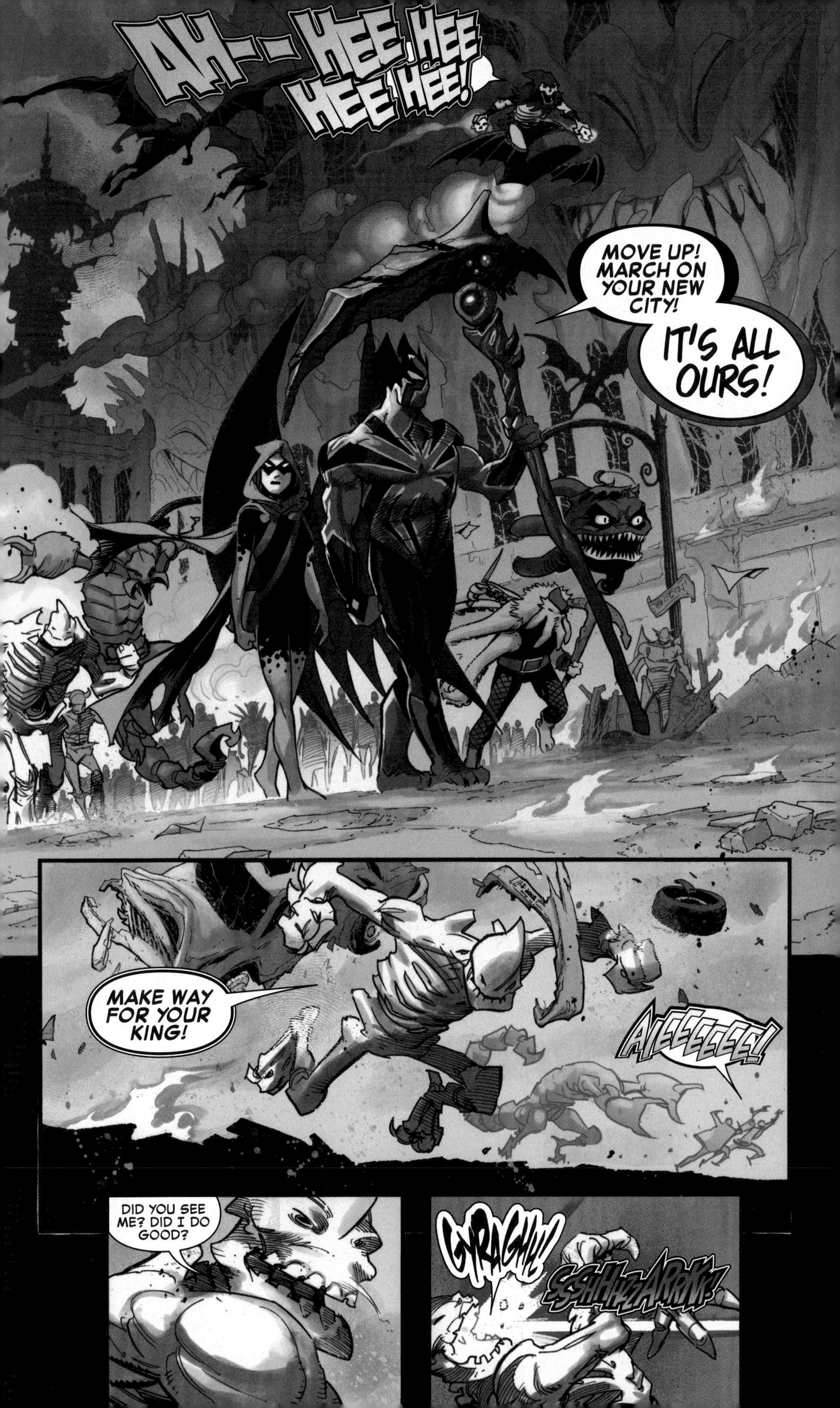
AH-- HEE HEE HEE HEE!
MOVE UP! MARCH ON YOUR NEW CITY!
IT'S ALL OURS!
MAKE WAY FOR YOUR KING!
AIEEEEEE!
DID YOU SEE ME? DID I DO GOOD?
GYRAGH!!
SSHHHZZARRKK!

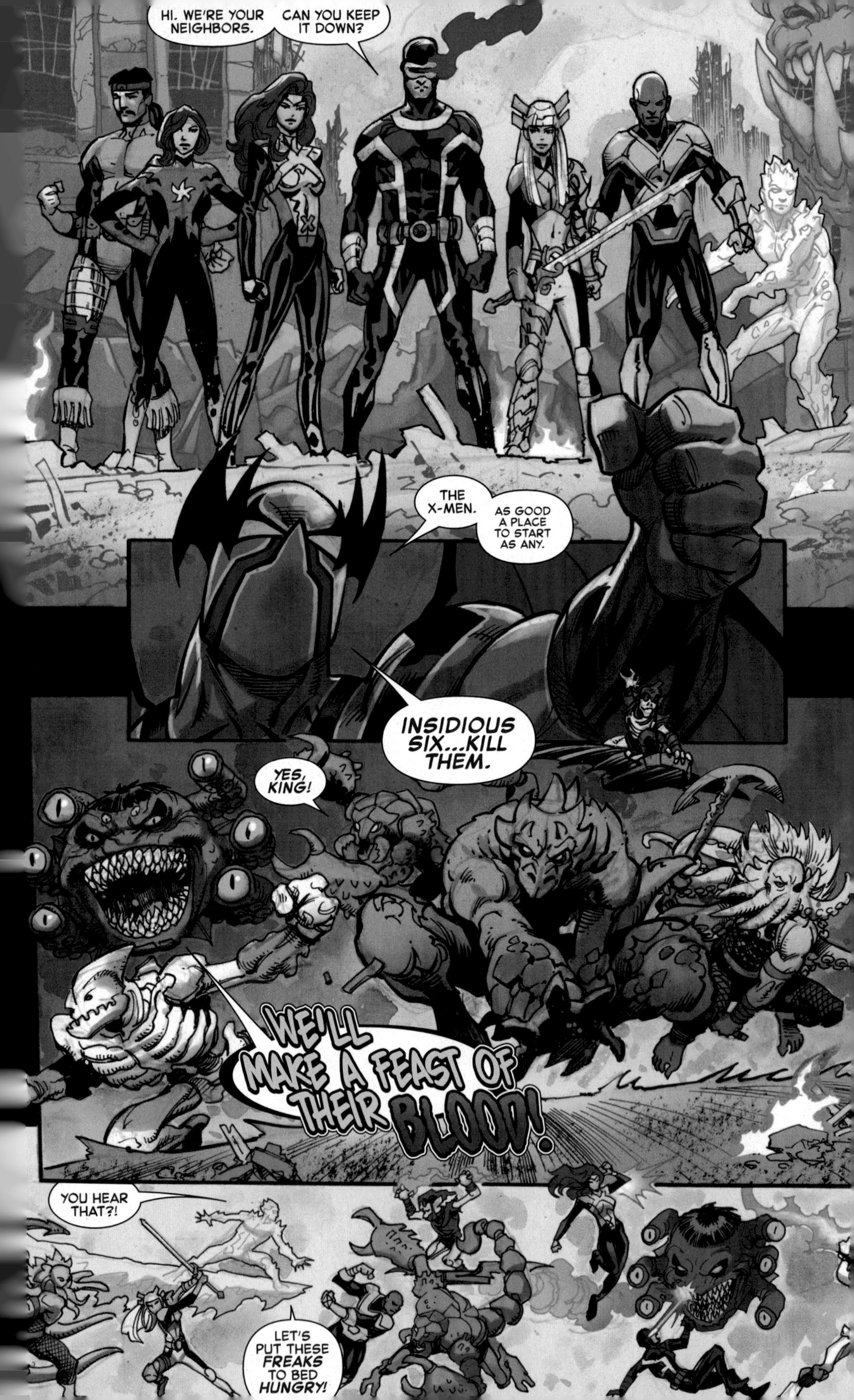

HI. WE'RE YOUR NEIGHBORS.
CAN YOU KEEP IT DOWN?
THE X-MEN.
AS GOOD A PLACE TO START AS ANY.
INSIDIOUS SIX...KILL THEM.
YES, KING!
WE'LL MAKE A FEAST OF THEIR BLOOD!
YOU HEAR THAT?!
LET'S PUT THESE FREAKS TO BED HUNGRY!

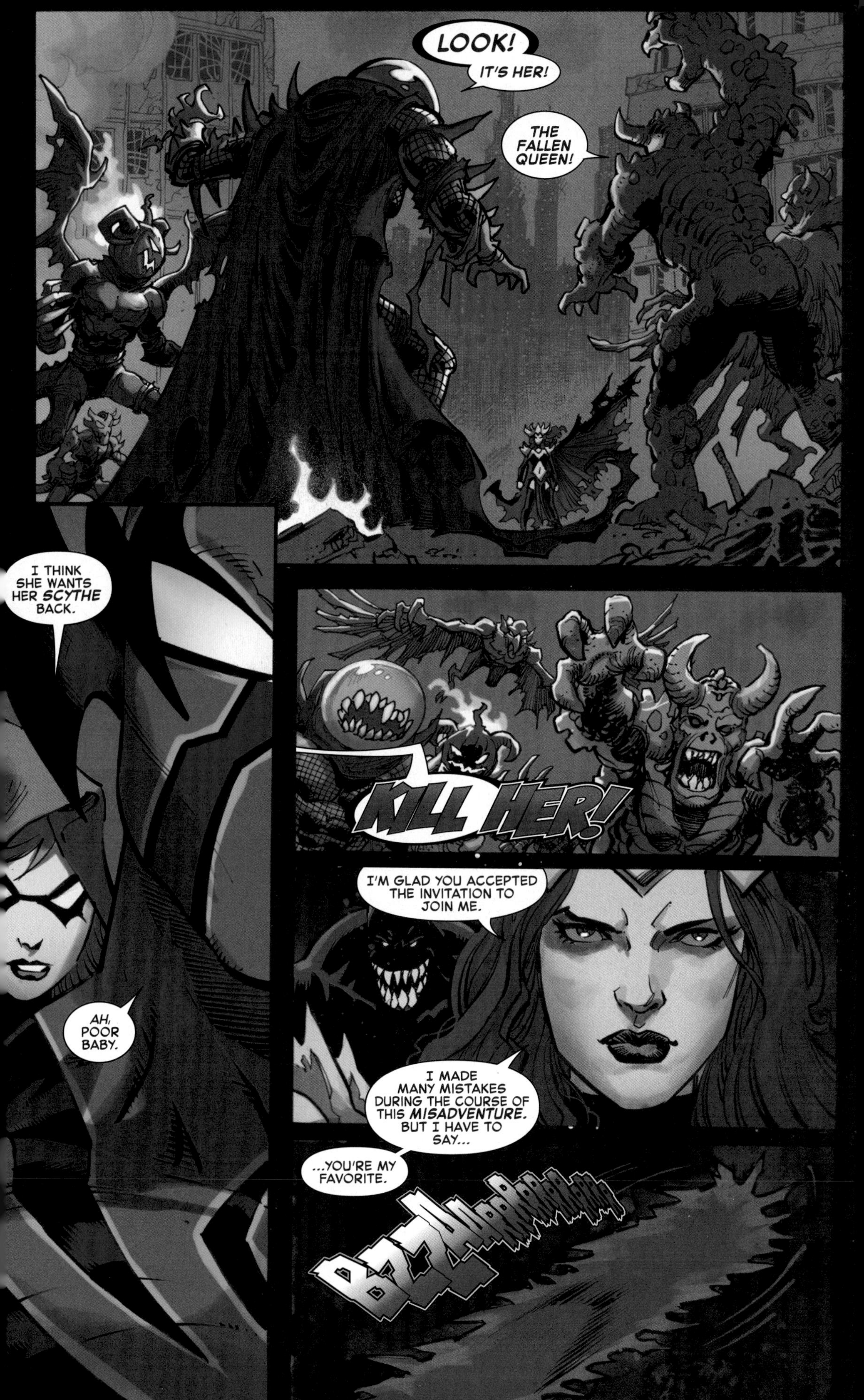
LOOK!
IT'S HER!
THE FALLEN QUEEN!
I THINK SHE WANTS HER SCYTHE BACK.
AH, POOR BABY.
KILL HER!
I'M GLAD YOU ACCEPTED THE INVITATION TO JOIN ME.
I MADE MANY MISTAKES DURING THE COURSE OF THIS MISADVENTURE. BUT I HAVE TO SAY...
...YOU'RE MY FAVORITE.

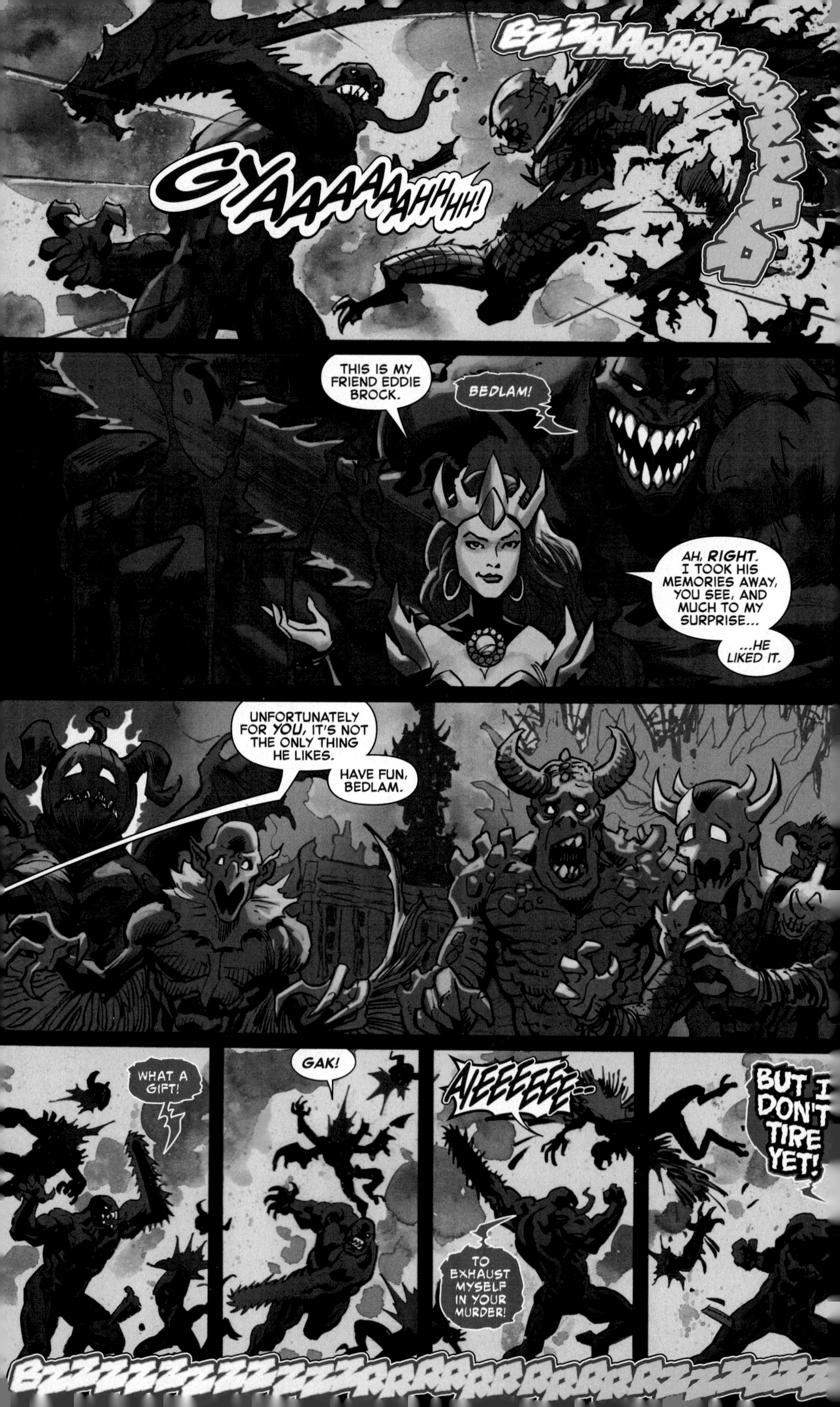

BZZAARRRRRRRRRRRRR
GYAAAAAHHHH!
THIS IS MY FRIEND EDDIE BROCK.
BEDLAM!
AH, RIGHT. I TOOK HIS MEMORIES AWAY, YOU SEE, AND MUCH TO MY SURPRISE...
...HE LIKED IT.
UNFORTUNATELY FOR YOU, IT'S NOT THE ONLY THING HE LIKES.
HAVE FUN, BEDLAM.
WHAT A GIFT!
GAK!
AIEEEEEE--
TO EXHAUST MYSELF IN YOUR MURDER!
BUT I DON'T TIRE YET!
BZZZZZZZZZZZZZRRRRRRRRRRRRRRZZZZZZ

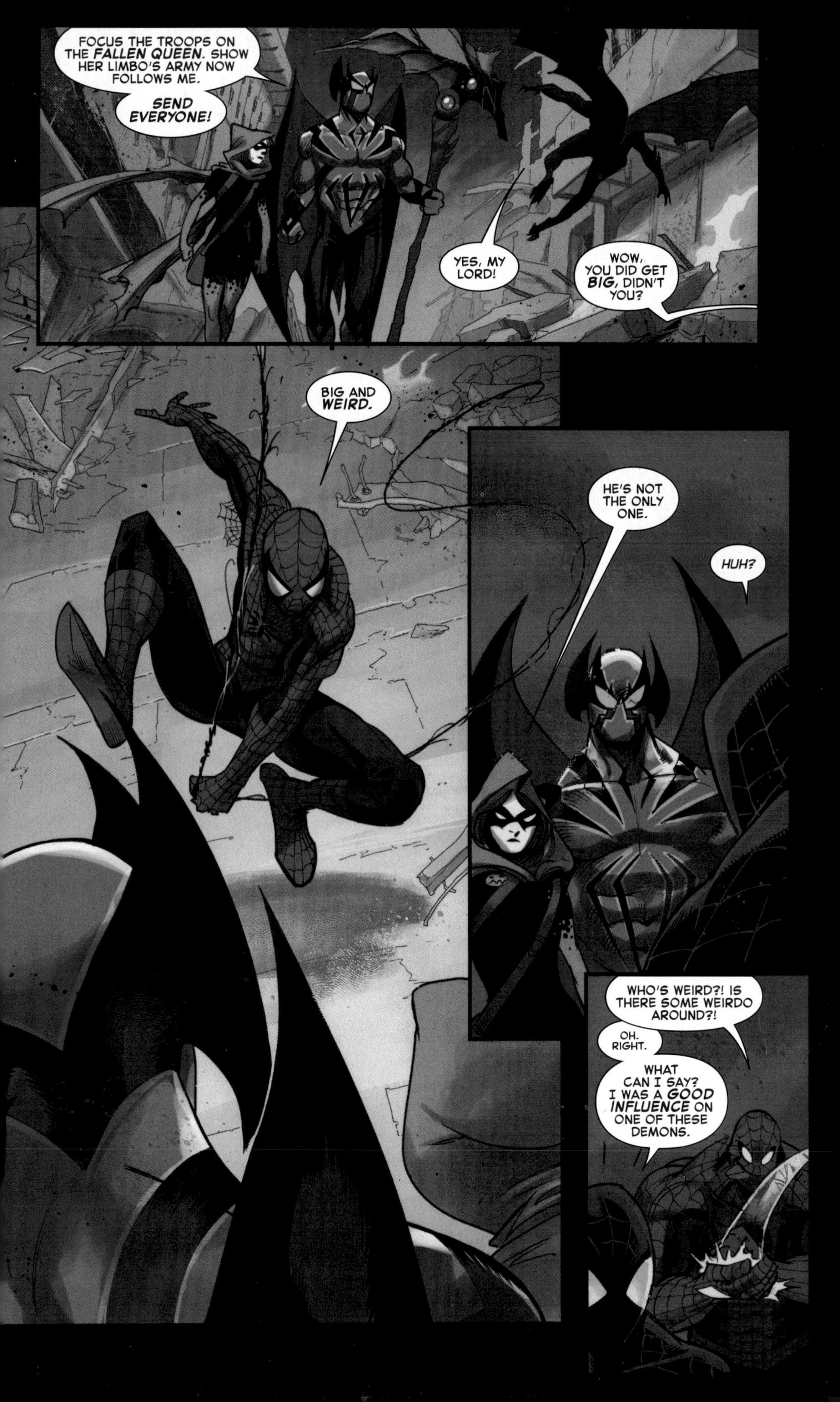
FOCUS THE TROOPS ON THE FALLEN QUEEN. SHOW HER LIMBO'S ARMY NOW FOLLOWS ME.
SEND EVERYONE!
YES, MY LORD!
WOW, YOU DID GET BIG, DIDN'T YOU?
BIG AND WEIRD.
HE'S NOT THE ONLY ONE.
HUH?
WHO'S WEIRD?! IS THERE SOME WEIRDO AROUND?!
OH. RIGHT.
WHAT CAN I SAY? I WAS A GOOD INFLUENCE ON ONE OF THESE DEMONS.

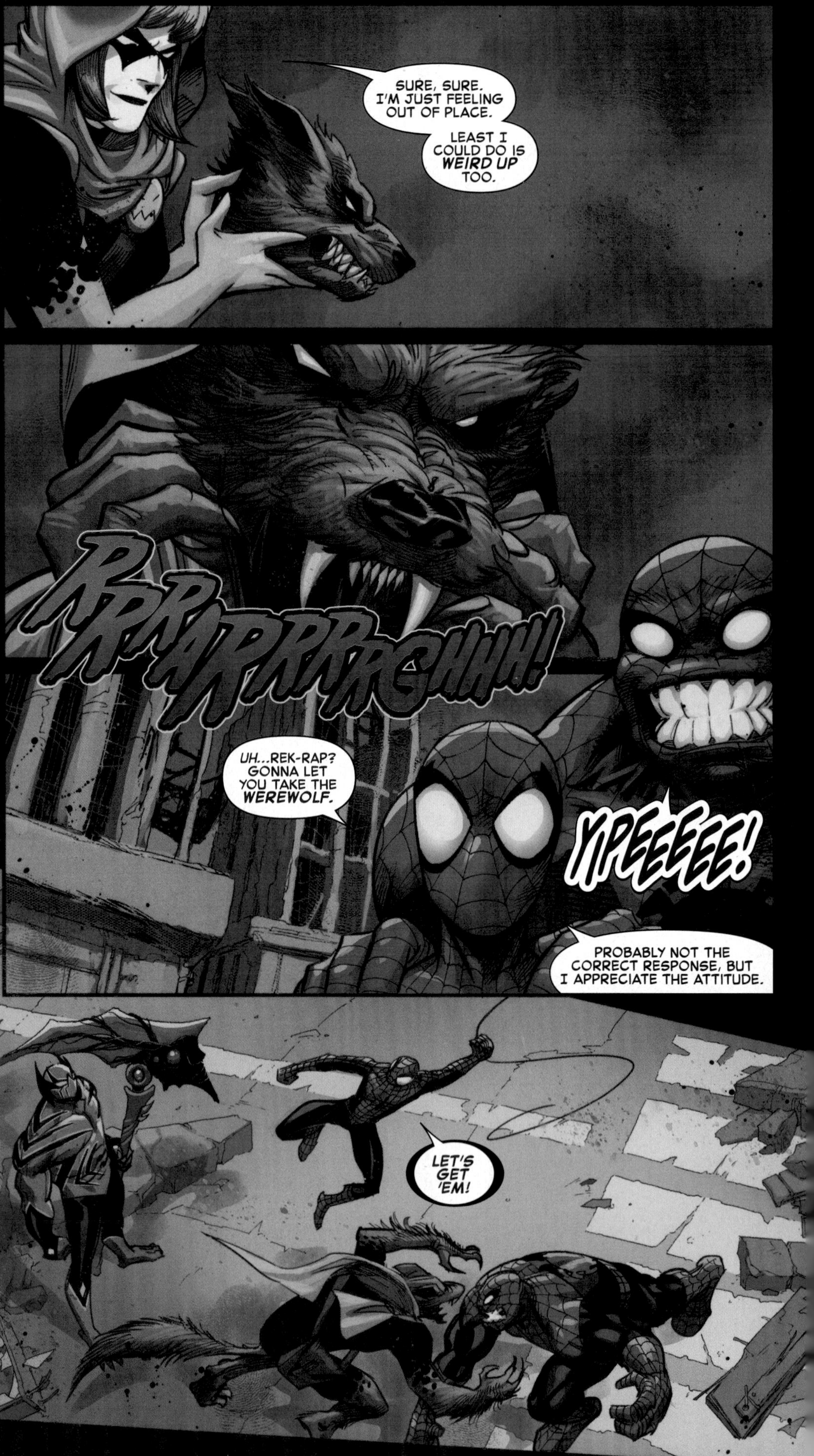
SURE, SURE. I'M JUST FEELING OUT OF PLACE.
LEAST I COULD DO IS WEIRD UP TOO.
RRRAARRRRRGHHH!
UH...REK-RAP? GONNA LET YOU TAKE THE WEREWOLF.
YIPEEEEE!
PROBABLY NOT THE CORRECT RESPONSE, BUT I APPRECIATE THE ATTITUDE.
LET'S GET 'EM!

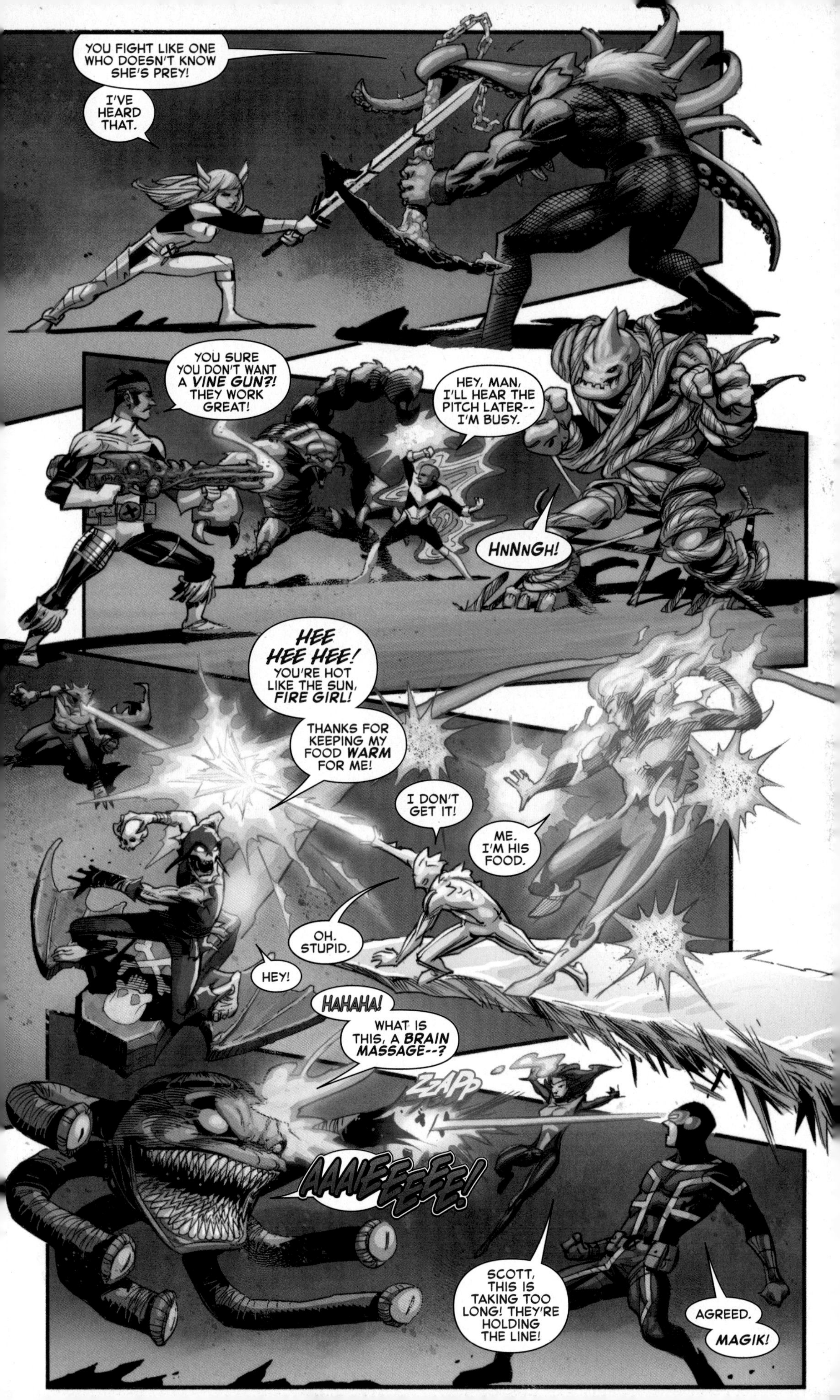

YOU FIGHT LIKE ONE WHO DOESN'T KNOW SHE'S PREY!
I'VE HEARD THAT.
YOU SURE YOU DON'T WANT A VINE GUN?! THEY WORK GREAT!
HEY, MAN, I'LL HEAR THE PITCH LATER-- I'M BUSY.
HNNNGH!
HEE HEE HEE! YOU'RE HOT LIKE THE SUN, FIRE GIRL!
THANKS FOR KEEPING MY FOOD WARM FOR ME!
I DON'T GET IT!
ME. I'M HIS FOOD.
OH. STUPID.
HEY!
HAHAHA!
WHAT IS THIS, A BRAIN MASSAGE--?
ZZAPP
AAAIEEEEE!
SCOTT, THIS IS TAKING TOO LONG! THEY'RE HOLDING THE LINE!
AGREED.
MAGIK!

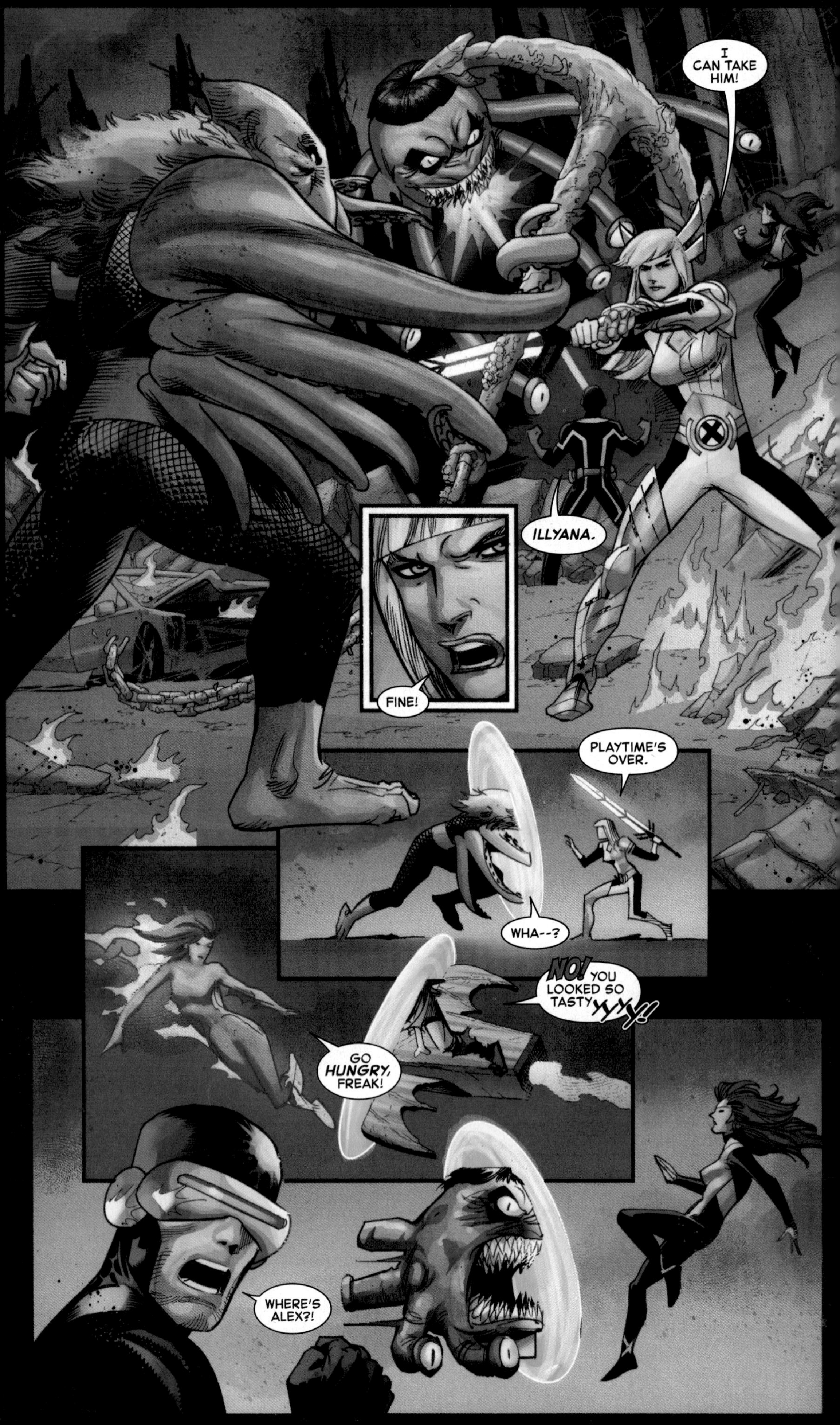
I CAN TAKE HIM!
ILLYANA.
FINE!
PLAYTIME'S OVER.
WHA--?
NO! YOU LOOKED SO TASTYYYY!
GO HUNGRY, FREAK!
WHERE'S ALEX?!

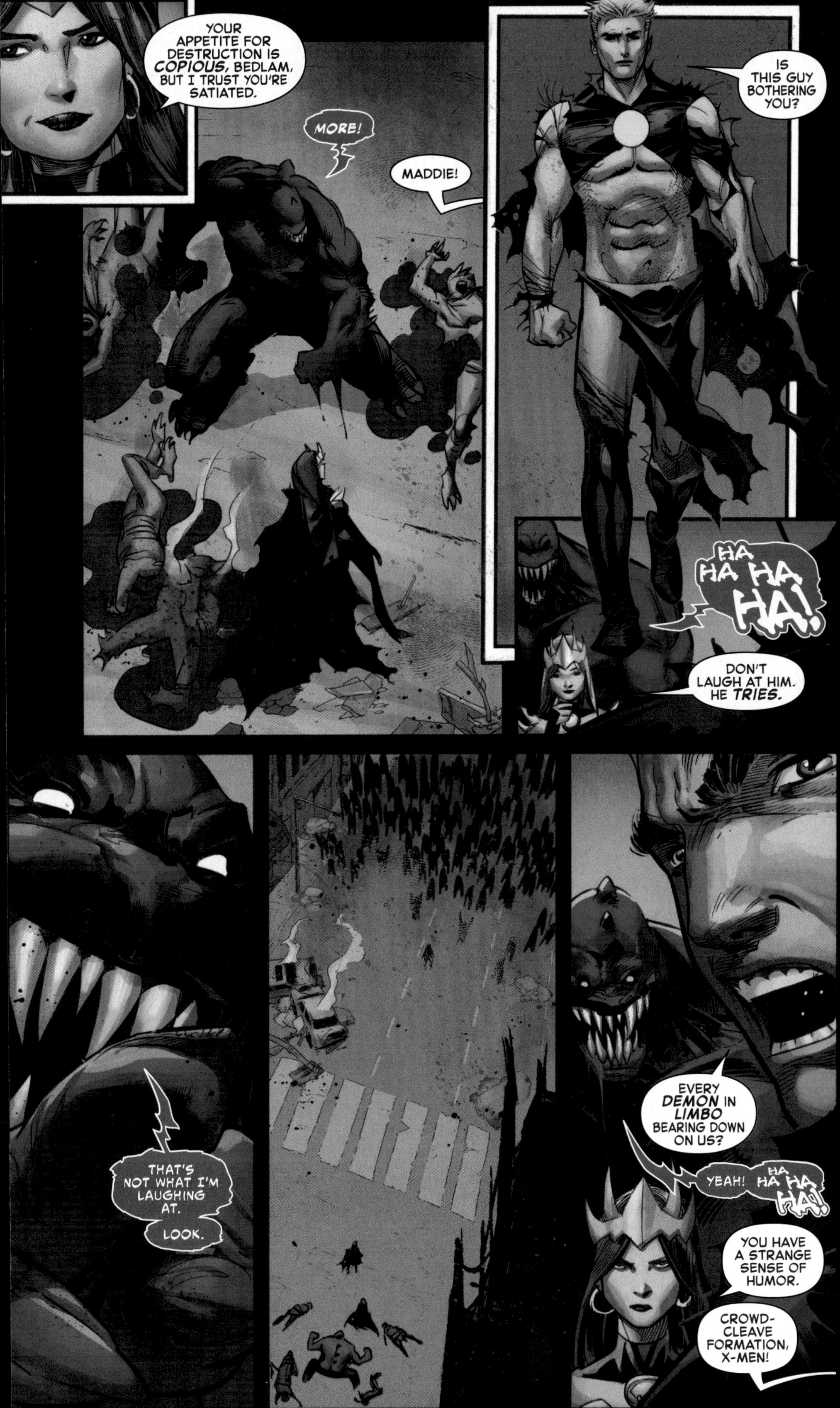
YOUR APPETITE FOR DESTRUCTION IS COPIOUS, BEDLAM, BUT I TRUST YOU'RE SATIATED.
MORE!
MADDIE!
IS THIS GUY BOTHERING YOU?
HA HA HA HA HA!
DON'T LAUGH AT HIM. HE TRIES.
THAT'S NOT WHAT I'M LAUGHING AT.
LOOK.
EVERY DEMON IN LIMBO BEARING DOWN ON US?
YEAH! HA HA HA HA!
YOU HAVE A STRANGE SENSE OF HUMOR.
CROWD-CLEAVE FORMATION, X-MEN!

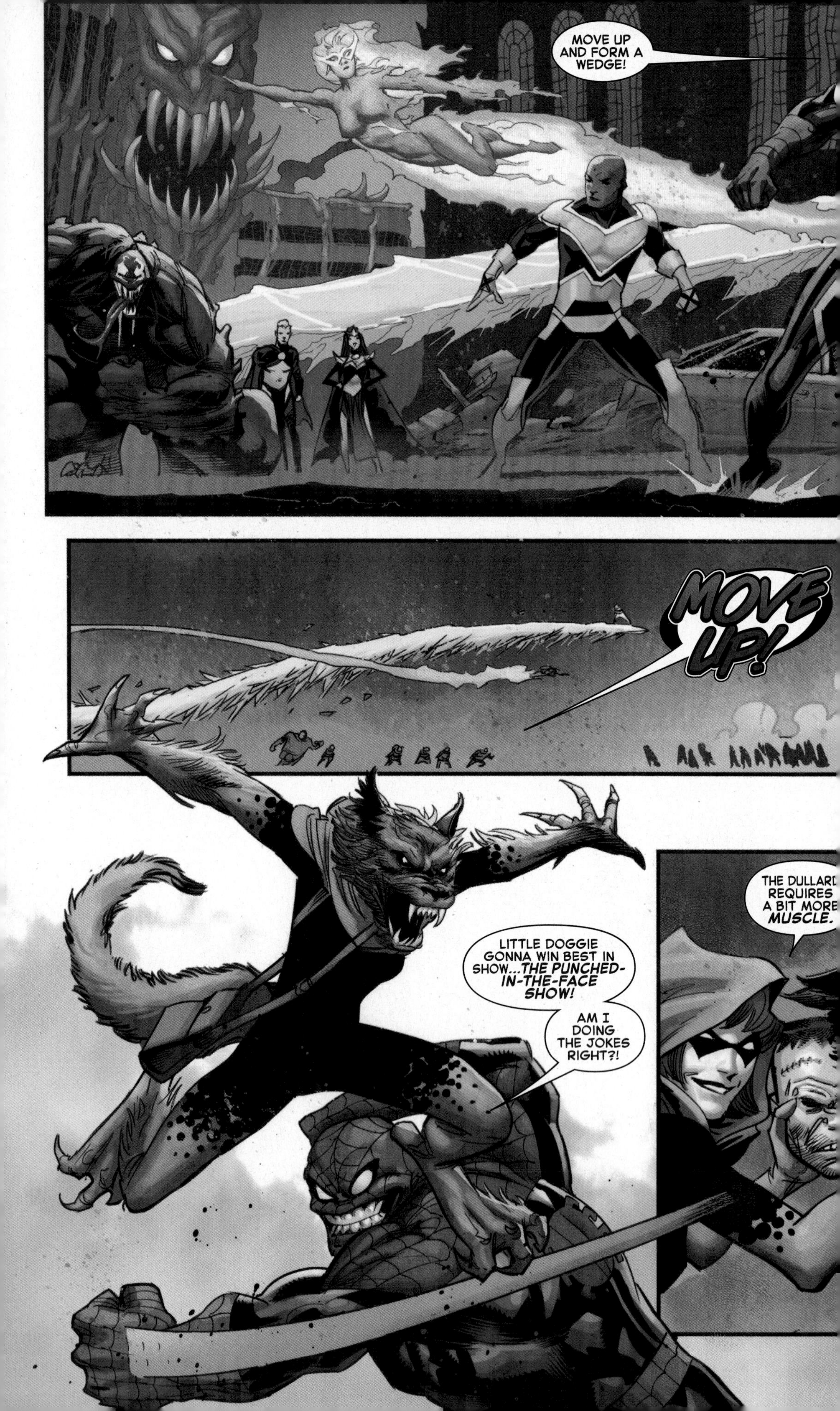
MOVE UP AND FORM A WEDGE!
MOVE UP!
LITTLE DOGGIE GONNA WIN BEST IN SHOW...THE PUNCHED-IN-THE-FACE SHOW!
AM I DOING THE JOKES RIGHT?!
THE DULLARD REQUIRES A BIT MORE MUSCLE.

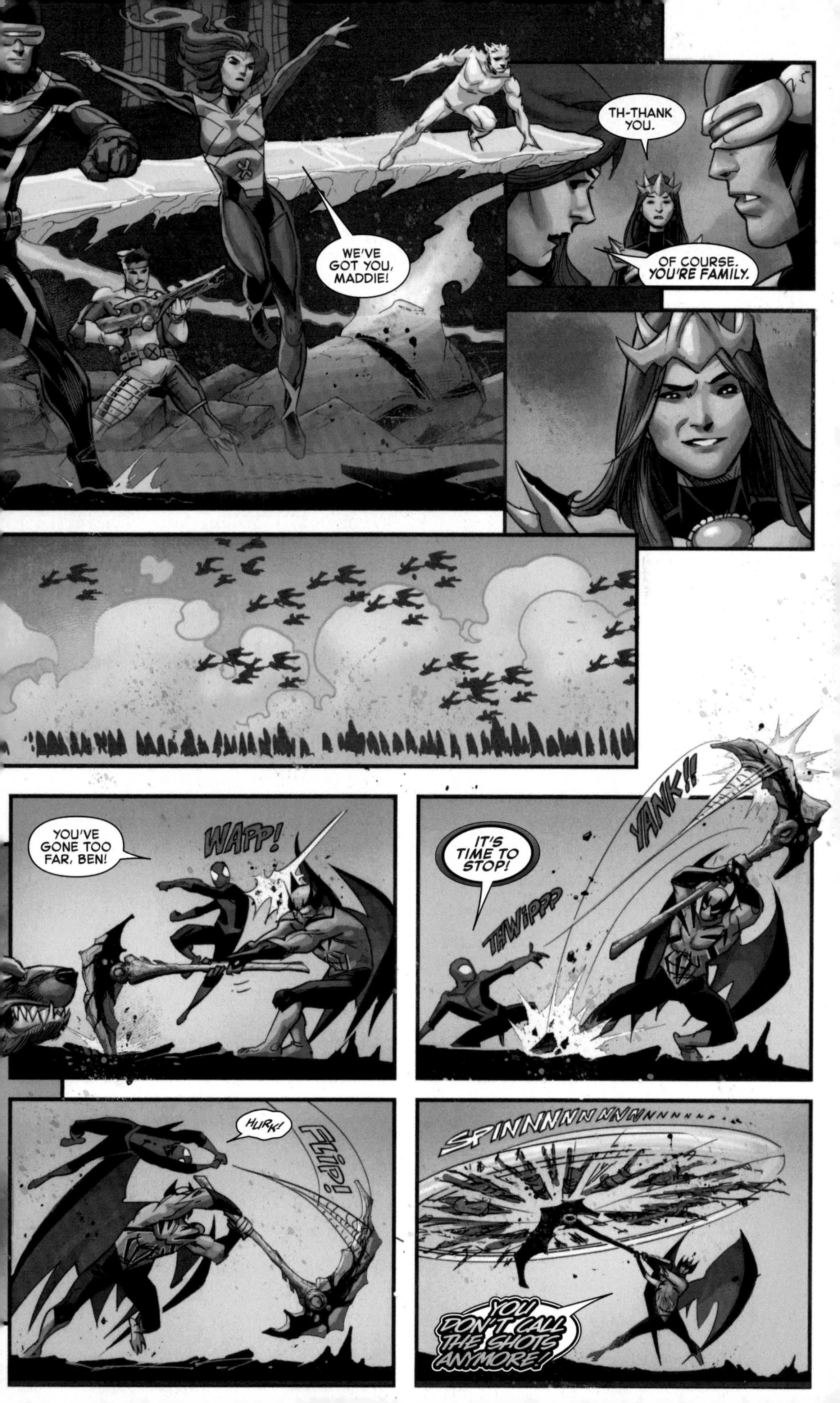
WE'VE GOT YOU, MADDIE!
TH-THANK YOU.
OF COURSE. YOU'RE FAMILY.
YOU'VE GONE TOO FAR, BEN!
WAPP!
IT'S TIME TO STOP!
THWIPPP
YANK!!
HURK!
FLIP!
SPINNNNNNNNNNNNNNNN
YOU DON'T CALL THE SHOTS ANYMORE!

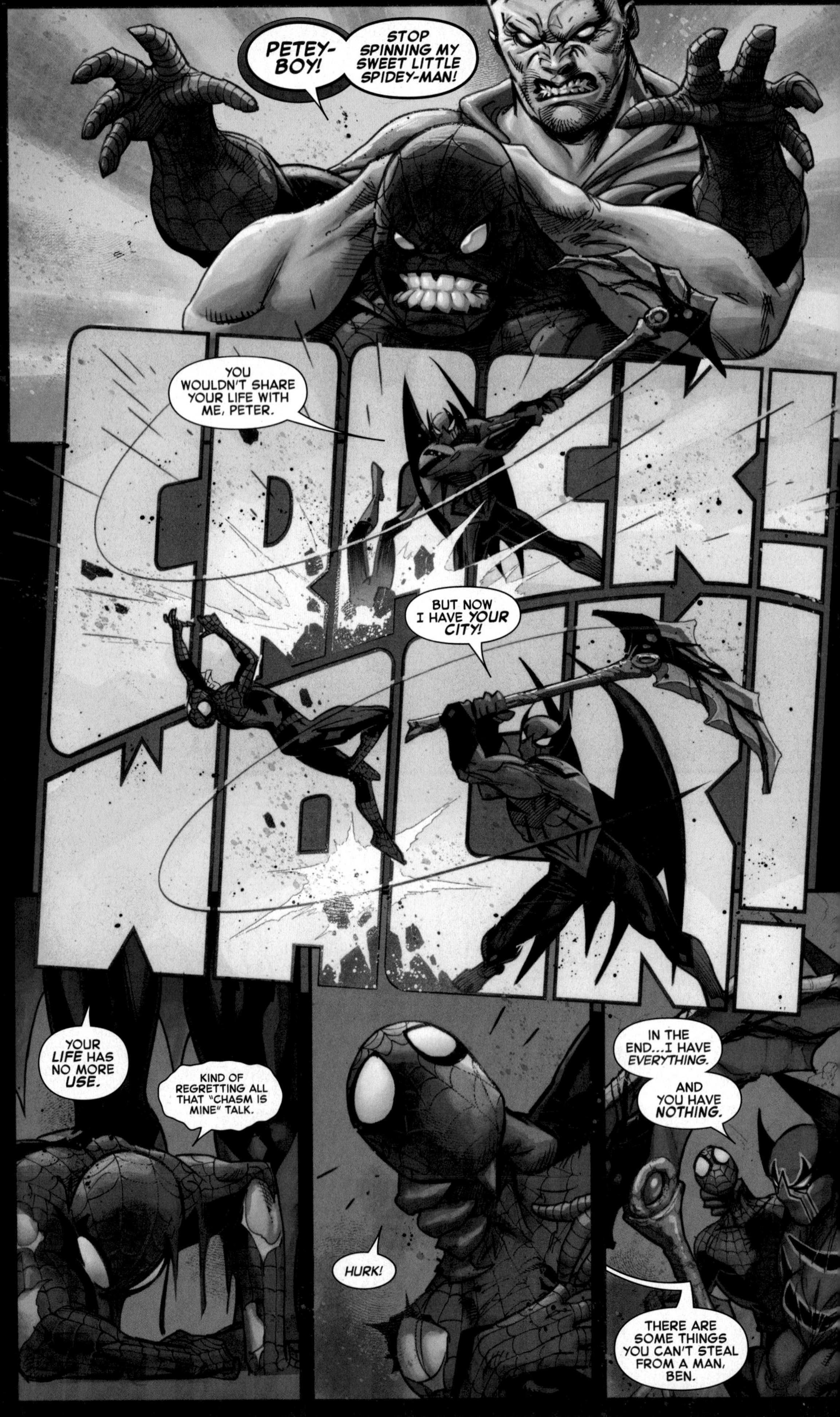

PETEY-BOY!
STOP SPINNING MY SWEET LITTLE SPIDEY-MAN!
YOU WOULDN'T SHARE YOUR LIFE WITH ME, PETER.
BUT NOW I HAVE YOUR CITY!
YOUR LIFE HAS NO MORE USE.
KIND OF REGRETTING ALL THAT "CHASM IS MINE" TALK.
HURK!
IN THE END...I HAVE EVERYTHING.
AND YOU HAVE NOTHING.
THERE ARE SOME THINGS YOU CAN'T STEAL FROM A MAN, BEN.

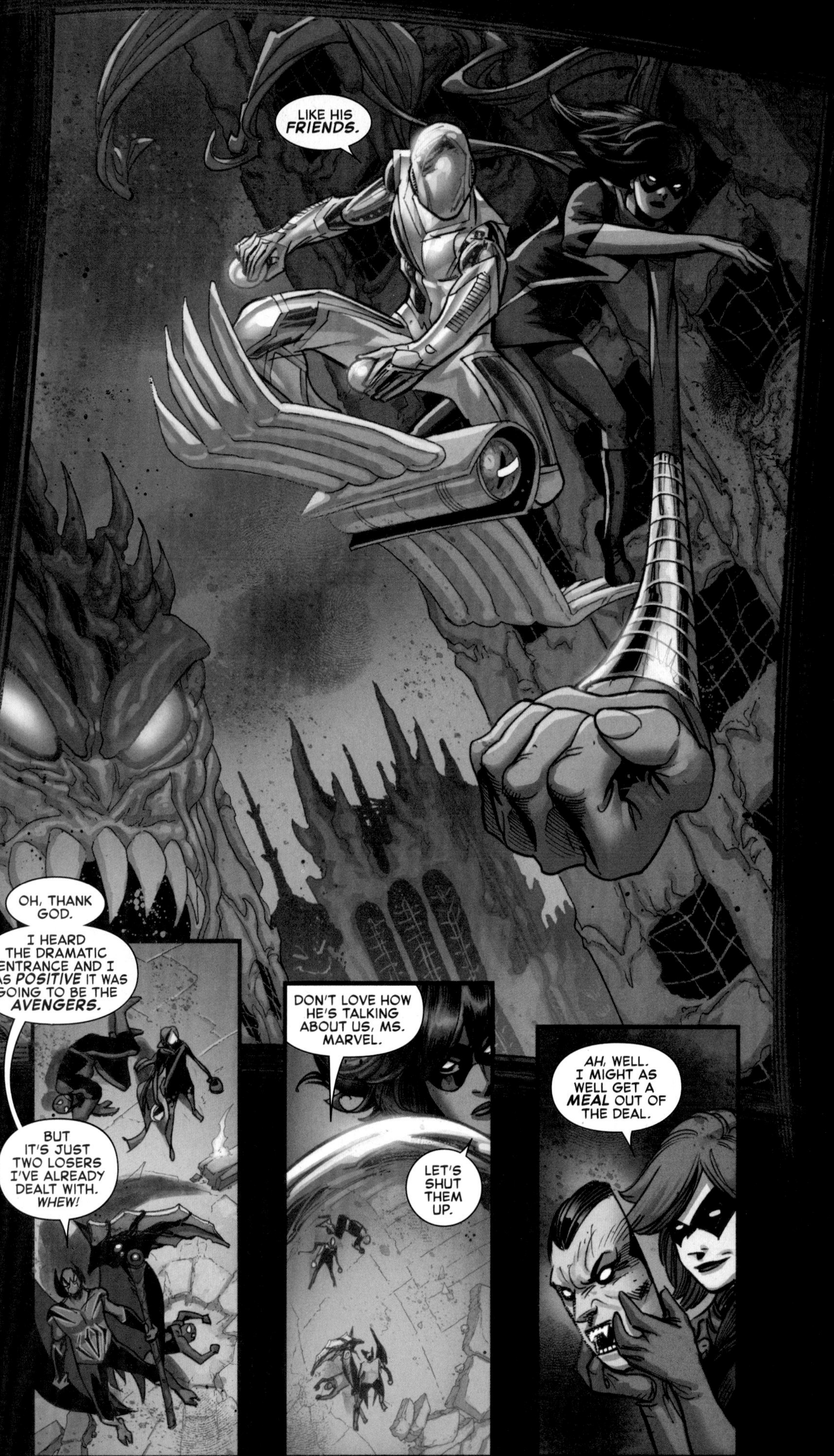
LIKE HIS FRIENDS.
OH, THANK GOD.
I HEARD THE DRAMATIC ENTRANCE AND I WAS POSITIVE IT WAS GOING TO BE THE AVENGERS.
BUT IT'S JUST TWO LOSERS I'VE ALREADY DEALT WITH. WHEW!
DON'T LOVE HOW HE'S TALKING ABOUT US, MS. MARVEL.
LET'S SHUT THEM UP.
AH, WELL. I MIGHT AS WELL GET A MEAL OUT OF THE DEAL.

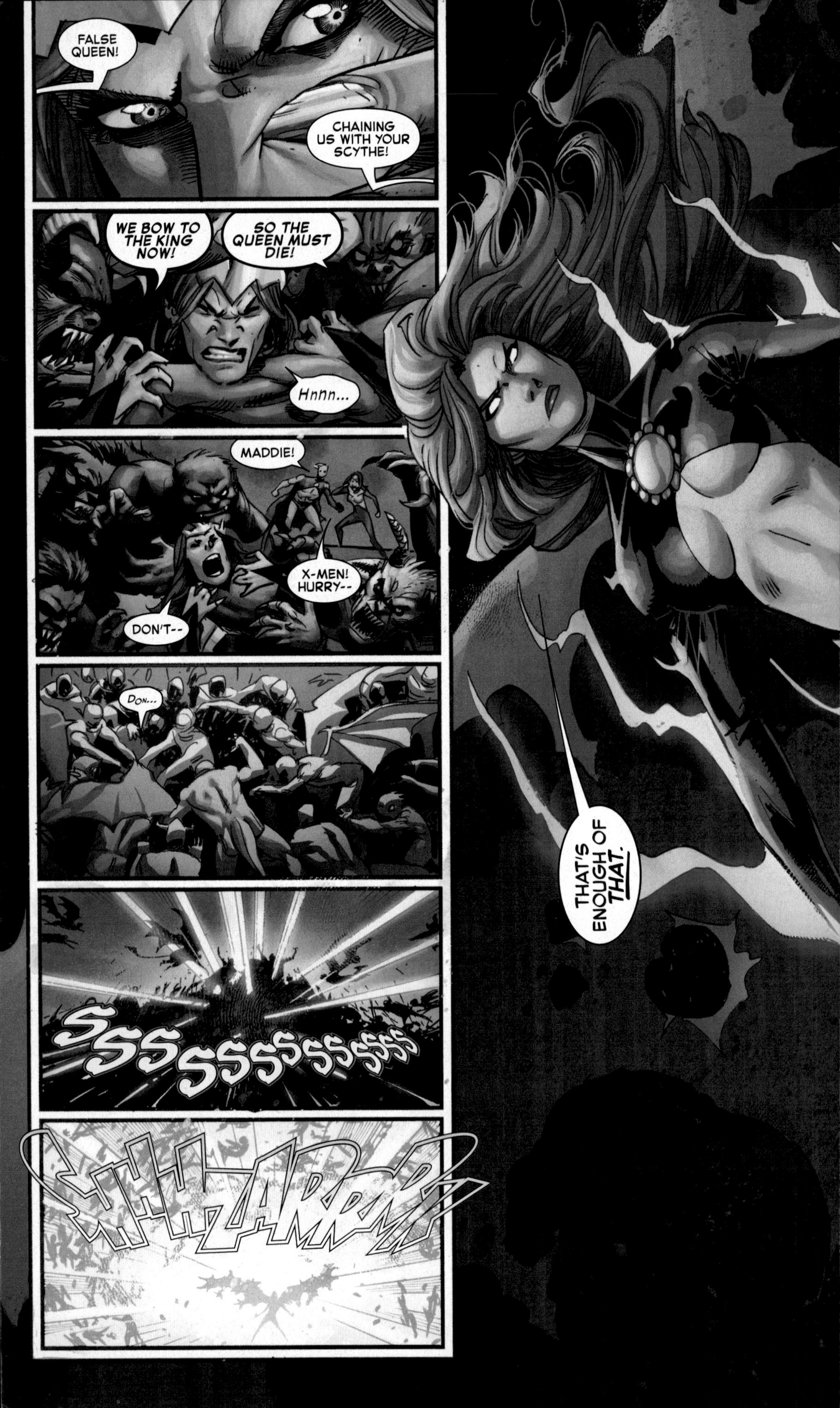
FALSE QUEEN!
CHAINING US WITH YOUR SCYTHE!
WE BOW TO THE KING NOW!
SO THE QUEEN MUST DIE!
Hnnn...
MADDIE!
X-MEN! HURRY--
DON'T--
DON...
THAT'S ENOUGH OF THAT.
SSSSSSSSSSSSS

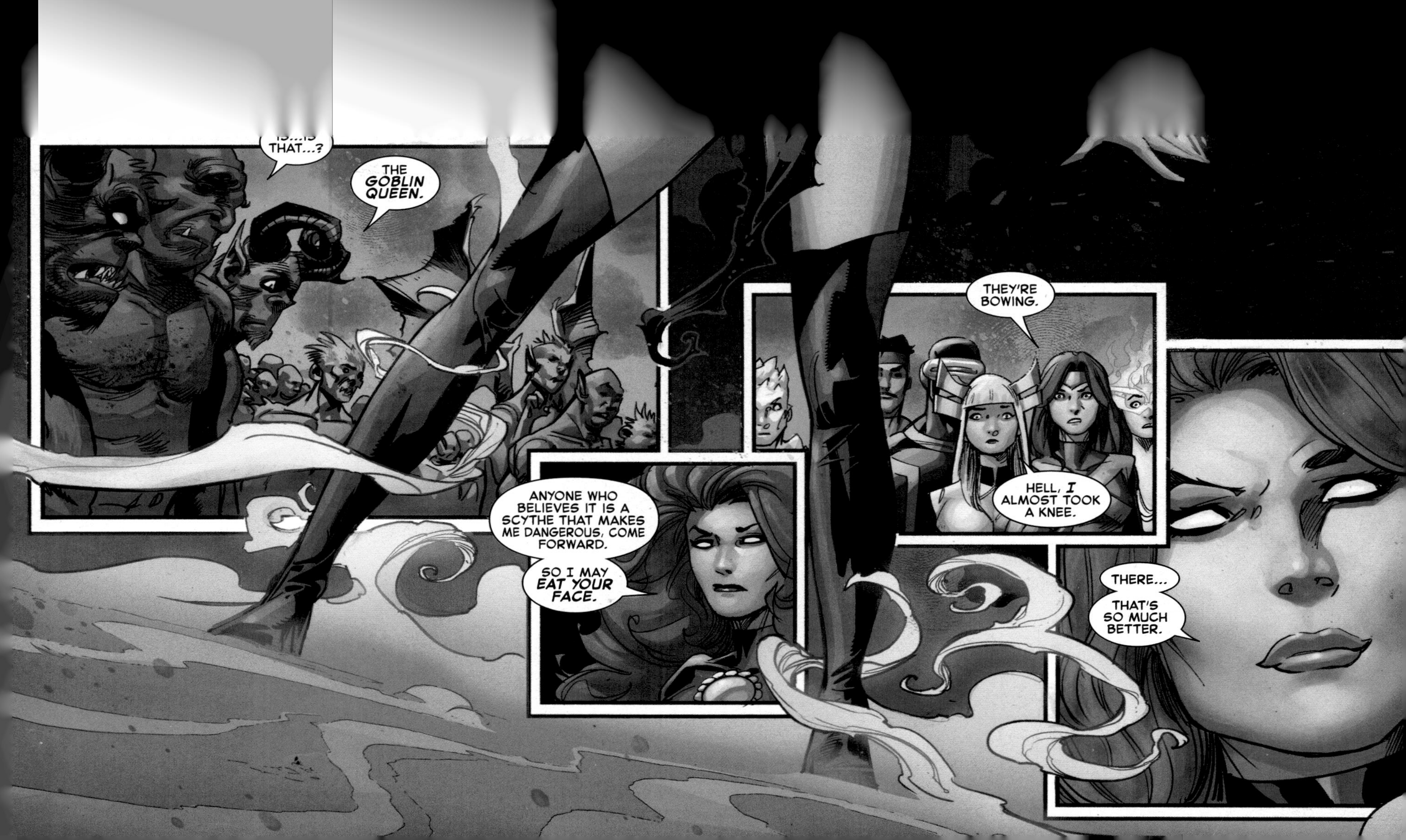
THAT...?
THE GOBLIN QUEEN.
ANYONE WHO BELIEVES IT IS A SCYTHE THAT MAKES ME DANGEROUS, COME FORWARD.
SO I MAY EAT YOUR FACE.
THEY'RE BOWING.
HELL, I ALMOST TOOK A KNEE.
THERE...
THAT'S SO MUCH BETTER.

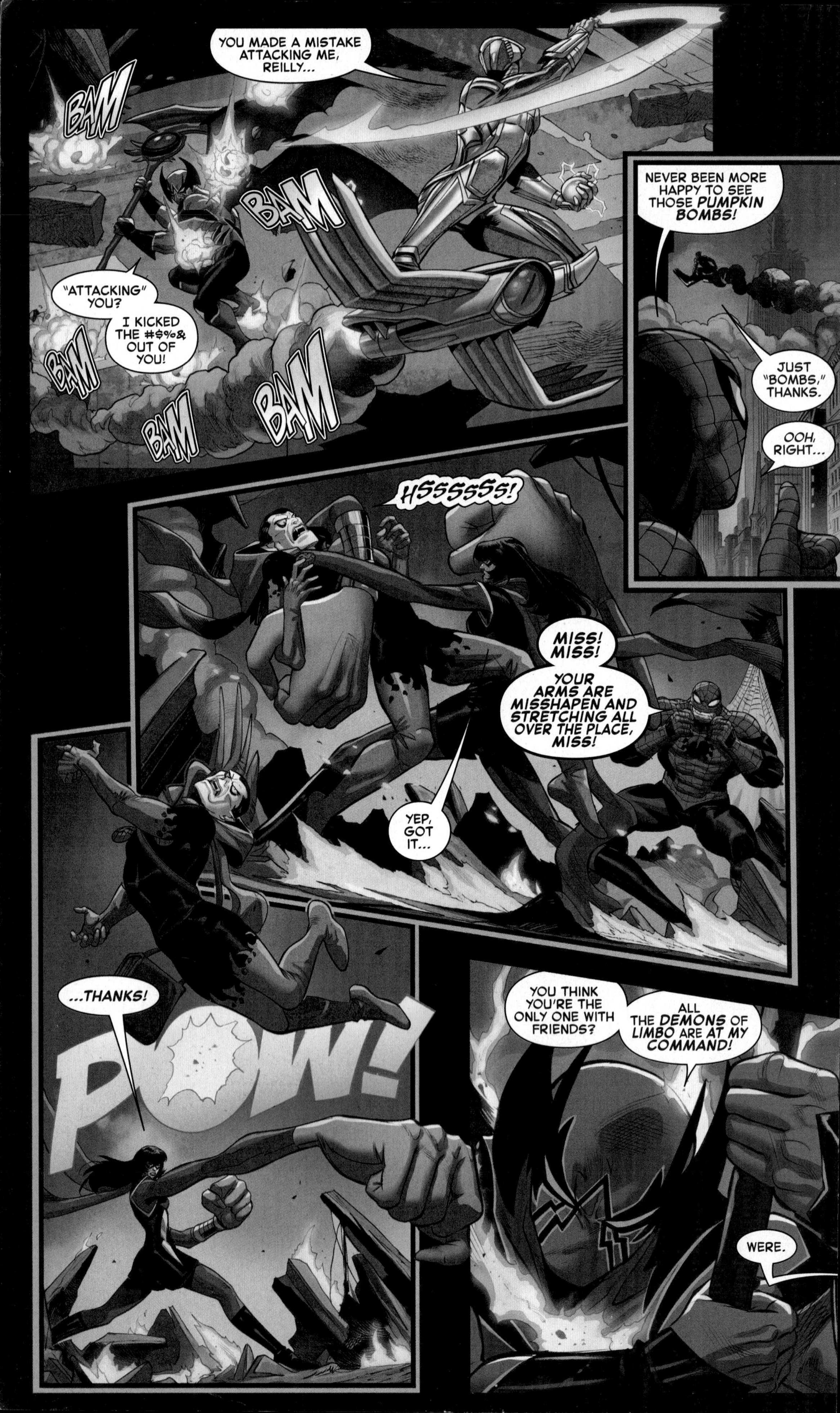
YOU MADE A MISTAKE ATTACKING ME, REILLY...
BAM
BAM
"ATTACKING" YOU?
I KICKED THE #$%& OUT OF YOU!
BAM
BAM
BAM
NEVER BEEN MORE HAPPY TO SEE THOSE PUMPKIN BOMBS!
JUST "BOMBS," THANKS.
OOH, RIGHT...
HSSSSSS!
MISS! MISS!
YOUR ARMS ARE MISSHAPEN AND STRETCHING ALL OVER THE PLACE, MISS!
YEP, GOT IT...
...THANKS!
POW!
YOU THINK YOU'RE THE ONLY ONE WITH FRIENDS?
ALL THE DEMONS OF LIMBO ARE AT MY COMMAND!
WERE.

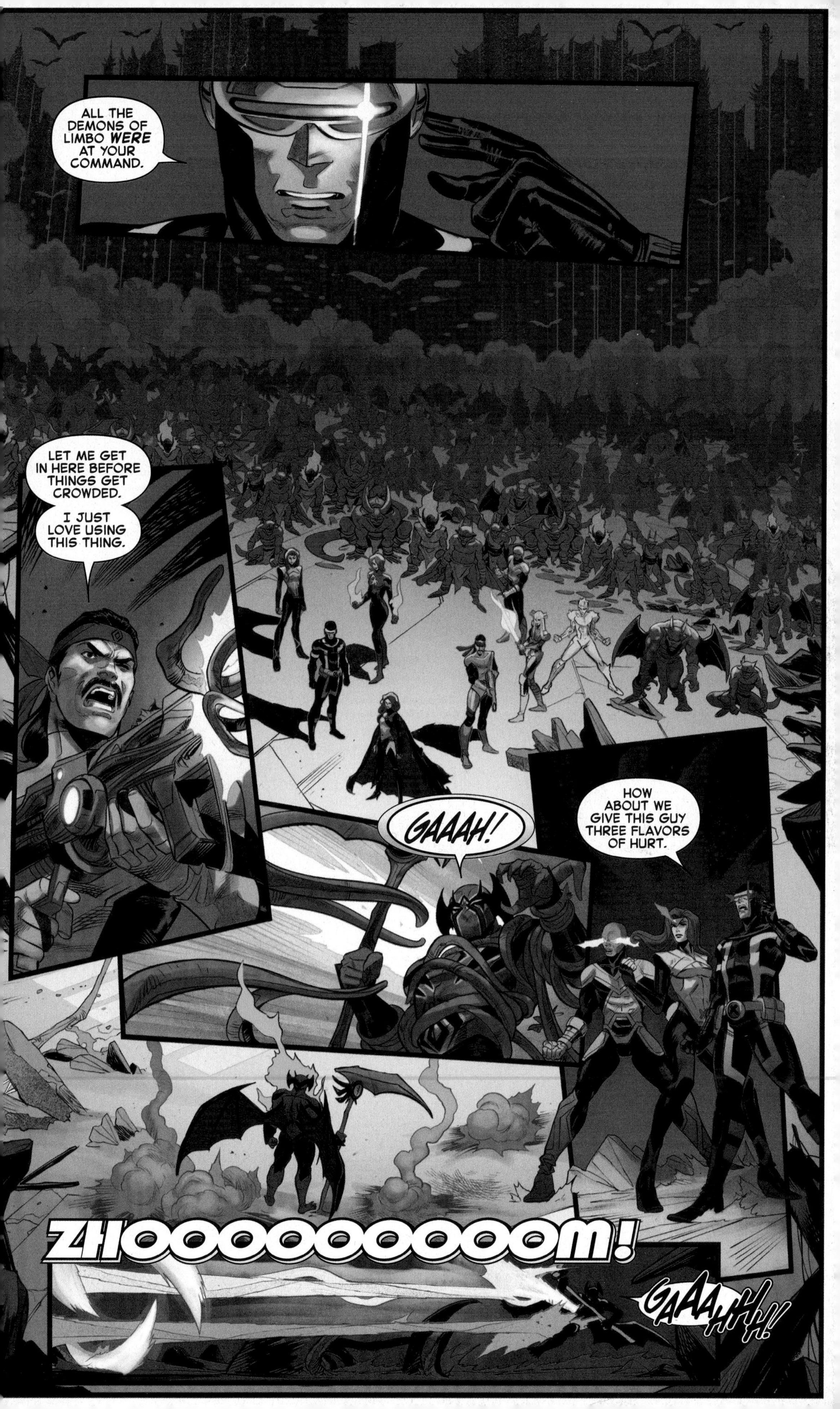
ALL THE DEMONS OF LIMBO WERE AT YOUR COMMAND.
LET ME GET IN HERE BEFORE THINGS GET CROWDED.
I JUST LOVE USING THIS THING.
GAAAH!
HOW ABOUT WE GIVE THIS GUY THREE FLAVORS OF HURT.
ZHOOOOOOOOOOM!
GAAAHHH!

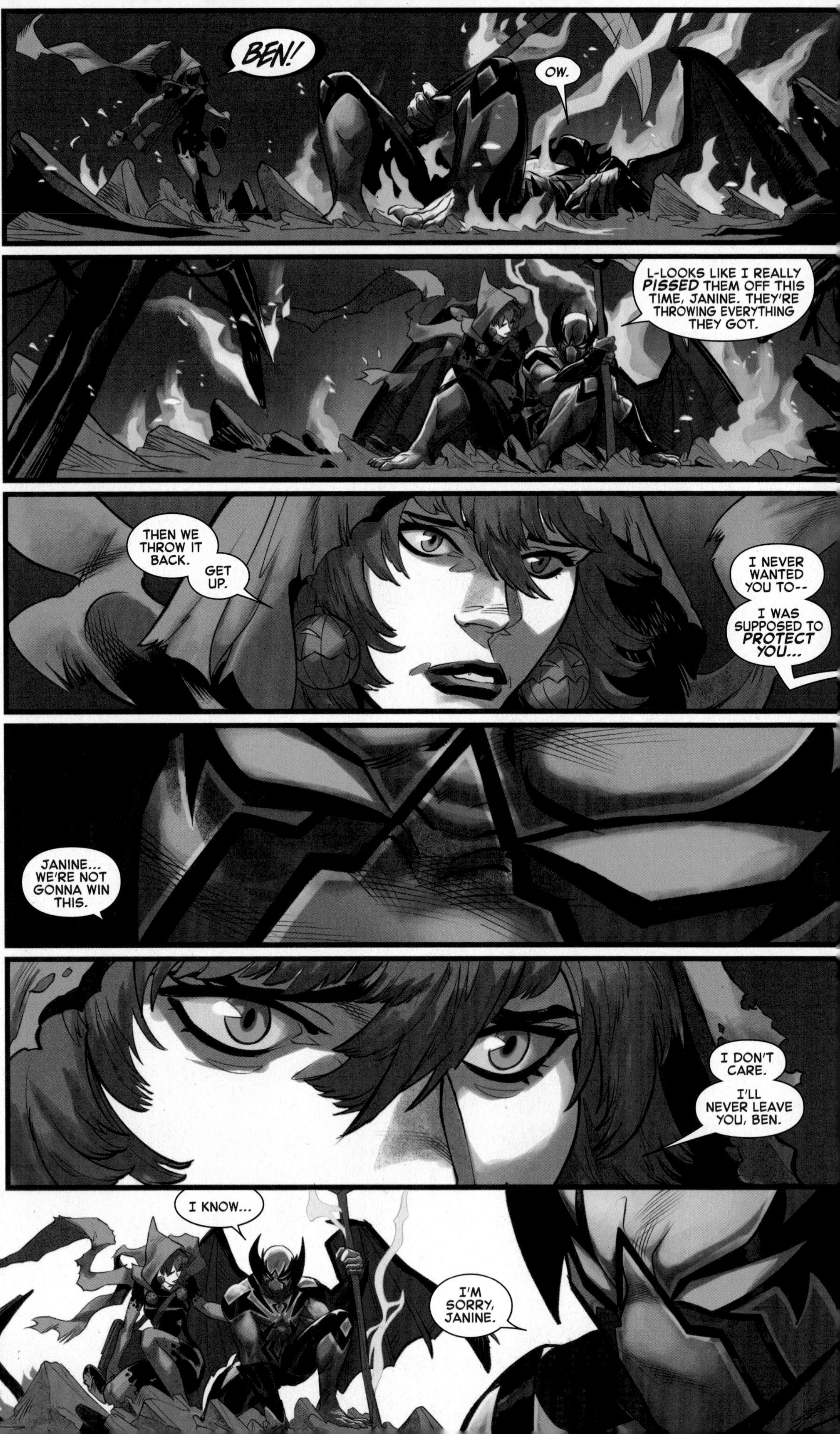

BEN!
OW.
L-LOOKS LIKE I REALLY PISSED THEM OFF THIS TIME, JANINE. THEY'RE THROWING EVERYTHING THEY GOT.
THEN WE THROW IT BACK.
GET UP.
I NEVER WANTED YOU TO--
I WAS SUPPOSED TO PROTECT YOU...
JANINE... WE'RE NOT GONNA WIN THIS.
I DON'T CARE.
I'LL NEVER LEAVE YOU, BEN.
I KNOW...
I'M SORRY, JANINE.

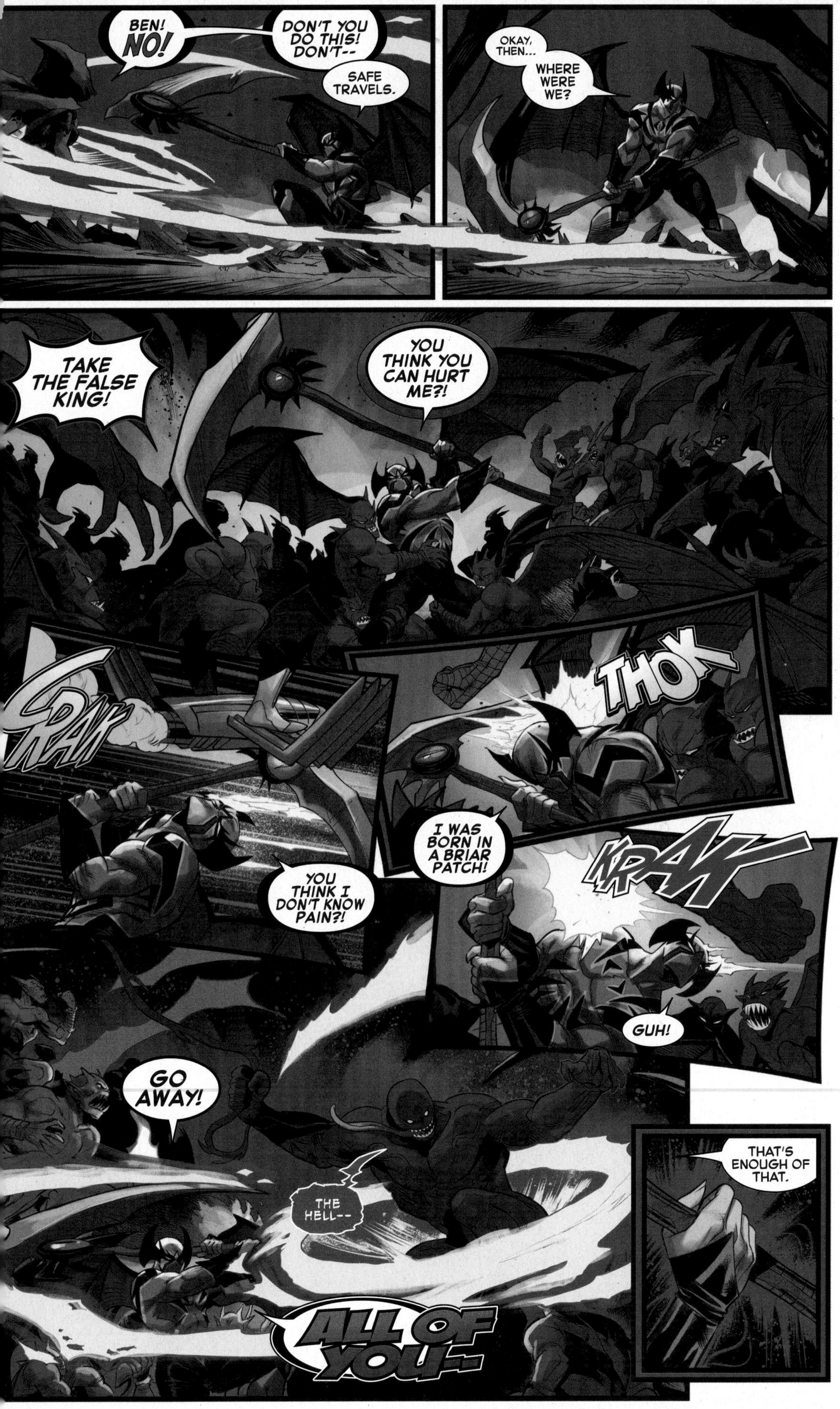

BEN! NO!
DON'T YOU DO THIS! DON'T--
SAFE TRAVELS.
OKAY, THEN...
WHERE WERE WE?
TAKE THE FALSE KING!
YOU THINK YOU CAN HURT ME?!
KRAK
THOK
YOU THINK I DON'T KNOW PAIN?!
I WAS BORN IN A BRIAR PATCH!
KRAK
GUH!
GO AWAY!
THE HELL--
ALL OF YOU--
THAT'S ENOUGH OF THAT.

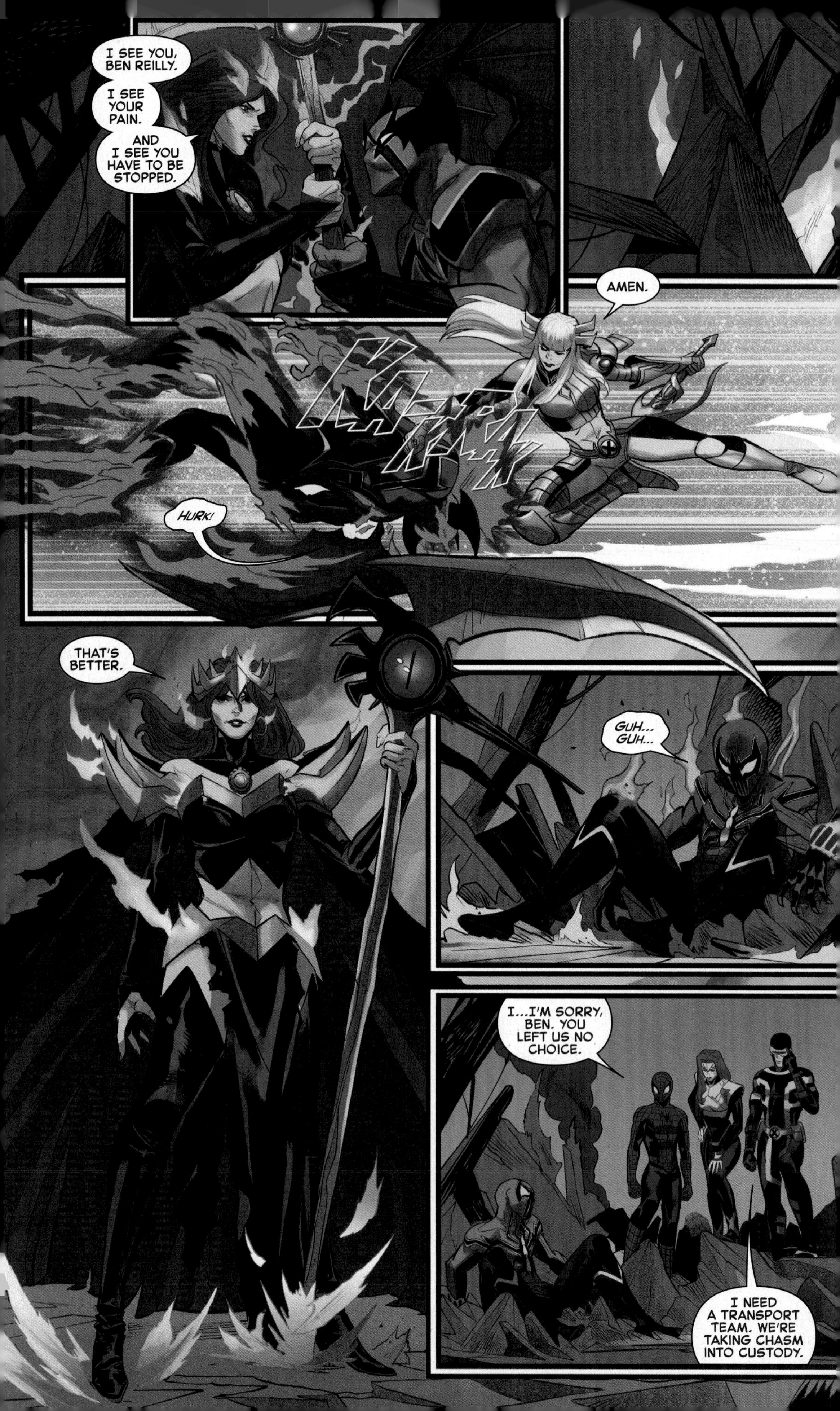
I SEE YOU, BEN REILLY.
I SEE YOUR PAIN.
AND I SEE YOU HAVE TO BE STOPPED.
AMEN.
HURK!
THAT'S BETTER.
GUH... GUH...
I...I'M SORRY, BEN. YOU LEFT US NO CHOICE.
I NEED A TRANSPORT TEAM. WE'RE TAKING CHASM INTO CUSTODY.

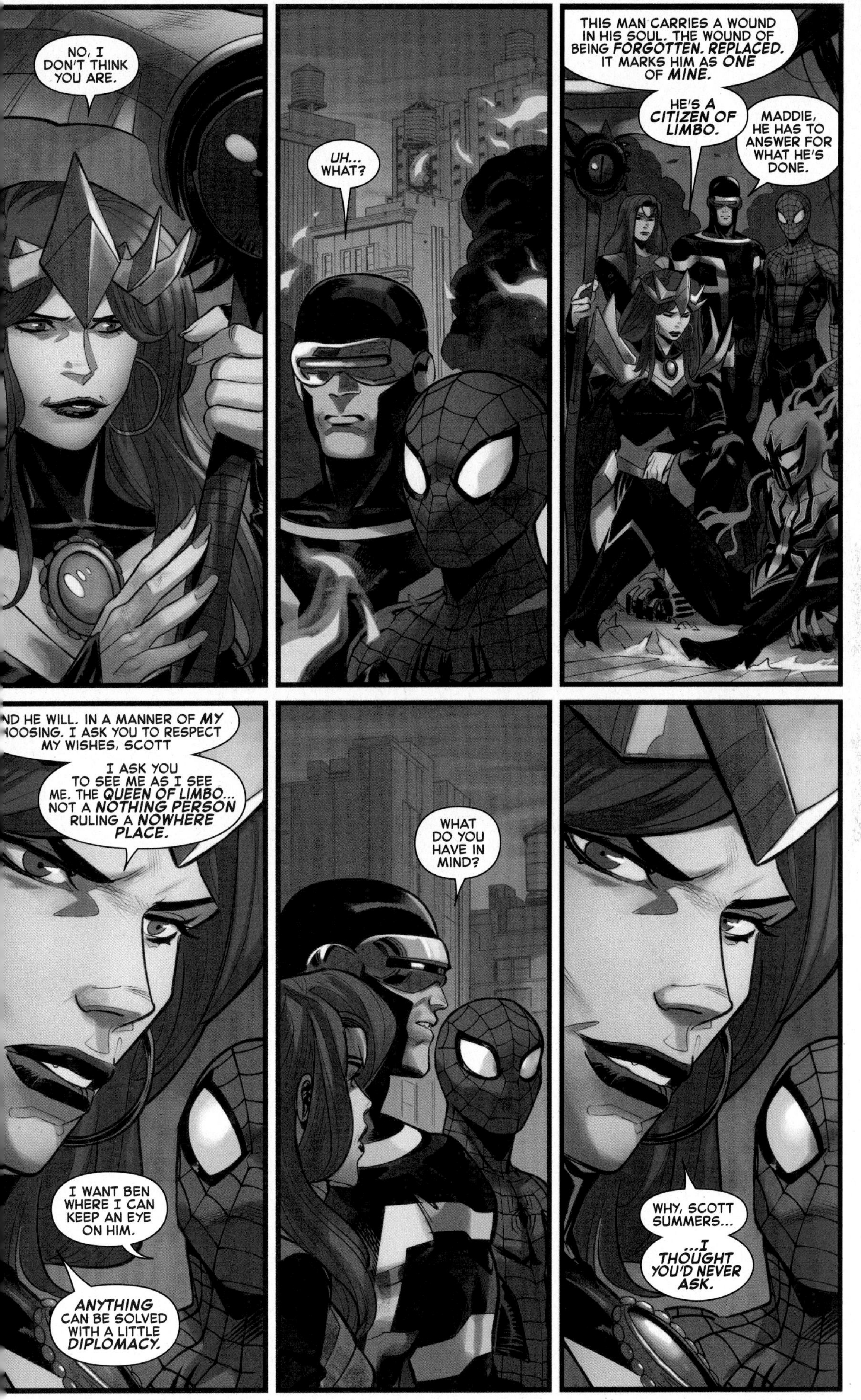

NO, I DON'T THINK YOU ARE.
UH... WHAT?
THIS MAN CARRIES A WOUND IN HIS SOUL. THE WOUND OF BEING FORGOTTEN. REPLACED. IT MARKS HIM AS ONE OF MINE.
HE'S A CITIZEN OF LIMBO.
MADDIE, HE HAS TO ANSWER FOR WHAT HE'S DONE.
ND HE WILL. IN A MANNER OF MY HOOSING. I ASK YOU TO RESPECT MY WISHES, SCOTT
I ASK YOU TO SEE ME AS I SEE ME. THE QUEEN OF LIMBO... NOT A NOTHING PERSON RULING A NOWHERE PLACE.
I WANT BEN WHERE I CAN KEEP AN EYE ON HIM.
ANYTHING CAN BE SOLVED WITH A LITTLE DIPLOMACY.
WHAT DO YOU HAVE IN MIND?
WHY, SCOTT SUMMERS...
...I THOUGHT YOU'D NEVER ASK.

SPRING

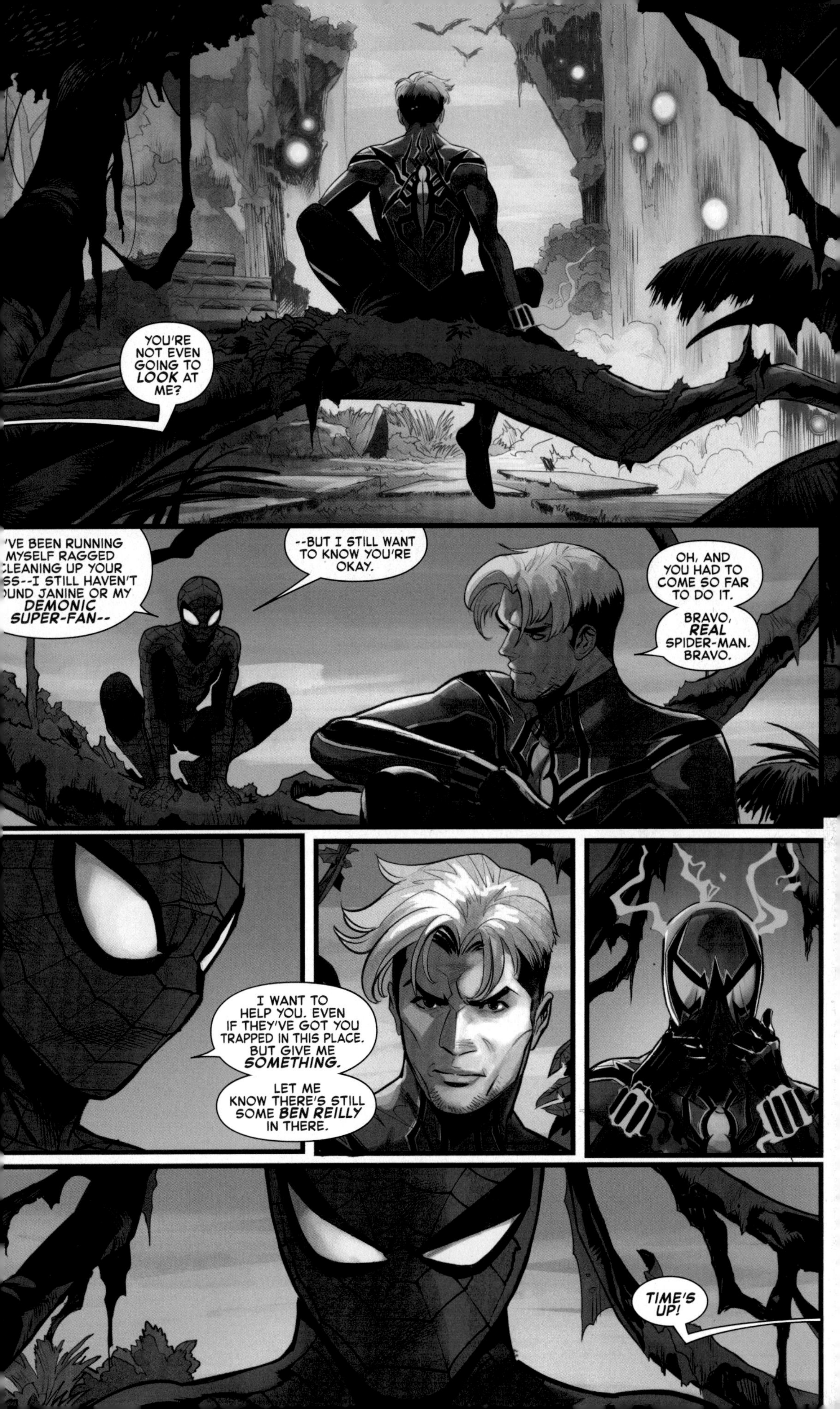

YOU'RE NOT EVEN GOING TO LOOK AT ME?
'VE BEEN RUNNING MYSELF RAGGED CLEANING UP YOUR SS--I STILL HAVEN'T OUND JANINE OR MY DEMONIC SUPER-FAN--
--BUT I STILL WANT TO KNOW YOU'RE OKAY.
OH, AND YOU HAD TO COME SO FAR TO DO IT.
BRAVO, REAL SPIDER-MAN. BRAVO.
I WANT TO HELP YOU. EVEN IF THEY'VE GOT YOU TRAPPED IN THIS PLACE. BUT GIVE ME SOMETHING.
LET ME KNOW THERE'S STILL SOME BEN REILLY IN THERE.
TIME'S UP!

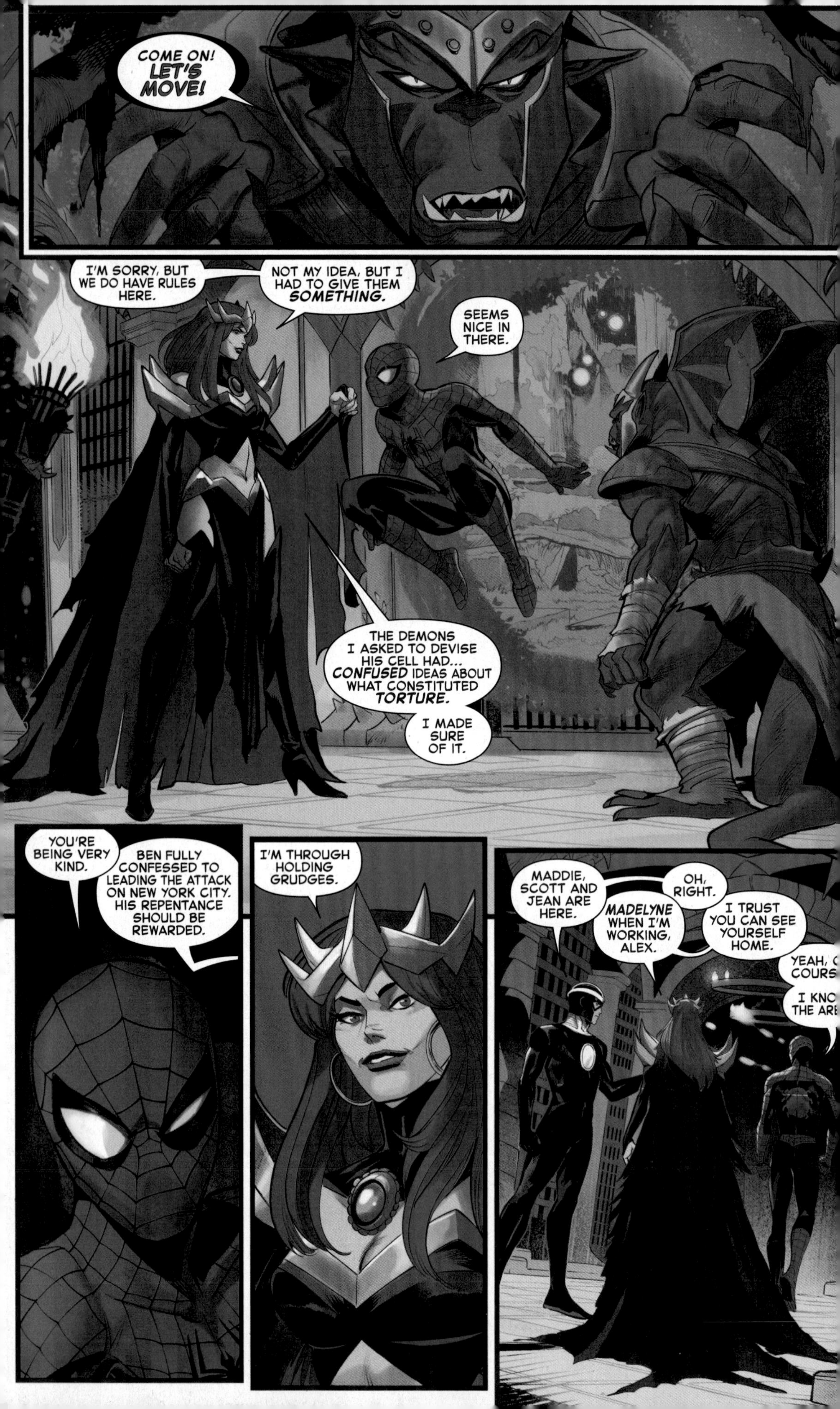
COME ON! LET'S MOVE!
I'M SORRY, BUT WE DO HAVE RULES HERE.
NOT MY IDEA, BUT I HAD TO GIVE THEM SOMETHING.
SEEMS NICE IN THERE.
THE DEMONS I ASKED TO DEVISE HIS CELL HAD... CONFUSED IDEAS ABOUT WHAT CONSTITUTED TORTURE.
I MADE SURE OF IT.
YOU'RE BEING VERY KIND.
BEN FULLY CONFESSED TO LEADING THE ATTACK ON NEW YORK CITY. HIS REPENTANCE SHOULD BE REWARDED.
I'M THROUGH HOLDING GRUDGES.
MADDIE, SCOTT AND JEAN ARE HERE.
OH, RIGHT.
MADELYNE WHEN I'M WORKING, ALEX.
I TRUST YOU CAN SEE YOURSELF HOME.

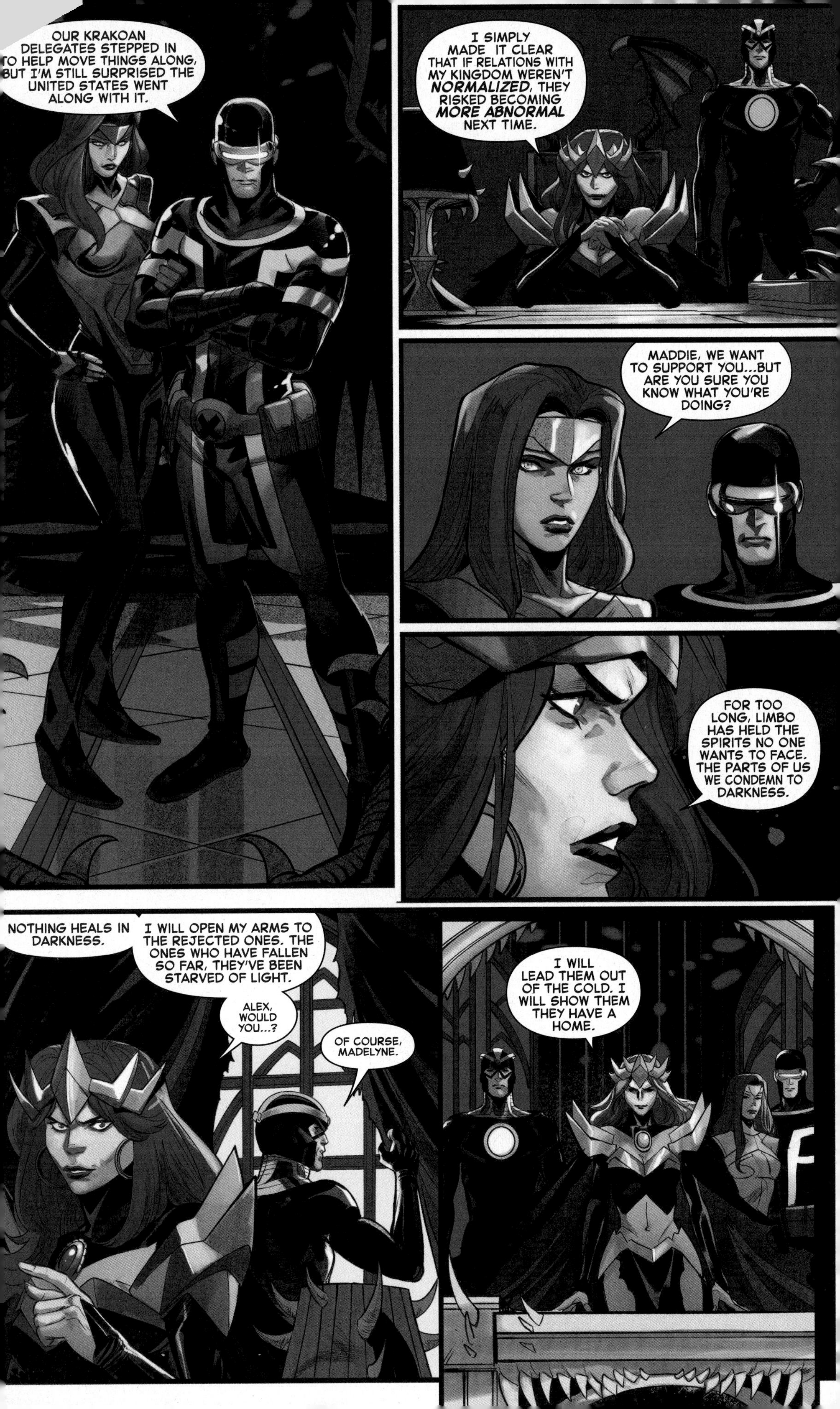
OUR KRAKOAN DELEGATES STEPPED IN TO HELP MOVE THINGS ALONG, BUT I'M STILL SURPRISED THE UNITED STATES WENT ALONG WITH IT.
I SIMPLY MADE IT CLEAR THAT IF RELATIONS WITH MY KINGDOM WEREN'T NORMALIZED, THEY RISKED BECOMING MORE ABNORMAL NEXT TIME.
MADDIE, WE WANT TO SUPPORT YOU...BUT ARE YOU SURE YOU KNOW WHAT YOU'RE DOING?
FOR TOO LONG, LIMBO HAS HELD THE SPIRITS NO ONE WANTS TO FACE. THE PARTS OF US WE CONDEMN TO DARKNESS.
NOTHING HEALS IN DARKNESS.
I WILL OPEN MY ARMS TO THE REJECTED ONES. THE ONES WHO HAVE FALLEN SO FAR, THEY'VE BEEN STARVED OF LIGHT.
ALEX, WOULD YOU...?
OF COURSE, MADELYNE.
I WILL LEAD THEM OUT OF THE COLD. I WILL SHOW THEM THEY HAVE A HOME.

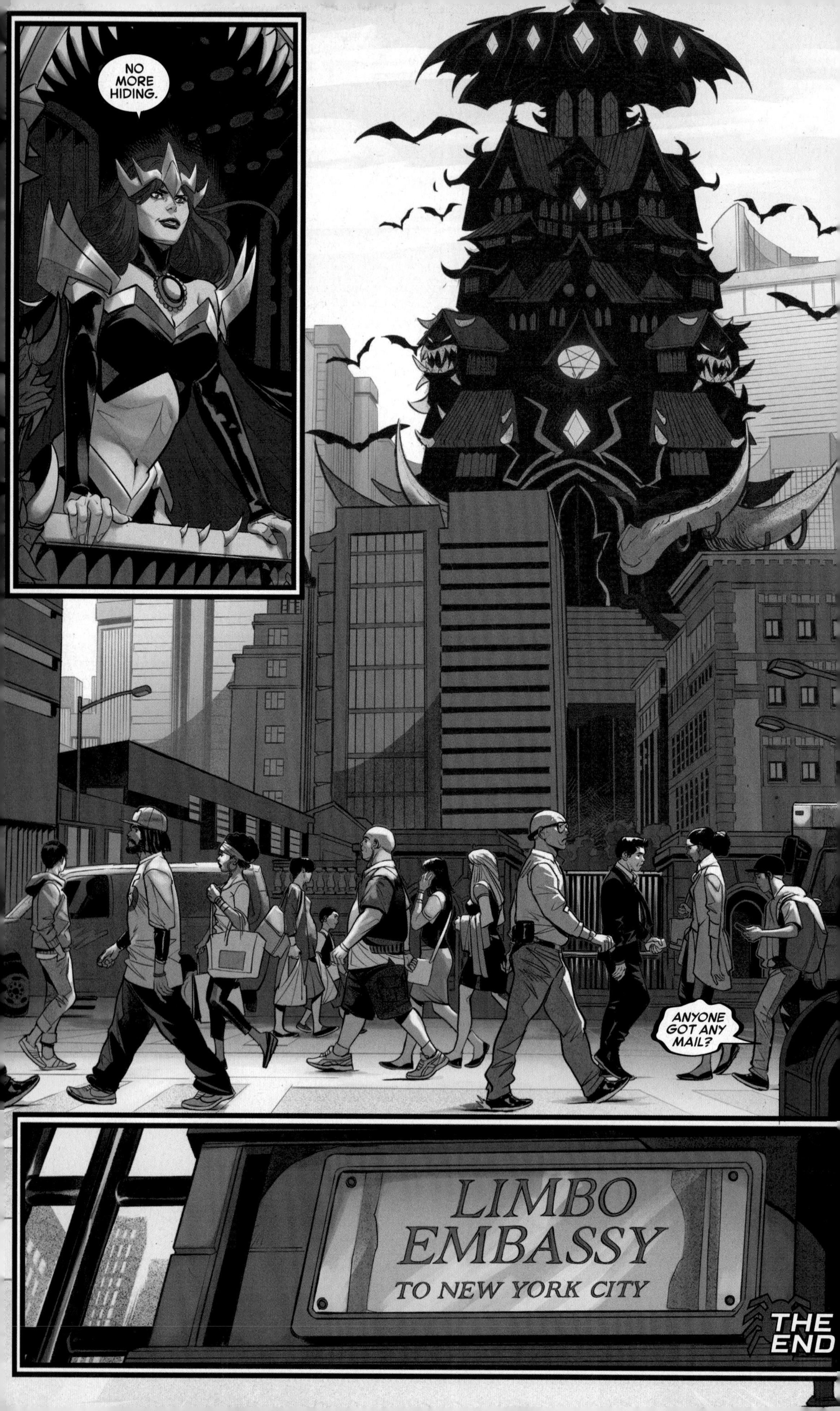
NO MORE HIDING.
ANYONE GOT ANY MAIL?
LIMBO EMBASSY TO NEW YORK CITY
THE END

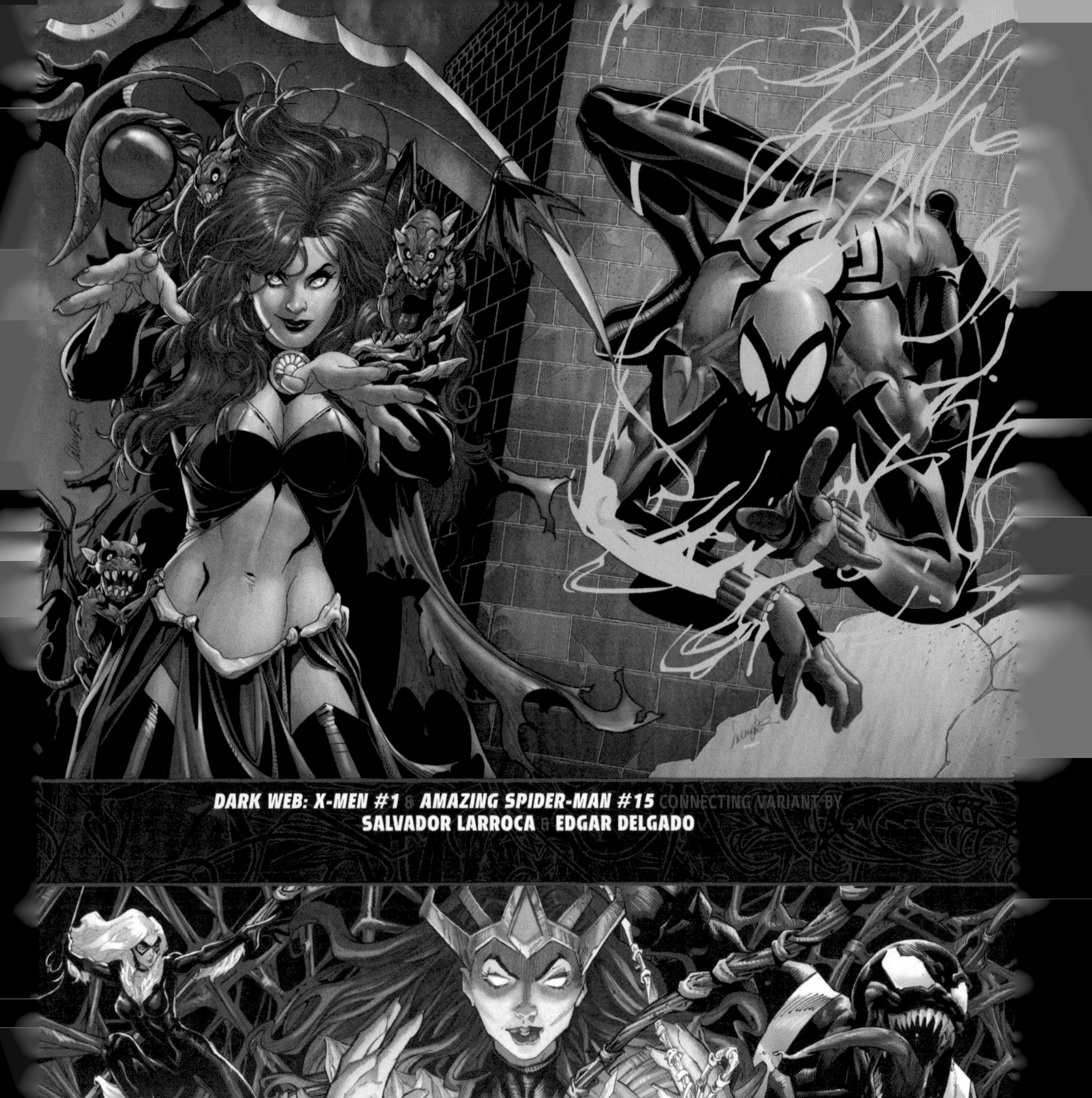

DARK WEB: X-MEN #1 & **AMAZING SPIDER-MAN #15** CONNECTING VARIANT BY
SALVADOR LARROCA & **EDGAR DELGADO**

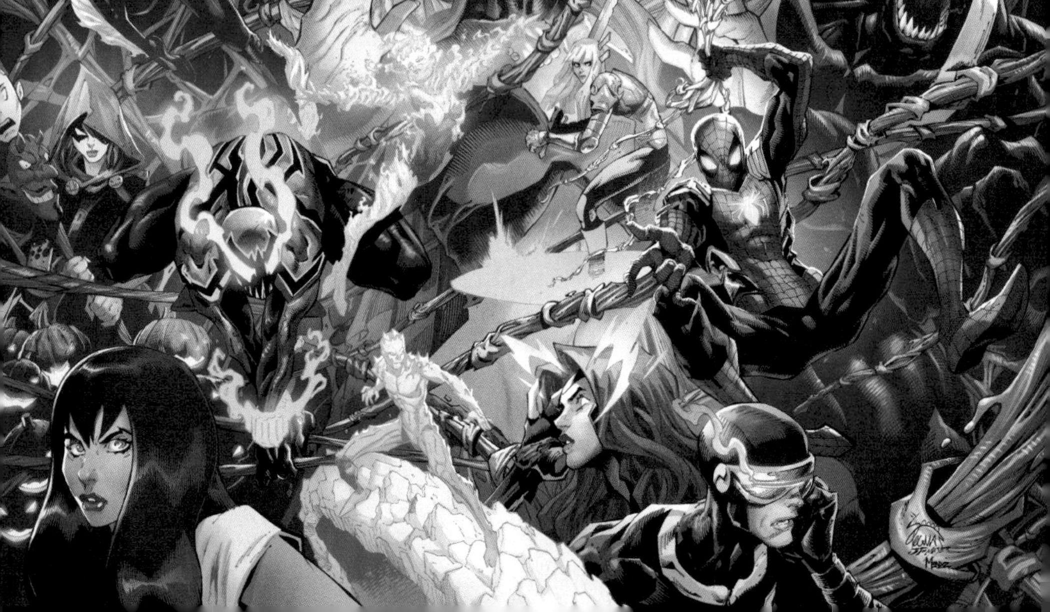

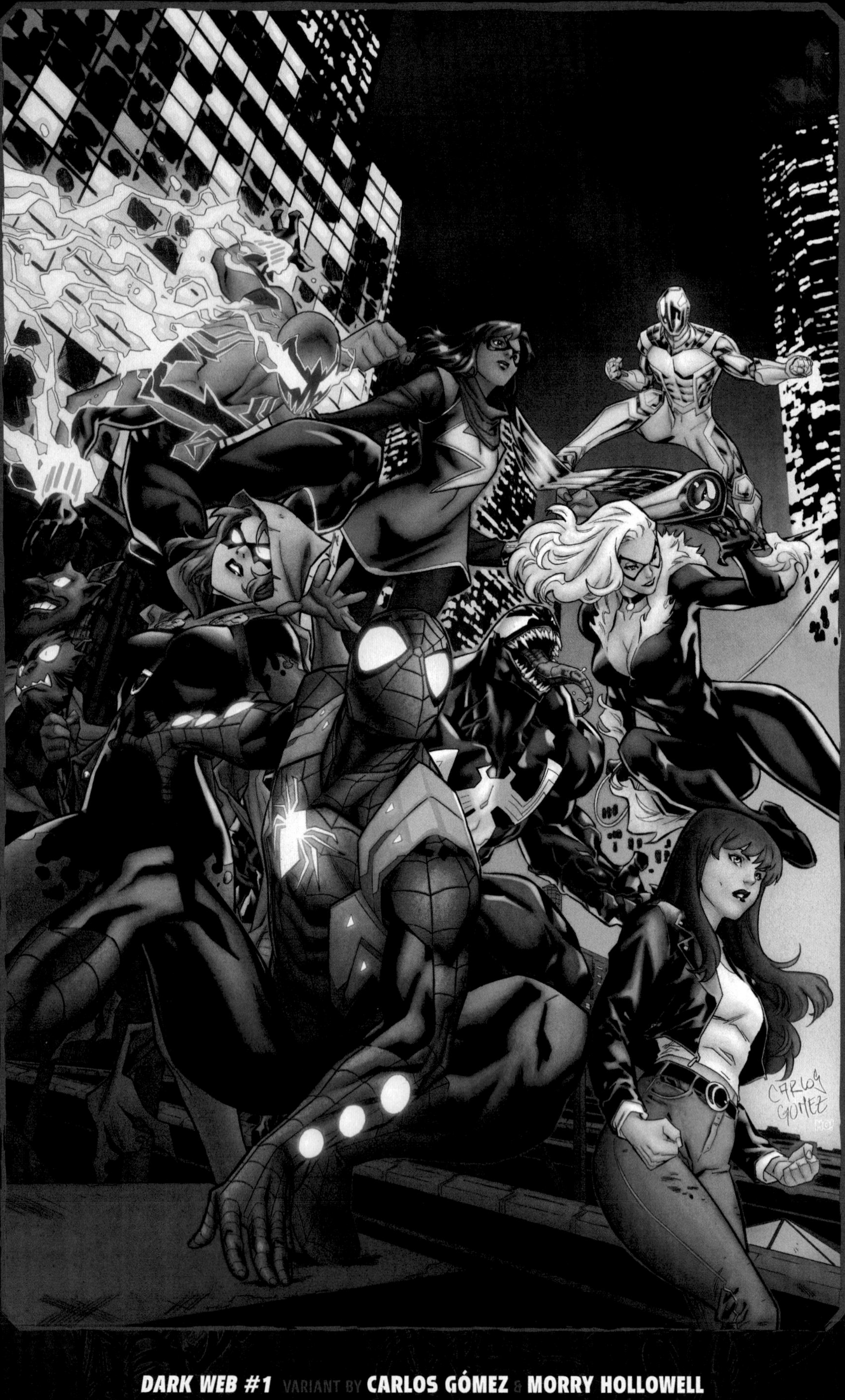
CARLOS GOMEZ

DARK WEB #1 VARIANT BY **CARLOS GÓMEZ** & **MORRY HOLLOWELL**

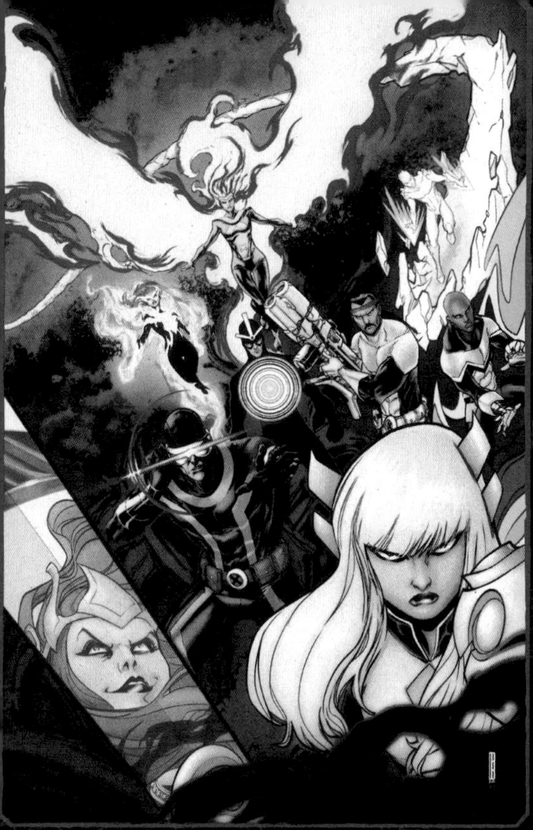

DARK WEB #1 VARIANT BY
DAVID BALDEÓN & **MORRY HOLLOWELL**

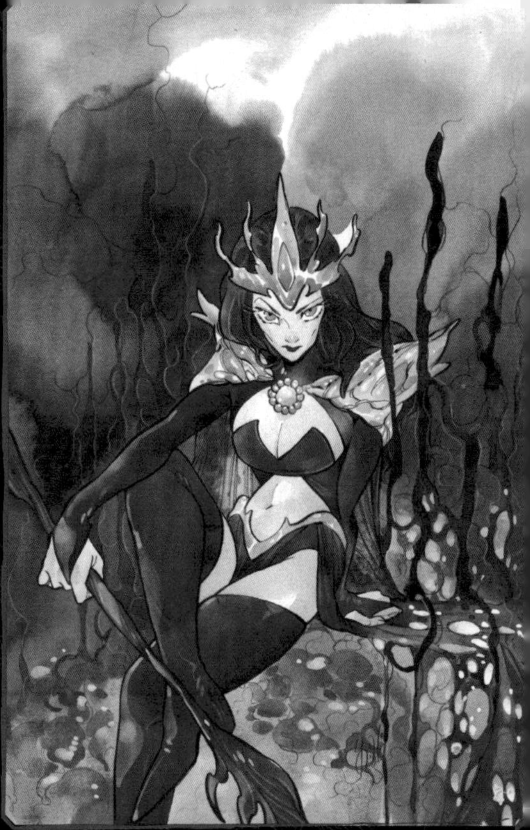

DARK WEB #1 MARVEL UNIVERSE VARIANT BY
PEACH MOMOKO

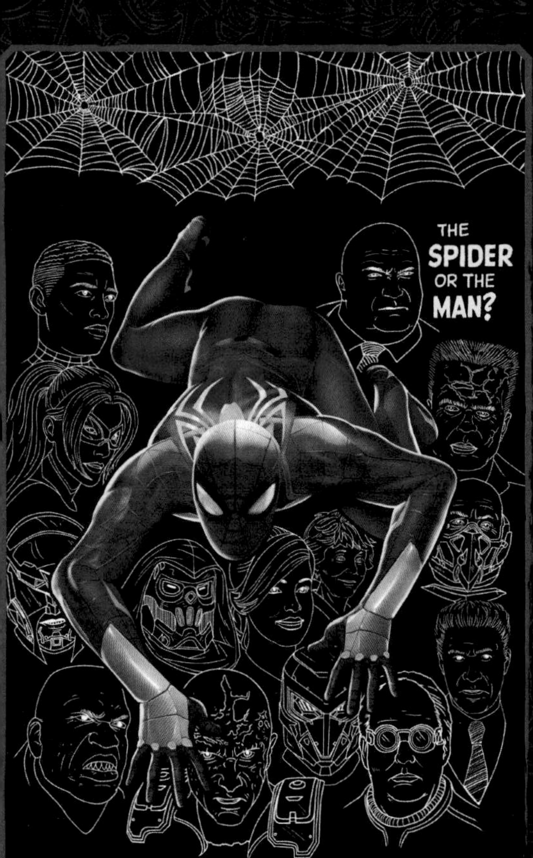
THE SPIDER OR THE MAN?

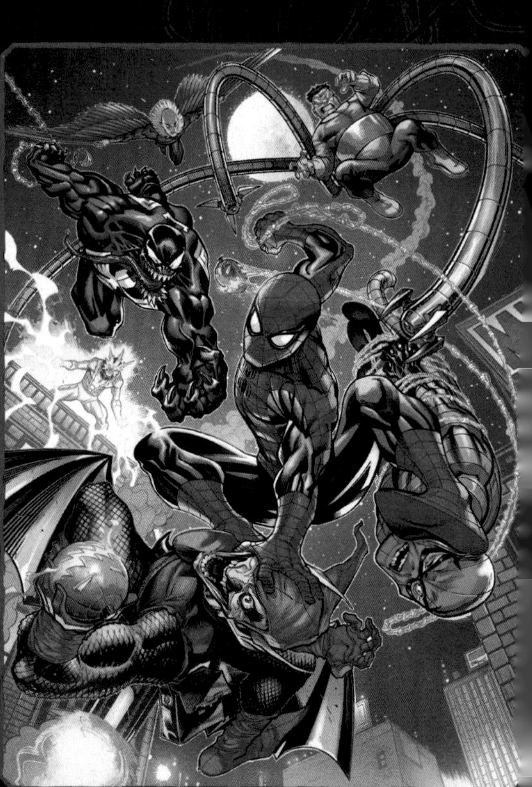

AMAZING SPIDER-MAN #15 VARIANT BY

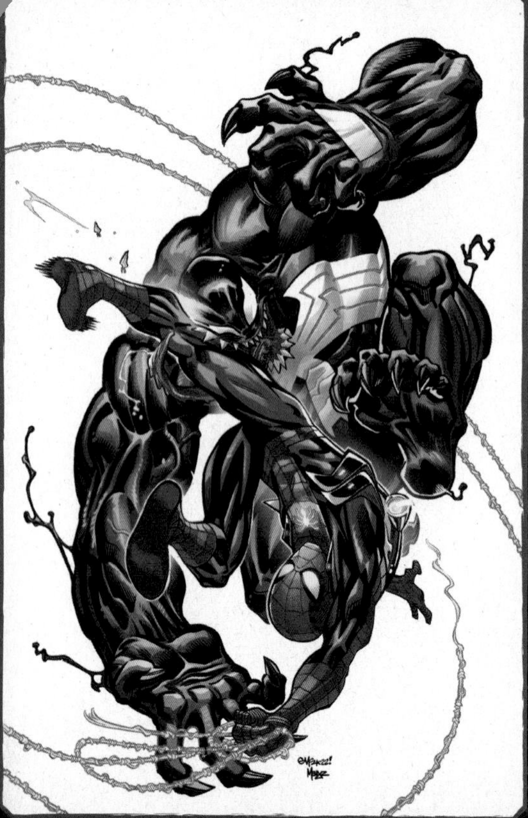

AMAZING SPIDER-MAN #15 DARK WEB VARIANT BY
ED McGUINNESS & **MARCIO MENYZ**

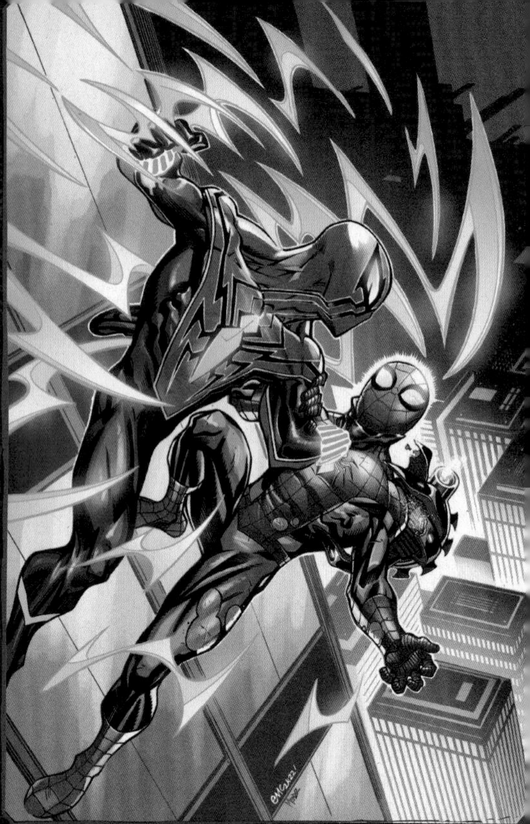

AMAZING SPIDER-MAN #16 DARK WEB VARIANT BY
ED McGUINNESS & **MARCIO MENYZ**

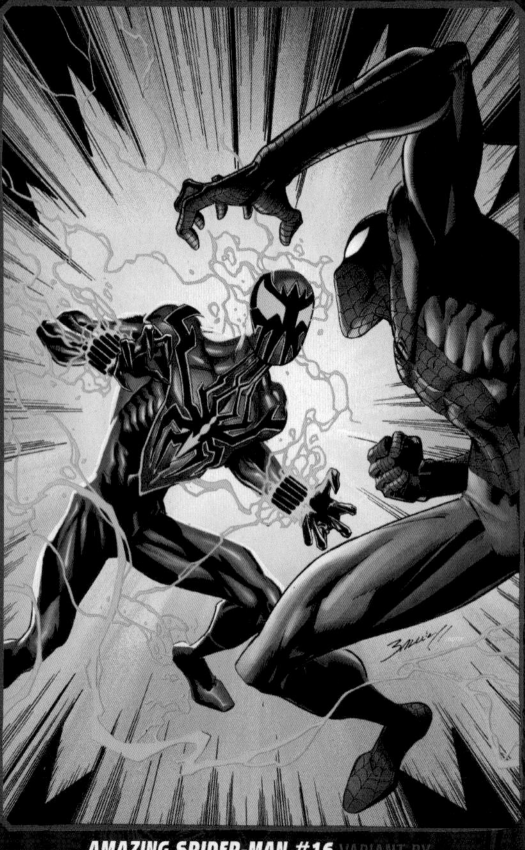

AMAZING SPIDER-MAN #16 VARIANT BY
MARK BAGLEY & **CHRIS SOTOMAYOR**

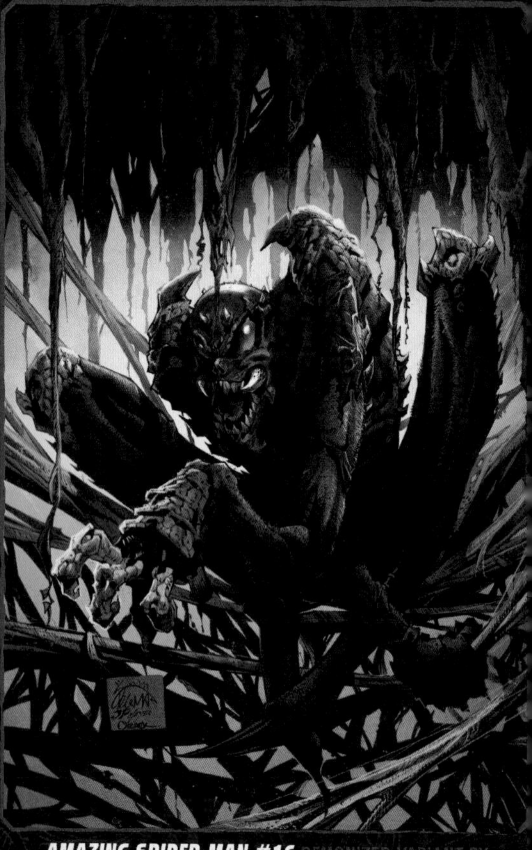

AMAZING SPIDER-MAN #16 DEMONIZED VARIANT BY
RYAN STEGMAN, JP MAYER & **SONIA OBACK**

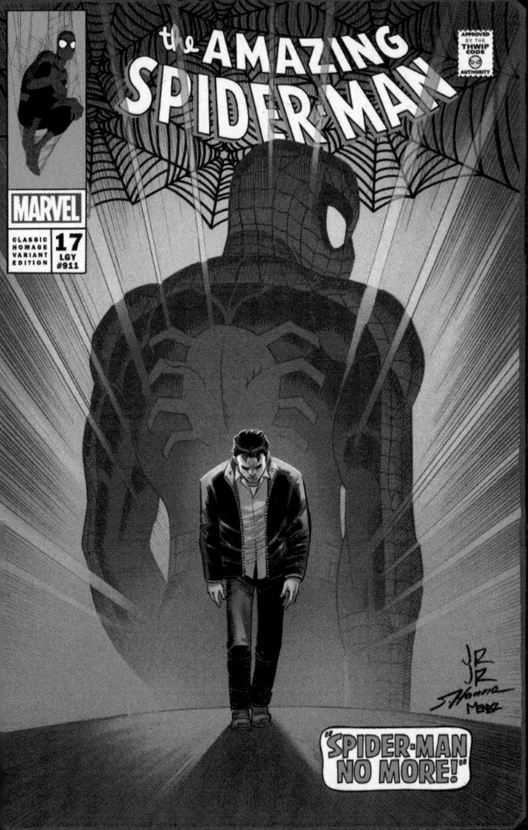
the AMAZING SPIDER-MAN
APPROVED BY THE THWIP CODE AUTHORITY
MARVEL
CLASSIC HOMAGE VARIANT EDITION
17 LGY #911
"SPIDER-MAN NO MORE!"

AMAZING SPIDER-MAN #17 CLASSIC HOMAGE VARIANT BY
JOHN ROMITA JR., SCOTT HANNA & MARCIO MENYZ

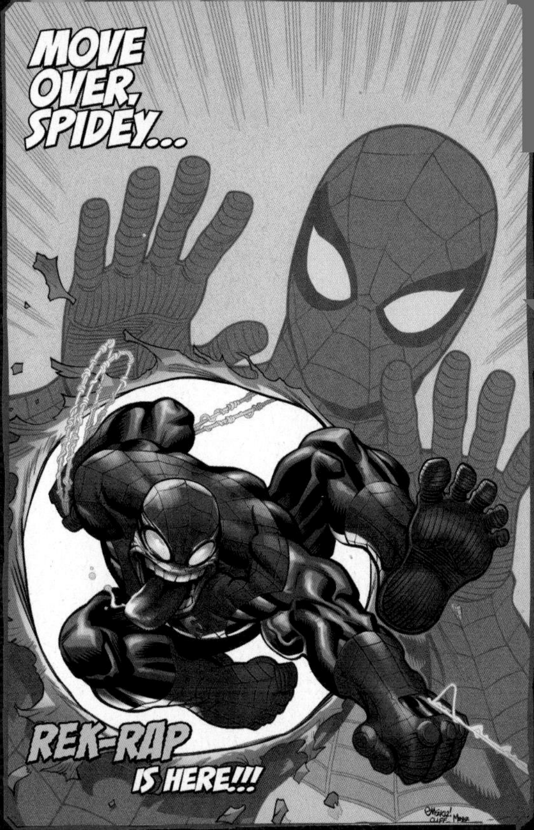
MOVE OVER, SPIDEY...
REK-RAP IS HERE!!!

AMAZING SPIDER-MAN #17 VARIANT BY
ED McGUINNESS, CLIFF RATHBURN & MARCIO MENYZ

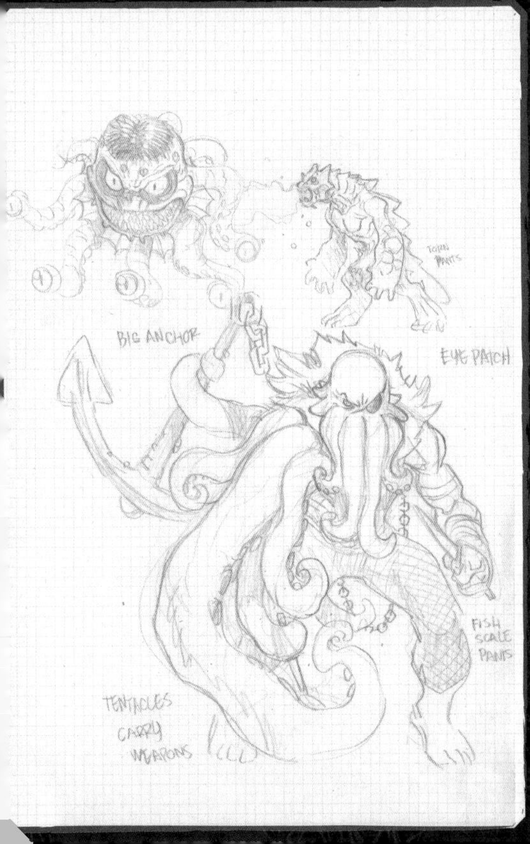
BIG ANCHOR
EYE PATCH
FISH SCALE PANTS
TENTACLES CARRY WEAPONS

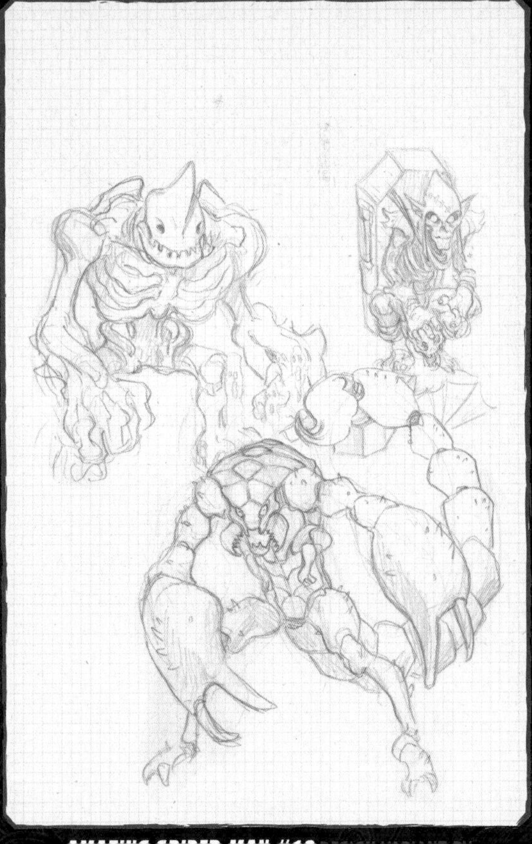

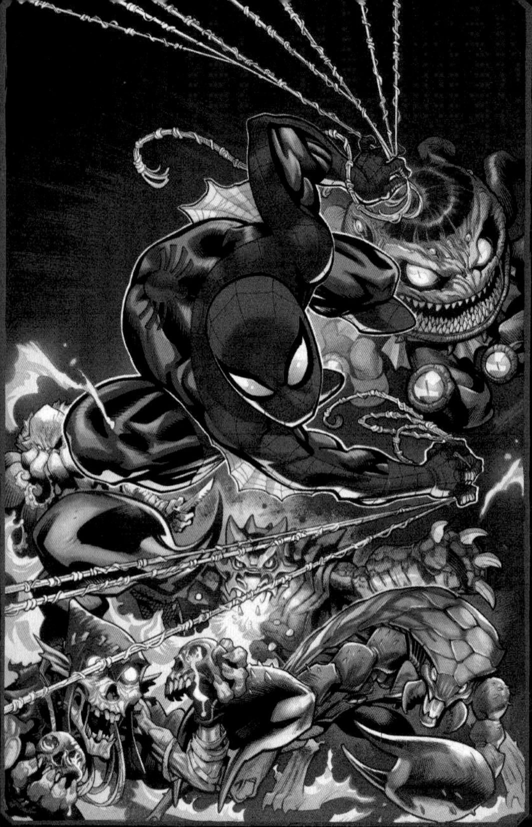

***AMAZING SPIDER-MAN* #18** VARIANT BY
ED McGUINNESS, CLIFF RATHBURN & MARCIO MENYZ

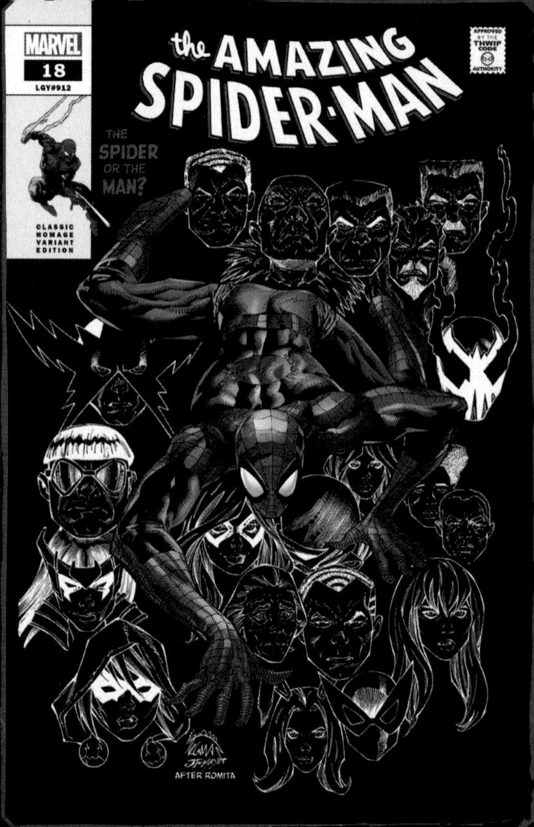
MARVEL
18
LGY#912
the AMAZING SPIDER-MAN
APPROVED BY THE THWIP CODE AUTHORITY
THE SPIDER OR THE MAN?
CLASSIC HOMAGE VARIANT EDITION
AFTER ROMITA

***AMAZING SPIDER-MAN* #18** CLASSIC HOMAGE VARIANT BY
RYAN STEGMAN, JP MAYER & SONIA OBACK

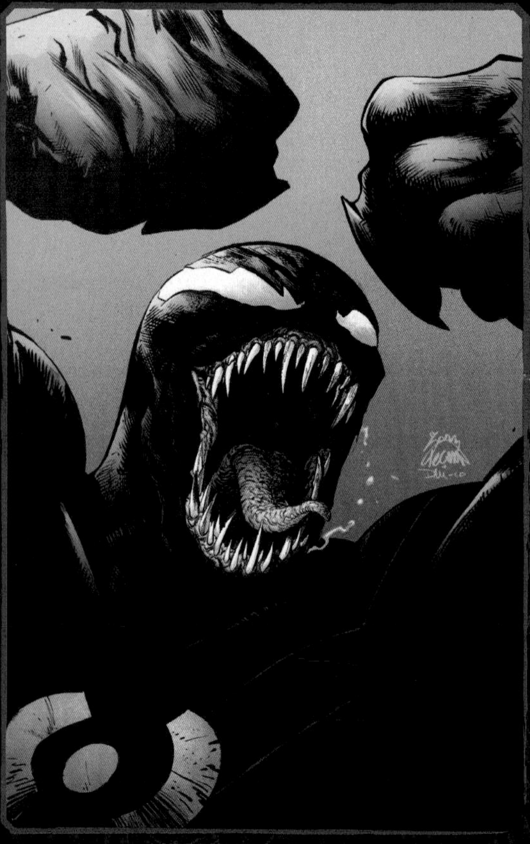

***VENOM* #14** VARIANT BY
RYAN STEGMAN & DAVE McCAIG

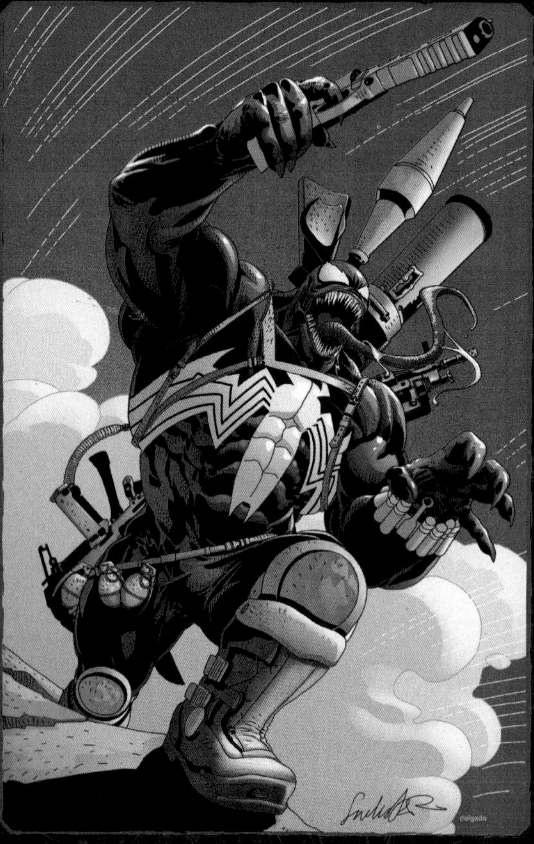

***VENOM* #14** X-TREME MARVEL VARIANT BY
SALVADOR LARROCA & EDGAR DELGADO

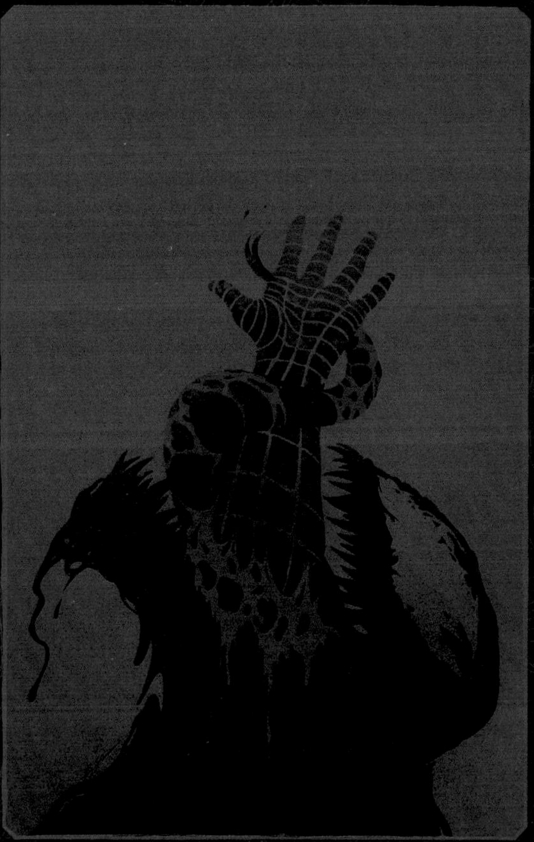

VENOM #15 VARIANT BY
BENJAMIN SU

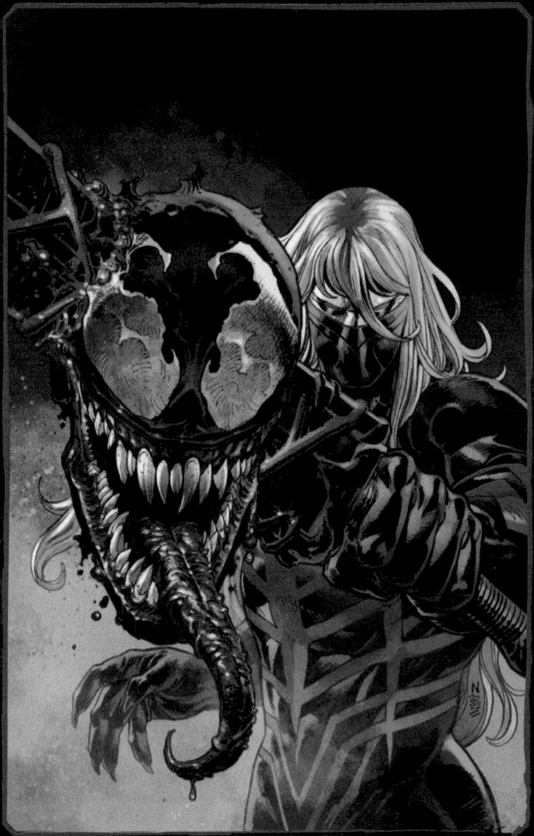

VENOM #15 VARIANT BY
NIC KLEIN

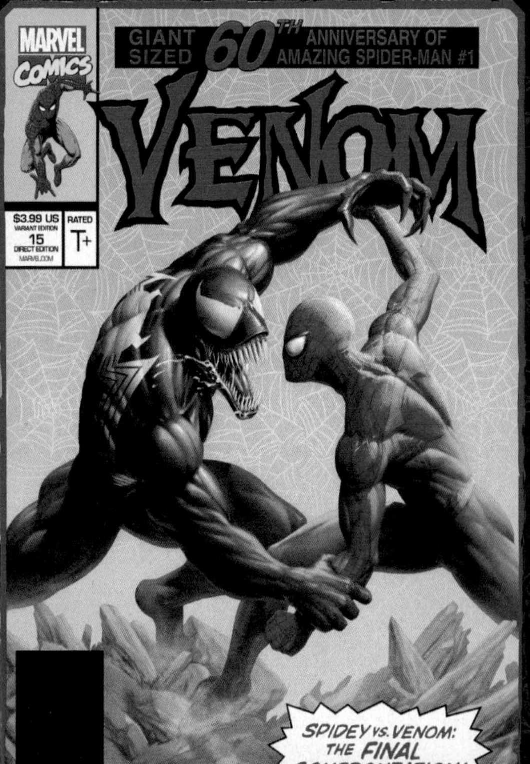

MARVEL COMICS
GIANT SIZED 60TH ANNIVERSARY OF AMAZING SPIDER-MAN #1
VENOM
$3.99 US VARIANT EDITION 15 DIRECT EDITION MARVEL.COM
RATED T+
SPIDEY VS. VENOM: THE FINAL CONFRONTATION!
after bagley

VENOM #15 CLASSIC HOMAGE DESIGN VARIANT BY
JOHN TYLER CHRISTOPHER

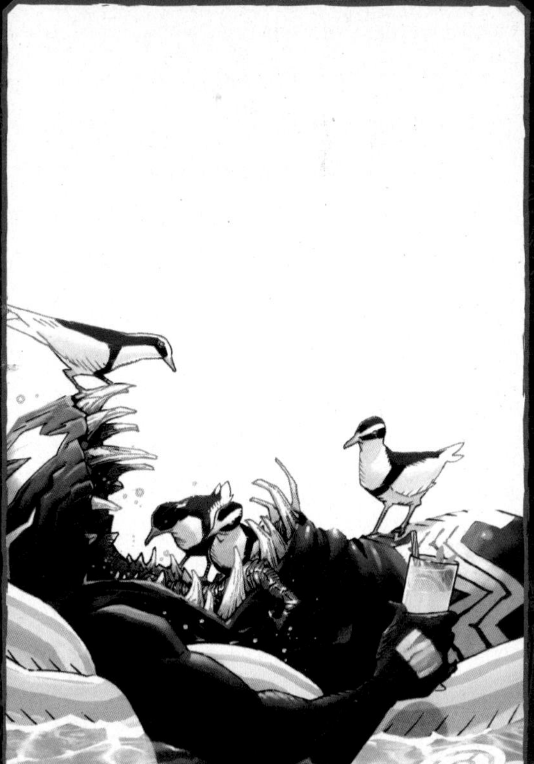

VENOM #16 VARIANT BY
CHRIS BACHALO

VENOM #16 STORMBREAKERS VARIANT BY
MARTÍN CÓCCOLO & **MATTHEW WILSON**

DARK WEB: X-MEN #1 VARIANT BY
TERRY DODSON & **RACHEL DODSON**

DARK WEB: X-MEN #1 VARIANT BY
RYAN STEGMAN JP MAYER & **MATTHEW WILSON**

DARK WEB: X-MEN #2 VARIANT BY
DAVID BALDEÓN & **ISRAEL SILVA**

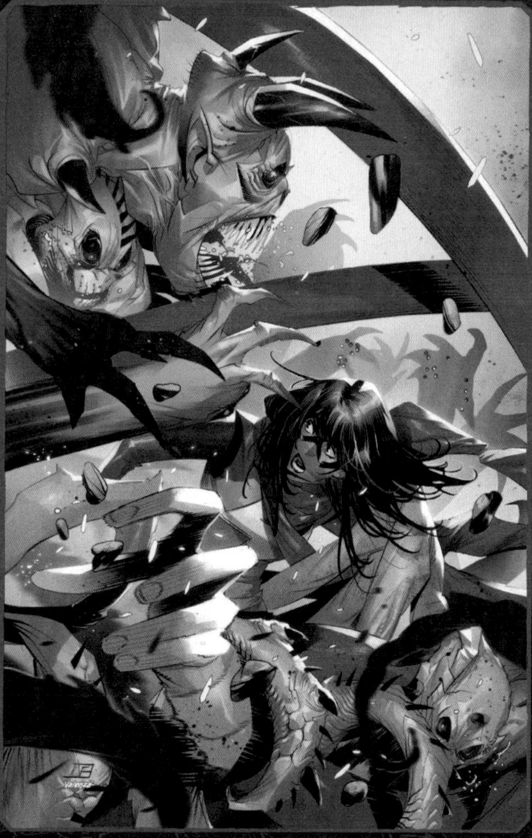

DARK WEB: MS. MARVEL #1 VARIANT BY
FEDERICO VICENTINI & **BRYAN VALENZA**

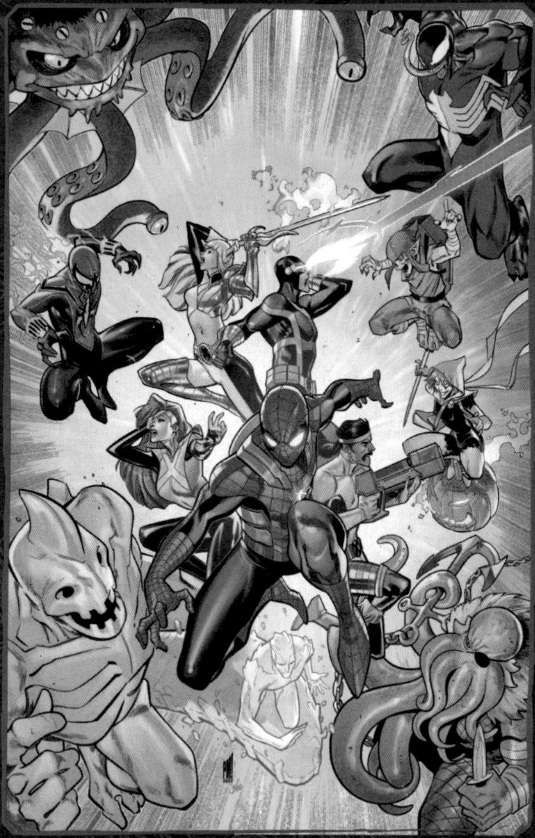

DARK WEB FINALE #1 CLASSIC HOMAGE DESIGN VARIANT BY
PACO MEDINA & **FEDERICO BLEE**

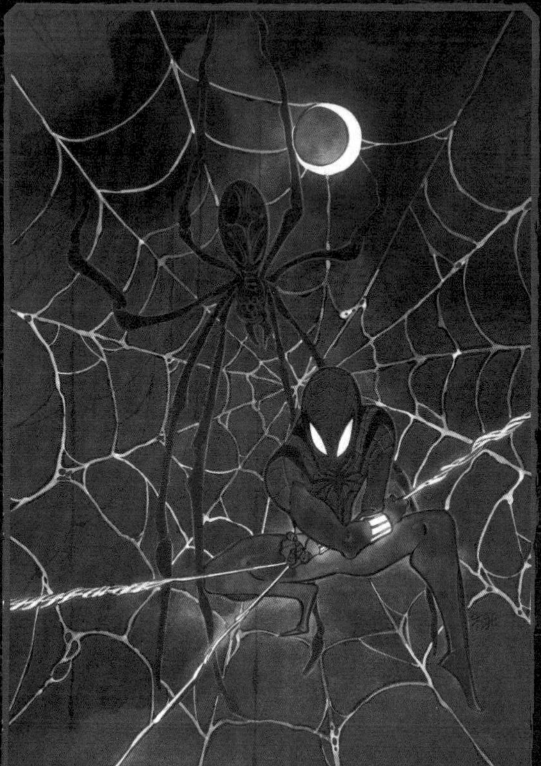

DARK WEB FINALE #1 VARIANT BY
PEACH MOMOKO

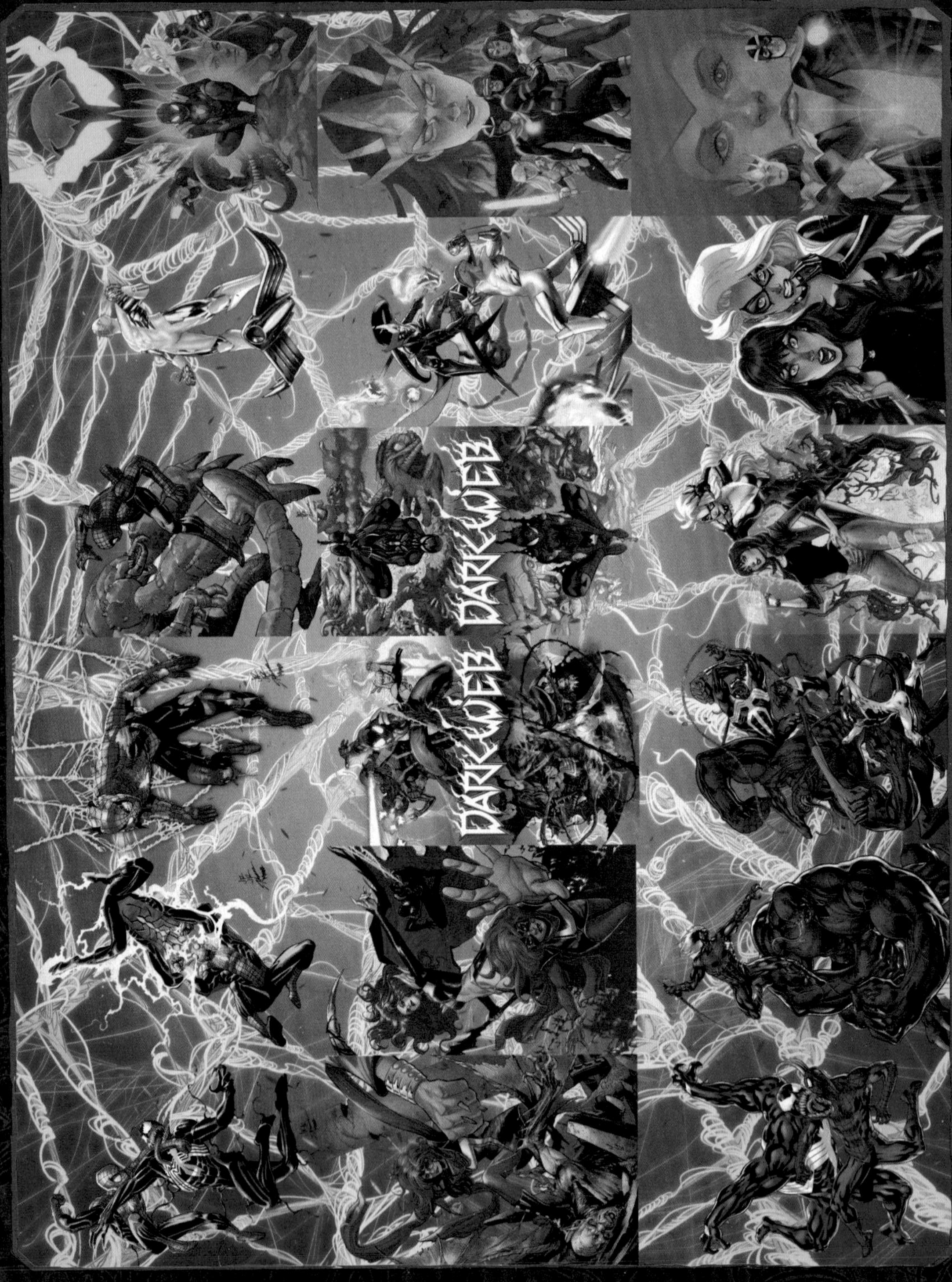
DARK WEB
DARK WEB

AMAZING SPIDER-MAN #15-18, DARK WEB #1, DARK WEB FINALE #1, DARK WEB: MS. MARVEL #1-2, DARK WEB: X-MEN #1-3, GOLD GOBLIN #2-3, MARY JANE & BLACK CAT #1-2 AND **VENOM #14-16** CONNECTING COVERS